OUT-OF-CONTROL

A Dialectical Behavior Therapy (DBT) -

Cognitive Behavioral Therapy (CBT) Workbook

For Getting Control of Our Emotions and Emotion-Driven Behavior

(targeting drug / alcohol abuse, bipolar disorder, borderline personality disorder,

depression, anger, cutting, and codependency recovery)

Melanie Gordon Sheets, Ph.D.

RECOVERY WORKS
PUBLICATIONS

Author's Note

This workbook is not designed to be a substitute for counseling or consultation with mental health professionals. When professional assistance or counseling is needed, the services of a competent professional should be sought.

 The DBT-CBT Out-of-Control Workbook

Printed in the United States of America

Printed on acid-free paper

10 9 8 7 6 5 4 3 2 1 813

To all the patients, friends, and family

    who have shared their stories

        of pain and trauma...

           and healing and recovery...

               and have taught me infinitely more

                   than could be learned through all the books, classes, and workshops.

Acknowledgements

The time has come to thank God for all the hurtful and difficult experiences I've gone through. Though, at times, I wondered why I had to go through so much...in my heart, I knew. I knew God would use my experiences to help others. I am now very aware that I would not be who I am today...if not for what I've been through. If it weren't for God pulling me through the pain, addictions, and destructive behavior during those times...it's doubtful I would have made it through. I thank Him and the special people He put in my life that led me through the pain. I believe in God's promise that He will make good rise out of the bad...for the benefit of His people.

I also thank God for his oversight of this work and for pressuring me to do this when I had many other things I wanted or needed to do. Even though I've called it a curse at times, I thank Him for giving me the drive and ability to persist at a task for seemingly endless hours, day after day. I thank Him for instilling in me the passion to care for His people...it is something that has shaped my life.

I owe a big thanks to my former colleague, Dr. Tom Dawson. If not for him leaving the State Hospital, DBT-CBT would have never come about! When he left, I inherited the DBT Group. I knew very little about DBT and had to come up with something fast. I began teaching what I already knew about recovery...and added DBT concepts to my presentations as I learned them...hence, DBT-CBT evolved. I also thank the founder of DBT, Dr. Marsha Linehan, for laying the groundwork for this program. What I knew about recovery when Dr. Dawson left would have resulted in "just another recovery group." A new understanding of human behavior and mechanisms of change unfolded as I began to learn DBT. What has evolved has been a tremendous gift for my patients...and for my friends and family...and myself. You have to know I use this in my personal life!

I owe a BIG thanks to the staff of Big Spring State Hospital for their ongoing support of the DBT-CBT program. I thank my former boss, Dr. John Pichitino, for coming up with the name, DBT-CBT, and for trusting me "to do my own thing" rather than forcing me to follow the established DBT curriculum. I thank him for allowing me to add extra groups during the week even though it put me behind in other work. I thank our hospital administrators, Ed Moughon, M.A., Olivia Flournoy, MSSW, and Lorie Dunnam, M.A., for their ongoing support and assistance and for allowing thousands of copies of the draft material to be produced and handed out to our patients. I thank everyone who pitched in to make and bind the copies...it was a B-I-G job!

I thank the treatment teams for referring their patients to Group and all the staff who encouraged the disheartened "to give it a try." I thank our unit staff for rounding up folks after lunch and getting them ready to go. I thank Martha Long, RN and the tram drivers for running an extra tram so they could arrive on time. I thank our ATD workers for their help getting the patients to the group room. Many of these people are my friends and I thank them for their love and support. Really, the success of the DBT-CBT program has been a team effort. I am deeply gratified by my work at Big Spring State Hospital and am blessed to have the opportunity to work with our patients and staff. My work at this facility fills my life with the people, activities, and experiences that provide a sense of purpose and meaning in life.

I also wish to thank my family for their support and assistance during all phases of this project. I thank my Mom, Merle Gordon, and my ex-husband, Clint Sheets, for being my "Chief Editors" and reviewing these chapters over and over...and continuing to do so, even though I did not make all the appropriate edits! I thank my kids, Mara and Cowboy, for all their sacrifices during this time and I thank my dear friend, Rebecca Arriola, for standing in the gap and providing so much extra help over the years. I thank my husband, David Carpenter, for his loving support and his daily efforts to ensure this material reaches those who can use it most.

On another note, I wish to thank my Dad, Noel Gordon, for his wisdom, love, and support, and despite all, for being the safety net when the world got scary. I thank my sisters, Lisa Phillips, Dawn Struble, and Janet Case, for their love and support and lifetimes of experiences and the memories that gave me "sister stories" to share!

I thanked the patients I have worked with on a preceding page for teaching me so much. Their stories of pain and suffering...and healing and recovery fill the pages of this book. I thank them for their life lessons. I also wish to share a special thanks to the patients who have participated in the DBT-CBT Group. If it weren't for them asking for more to read outside of group and materials to take to their families, this workbook would not have been written...not a chance! I thank them for the inspiration and motivation to write this book.

~ *Statements of Support and Encouragement* ~

Ask the people who support your recovery to write statements of support and encouragement

for your journey through the Pathways of Recovery.

An Expanded and Selected
~ Table of Contents ~

Section Three
Tolerating and Coping with Distress: "How Do I Stay in Control?" — 287-419

~ INTRODUCTION ~

Welcome to DBT-CBT! This is an exciting time! You're about to embark[1] on a journey that CAN change your life! The original DBT program developed by Marsha M. Linehan, Ph.D.[2] was designed to treat some of the MOST DIFFICULT to treat individuals...and the results have been ASTOUNDING![3] This program, DBT-CBT, is based on Dr. Linehan's work, but it has been GREATLY modified! It includes many original concepts, principles, and techniques developed during 24 years of patient care. MANY PEOPLE have described DBT-CBT to be LIFE-CHANGING, so HAVE GREAT HOPE! Applying the principles of DBT-CBT to your life CAN BE LIFE-CHANGING...but only if you're WILLING TO MAKE CHANGES in your life.

I assume you have great interest in changing your life...in feeling better, in responding to the world better, and having better life outcomes and experiences... else, you wouldn't be reading this book...especially an intro!! You've already taken the first step on this journey...and the Road to Recovery! **WELCOME ABOARD!**

1- Embark – (em-bark) – to start, to set out on.

2- From her *Skills Training Manual for Treating Borderline Personality Disorder* (1993) and *Cognitive-Behavioral Treatment of Borderline Personality Disorder* (1993).

3- Astounding – (uh-stound-ing) – surprising, amazing.

Happiness is not given to us, nor misery imposed. At every moment, we are at a crossroads. We must CHOOSE the direction we will take.
M. Richard

4- Many become great motivators and teachers because they're filled with the excitement and joy of recovery and they want everyone to experience New Life!

5- Self-mutilation - (mute-till-a-shin) – harming one's body by cutting, burning, scratching, or other forms of self-abuse.

This workbook is written for people who are hurting and suffering the pain of life. It's about bringing hope and peace and the life-changing gift of healing and recovery. I hope you heal and recover. I hope this workbook leads you there. Even if it's just about "planting seeds" or watering the seeds of recovery that were planted before, then, IT IS GOOD. This workbook CAN BE life-changing...AND HOW I HOPE...it is YOUR LIFE that is changed!

Think about this...if we do not make positive changes in our life, our life will NOT change for the positive. Please remember this. Repeat it over and over..."IF I DO NOT MAKE POSITIVE CHANGES IN MY LIFE...MY LIFE WILL NOT CHANGE FOR THE POSITIVE." Let that penetrate your soul. Making major life changes is hard to do, BUT with effort and support, MANY people RECOVER! We all know these people or we've heard their stories.[4] They're RECOVERED drug addicts, alcoholics, career criminals, "treatment failures," and "hopeless cases." They're people with long histories of depression, anger, anxiety, suicide attempts, self-mutilation,[5] abusive relationships, aggression, eating disorders, Bipolar Disorder, codependency, Borderline Personality Disorder, and other major life issues. Something Happened and they became disgusted enough or slowed down long enough to Think Things Through. They set their heart, mind, soul, and spirit on recovery...and THEY RECOVERED.

2

Tomorrow is the future. Today, we'll focus on the things we can do to bring about a brighter tomorrow. Today, we'll set a foundation for recovery and tomorrow, we'll build on it.

Think about people you know who have recovered...or recovery stories you've heard. How did they do it? What changes did they make in their life? _____

_____

_____

_____

_____

_____

6- Life-enhancing – (in-han-sing) – to enhance or improve life.

Change isn't easy, that's why we struggle with it. If change were easy, we'd all be doing it and we wouldn't need programs, rehabs, classes, workbooks, sponsors, psychologists, pastors, and support systems to help us through it!

Recovery Requires Us...

...to make major life changes...including changes in how we think and respond to life... our life in the past, the present, and the future.

...to turn away from old ways and respond to life in new ways.

...to use Life-Enhancing[6] Coping Skills to deal with tough and trying times rather than our preferred Self-Destructive Coping Behaviors.

...to make changes in what we allow in our life and what we allow ourselves to be involved in.

...to remove toxic people and situations from our life... and add life-enhancing, recovery-supporting people and situations.

...to fill our life with meaningful activities and relationships... things that give life meaning and value.

...to have hope and faith that things will get better as we get better.

...to accept that life isn't easy or always enjoyable.

...to accept and deal with the difficult things that Come Our Way.

...to give ourselves time to grow into and be... more and more the person we were designed to be.

7- Perseverance – (per-suh-veer-ance) – sticking to it and Getting Through it!

Through hope, self-discipline, and perseverance, we CAN radically change our lives.

People who recover make many changes in their life. They realize recovery is a process...a lifestyle...and NOT a one-time event! Recovery requires work. It's work worth doing...because we're worth the work and the people who love us and depend on us are worth our work and sacrifices! Recovery requires dedication and perseverance[7] to live, eat, and breathe the principles, concepts, and skills for living a Recovery Lifestyle. This workbook also requires dedication and perseverance to work through. It'll teach many principles, concepts, and skills for living a Recovery Lifestyle.

People who have major problems in living…tend to have experienced major problems in living.

We weren't born this way. We became this way. We're a product of our experiences.

Many of our "abnormal" behaviors are actually normal given our experiences. In many cases, these behaviors served as survival skills. However, their period of usefulness is long over. We've overused these behaviors and now they're causing us tremendous pain… and they're destroying our lives.

8- The book, *Getting Started in AA,* credits "The Serenity Prayer" to Friedrich Oetinger. Other sources credit Reinhold Niebuhr.
9- Minimize – (men-uh-mize) – to reduce to the lowest degree possible.
10- Studies show the average number of recovery attempts from drugs and alcohol is 8 – 18 tries. If we're just getting started in recovery, this doesn't (continued)

Our Humanity

It's important to accept we're human…and because of our humanity, we've made many errors and bad decisions. Most of us have done some pretty stupid and shameful things…and many self-defeating things over and over! We're human and we have a record of our life to prove it! If you find yourself wearing these shoes, realize you're not the trailblazer. Many have come before you…and many are walking the same path right now. You might say, "Yeah, some more than others!"…and you're right!

We're a product of our past experiences and the environments we were raised in. It's RARE that a kid with a stable home environment, emotionally healthy parents, positive role models, and good self-esteem begins to live a troubled life. Something generally happened that led the kid off course. RARELY do kids with "good enough upbringings" just "go bad." This isn't meant to minimize OUR RESPONSIBILITY for our behavior and choices, but it's important to understand "why we are the way we are" is because Something Happened in our life, be it one very difficult situation or many.

On Acceptance

Recovery requires us to accept what has happened…has happened…and what we've done, we've done. These things are of the past. They're over and they're done. Nothing we can do now will change the past. It's history. It's our history. Today is the present…and the things we do today CAN CHANGE our life…our today and our tomorrows. Focus on today and plan for tomorrow…and live the wisdom of "The Serenity Prayer" - "God, grant me the serenity to accept the things I cannot change, the courage to change the things I can, and the wisdom to know the difference."[8]

This workbook will help us develop skills to manage our life in the here-and-now. We'll learn skills to cope effectively with our problems, to set boundaries to prevent and minimize[9] emotional distress and problems, to gain peace and acceptance, and to make lifestyle changes which will gradually lead to relief, peace, then satisfaction, and finally, joy. Some people recover on the first try; however, recovery usually takes many attempts over many years.[10] Some days may be easy…and some more difficult. Recovery hinges on minute-to-minute and hour-to-hour decisions to remain on the Recovery Path. We can help ourselves along the way by seeking people who will support and encourage us along the path of recovery…AND BY AVOIDING people who are critical or negative BECAUSE THESE PEOPLE ARE TOXIC TO OUR RECOVERY.

4

(10 – continued) mean we have permission to relapse 17 times on purpose just so we can be normal!! 8-18 is just an average! Some do it on the 1st, 2nd, or 3rd try...and others on the 30th or 31st try. After reading this workbook, it'll be clear why recovery can take so many tries!

On Recovery

We can be "straight A" therapy students. We can earn extra credit on every assignment. We can have all the answers and understandings possible. However, to recover, WE'VE GOT TO BE WILLING TO APPLY THE PRINCIPLES OF RECOVERY TO OUR LIFE! Knowing what to do is one thing...actually doing it is another! We must DO recovery things and LIVE a Recovery Lifestyle. This often requires us to STEP OUT OF OUR COMFORT ZONE AND TAKE THE STEPS NECESSARY TO CHANGE OUR LIFE. The question is..."WHAT ARE YOU WILLING TO GIVE UP OR CHANGE IN ORDER FOR YOUR LIFE TO CHANGE...FOR THE BETTER?!!"

11- Reflect – to really think about!

That's a difficult question. Honestly reflect[11] on it a minute. What are you WILLING to give up or change in order for your life to change? _____

_____

_____

_____

Recovery is a process. It's decision by decision, step by step, gain by gain, day by day, month by month, and year after year.

Knowing and doing are two very different things. We can be WISE and have all the knowledge; however, there's nothing wise about not doing what we know NEEDS to be done!!!

No doubt you have some things in mind...and heart...that YOU KNOW MUST CHANGE...in order for YOUR LIFE to CHANGE and your LIFE SITUATIONS to IMPROVE. There are many things we need to give up and change. These are often things we have NO DESIRE to give up or change. That's where we run into problems. We have the gut wisdom TO KNOW what these things are...they're just hard to look at and deal with! What do you NEED TO CHANGE? This question will come up many times during this study. The answer you write today may be very different from your answer later. That's because this study will help you gain insight and learn more about the things that mess up our lives and keep our lives messed up.

Take a few moments and reflect on your thoughts and feelings about this opening reading. Does it make you excited? Uneasy? Anxious? Does it bring a sense of hope and peace...and light at the end of the tunnel...or does it bring a sense of dread...or some of both? _____

_____

_____

_____

_____

_____

_____

1- Dialectical – (di-uh-lec-tuh-cole) – finding balance or making sense out of very different or opposite things. Consider "black and white thinking" and the need to see things in shades of gray! Consider Bipolar Disorder and the need to balance the highs and lows.

2- Mindfulness refers to attention or awareness.

3- Interpersonal Effectiveness - being skilled or effective in relationships.

4- Emotion Regulation - managing, regulating, and controlling our emotions.

5- Distress Tolerance - willingness to tolerate or put up with upsetting feelings and situations without doing destructive things to relieve distress, like drinking, cutting, overdosing, or yelling.

6- DBT respects that our past experiences drive our intense emotions and dysfunctional behaviors. However, working through the past is NOT the focus of the program.

7- To learn more about DBT, review Dr. Linehan's books and videos. A lot of info about DBT can be found on the internet.

8- An argument with a loved one may seem like a life-shattering crisis for one person...and a minor stressor for another. Likewise, what may be "brushed off" and not responded to by some people may be the trigger for a major emotional response for others.

9- DSM-IV - *Diagnostic and Statistical Manual - Fourth Edition.* This is the official reference book for psychiatric symptoms and disorders.

10-11 (see the next page)

You've Gotta Be Kidding...400+ Pages?

Don't panic yet, we'll have lots of opportunities for that later! Believe it or not... I have major problems getting into books with a lot of words on each page. Books with single spacing and small print are particularly overwhelming! This workbook is designed to reach those who love to read AND folks who are overwhelmed by too many words on a page! To make this workbook more readable, the print is larger and the lines are further apart than most books...so, it seems longer than it really is!

What Is DBT?

Dialectical[1] Behavior Therapy (DBT) is a highly respected skills training program developed by Dr. Marsha Linehan to treat Borderline Personality Disorder (BPD). BPD is a severe disorder that's very difficult to treat. Many studies show DBT to be an effective treatment program for BPD. DBT addresses four major skill areas. The Mindfulness[2] unit teaches skills to increase awareness of our thoughts, feelings, behaviors, and experiences. The Interpersonal Effectiveness[3] unit teaches skills for developing and maintaining fulfilling relationships. The Emotion Regulation[4] unit focuses on labeling emotions, increasing positive emotions, and decreasing upsetting emotions. The Distress Tolerance[5] unit focuses on dealing with uncomfortable feelings and situations in positive ways. Crisis survival skills and acceptance are also discussed.

DBT teaches skills for managing stress and difficult emotional states. It wasn't designed to work through the traumas, losses, and difficult experiences in our past.[6] DBT focuses on the here-and-now...today's problems and concerns that lead to problematic emotions and behavior.[7]

What Is Borderline Personality Disorder (BPD)?

People with BPD have MAJOR problems controlling their thoughts, feelings, and behavior when upset. They're very sensitive to rejection and abandonment and they often respond to relationship problems in intense and desperate ways. Their lives are very unstable and they live in an almost constant state of distress or crisis.[8]

The DSM-IV[9] lists the symptoms of BPD.[10] They include desperate attempts to avoid abandonment; intense and unstable relationships; identity problems; impulsive behavior; suicidal behavior, gestures, and threats; self-mutilation; mood swings; intense emotional reactions; feelings of emptiness; intense anger or difficulty controlling anger; and paranoia or severe dissociation.[11]

What Is DBT-CBT? What Is This Workbook All About?

DBT-CBT is a psychoeducational,[12] skills training program. It combines traditional DBT and Cognitive-Behavioral Therapy (CBT)[13] principles. IT ALSO INCLUDES MANY NEW[14] Cognitive-Behavioral concepts and techniques. DBT-CBT addresses REAL LIFE and the problems and experiences common to people with Self-Destructive Coping Addictions and habits. This workbook is FILLED WITH THOUGHT-PROVOKING WORKSHEETS AND ACTIVITIES which explain major principles and concepts. The worksheets also PROMOTE INSIGHT, LIFE APPLICATION, AND A PERSONAL CONNECTION with the material. Alike DBT, this workbook is NOT designed to fully process or resolve specific traumas from the past. ITS PURPOSE is to address the emotions, behaviors, thought patterns, and Destructive Coping Responses that have developed IN RESPONSE TO trauma, loss, and other difficult experiences.[15] MAJOR GOALS OF THIS STUDY are self-awareness, self-understanding, self-respect, tolerating and accepting difficult times, effective coping, goal-directed behavior, life management and stability, and the experience of relief, peace, acceptance, and healing.

Over time, the use of DBT has expanded. It's not just for BPD anymore. It's now used to treat many problems like depression, anxiety, anger, substance abuse, and eating disorders.[16] Likewise, DBT-CBT addresses the needs of people WITH and WITHOUT BPD. This program will teach us ways to manage our emotional states and reactions to DAILY STRESS and MAJOR LIFE ISSUES...both past and present.

10- Many books have been written on BPD and a lot of information can be found on the internet.

11- Dissociation - (dis-so-see-a-shin) – feeling things are not real...or feeling separated from our body or experiences.

12- Psycho-educational - education about our psychological functioning.

13- CBT is a highly respected and widely used therapy which focuses on changing the way we think about things to change the way we feel about them.

14- DBT-CBT contains a lot of original material developed during 24 years of clinical work... and having to deal with myself, my friends, and my family for much longer!

15- DBT-CBT respects that our past experiences drive most of our dysfunctional behaviors and intense emotions. However, working through the past is NOT the focus of this program. Gaining the insight, knowledge, and skills to improve our current life and our future is the focus!!! DBT-CBT focuses on the here-and-now... the problems, situations, and concerns of TODAY that lead to troublesome emotions and behavior.

16- Eating disorders - like anorexia, bulimia, and overeating.

When we're filled with upsetting emotions, we often do things for quick relief...like drugs and alcohol; suicide attempts, gestures and threats; cutting and other forms of self-harm; overtaking medication; verbal and physical aggression; temper tantrums; walking off and leaving the situation; withdrawal; overeating or not eating enough; overshopping; "sleeping around;" rebound relationships; gambling; and other risky and reckless behaviors. THE NATURE OF THE PROBLEM IS...THE THINGS WE DO TO FEEL BETTER END UP MULTIPLYING AND INTENSIFYING OUR PROBLEMS. Our Destructive Coping Behaviors help us to cope in the Heat-of-the-Moment...but, they have many negative consequences. They make our CURRENT PROBLEMS MORE SEVERE...and they CREATE MANY NEW PROBLEMS for us to struggle with. The importance of this workbook is best understood by recognizing how our Destructive Coping Behaviors impact AND DESTROY the Big Picture of Our Life. DBT-CBT IS ALL ABOUT THE NATURE OF THE PROBLEM AND WHAT TO DO ABOUT IT!

17- Our emotions and behaviors are fairly normal and understandable given our experiences. However, some are highly dysfunctional and self-defeating!
The goal of DBT-CBT is to develop and USE skills to effectively respond to upsetting situations, including daily hassles! The prevention of problems is also a MAJOR GOAL!

What we do hurts us…hurts others…hurts the quality of our lives…and then, it hurts us even more.

18- Stamina – (stam-in-uh) – strength, the ability to endure or to keep going.
19- Chaos - (kay-aus) – (like Aus-tralia) - craziness and turmoil, things are a mess and Out-of-Control.
20- Bipolar Disorder was once called Manic-Depression. It causes severe mood swings…from the depths of depression to the heights of mania or extreme happiness. In some cases, people are angry and impatient instead of happy.
21- PTSD is a severe anxiety disorder. It's a response to trauma (war, abuse, a tornado, being at gunpoint, etc). Symptoms include nightmares; unwanted thoughts about the trauma; flashbacks; being overly alert, "on guard," or paranoid; and a great deal of anxiety.
22- Schizoaffective (ski-zoh-aff-feck-tive) – Disorder - it's a blend of Schizophrenia and mania and/or depression.

It may seem wild to say that Self-Destructive Coping Behaviors are normal![17] However, we've all responded to distress and conflict in overly intense and self-defeating ways. We ALL do these things…some more often than others…and some behaviors are much more destructive than others. Most of us struggle with stressful lives and many of us struggle with traumatic or otherwise difficult experiences. These things take their toll on our physical and emotional stamina.[18] Sometimes, when we've HAD ENOUGH or we've had MORE THAN WE CAN BEAR, WE BLOW. WE LOSE CONTROL. We do something DESPERATE and IMPULSIVE…and OFTEN REGRETTABLE. This type of response causes us GREAT PAIN AND SUFFERING.

This workbook is about HOW TO STOP THE PAIN…
and HOW TO TURN PAIN AND SUFFERING that we cannot tolerate…
INTO A RECOVERY EXPERIENCE we can tolerate…
one that BRINGS PEACE AMIDST THE CHAOS.[19]

How Was DBT-CBT Developed?

DBT-CBT came into existence when I was asked to take over a traditional DBT Group. Very few people attended because it was for severe Borderline patients only. My department was short-staffed at the time and we were pressured to provide services to as many patients as possible. In response, the DBT Group was expanded to include folks WITH MAJOR LIFE PROBLEMS with or without BPD. Most Members were diagnosed with Major Depression or Bipolar Disorder,[20] some had PTSD (Post Traumatic Stress Disorder)[21] and some had Schizoaffective Disorder.[22] Some of these patients had full-blown BPD, others had a few features of BPD, and some did not have a personality disorder. Most were hospitalized for suicidal behavior or gestures, or serious thoughts or threats to suicide. Others were hospitalized for physical aggression or serious thoughts or threats of aggression. About 80% had substance abuse problems and about 80% had history of some form of abuse. 100% were suffering from major life issues, problems, and losses. A common theme was noted among Group Members - HIGHLY DESTRUCTIVE RESPONSES TO EMOTIONALLY CHARGED SITUATIONS. As such, about 60% found themselves "starting over" to a significant degree. The material for the traditional DBT Group changed to meet the needs of these new Members.

Another reason the material changed is that I was "thrown into" leading the Group before I knew much about DBT! Naturally, I began teaching what I already knew

8

about human nature and the mechanisms of change and recovery! As I studied DBT, I found Dr. Linehan's work to be brilliant for understanding addictions and self-destructive behavior. The DBT concepts and principles that best targeted Members' needs were added to the Group material as I learned them. What resulted was a blend of DBT, CBT, Psychodynamic theory,[23] and a bunch of other stuff I had learned from over 20 years in the mental health profession. My boss, Dr. John Pichitino, suggested renaming the Group "DBT-CBT" to highlight the major changes.

23- Psycho-dynamic - (die-nah-mick) - a highly respected therapy which focuses on how our past experiences affect us over time.

> The new name, DBT-CBT, emphasizes that this program is
> AN OFFSHOOT[24] of traditional DBT that RESTS HEAVILY on
> Cognitive-Behavioral traditions and MANY NEW concepts and principles.

24- DBT-CBT is an "OFFSHOOT" of DBT. This means that DBT is the inspiration and foundation for DBT-CBT...but, DBT-CBT goes off in a different direction. This program can also be considered to be an OUTGROWTH of DBT...meaning that something new has grown or developed...something rooted in DBT! As such, DBT-CBT includes SOME but NOT ALL the principles or concepts of DBT. It also includes many different things. Also, some DBT concepts and principles are reinterpreted or tailored to better fit the needs of the new Group. If you've studied DBT, you'll recognize traditional DBT content... but, you'll also notice that some DBT concepts are "twisted" or used in different ways. You'll also notice a lot of new material! I certainly hope Dr. Linehan is flattered and not MAD!

Another reason the Group material changed is that the new Members had short hospital stays (1-2 weeks) whereas the severe borderlines in the traditional DBT Group had much longer stays (2 or more months). Their short stays created great pressure to provide a Big Picture approach...fast! The material had to quickly "hit home" and make sense. Many chalkboard illustrations, worksheets, and activities were developed to provide a visual presentation of major concepts and principles to go along with the discussion. These were designed to be attention grabbers and to lead Members to look at and process the major issues and situations that led to hospitalization. Most Members are very active in Group and blurt out answers to the worksheets and activities so it is THEIR lives that are illustrated on the board.

> DBT-CBT EVOLVED as a FAST-TRACK PROGRAM to provide PRACTICAL TOOLS
> and INSIGHTS to PROMOTE RECOVERY for people SUFFERING from
> PAINFUL EXPERIENCES and major EMOTIONAL ISSUES AND CONCERNS.

Who Is This Workbook Designed For?

DBT-CBT is designed to address six major problem areas:

1. Relationship Problems
2. Mood Swings - Depression - Anxiety - Anger
3. Unhealthy Thinking
4. Unhealthy Coping Behaviors
5. Other Impulsive Behavior – Bad Choices
6. Quality of Life Problems

Examples of the types of problems we experience in each area are listed in the six textboxes below. These examples highlight the range of issues and concerns that DBT-CBT can help with. This workbook is tailored to meet the needs of people who suffer from problems in some or all of the six areas.[25]

The Six Major Problem Areas Addressed by DBT-CBT

As you read through these problem areas, circle or highlight the types of issues and problems you CURRENTLY experience in each area...AND those you've experienced over THE LAST YEAR OR TWO. For example, you might circle "Stormy Relationships," "Fear of Rejection," and "Can't Tolerate Being Alone" in the Relationship Problems textbox.

25- Having been hospitalized before for psychiatric treatment is not a requirement!

---

1. RELATIONSHIP PROBLEMS

Conflict-Filled or Stormy Relationships -+- Abusive Relationships -+- Mistrust

Relationship Disappointments or Frequent Ups and Downs -+- Mad at Everyone

Unfulfilling Relationships -+- Love - Hate Relationships -+- Short-Term Relations

Fear of Rejection / Actual Rejection / Family and Friends Have Pulled Away

Co-Dependency / Dependency -+- Fear of Abandonment / Actual Abandonment

Loneliness / Can't Tolerate Being Alone -+- Attention-Seeking Behavior

Shyness/Fear/Major Discomfort in Social Situations -+- Few or No Close Relations

---

26- Pessimistic - (pess-uh-miss-stick) – having a negative outlook or bad expectations.

27- Stewing on things – to dwell on, to keep thinking about, or to ruminate.

28- Preoccupied - (pre-ock-cue-pie-d) – totally focused on.

2. MOOD SWINGS - DEPRESSION - ANXIETY - ANGER

Moodiness / Major Mood Swings -+- Easily Angered -+- Rage

Being a "High Drama" Person/Drama Queen -+- Unbearable/Very Intense Emotions

Anxiety / Panic -+- Depression / Helplessness / Hopelessness / Worthlessness

Feeling Like Things Will Never Work Out / Wanting to Give Up / Feeling Suicidal

Feeling Overwhelmed or Out-of-Control -+- Guilt / Shame

29- Catastrophizing - (cuh-tass-stro-fiz-zing) - feeling like everything is a major disaster or catastrophe.

30- Blowing things out of proportion – (pro-poor-shin) - exaggerating, feeling like things are much worse than they truly are...but not to the extent of a catastrophe!

31- Black and white...and all-or-none thinking – two terms for the same thinking style. Seeing things as all one way or another...like "all good" or "all bad" with no middle ground. Things are either black or white with no shades of gray!

3. UNHEALTHY THINKING

Worrying / Overthinking -+- Pessimistic[26] Thinking / Negative Expectations

Denial / Avoiding Thoughts About Something / Stuffing Feelings

Dwelling on the Past -+- Stewing On Things[27] -+- Preoccupied[28] with Revenge

Catastrophizing[29]/ Blowing Things Out of Proportion[30]

Black and White Thinking / All-or-None Thinking[31]

Putting Ourselves Down / Focusing on Our Worst Qualities -+- Irrational Beliefs

---

4. UNHEALTHY COPING BEHAVIORS

Substance Abuse - Alcohol, Drugs, Prescription Medication, Over-the-Counter Meds

Suicidal Behavior/Gestures/Threats -+- Self-Mutilation/Injuring Self on Purpose

Verbal / Physical Aggression -+- Tantrums / Throwing Fits -+- Rage Episodes

Overshopping -+- Anorexia / Bulimia[32] -+- Overeating / Comfort Eating

Living Crisis-to-Crisis -+- Sleeping Around / Affairs / Rebound Relationships

Avoidance / Withdrawal / Isolation / Leaving -+- Criminal Acts -+- Gambling

32- Two well-known eating disorders. Anorexia – (an-ner-rex-ee-uh) – not eating or eating VERY little.
Bulimia – (bull-lee-me-uh) – eating large amounts of food and forcing oneself to throw up…
"to scarf n' barf."

5. OTHER IMPULSIVE BEHAVIOR - BAD CHOICES

Doing Things "On a Whim" / Making "Snap Judgments" / Not Thinking Things Through and Having Negative Consequences as a Result

6. QUALITY OF LIFE PROBLEMS

"Burnt-Out" / Life Is a Chore -+- Emptiness / Meaninglessness / Boredom

Nothing to Live For -+- More Problems than I Can Bear -+- Having to Start Over

Financial Problems / Bankruptcy -+- Job Loss / Can't Keep a Job

Loss of Career or Professional License -+- Demotion / Probation at Work

Loss of Relationships -+- Family Pulled Away -+- Can't See Children

Loss of Trust from Others -+- Reputation Damaged

Loss of Self-Respect and Integrity[33] -+- Loss of Self-Confidence

Problems Getting an Education / Not Completing Semesters[34]-+- Underachievement

Loss of Housing -+- Loss of Transportation -+- Loss of Possessions

Loss of Freedom -+- Legal Problems / Probation or Imprisonment

Loss of Pets -+- Health Problems / New Medical Diagnosis

33- Integrity – (in-teg-gritty) – feeling like a "good" person with good morals and values. Feeling whole and "okay."

34- In this section, we're referring to educational problems caused by our behavior or choices… NOT from other issues like brain-related learning problems or being a single parent with three kids to support.

How many of the six problem areas did you mark something in? _____

Most readers mark something in all six areas. That's because these problems and issues tend to cluster. For instance, if we have problems in one area, we often have problems in other areas, too! Feel fortunate if you marked something in four or less areas! The MORE AREAS you marked something in and the MORE PROBLEMS IN EACH AREA that you marked, the closer this program will come to meeting your recovery needs…and the more likely you are to find your story told in these pages.

How Is This Program to Be Delivered?

This workbook was written to provide program materials for group members to study outside of group and as a take-home study. The workbook format provides members the opportunity to review and reflect on the material and to complete the study at their own pace. This encourages in-depth processing and application.

This workbook can be completed as part of an Individual or Group Therapy program, a support group,[35] or as an independent home-based study.

35- A support group is always good, not only for ongoing encouragement and support, but also to realize how common our experiences, problems, emotions, behaviors, and responses are! For instance, we'll come to realize that the things we've felt so much shame, guilt, and anger about are experiences others have gone through...and our feelings and behaviors are quite normal for people with these experiences. This understanding can be quite healing in itself.

36- Alike DBT, this workbook is not designed to FULLY process specific traumas, issues, or experiences; but to address some of the emotions, behaviors, thought patterns, and destructive coping responses which DEVELOP as a result of difficult experiences. This workbook will help us to Get Control of our Out-of-Control emotions, thoughts, and behaviors... and to find peace and healing along the Recovery Path.

37- Trusted others include TRUSTWORTHY and SUPPORTIVE family, friends, counselors, treatment providers, clergy, etc.

Words of Warning

THIS WORKBOOK IS **NOT** AN EMOTIONALLY EASY STUDY.
IT PACKS A PUNCH...AND IT HITS HARD AND QUICK.
It addresses destructive coping behavior AND the difficult emotions and life experiences that lead to self-destructive behavior.[36]

IF YOU HAVE DIFFICULT ISSUES WHICH SIGNIFICANTLY BOTHER OR OVERWHELM YOU, IT'S RECOMMENDED THAT YOU SEEK PROFESSIONAL HELP.
A professional can help you process and work through your experiences AND the material in this workbook.

BEFORE STARTING THIS STUDY, IT'S RECOMMENDED THAT YOU INFORM TRUSTED OTHERS[37] THAT YOU'LL BE DEALING WITH DIFFICULT EMOTIONS, EXPERIENCES, SITUATIONS, AND BEHAVIORS. IT'S ALSO RECOMMENDED THAT YOU SHARE THE INFORMATION YOU'RE LEARNING WITH THEM.
This will create a knowledgeable support system and you'll have discussion partners who can give you ideas and feedback for responding to the activities and worksheets! MOST folks find this material very interesting...so they should be interested in learning this information, too!

What Are Some Goals of This Study?

* Starred items are classic DBT goals and concepts.

38- Self-monitoring - watching and monitoring ourselves.

* 1. To increase self-awareness and self-monitoring[38] skills (**Mindfulness**)

* 2. To gain a better understanding of our emotional lives, including skills to recognize and describe our emotions and to effectively respond to troubling emotional states (**Emotion Regulation Skills**)

12

* 3. To gain skills for effectively dealing with difficult experiences and situations as well as daily hassles and frustrations (**Life-Enhancing Coping Skills, Behavioral Control Skills,** and **Distress Tolerance Skills**)

* 4. To achieve acceptance, healing, and peace with the troubling experiences in our life, both past and present (**Recovery and Healing**)

* 5. To gain knowledge and skills to improve our relationships and social functioning (**Interpersonal Effectiveness Skills**)

6. To understand we're human and in our humanity we make mistakes and bad decisions...and sometimes, we behave in ways which hurt ourselves and others (**Acceptance and Self-Forgiveness Skills**)

7. To understand that many of our "abnormal" and self-destructive behaviors are normal given our history of abnormal, difficult, or traumatic experiences (**Acceptance and Self-Forgiveness Skills**)

8. To understand that impulsive, quick-fix coping behaviors work for a short period of time (minutes, hours, or days)...but lead to awful consequences and many more problems...AND to understand these behaviors are very self-defeating and make our lives MORE unmanageable and our life circumstances HARDER TO BEAR (**Insight and Understanding**)

*9. To have the serenity to accept the things we cannot change, the courage to change the things we can, and the wisdom to know the difference[39] (**Wisdom, Distress Tolerance Skills,** and **Goal-Directed Behavior**)

Saving Face: DBT-CBT in Action

You've heard the saying about "stepping in it." Well, I sometimes "step in it"... and the work of this book is no exception! I spoke to a professor at Texas A&M, Dr. Brian Stagner, about reviewing this workbook. He was my mentor during graduate school and he graciously agreed. Although I'm proud of this work, at the same time, I'm a little embarrassed by it! That's a dialectical problem by the way! I figured he'd be impressed by the content, but stunned[40] by the language and grammar...so, I never sent it to him!

Part of DBT-CBT is Choosing Our Battles and Taking a Stand and Fighting for what's MOST IMPORTANT to us...NOT EVERYTHING in life. It's also about being prepared for and accepting the consequences of our behavior and choices. It's also about being wise...and we'll see if I made a wise choice! I expect to take some hits on

39- From "The Serenity Prayer."

40- Stunned – shocked.

grammar, like dangling participles, commas instead of semicolons, overuse of contractions, pronoun and antecedent disagreement, Texas slang, and other informal language and grammar. The truth, I wrote this for the average person and in a language many people speak…except for some southern slang! It wasn't written for a professional audience,[41] though I hope many in that audience will read it. I'm an informal, "down-home girl"[42] and I wrote this for "down-home people." I CAN BE formal if I have to be, but I certainly PREFER NOT!

Another criticism I expect is repetition in the workbook. I tried to write this as I would speak it and teach it in Group. When I teach important principles and concepts, I often repeat myself by explaining the same thing in different words…one sentence right after another. Sometimes, hearing something said in different ways helps us to understand and remember it better…and if our minds have wandered, maybe we'll get it the second or third time around! I'm very invested in the people I work with…and I'm passionate about doing my part to change lives. I drill home SOME points because this is intended to be a learning AND recovery experience. It's NOT designed for casual reading or entertainment purposes!

> You'll notice some repetition across chapters. My belief, most people don't have audiographic memories[43]…like they hear something once and remember it. My goal is for people to understand and remember these life-changing principles, concepts, and skills…so they'll be equipped to apply them in Real Life. Many of us are hard-headed and need this information drilled into our minds. We may not WANT to hear some things and we may not be ready to look at or process some things. We usually have to be emotionally MOVED before we DECIDE to make difficult life changes. Being MOVED often involves looking at the Big Picture of Reality until our eyes are opened and the truth sinks in. Further, to learn how to carry out these skills and to live these concepts…we need to live, eat, and breathe this information until we know it so well we can repeat it back to ourselves. We LEARN by repetition.

Also, everyone doesn't read a book cover to cover in a few days. When time goes by, a review of important principles and concepts helps us to get the most out of what we're reading. Further, when we're stressed out by life, our brain is working full capacity to survive and meet here-and-now demands…and it isn't always so able to fully process and learn new information. On top of all this, some of us have used a lot of drugs and alcohol, are aging, on medications, or have had head injuries…and our

---

Sidebar notes:

41- A professional audience…like university professors and editors.

42- "Down-home" – down-to-earth.

Don't panic! Everything isn't repeated…just some of the most important things!

43- Audiographic memories – (ah-dee-oh-graf-ick) – like a photographic memory is a great memory for what we see, the term "audiographic memory" refers to a great memory for what we hear. I think I just made up a word!

We've all heard the saying, "The truth hurts," but, we've also heard, "The truth shall set you free."

attention, concentration, and memories aren't like they used to be! Also, some folks have had learning problems all their lives. Others may have symptoms of mental illness[44] which affect their ability to concentrate. In my mind...REPETITION IS GOOD!

44- Symptoms like depression, racing thoughts, anxiety, or hearing voices.

Some folks don't like how I've used CAPITAL LETTERS. I took some out, but left many. Again, I'm trying to drill home points. The capital letters are intended to draw attention to important principles and concepts...things I really want folks TO GET and be aware of! Sometimes, they're for emphasis (like to say louder when we're reading), but most often they're there to highlight a point. The capital letters may make reading a little difficult until you get used to the writing style.

The last point of embarrassment is...there WILL BE errors and typos...and Lord, I hope not...lost lines...where they disappear when the document is printed. I know I'm obsessive-compulsive...a perfectionist in many ways. I could review this book for ANOTHER year...and continue to make changes. However, if I don't GET 'ER DONE... it'll be half of forever before it's in print and can be helpful to people who are HURTING and SUFFERING. Getting this in print is much more important than perfection and my ego. The website, **www.dbt-cbt-workbook.com**, will be online shortly after publication. If your heart is there, let me know about the errors you find! I know as soon as it's in print...errors I've missed will jump right off the page!

So, I resolve my dialectical problem of being both proud of this work and embarrassed by it. I realize I want to print the PERFECT book to please a professional audience...however, I also recognize this book is for the average person who desperately seeks recovery. THAT IS its value and purpose. I ACCEPT that no matter how obsessive-compulsive and perfectionistic I am, I'm not perfect and I'll make errors despite my best efforts to avoid them. I also understand that although I'm a highly educated professional, it's not my spirit to interact with the world in a formal manner. I'm different, I'm down-to-earth, I am ME...and I'm okay. Some people will accept and embrace this work...others will criticize it. I understand some people will find fault no matter what...but, I've "stepped in it" and have set myself up for criticism because I haven't used proper grammar or writing rules. I'll take my hits, do Damage Control, fix things as I see appropriate, and I'll move on down the Recovery Path...and on with life! Perhaps our paths will cross as we journey through the Pathways of Recovery. Hope to see you there.

~ BEFORE YOU GET STARTED ~

1. READ THE "WORDS OF WARNING" section in the FAQ's (page 11).

2. HAVE A PEN AND HIGHLIGHTER available. You'll have writing to do and you'll be asked to highlight, underline, or otherwise mark some things!

3. MAKE COPIES of blank worksheets and tracking sheets. Multiple copies may be needed and you may want to re-do the worksheets and tracking sheets for problem solving, as a coping tool, and to update them to reflect your life as you make life changes! Photocopies of the worksheets and tracking sheets are allowed for personal use only.

4. Know that this is NOT an emotionally easy study. The first two chapters are rather difficult. Many group members find this material to be life-changing and I encourage you to work through it AS YOU'RE ABLE TO. It's about Real Life... and the more difficult your life is and has been, the more difficult this material may be for you. Being aware of...and processing the things in this workbook will help you to recover. We need to understand why things are the way they are... and what we can do to change them.

5. If you find something too hard to understand, too hard emotionally, or too boring, SKIP IT! Go back to it later if it's important.

6. To get the most out of this program, READ IT MORE THAN ONCE. There's so much material, it's unlikely that all the important things will be absorbed, learned, and fully processed during the first read through!

7. The first letter of some words are CAPITALIZED because they're major concepts or principles in this program. Some entire words, phrases, and sentences are capitalized to draw your attention to them.

8. As needed, masculine pronouns (him, his) will be used for general reference.

9. Check out the website **www.dbt-cbt-workbook.com** for more information about this program and to post feedback, comments, and suggestions.

There is pain in change...and suffering in stagnation.[45]

45- Stagnation – (stag-nation) – when something goes bad from lack of movement (like water) or from being stuck in an unchanging situation.

An Overview of the Three Mind States

Raw Emotions	Emotion-Driven Thoughts	EMOTIONAL MIND	RATIONAL MIND	WISE MIND
		When we're in Emotional Mind, we're in an emotional state! Emotional Mind is made up of Raw Emotions and Emotion-Driven Thoughts. Our Raw Emotions are our feelings. Emotion-Driven Thoughts are the thoughts that go through our mind when we're in an emotional state. They're driven by or are caused by the emotions we're experiencing. For instance, if we're angry, we have angry thoughts about hurting someone, getting even, etc. If we're depressed, we have depressed thoughts.	When we're in Rational Mind, we're thinking rationally and logically. We're dealing with reality and seeing things as they truly are. When we're in Emotional Mind, we see things and think about things based on how we're feeling. Like when we're depressed, we see everything as depressing...we see the world through dark colored glasses. When we Turn On Rational Mind, we see things clearly. We're dealing with the facts and reality as they truly are.	When we're in Wise Mind, we're focused on problem-solving. Wise Mind Turns On when we're dealing with our problems based on what's going on in our Emotional Mind and what Rational Mind has to say about the situation. Wise Mind isn't just about knowing what to do...it's about following through with what we know to do! Wise Mind is ACTION-ORIENTED...wise actions!
Angry	I don't get mad...I get even.		Getting even would feel good, but it would cause me a lot more problems.	Getting even isn't the way to go. I've got to move on and not allow myself to get in this type of situation again.
Depressed Hopeless Helpless Worthless Empty	I'd be better off dead.		I really don't want to die, I just want the pain to go away.	I'm too depressed right now to think realistically about my situation. It's no time to make any major decisions other than the decision to get some therapy and anti-depressants! I'll have to allow some time to feel better again and to get a new direction for my life.
	My family would be better off without me.		Destroying myself would destroy my family. They'd be better off if I got my life in order.	
	There's no reason to live now.		Things HAVE changed and my life is going a different direction now.	
	I don't deserve any better than this.		I DESERVE good things...but, I must DO THINGS to bring them about! When I'm good to people, I deserve people to be good to me.	
Betrayed Rejected Hurt Alone Lonely	Nobody understands me.		Folks don't understand me when I'm Big-Time in Emotional Mind. I don't understand myself either when I get that way.	I'll apologize to my family and let them know I'll go back in rehab and get my life in order again! They've always welcomed me back into their lives when I'm living a Recovery Lifestyle.
	No one will ever love me. Nobody cares about me.		My family loves me and has helped me a lot over the years. They're just burnt out and angry because of what I've done...over and over.	
	I'm a social reject.		People I want to be around reject me when I do things that aren't acceptable to them.	

From "Out-of-Control: A Dialectical Behavior Therapy (DBT) - Cognitive-Behavioral Therapy (CBT) Workbook for Getting Control of Our Emotions and Emotion-Driven Behavior"
Copyright © 2009 by Melanie Gordon Sheets, Ph.D.   (www.dbt-cbt-workbook.com)

Abused Used Mistreated Paranoid Mistrusting	She'll screw me over just like everyone else.	She's not everyone or everything that has ever hurt me. She's been good to me and she'll probably continue to be good to me... if I'm good to her. She may disappoint me now and then...that's normal for any relationship.	When I start thinking she's going to hurt me like many people have in my life, I'll remind myself of the truth about her. I'll Turn My Mind to focus on how loyal and kind she's been to me.
Scared Worried Confused Paralyzed Anxious Panicky	I can't deal with this. I'll never get over this.	I CAN deal with this. I'm just not in any mood to do so. Getting through this requires me to do things I don't feel like doing... and things I'm not comfortable doing. I CAN deal with this...though it will be one of the hardest things I've ever done. This will be a major challenge to get through and I'll need support and help.	I'll remind myself of my strengths and how I've gotten through tough times before. I'll contact my sponsor and get counseling at the clinic. I'll use Distress Tolerance skills and positive coping skills to get through this tough time. I'll write-up a Game Plan for how I'm gonna do it!
	Recovery hasn't done me any good. Life will never be better. Screw EVERYTHING. There's no way out. Nothing stays good for long. There's no hope for me.	Six months in recovery has brought about many great changes, like a job, housing, cash flow, better relations with my family, etc. Life got better as I got better. Life is going to happen and normal life problems will come my way even when I'm in recovery. I created this bad situation by getting involved with someone who wasn't really into recovery...because I was lonely.	I will Say NO to temptation and impulses to relapse. I WILL CALL MY SPONSOR and use my support system if I start wigging out. I will use positive coping skills and I will NOT get involved in another relationship until I have at least one year in recovery. I'll listen to everyone that warns me about an unhealthy relationship! I knew better and I was warned, but I got involved anyway!
Desperate Out-of-Control Overwhelmed	I'd be better off a drunk. I'm happy when I'm using.	I was NOT happy when I was drinking and drugging. My life was miserable. I lost everything and my life was a grand example of the Cycle of Suffering.	
Stupid Like a failure	I'm a worthless piece of crap. I screw everything up.	I feel worthless when I focus on my worst qualities and mistakes. The truth, I have many positive qualities and I've done many positive things for others. Many people depend on me and value me. I've made mistakes and have hurt people when I've lived in Emotional Mind. When I've been clean n' sober and on my Bipolar meds, I've made many good decisions.	When I begin to think negative, I'll remind myself of my positive qualities, the good decisions I've made, the positive things that go on in my life when I'm in recovery, and how I'm valued by others. I'll Turn My Mind from the painful lies and perceptions to the healing truth.

18

An Overview of the DBT-CBT Process and the Pathways of Recovery and Relapse

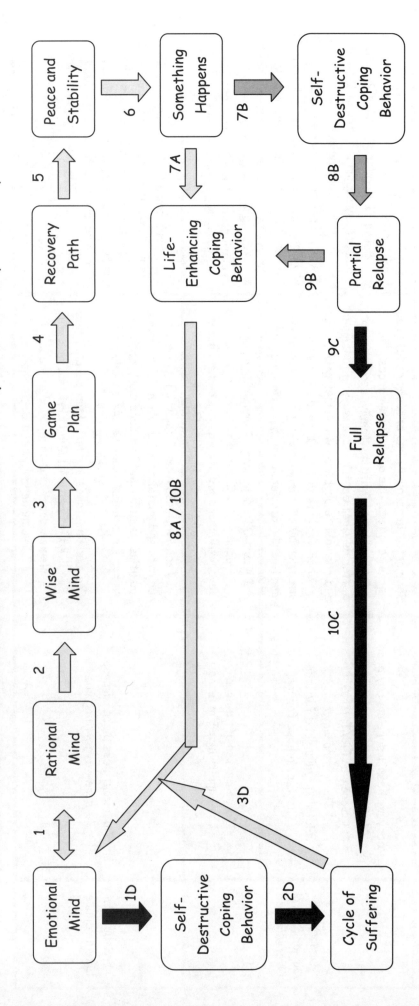

The text below will walk you through the flowchart and explain the DBT-CBT process.

The lightest arrows point out **the best route for recovery.** Our healing and recovery has a lot to do with **how we deal with our issues and problems and how we deal with temptation.** The best route starts at Point 1 and goes through 6, then 7A, 8A, and back to 1. **It's "The Pathway of Recovery."** The gray arrows go from 7B to 8B point out the path when Something Happens and we relapse into Self-Destructive Coping Behaviors (like drugs, alcohol, cutting, suicide attempts, aggression, etc). We can have a **partial relapse** (gray arrows) or a **full relapse.** The black arrows point out the path of a full relapse that takes us to "The Cycle of Suffering." That's the pit of destruction...where our life fills with pain, depression, and losses. This is where life spirals Out-of-Control and gets worse and worse. This is where people bottom-out if they don't get out.

From "Out-of-Control: A Dialectical Behavior Therapy (DBT) – Cognitive-Behavioral Therapy (CBT) Workbook for Getting Control of Our Emotions and Emotion-Driven Behavior" Copyright © 2009 by Melanie Gordon Sheets, Ph.D. (www.dbt-cbt-workbook.com)

The DBT-CBT process starts at Emotional Mind. It begins when we're upset or tempted to relapse for other reasons. There's two ways to go at this point. We can do a Self-Destructive Coping Behavior to try to feel better (route marked by 1D)...or we can work hard to Turn-On Rational Mind to think through our situation and to find a wise way of handling it (route of 1 -> 2 -> 3, etc). If we use Self-Destructive Coping Behaviors, we'll end up in the Cycle of Suffering (2D). If we deal with our problems rationally and wisely (1 -> 2 -> 3, etc), we'll get on or stay on the Recovery Path. You'll notice the arrow between Emotional Mind and Rational Mind is a double-sided arrow. It goes both ways. That's because we go back and forth between Emotional Mind and Rational Mind in the Heat-of-the-Moment. We often struggle with the temptation or desire to do a DESTRUCTIVE coping mechanism...and the desire NOT to. It's the struggle between our desire to remain in control of our life and on the Recovery Path...and our desire for quick relief and old ways of avoiding our pain and problems. The Emotional Mind way is to respond to the situation using a quick relief, Self-Destructive Coping Behavior (1D). We're often tempted to use Self-Destructive Coping Mechanisms so we can Numb-Out our upsetting feelings and White-Out our painful thoughts (like Liquid Paper). Self-Destructive Coping Mechanisms are generally very powerful and they work quickly. That's why we do them. "The Nature of the Problem" is...the things we do to feel better...end up making us feel worse. They cause us more pain and problems and they destroy our life. We lose many things we cherish and love...and sometimes, we lose everything.

DBT-CBT is all about choices...and, we have a choice. When we're Big-Time Emotional Mind, we can choose recovery. We can Turn On Rational Mind and think through the situation. Rational Mind helps us to look at our problem and "The Big Picture of Our Life" in a rational and realistic way. Rational Mind tells us the TRUTH and it challenges the lies that come out of Emotional Mind...lies like, "I'm worthless, my life is over, life will never get better, I just want to die, why try, I don't deserve any better, and no one cares about me." Rational Mind will remind us of the facts about what we REALLY want...the positive things about ourselves...and the positive things that are going on in our life. Rational Mind will remind us of truths that will help talk us out of doing destructive things...and into doing positive, life-improving things.

When we're dealing with our emotional issues and concerns through Rational Mind, Wise Mind Turns On (Point 2). Wise Mind helps us to come up with a plan of action to deal with our pain and problems (Point 3). Wise Mind offers suggestions about how best to deal with our problem with RESPECT for what's going on in our Emotional Mind and what Rational Mind has to say about things. A Recovery Goal is to review these Wise Mind suggestions and to come up with a Game Plan for dealing with our problems in a life-enhancing way...a way that enhances or improves our life. When we follow through with a Wise Mind Game Plan, we're dealing with life in a positive way. We're living a Recovery Lifestyle...and we're on the Recovery Path (Point 4).

When we've just begun recovery or when we're dealing with a very upsetting event...even though we're dealing with life in a recovery way...we still have problems and issues to deal with. Life is tough at these times. We may be making a lot of changes and we're dealing with our pain and problems WITHOUT the old coping mechanisms that give us comfort and quick relief. However, as time passes, we get through some of the tough times and many good things are happening in our life. We finally begin to feel some peace...and we're finally having some stability in our life (Point 5).

From "Out-of-Control: A Dialectical Behavior Therapy (DBT) - Cognitive-Behavioral Therapy (CBT) Workbook for Getting Control of Our Emotions and Emotion-Driven Behavior" Copyright © 2009 by Melanie Gordon Sheets, Ph.D. (www.dbt-cbt-workbook.com)

20

At this point, we're living a Recovery Lifestyle...and life is going pretty well. Then, **Something Happens** (Point 6). It's like a boulder falls out of the sky and slams right in the middle of our Recovery Path. Something Happened. No matter how great a life we're living...life happens. Bad things will come our way. Bad things happen to good people. Something Happens like our loved one is being tested for cancer, the apartment building we're living in gets sold and we have 30 days to leave...or we get laid off from our job, no fault of our own. All kinds of things happen to people.

When Something Happens, we have two choices how to respond. The best choice is to **fight hard to stay on the Recovery Path** (Point 7A) by using every **Life-Enhancing Coping Behavior** known to man. We choose to struggle through our problem in a recovery way. At times during this struggle, we'll find ourselves **going back into Emotional Mind** (Point 8A). We'll be filled with upsetting feelings...and we'll have all kinds of angry, hopeless, things never work out types of thoughts. Instead of trying to Numb-Out or White-Out, **we go back through the DBT-CBT process.** We get **Rational Mind Turned On** to deal with the situation and our emotional thoughts and feelings in a rational, logical way (Point 1...once again). The same process occurs. **Wise Mind Turns On** and we come up with a **Game Plan** for dealing with our situation in a life-enhancing way. We follow through with our Game Plan and we stay on the **Recovery Path. Life improves some more...things settle down...and we have some peace and stability...for awhile.** Then of course, as time goes by, life happens. **Something Happens again and we go through the process again! That's life... and we have to continue to deal with life if we are to stay on the Recovery Path.** No one ever promised life would be easy. But, the truth is... if we deal with life in a productive way, it's a lot less painful than the Cycle of Suffering. When we're in recovery and doing recovery things...life gets better and better. Life gets better **as we get better.**

When Something Happens, the bad choice is to **respond using our old destructive coping skills** (7B, 8B). If we go back to our old self-destructive ways, we can make it a **Partial Relapse** by getting right back on the Recovery Path (Point 9B) by using Life-Enhancing Coping Mechanisms. Then, we go back through the process (10B) of dealing with our emotional stuff through Rational Mind and Wise Mind...and we get a Game Plan. **If we don't get back on track, we're headed for a Full Relapse** (Point 9C). We know where that leads...right back into the **Cycle of Suffering** (10C)...and the pattern of losing many of the things we worked so hard for in recovery. When we're in the Cycle of Suffering, **we DON'T HAVE TO STAY THERE.** We can go the route of the arrow at Point 3D. We can **choose to work through our relapse** and all the pain and problems...**starting back at Emotional Mind and Rational Mind.** We can follow Wise Mind suggestions...**and we can get BACK ON the Recovery Path!**

Take a few minutes to review the Table of Contents or flip through the workbook. You'll see that the chapters focus on the points we just discussed. **The first section in the workbook,** Chapters 1-5, addresses the Cycle of Suffering and **"Why is my life so Out-of-Control?"** The Cycle of Suffering is discussed in detail, including the types of losses we experience and why...as well as the pathways of relapse and recovery we've just discussed. **The second section,** Chapters 6-10, addresses the three mind states in detail...and **"How do I get control of my life?" The third section,** Chapters 11-14, addresses **"How do I stay in control?"** These chapters focus on positive coping skills, how to accept and deal with the difficult things in our life, and the development and use of a Game Plan. So, what you have before you is a **recovery program that gives you some powerful tools for Getting On and Staying on the Recovery Path!**

From "Out-of-Control: A Dialectical Behavior Therapy (DBT) – Cognitive-Behavioral Therapy (CBT) Workbook for Getting Control of Our Emotions and Emotion-Driven Behavior"
Copyright © 2009 by Melanie Gordon Sheets, Ph.D. (www.dbt-cbt-workbook.com)

How Bad Do I Really Want Recovery?

Here's some questions to think about as you start this study. They'll help you to know how tired you are of living like you're living…and how ready you are to recover. We'll be asked these types of questions throughout this workbook. You'll probably notice that your feelings and attitudes about these things will change as you process the material in this workbook. That's because you'll be gaining many understandings about why things are the way they are in your life…and what it takes to change the way things go for you in life.

How tired are you of living like you're living? How tired are you of all the pain and problems? How tired are you of going through all the negative things you've been going through? _____

_____

_____

Are you tired enough to acknowledge the truth to yourself about why things are the way they are? Are you tired enough to talk about it honestly with a support person? _____

_____

_____

Are you tired enough to actually do what it takes to change your life? How far are you willing to go? What are you willing to give up or change in order for your life to change? _

_____

_____

_____

What are you willing to change about yourself? _____

_____

_____

What are you willing to do differently that you've resisted doing all along? _____

_____

_____

What uncomfortable feelings are you willing to Go Through to make the life changes that will change your life? Are you willing to deal with the anxiety that accompanies change? Are you willing to deal with the pain of change? _____

_____

22

_____

_____

_____

_____

_____

Are you willing to end an unhealthy relationship? Are you willing to be lonely for six months or a year or for however long it takes to find someone that can offer you a satisfying and healthy relationship? _____

_____

_____

_____

_____

Are you willing to tolerate life distress clean n' sober or without using other Self-Destructive Coping Mechanisms? Are you willing to give up your favorite Self-Destructive Coping Mechanisms? _____

_____

_____

Are you willing to give up part of your identity to change your life for the better…such as no longer being the bad-ass, the rebel, the nice one, or the one who takes care of everybody? ___

_____

_____

Are you willing to let some things go…instead of responding to everything that upsets you? _

_____

_____

Are you willing to take time-out to Think Through your situations BEFORE you respond? _

_____

_____

What ARE YOU willing to give up or change in order to bring peace and stability into your life…and to LIVE A RECOVERY LIFESTYLE? _____

_____

_____

_____

_____

Section One

The Cycle of Suffering:

"Why Is My Life So Out-of-Control?"

~ 1 ~

THE NATURE OF THE PROBLEM

1- Most of the material in this workbook is easy to understand because it's common sense and it describes things we're familiar with...the things WE DO and the things OUR PEOPLE DO. This workbook is also very interesting because it describes WHY we do the things we do and WHY WE KEEP DOING THESE THINGS when they cause us so many problems! Group Members with years of experience in treatment say they've heard a lot of this material before...but the way it's presented helps them more than anything in the past. They say it's down-to-earth and real ...that it's applied vs. clinical...and it describes them...and tells their story. This material is TRUTH, it's REALITY ...and it really applies to our lives. It's insight building, motivating, and it brings hope, peace, and acceptance of ourselves... and others.

Why we do the things we do...and why we keep doing these things when they cause us so many problems in living and so much pain and suffering.

2- Mindful - aware or paying attention to something. Mindfulness refers to a state of awareness or attention.

If you've ever thought, "Why try? Everything gets screwed up anyway." or "The world would be better off without me." or "I'm going to hurt them worse than they hurt me." or "I don't deserve any better than this."...then, you'll find this workbook to be about you. It's about our emotional ups and downs and how we try to cope with difficult feelings and life experiences. It's about the problems in living caused by our Self-Destructive Coping Behaviors.

We'll begin this journey with a discussion of "The Nature of the Problem." We'll first learn what causes most of our problems and later, what to do about them. This journey is NOT going to be a joyride. It'll be uncomfortable at times, difficult at other times, but interesting most of the time. You'll come to great emotional insight and psychological growth...and you'll be motivated to return to...or to stay on the Recovery Path. Hope, peace, and acceptance will come out of this study. Many people have described this material to be life-changing. They say it's REALITY and makes great sense.[1] Many people say, "It's how I am! It's all about me!" This material describes why we do the things we do! So, know this study may be emotionally hard, but know it'll be well worth your time and effort. I write this HOPING IT'LL BE A TURNING POINT FOR YOU.

You can make this an academic or educational study by just reading the material and thinking A LITTLE about it, OR you can make it a MAJOR THERAPEUTIC STUDY by TAKING TIME TO REFLECT on the material and by SERIOUSLY and THOUGHTFULLY COMPLETING the worksheets and answering the questions. You can increase your benefit by PRACTICING and REMAINING MINDFUL[2] of these principles and concepts AND by applying them to your life as you learn them.

"Answers" and comments about many of the workbook questions can be found in the text following each question. If these answers or comments lead you to new answers, take the time to write them down. The more effort you put into this study, the more you'll learn, the deeper you'll process the material, and the greater the therapeutic benefit! Don't miss the information in the margins, that's good stuff, too! Please note that this first chapter is an overview. Many concepts are just introduced...but, they'll be discussed in detail throughout the workbook. Don't worry if it all doesn't make sense at first. It will as you read on! Enough preamble! Let's get on with the program!

Figure 1.A:[3] **The Two Parts of Emotional Mind**

3- **The "1" in "Figure 1.A"** means it's a figure for Chapter 1.
The "A" means it's the first figure for the chapter.
The second figure for Chapter 1 will be "Figure 1.B." The third will be "Figure 1.C" and so on.

4- Incompetent - (in-com-pet-ant) - not capable, competent, or able...not having what it takes to succeed.

5- Her landmark works include the *Skills Training Manual for Treating Borderline Personality Disorder* (1993) and the companion text, *Cognitive-Behavioral Treatment of Borderline Personality Disorder* (1993). She has authored many books and articles on DBT. A great deal of information about her publications can be found on the internet.

6- Psyche – (sigh-key) - psychological mind.

7- Dr. Linehan uses the term "Reasonable Mind" and I use the term "Rational Mind" because... I've forgotten why. I'm sure I had a good reason at the time!

8- "Emotion-Driven Thoughts" is a new term introduced in this DBT-CBT program. It describes the types of thoughts that come out of Emotional Mind. These thoughts have been described in the Cognitive-Behavioral Therapy (CBT) literature over the years.

Raw Emotions	Emotion- Driven Thoughts
Depression	The world would be better off without me.
Hopelessness	Nothing ever works out. Why try? I'd be better off drinking again (drugging, cutting, overdosing...).
Desperation	I should just kill myself and get it over with.
Anger / Rebellion	Screw everyone, screw everything. I'm gonna do as I please.
Anger / Disgust	I'm leaving. I don't care what happens.
Anger / Aggression	He deserves to have the taste slapped right out of his mouth and I'm just the one to do it.
Alone / Misunderstood	No one understands me.
Aloneness / Unloved	No one really loves me.
Worthlessness	I'm a worthless piece of crap.
Worthlessness / Undeserving	I don't deserve any better than this.
Worthlessness / Defective	No other man/woman would ever want me.
Despair / Helplessness	I'll never get over this. There's no fixing this.
Incompetent[4] / Defective	I'm such a screw-up. I screw everything up.
Hopelessness / Defeated	My life is over. Things will never be the same.
Sadness / Grief	I can never love anyone else.
Anxiety / Loneliness	I can't deal with being alone.
Desperation	A bad relationship is better than no relationship.
Shame / Guilt	They'll never forgive me.

The Two Parts of Emotional Mind

Marsha M. Linehan, Ph.D., the founder of DBT,[5] discussed three states of mind that make up the human psyche:[6] Emotional Mind, Reasonable Mind,[7] and Wise Mind. Because the Nature of the Problem lies in Emotional Mind, this will be our starting point. Figure 1.A shows the two parts of Emotional Mind - RAW EMOTIONS and EMOTION-DRIVEN THOUGHTS.[8] When we're upset, we're troubled by our Raw Emotions AND the Emotion-Driven Thoughts that run through our minds!

RAW EMOTIONS ARE FEELINGS...like feeling angry, depressed, scared, anxious, rejected, lonely, empty, confused, frustrated, abused, and used.

Check out Figure 1.B below. Highlight or circle the emotions you've experienced during the last 2-3 months.

What are some of the most difficult Raw Emotions you experience? _____

_____

_____

9- A case could be made that some of the "emotions" listed in this figure are not really emotions. However, they're listed here because they express how we feel at times. Consider these to be examples of Raw Emotions.

Figure 1.B: A List of Negative Emotions[9]

Humbled Moody Sad
Unhappy Self-Pity
Despondent
Disheartened
Disappointed
Discouraged
Depressed Disgusted

Undeserving Worthless
Weak Helpless Unable
Hopeless Defeated
Broken Like a Failure
Incapable "Less Than"
Defective

Misunderstood Vulnerable
Disrespected Picked-On
Singled-Out Mistreated
Used Abused Hurt
Wounded Victimized
Terrorized

Not Trusted
Pushed Away Alone
Lonely Uncared For
Unloved Rejected
Dumped Abandoned
Betrayed Alienated
Withdrawn Isolative

At Fault Blamed Guilty
Ashamed Shameful
Sorrowful Regretful

Lifeless Empty
Meaningless Lost
Worn-Out Tired "Done"
Had Enough Used Up
Beaten Exhausted
Miserable Anguished
Tormented

Unfocused At-a-Loss
Lost Mindless
Bewildered Confused
Disillusioned Disbelief
Shocked Stunned Numb
Unreal Dissociated

Apprehensive Uneasy
Uncertain Concerned
Worried Preoccupied
Anxious Insecure Needy
Troubled Unstable
Unsafe Scared Fearful
Panicky Terrorized

Stressed-Out
Burdened Pressured
Overwhelmed Exasperated
Out-of-Control
Desperate Crazy-like
Freakin'-Out
Manic Frantic

Restless Impatient
Uncomfortable
Irritated Frustrated
Aggravated Agitated

Resentful Bitter Mad
Angry Pissed Off Furious
Hatred Hostility Rage
"Hot" About to Go Off

Willful Reckless
About to Lose It
Mean-Spirited
Wanting Revenge
Aggressive Destructive
Suicidal Self-Harmful
Violent Dangerous

Bored Uncaring
Unmotivated Stuck
Boxed-In Constrained
Restrained Giving Up
Apathy Paralyzed

Gullible Made Fun Of
Not Taken Seriously
Ridiculed Manipulated
Stupid Foolish
Embarrassed Humiliated

Mistrusting Defensive
Guarded Paranoid
Suspicious Jealousy

Unattractive
Undesirable Fat Ugly
Damaged

Intimidated
Threatened
Plotted Against
Persecuted
Pushed Provoked

10- Emotion-Driven Thoughts are sentences. "Suicidal" is not an Emotion-Driven Thought. It's a feeling. An Emotion-Driven Thought related to feeling suicidal, would be "I'd be better off dead." or "Suicide is my only option."

11- Like "I can't do anything right.", "Life sucks and then you die.", "People only care about themselves.", and "Everybody treats me like crap."

12- When we're in a positive mood, our Emotion-Driven Thoughts tend to be positive. For instance, "I can do anything I put my mind to." or "Things are looking up for me!"

13- Like "I'll get my revenge. This isn't over.", "I'm going to tell her husband how she flirts with everyone.", and "I'll get so plastered, I won't be thinking about her or anything else."

Emotion-Driven Thoughts are thoughts that are "DRIVEN BY" or are CAUSED BY our emotions. They're SENTENCES[10] that run through our mind...though sometimes we say them aloud. When we're upset, our Emotion-Driven Thoughts often express negative beliefs about ourselves, others, and life in general...[11,12] AND how we FEEL LIKE responding.[13] If we're depressed, we may have thoughts like, "Life sucks. I'd be better off dead." or "Why try? Nothing ever gets better." If we're angry because someone really hurt us, we may think, "This isn't over. I'll get even." or "I'm going to knock the crap out of her the next time I see her." If we're angry with ourselves for a big mistake, we may say, "I've got to be the STUPIDEST person alive. I screw EVERYTHING up." If we're angry someone isn't meeting our needs fast enough or well enough, we may have thoughts like, "He's doing this on purpose. I'll do the same thing to him next time he wants something." or "My needs aren't important to others." or "Nobody cares about me or what I want."

Our Emotion-Driven Thoughts are based on OUR BELIEFS and IMPULSES IN-THE-MOMENT...in the EMOTIONAL moment! Sometimes, they're based on truth and the way things really are...BUT USUALLY, they're not! THEY'RE JUST HOW WE FEEL BECAUSE WE'RE UPSET. We tend to have CERTAIN Emotion-Driven Thoughts that WE SAY when we're upset. We use some of the same ones over and over. They're OUR BELIEFS and UNDERSTANDINGS...and how WE THINK and what WE FEEL LIKE DOING when WE'RE UPSET.

List some Emotion-Driven Thoughts you have when you're depressed. Make sure they're sentences! _____

_____

_____

14- Irritation – (ear-it-tay-shin) – when we're very bothered by things.

15- Distress – (dis-stress) – stress that causes us to be upset. When we're distressed, we're UPSET!

APPLICATION: Why Do We Become So Overwhelmed with Our Emotions?

One reason is that we're experiencing TWO SOURCES OF IRRITATION[14] AT ONCE! When we're in an emotional state, we're HIT BY RAW EMOTIONS AND EMOTION-DRIVEN THOUGHTS. That's double the distress![15] THEY FEED OFF EACH OTHER, TOO! For instance, the more depressed we become, the more hopeless and depressing our thoughts become. As our mind fills with depressing and hopeless thoughts, WE FEEL MORE DEPRESSED AND HOPELESS! This works the same for other emotions. Consider how anger and jealousy build up. The more we think about what happened, the angrier we get. The angrier we get, the more our angry thoughts intensify and rage through our mind...AND the madder and more jealous we become. Our angry feelings and thoughts feed off each other and become more and more intense...UNTIL WE GET CONTROL OR WE BLOW!

To make things even more challenging, when we're in an emotional state, we're NOT ONLY dealing with here-and-now stuff, but WE'RE ALSO HIT BY UNRESOLVED[16] EMOTIONS and SITUATIONS FROM THE PAST that are brought up by the current situation. That makes things even worse!

> FURTHER, when we're upset, we experience MANY EMOTIONS AT ONCE. For instance, if we're going through a break-up, we tend to feel depressed and angry. Right? Well, what about feeling lonely, lost, betrayed, anxious, worried, rejected, empty, abandoned, mistrusting, suspicious, frustrated, and overwhelmed! We're often FULL OF EMOTIONS when we're going through a difficult time. Sometimes we get so overwhelmed by our emotions that we're in a state of emotional upheaval.[17] We CAN'T THINK STRAIGHT. We may not even know how we're feeling. We may feel like we're going to FALL APART or EXPLODE. We're SO FULL OF FEELINGS that our MIND IS RACING...thoughts are FLYING THROUGH OUR HEAD. We're so AGITATED,[18] so FULL, so PRESSURED, and SO DESPERATE FOR RELIEF.

APPLICATION: What Happens if We Act on These Intense Feelings?

What do you think happens when we allow Emotional Mind to control or drive our behavior when we're upset? What is our behavior like? What are we likely to do? ___

_____

_____

_____

When we're filled with difficult emotions, we often act on them through Emotional Mind. We're desperate for relief so we do things that provide IMMEDIATE RELIEF. We often do the things that have worked for us in the past. Some of our "favorite" or most preferred coping responses include drugs and alcohol; suicide attempts, gestures, and threats; cutting ourselves; overtaking medication; walking off and abandoning the situation; withdrawal; and verbal and physical aggression.[19]

What other types of Self-Destructive Coping Behaviors can you think of? _____

_____

_____

See Figure 1.C for "A List of Common Self-Destructive Coping Behaviors."

16- Unresolved – (un-ree-zolved) – not fully dealt with yet!

Why do our emotions become so overwhelming?
1. Because we're hit by emotions AND Emotion-Driven Thoughts. These two sources of distress feed off each other, too!
2. Because our current emotional state is driven by the here-and-now situation AND unresolved situations from the past.
3. Because of the number of underlying emotions. We're not hit by just one unpleasant feeling...but sometimes 10-20 AT ONCE! Together, these three things make for a triple whammy of distress! No wonder we get so overwhelmed! NO WONDER WE FEEL SO OUT-OF-CONTROL!

17- Upheaval – (up-heave-ull) – when everything is all messed up and Out-of-Order! When our lives become totally messed up for awhile.

18- Agitated - (add-juh-tay-tid) – when we're so bothered or disturbed by something that we feel restless and emotionally pressured to do something. We're stirred up and energized to respond.

19- Verbal and physical aggression includes temper tantrums, being verbally abusive or hostile, telling people off, and physically harming people, animals, property, and objects.

Sometimes, we just react to the pressure of the emotional moment. We don't Think Things Through, we just react. At times, we "think about" a situation and DECIDE how to respond, but what we come up with is a VERY BAD IDEA!

20 - Passive-aggressive behaviors express anger in indirect ways. They're not direct or upfront. For instance, we may "accidently" do things or "forget" to do things because we're angry with someone and we want to get even! If we're mad at our spouse for not spending time with us, we may "forget" to tell them that the time for their meeting was changed or we may "accidently" spill coffee all over their hand-outs for the meeting. If we're mad at a friend, we may "accidently" tell a secret.

21- Some people pride themselves on ALWAYS speaking their mind. Truly, part of being assertive is choosing when and when not to be assertive! ALWAYS speaking our mind is an Emotion-Driven Behavior because we do it even when it's NOT in our best interests. We're not Thinking Through Before We Do...we're just saying something because we feel like it!

Figure 1.C: A List of Common Self-Destructive Coping Behaviors

Avoidance	Denial Flight into Activity (staying too busy to think about personal matters) Oversleeping Procrastination Stuffing Our Emotions Walking Off - Leaving Withdrawal - Isolation
Eating Disorders	Anorexia Bulimia Overeating
Passive-Aggressive Behavior[20]	"Accidents" (accidently doing something on purpose!) "Forgetting" (forgetting on purpose!) "Harmless" Jokes Procrastination Sarcasm - Talking Behind Someone's Back – Gossiping
Physical Aggression	Towards People, Animals, Objects, and Property
Self-Harmful Behavior	Self-Mutilation (cutting, burning, scratching, hair pulling, and other forms of self-inflicted body damage) Suicide Threats Suicide Gestures Suicide Attempts
Substance Abuse / Dependence	Alcohol Illegal Drugs Over-the-Counter Drugs Prescription Drugs
Vengeful Acts	Taking Revenge (getting even...or ahead!)
Verbal Aggression	"Always Speaking My Mind"[21] – Bluntness (saying what we think without trying to find a positive way to say it) Hostile - Threatening Remarks Saying Hurtful Things to Others Telling People Off Screaming Fits - Temper Tantrums
Other	Criminal Acts (stealing, property damage, setting fires, etc.) Gambling Habitual Lying High Risk Behavior (high speed driving, "playing chicken," road rage, etc.) Overshopping – Spending Money We Don't Have Promiscuity (sleeping around!) – Affairs Rebound Relationships Taking a Stand on Everything! - Confronting Everything! Being the Drama King or Queen Getting Involved in Other People's Problems

From "Out-of-Control: A Dialectical Behavior Therapy (DBT) – Cognitive-Behavioral Therapy (CBT) Workbook for Getting Control of Our Emotions and Emotion-Driven Behavior" - Copyright © 2009 by Melanie Gordon Sheets, Ph.D. (www.dbt-cbt-workbook.com)

THE NATURE OF THE PROBLEM:
We seek quick relief from our upsetting emotions…and the things we choose to do to feel better end up causing us more and more problems!

THE NATURE OF THE PROBLEM is the things we do to FEEL BETTER end up causing us MORE PAIN AND SUFFERING. We're hurting…we're desperate for relief…and we're dealing with our situation through Emotional Mind. We make an EMOTIONAL DECISION how to respond, NOT A RATIONAL ONE! We follow our heart and not our head! We do impulsive, irrational, and self-destructive things. The consequences of our Emotion-Driven Behavior[22] often result in serious problems across many areas of our life…and MANY LOSSES…and LONG-TERM pain and suffering.

22- Emotion-Driven Behavior is driven by our emotions. It occurs when we act on our emotions without Thinking Through Before We Do. Group Members describe this behavior to be impulsive, irrational, poorly planned, of poor judgment, selfish, childish, hurtful, destructive, and Out-of-Control.

23- Emotion-Driven Coping Behaviors are coping mechanisms that are driven by our emotions. They're not well thought out or rational. We do them because they help us to feel better NOW…and since it feels good, we do it! They're also called Emotion-Driven Coping Responses and Self-Destructive Coping Behaviors.

24- "Probs/Conseq's" on Figure 1.D stands for "problems and consequences."

25- The Original Problem hasn't been dealt with so, it's still there. Our problems don't go away because we don't deal with them! We must deal with them effectively or at least adequately to get them to go away…or to get passed or through them!

Emotion-Driven Coping Behaviors[23] ARE coping mechanisms because they provide us relief…and often immediate relief. However, we have hell to pay because of their consequences. They make our CURRENT PROBLEMS WORSE and cause us even MORE PROBLEMS. They're coping mechanisms, just some very SELF-DEFEATING ones! When you're really upset, which Self-Destructive Coping Behaviors do you do? _____

_____

_____

What sort of problems have these coping mechanisms caused you? _____

_____

_____

If you continue to use these coping mechanisms, what other life problems might they cause? _____

_____

APPLICATION: "The Cycle of Suffering"

Check out Figure 1.D, "The Cycle Of Suffering." This cycle starts when Something Happens to upset us (noted by *). In response, we do Self-Destructive Coping Behavior** to feel better. Then, painful consequences and life problems[24] result.*** What comes next? _____

WE USUALLY FEEL A WHOLE LOT WORSE! Not only are we STILL UPSET about the ORIGINAL SITUATION[25] because we haven't effectively dealt with it yet…BUT, we're ALSO UPSET about the CONSEQUENCES and PROBLEMS OUR COPING BEHAVIOR HAS JUST CAUSED! That's double the distress and we now feel WORSE. So, what do we usually do now? _____

_____

We KEEP USING Emotion-Driven Coping Responses TO TRY TO feel better! Then what happens? _____

_____

We usually have EVEN MORE negative consequences and life problems.

Do you see a pattern? What do you notice? _____

_____

It's called "The Cycle of Suffering" because the more times we do Self-Destructive Coping Behaviors, the worse our problems become… and the worse we feel. Because we still feel bad, we do self-destructive behaviors again. Our problems worsen even more… and we feel even worse than before. The worse we feel, the more desperate we are for relief. The cycle continues and we suffer through the pain and destruction. This suffering is… "The Tragedy of the Problem."

Figure 1.D: "The Cycle of Suffering"

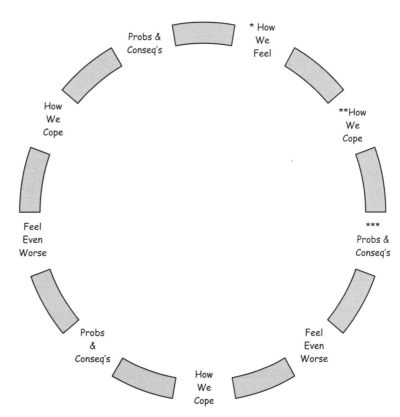

If we continue in the cycle of **UPSETTING LIFE EVENT → FEEL BAD → DESTRUCTIVE COPING → NEGATIVE CONSEQUENCES → FEEL WORSE**…what will be the result of this pattern over time? _____

_____

_____

"The Tragedy of the Problem"

Over time, things get worse and worse in our lives. When we keep responding to normal human emotions in desperate and destructive ways, we end up causing ourselves more and more problems. Our problems multiply and intensify as this cycle runs its course. Most, IF NOT ALL the important parts of our lives are affected. We find our lives filled with problems and the things we cherish messed up or destroyed. We become overwhelmed by the pain of our losses. This Cycle of Suffering is THE TRAGEDY OF THE PROBLEM. It's a tragedy when precious lives are destroyed by desperate attempts to deal with painful life situations and events.

Have you ever been in a Cycle of Suffering? Mention how your experiences have fit this pattern? _____

_____

_____

Once we're in the Cycle of Suffering, how do we get it to stop? _____

_____

_____

This cycle continues until it stops...until we stop it or others stop it for us.

The Cycle of Suffering continues...UNTIL WE STOP our destructive behaviors...or WE ARE STOPPED. If we DON'T STOP ON OUR OWN, Something Will Happen and WE WILL BE STOPPED! Something like being jailed, hospitalized, or otherwise institutionalized! Either we control ourselves or we WILL BE controlled by others!

26- We often change our behavior because of relationship pressure... like "Either lose that behavior or lose me. I'm done. Make your choice." Sometimes, it's a cherished profession or job. Sometimes, it's "freedom vs. locked up." Sometimes, it's a major health problem and the choice is "life or death" or "pain or no pain." Sometimes, our addictions become so severe or go on for so long that our health is jeopardized. Consider liver problems from drinking. It comes down to a choice between "life and death." With alcohol related pancreatitis, it's a choice between "severe pain or not." Think about someone who becomes pre-diabetic due to their weight. They're faced with a choice "lose weight or get diabetes." We're VERY willful creatures and we often push things so far...for so long...that we're faced with awful consequences. We're FORCED to change our behavior. It's like we don't have a choice anymore and the decision is MADE FOR US.

What do you think causes people to stop it on their own? _____

_____

_____

SOME people stop when they're faced with a demand like, "You STOP or I'll leave." They're faced with a choice to continue their behavior or to lose something precious and dear to them.[26] Some stop when they become totally disgusted with themselves and they realize it's their behavior they're so disgusted with! This moment of utter disgust becomes their Turning Point.

If you haven't already reached your Turning Point, how bad will things have to get before you become committed to recovery? _____

_____

_____

Have you ever been so entirely disgusted with yourself that you made a major life change because of it? If so, explain. _____

_____

_____

OUCH, I know these questions hurt! But wouldn't it be nice to STOP NOW before things have to spiral completely Out-of-Control and the consequences become so severe that you're FORCED to change? If you've already reached the point of life spiraling completely Out-of-Control, DON'T YOU WISH YOU WOULD STOP YOURSELF NOW before things get even worse? YES / NO

> We all know WISHING and DOING ARE TWO DIFFERENT THINGS!
> WE WISH WISHING WOULD WORK THOUGH! Gladly, this workbook will help us
> reach the point of WISHING things would change and it'll give us the tools for
> DOING what we need to do to make those changes. It'll help turn WISHING into
> ACTION! So, keep reading! This workbook will help you to REACH YOUR
> TURNING POINT...AND TO MOVE ON DOWN THE RECOVERY PATH.

APPLICATION: A Detailed Look at the Cycle of Suffering

Look at Figure 1.E. As you review it, HIGHLIGHT things you've experienced that have been part of your Cycles of Suffering. This figure presents a list of common events, feelings, and behaviors that drive the Cycle of Suffering. Common consequences of our actions are also listed. These consequences are EVENTS that keep the cycle going, too.

How to Make Sense of Figure 1.E

Column 1. The cycle begins with upsetting "Events or Situations." Some common trigger events for "The Cycle of Suffering" are listed.

Column 2. This column notes "How We Feel" because of an upsetting event or situation.

Column 3. "How We Cope" lists some common Emotion-Driven Coping Behaviors we do to TRY to quickly relieve our distress and pain.

Column 4. The "Consequences" column lists the type of problems we commonly experience because of our Self-Destructive Coping Responses.

Column 5. "How We Feel" lists the feelings we STILL HAVE because of the event we haven't dealt with yet...AND the feelings we have due to the negative consequences of our Destructive Coping Behavior.

Column 6. "How We Cope" lists some common Emotion-Driven Coping Responses we do to TRY to relieve upsetting feelings about the event AND our consequences.

Column 7. "Consequences" lists the type of problems we experience because of our continued use of Self-Destructive Coping Mechanisms.

Column 8. "How We Feel" lists the feelings we still have about the event AND the increasingly severe consequences of our Destructive Coping Responses.

Check out the bottom row. The column titles aren't filled in for Columns 12-16. FILL IN THOSE TITLES following the pattern of the Cycle of Suffering in Columns 1-8. They're there because we often repeat this cycle over and over!

Figure 1.E: A Detailed Look at the Cycle of Suffering

1. EVENTS OR SITUATIONS →→→	2. HOW WE FEEL →→→		3. HOW WE COPE →→→	4. CONSEQUENCES →→→	5. HOW WE FEEL →→→	6. HOW WE COPE →→→	7. CONSEQUENCES →→→	8. HOW WE FEEL →→→
Aloneness	Depressed	Sad	Drugs - Alcohol	Legal Problems	More Depressed	More Drugs and Alcohol	Arrested - Prison	More Depressed
Big Relationship Blow-up	Hopeless	Empty	Overtaking Prescriptions	DWI - Arrested	More Guilty	Self-Medicating at Doses Higher	Lose Probation	More Guilty
Divorce-Separate	Helpless	Suicidal	Overdosing	Lose Freedom- Go to Jail or Treatment	More Ashamed	More Severe Suicide Attempt or Self-Harm	Lose Freedom	More Ashamed
Death - Dying of Loved One	Angry	Vengeful	Suicide Attempt - Gesture - Threats	Lose Respect and Trust from Others	More Hopeless	Worse Sexual or Relationship Choices	Hospitalized	More Hopeless
Kids Taken Away	Overwhelmed		Self-Mutilation	Lose Self-Respect	Disgusted	Riskier Behavior	Hot Checks	Disgusted
Fired - Laid Off	Lost	Confused	Impulsive Sex - Affairs - Rebound Relationships	Relationship Stress	Overwhelmed	Verbal Aggression	Lose Respect and Trust of Others	Overwhelmed
Passed up for a Promotion	Anxious	Worried	Reckless Behavior	Friends and Family Pull Away	Angrier	More Frequent Physical Abuse Towards Others	Lose Self-Respect	Angrier
Money Problems	Ashamed	Guilty	Verbal Aggression	Kicked out of House	Abandoned	Leave Job- Home	Lose Relationships	Abandoned
Rejection	Alone		Being Rude - Ugly	Behind on Bills	More Empty	Criminal Acts	Lose Housing	More Empty
Betrayal	Abandoned		Temper Tantrums	Pawn Stuff	More Alone	Gambling It All Away	Lose Car	More Alone
Major Loss or Disappointment	Betrayed		Hit People	Demotion - Probation at Work	Overwhelmed	Eating Disorder Worsens	Lose Possessions	More Desperate
Major Car Problems	Abused	Used	Destroy Property	Health Problems	More Desperate		Lose Job	Totally Defeated
Major Embarrassment	Rejected		Overspending	Scars	Even More Devastated		Lose Career - Profession	Devastated or Wiped Out
Bad Health News	Scared		Gambling	Child Custody Stress	Out-of-Control		Lose Sobriety	Like a Complete Failure
Pain - Injury	Terrified		Leaving It All	Lose Recovery Time	Suicidal		Full Relapse	Bottomed-Out
Legal Problems	Worthless		Avoidance- Denial	Symptoms of Mental Illness Worsen	Like a Failure		Health Problems	Disgusted
Having to Give Something Up	Desperate		Isolation	Treatment Providers Are Disappointed			Brain Damage	Paralyzed
BAD Decision	Mistrusting		Reckless Driving	Education Problems			Family Pulls Away	Totally Out-of-Control
	Devastated		Overeating				Lose Kids	Suicidal
	Out-of-Control		Anorexia - Bulimia				Lose Support of Treatment Team	
	Defeated						Spiritual Problems	
	Paralyzed						Must Start Over	
9. HOW WE COPE	10. CONSEQUENCES		11. HOW WE FEEL	12.	13.	14.	15.	16.

How does the information in Figure 1.E reflect your life and experiences? _____

_____

_____

What things are not mentioned that you've experienced in a Cycle of Suffering? ____

_____

_____

An Overview of "The Cycle of Suffering in My Life Worksheet"

Step 1. This worksheet is easy to explain in Group...and quite a challenge to explain on paper! Read this overview and the instructions on the next page before starting your worksheet (Figure 1.G).

Step 2. Look over Figure 1.F. It's a sample of a completed "The Cycle of Suffering in My Life Worksheet."

Step 3. Notice there's room for three cycles on the worksheet. Look for the shaded subtitles "Start Cycle 1," "End Cycle 1 - Start Cycle 2," and "End Cycle 2 – Start Cycle 3."[27]

Step 4. Notice Sections 11 and 12 in the bottom row. The "How I Feel NOW" section gives space to comment on how we feel NOW because of the Cycle of Suffering in our life (at the END OF CYCLE 3). The "How I'll Cope NOW!" section provides space to comment on our plans for breaking this cycle and using Life-Enhancing Coping Mechanisms to deal with our current situations and problems (Starting New Life!).

Step 5. There are several ways to do this worksheet. Choose the option below that will make completing this worksheet the most meaningful to you and a GOOD EXAMPLE of the Cycle of Suffering in YOUR life.

Option 1. Do it like Figure 1.F. Use the three cycles to comment on an early stage, a middle stage, and the most recent stage that has led up to you feeling the way you do now. In this example, the first cycle began when the person began to use Self-Destructive Coping Behavior at age 13.[28] The second or middle cycle began in the person's early 20's (Section 5). The third or most recent cycle began in their late 20's – 30's (Section 8). They used the "How I Feel Now" Section 11 to describe how they feel in at this point in their Cycle of Suffering. It's called "Recent Times" in the shaded text. Your ages will probably be different from those given in this example.

Option 2. Use the three cycles for three specific periods in your life. For example,

27- The first cycle begins in Section 2, "How I Felt." It begins AFTER the upsetting events or situations in Section 1. **The first cycle** runs from Section 2, "How I Felt" to Section 3, "How I Tried to Cope," to Section 4, "Consequences and Problems," to Section 5, "How I Felt." It runs from feeling bad to feeling worse! **The second cycle** begins with "How I Felt" in Section 5 and goes to Section 6, "How I Tried to Cope," to Section 7, "Consequences and Problems," to Section 8, "How I Felt." **The third cycle** follows the same pattern and runs from Section 8 to Section 11. You'll notice that **each cycle starts and ends with a "How I Felt" section.** That's because we're going FULL CIRCLE ...from feeling bad to worse. So, where one cycle ends is where one cycle begins. Avoid getting confused by this detail. If it doesn't make sense to you...Let it Go... and Move On!

28- "13 YEARS OLD" is the shaded text in the "How I Felt" Section 2.

Figure 1.F: The Cycle of Suffering in My Life Worksheet (Completed)

1. EVENTS OR SITUATIONS I FACED --------------------→	2. HOW I FELT ------------------→ (Start Cycle 1)	3. HOW I TRIED TO COPE --------------------→	4. CONSEQUENCES AND PROBLEMS --------------------→
Parents divorced Grandpa died Sexual abuse New school Rejected – Bullied Loneliness	**13 YEARS OLD** Lost – Alone - Depressed Empty - Rejected Defective - Different Hurt - Undesirable Broken - Ashamed Guilty – Ugly - Stupid Overwhelmed Stressed-Out - Anxious	Pot – cigarettes - beer Friends with anyone who would accept me Sexual with almost any boy that wanted me Fighting Broke family rules Skipped school Running away Cutting on myself Bad things with friends – stealing - vandalism	Failing grades Suspended Major family conflict Teen pregnancy Depression - Panic Attacks Juvenile criminal record Probation Dropped out of school Rejected by church youth group

5. HOW I FELT ------------------→ (End Cycle 1 – Start Cycle 2)	6. HOW I TRIED TO COPE --------------------→	7. CONSEQUENCES AND PROBLEMS --------------------→	8. HOW I FELT ------------------→ (End Cycle 2 –Start Cycle 3)
IN MY EARLY 20's Depressed - Scared Like a total loser or screw-up Rejected - Alone Given up on - Abandoned Unloved - Uncared for Suicidal Ashamed Overwhelmed Angry – Lost - Empty Trapped - Stuck	Desperately married 1st husband despite his abusiveness Self-medicated – heavy drinking, drugs, and prescriptions Cutting Suicide threats Temper tantrums Gave up - Didn't try Withdrawal - Avoidance Numb-Out The affair	Became an addict, alcoholic No diploma Couldn't keep a job No car - no money 22 years old with 4 kids, tied down Trapped in a bad marriage – crazy fights and physical abuse Bad family conflict Isolated Scars Hospitalizations	**LATE 20'S – 30'S** Suicidal Trapped Desperate Helpless - Hopeless Worthless Stupid - Defective Incompetent Like a total screw-up Alone - Empty Overwhelmed Unloved ANGRY Pent-up - Anxiety -Worry

9. HOW I TRIED TO COPE --------------------→	10. CONSEQUENCES AND PROBLEMS --------------------→	11. HOW I FEEL NOW ----------------------→ (End Cycle 3)	12. HOW I'LL COPE NOW (Starting New Life!)
Drugs - Alcohol Overdosing Suicide Attempts Cutting Overeating, Bulimia Yelling – Hitting Kids Withdrawing in bed Hospitalizations Gave up – Didn't try Lying – Stealing Throwing fits	Possession – DWI arrests Jail time – Probation Kids taken away Hospitalizations Bad memory Health problems – Scars Divorces Many short relationships Lost everything Family pushed me away Very overweight	**RECENT TIMES** Depressed - Suicidal Disgusted with life Worthless – Hate myself Undesirable - Ugly Like a total failure Angry - Bitter - Resentful Racing thoughts – Worry Anxiety - Panic Guilt – Shame Empty – Unfulfilled Miserable	I MUST TRY NEW ways, Life-Enhancing ways. I can no longer do things the old self-destructive way. It's killing me and making me miserable. I used to think these things made me happy. They've only made me miserable and worse off. I will cope by AA, painting again, therapy, baths, the internet, and by reading this workbook over and over!

37

Figure 1.G: The Cycle of Suffering in My Life Worksheet

1. EVENTS OR SITUATIONS I FACED ----------------------→	2. HOW I FELT ------------------→ (Start Cycle 1)	3. HOW I TRIED TO COPE -------------------→	4. CONSEQUENCES AND PROBLEMS -------------------→
5. HOW I FELT -------------------→ (End Cycle 1 – Start Cycle 2)	6. HOW I TRIED TO COPE -------------------→	7. CONSEQUENCES AND PROBLEMS ----------------------→	8. HOW I FELT ------------------→ (End Cycle 2 –Start Cycle 3)
9. HOW I TRIED TO COPE -------------------→	10. CONSEQUENCES AND PROBLEMS ----------------------→	11. HOW I FEEL NOW ----------------------→ (End Cycle 3)	12. HOW I'LL COPE NOW (Starting New Life!)

From "Out-of-Control: A Dialectical Behavior Therapy (DBT) – Cognitive-Behavioral Therapy (CBT) Workbook for Getting Control of Our Emotions and Emotion-Driven Behavior" - Copyright © 2009 by Melanie Gordon Sheets, Ph.D. (www.dbt-cbt-workbook.com)

29- Specific periods may be when you were in your 20's, 30's and 40's. You could also do it for other age spans, like from age 15-20, 21-23, and 24-28. The time periods don't have to be the same number of years. The purpose is to choose the age groupings that best represent stages or cycles in YOUR LIFE. So, tailor this worksheet to reflect YOUR life.

30- Like from business owner...to a manager at someone else's business... to a non-management position at another job.

31- In this case, list the events or situations that triggered your relapse in Section 1. Then, complete the worksheet for the cycle or cycles that followed.

32- If you're having a hard time identifying the feelings you had, review the list of negative emotions in Figure 1.B.

33- Note that this marks the end of one cycle and the start of another! You've gone full circle... from feeling bad... to feeling worse!

use a cycle for each 2, 5, or 10-year period in your life.[29] You can also break the cycles down by relationships, like 1st, 2nd, and 3rd marriage. You can do it by types of jobs,[30] what town you lived in, etc.

Option 3. Start the worksheet based on a time when you were in recovery and things were going pretty good for you AND THEN...Something Happened and you relapsed AND suffered great losses and consequences...and go from there.[31]

Option 4. Any way that's meaningful to you!!!!

SKILL BUILDER: Using "The Cycle of Suffering in My Life Worksheet"

Step 1. Make a copy of the blank worksheet for your personal use.

Step 2. Decide how you want to do it...which of the four options just discussed will you choose? Base your decision on how to make it meaningful to you and how best to show the Cycle of Suffering in your life.

Step 3. In the "Events or Situations I Faced" section, list the difficult ones which triggered your upsetting emotions and Destructive Coping Behavior.

Step 4. Take a few minutes and reflect on the feelings you had that triggered your Self-Defeating Coping Responses. List them in the "How I Felt" Section 2.[32]

Step 5. In the "How I Tried to Cope" Section 3, list the Self-Destructive Coping Behaviors you did to TRY TO NUMB-OUT your painful feelings.

Step 6. In the "Consequences and Problems" Section 4, list ones that were caused by the Self-Destructive Coping Behaviors you did. Be honest!

Step 7. In the "How I Felt" Section 5, list how you felt as a result of those negative consequences AND the unresolved problems and emotions you were still running from.[33]

Step 8. Complete the remainder of the worksheet following the steps above until you reach the "How I Feel NOW" Section 11.

Step 9. In the "How I Feel NOW" section, list how you feel NOW because of this Cycle of Suffering. If you're in recovery, life is no doubt much better now than it was at the end of the Cycle of Suffering...so in this section, comment on how you felt at the end of the cycle when you felt really bad.

Step 10. In the "How I'll Cope Now!" section, list the LIFE-ENHANCING Coping Mechanisms you'll use to deal with the difficult emotions you have NOW... so you can break this Cycle of Suffering. If you're in recovery now, make note of the Life-Enhancing Coping Behaviors you used early in recovery.

What was that worksheet like for you to do...how did it hit home? Also comment on what you learned and how you can use this information to better your life. _____

_____

_____

_____

_____

If you continue to respond to life using Emotion-Driven Coping Responses, what will your life be like in the next year? What additional losses and problems might you experience? _____

_____

_____

Each cycle goes from feeling bad to feeling worse! We just thought things were bad in the early days of the Cycle of Suffering.

What additional losses and problems might you experience in 5 years? _____

_____

_____

What additional losses and problems might you experience in 10 years? _____

_____

_____

> This material can be VERY painful to process. Most folks feel emotionally drained at this point. However, the GIFT IS...THIS MATERIAL CAN BE LIFE-CHANGING. It's Real Life. It's truth...and it'll lead to understandings that will help us on our journey to and through recovery. Understanding why we do the things we do and what we can do to Get Control of our Out-of-Control lifestyle...will give us the HOPE we need and the KNOWLEDGE and SKILLS to LIVE RECOVERY! The light at the end of this journey is THE PEACE that comes from UNDERSTANDING, HEALING, and RECOVERY. I hope this study touches you in a way that motivates you to stay on the Recovery Path or to turn towards that path to be...ON THE ROAD TO RECOVERY!

~~~~~~~~ CHAPTER REVIEW ~~~~~~~

1. What are the two parts of Emotional Mind? _____

_____

2. What are Emotion-Driven Thoughts? Describe what they are rather than just giving examples. _____

_____

_____

The Nature of the Problem is the things we do to feel better end up causing us many more problems. Our Emotion-Driven Coping Responses are an Emotional Reflex and sometimes an emotional explosion. They're the fuel for the Cycle of Suffering. This cycle of pain and suffering is… "The Tragedy of the Problem."

3. List some Destructive Emotion-Driven Thoughts you have when you're upset. _____

_____

_____

_____

4. What are three reasons why our emotions can become so overwhelming? _____

_____

_____

_____

_____

5. What are Emotion-Driven Coping Responses? Describe what they are rather than giving examples of specific ones. _____

_____

_____

6. Are Emotion-Driven Coping Responses the same thing as Self-Defeating Coping Responses and Emotion-Driven Coping Mechanisms? YES / NO

7. List eight types of Self-Destructive Coping Behaviors.

1. _____   2. _____
3. _____   4. _____
5. _____   6. _____
7. _____   8. _____

34- The snowballing effect: Do you remember the Suave shampoo commercial, "She told two friends, who told two friends, who told two friends" and quickly about two dozen people had been told?! Our Self-Defeating Coping Behavior affects several areas of our lives which affects several other areas...and several more…

35- Avalanche – (ave-uh-lanch) – when the snow on a mountain comes tumbling down with great force…and wipes out everything in its path.

36 – Strewn – (st-ruin) - scattered about and in pieces.

37- Debris - (duh-bree) - the rubble, the pieces of destroyed things, the broken and scattered parts…like the debris around a train wreck.

The Nature of the Problem lies in our use of EMOTION-DRIVEN Coping Responses to deal with life issues, stressors, and events. These Destructive Coping Behaviors cause many more problems for us…far beyond the problems we had in the first place. We feel worse…and use Destructive Coping Responses even more…and we end up with severe problems across many areas of our life. In Group, I once described the Cycle of Suffering to be like a "snowballing effect"[34] where one problem leads to more problems…and these problems lead to even more problems. Members said it's more like "an avalanche,"[35] and many age 40+ men, especially our veterans, said it's more like "a train wreck." It's wild how often "train wreck" is mentioned. It's obviously an expression of the devastation our Destructive Coping Responses cause. Over time, our problems snowball, then avalanche, and everything we've loved and valued is destroyed…and the pieces of our life are strewn[36] about like the debris[37] of a train wreck. That is a tragedy…the Tragedy of the Problem.

8. Describe the Nature of the Problem in your own words. _____

_____

_____

_____

9. Describe the Cycle of Suffering in your own words. _____

_____

_____

_____

_____

10. What are the five parts of the first cycle in the Cycle of Suffering?

   1. _____

   2. _____

   3. _____

   4. _____

   5. _____

11. What's my hope for you? What's the purpose behind this workbook? _____

_____

_____

_____

12. What's YOUR hope for this study? _____

_____

_____

_____

~~~ For Reflection ~~~

FOR REFLECTION:
Take a few moments to reflect on this chapter.
Some questions are listed in the margin on the next page to guide your reflection.
Feel free to reflect on whatever your heart brings to mind.

_____

_____

_____

_____

_____

_____

_____

42

What are your reactions to the material? _____
_____

Which parts hit home or relate to you the most? _____
_____

Which parts have helped you the most? _____
_____

Which parts have helped you to understand yourself the most? _____
_____

How will you use this information to feel better about yourself? _____
_____

How will you use this information to improve the quality of your life...or to change how things work out for you in life? _____
_____
_____
_____

What will you do differently based on this material? _____
_____

How has this information changed the way you feel about your patterns of relapse and recovery... and your overall response to life? _____
_____
_____
_____

What does this material motivate you to do? _____
_____
_____
_____
_____
_____
_____
_____
_____
_____
_____

```
┌─────────────────────────────────────────────────────────────────────┐
│          A Little Extra: "The Concepts and Skills Tracking Sheets"    │
│   You'll find "The Concepts and Skills Tracking Sheets" at the end of chapters 1-13.  These worksheets │
│   identify the major concepts, principles, understandings, and skills presented in each chapter.  These │
│   tracking sheets are a tool to help us learn, practice, and apply this information.  They'll help us to │
│   REMEMBER what we've read and they offer us a way to TRACK our practice and Real Life use of the │
│   RECOVERY SKILLS AND UNDERSTANDINGS presented in this workbook. │
└─────────────────────────────────────────────────────────────────────┘
```

Instructions for Completing "The Concepts and Skills Tracking Sheets"

Step 1. **Make copies of** Figure 1.H and Figure 1.J before you use them. They're designed for repeat use.

Step 2. Check out Figure 1.H. It's **"The Concepts and Skills Tracking Sheet"** for Chapter 1. It lists some of the most important concepts, principles, understandings, and skills presented in Chapter 1. (In the remainder of this workbook, the "concepts, principles, understandings, and skills" listed on the tracking sheets will be called "concepts and skills" for reading ease).

Step 3. Look at Figure 1.I.1. It's **a sample of a completed tracking sheet for Week 1.**

   A. Notice the week number is written on the left hand side of the top row of the worksheet.

   B. Notice the days of the week and the dates of the month are written in, too.

   C. Notice the Rating Scale at the bottom. It's a 1-5 rating scale with a DD "Didn't Do" option.

   D. Notice the first concept or skill is "I reminded myself of the two parts of Emotional Mind." Notice this person rated himself 4 or 5 during the week when he practiced naming the two parts of Emotional Mind. HE FELT he did a "Pretty Good" or "Excellent" job of remembering this information.

   E. Notice he reminded himself of the two parts of Emotional Mind four days in a row (rated 4 or 5). Notice the "DD" ratings on 7-24 and 7-26. Those show that he didn't practice this concept on those days.

   F. Notice the ratings he gave himself on the second item, "1B." It's the one that reads, "I became aware of the different types of emotions I was experiencing today."

   G. Notice the "Notes" section at the bottom of the tracking sheet. He used this section to make comments about his use of the tracking sheet during the first week. He also wrote down his plan for making a tracking sheet notebook. It's up to you how you use the Notes section.

Step 4. Take a look at Figure 1.I.2. It's a sample of a completed **tracking sheet for Week 2.** It's completed in the same way as the Week 1 tracking sheet. Notice what he wrote in the "Notes" section. He commented on his progress and noted his therapist was impressed with his practice. He noted his plan to put extra paper in his tracking sheet notebook for journaling. He also commented on how he used the Cycle of Suffering to refuse an offer to go out partying. Obviously, he thought about how a relapse would lead to negative consequences in his life and another Cycle of Suffering.

Step 5. **Begin using "The Concepts and Skills Tracking Sheet** for Chapter 1." It's Figure 1.H.

A. When you're ready to start, fill in the week number (start with Week 1), the days of the week, and the dates. You don't have to start with Sunday...a principle in DBT-CBT is to start where you're at! So, if it's Tuesday, start your worksheet on Tuesday. The start date is totally up to you!

B. Begin to practice and use the concepts and skills listed on the tracking sheet.

C. Take note of how well you're remembering and using the concepts and skills you're learning. Use the Rating Scale to track your progress during the week.

D. At the end of Week 1, make a Week 2 tracking sheet and continue to practice! Do your best to get these recovery concepts and skills drilled into your head...so you can make a habit of using them in Real Life situations!

Step 6. Check out Figure 1.J. It's a **Concepts and Skills Tracking Sheet that's BLANK**. This tracking sheet is basically the same as the ones we've been working with in Figures 1.H, 1.I.1, and 1.I.2. The only thing that's different is YOU GET TO CHOOSE which concepts, principles, understandings, and skills to write-in and practice. Some folks use it to practice things in the workbook that are important to them, but aren't listed on the tracking sheets. They also add things they're learning and working on from other recovery programs. Some people use it to list the concepts and skills they're having trouble with...and really need to practice...liking SAYING NO when they need to... and walking away from unnecessary drama and people who are toxic to their recovery.

SOME TIPS FOR USING THESE TRACKING SHEETS

Make several copies of each tracking sheet (1.H, 1.J, and the ones for the other chapters) and put them in a notebook.

Try to PRACTICE and USE the concepts and skills for each chapter **5-7 times a week for the first two weeks** after you complete a chapter. When you're doing "pretty good" to "excellent" with the concepts and skills, begin to rate yourself **once a week**. When you continue to do well, rate yourself **once every two weeks**. When you have really learned these concepts and skills and you continue to do well...rate yourself **once a month**.

Use these tracking sheets as **a coping tool**...to focus on recovery when you really need to!

Complete these tracking sheets during a devotional, journaling, or meditation time... WHEN YOU TAKE TIME EACH DAY to remind yourself that **"Recovery Is My #1 Priority"**... and when you reflect on your daily recovery efforts and progress.

Figure 1.H: The Concepts and Skills Tracking Sheet – Chapter 1

Week # _____

Day of Week →

Date →

1A. I reminded myself of the two parts of Emotional Mind.

1B. I became aware of the different types of emotions I was experiencing today.

1C. I became aware of the Emotion-Driven Thoughts I was having today.

1D. I became aware that some of the emotions I was having today were based on here-and-now situations AND some situations from the past.

1E. I became aware of the self-destructive behaviors I DID today and THOUGHT about doing.

1F. I stated "The Nature of the Problem." I wrote it out, said it aloud, or said it in my mind.

1G. I described the Cycle of Suffering AND named off the parts that make up one cycle.

1H. I helped myself to avoid self-destructive behavior today by reminding myself of the Cycle of Suffering or the Nature of the Problem.

Notes:

RATING SCALE
5 – Did Excellent in this area today
4 – Did Pretty Good in this area today
3 – Did Alright in this area today
2 – Did Only Fair in this area today
1 – Didn't Do Well in this area today
DD – Didn't Do today

Figure 1.I.1: The Concepts and Skills Tracking Sheet (Sample - Week 1)

Week # __1__

	W	Th	F	Sat	Sun	M	T
Day of Week → / Date →	7-20	7-21	7-22	7-23	7-24	7-25	7-26
1A. I reminded myself of the two parts of Emotional Mind.	4	5	5	5	DD	5	DD
1B. I became aware of the different types of emotions I was experiencing today.	4	5	4	3	4	3	5
1C. I became aware of the Emotion-Driven Thoughts I was having today.	2	3	3	3	3	2	4
1D. I became aware that some of the emotions I was having today were based on here-and-now situations AND some situations from the past.	DD	DD	DD	2	3	DD	3
1E. I became aware of the self-destructive behaviors I DID today and THOUGHT about doing.	DD	3	4	2	3	3	4
1F. I stated "The Nature of the Problem." I wrote it out, said it aloud, or said it in my mind.	3	4	4	DD	DD	4	5
1G. I described the Cycle of Suffering AND named off the parts that make up one cycle.	2	3	4	DD	DD	3	4
1H. I helped myself to avoid self-destructive behavior today by reminding myself of the Cycle of Suffering or the Nature of the Problem.	2	3	4	2	3	3	4

Notes: Never thought I'd be doing something like this! I feel good about myself for keeping up with this. I think I'll make some copies of the tracking sheets for each chapter and put them in a notebook. I'll copy all the worksheets, too so I'll have those ready when I need them. That's all for now!

RATING SCALE
5 - Did Excellent in this area today
4 - Did Pretty Good in this area today
3 - Did Alright in this area today
2 - Did Only Fair in this area today
1 - Didn't Do Well in this area today
DD - Didn't Do today

47

Figure 1.I.2: The Concepts and Skills Tracking Sheet (Sample - Week 2)

Week # ___2___

Day of Week →	W	Th	F	Sat	Sun	M	T
Date →	7-27	7-28	7-29	7-30	7-31	8-1	8-2
1A. I reminded myself of the two parts of Emotional Mind.	DD	5	DD	DD	DD	DD	5
1B. I became aware of the different types of emotions I was experiencing today.	DD	4	5	DD	5	DD	5
1C. I became aware of the Emotion-Driven Thoughts I was having today.	3	4	4	4	5	5	5
1D. I became aware that some of the emotions I was having today were based on here-and-now situations AND some situations from the past.	4	3	4	4	5	4	4
1E. I became aware of the self-destructive behaviors I DID today and THOUGHT about doing.	4	4	5	4	5	5	5
1F. I stated "The Nature of the Problem." I wrote it out, said it aloud, or said it in my mind.	DD	4	5	DD	DD	5	DD
1G. I described the Cycle of Suffering AND named off the parts that make up one cycle.	DD	4	5	DD	DD	5	DD
1H. I helped myself to avoid self-destructive behavior today by reminding myself of the Cycle of Suffering or the Nature of the Problem.	4	4	4	5	5	5	5

Notes: I did good! Another week done! My therapist is impressed with this! She wants me to journal a little bit each day. I'll get some paper and put it in the notebook and write something in the evening before bed. I can do some of the tracking sheets at the same time. I actually thought about the Cycle of Suffering when Jennifer called and wanted to go out. I did good not to give in to her, but I wasn't honest about why! I told her I had diarrhea rather than I was fighting hard to stay on the Recovery Path! At least I said NO and stuck with it! This will count as my journal entry at the end of the week!

RATING SCALE
5 - Did Excellent in this area today
4 - Did Pretty Good in this area today
3 - Did Alright in this area today
2 - Did Only Fair in this area today
1 - Didn't Do Well in this area today
DD - Didn't Do today

48

Figure 1.J: The Concepts and Skills Tracking Sheet – Blank

Week # _____	Day of Week →	Date →													Notes:

RATING SCALE

5 – Did Excellent in this area today
4 – Did Pretty Good in this area today
3 – Did Alright in this area today
2 – Did Only Fair in this area today
1 – Didn't Do Well in this area today
DD – Didn't Do today

~ 2 ~
THE BIG PICTURE OF MY LIFE

This isn't just about Mindfulness of the things that make up the Big Picture of Our Life…it's also about learning to protect and maintain the things we cherish…and about putting the meaning back into our lives!

We're going to look at the precious parts that make up THE BIG PICTURE OF OUR LIFE. These are the things we cherish and value, the things that give life meaning. These are the treasures that get broken, scattered, and lost when our lives spiral Out-of-Control. THESE ARE THE PRECIOUS THINGS THAT GET WRECKED BY OUR RECKLESS BEHAVIORS.

SKILL BUILDER: "The Big Picture of My Life Worksheet"

Step 1. Check out Figure 2.A, "The Big Picture of My Life Worksheet."[1,2] Avoid looking at the completed one at this point (Figure 2.C)!

Step 2. In the bubbles, write things that are VERY PRECIOUS and IMPORTANT to you, things that provide meaning and satisfaction in your life, THINGS THAT MAKE UP THE BIG PICTURE OF YOUR LIFE. These may be things you've lost and you'd like to regain, like a spouse, a driver's license, a job, etc. They may be things you've never really had…but are important for recovery and life satisfaction like hobbies, a support system, or a same-sex friend. They may be other things like an education, a career, a romantic relationship, time with parents and family,[3] housing, and pets. List all the things YOU value…things that add meaning to life.

Step 3. When you're totally out of ideas, review Figure 2.B. It's a list of the cherished parts that make up the Big Picture of Our Life. Add some of these and others that come to mind…and fill ALL your bubbles!

Step 4. When you're done, see the completed worksheet.[4] Of course, yours will be different because it'll reflect the Big Picture of YOUR Life!

1- If you haven't made a copy for personal use, you might want to do so before writing on the blank one!

2- In Group, this worksheet is completed on the board while Members blurt out responses. Members complete one on their own as we go along. The material for this session is hard to "write-up" and capture on paper…so, we'll do the best we can…because the best we can is the best we CAN DO!

3- Group things of the same category, like Mom, Dad, and sister into "Family," and gardening and golf into "Hobbies and Interests." Else we'll run out of bubbles!

4- See Figure 2.C, "The Big Picture of My Life Worksheet – A Full Life."

How did this worksheet impact or affect you? _____

_____

_____

_____

_____

_____

_____

_____

Figure 2.A: The Big Picture of My Life Worksheet

The Big Picture of My Life Worksheet

Figure 2.B: The Cherished Parts in the Big Picture of Our Life

We need to be KEENLY AWARE of the things in our life that are meaningful and valuable to us… ESPECIALLY WHEN we're going through tough times. To Talk Ourselves Out Of the Self-Defeating Coping Behaviors WE REALLY WANT TO DO, we're going to need some pretty powerful reasons why we really don't want to do those things! These precious parts of our lives are OUR "HOLDS ON LIFE," the reasons to keep going and to Stand in the face of our troubles…rather than to fall into the pit of destruction.

5- List as many as you can on your own. Then see Figure 1.C in Chapter 1 for "A List of Common Self-Destructive Coping Behaviors."

Romantic Relationship	Finishing School	Hobbies and Interests	Housing
Family	Job – Career - Profession	Possessions	Utilities (water, gas, etc)
Seeing My Kids	Financial Status - Cash Flow	Legal Status	Privacy
Friends	Church and Church Relations	Transportation	Freedom
Pets	Spiritual Condition - Relationship with God	Good Brain Functioning - Intelligence - Memory	Independence – Not Controlled by Others – Make Own Decisions
More Trust from Others - Relationships Improving	Length of Sobriety - Clean Time - Habit-Free Time	Relationship with Treatment Providers – Special Programs	Self-Respect – Dignity – Integrity - Self-Esteem – Self-Worth
Reputation - Respect from Others	Emotional Stability – Peace - Well-Being	Able to Get Meds	Self-Discipline - Self-Control
Hopes - Dreams - Goals	Mental Illness Under Control	Safety – Safe Environment and Lifestyle	Having a Routine - Structure
Hope - Motivation	Physical Appearance	Health Status	Productivity - Accomplishing Things
Time	Having a Sponsor	Having a Support System	

SKILL BUILDER: Part II of "The Big Picture of My Life Worksheet"

Step 1. Be totally honest and list the Self-Destructive Coping Behaviors you've been using.[5] _____   _____

_____   _____

_____   _____

_____   _____

Step 2. Think about how Self-Destructive Coping Behaviors affect your life NOW and the effect THEY WILL HAVE if you continue to cope with your issues and problems in the same self-destructive ways.

Step 3. Using "The Big Picture of My Life Worksheet" you completed, draw an "X" over the parts of your life that'll be messed up or destroyed if you continue to use Destructive Coping Behaviors. Go bubble by bubble, one by

52

The Big Picture of My Life Worksheet

Figure 2.C: The Big Picture of My Life Worksheet – A Full Life

- Make Own Decisions - Not Controlled
- More Trust from Others
- Church and Church Friends
- Job and Career
- Nursing License
- Seeing My Kids Daily

- Long-Term Romantic Relationship
- Transport-ation
- Privacy
- Things Better with Family
- Getting Caught Up on Bills
- Legal Problems Almost Over

- Length of Recovery
- Emotional Peace and Stability
- Can have Pets
- Quality of Reputation
- Adequate Housing
- Freedom

- Quality of My Witness
- Going to School
- Possessions
- Relations with Treatment Providers
- Physical Status - Health
- Hobbies and Activities

Footnotes (left margin):

6- An example of how to do this is found in Figure 2.D, "The Big Picture of My Life Worksheet - The Tragedy of the Problem."

Many of us are good at Starting Over. It's maintaining the good start that's the problem! That's because Something Always Happens and we relapse into old ways…and the SAME THING ALWAYS happens. Our lives fall apart and we lose everything AGAIN.

Our lives feel meaningless because our behaviors have wiped-out all the things that give life meaning. It's because of OUR BEHAVIORS. It's because of the things we do. It's because of our destructive responses to life situations.

7- "The Nature of the Problem" chapter.

8- This worksheet shows that the quality of our life is based on many things. That's why we're encouraged to get involved with activities, people, and organizations. These things give our lives meaning. Without them, we feel empty.

Main body:

one, and cross out things you've already lost because of your coping behaviors and things you face losing if you continue to deal with life in the same way.[6] What did you notice? How many of your bubbles were crossed out? Were most of them? All of them? _____

_____

When we do this in Group, most Members find ALL their bubbles get crossed out or WILL GET crossed out in the near future if they continue in their ways. Many age 40+ Members comment that their lives have been wiped out MANY TIMES, they've Started Over MANY TIMES, AND AGAIN, FIND THEMSELVES AT SUCH A TIME. People are hurting. It's heartbreaking.

How many times have you Started Over? _____

Do you feel you're pretty good at Starting Over, but have trouble maintaining the good start for any significant period of time? Explain. _____

_____

_____

In your life, which situations or events have led to bottoming-out and having to Start Over? _____

_____

The Purpose of "The Big Picture of My Life Worksheet"

What does this worksheet have to do with the Big Picture of DBT-CBT and the material discussed in Chapter 1?[7] _____

_____

_____

How does this worksheet relate to "The Cycle of Suffering Worksheet"? _____

_____

We learned that "The Nature of the Problem" is the things we do to feel better end up causing us to feel worse and worse over time. "The Cycle of Suffering in My Life Worksheet" lists the consequences we suffer because of our Self-Destructive Coping Behaviors. "The Cycle of Suffering" helps us to understand how and why we're suffering so many losses and why we feel worse over time. "The Big Picture of My Life Worksheet" identifies the many things which bring meaning and value to our lives.[8] We saw what happens to these cherished parts of our life when the consequences of our behaviors hit. It shows WHAT WE LOSE OR STAND TO LOSE because of our

The Big Picture of My Life Worksheet

Figure 2.D: The Big Picture of My Life Worksheet - The Tragedy of the Problem

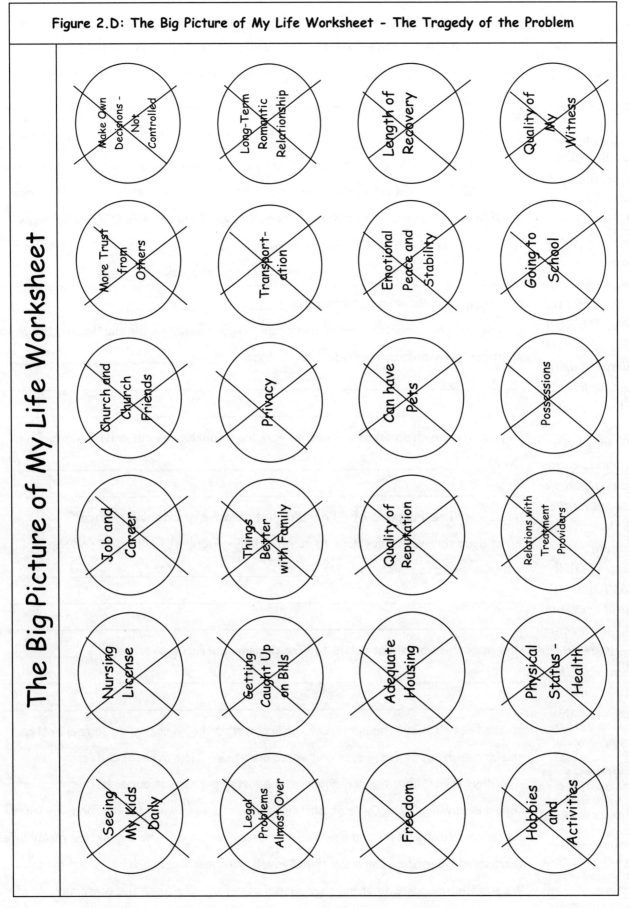

Out-of-Control behaviors. It also explains WHY LIFE LOSES ITS MEANING and we FEEL EMPTY. These concepts and worksheets help to understand WHY WE'RE SUFFERING SO MUCH and why our lives are so Out-of-Control. It has a lot to do with the way we respond to upsetting life events. Self-Destructive Coping Behaviors are just that…destructive. They destroy many, if not all, the important parts of our life.

APPLICATION: How Emotion-Driven Behaviors Affect the Big Picture of Our Life

In the upcoming sections of this chapter, we'll take a closer look at the effect certain behaviors have on the Big Picture of Our Life. We'll see how our behavior causes problems and losses in some parts of our life…and then, like a DOMINO EFFECT,[9] these problems and losses spill over to cause problems and losses in other areas of our life…until the Big Picture of Our Life is messed up or destroyed. AS YOU READ THESE UPCOMING SECTIONS, underline, circle, or highlight problems and issues you've experienced because of these Emotion-Driven Coping Behaviors.

The Impact of "Drinking Again" on the Big Picture of Our Life

Although this is about drinking again, this material applies to relapsing into drug usage as well. If you don't have substance abuse problems, read this section for educational value and apply as much as you can to your life!

> If you've been "clean n' sober" for a year or more, good things have probably began to happen in your life (a job, relationships getting better, more cash flow, adequate housing, feeling better physically, increased self-respect and self-confidence, etc).

Consider now the effect on the Big Picture of Your Life if you begin to drink or use drugs again. Which areas of your life would be negatively impacted or hurt? If you don't have substance abuse issues, respond to this question based on what you think would happen! _____
_____
_____

If we pull a drunk and show up to work smelling of alcohol or don't show up at all, we may lose our job. If we've relapsed into drinking and especially if we lose our job, our people are going to be very angry and disappointed. We immediately lose their trust… THAT WAS JUST BUILDING UP AGAIN. If this is a pattern for us, they'll be disgusted. We may get kicked out of our living situation and we might find ourselves hit with divorce papers. Our people may push us away…AGAIN. They'll probably

We feel empty because the Big Picture of Our Life empties out. We lose everything or nearly everything. That's why life feels meaningless. We've lost the things that give value and meaning to life. A Recovery Goal is to fill our lives up with meaningful people and activities. Then we'll begin to experience meaning and value in our lives. Our lives will be full and fulfilling …and will no longer seem empty and meaningless.

9- "The Domino Effect" of life losses. It's how a loss in one area causes losses and problems in other areas…AND how these losses affect other areas of our life. That's what quickly wipes out all the things we cherish. When we make a decision how to respond to a situation in our life, we need to consider the Domino Effect and not just the IMMEDIATE CONSEQUENCES.

remind us, "I told you if you started drinking again I was done. I'm done. I've had it. I'm tired of living like this. I'm not going through this again. It's over."

Have things been so bad in your life that you've heard something like that before? If so, what brought it on? _____

_____

10- Possessions – our personal belongings.

11- If we don't have money to pay for our hobbies and supplies, we can't do them.

12- Deteriorates – (dee-teary-ates) – gets worse and worse.

13- Aggravate – (ag-ruh-vate) – to stir up or bother, to make worse.

> Process this further. If we're drinking again, lose our job, make our people mad, get kicked out of the house, and get hit with divorce papers, we may feel so angry and reckless that we go out, get plastered, get behind the wheel, and get pulled over. Hello DWI or PI and spending the night in jail. If we lose our job, have legal fees and fines, and an alcohol habit to support, we don't have money to pay bills. Our utilities get turned off, we lose our housing, our car gets repossessed, and we lose many possessions.[10] If we can't pay child support, we lose the opportunity to see our kids regularly. We lose our hobbies and interests[11] because we don't have the money or lifestyle to do them anymore. We then lose enjoyment and socialization opportunities. As this Domino Effect occurs, our precious lives fall apart. People who haven't been through this…may think this is an exaggeration. Folks who've been through this…know it's a HARSH REALITY!

Whatever we did, WE did something destructive to our life. That's what happened. That's why things went to hell. It's not what anybody else did… granted they may have upset us. It's what WE did, how WE reacted, and the consequences of OUR BEHAVIOR. It's what happens when Emotional Mind drives and our better judgment takes a back seat. We wreck-out and our life becomes a total wreck.

Through this process, we become filled with anger, depression, and desperation. We lose our emotional peace. We lose our self-discipline and recovery time. Symptoms of mental illness return, we drink more, care less, and life further deteriorates.[12] We lose our self-confidence and self-respect. Our reputation suffers and our people are disappointed and upset with us. We lose motivation to take care of ourselves and our lives. Our spiritual condition deteriorates. We may develop health problems from drinking or aggravate[13] health conditions that improved during our sober time. And…the list of losses and problems lengthens and lengthens.

What things have you lost when you've relapsed into Self-Destructive Coping Behavior?

_____

_____

_____

_____

THINGS DONE IN THE HEAT-OF-THE-MOMENT…BACKFIRE.

That's the Nature of the Problem. Our problems lie in the choices we make in the Heat-of-the-Moment…when we act on the impulses and urgings of Emotional Mind.

14- It's like Emotional Surgery to remove something malignant that's causing us great pain...and is killing us. Like physical surgery, Emotional Surgery is painful, scary, and unknown territory for many of us. Both types of "surgeries" are painful and take time to heal and recover from. To live, minimize pain, and have life satisfaction, WE MUST COWBOY UP and deal with our problems... and do whatever is needed to get on and stay on the Recovery Path.

In order to heal and move on with our life, we must process and learn from where we've been, what we've done, and what we've been through. It doesn't mean we dwell there. It doesn't mean we beat ourselves up over it. It means we reflect on what happened and extract the life lessons!

15- Years ago, the bad sexually transmitted diseases (STD's) were gonorrhea and syphilis. Folks got a shot and went on with life. No real big deal other than a doctor bill and embarrassment. In the early 80's, herpes became popular! A social disgrace, no cure, painful sores now and then, but, people get to live with it! Herpes wasn't bad enough. It didn't stop us from sleeping around. (continued)

We had a problem and were really upset. We thought, "Drinking would make me feel better." or "One drink won't matter."...and we drank. Maybe we thought, "Screw it. Why try? Everything gets screwed up anyway."...and we gave up and relapsed into our preferred coping behaviors. Maybe it wasn't drinking we relapsed into, maybe it was another suicide attempt, an affair, violence, or gambling. WHATEVER WE DID to feel better...BACKFIRED...AND CAUSED US TO FEEL WORSE BECAUSE OF ALL THE PROBLEMS OUR COPING BEHAVIOR CAUSED. That's what happens when we act on the pressures and urgings of Emotional Mind. Though it's disheartening, discouraging, and overwhelming to read this...it's even more devastating to live it.

THIS DEVASTATION IS...THE TRAGEDY OF THE PROBLEM.

How does this information hit you? Does it reflect your life and experiences in any way? Explain. _____
_____
_____

I know this stuff is painful to look at and experience.[14] However, the only way to heal and recover is to confront what's going on, deal with it, and learn from it.

The Effects of an Affair on the Big Picture of Our Life

Let's look at how "The Cycle of Suffering" can play out when we act-out...and have an affair while we're married or in a "committed" relationship. If we're mad or bored or have other relationship problems and have an affair "to get our needs met," to "get even" for something, or just to have some "fun n' excitement"...once we get caught, we stand to lose so much of what we value.

What do we stand to lose because of an affair? _____
_____

Have you noticed the effect a loss in one area has on other areas? YES / NO

We certainly lose our partner's trust and respect. We may also lose our marriage or our "committed" relationship. If so, we may lose housing, time with the kids, and financial strength (less money, more expenses). If our partner stays with us, we often lose a very sweet part of our relationship. If people find out about our affair, our reputation may sour and we may get pushed out of certain social circles and positions. We lose friendships because people take sides. Our family and kids are mad at us. We may suffer spiritually and with the church family. We lose dignity and self-respect. We lose our peace and stability. We risk sexually transmitted diseases.[15] If we've continued to have sex with our spouse, we could infect them. Talk about BIG

58

(15- continued)
Now we have HIV-AIDS. There's no cure, treatment only slows the process. AIDS is killing our people...but this still hasn't stopped our risky sexual behavior. We're still a promiscuous society. How bad do things have to get before we change our behavior? We're hard-headed, willful people. I wonder if the next generation of STD's will be bad enough to change our behavior.
16- If we lose our job, we'll have money problems and we often lose our health insurance. This not only affects our physical health...but also our emotional health if we can't get our psych meds! Hello relapse!
17- The stress causes ulcers, high blood pressure, migraines, etc.

For some people, treatment facilities provide a safety net. They push life to the limit...knowing they can fall into the hands of a familiar facility and well-liked caregivers. For others, these facilities serve as a Life Repair Station, a depot where healing begins and strength is gained for a fresh start.

18- Stigma - (stig-muh) - negative beliefs shared by "society" or "most people" about something being "bad" or disgraceful ...like the stigma of mental illness or going into a psych hospital.

TROUBLE. If it's HIV, it could kill them and orphan our kids. If it's an office affair, we may be demoted, moved to a different position, or fired.[16] We lose office friendships, too. If we lose our job, we lose cash flow, insurance, and sometimes our retirement.

Consider the severe stress, problems, and losses of divorce. These are things like child custody and visitation issues, financial and housing problems, loss of possessions and pets, and major emotional and physical problems.[17] Financial problems cause many problems, too...even physical ones. If we relapse into Emotion-Driven Coping Behaviors because of the stress, we'll suffer even more losses! It's the Domino Effect again.

The Effects of Going into Rehab or a Psychiatric Hospital

For some people, treatment facilities are used as a coping mechanism. They seek time-out from problems. Some seek a place for fun, socialization, and meeting the next romantic partner! These folks tend to be in-and-out of facilities. Many don't take treatment seriously. They're there for all the wrong reasons.

For many, a treatment stay WAS NOT their goal. It's NOT what they had in mind! They ended up in treatment because they hit rock bottom and gave up on themselves. Once in treatment, it may take awhile before a SPARK OF HOPE is ignited and they believe recovery is possible for them. When this occurs, they become involved in their treatment. It becomes a time when ANOTHER TREK DOWN THE RECOVERY PATH occurs and NEW LIFE begins. Although the outcome is good, they experience negative consequences because of their stay...just like folks who are in treatment for all the wrong reasons.

What are some of the negative consequences associated with a treatment stay? _____

_____

_____

_____

For many folks, being in a treatment facility for 2-4 weeks causes many losses and problems. People lose jobs and suffer the problems of lost income, INCLUDING relationship stress. If they can't pay rent, they lose housing...and their possessions may be taken by the landlord. If "friends" and neighbors know they're gone, their possessions may be stolen. They may not see their kids, family, or friends during their stay. They often have more relationship conflict due to the stress caused by their absence. They may lose relationships. Their reputation may be damaged by gossip and the stigma[18] of treatment. They may lose self-respect. They lose privacy and

19- When folks are in jail or a treatment facility, they lose their freedom and independence. They have rules to follow and lose choices about many things, such as what they eat, when they leave, and what they do.

20- If no one cares for their pets, an agency will remove them.

21- Widespread – (wide-spread) – spread across a larger area...like more areas in the Big Picture of Our Life!

22- Jeopardized - (jep-per-dized) - put at risk for loss or harm.

23- Our people finally "have enough." They love us but they can't deal with all our drama...and all the stress and heartache our drama and problems cause them. We push them to their limit and they can no longer meet or deal with our demands. TO PROTECT THE BIG PICTURE OF THEIR LIFE, they push us away.

24- Our landlord may want us out because the blood from our cuts stained the carpet. Our family may want us out because they missed work and lost their job dealing with us, or our dad's new wife will leave if we don't leave, or they have migraines because of the stress, or their kids have nightmares of the blood all over or finding us and we looked dead.

25- Facilities don't feel equipped to deal with our severe problems. They don't want the extra work and worry, the liability and risk, or the problems and trauma our behavior caused the other residents.

26-29 - (see the next page)

freedom.[19] They lose the ability to do hobbies. They may lose their pets.[20] What losses and problems have I left off? _____

_____

> Going into treatment is an example of how THE CONSEQUENCES OF OUR BEHAVIOR CAN QUICKLY STACK UP AND MULTIPLY...and we suddenly find ourselves WITH MORE TROUBLE, ANXIETY, AND DEPRESSION. Folks come into treatment overwhelmed with life problems...and then, being in treatment results in more problems. The problems in the Big Picture of Their Life tend to become MORE INTENSE and WIDESPREAD.[21] Thank God the outcome of treatment is a blessing and well worth the sacrifices for most people.

The Effects of a Suicide Attempt on the Big Picture of Our Life

As mentioned, many folks wind up in the hospital because of a suicide attempt, be it by overdosing, cutting, hanging, gunshot, or other means. Consider how this Self-Destructive Coping Response affects the Big Picture of Our Life. Turn back to "The Cherished Parts in the Big Picture of Our Life" (Figure 2.B) and mark the areas that are likely to be seriously affected or jeopardized[22] by suicidal behavior.

If a suicide attempt is due to relationship problems, our relationship may be seriously jeopardized or lost. If suicide attempts are frequent and especially if they're just one type of Emotion-Driven Coping Behavior we do, many of our relationships may be impacted and our people may pull away from us.[23] We may also lose housing because of the trauma, drama, and heartache a suicide attempt causes the people we live with.[24] We may lose the privilege of staying in special housing programs (halfway houses, group homes, rehabs) for similar reasons.[25] We may lose jobs and careers.[26] We may cause our bodies physical damage from scarring or disfigurement[27] and damage to our brain, organs, and nerves.[28]

All in all, the losses and problems caused by suicidal and parasuicidal[29] behaviors are similar to those caused by substance abuse and being hospitalized or in rehab. Most, if not all, the areas listed in the chart would be affected, especially when suicide attempts and gestures occur frequently.

APPLICATION: When We Over-Respond to One Part of Our Life, the Effect on Other Parts Can Be Tragic

Group Members are usually hospitalized because of violence, threats of violence, suicidal behavior or threats, and cutting. Relationship problems are the biggest

60

We erupt like an ocean floor volcano. Then the tsunami[31] wave comes and wipes out everything in our lives. Total destruction. The Big Picture of Our Life is like a little village by the ocean and all the bubbles are the little huts. Everything we love, cherish, and value is in those huts. When the tsunami wave hits shore, waves of disaster follow. Everything we cherish, hut by hut, is washed away.

31- Tsunami - (sue-nah-me) - a huge ocean wave.

32- Underline, circle, or highlight!

33 - (see the next page)

reasons these behaviors occur.[30] Drugs and alcohol are often involved, but that's not what lands them in the hospital. It's WHAT THEY DO ON DRUGS AND ALCOHOL that lands them in the hospital!

Since we're Mindful of the Big Picture of Our Life, we know this one relationship is NOT the ONLY cherished part of our life. It's ONE OF MANY! When Something Big Happens in this ONE area, OUR RESPONSE is often SO INTENSE that it causes problems in most, IF NOT ALL, the other parts of our life. WE OVER-REACT. WE OVER-RESPOND. We do something REALLY DRAMATIC...A BIG, EXAGGERATED RESPONSE that has AWFUL CONSEQUENCES and AFTER-EFFECTS.

When we're faced with problems in one part of our life, we need to be Mindful that this one part is...ONE PART of our life. When we respond to this one part, we NEED to act in ways to PRESERVE or PROTECT ALL THE OTHER AREAS of our life... that is, the Big Picture of Our Life. WE CANNOT ALLOW our response to this ONE AREA to WIPE OUT or MESS UP EVERYTHING in our life...EVERYTHING we value and cherish...EVERYTHING that gives MEANING to our life.

Have you ever done that? Have you over-responded to ONE area of your life and caused yourself problems in MANY OTHER areas of your life? Explain. _____

_____

_____

Our Recovery Goal is to Think Through Before We Do. This involves Mindfulness of the Big Picture of Our Problem...and Our Life. We need to be aware that any intense or overly dramatic response may "seal the deal" and lead to permanent damage to that area of our life...or a whole lot more unwanted conflict in that area. For instance, we may permanently lose a relationship because of our response...or we may make someone so mad that it won't take much more to lose it. We also need to be Mindful that the OVERALL QUALITY OF OUR LIFE IS IMPACTED when we over-react. We may not only lose our relationship, but many other things as well.

APPLICATION: Teri's Life Story

It's Big Picture application time! To show how the concepts and principles we've been discussing play out in Real Life, let's go through a common life story for Group Members. As you read "Teri's" story, MARK[32] THE PARTS OF HER LIFE THAT ARE SIMILAR TO YOURS. IF YOURS IS A BIT DIFFERENT, make a note of that, too![33]

33- Make note of any minor differences. For instance if you have Depression, write Depression above Bipolar. If you have been certified as a teacher, write teacher above LVN.

Teri has Bipolar Disorder and a substance abuse problem. She is on probation for a DWI and possession of cocaine. She is bright, has worked as a LVN, and has tried many times to complete an RN program. Something Always Happens and she has to drop her courses. Her LVN license has been suspended due to legal problems. She has had many jobs. She loses jobs due to using too much sick time or not showing up for work. Her family is angry with her for all the trouble and heartache she has put them through. They have tried to help her many times, but she continues to have more and more problems. THEIR HELP ISN'T HELPING…IT HAS NO LASTING EFFECT. Their phone calls and visits are filled with conflict. She is often broke and asks friends and family for money to pay for food, medical care, rent, etc.

She's twice divorced and has two kids. One is with the father, the other is in foster care. She is behind on child support and cannot see her child until she catches up. She chooses abusive men. She is abusive to the men, too. She "can't stand to be alone" and jumps from one relationship to another. She had a difficult childhood. Her father left when she was two. Her mother drank and was physically and emotionally abusive. She thinks her mother is Bipolar. She was molested by an uncle until age 12 and was raped by a boyfriend at age 20.

She believes in God and attends church when she is clean and living a Recovery Lifestyle. She's been through many rehab programs and has been hospitalized several times for mania, depression, and suicidal behavior. After treatment, she does well for 3-6 months. However, Something Always Happens and she returns to drugs and alcohol, stops her Bipolar meds,[34] has a relationship blow-up, and overdoses or cuts herself. This cycle generally ends with hospitalization or another rehab stay.

34- Medication!

SKILL BUILDER: Teri's "The Big Picture of My Life Worksheet"

Step 1. Check out Teri's "The Big Picture of My Life Worksheet."[35]

Step 2. Review Teri's story and cross out[36] the areas of her life that are seriously affected by her lifestyle and behavior…or will be in the near future if she continues along the same destructive path.[37]

Step 3. Now, consider the areas that weren't addressed in the story and make your best guess whether these areas are likely to be seriously affected now or in the near future if she doesn't gain control of her Emotion-Driven Behavior. Cross out those areas, too!

35- See Figure 2.C, "The Big Picture of My Life Worksheet - A Full Life." We looked at this earlier in the chapter.

36- Put an "X" over!

37- You may be unsure of some areas because we haven't discussed all of them yet!

SKILL BUILDER: The Impact of Self-Destructive Behavior on Teri's Life

> Let's go bubble-by-bubble and discuss the impact Teri's Emotion-Driven Behavior has on the precious areas of the Big Picture of Her Life. This will take a while to do, but UNDERSTANDING how this process works is VERY IMPORTANT. IF YOU ARE TIRED, DON'T DO THIS RIGHT NOW. It'll take concentration and a lot of thought. It's important for you to "GET" this process so you can EASILY APPLY IT to your life and UNDERSTAND WHY THINGS CAN GET SO BAD SO QUICKLY. This process will show how it happens.

Let's start with the first bubble. Would an "X" go over "Seeing My Kids Daily"? Explain. _____

_____

This area is crossed out because she has no visits with her child in foster care and she can't see the other until she catches up on child support. If she continues in her ways, she may permanently lose parental rights and visitation.

Would an "X" go over "Nursing License" and "Job/Career"? Explain. _____

_____

_____

38- A urine test that comes up positive for drugs or alcohol.

> Her LVN license is suspended, but she can regain it IF she completes probation. However, her pattern is to relapse after 3-6 months of clean time. If she has a dirty UA[38] during a probation visit or is arrested again, her nursing license may be suspended longer or she may lose it completely. Another issue is she'll continue to have job and career problems if she doesn't get her Emotion-Driven Behavior under control! She loses jobs by abusing sick time or not showing up to work and she has lost many jobs when she has gone into treatment. The more jobs she loses, the worse her job history becomes, and the harder it is to get new jobs.

39- We're not going in order. We're skipping around on Figure 2.C...but, we'll discuss each bubble.

Would an "X" go over "School"?[39] Explain. _____

_____

_____

She has tried to finish her RN degree many times, but Something Always Happens and she has to drop courses. It's often because of relationship blow-ups, drug and alcohol binges, symptoms of Bipolar Disorder, and being institutionalized. If she has a relationship blow-up and loses housing, this crisis affects her school attendance and her ability to focus on schoolwork. If she loses her car, she has trouble getting to and

When our lives are falling apart because of all the consequences of our bad choices, isn't it funny that we blame others AND God for our troubles and problems?!

It takes a lot of insight and humility to finally say, "God, I've got a problem ...it's me."

This is the point when recovery begins...when we finally understand what's causing our pain and suffering.

A Law of Trust is ...the more we break someone's trust, the harder it is to regain. It can take months or years to regain trust and only one moment to lose it...the moment we enact Emotion-Driven Coping Behavior.

40- Autonomy - (ought-tawn-uh-me) - (tawn like dawn) - having to do with self-rule or independence. "It's my life. I'm going to live it like I want to. No one's gonna tell me what to do." That's a definite expression of a desire for autonomy!

from school. Overall, her lifestyle gets in the way of finishing school.

Would an "X" go over "Church and Church Friends"? Explain. _____

_____

_____

I hate to say it, but if she continues in her ways, it's likely that her church will NOT be so welcoming over time. Further, the more she falls into a destructive lifestyle, the more likely SHE IS to pull away from church and spirituality. Many people pull away because they blame God for their problems. Some pull away because they feel so much shame and guilt and they think they're unforgivable.

Would an "X" go over "More Trust from Others" and "Things Better with Family"? Explain. _____

_____

_____

She continues to ask friends and family for money. In time, they'll become resentful and her requests will cause great conflict. She's at the point now that every time she speaks with her family, it turns into a big argument. It sounds like her people are losing trust in her and are tiring of her behavior and instability. It's UNLIKELY things will get better with her family while this cycle continues. It's expected they'll become more and more angry and burnt-out...and they'll finally pull away from her.

Would an "X" go over "Make Own Decisions," "Privacy," and "Freedom"? Explain. ____

_____

_____

_____

_____

She loses the freedom to make decisions and control her life when she winds up in hospitals, rehabs, and jail. She loses autonomy[40] when she becomes MORE AND MORE DEPENDENT ON OTHERS AND LESS ABLE TO MEET HER OWN NEEDS. When we move back in with our parents, they begin to set "house rules" and treat us like a child. Our people agree to do things for us "on one condition" and they set rules for us. How many times have you heard, "You can stay here, but you've got to..." or, "I'll do this for you, but you've got to do..."

Privacy is lost when we share living quarters or when we stay on someone's couch. Ever been in jail and have a private toileting area? In most jails, phone calls are even recorded and in a psych hospital, there's lots of people around to overhear personal

64

We lose the ability to control our lives and make our own decisions when we put ourselves in a position to be controlled by others.

All in all, we lose our freedom when we get locked up in an institution, when we come under the control of friends or family, and when we don't have resources to take care of ourselves.
The more needy and dependent we become, the more personal freedoms we give up...and the less control we have over our own life.

phone calls! When we're in institutions, we lose many personal freedoms. People decide what we eat, when we eat, when and if we go outside, what we can have for personal belongings, and overall, what we can and cannot do. Most institutions are smoke-free too! No doubt Teri takes many hits to her privacy and autonomy.
Would an "X" go over "Legal Problems Almost Over"? Explain. _____

_____

_____

Legal problems will likely continue if she relapses into drugs and alcohol and continues to have violent relationships. These days, women get arrested for domestic violence, too. Further, she may violate probation if she has a dirty UA or if she's arrested again. Failing to hold down a job may cause problems with probation as well.
Would an "X" go over "Getting Caught Up on Bills"? Explain. _____

_____

_____

It's unlikely she'll get caught up on bills if she's buying drugs and alcohol and is in and out of jobs. Further, she currently has extra expenses with probation, legal fees, and getting caught up on child support payments.
Would an "X" go over "Transportation"? Explain. _____

_____

_____

Transportation is likely to be a major issue because of her DWI. Once she finishes her DWI license suspension period, it'll be a challenge to maintain a car in her current financial condition (gas, repairs, insurance, tags, etc). Further, as friends and family pull away, it'll be harder to get rides.
Would an "X" go over "Housing"? Explain. _____

_____

_____

41- It's got to be awful to NOT know what the next day will bring. Some people say stability is boring. Man, I'd rather be bored any day and have a good idea where I lay my head tomorrow!

With her lifestyle, she's had trouble keeping an apartment. She's been living with other people. If her people start pulling away, she'll have fewer options. If she gets her own place, it'll be hard to keep if she relapses into drugs and alcohol, loses her job, or ends up in an institution. If she begins to live in halfway houses, she'll get kicked out when she starts using again. If she lives with boyfriends, she'll lose housing when those relationships end. The instability in her life is overwhelming.[41]

42- This wasn't addressed in her story, but it's one area listed on her worksheet. You decide.

Would an "X" go over "Pets"?[42] Explain. _____

_____

_____

If she's in jail, rehab, a hospital, or is living with friends or in a halfway house, it's unlikely she'll be able to keep her pets. As she goes from place to place, her pets are likely to be abandoned in the shuffle. HOPEFULLY, they'll end up with family or friends, else, they'll end up in an animal shelter.

Would an 'X' go over "Long-Term Romantic Relationship"? Explain. _____

_____

_____

Sometimes, we want a relationship so bad that we'll take one of the first ones offered to us. We don't pick and choose and seek someone compatible or someone with good relationship skills. We're desperate. We take what we can get. We adjust ourselves and change our values and interests as we try to merge and make the best of what comes our way. It's no doubt these relationships end quickly…they weren't a good fit to start with!

She tends to have violent, stormy, conflict-filled, high drama relationships that are intense and short-term. She doesn't like to be alone so she isn't too picky about who she hooks up with. When she's using, she chooses a partner who's using. She often meets people during rehab and hospital stays and hooks up with them. Both are obviously going through difficult times and are just coming out of a time of life crisis and chaos. Neither one is stable, so their relationship is very unstable. She tends to jump from one relationship to another…like out of the frying pan and into the pot. So, the likelihood for a long-term relationship seems far off.

Does this Big Picture stuff seem unreasonable? Exaggerated? Overwhelming? Is it a story about your life? Explain. _____

_____

_____

_____

Most Members comment, "Been there, lost that…and that…and that." It's the Cycle of Suffering and loss…one precious thing after another. Sadly, we're not EVEN finished with Teri's life. We still have a ways to go! Take a break from this if you need to. It's pretty heavy writing for me…and I expect it's heavy reading and emotionally draining for you. It's so important though…

43- Deliberate behavior - (dee-lib-er-it) - behavior that is thought through and done on purpose. The opposite of impulsive!

It's SO IMPORTANT TO "GET" THIS. Letting this penetrate our soul will help us to choose differently in the future. Being Mindful of how one decision or behavior can cause so much life damage will help us to be much more deliberate[43] in our responses to life situations. THAT'S HOW WE CHANGE OUR LIVES… ONE MINDFUL DECISION AFTER ANOTHER!

66

44- We may say "It doesn't matter to me what people think. They can think whatever they want." That's a hardened attitude that's NOT helpful in recovery. That's because IT MATTERS what people think. People are our bosses, co-workers, treatment providers, neighbors, parents of our children's classmates, etc. Their opinions matter. We need jobs and promotions and it's nice to have a friendly work environment. We want our treatment providers to choose us for special programs and benefits. We want a cop to give us a warning and NOT to arrest us. We actually prefer cops aren't familiar with us and aren't interested in what we're doing! We want our kids to have friends over and to be invited to parties and activities. We want our neighbors to have mercy on us and not call the cops on us all the time. We want the lady at Wal-Mart to accept our returns. We want friends. We want our family to invite us over. We want a judge to go easy on us and a Child Services worker to believe us. We want the world to give us the benefit of a doubt. We want people to believe us even though the truth is hard to believe. It really matters what people think. Many doors are closed and some are slammed shut when we have a bad reputation and a care less attitude. Many doors open and stay open if we have a decent reputation and attitude ...and how we need those open doors!!!!

Would an "X" go over "Quality of Reputation"? Explain. _____

_____

_____

It's expected that her reputation[44] in the community is hurt by her behavior. No doubt her reputation in the medical community is hurt by poor work habits and having her nursing license suspended. Treatment providers are familiar with her since she is in and out of programs. Some may be getting pretty discouraged with her by now. However, it's important to be Mindful that EVEN THOUGH she cycles, she MAINTAINS WELLNESS and PRODUCTIVITY FOR 3-6 MONTHS after treatment. Months of clean time and good functioning are a MAJOR BIG DEAL! She obviously knows HOW TO GET STARTED IN RECOVERY. Her Recovery Challenge is to THINK before she acts, to use Life-Enhancing Coping Skills, and to set up a lifestyle that'll give her what she needs to STAY ON THE RECOVERY PATH!

Would an "X" go over "Emotional Peace and Stability"? _____

_____

Her emotional peace and stability is CONSTANTLY CHALLENGED by severe family conflict, inability to see her kids, and financial, transportation, employment, and legal problems. Her life is FILLED with problems, losses, and stressors. To make matters worse, she often has to deal with the stress of major life changes (relationship losses, new jobs, changes in housing and placements, Starting Over, etc.). It's HARD to have emotional STABILITY when our lives are SO UNSTABLE. If she continues to abuse substances and doesn't stay on her psych meds, she'll suffer the instability of major mood swings and symptoms of her Bipolar Disorder, too.

When she's in a time of recovery and is WORKING HARD to apply DBT-CBT skills and understandings, SHE CAN EXPERIENCE PEACE AMIDST THE CHAOS. Keep reading to learn how this is done! It's a way to BE "AT PEACE" DESPITE all the chaos and troubles in our lives.

Would an "X" go over "Length of Recovery"? Explain. _____

_____

_____

She tends to have 3-6 months of recovery time after treatment. Something Always Happens and she relapses into substance abuse, depression, mania, suicide attempts, and self harm. She'll continue in the Cycle of Suffering with frequent relapses into self-destructive behavior and symptoms of mental illness. I'd put an "X" on this one. Would an "X" go over "Hobbies and Activities"? Explain. _____

_____

_____

She'll be unable to do her hobbies and favorite activities if she is without money and transportation...and if she is institutionalized.[45] Further, she likely loses possessions and hobby supplies due to frequent moves and treatment stays.

Would an "X" go over "Physical Status/Health"? Explain. _____

_____

_____

Her physical condition deteriorates when she's drinking and using drugs. She doesn't eat well, loses weight, and becomes anemic.[46] With continued substance abuse, major health conditions[47] are likely. Further, she puts herself at risk for HIV, Hepatitis,[48] and other diseases when she's shooting up cocaine and sleeping around. She puts herself at risk for broken bones and disfigurement because of violent relationships. In addition, her overdoses may cause permanent brain and organ damage.[49] Her arms are already pretty scarred up from cutting. Also, the more relapses into full-blown Bipolar symptoms, the worse her illness will become over time.[50]

Would an "X" go over "Relations with Treatment Providers"? Explain. _____

_____

_____

If she keeps returning to drugs and alcohol, continues with suicide attempts, gestures, and cutting, continues to stop her Bipolar meds, and continues this cycle, treatment providers will tire...just like family and friends. She'll no longer be offered the best programs and special assistance. They'll save these programs for folks they think will benefit most from them.

Would an "X" go over "Possessions"?[51] Explain. _____

_____

_____

She loses her possessions when landlords lock her doors due to nonpayment of rent and when she pawns off her belongings to pay for necessities, drugs, and alcohol. She loses her belongings when "friends" steal from her to pay for their habit. She loses

---

45- Most jails and hospitals don't allow folks to leave the facility or to have much in the way of personal belongings. So, hobbies like beading, painting, fishing, and bowling are out. We tend to lose the ability to do our hobbies and favorite activities when we're institutionalized.

46- Anemic - (uh-knee-mick) - having anemia, or low red blood count. Folks are pale and lack energy. They usually need more iron.

47- Like cirrhosis and pancreatitis. (sir-row-sis) – a liver disease caused by long-term alcohol use. (pan-cree-uh-tie-tiss) - swelling of the pancreas (an organ in our body). A very painful disease caused by drinking.

48- Hepatitis - (hep-uh-tie-tiss) – swelling of the liver. A very serious disease.

49- Like with the heart, liver, kidneys, and stomach.

50- Research shows that the more relapses people have into major symptoms of Bipolar Disorder and Schizophrenia, the longer it takes to get well each time...AND the more severe symptoms become over time. It's believed this is due to brain changes.

51- Our possessions are our "stuff"...like stereos, TV's, clocks, kitchen goods, clothing, furniture, collectibles, etc.

68

52- Abruptly –
(uh-brupt-lee) - quickly,
all of a sudden,
unexpectedly.

stuff when she is abruptly[52] institutionalized and doesn't have time to pack and store her things. She loses belongings when she has to abruptly leave an abusive boyfriend. She also loses stuff when she goes from house-to-house and from one treatment program to another.

53- The "quality of her
witness" refers to how
good of an example
she is...of what she
believes in.

Would an "X" go over "Quality of My Witness"?[53] Explain. _____

_____

_____

_____

This area is challenged as shame and guilt grow and as she feels worthless and believes she'll lose her salvation due to everything she has done. Further, as anger and hopelessness build, she blames God for her problems and losses AND feels God has abandoned her. With her lifestyle and these feelings, the quality of her witness to others is likely to suffer.

> We're finally to the end of this detailed discussion about WHAT HAPPENS that our lives get SO OUT-OF-CONTROL...SO FAST. It's the Domino Effect. It's how one thing affects another and how our behavior impacts the Big Picture of Our Life. It's about the Nature of the Problem.

How has Teri's story and this in-depth look at the Big Picture of Our Life impacted you? _____

_____

_____

_____

Have you experienced a Cycle of Suffering like Teri's? If so, in what ways is her Cycle of Suffering and pattern of losses similar to yours? _____

_____

_____

_____

54- Consider "1" to be:
"I'm absolutely NOT
willing to make any major
changes in my life right
now. I have no interest in
doing so! I'm going to live
my life like I WANT
to live it."

Consider "10" to be:
"I'm SO TIRED of living
this way. I'll do whatever
I have to do to stop this
Cycle of Suffering. I've
HAD ENOUGH of living
like this. I AM DONE
living this way."

What needs to change in YOUR life to stop your Cycle of Suffering? Be specific. ___

_____

_____

_____

On a scale of 1-10,[54] HOW WILLING ARE YOU to make these changes? _____

Write some statements[54] to describe how you feel? _____

_____

We're hurting and we want to know WHY things are the way they are in our life. We're in a state of shock. We can't believe what has happened. We're devastated…but we seek hope for what seems hopeless and insurmountable.[55]

55- Insurmountable - (in-sir-mount-able) - can't be overcome or managed.

We now know HOW and WHY this happens. It's because of how we respond to troubling life events. When we respond in a rational, Life-Enhancing way, things go pretty well in our life. When we respond in a reckless, Emotion-Driven way, the Big Picture of Our Life is overtaken by one loss after another. This is the Nature of the Problem. To stop the problems and negativity, we MUST CHOOSE to respond in new ways…to protect the Big Picture of Our Life.

IF YOU FIND YOURSELF WILLING TO MAKE LIFE CHANGES, on a scale of 1-10, how likely do you think you are to FOLLOW THROUGH WITH WHAT YOU NEED TO DO to stay on the Recovery Path? Consider 1 to be "Not a chance at all" and 10 to be "COME HAIL OR HIGH WATER, I'LL MAKE IT THIS TIME. I'M NOT LIVING LIKE THIS ANYMORE." List a number 1-10 and a statement to go along with it. _____ _____ _____

APPLICATION: Teri's Story: A Story of Real Life

Her story is Real Life. It's life after life, Member after Member. The number of life problems and the types of problems are similar across stories. It's heartbreaking to hear the stories and to witness the pain, face after face, and life after life. It's very sad to be stuck in the Cycle of Suffering. We suffer so many painful losses because of our attempts to soothe ourselves. How we've been driven to find temporary comfort and relief has caused us so many losses and LONG-TERM PAIN AND SUFFERING.

> *It's the Domino Effect. One loss leads to another…and another. Our problems snowball and avalanche until our lives are like a train wreck with all the precious parts of our lives strewn about. We're broken. Our lives are in pieces. Everything we care about has fallen apart. Our world has blown-up. We have self-destructed. We can't believe the state our life is in. We're shocked. We're filled with anger. We're looking for someone or something to blame for all the destruction and hell we've gone through AND are still going through. We're asking, "How?", "Why?"*

With what you know now, how would you respond to someone asking those questions?

_____
_____
_____
_____

The biggest thing that has caused our problems has been the WAY WE HAVE RESPONDED to our problems. It's HOW WE HAVE RESPONDED to conflict, stress, and major life events that's THE SOURCE of MOST of our problems. Our problems became REALLY PROBLEMATIC because of the Destructive Coping Mechanisms we have used to feel better. When we desperately seek immediate relief for our intense emotions...when we act-out to Numb-Out or White-Out our emotions and pain... all we gain is temporary relief...and a BOAT LOAD OF NEW PROBLEMS to deal with... when we FINALLY "COME TO."

The quality of our life won't change UNLESS we make life changes. If we don't change, our life won't change.

If we don't change, nothing changes. We'll remain in the Cycle of Suffering and we'll be stuck in the Pathways of Destruction.

There's No Other Way Out

No matter what therapy we do, THE ONLY WAY OUT of our pain and suffering is to REFUSE TO ALLOW OURSELVES to respond to life in the same self-defeating ways. WE'VE GOT TO CHANGE THE WAY WE RESPOND. We CANNOT continue to live, eat, and breathe Emotional Mind. We must TURN ON RATIONAL MIND and THINK THROUGH BEFORE WE DO! We must make RATIONAL DECISIONS about how to BEST RESPOND to our life situations...BEST in terms of ADDRESSING THE PROBLEM and PROTECTING THE BIG PICTURE OF OUR LIFE! WE MUST RESPOND TO LIFE...IN LIFE-ENHANCING WAYS.

How we do this is a major part of this workbook. This study is hard to read and process emotionally. It's painful. It really hits home for a lot of people. It also takes a lot of concentration and energy to do...and it's time-consuming. HOWEVER, I'd rather suffer through THIS WORKBOOK than suffer THE REST OF MY LIFE. GETTING CONTROL of our emotions and STOPPING THE EMOTIONAL PAIN is what this workbook is all about. That's why it was written and no doubt that's why you're working through it...even if it's painful and draining at times.

56- Another tool in our arsenal is INSIGHT AND UNDERSTANDING. We've just learned about the things that make up the Big Picture of Our Life and what we stand to lose by relapsing into destructive behavior. We've also learned about "The Nature of the Problem" and "The Cycle of Suffering." This information will help us to Talk Ourselves Out Of Self-Destructive Coping Behavior and into Life-Enhancing Behavior. We'll add more tools to our arsenal as we journey through the pages of this workbook!!!!!

57- Arsenal - a place where weapons are kept. It also refers to a collection or supply of something!

APPLICATION: The Importance of "The Big Picture of My Life"

"The Big Picture of My Life" is a major DBT-CBT concept. It's very important that we REMAIN MINDFUL and ALWAYS AWARE of the Big Picture of Our Life. We need to be RATIONAL. We need to THINK. We need to THINK THINGS THROUGH. We need to MAKE DECISIONS about HOW BEST TO respond to life, rather than just emotionally or impulsively REACTING TO LIFE. One major tool[56] in our recovery arsenal[57] is MINDFULNESS of "The Big Picture of Our Life." That's why you've been asked to work so hard on this one concept in this chapter!

SKILL BUILDER: Drilling It into Our Mind

"The Big Picture of My Life" is a major DBT-CBT tool which can be used to GUIDE OUR DECISIONS in the Heat-of-the-Moment. We must Turn On Rational Mind to BECOME MINDFUL of the problems and losses WE'LL CAUSE OURSELVES if we do what we feel like doing. Using "The Big Picture of My Life" in the HEAT-OF-THE-MOMENT is a skill. Skills take PRACTICE TO LEARN TO DO and to GET GOOD AT

The more Mindful we are of the Big Picture of Our Life, the more ammunition we'll have in our battle to be rational and to fight our Emotion-Driven impulses to defend our recovery!

58- Figure 2.E, "The Concepts and Skills Tracking Sheet" for this chapter. Notice the SAMPLE in the grey region. It offers a suggestion for tracking the number of areas you can remember. As always, BE SURE TO MAKE SOME COPIES of this tracking sheet before you use it!

It's the Big Picture of YOUR Life and that's BIG-TIME IMPORTANT!

We CANNOT CONTINUE to allow Emotional Mind to drive our behavior. We've got to take the wheel and steer our lives in a different direction. We do that by putting the brakes on and Stopping Ourselves right in our tracks…and not allowing ourselves to drive down the same Path of Destruction.

DOING. We need to practice and prepare ourselves to use this COPING TOOL. We do it by DRILLING "The Big Picture of My Life" into our HEAD and our HEART! We need to know this information SO WELL…that even if WE'RE FREAKIN' OUT, we can remember it and apply it to our life. So, PLEASE do the following.

Step 1. Review "The Big Picture of My Life Worksheet" YOU filled out based on YOUR life. Is there something you'd like to add or change? If so, make those changes now. Get it fixed up so it BEST reflects the Big Picture of Your Life.

Step 2. Make copies of YOUR "The Big Picture of My Life Worksheet" and post it in places where you'll see it often, like on the fridge, the bathroom mirror, at your bedside, on your desk, etc.

Step 3. Take time every day (for awhile) to list the things that make up the Big Picture of YOUR Life. You can do this on paper or mentally. Count the areas you can remember and note this on the tracking sheet.[58]

Step 4. Compare what you can remember with what's on your worksheet…and work to remember more and more of it. Memorizing and reciting the whole thing each time ISN'T necessary. Our goal is to remember ENOUGH OF IT so we can apply this knowledge to COUNSEL and HELP OURSELVES whenever needed!

Step 5. When it becomes easy to QUICKLY list many areas, practice running them through your mind 2-3 times a week rather than daily. As it remains easy, practice once a week, then twice a month, and monthly thereafter. Keep fresh…these are TOO IMPORTANT to forget.

Step 6. Begin to PRACTICE USING your completed worksheet. Some suggestions for use are listed on the tracking sheet. Use this tracking sheet to track your use and progress!

~~~~~~~ CHAPTER REVIEW ~~~~~~~

1. How would you describe "The Big Picture of My Life Worksheet" to someone? What would you say is its purpose? _____

_____
_____
_____
_____

2. How does "The Nature of the Problem" relate to "The Big Picture of My Life"? ___
_____
_____

72

3. What is meant by "The Tragedy of the Problem"? _____

_____

_____

4. How does "The Domino Effect" relate to "The Big Picture of My Life"? _____

_____

_____

5. What do we have to do to get the Cycle of Suffering to Stop? What's the only way out? _____

_____

_____

FOR REFLECTION:
Take a few moments to reflect on this chapter. Some questions are listed to guide your reflection. Feel free to reflect on whatever your heart brings to mind.

What are your reactions to the material?

Which parts hit home or relate to you the most?

Which parts have helped you the most?

Which parts have helped you to understand yourself the most?

How will you use this information to feel better about yourself?

How will you use this information to improve the quality of your life...or to change how things work out for you in life?

What will you do differently based on this material?

How has this information changed the way you feel about your patterns of relapse and recovery... and your overall response to life?

What does this material motivate you to do?

~~~ For Reflection ~~~

_____

_____

_____

_____

_____

_____

_____

_____

_____

_____

_____

_____

_____

_____

_____

_____

_____

_____

_____

73

Figure 2.E: The Concepts and Skills Tracking Sheet – Chapter 2

Week # _____

Day of Week →
Date →
Rating → Number of areas remembered →
Rating → Number of areas remembered →

	3 (16)	3 (15)	4 (18)	DD	5 (20)	5 (21)	DD
2A-SAMPLE List the things that make up the Big Picture of My Life?							
2A. Today, I listed the things that make up the Big Picture of My Life.							
2B. Today, I thought about my life and how my Destructive Coping Behavior has caused many losses and problems across the Big Picture of My Life.							
2C. Today, I thought about my life and the SPECIFIC losses and problems I'd have NOW or would have SOON if I did my preferred self-destructive behavior.							
2D. Today, I thought about "The Domino Effect" and how my behavior can cause losses or problems in some areas of my life fairly quickly...AND HOW THE LOSSES AND PROBLEMS IN THESE AREAS can cause losses and problems in OTHER PARTS of my life.							
2E. Today, I helped myself to avoid destructive behavior IN-THE-MOMENT by thinking about the losses and problems it would cause across the Big Picture of My Life. I used this as a COPING SKILL when temptation hit!							
2F. Today, I thought about a certain area of my life and realized it was MY CHOICES and BEHAVIOR that led to problems, not anyone else's.							
2G. Today, I did something to fill up a bubble in the Big Picture of My Life or to improve that area (like inviting someone for coffee to build a friendship, attending a support group to build a support network and friendships, setting up a pill organizer box to keep up with my medication, or doing a hobby or activity I haven't done in awhile).							

Notes:

RATING SCALE
5 - Did Excellent in this area today
4 - Did Pretty Good in this area today
3 - Did Alright in this area today
2 - Did Only Fair in this area today
1 - Didn't Do Well in this area today
DD - Didn't Do today

~ 3 ~
THE PATHWAYS OF RECOVERY

Why Try? Nothing Ever Changes

"Why try? I'm tired of trying. I might as well relapse. I'm going to end up doing it sooner or later." "Why change? Nothing ever changes?" We see no reason to change our life. We think life will never change, that it'll always be this way.

This hopelessness, this sense of utter helplessness is incredibly common.

This type of statement comes up almost every time we get to this point in Group.

There's many ways we express these feelings. Consider the following statements.

> "Why try, everything gets screwed up anyway?"
>
> "Nothing will help for long."
>
> "Things that are going good today, won't last."
>
> "Why go through all the pain of change, life won't get any better?"
>
> "Why should I give up something I enjoy? It's my only source of pleasure and giving it up isn't going to change anything. Life will still be miserable."

Have you ever said these types of things about your recovery? YES / NO

Write the sentences you use to express these feelings? _____

_____

_____

SADLY, MANY FOLKS LIVE AND BELIEVE THESE SELF-DEFEATING, SUFFERING-INDUCING, RECOVERY SABOTAGING STATEMENTS.

Many believe NOTHING will ever get better. Others believe things will get better, but only TEMPORARILY! Many expect that when things are going well, SOMETHING WILL HAPPEN and ruin everything...the bottom will fall out again and they'll end up in the same position or worse. These folks have trouble believing recovery will make a real difference in their life. THESE BELIEFS ARE VERY SELF-DEFEATING AND THEY'RE NOT OKAY TO CONTINUE TO LIVE WITH.

Do you believe things will NEVER get better...or things WILL GET BETTER, but relief and satisfaction will ONLY BE TEMPORARY...and things will get bad again? If so, explain why you feel this way. _____

_____

_____

Do you think SOMETHING WILL ALWAYS HAPPEN and the bottom will fall out AGAIN and you'll end up in the SAME position or worse? If so, explain why you think that happens. _____

_____

_____

How can we make this STOP? How can we end this SEEMINGLY ENDLESS Cycle of Suffering? _____

_____

_____

The Truth Behind the Lies

1- Pessimistic – (pess-uh-miss-tic) – thinking the worst… being negative.

2- Suffering-inducing – something that causes suffering.

There's a LOT of truth in the hopeless, pessimistic[1] suffering-inducing[2] statements listed on the previous page. These statements are REALITY. They reflect THE TRUTH about what MANY people experience.

You may wonder then, how these statements can express truth, but also be lies. Got any idea how to support both sides of this argument?! Think about the parts of these statements that are true and the parts that are false. Share your thoughts. _____

_____

_____

_____

3- Sabotage - (sab-oh-todge) "todge" sounds like Dodge! Sabotage means to ruin or destroy something.

This topic is CRITICAL because these beliefs SABOTAGE[3] RECOVERY once it's underway. We SAY these things. We BELIEVE these things. The answer to the question above is a MAIN THEME of this chapter. Read on! You'll come to understand the truth about the lies!

APPLICATION: A Walk Through the Pathways of Recovery

RECOVERY IS A PROCESS. It's NOT something that happens in a day. It's STEP-BY-STEP, DECISION BY DECISION, and DAY AFTER DAY. Figure 3.A illustrates the process of Recovery. **As we go from Point A to G**, time passes. **As the lines go upward**, our life is improving and the Big Picture of Our Life is filling back up! **As the lines go downward**, the quality of our life is decreasing. We're having problems and the Big Picture of Our Life is impacted. Some parts of our life may be challenged, others may be in turmoil.[4]

Recovery is NOT one action. It's a lifestyle…and a life-long endeavor!

4- Turmoil - (ter-moil) – when life is turned "upside-down" and is in total disorder…and full of pain and problems.

Figure 3.A: The Pathways of Recovery

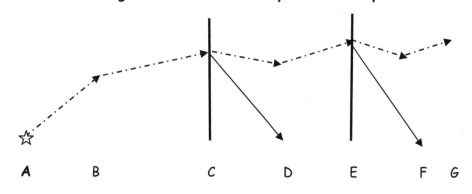

A   B   C   D   E   F G

76

5- Trek - a slow, difficult walk....a difficult journey.

6- A Texas A&M professor cited a study about ten survivors of a type of suicide attempt that almost always ends in death. EVERY survivor reported that during the seconds between life and expected death, they regretted their decision. EACH experienced a spark of hope and a desire to live. It's sad to think of the hundreds of people who experienced this spark of life, but didn't live...to live it out.

7- We're physically, mentally, and emotionally recovering from our Destructive Coping Responses. For example, the physical effects of drugs and alcohol have lessened and we're starting to feel better OR we're getting over the physical effects of an overdose OR we're healing from a gunshot wound OR we're otherwise rested and our body is strengthened by good nutrition, sleep, etc!

8- A Game Plan is a treatment plan. It's a Recovery Plan WE develop. It lists what WE need to do to be okay...and to live a Recovery Lifestyle.

9- We may find out we have options for housing or placement or a loved one returns our call or sends a card. We may make a decision about a problem and feel the relief that comes from finally making a decision! Maybe we learn we'll serve 30 days in jail rather than "going back to the pen." From Point A to B, good stuff begins to happen in our life!!!

WE START THE TREK[5] OF RECOVERY AT POINT A (see the ☆ on Figure 3.A). *For most of us, this is when things are REAL BAD in our life. We've bottomed-out. We often find ourselves in treatment. With some therapy, treatment, and time, we start to feel better AND a tiny spark of hope[6] flares. We're eating 2-3 meals a day, we're back on psych meds, and we're recovering from the physical effects of our self-destructive behavior.[7] We're learning coping skills, gaining insight, and looking at our problems more realistically and rationally. The intensity of our emotional pain has decreased some. We've come up with a Game Plan[8] for DEALING WITH and MANAGING our life AND...WE MAKE A COMMITMENT TO OURSELVES TO LIVE A RECOVERY LIFESTYLE. That's where **Point A turns into Point B.***

Notice **the line goes up from Point A to B**. That's because our life is improving. We're LIVING a Recovery Lifestyle and DOING recovery things! Life is LOOKING UP and GOOD STUFF IS COMING OUR WAY. We see LIGHT AT THE END OF THE TUNNEL and some BRIGHT SPOTS in the Big Picture of Our Life![9]

From Treatment to Pavement...Hitting the Road to Recovery

POINT B STARTS when we leave treatment OR make a decision to step onto the Recovery Path if we didn't go into treatment. We have a Game Plan and begin to do recovery things, like being clean, going to meetings, getting a sponsor, looking for work, hanging around positive people, saying "NO" to relapse people and situations, following the rules of the house so we can maintain housing, dealing with life problems, taking prescribed medications, etc. Most everyone reading this has been at Point B before. It's a familiar place.

What sort of "recovery things" do you do at this point? What actions have been a part of your early recovery periods in the past? _____

_____

_____

Note the positive things that began to happen in your life when you were living a Recovery Lifestyle. _____

_____

_____

At this point in Group, folks easily see that THINGS GOT BETTER in their lives when they were on the Recovery Path. THAT'S A TRUTH. When we're living a Recovery Lifestyle things GET BETTER in our life. In fact, NOT ONE MEMBER has EVER clung to their belief THAT THINGS NEVER CHANGED!

When we're busy in recovery, it doesn't take long before the Big Picture of Our Life starts filling up. Soon, we go from experiencing relief to experiencing some life satisfaction. Then, periods of joy occur and meaning returns to our life! It's a process… the recovery process!

If we Allow Time for Our Changes to Take Root, good things will happen. At first, one or two good things happen. These things serve as a foundation. When we build on these improvements, several more good things happen…then several more…and several more.

Just like one thing led to another and our life fell apart, it comes back together the same way… bubble by bubble, piece by piece. It's a reverse Domino Effect. Once some areas improve, others improve as well.

When we're living a Recovery Lifestyle, we're doing the things that add meaning and satisfaction to life… things that fill our emptiness. That's because we're FILLING UP our life with meaningful activities and relationships.

AS RECOVERY TIME INCREASES, the Big Picture of Our Life begins to come together and MANY GOOD THINGS HAPPEN. For instance, we have adequate housing and sometimes our own place to live! We land a job. We get enough money for a down-payment on an ugly $500 car that runs. Our family invites us over for Thanksgiving for the first time in years. We get to see our kids. We acquire possessions like a bed, a sofa, a TV, a DVD player, kitchen goods, clothes, and hobby stuff. We have six months on the job and we get a raise. We join a volunteer group or a church and are involved in the on-goings. We make new friends who invite us to other positive activities. Maybe we're dating someone who lives a healthy lifestyle. Maybe we filled out papers for financial aid and we go back to college or get our GED. We're STARTING to feel PRETTY GOOD about OURSELVES and OUR LIFE. **THESE ARE THE GOOD THINGS THAT HAPPEN BETWEEN POINT B AND C.**

The Truth About the Lies

With all this said…WHAT IS THE TRUTH behind the Self-Defeating, Suffering-Inducing Lies we tell ourselves…the lies about how things will NEVER get better even though we TRY to make things better? What's the truth behind "Why try, things never get better?" _____

_____

_____

The TRUTH…THINGS GET BETTER WHEN WE GET BETTER. THINGS CHANGE WHEN WE CHANGE. However, Group Members respond, "Things may get good FOR AWHILE, BUT SOMETHING HAPPENS and they GET BAD AGAIN."

When a Boulder Lands on Our Recovery Path

From Point B to C, things rock along okay for awhile…3 months, 6 months, sometimes longer. We're DEALING WITH STUFF that Comes Our Way…and we're MAKING GAINS day by day…and then, **SOMETHING HAPPENS. BOOM!** It's

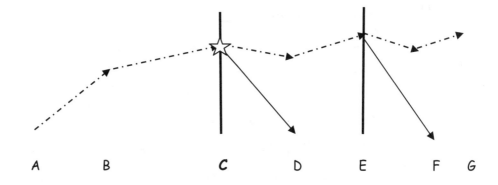

| A | B | C | D | E | F | G |

From "Out-of-Control: A Dialectical Behavior Therapy (DBT) – Cognitive-Behavioral Therapy (CBT) Workbook for Getting Control of Our Emotions and Emotion-Driven Behavior" - Copyright © 2009 by Melanie Gordon Sheets, Ph.D. (www.dbt-cbt-workbook.com)

We're always better off trying...because when we try, good things happen. If we don't try, good things rarely happen.

The truth...LIFE IS GOING TO HAPPEN. Difficult things WILL Come Our Way and boulders WILL land on our Recovery Path.

Our world gets rocked when Something Happens. It's either something WE CAUSED or something that just happened... something we had NO CONTROL OVER. Sometimes, the Something that Happens is good, like a promotion, new friends, or moving to a nice area. Though they're positive changes, they can become a boulder. They may cause anxiety and self-doubt or they may bring up old issues...and Something Happens and we don't deal with them well...and, we relapse.

like a boulder falls out of the sky and smashes right into the middle of our Recovery Path. We're now faced with a huge stumbling block...something BIG...and something HARD TO GET AROUND.

The **HEAVY line at Point C marks the point when WE GET HIT WITH A BOULDER!** That's when...SOMETHING HAPPENS...when something difficult Comes Our Way...something very undesirable and upsetting. For example, since we're clean and have changed, maybe our best friend or romantic partner leaves us to be with someone who parties. Maybe our great job ends because of a lay-off of the most recent hires. Maybe the engine in our car burns up and we lose our transportation. Maybe we get evicted from our affordable apartment because the building was sold. Maybe our spouse or parent is diagnosed with cancer, our dog gets hit by a car, or an old friend suicides. Maybe we become over-confident about our recovery and we get BLIND-SIDED by temptation and it knocks us off our feet and off the Recovery Path. ALL KINDS OF THINGS CAN HAPPEN and DO HAPPEN in people's lives.

> *The boulder that SLAMS INTO our Recovery Path may be an old friend who shows up one day, maybe someone we've been in love with before. We're feeling all the FUN and EXCITEMENT of the GOOD OL' TIMES. We're TEMPTED to spend time with them to relive old times and cherished memories...HOWEVER, THEIR SITUATION OR LIFESTYLE CONFLICTS WITH OUR RECOVERY PLAN. Maybe they still drink or use drugs, or cut, or shoplift...maybe they have a bad attitude or they don't have steady work and want to stay with us for awhile...maybe they're moody and get very critical and ugly...maybe they've abused us before.*

If we spend time with someone on Relapse Road, what will likely happen to us? _____
_____
_____

What boulders have landed on your Recovery Path in the past or ARE on your Recovery Path right now? Make note if they NEARLY knocked you off course or if they DID lead you into relapse. _____
_____
_____

To Flee or Not To Flee

At Point C, we're faced with a major life event or stressor. We have two choices how to respond. What do you think they are? _____
_____

The direction our life goes depends on the choice we make when we're faced with difficult situations. It's like we come to a fork in the road. We can keep on the right path or we can go down the wrong road. No matter what we do, WE ALWAYS HAVE A CHOICE… to stay on the Recovery Path or to go down Relapse Road.

We get on the wrong track when we try to shortcut the process by running to old Self-Destructive Coping Behaviors to Numb-Out and White-Out reality.

Getting around, through, and passed a boulder takes time. We're impatient creatures…especially when we're expected to tolerate discomfort, inconvenience, pain, and suffering. WE DON'T WANT TO TOLERATE DISTRESS and it's VERY TEMPTING to give up…and give in to old ways…the ways of relapse.

10- Especially when more than one boulder hits at the same time. It seems like they come in waves of two's and three's.

This is pretty cut n' dry. One is TO STAY ON the Recovery Path, the other is TO RELAPSE. If we choose to stay on the Recovery Path, we'll probably have a tough time dealing with the situation AT FIRST. Emotional Mind will be hitting us HARD. We'll likely feel confused, overwhelmed, and upset…with lots of other feelings, too. That's why the **ARROW goes down some** (upper arrow - Point D).   To Get Through this tough time, we'll HAVE TO give ourselves TIME to adjust to the situation. We'll need TIME to process the whole thing. We'll need TIME and SPACE to PROCESS AND EXPERIENCE ALL THE NORMAL HUMAN EMOTIONS which go along with a difficult situation. **THEN,** we'll need TIME to develop a Game Plan for dealing with it. **THEN,** we'll need TIME to follow our Game Plan…**AND THEN,** we'll need TIME to Work Through It and Get Through It!

This whole process of processing stuff TAKES TIME…and we don't want to take the time IT TAKES…to process our stuff!! WE WANT THE PAIN AND DISCOMFORT TO GO AWAY…FAST. We DON'T WANT to deal with it. We DON'T WANT the stress. We DON'T WANT the heartache. We just want to BE HAPPY. We want life to go smooth…and when it DOESN'T, we get discouraged. We want to call it quits. If life has to be like this, WE DON'T WANT ANY PART OF IT. Sounds like Emotional Mind kicking up its heels! Sounds like STINKIN' THINKIN' and the grand entry to Relapse Road.

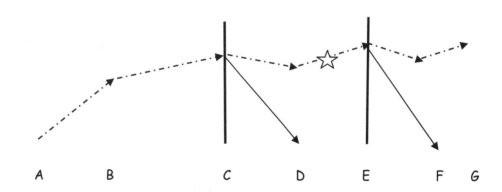

A   B   C   D   E   F   G

SOMETIMES, WE HAVE TO FIGHT REAL HARD TO STAY ON THE RECOVERY PATH WHEN THE BOULDER HITS.[10] When we Fight to stay on the Recovery Path, things continue to improve in our life. **Notice the arrow goes up again from Point D to E!**   Things improve in our life not only because we stayed on the Recovery Path…but for another VERY important reason. What do you think it is? Why else would life continue to improve at this point? _____

_____

11- Astray – (uh-stray) - to go off the right path...to go the wrong way.

> BECAUSE WE FOUGHT HARD AND WON. WE KEPT OURSELVES ON THE RECOVERY PATH despite all pressure to go astray.[11]
> BECAUSE WE MADE IT THROUGH the huge obstacle in our path.

Why would this be such a big therapeutic event? How does such a challenge or setback IMPROVE our life? _____

_____

_____

12- Empowered – (em-powered) – to feel great strength or power.

> Because WE DID IT! We've had a MAJOR SUCCESS! We GOT THROUGH SOMETHING BIG that would have been a Relapse Point for us before. WE FEEL EMPOWERED![12] We can't believe WE DID IT! We're SO AMAZED and PROUD of ourselves! We have RENEWED CONFIDENCE! We now know WE CAN!!!!

Other than this major psychological boost, we have gained something else VERY valuable. What do you think it is? _____

_____

_____

We learn a lot by Going Through AND Working Through trying times...and by OVERCOMING THEM!!!

We've been there, done that, and are reading the book... and it's just made us a more confident and more skilled person...skilled at MANAGING LIFE!

> *We've gained KNOWLEDGE AND EXPERIENCE. We used the skills we've been learning and tried new ones. We ALLOWED ourselves to experience NORMAL HUMAN DISTRESS and NEGATIVE EMOTIONS WITHOUT DOING our favorite Self-Destructive Coping Mechanisms to take away the pain and distress. We came up with a Game Plan. We did things to deal with the boulder in a way that allowed us to stay on the Recovery Path and to protect the Big Picture of Our Life.*
> *WE TOLERATED THE DISTRESS adequately and ALLOWED TIME TO GO BY.*
> *We WORKED THROUGH the situation. WE DID SOMETHING REAL BIG!!!!*
> *That's why the line goes up again! WE'VE GROWN! SOME BIG, MAJOR, THERAPEUTIC THINGS ARE HAPPENING in our life...and LIFE IS GOOD!*

Getting Through life is a process and we've got to allow ourselves time to process life!

Write about two times when you PULLED THROUGH something YOU THOUGHT YOU'D NEVER GET THROUGH...and you felt the EMPOWERMENT that comes with a major success. _____

_____

_____

_____

_____

_____

What's That Major Downer at Point D?

We've got to deal with life, so we're going to deal with the downer at Point D!

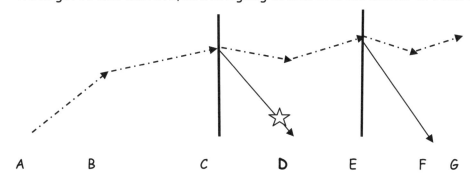

A   B   C   **D**   E   F G

"Happiness is not given to us, nor misery imposed. At every moment, we are at a crossroads. We must choose the direction we will take."
M. Richard

Either we steer straight or we go off course.

Either we didn't try...we didn't try HARD enough... or we didn't try LONG enough.

13- The Fight OF our life refers to "The Big Fight," the real important one, the one that's going to be the biggest fight of our life. The Fight FOR our life refers to fighting FOR our life...we want to have a life...a good life... and we're going to fight hard to make that happen. No one or nothing is going to get in our way of that! The Fight FOR LIFE refers to a fight that's for life itself...when the fight seems to be one that determines life or death.

> At Point C, when the boulder slammed into our Recovery Path, we were faced with a decision. We had exactly two choices. One was to fall into relapse and the Cycle of Suffering. The other was to FIGHT to stay on the Recovery Path.
> For some, this is the Fight OF our life,
> for others, it is the Fight FOR our life,
> and for others, it is a Fight FOR LIFE.[13]

What kind of Fight is it for you? Explain. _____
_____
_____

At Point C, we have a choice. If we allow Emotional Mind to drive and we give in to impulses for instant relief, we'll relapse into Self-Destructive Coping Behaviors. What will happen to our life if we do that? _____
_____

Yep, that's the MAJOR DOWNER at Point D. **The line going down** represents how bad our life gets when we relapse. We go back to where we were when we landed in rehab or a psych hospital back at Point A. WE BOTTOM-OUT AGAIN. That's the downside to relapse. Our life will fall apart again. Everything we had going for us...everything we've been WORKING for, STRUGGLING for, and FIGHTING for... will get messed up AGAIN because of the AWFUL consequences of Destructive Coping Behaviors. The Cycle of Suffering starts again...and the Big Picture of Our Life gets wiped out again.

The Truth...Life Got Better Until We Relapsed

Life was good FOR A WHILE when we were living a Recovery Lifestyle. HOWEVER, when we relapsed into Self-Destructive Behavior, BAD THINGS HAPPENED AGAIN. Our belief, "Why try, things get screwed up anyway?" seems to ring true, but it's NOT the WHOLE Truth!!!

82

The whole truth…WHEN WE STAYED ON THE RECOVERY PATH, LIFE BEGAN TO GO WELL. The Big Picture of Our Life was filling up. We were DOING GOOD and things were GOING GOOD. Then, SOMETHING HAPPENED. Some upsetting life event happened. A boulder landed on our Recovery Path. We GOT TIRED of dealing with it and we relapsed into old coping behaviors like drinking, drugs, a suicide attempt, cutting, a bad relationship…something destructive. OF COURSE, life got bad again BECAUSE OF OUR BEHAVIOR and we walk away saying, "Why did I even try? I ALWAYS RELAPSE and things GET BAD AGAIN."

The Truth…Things Get Bad Again Because We Make a Bad Choice

We TWIST things around. We say, "Why try, things get screwed up anyway?" To us, this means, why try, nothing will ever get better EVEN IF I try. That's the part that's THE LIE…because…THE TRUTH IS…things GET BETTER when WE TRY…and they GET BAD AGAIN when we GIVE UP and RELAPSE. If we try and continue to try …and we KEEP TRYING and TRYING and TRYING, life will get BETTER and BETTER. IF WE KEEP TRYING, WE WILL GET THROUGH…PASSED…OVER…AND AROUND THAT BOULDER AND ANY OTHER BOULDER THAT LANDS ON OUR PATH. If we keep trying, WE WILL MAKE IT. That's how people recover. They don't give up… or they don't give up for long!

When we choose to give up…that's the breaking point. That's when our life really falls apart. We may be holding on by a thread, but we're holding on. It's only when we let go, that we fall. It's like the saying, "You never fail until you stop trying."

Why try? Because life GETS GOOD WHEN WE TRY and EVEN BETTER when we KEEP TRYING and REFUSE TO GIVE UP! The SOMETHING that happens that destroys our life is OUR DECISION TO RELAPSE. The THING that REALLY BREAKS US and causes us to bottom-out emotionally and spiritually is a BROKEN PROMISE to ourselves…the promise we make at the start of recovery. It's the promise that, "I'll do WHATEVER IT TAKES to be okay…because I'M TIRED OF LIVING THIS WAY. COME HAIL OR HIGH WATER, I'll do WHATEVER I HAVE TO DO to be okay…because I REFUSE to live like this anymore."

Do you agree with the understanding in the above textbox? YES / NO.

In what ways do you think it's true or false? _____

_____

_____

14- About the only thing that really breaks us is our broken promises to ourselves.

I expect some readers with HORRIBLE life situations to be screaming right now, perhaps throwing this book across the room, angry with what I just said[14]…and

15- This can happen in Group when new Members come in late and they hear something like this! One lady read only part of the Distress Tolerance chapter and became VERY angry. However, like this lady, once folks are in Group longer and get the Big Picture of DBT-CBT, the "unacceptable" material comes to make sense. These folks often report healing to degrees they haven't experienced before. So, know it's normal to be upset by this material now and then, but, TRY hard to stick with it. DON'T GIVE IN TO GIVING UP! As my daughter would say, "Breathe, Momma, breathe!" Take a breather and continue on. This is all about Working Through difficult things and staying on the Recovery Path… no matter what!

16- A Self-Fulfilling Prophecy comes about when we believe something like, "Why try, things never work out anyway?" Since we believe it's true, we act in ways that help it come true. For instance, IF WE SEE NO HOPE in changing our life, we DON'T TRY LONG ENOUGH…and our life DOESN'T CHANGE! If we stop trying, things won't work out for us! We thought it, believed it, and acted in ways to make it come true!

When the going got tough…we got going. We left the Recovery Path and high-tailed it to Relapse Road.

believing I'm seriously disconnected from Real Life.[15]   What I'm saying is a VERY HARD TO ACCEPT TRUTH. IF you continue this workbook, you'll come to understand this truth. This workbook will GUIDE you to a level of PEACE and HEALING that'll MOVE YOU BEYOND whatever LEGITIMATE pain and suffering you're experiencing. It'll teach you HOW TO BE OKAY EVEN WHEN LIFE IS NOT OKAY. It'll teach you HOW TO ACCEPT THINGS that are NOT ACCEPTABLE. It'll teach you HOW TO BEAR THINGS that are UNBEARABLE. If you're really having trouble with this, back up a few paragraphs and highlight the parts that make sense to you, parts you can accept or pretty well accept AND leave the unacceptable parts alone FOR NOW and just move on with the study. By the end of this workbook, you'll be better able to accept it…as BITTER TRUTH. Consider this a Recovery Path Challenge!

A Self-Fulfilling Prophecy

The Self-Defeating, Suffering-Inducing, Recovery Sabotaging statements we've discussed in this chapter are Self-Fulfilling Prophecies.[16] These statements BECOME TRUE because WE ACT IN WAYS THAT MAKE THEM COME TRUE.

These "Why try" statements COME TRUE because we don't believe that STANDING TOUGH and GETTING THROUGH the rough times…COME HAIL OR HIGH WATER will make any real difference. So, we GIVE UP and bad things begin to happen AGAIN. Had we FOUGHT and STAYED on the Recovery Path, we would have EVENTUALLY GOT THROUGH IT and the quality of our life would be CONTINUING TO IMPROVE. Instead, things went downhill FAST because we relapsed. The TRUTH…it didn't have to happen that way. It happened because we believed a lie. WE DIDN'T HAVE FAITH that OUR STRUGGLE TO GET THROUGH TOUGH SITUATIONS WOULD PAY OFF…so we gave up. We stopped trying.

When we say, "SOMETHING ALWAYS HAPPENS and things get bad again," what is the SOMETHING that always happens? What is it that REALLY HAPPENS that causes our life to get messed up again? _____

_____

That SOMETHING is…we cut n' run. We give up. We walk off the Recovery Path and RUN TO THE OLD COMFORTS on Relapse Road. We stop trying. THAT'S WHY OUR LIFE GETS SO BAD AGAIN. WE MAKE A BAD CHOICE AND WE RELAPSE…and the Cycle of Suffering starts over again. Thus, the QUALITY of our life COMES DOWN TO **TWO CHOICES** at Point C – the Recovery Path or Relapse Road.

From "Out-of-Control: A Dialectical Behavior Therapy (DBT) – Cognitive-Behavioral Therapy (CBT) Workbook for Getting Control of Our Emotions and Emotion-Driven Behavior" - Copyright © 2009 by Melanie Gordon Sheets, Ph.D. (www.dbt-cbt-workbook.com)

It was the Fight FOR our life and we walked out of the ring.

Whatever route we choose brings us to Point D. **Point D marks the outcome** of OUR choice. We EITHER FIGHT TO STAY ON THE RECOVERY PATH **(upper line, Point C to D)** and life CONTINUES TO IMPROVE **("the high road", the upper line from Point D to E)** or we RELAPSE and life GOES DOWNHILL and we BOTTOM-OUT AGAIN **(lower line, Point C to D).**

The Recovery Path Is a Rocky Road

Life goes on... and time goes by. Either things will get better n' better or worse n' worse.

We need to remind ourselves that when we're on the Recovery Path, good things happen. Things will improve when we're doing things that bring people relief, stability, peace, and happiness. It's when we relapse into self-destructive behavior that the Cycle of Suffering starts again and devastates the Big Picture of Our Life...and bad things happen again.

Even though we "TAKE THE HIGH ROAD" and FIGHT TO STAY ON COURSE and to deal ADEQUATELY with the boulder at Point C, OVER TIME, ANOTHER BOULDER IS GOING TO ROCK OUR WORLD. It's guaranteed. Over time, other difficult situations will Come Our Way. **Point E marks when** THE NEXT METEOR STORM HITS and SOMETHING HAPPENS AGAIN. We know this process...we've lived it. This IS Real Life. We're challenged AGAIN by ANOTHER upsetting situation. As before, we're faced with a MAJOR DECISION...and we have TWO choices. We can FIGHT TO STAY ON THE RECOVERY PATH and WORK TO DEAL WITH THE SITUATION PRODUCTIVELY, or we can relapse into old behaviors and habits to Numb-Out and White-Out the pain and distress. As before, if we choose to stay on the Recovery Path, we may have a tough time AT FIRST dealing with the situation. That's why **the top arrow goes down a little at Point F.**

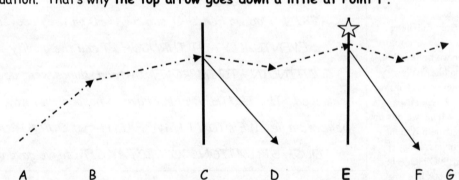

A   B   C   D   E   F   G

How might getting passed the boulder at Point C help us when we're faced with ANOTHER boulder at Point F? _____

_____

_____

It helps because we have all the skills and understandings we gained from coping ADEQUATELY from Point C to E. Though we're challenged again, we have the faith, hope, and experience TO KNOW we can make it through if we stay on course. So, IT'S TOUGH, but this time we're BETTER PREPARED. That's a gift. Like before, we have to give ourselves time to process the event AND our emotions, to adjust to the situation, to get a Game Plan, and to Work Through it. Through our effort and determination to stay on the Recovery Path, we gain LIFE STABILITY and IMPROVED LIFE OUTCOMES (**Point G**)!

How would you respond NOW to the Emotional Mind question, "Why try, things will get screwed up anyway...the good ALWAYS turns bad?" _____

_____

_____

APPLICATION: Why Bad Things Happen to Good People

17- The bible tells about human nature and what we Go Through when we don't control our impulses. The bible is full of stories about people who drink too much, sleep around, harm themselves, gamble, suicide, etc. It's all about US!

In fact, most major biblical figures suffered greatly. They suffered death of children and other loved ones, rape, incest, abandonment, betrayal, chronic pain, severe physical illness, business loss, imprisonment...all kinds of things. God told us how difficult life is when we live in the world. He did NOT promise an easy life here on earth.

We have bad experiences when we don't manage ourselves effectively. Remember, when Emotional Mind drives…bad things are more likely to happen.

Very often in Group, the question comes up, "Why do bad things have to happen?" and the subject of God follows. To be honest, the hard to swallow Law of Life is NOBODY EVER PROMISED life would be easy, NOT EVEN GOD. In fact, the bible tells us we'll have times of trouble and heartache...that living in the world will be difficult and full of woe, sorrow, pain, and temptation.[17]

> *The truth...all people will have times of trouble and distress WHETHER THEY'RE LIVING RECKLESSLY or are CAREFULLY GUARDING THEIR PEACE AND STABILITY. We ALL will have life-changing traumas and events to Go Through... THROUGHOUT our life...in addition to daily hassles and disappointments. Life WILL happen. Bad things and difficult times WILL Come Our Way.*

In the Big Picture of Life, bad things happen for two reasons. What do you think these reasons are? _____

_____

> *One reason bad things happen...is because...BAD THINGS HAPPEN. Some things happen that are OUT OF OUR CONTROL. NOTHING WE DO causes the event. MOST OFTEN though, bad things happen because of something WE HAVE SOME CONTROL OVER. Either we DO SOMETHING to cause a bad outcome or we DON'T DO WHAT IS NEEDED TO PREVENT ONE.*

What are some of the most upsetting things that have happened to you that YOU HAD LITTLE OR NO CONTROL OVER? Try to list at least five things. _____

_____

_____

Now list five of the most upsetting things that have happened to you that YOU HAD A MAJOR ROLE in bringing about. _____

_____

18- Victimization – when someone is an innocent victim. Examples include being robbed or mugged, being an Enron employee and losing our retirement investment, and being physically, sexually, or emotionally abused by a trusted person.

19- However, if we fall asleep smoking and our house catches fire, I'd say we caused that one. If we get in a car wreck because we're "road raging," I'd say we caused that one! If we have a family history of diabetes and get it when we're over 40, obese, and eating a lot of sweets, I'd say we had SOME control over that one! If we're still in the party mood at 4AM and leave the bar with folks we JUST met to party some more...and Something Bad Happens, I'd say we caused that one, too.

We can MINIMIZE pain and suffering, by decreasing the number of bad things we have to go through. The only things we can do anything about are ones we have SOME CONTROL over! We must use self-control and self-discipline and force ourselves to do THE THINGS we NEED TO DO to be okay. This includes using positive coping skills to calm our emotions to help prevent Emotion-Driven Behavior. We can MINIMIZE pain and suffering by Fighting to stay on the Recovery Path...so we can steer clear of Relapse Road.

Many things happen to us that we have NO CONTROL OVER, things like death, "freak accidents," some car accidents, genetic diseases, HIV from a blood transfusion, some lay-offs (business closure, last 50 hires), victimization,[18] a house fire,[19] a tornado, etc.

> *SOME bad things happen NOT BECAUSE OF anything we've done, but just because bad things happen in this world we live in. Unfortunately, bad things seem to come in multiples, one thing after another, EVEN FOR "good people who are living right." No matter how PERFECT a life we live, no matter how GREAT OR STABLE WE ARE, we'll NEVER HAVE A DISTRESS-FREE LIFE. Things will ALWAYS happen that upset us. EVERY DAY we have MANY OPPORTUNITIES to become upset... whether it's daily hassles and aggravations or big, traumatic, life-changing events.*

We GREATLY INCREASE the NUMBER OF upsetting situations in our lives WHEN WE ACT ON EMOTIONAL MIND...when we respond to life in an Emotion-Driven way. Impulsive or otherwise reckless behavior causes us A LOT OF UNNECESSARY LIFE PROBLEMS. THESE ARE the bad things we have SOME CONTROL OVER!!

> GAINING CONTROL over our Emotion-Driven Behavior IS THE ONLY WAY to MINIMIZE negative life outcomes and to have the MOST stable life POSSIBLE. We can only MINIMIZE negative outcomes because WE CAN'T MAKE THEM GO AWAY entirely. That's because BAD THINGS and DIFFICULT TIMES WILL Come Our Way...NO FAULT OF OUR OWN.

MOST of our problems happen because of HOW WE RESPOND when we're Big-Time in Emotional Mind. Therefore, WE CAN AVOID MANY negative life events and problems by DEVELOPING SKILLS TO MANAGE our emotions and Emotion-Driven Behavior...skills to help us THINK CLEARLY and to THINK THROUGH BEFORE WE DO. This involves MAKING RATIONAL DECISIONS about how BEST to respond with THE GOAL OF MAINTAINING life stability and PROTECTING the Big Picture of Our Life. This includes MAKING DECISIONS TO KEEP OURSELVES AWAY FROM relapse triggering people, places, situations, and things...no matter what!

APPLICATION: The Least We Can Do...Should Be the Most That's Expected

> *When bad things Come Our Way, whether or not we caused them, OUR JOB IS TO DO THE BEST WE CAN. Sometimes this means we just focus on surviving and functioning ADEQUATELY.*

When we're hit with really big stuff or just a whole bunch of stuff at once, OUR JOB is to PUSH OURSELVES to meet BARE MINIMUM LIFE DEMANDS. These are the MAJOR PRIORITIES…the MUST DO's of life. For example, if something difficult is happening, like a loved one dying or a sudden and unexpected divorce, our task is NOT to be Superman or Superwoman. We should NOT expect ourselves (or anyone else in our situation) to meet ALL the demands of daily life PLUS THE EXTRA and often OVERWHELMING DEMANDS of the stressful situation. During a difficult time in our life, a cooked breakfast for the kids (who can pull this off anyway??) might be replaced with Pop-Tarts FOR THEM TO PUT IN the toaster. The kids may miss a bath or two and their hair may not be dressed up, but…THEY GET TO SCHOOL. It may mean their homework doesn't get checked every night and their grades may suffer, but…THEY'RE IN SCHOOL and WE DON'T GET ARRESTED because they're not. It may mean the coach or another parent will have to take them to games and practices and we'll WORK to throw their uniform in the washer ONLY IF IT REALLY HAS TO BE WASHED! It may mean completing JUST TWO HOURS of "Must Do" tasks at work and not even trying to do other things. It may mean we miss bowling night or Room Mother events for awhile, but WE MAKE SURE WE DON'T MISS AA MEETINGS, THERAPY SESSIONS, AND MEDICATION APPOINTMENTS. Lord knows it's times like these when we need support, therapy, and meds…THE MOST!

When life is difficult, we're doing VERY WELL when we maintain recovery and meet basic life demands. That way, at the end of the day, we still have a job and income, our kids don't miss school, they eat, we stay on the Recovery Path, AND…we've protected the Big Picture of Our Life!

When we're going through tough times, we need to focus on bare minimum life essentials…the "MUST DO'S"… not the "Would Be Nice To Do's!"

Folks say, "I was too depressed to go to therapy." I say, "That's when you need it the most!"

In other words, when things are really rough in life, we need to WORK TO PROTECT the Big Picture of Our Life. We need to PUSH OURSELVES to function ADEQUATELY to meet BARE MINIMUM life demands. That way, we MAINTAIN our job, we MAINTAIN housing, we MAINTAIN adequate health, we MAINTAIN basic family and household functions, and…WE MAINTAIN OUR RECOVERY.

If something BIG happened in your life, what would be the BARE MINIMUM LIFE DEMANDS you'd NEED to do TO PROTECT the Big Picture of Your Life? _____

_____

_____

_____

APPLICATION: A Partial Relapse?

It's been said that we ONLY FAIL WHEN WE STOP TRYING. Have we failed or relapsed when Something Big Happens and we decide we DON'T WANT TO deal with it and we stop trying? Maybe we drink heavily for a few days, but we come to our senses and go back to AA and get back on track? Is this a failure? Is this relapse? Explain.

_____

_____

_____

What if we're talking about cutting for a few days, or binging and purging (bulimic behaviors), or we withdraw and stop taking care of ourselves and our life activities for a few days. Is that a failure? Relapse? Explain. _____

_____

_____

My opinion…yes, it's a relapse…a Partial Relapse, not a full relapse. It's a slip, not a complete failure. This applies to any of our Self-Destructive Coping Behaviors.

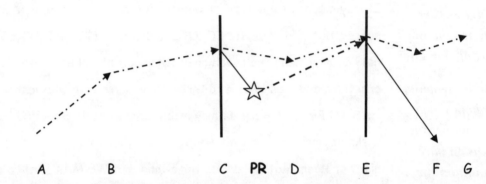

On the figure above, **the letters PR** refer to a Partial Relapse. Notice **the PR line** doesn't go all the way down…like the "F line" for a full relapse. That's because we generally DON'T bottom-out from a Partial Relapse. The PR line goes down a bit because we'll have SOME consequences and problems. However, the impact on the Big Picture of Our Life is USUALLY…ONLY partial. We haven't messed EVERYTHING up BECAUSE WE QUICKLY RETURN TO THE RECOVERY PATH. That' why **the PR line goes right back up**! Our life gets BACK ON TRACK and CONTINUES TO IMPROVE.

Bear in mind that a Partial Relapse may result in VERY SERIOUS consequences and a very destructive impact of the Big Picture of Our Life. Consider if our spouse files for divorce because we relapsed AGAIN, if a 4th DWI occurs and we face prison, if we get arrested for something else, if a serious injury occurred, or a job or career was lost. A Partial Relapse CAN HAVE DEVASTATING EFFECTS on our life…and it CAN LEAD to a TOTAL BOTTOMING-OUT and a FULL RELAPSE.

Have you ever told yourself that you could do a Partial Relapse and then STOP WHEN YOU PLANNED TO…just so you could do what you felt like doing? YES / NO

If so, how did it work out for you? We're you able to stop as planned or did you end up in a full relapse? Explain. _____

Getting back on track is what it's all about…NOT a one-man butt-kicking contest! Revising our Game Plan and then Following Through With It will get us back on the Recovery Path… and on with our life.

Recovery is a lifestyle and our lifestyle may have to radically change… or undergo a complete overhaul. Some of us are willing to make ALL the necessary changes on Attempt 1 or 2, but most of us are only willing to make changes a little at a time…and it takes us many more attempts.

20- Productive activities like baseball, joining an acting club, volunteering at the VA, going to church, etc.

It's when the pain of living like we're living is greater than the pain of change…do we FINALLY make ALL the required changes.

Application: A Successful Failure?

A Partial Relapse CAN BE a successful learning experience…IF WE LEARN FROM IT…and the COMMITMENT FOR RECOVERY IS QUICKLY REGAINED… and RECOVERY BEHAVIOR FOLLOWS. Because THE KEY TO RECOVERY IS RELAPSE PREVENTION, we must take RESPONSIBILITY for our actions and have some "HEART-TO-HEART" TALKS with ourselves and others aimed at understanding our behavior. After taking an honest look at what led to relapse, we must PROBLEM-SOLVE and REVISE our Recovery Plan so the same thing doesn't happen again! Recovery often takes 8-18 TRIES because we're hard-headed creatures and WE HAVE TO LEARN FROM OUR EXPERIENCES. We're certainly too hard-headed to learn from others' experiences!

During our EARLY RECOVERY attempts, we THINK we know it all and we're DETERMINED TO DO IT OUR WAY. Most of us relapse MANY TIMES this way! Over time, when we REALLY WANT recovery, we begin to do recovery like recovery people suggest. We try new things and make SOME changes. WE DON'T DO EVERYTHING that's suggested, just SOME THINGS. More relapses occur because WE HAVEN'T CHANGED EVERYTHING that NEEDS to be changed, just SOME THINGS. Relapses often occur because WE STILL HAVE some relapse triggers in our life and we DON'T HAVE ENOUGH of the "right stuff" to FILL OUR TIME and to BRING MEANING and SATISFACTION to life. As more time goes by and our heart is TRULY SET on recovery, we begin to do ALL THE OTHER THINGS suggested by recovery people, THE THINGS WE DIDN'T WANT TO DO BEFORE…like 90 meetings in 90 days (AA, NA), staying out of a romantic relationship during the first year of recovery, doing a daily devotional, leaving abusive or otherwise toxic relationships, and filling our day with productive activities,[20] etc.

We're WILLFUL creatures. We HAVE TO relapse MANY TIMES before we HUMBLE UP and become WILLING to make ALL the NECESSARY CHANGES. That's why it takes so many tries…because WE LEARN as we go…and we BECOME MORE WILLING to make changes over time! Unfortunately, we have to hurt MORE AND MORE before we make MORE AND MORE changes. When we REALLY want recovery, we look at what has lead to our relapses and we ALL make the necessary changes. We FINALLY come up with a RECOVERY PLAN THAT WORKS...for a long time!

If We're Contemplating if We Can Safely Relapse, We've Already Relapsed

We're deceiving ourselves if we think we can turn our Life-Destroying Addiction on and off. To think this way, we'd have to be Big-Time in Emotional Mind!

If Partial Relapses are beginning to happen, then, we're in the early stages of a FULL BLOWN RELAPSE.

The Partial Relapse just described refers to A ONE-TIME or a ONCE EVERY 2-3 YEARS type of event. IF PARTIAL RELAPSES ARE HAPPENING TWICE A YEAR, WE'RE IN SERIOUS TROUBLE. WE'RE NOT FAR FROM A FULL RELAPSE...JUST A TIME OR TWO AWAY. If we're tempted to relapse for a special weekend or because of some horrible-rotten event...then, WE'VE ALREADY RELAPSED. We've lost our Mindfulness and insight about "The Nature of the Problem," "The Cycle of Suffering," the addictive nature of our self-destructive behavior... and OUR COMMITMENT TO RECOVERY. Full Relapse is right around the corner.

~~~~~~~~ CHAPTER REVIEW ~~~~~~~~

1. Give three examples of "Self-Defeating, Suffering-Inducing, Recovery-Sabotaging" statements. Think of some of your own rather using the ones in this chapter. _____
_____
_____
_____

2. In what way are these "Self-Defeating, Suffering-Inducing" statements true? ___
_____
_____

3. Why are these "Self-Defeating, Suffering-Inducing" statements really lies we tell ourselves? In what way are they false? _____
_____
_____
_____

4. What is meant by "a boulder landing on our Recovery Path"? _____
_____
_____

5. Give five examples of common "boulders" that fall on our Recovery Path. _____
_____
_____
_____

6. When our world gets rocked by a boulder falling on our Recovery Path, what are our

two choices? _____

_____

_____

21- The arrow from Point C to Point D.

7. Why does the arrow[21] go down a little bit after the boulder hits EVEN THOUGH we stay on the RECOVERY PATH? _____

_____

_____

8. Why is it we relapse? What were some reasons discussed? _____

_____

_____

_____

9. After the boulder hit, the arrow on the RECOVERY PATH went down. WHAT CAUSES THIS ARROW TO GO BACK UP?[22] Provide three or more reasons. _____

22- The arrow from Point D to Point E.

_____

_____

_____

_____

10. After the boulder hit, the arrow for the RELAPSE ROUTE went WAY DOWN. What does this illustrate…what does it show that happens in our life? _____

_____

_____

11. Does it ALWAYS have to happen this way? Do we ALWAYS HAVE TO relapse when life takes a sharp turn into DIFFICULT? Explain. _____

_____

_____

12. What is the "Something That Happens" that causes our life to get all messed up again? What really happens that causes things to get real bad again? _____

_____

_____

13. What is meant by, "The Recovery Path is a rocky road"? _____

_____

_____

14. What are some reasons why bad things happen? _____

_____

_____

15. What was stated to be the ONLY WAY we can minimize or lessen our chances of bad things happening to us? What can we do to minimize our pain and suffering? ____

_____

_____

16. What should be our goals when bad things happen? What defines SUCCESS when we're going through a tough time...what two specific things were mentioned? _____

_____

17. How can we turn a relapse into a "Successful Failure"? _____

_____

_____

18. Why might it take 8-18 tries to recover? _____

_____

_____

19. Some people recover on the 1st or 2nd try? What do they do that most people don't do?! _____

_____

FOR REFLECTION:
Take a few moments to reflect on this chapter. Some questions are listed in the margin to guide your reflection. Feel free to reflect on whatever your heart brings to mind.

What are your reactions to the material?

Which parts hit home or relate to you the most?

Which parts have helped you the most?

Which parts have helped you to understand yourself the most?

How will you use this information to feel better about yourself?

How will you use this information to improve the quality of your life...or to change how things work out for you in life?

What will you do differently based on this material?

How has this information changed the way you feel about your patterns of relapse and recovery... and your overall response to life?

What does this material motivate you to do?

~~~ For Reflection ~~~

_____

_____

_____

_____

_____

_____

_____

_____

_____

_____

_____

_____

Figure 3.B: The Concepts and Skills Tracking Sheet – Chapter 3

Week # _____	Day of Week →							
	Date →							
3A. I caught myself making a "Self-Defeating, Suffering-Inducing, Recovery-Sabotaging" statement today.								
3B. I thought about that statement and realized it would only come true if I acted in ways to make it come true.								
3C. Today, I reminded myself of the good things that have happened in my life when I was on the Recovery Path.								
3D. Today, something bad or upsetting happened. I took notice if this upsetting event was something I caused or something that just happened that was out of my control.								
3E. Today, I reminded myself that I have two choices when something difficult happens. I can FIGHT HARD to stay on the Recovery Path or I can relapse.								
3F. Today, I reminded myself that life is tough when bad things happen, but it gets EVEN TOUGHER if I respond in self-destructive ways.								
3G. Today, I reminded myself that bad things will Come My Way and my job is to do the best I can to Work Through them so I can Get Through them... WITHOUT acting in self-destructive ways.								
3H. Today, I FOUGHT HARD to deal with a difficult situation in a positive way and I did a pretty good job of dealing with it!								
3I. Something Happened today and I didn't do such a great job of dealing with it. I thought about the situation and my response...and I came up with a plan for dealing with the next situation better. I realize I'm a Work in Progress.								
3J. Today, I was tempted to relapse "a little." I reminded myself that a partial or temporary relapse often becomes a full relapse.								

Notes:

RATING SCALE
5 – Did Excellent in this area today
4 – Did Pretty Good in this area today
3 – Did Alright in this area today
2 – Did Only Fair in this area today
1 – Didn't Do Well in this area today
DD – Didn't Do today

> ~ 4 ~
>
> # MINDFULLY PROTECTING
>
> # MY PEACE AND STABILITY

MINDFULNESS is a FUNDAMENTAL SKILL[1] in DBT and DBT-CBT. When you hear the word "Mindfulness," what does it mean to you? _____ _____

1- Fundamental skill – (fun-duh-mental) – a very basic and important skill we must learn BEFORE we can carry-out other skills. Mindfulness is a CORE SKILL in Dr. Linehan's DBT.

Mindfulness is a state of awareness and attention. It ENABLES us to TAKE IN and PROCESS what's going on so we CAN MAKE **WISE** DECISIONS about HOW BEST TO RESPOND to our life situations. A MAJOR Recovery Goal is to become Mindful of what's going on AROUND US, WITHIN US, and IN OUR LIFE. We do this by paying attention to and being aware of:

- How we're FEELING
- Our EMOTION-DRIVEN THOUGHTS
- What we're DOING
- What we're THINKING ABOUT DOING
- The CONSEQUENCES of our actions
- THE BIG PICTURE OF OUR LIFE
- Our LIFE GOALS
- The RATIONAL TRUTH about our situation
- OPTIONS FOR EFFECTIVELY DEALING WITH our situation

Mindfulness tames Emotional Mind. It brings control to our Out-of-Control emotions and behavior. Mindfulness enables us to GAIN and MAINTAIN CONTROL over our life and our life outcomes.

Mindfulness provides us with the space and time to Think Through Before We Do!

With this in mind, do you tend to be more MindFUL or MindLESS when dealing with your life situations? _____

Mindfulness is AWARENESS IN-THE-MOMENT, in the HERE-AND-NOW. For example, if we just had an argument, being Mindful is being **AWARE of HOW WE'RE FEELING** (angry, frustrated, hurt, overwhelmed, anxious, etc.) and **AWARE of the EMOTION-DRIVEN THOUGHTS** flying through our mind, such as, "What's wrong with me? Why do I always mess up my relationships?", "I don't get mad, I get even.", "I'll take every pill in the house and show him!", or "Screw it, I'd rather be a drunk."

Mindfulness takes Emotional Mind out of the driver's seat and puts us behind the wheel so we can steer clear of the road hazards on the Recovery Path.

Being Mindful also involves being **AWARE of WHAT WE'RE DOING** and **WHAT WE'RE THINKING ABOUT DOING.** For instance, "I'm searching the house for money. I've got keys in hand. When I'm doing this, I'm on my way to the beer store." or "I'm sitting on the floor in the bathroom. I've been holding this razor blade for twenty minutes. If I don't change what I'm doing, I'm gonna end up cutting myself."

APPLICATION: Using Mindfulness of the Big Picture of Our Life to Talk Ourselves Through a Difficult Situation

Being Mindful also involves being **AWARE of THE BIG PICTURE OF OUR LIFE and OUR LIFE GOALS.** Being aware of the POSITIVE and PRECIOUS things in our life is of GREAT HELP when we try to TALK OURSELVES OUT OF the destructive behavior we STRONGLY DESIRE to do.[2] "Dan's Story" below is an example of how we use Mindfulness to Talk Ourselves Through an upsetting situation. Dan just got off the phone with his ex-wife who is "pulling some crap again" to upset him. He's VERY angry. This is HOW he Talks Himself Through the ANGER so he DOESN'T DO SOMETHING to mess up his NEW life!

2- We can Talk Ourselves Through the situation by being Mindful of how we're thinking and feeling, the consequences of our desired behavior, the Big Picture of Our Life, our life goals, and Life-Enhancing Coping options.

If we really want to make major life changes, we have to change how we react when we're Big-Time in Emotional Mind…because this is when we do things that have a devastating impact on the Big Picture of Our Life.

We have to use Self-Talk to chill-out when we're in the Heat-of-the-Moment.

3- Delirious – (duh-leer-e-us) – out of one's mind.

"Dan's Story"

"I'm so angry right now. I'm fixin' to blow. I can't deal with this crap. I can't take it anymore. I'm fixin' to do something drastic. God, I just can't relapse AGAIN. I need some big help right now. I've been clean for months and Cindy will leave me if I start drinking again. She's serious this time. I've been working so hard at this. I'm up for a promotion. My blood sugars are finally good. I've got way too much to lose to blow it right now…but man, a drink would sure calm me down. Lord help me…I've got to pull myself together. I've got to get some relief. What am I going to do? I'm filled with anger. I just want to hit something right now. I want to drink myself delirious.[3] I'm fixin' to lose it. What am I going to do? Okay, I remember that lady told me to get my calendar and find an activity or someone to call so I can distract myself. She told me to call the Crisis Line or 911 if I was TOTALLY losing it! I'll get my calendar out to see what I can do. Relapsing would mess things up SO BAD, it's not even an option. Okay, it's 6:15, Tuesday evening. There's an AA meeting at 7 at Hillside Church. My brother should be home tonight…but he has the grandkids over on Tuesday's. This would not be a good night for me to show up in this condition! I really need some support and help right now…a meeting would do me good. I'll put on a clean shirt and head that way…else I'm headed for disaster. A meeting will give me time to chill-out and get some perspective on this crap. I really don't want to blow it again. How I hate dealing with her. She ALWAYS knows what to say to twist me all up. Maybe we need a go-between. I'm so tired of going through this every month. I've had enough. She's not worth my marriage and my recovery. I'm gonna work on not allowing her to get me so wigged out anymore."

SKILL BUILDER: Using Mindfulness in the Heat-of-the-Moment

4- This Skill Builder is
also a demonstration of
how we use the three
Mind States to Work
Through a problem.
It's DBT-CBT in action!
Steps 2 and 3 address
Emotional Mind. Step 4
addresses Rational Mind
and Step 5, Wise Mind.
Chapters 6-10 will discuss
these Mind States in
MUCH greater detail.
This is just a preview!

5- Instead of underlining,
you can use different
colored highlighters.
Light colored crayons also
work well.

Dan's story shows HOW we BECOME MINDFUL and TALK OURSELVES THROUGH the HEAT-OF-THE-MOMENT.[4] This skill IS A LIFELINE...so, let's take a closer look at how to use this Mindfulness Self-Talk Technique.

Step 1. Re-read the story and complete Steps 2-5. You can do one step at a time or all of them at the same time. Read the steps below before getting started.

Step 2. Underline[5] the FEELINGS Dan makes himself aware of.

Step 3. Double underline the EMOTION-DRIVEN THOUGHTS he expresses. In this story, they're statements about what he FEELS LIKE doing because he's MAD! They're the self-destructive thoughts that FLEW THROUGH his mind.

Step 4. Circle his statements about THE BIG PICTURE OF HIS LIFE. These are statements about the precious things in his life that'll be messed up if he does what he FEELS LIKE doing.

Step 5. Put a box around the LIFE-ENHANCING COPING and PROBLEM-SOLVING IDEAS he comes up with...the POSITIVE things he thinks about doing.

Step 6. See Figure 4.A for a worked-out version of "Dan's Story."

> Most of the time, we act on our emotions WITHOUT Thinking Things Through. We just react. We FEEL LIKE doing something, so we DO it! Mindfulness skills are important because they help us become AWARE of WHAT WE'RE DOING and WHAT WE'RE GETTING READY TO DO! This gives us the space and time to THINK THROUGH BEFORE WE DO!

No matter what therapy program we do, the quality of our life comes down to WHAT WE DO in the Heat-of-the-Moment when our emotions are running hot! If we mindlessly respond to the world, we're going to have a lot of bad outcomes!

We've got to Talk Ourselves THROUGH it...to GET THROUGH it.

Did you notice that Dan STRUGGLED with his DESIRE TO ACT ON HIS ANGER by doing something self-destructive? YES / NO

Did you notice he went back and forth between self-destructive desires...and desires to remain on the Recovery Path.? YES / NO

Notice the shaded areas in Figure 4.A. The first shaded area is when he was Big-Time in Emotional Mind. The shading stops at the MOMENT OF MINDFULNESS, when he GAINED AWARENESS of his emotional state and REALIZED HE WAS HEADED FOR DISASTER, "God, I just can't relapse AGAIN..." THIS IS WHEN RATIONAL MIND TURNED ON and he BEGAN TO THINK THINGS THROUGH.

Did you notice he was ONLY able to Think Straight for A FEW SECONDS and then, EMOTIONAL MIND FLARED BACK UP and tried to have the last word! YES / NO

That's where the shading starts again. Dan STOPPED this train of thought REAL

QUICK and REGAINED MINDFULNESS. He became Mindful ONCE AGAIN of the intensity of his emotions and the emotional pressure to relapse into self-destructive behavior, "I'm filled with anger. I just want to hit something right now. I want to drink myself delirious. I'm fixin' to lose it." Dan is serious about recovery and was FIGHTING FOR HIS LIFE...the quality of his life. At this point, he was able to REMAIN recovery-minded. RATIONAL MIND was helping him to Think Things Through and WISE MIND TURNED ON to provide him with some Life-Enhancing Coping options. He DEALT WITH this intense emotional situation through WISE MIND and he Followed Through with what He Knew to do!

Underline the FEELINGS Dan makes himself aware of. It looks like this.

Double underline his EMOTION-DRIVEN THOUGHTS. It looks like this.

Circle his statements about THE BIG PICTURE OF HIS LIFE. I'VE USED SMALL CAPS.

Put a box around the LIFE-ENHANCING COPING and PROBLEM-SOLVING IDEAS he came up with. I've used a broken underline.

Some underlined emotions may not seem like emotions...such as feeling like he's going to blow...or lose it...or that he's had enough. I think they're emotional expressions. They express feeling Out-of-Control, totally overwhelmed...highly agitated...and crazy-like. Some things will be a judgment call.

Figure 4.A: "Dan's Story" Worked Out

"I'm so angry right now. I'm fixin' to blow. I can't deal with this crap. I can't take it anymore. I'm fixin' to do something drastic. God, I just can't relapse AGAIN. I need some big help right now. I'VE BEEN CLEAN FOR MONTHS AND CINDY WILL LEAVE ME IF I START DRINKING AGAIN. She's serious this time. I've been working so hard at this. I'M UP FOR A PROMOTION. MY BLOOD SUGARS ARE FINALLY GOOD. I'VE GOT WAY TOO MUCH TO LOSE TO BLOW IT RIGHT NOW...but man, a drink would sure calm me down. Lord help me...I've got to pull myself together. I've got to get some relief. What am I going to do? I'm filled with anger. I just want to hit something right now. I want to drink myself delirious. I'm fixin' to lose it. What am I going to do? Okay, I remember that lady told me to get my calendar and find an activity or someone to call so I can distract myself. She told me to call the Crisis Line or 911 if I was TOTALLY losing it! I'll get my calendar out to see what I can do. RELAPSING WOULD MESS THINGS UP SO BAD, it's not even an option. Okay, it's 6:15, Tuesday evening. There's an AA meeting at 7 at Hillside Church. My brother should be home tonight...but he has the grandkids over on Tuesday's. This would not be a good night for me to show up in this condition! I really need some support and help right now...a meeting would do me good. I'll put on a clean shirt and head that way... ELSE I'M HEADED FOR DISASTER. A meeting will give me time to chill-out and get some perspective on this crap. I really don't want to BLOW IT AGAIN. How I hate dealing with her. She ALWAYS knows what to say to twist me all up. Maybe we need a go-between. I'm so tired of going through this every month. I've had enough. She's not worth MY MARRIAGE AND MY RECOVERY. I'm gonna work on not allowing her to get me so wigged out anymore."

As shown in Dan's story, when we become Mindful that we're losing control, we CAN DO SOMETHING to GAIN CONTROL! We do this by considering the Big Picture of Our Life and all the good things we have going for us and WHAT WE STAND TO LOSE by acting on a HEATED Emotional Mind. This insight motivates us to consider Life-Enhancing Coping options and to DO SOMETHING to PULL US THROUGH the difficult time. DBT-CBT is all about GETTING and MAINTAINING Peace and Stability...and, it STARTS WITH MINDFULNESS!

Mindlessness

The opposite of Mindfulness is mindlessness. What do you think mindlessness means? _____

_____

A very common example of mindlessness is walking into a room and thinking, "Why did I walk in here?" Consider, "I just had my keys. Where did I put them?" Consider when we meet someone and immediately forget their name! These things happen because we're NOT FOCUSED on what's going on IN-THE-MOMENT. WE'RE NOT PAYING ATTENTION! We usually have other things on our mind or we're trying to do several things at once. We're DISTRACTED. We're MINDLESS of what we're doing! MindFULness involves KEEPING our mind FOCUSED ON WHAT WE'RE DOING... like MAINTAINING AWARENESS we're going to the kitchen to get a light bulb![6] What percentage of time during a NORMAL day do you spend in mindlessness?[7] _____

MOST OF US SPEND A LOT OF TIME BEING MINDLESS! The amount of time we spend in mindlessness depends on many factors...like how much we have going on, how important it is that we're focused, how familiar we are with what we're doing, how we feel, etc. For instance, if we're sleepy, depressed, in pain, or are worried about something, we're going to be more mindless than if we feel well and are at peace. Further, a parent with a special needs child will be more Mindful in parenting than most parents. Workers with highly complex jobs (like surgeons) or high pressure jobs (stock trader, McDonald's drive-thru window worker) will have fewer mindless moments than a worker who completes the same task over and over (assembly line worker). Someone with an Obsessive-Compulsive germ phobia will be more Mindful of their environment than others. When we live with an abusive person, we're VERY Mindful of THEIR environment and mood. We're SO MINDFUL...we call this "walking on eggshells." We're VERY aware of them and we TRY VERY HARD to MAKE them happy and KEEP them happy.

6- When I get fed up with my mindlessness, I do things to increase MindFULness. For instance, I say to myself, "I'm going for a light bulb...I need a light bulb." I also TRY to put my keys in the same place all the time. I've read that we spend six years of our life looking for things! At work, I can forget something from the time I leave my boss' office to when I walk into my office. It's not because I'm stupid or have a poor memory, it's because I'm pressured and have five other things on my mind to do...and by the time I get to my office, I've been distracted by a conversation or three! So, I've learned to write things down! The other day, I wrote down what my boss asked me to do on a sticky note. I stuck it on my shirt when I went into the bathroom. It sure was funny when a co-worker told me HOURS LATER that I had a sticky note on my shirt! I wonder what the patient thought that I had just interviewed! FUN-NY!

7- For instance, 70% would be about 70% mindless and 30% Mindful. Perhaps you're 60% mindless and 40% Mindful...is it 50-50? Just guess... based on a normal day!

"Normal Mindlessness?"

I decide to do the dishes. I fill the sink with warm soapy water and begin filling it with dishes. I decide to walk around the house to get other dishes. While getting the cup from my bedside, I decide I could be real efficient and wash my bed linens while doing the dishes. I put the dishes I was holding on my dresser and I remove the linens and carry them to the laundry room. I load the washer and find no soap. I remember I left it in the car. I run to my room to put my shoes on so I can get the soap. The phone rings. Just two rings and they hung up! I notice my battery's low, so I go to the computer room to plug it in. Seeing the computer, I remember I had an Ebay item closing and get online to check it. Still two hours. I decide to check my email while online. I notice an email regarding a late payment, no way. I get my bill folder out and go through it. I find the stub and there's payment info on it. I call the company and they're closed on the weekend. I go back to the kitchen to do the dishes and remember I was washing the linens. I go back to the bedroom to put my shoes on and notice my toenails need trimmed. Of course, the clippers are not where I left them. I look all over and while going through my purse, I see the unusual postage stamp I had tucked away and start to the kitchen to put it in the stamp envelope. The phone rings. It's my sister. She needs me to try on the bridesmaid dress, shoes, and hosiery she sent. She wants me to do it NOW because it's the last day to make changes, but I'm think I'm starving to death. I throw a Lean Cuisine in the microwave for a quick lunch before I try on ALL those clothes. The doorbell rings. The postman has a package! It's the computer game I bought for my son's birthday. I take it to the gift closet to put it away before he gets home. The gift closet is a mess. I decide to straighten it a little so I have room for his other stuff when it arrives. I start sorting the items and realize I need some boxes to sort everyone's stuff so I can tell what I have and won't overbuy this year at Christmas. I go to the garage to get the extra boxes. I hear the phone ringing and run inside to get it. It's my sister. Oops, I forgot to try on the clothes. I remember I got distracted because I started lunch. I go to the microwave and the food has cooled! I turn it on for two minutes to reheat it. The dog is scratching on the door. I open it and he pushes his way past me. He's obviously been for a swim in the pond and a roll around the pasture. He's wet n' muddy! He doesn't want to go back outside and runs around the kitchen and mud is going everywhere. I finally catch him and get him locked in the bathroom. I'm going to have to bathe him. I find the mop and start to clean the floor. My sister calls back. She needs me to try the clothes on NOW. I'm about to lose it! I'm starving to death, my food is probably cold again, the dog is scratching on the bathroom door, the floor is a mess, my Ebay item closing alert is going off, there's still dirty dishes on the counter, the linens are in a ball on the floor, the gift closet is spread all over the living room, my boy's on the way home, and no doubt my sister will be calling AGAIN! I've had enough. I've been running myself crazy ALL DAY and nothing is taken care of...and I still have to find those darn clippers. I've gotta trim my toenails before I try on those fancy hose...my sister would have a flippin' fit if I snagged them with that jagged toenail!!!!

APPLICATION: Normal Mindlessness?

I enjoy a low stress day when I can be relaxed and "clean" the house...mindlessly

wandering through the house...getting distracted as I go. I can work on whatever

8- Prioritizing –
(pry-or-it-eye-zing) –
deciding which things are
more important than
others. A High Priority
(pry-or-it-tee) is
something that's VERY
important. A low priority
is something that is much
less important than other
things. When we're
overwhelmed, it's
important to decide
which things are High
Priorities and which are
not. We need to focus on
the High Priorities and
let other things go…
for the time being.

*To Get Control of
my world, I'd have
to TURN ON
MINDFULNESS
TO PRIORITIZE
"MUST DO'S"
while putting other
things on "hold."
Then I'd have to
keep my mind on
ONE TASK AT A
TIME until I GOT
'EM DONE!*

*When we react
without Thinking
Through, we're
acting on our
emotions and desires
IN-THE-MOMENT.
Our behavior is not
Mindfully guided
and we often end up
with a mess of
undesirable
consequences.*

interests me in-the-moment. It's nice to be mindless and WITHOUT DEMANDS. But darnit, having to try on that bridesmaid dress was just too much of a demand! Read the story, "Normal Mindlessness?" Do you find yourself there? Are you like that at all? Explain! _____

_____

When can you be mindless and it doesn't really matter? _____

_____

_____

When does mindlessness become a problem for you? _____

_____

SKILL BUILDER: Mindfully Prioritizing[8] the Must Do's

Mindlessness becomes a problem when we're required to do things in a timely and orderly fashion and we have trouble controlling our attention! In the story, what began as a relaxing day became a stressful nightmare! Several lazy-day tasks became MUST DO's that HAD TO BE dealt with…like the wedding outfit, the bed linens, and the gifts all over the room! They BECAME High Priority, Must Do NOW tasks! Which ones were LOWER PRIORITY tasks that COULD BE put off until later that day or the next day so I could CHILL-OUT and REGAIN MY peace and stability? _____

_____

_____

On a stressful day like this, I would put the dishes on hold, let the stamp lay where it lies, sort the gift closet another day, and the mud on the floor would be dry already, so it could just wait, too! I couldn't do anything about the bill until Monday, so I would CHOOSE not to worry about it until then!

APPLICATION: When We're Not Minding Our Emotions

Another problem with mindlessness occurs when we're Big-Time in Emotional Mind and we MINDLESSLY REACT to the EMOTIONAL PRESSURE in the HEAT-OF-THE-MOMENT. Our impulsive reactions can cause serious problems that affect the Big Picture of Our Life…both now and down the road.

When the emotional heat is turned up a few notches, do you tend to Think Things Through and make a DECISION how to respond OR do you tend to respond impulsively or mindlessly? _____

_____

When we're acting mindlessly, we often act on our feelings and do what we're emotionally pressured to do… rather than what's in our best interests.

When we're not being Mindful, when we're not thinking…we're just doing…and how we do some very regretful things!

People who are more mindless tend to have more problems in life than folks who are more Mindful…like legal problems, financial problems, drug and alcohol problems, broken relationships, lost jobs, etc.

9- Ruminate – (ru-men-ate) - to keep thinking about something over and over and over… It's when we "stew over" something…or when thoughts "churn through our mind." We just keep thinking about it and we DON'T Let It Go.

We can't allow ourselves to stew over or dwell on painful Emotion-Driven Thoughts! That just makes us sick.

Mindlessness causes problems when we respond to life WITHOUT being AWARE of the things we NEED to be aware of…and WITHOUT PAYING ATTENTION to what we REALLY NEED to be paying attention to! When we're CAUGHT UP in the Heat-of-the-Moment, we DON'T pay much attention to THE BIG PICTURE of what's going on OR we just attend to SOME PARTS of the situation…and NOT others. When we're UNDER THE INFLUENCE of an EMOTIONAL STATE (anger, anxiety, desire) or an ALTERED STATE OF MIND (high, drunk, spaced-out, manic, mindlessness), we do things WITHOUT THINKING MUCH about what we're doing…and we OFTEN end up doing some VERY PAINFUL THINGS!

Consider when we get messed up on drugs and alcohol and have a one-night stand with someone we WOULD NOT HAVE BEEN WITH had we been Mindful. Consider when we want to party so bad, we get ourselves in a dangerous situation…just so we can party. Consider when we get in a car wreck or have an on-the-job accident because we're angry and distracted by what made us angry. Consider when we spout off at work or in a social gathering and we say something we SHOULDN'T have said. Consider when we're totally aggravated and slap our child too hard or hit our romantic partner…or throw something we value. Consider when we're upset about something and we binge eat or wolf down a big bag of chips or cookies while we watch TV. Consider when we're in a manic state and we go shopping and spend more money than we have…with checks we cannot cover.

What types of emotional situations GET THE BEST OF YOU and lead to mindless reactions and painful consequences? _____

_____

_____

APPLICATION: When We Keep Hurting Ourselves…Mindlessly

When we're NOT IN CONTROL of what we pay attention to, sometimes, we LET OUR MIND RUN…and we ruminate.[9] We keep thinking about the same things over and over…and very often, these are the things that HURT US THE MOST…AND KEEP US HURTING…MINDLESSLY.

What sort of things do you ruminate about that causes you to feel worse n' worse? Mention how long you typically dwell on such things…minutes, hours, days, weeks? ____

_____

_____

We've got to become Mindful of Painful Rumination and STOP ourselves! Else, we'll become more and more angry, more and more depressed, more and more hopeless, and, more and more likely to do something impulsive and desperate...like one of our favorite coping behaviors that'll end up causing a whole lot more pain and suffering.

Below are examples of PAINFUL RUMINATION...the type of rumination that often results in Self-Destructive, Emotion-Driven Behavior.

> "Man, I've been pacing back and forth for over 30 minutes stewing over that idiot. I'm getting angrier and angrier by the minute. I'd like to rip his head right off his shoulders. How dare him. I'm gonna find a way to get even. Actually, I should find a way to hurt him twice as bad as he's hurt me. He's gonna pay BIG. I should call his girlfriend and tell her about his little office affair. That would really fix him! I could tell his boss what he says behind her back. That would be good, too! I could have his car towed. He's always parking where he shouldn't. I could..."

> "I can't believe I said that. How could I be so stupid? What an idiot I made of myself. Everybody heard me. Why do I do such stupid things? Why don't I think before I say things? Why can't I do anything right? They're going to think I'm such a fool. I either say stupid things or do stupid things. And last week, I can't believe I said that. He looked at me like I was the biggest idiot. And what a fool I made of myself last month. I must be the stupidest person alive. Why am I even taking that class? I'll make a fool out of myself there, too. I'm so stupid, I don't deserve to be alive. I should just end it all right now. This is too painful. I'll never change. I'll ruin everything that's going good by being so stupid. I can't deal with this anymore."

Do you find yourself in these stories...or something like one of these stories? Explain.

_____

_____

_____

How often do you respond to Painful Rumination in a self-destructive manner? What do you end up doing? _____

_____

_____

Ever think about how our TODAY'S are burdened when we ruminate about YESTERDAY'S misdeeds and what might happen TOMORROW?

Don't you think our TODAYS would be much better if we'd Let Go of our YESTERDAYS... and Follow Through with a Game Plan for a better TOMORROW instead?

SKILL BUILDER: Turning On Mindfulness to Turn Off Mindless Rumination

Below are two examples of BECOMING MINDFUL of Painful Rumination. They show HOW TO TAKE CONTROL of Emotional Mind by TALKING OURSELVES THROUGH what could end up being a crisis situation.

> "I've been sitting here FOR HOURS, smoking and drinking...beer after beer. The TV's on, but I couldn't say what's been on. I can't stop thinking about this. I can't get it off my mind. I've gone from angry to depressed to hopeless, and now, all I'm doing is thinking about ways to hurt them and kill myself. God, I'm getting more and more depressed by just sitting here. Why can't I let things go? Why do I let things get this bad? I can't do this for the rest of the night or I'm gonna end up doing something drastic. I've got to get control before I lose it. I've got to do something to stop this painful rumination. I've got to find a way to get out of this mood. The lady said to phone a friend, call your sponsor, call your pastor, go to an activity...or call 911 if it gets too bad. I'm not quite there yet, but close! I'll make some calls and see who's available. I can't do this to myself again. I've got to take control."

> "I should NOT have watched that movie. I knew better. I can't get the memories of what happened to me off my mind now. I can't sleep thinking about it and I'm crying a lot again. I'm isolating again, too. These are my warning signs. I guess my depression is coming back. I've got to get out of the house and get this off my mind. I've got to do something to distract myself. I've gotta nip this in the bud before I totally relapse and my life falls apart...and I end up in the hospital again. I'll never watch that kind of movie again. God, what was I thinking?"

Sometimes we CHOOSE to pay attention to things that get us all stirred up...things that take away any calm or peace we might feel...things that create chaos in our day and our life. These things are NOT a priority in our life and we DON'T NEED to be involved in them.

Think about a recent period of Painful Rumination. Using the examples above, write a story. Show how you CATCH yourself in Painful Rumination and what you can say to Talk Yourself Out of Painful Rumination and into Life-Enhancing Coping Behavior. ___

_____

_____

_____

_____

_____

_____

_____

_____

The High Drama person lives a highly charged life filled with intense emotion and lots of emotional ups and downs.

APPLICATION: Mindlessly Allowing Ourselves to Get All Stirred Up

Some people become SUCKED INTO emotionally charged situations...mindlessly. Before they're aware of what's going on, they're in the middle of something upsetting and they've lost their peace. Some folks LOOK FOR emotionally charged situations to GET involved in. This is so common...the terms "HIGH DRAMA" and "DRAMA QUEEN" have become part of our language! These people LIVE IN Emotional Mind...they live, eat, and breathe Emotional Mind. They may CREATE situations or EXAGGERATE their emotional experiences for the sake of drama, excitement, and attention. They're quick to GET involved in other people's problems and the latest gossip and nasty rumors. They're quick to TAKE ON and FIGHT ANY battle, conflict, or injustice that Comes Their Way! THE MORE DRAMA, THE BETTER...FOR THEM!

We CHOOSE to get involved in things that are NOT our problems. They belong on someone else's "To Deal With" list!

Are you a Drama King or Queen? If so, what effect does all the drama have on your life? _____

_____

We would NOT choose to be involved in these things if we were trying to limit the chaos, drama, and stress in our life!

What percent of your upsetting Emotional Mind time is related to things that DON'T BELONG in YOUR life...things that are NOT YOUR ISSUES...things YOU CHOOSE to be involved in that are NOT A PRIORITY in YOUR life? _____

10- We feel a sense of value, self-esteem, and mastery by helping others. It's easier to help other people with THEIR problems because we're not so emotionally involved. Having some emotional distance helps us to think rationally and to come up with some wise suggestions, It's funny how we're good at helping others...but when it comes to our own life, we feel helpless and we can't solve our own problems!

11- Ranting n' raving – fussing and throwing a fit.

12- Perceived injustice – something WE THINK is not fair or right. Like we believe a rule is unfair, but we don't understand the Big Picture of why the rule exists. We PERCEIVE it to be an injustice because it inconveniences us... but, it may save lives!

An opportunity to become upset and to act-out Came Our Way. We took advantage of it. We came upon a trigger situation on our Recovery Path. Instead of protecting our peace and stability, we CHOSE to get involved in drama that had nothing to do with the Big Picture of Our Life other than to upset it!

> *We CHOOSE to get involved in drama for many reasons. Some folks like to stir things up when life is calm and "boring." Chaos and drama is all they know and they don't feel comfortable without it. Some say drama makes them feel alive... that it fills the emptiness. Some take on other people's problems to distract themselves from their own pain and problems. Others believe the people and causes they're fighting for need them and wouldn't get along without them. This gives them a sense of value and purpose.[10]*

If you're a DRAMA SEEKER, why do you think you CHOOSE to get involved in drama?

_____

_____

In the following sections, we'll look at some ways we mindlessly GET involved in upsetting things that take away our peace and stability. As you read each section (like "The Joiner"), MARK OR HIGHLIGHT PARTS that describe things you do.

The Joiner

A common hospital example of mindlessly becoming involved in a negative situation is when folks return to the unit after a day of therapies. They're feeling pretty good and hopeful about life and they're focused on recovery. They get to the unit and another patient is upset and ranting n' raving[11] about some perceived injustice[12] on the unit or with their treatment team.

What do you think happens when they walk into this high drama situation? _____

_____

> *Many lose Mindfulness of THEIR recovery and turn their attention to the conflict and cause of the upset peer. They jump in the middle of it! They become upset, rant n' rave, and feed off the peers' emotions. The result, they lose their peace and stability and their focus on recovery. They become involved in conflict that's NOT a PRIORITY in THEIR life. This distracts them from their own life and recovery.*

Are you a "Joiner"? Do you get involved in drama in this way? If so, explain. _____

_____

_____

The Fixer

Consider the "codependent" person who CHOOSES to become involved with people who have a lot of problems and drama in their life. They want to "fix" or help them. Instead of focusing on their OWN recovery or life, they mindlessly get involved in relationships and situations that are NOT life-enhancing or recovery-focused. They

13- Destabilizing (dee-stay-bill-eye-zing) – causing us to lose our stability and balance.
14- Injustices – things that aren't fair or just.
15- Absorbs – takes in. Like a sponge absorbs water, we absorb all their complaints!

Every time the phone rings… every time we're with them, we MINDLESSLY make a DECISION to dance with them. We carry out the same moves and behaviors. They say this…so we say that. They bring this up…so we respond with that. Then, they say this…so we say that …time after time. The same dance. The same moves. The same outcome… conflict, misery, and upset.

We have a role in it. We play the game. We dance with them. We allow ourselves to get involved in the same song and dance over and over. They're like a broken record that we allow to play over and over…and it's NOT music to our ears.

fill their time and apply their energy to destabilizing[13] people and situations. This leads to depression, anger, unmet personal needs, and quite often…relapse.

Are you a "Fixer"? Do you CHOOSE relationships that BRING YOU DOWN and TAKE AWAY YOUR peace and stability…and YOUR focus on YOUR LIFE and recovery? If so, what types of people do you get involved with and how do they GET IN THE WAY of your life and recovery? _____

_____

_____

The Complainer's Ear

Think about the friend or family member who is "always" negative, angry, and critical of "everything." When you're around them, all it is…is whining, fussing, and moaning. All they talk about are the injustices[14] of life and their problems…which of course are caused by everyone but them. If you were feeling pretty good and were focused on positive things, this person can "Turn your Mind" and put you in a depressed or angry mood quick, fast, and in a hurry!

Are you "The Complainer's Ear"? Are you the one who LISTENS TO and ABSORBS[15] THEIR complaints? If so, who challenges YOUR POSITIVE MOOD by THEIR BAD MOOD? What happens to your peace and stability when you're around them? _____

_____

_____

The Dance Partner

This one comes up in almost every Group. It involves the awful phone calls or visits with family or ex-spouses. The visits may start off good, but they soon sour and are filled with great conflict and ugliness. The conversation turns to all our mistakes, how we've hurt others, all the things we're doing wrong, how we've made a mess of our life, and how we're irresponsible and will never grow up or take responsibility for our life. A big fight and great upset occurs almost every time we talk with them. We often lose our peace and stability and sometimes…our hopefulness…and our focus on recovery. It's the same conversation…the same topics over and over.

Do you have a relationship like this in your life? Is there someone who upsets you almost every time you talk or visit with them? If so, how does this affect your peace and stability? What does it make you feel like doing? _____

_____

_____

106

APPLICATION: Which Type Are You?

Which of the four ways of mindlessly getting involved in conflict and drama are MOST like you? _____

Are any of the other types like you? Which ones? _____

_____

What usually happens to you as a result of getting involved in these situations? How do you end up FEELING, THINKING, and REACTING? _____

_____

_____

Do you think that mindlessly allowing yourself to get involved in upsetting situations is a problem? If so, HOW MUCH MORE peace and stability would you have if you Mindfully protected your peace and stability and AVOIDED or MANAGED these situations? _____

_____

APPLICATION: The Infant Analogy

> To have peace and stability, we NEED to be MINDFUL and PROTECTIVE of OURSELVES and OUR LIFE. We need to be cautious about what we ALLOW ourselves to be AROUND and INVOLVED IN. We need to PROTECT and CARE FOR OURSELVES and OUR LIFE with the SAME MINDFULNESS AND DEDICATION WE HAVE FOR AN INFANT. Consider how protective and careful we are about the environment and situations we allow a baby to be in.

If an infant's environment becomes loud, smoky, or dangerous, what do we do? _____

_____

We get the baby out of there and take the baby to a safe place. If people are arguing or fighting, we take the baby out of the area. If it's loud or noisy, we move the baby to a quieter environment. If it's a questionable or potentially dangerous environment, we don't take the infant there. If we're already there, we get the kid out of there!

> We protect our babies because they're precious to us. WE ARE PRECIOUS, TOO… AND WE NEED TO CARE FOR OURSELVES IN THE SAME WAY.
> We must AVOID destabilizing situations and QUICKLY REMOVE OURSELVES from upsetting situations that are NOT A PRIORITY in our life. We must be protective of our physical AND emotional environment so we can MAXIMIZE peace and stability and MINIMIZE upsetting situations and problems.

If our baby begins to cry in a disturbing environment, what do we do? _____

_____

What do we do if the baby is still crying once we get them to a calmer place? _____

_____

16- Nurturance –
(nur-chur-ents) – when we
care for and protect
someone or something in
a loving way.

17- If you get stuck and
aren't sure what to put in
the circles, see Figure
4.C for a list of things
Group Members commonly
put in their Inner Circle.

18- For instance, instead
of listing "Mom" in one
circle and "Dad" in
another, list "Parents" or
better yet, "Family and
Friends."

19- The circles outside
the big circle.

20- A comet hitting our
home would be a major
threat to our emotional
stability. However, it's a
very unlikely event we'll
choose NOT to worry
about!

21- Intrude – (in-trude) –
to push into...in an
unwanted manner.
If something is intrusive,
it comes into our life
when we don't want it to.
It pushes real hard to
get in! It intrudes upon
our life!!!

22- Once you list as many
as you can think of, See
Figure 4.D for a list of
things Group Members
commonly put in their
outer circles.

23- Your completed
worksheet will include
some of the things on
this one. This completed
one will give you ideas for
filling out yours. Pick n'
choose things to add that
relate to your life!

> We get them out of there!!! We pat, rock, and soothe the baby. We talk softly,
> "It's okay. You're alright. You're safe now. Daddy's gonna take care of you.
> It's okay, don't cry..." We do everything we can to soothe the baby and help the baby
> return to a calm, peaceful state. You know what...WE'RE NO DIFFERENT FROM
> THAT BABY! WE, TOO, DESERVE OUR BEST NURTURANCE[16] AND CARE...AND
> OUR BEST SOOTHING METHODS APPLIED TO US...TO HELP US SETTLE DOWN!

Skill Builder: "The Mindfully Protecting My Peace and Stability Worksheet"

Step 1. Check out the worksheet (Figure 4.B). The big circle...that's YOUR Inner Circle...your world. Notice you're in the center and you're happy!

Step 2. Inside your Inner Circle are twelve small circles. In these circles, list the things that are the MOST precious and dear to you...the MOST IMPORTANT PARTS of the Big Picture of Your Life. These are the things you value THE MOST, things you want to remain GOOD in your life, the things you want to PROTECT, MAINTAIN, and KEEP...the things that make up YOUR WORLD. List these things...one in each small circle.[17] Group things like we did with "The Big Picture of My Life Worksheet."[18] If the circles are too small, your writing may go outside the circle. If you need an extra circle or two, draw 'em in! TAKE YOUR TIME to complete this worksheet. It's VERY important.

Step 3. In the outer circles,[19] list the things that COME AT YOU...the things that upset and burden you...that CHALLENGE or THREATEN YOUR RECOVERY and YOUR PEACE AND STABILITY. Include things that are relapse triggers for you, too. List things that are realistic and likely to be present in your life.[20] The issues and situations you list are things YOU NEED TO MINDFULLY PROTECT YOURSELF AGAINST. They're things you cannot allow to intrude[21] upon your peace and stability and take it away.[22]

Step 4. See the completed worksheet (Figure 4.E).[23]

What would you say is the purpose of this worksheet? _____

_____

_____

Figure 4.B: The Mindfully Protecting My Peace and Stability Worksheet

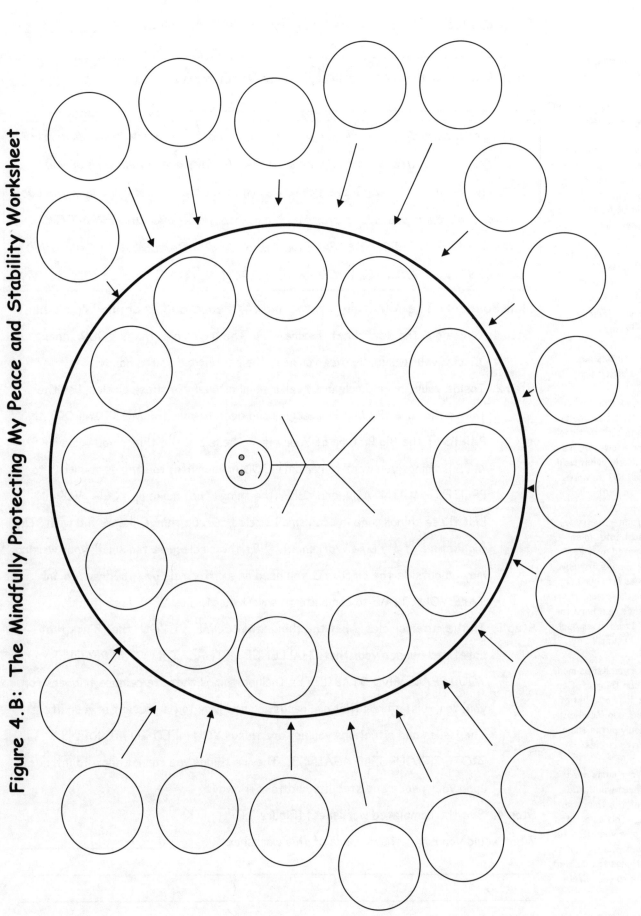

Figure 4.C: Examples of Things in Our Inner Circle

Housing	Family and Friends	Kids	Romantic Partner	Emotional Well-Being
Spiritual Well-Being	Pets	Cash Flow – Financial Stability	Legal Status	Freedom
Career – Job	Health	Transportation	Recovery	Hobbies and Activities
Good Brain Functioning	Possessions	Utilities – (phone, heat, water, etc.)	Safety	Treatment - Medication

Figure 4.D: Examples of Things Coming At Us

Temptation - Relapse Triggers – Impulses to Relapse	People Using Around Us or Trying to Get Us to Use Again	Difficult or Critical Co-Workers or Boss	Job Issues in General
Unemployment – Job Rejections	Bill Collectors - Financial Problems	Kid Problems	Dealing with the "Ex"
Upsetting Calls and Visits	Loved One in a Dangerous Situation	Loved One in a War Zone or Going to It	Problems of Loved Ones
Sick or Dying Loved Ones	Separation from Loved Ones	Marital or Relationship Stress	Divorce
Loneliness	Moving	Bad Memories – "The Past"	Grudges – Stuffed Anger
Disappointments – Criticism - Rejection	Rude People in General	Daily Hassles – Stress - Inconveniences	Traffic - Rude Drivers
Deadlines – Too Many Demands	When Things Break – (washer, A/C, etc.)	Transportation Problems	Bad News
Big Tests or Exams	Overcrowded or Noisy Environment	Depressing or Anger Arousing Music, Books, or Movies	Being in a Dangerous Situation
Too Much Free Time	Pressure to Change	Stress from Making Life Changes	New Activities - Environments
Medical Problems - Physical Disability	Symptoms of Mental Illness	Getting Medication - Med. Side-Effects	Bad Medical Findings

APPLICATION: The Purpose of "The Mindfully Protecting My Peace and Stability Worksheet"

This worksheet HELPS US to be MINDFUL that we EXPERIENCE peace, stability, meaning, and satisfaction in life when the things we cherish and value ARE PRESENT in our life and things are OKAY with them. A Recovery Goal is to be MINDFUL OF WHAT THESE THINGS ARE…AND TO ACT IN WAYS TO PROTECT THEM.

This worksheet helps us to KNOW and ACCEPT that things WILL BE Coming At Us that will challenge our peace and stability…and our recovery. We MUST put up a

The things that make up our Inner Circle serve as the foundation of our recovery.

110

Figure 4.E: The Mindfully Protecting My Peace and Stability Worksheet (Completed)

Making Changes

Loneliness

When Things Break

Grudges

Temptation

Symptoms Return

The Past

Transport-ation

$ Cash Flow

Job - Career

The "Ex"

Kids

God - Church

Kid Problems

Housing

Family

Jane's Cancer

Health

Recovery

Daily Hassles

Friends Who Use

Romantic Relation-ship

Hobbies and Activity

Peace

Bill Collectors

Med. Side Effects

Too Many Job Demands

Critical Boss

Upsetting Calls

Rude People

Health Problems

For many of us, the Fight for recovery is the FIGHT OF OUR LIFE. It's the big Fight. It's also the FIGHT FOR OUR LIFE and for many, it's the FIGHT FOR LIFE ITSELF.

We have to learn to live with these things and TO LIVE in spite of them.

THICK BOUNDARY or shield to DEFEND our Inner Circle...to protect the things we cherish and value. We MUST REFUSE TO ALLOW THE DESTABILIZING THINGS COMING AT US...TO GET TO US. We must PREVENT them from breaking into and entering our Inner Circle. IF they get INTO the middle of our world, they can mess up or DESTROY all that's precious and dear to us. We must refuse to let things TAKE AWAY our peace and stability...and our happiness. We must SET LIMITS for what we'll ALLOW in our life and HOLD TO these limits...with ALL THE STRENGTH and FIGHT we have. This is the FIGHT FOR OUR LIFE...because when we lose our peace and stability, our world becomes filled with distress, chaos, and turmoil. This is a major trigger point for relapse. Some will lose their recovery...and some will lose their life.

SKILL BUILDER: Dealing With the Things Coming At Us

It's important to realize that many of the things Coming At Us are a NORMAL part of life. As such, many are UNAVOIDABLE...and they're JUST GOING TO HAPPEN. Most people experience many of the things in Figure 4.D at some point in life.[24] Therefore, we must learn ways to MANAGE and DEAL WITH difficult life events so they DON'T GET INTO our INNER CIRCLE and OVERTAKE our WORLD! A Recovery Goal is to be MINDFUL of what's Coming At Us and what's LIKELY to Come At Us... and to DEAL WITH these things in an EFFECTIVE manner. We do that by getting a GAME PLAN for dealing with these things. Our plan may be to CONFRONT some things head on or to AVOID, IGNORE, or WALK AWAY.

24- Many of these things are part of everyday life and we'll have to deal with them as they Come Our Way. Our Recovery Task is to deal with these things in a life-enhancing way. Therefore, we MUST LEARN healthy ways to respond to them.

We must be Mindful that these DISTRESSORS can EASILY lead to self-destructive behavior and relapse. These things can really upset us and throw us off course. They can trigger a MAJOR Emotional Mind experience... and we certainly want to prevent THAT!

Some things Coming At Us will be VERY IMPORTANT to us. They'll be HIGH PRIORITIES in our life, like kid problems, car problems, temptations to relapse psychiatric symptoms, etc. Other things will be LESS IMPORTANT. We PROTECT our peace and stability by being MINDFUL of which things are HIGH PRIORITIES and WHICH ARE NOT! We must CHOOSE TO FOCUS ON the High Priorities and to do WHAT WE NEED TO DO to manage and deal with them. The upsetting things Coming At Us that are a NO or LOW priority for us...we must CHOOSE to AVOID them the BEST WE CAN...and to RID THEM FROM OUR LIVES as much as possible. We shouldn't just SAY "NO"...we should say, "AH...HELL NO!" and HOLD to our limits and boundaries. We must REMAIN MINDFUL that RECOVERY IS OUR NUMBER ONE PRIORITY...and WE MUST ACT IN WAYS TO MAKE IT SO!

To Mindfully Protect Our Peace and Stability, we must maintain a firm boundary around our Inner Circle...so the people, circumstances, and events that cause us

We must CHOOSE WHAT to pay attention to and focus on…WHAT to allow in our life… and WHAT to push out or avoid.

We must LIVE the mentality, "I WILL NOT ALLOW THIS TO RUIN MY DAY!"

25- "LP" stands for "Low Priority." These are things that aren't real important in our life. We're better off pushing these out of our life since they're things Coming At Us and cause us to be upset. On the completed worksheet, some of these may be "Friends Who Use," "Grudges," "Rude People" and "Temptation" we can avoid.

26- Higher Priorities – things that are more important in our life, like kid problems, marital problems, job issues, etc. Higher Priorities also include things we have no choice but to deal with like financial problems, health problems, upsetting phone calls, etc.

27- Adequately – (add-duh-quit-lee) - to meet the bare minimum standards of okay! To do the least possible to take care of something… to do an "okay" job!

28- This topic OFTEN comes up in Group. It led to the development of "The Mindfully Protecting My Peace and Stability" concept and worksheet.

unhappiness, anger, or instability can't get into our Inner Circle and wreck our world! We must control and manage our distressors to MINIMIZE the NEGATIVE IMPACT they have on us. We MUST NOT ALLOW them to upset us very much! We must develop an ATTITUDE THAT WE'LL DEAL WITH what we NEED to DEAL WITH and we WILL NOT ALLOW these things to RUIN OUR DAY or MESS UP OUR LIFE! Review the things Coming At You that you listed on your worksheet. Write "LP" next to ones that are Low Priorities[25] for your life…ones you can PUSH OUT or REMOVE from your life SO YOU CAN HAVE MORE peace and stability. Also note which ones are Higher Priorities[26] that you must find a way to deal with so they don't take away your peace and stability all the time. Write "HP" next to these. A Recovery Goal is to LEARN WAYS TO MANAGE these things and to BE OKAY EVEN AT TIMES when we're CHALLENGED TO THE MAX.

What do you think "being okay" means…when "we're challenged to the max"? _____

_____

_____

Being "okay" means we maintain the things that are important to us. It means we have SOME peace and stability despite the storm we're going through. It means we weather the storm during the tough times when we're challenged to the max and are faced with more than we feel we can bear. We do this by WORKING HARD to function ADEQUATELY.[27] We do our VERY BEST to meet BASIC LIFE DEMANDS and any other MAJOR PRIORITIES in our life. We PUSH OURSELVES to PARTICIPATE EFFECTIVELY in our life. We STAY IN THE RING…we STAND and FIGHT FOR our life. We use every coping skill and support available and we Fight for our peace and stability in an effective and life-enhancing manner. We SET LIMITS, HOLD OUR BOUNDARIES, and PROTECT OUR RECOVERY… and all the things we cherish and hold dear.

In the upcoming chapters, we'll discuss ways to manage and deal with the issues and problems Coming At Us. We'll discuss ways to Think Through our problems so we can come up with wise ways to handle them. We'll also discuss how to develop a Game Plan for dealing with these things. So hang on and read on!

APPLICATION: The Upsetting Phone Calls and Visits

These are the awful phone calls from family, ex's, and others…the ones which end up in big fights, anger, hurt, depression, extreme aggravation, and utter frustration.[28]

This continual conflict is toxic to our peace and stability AND our recovery.

These calls are soooo destructive. They make us want to self-destruct. They're sometimes "the last straw" and we end up doing something very desperate and self-destructive.

We must CHOOSE to allow things in our life that are helpful, supportive, and recovery based... and we must avoid and push out things that are hurtful and destabilizing.

Setting healthy boundaries involves taking control and CHOOSING what we'll allow in our life and what we WILL NOT allow. It's about CHOOSING what we'll tolerate and what we will NOT tolerate in our life.

We will NOT allow bad stuff to get too close to us and we will NOT allow bad stuff to get the best of us.

These people keep rubbing our nose in things. They're always reminding us of everything that's wrong with us and all the rotten things we've ever done, how stupid and irresponsible we are, how we screw up our life, and how we need to do this n' that. It's the same stuff every time.

Is this something you go through? Does someone call you and upset you all the time? If so, what is spoken about that's so upsetting to you? _____ _____

Do these conversations put you Big-Time in Emotional Mind? YES / NO

How do these conversations make you feel? Which emotions are triggered? _____ _____ _____

What destructive Emotion-Driven Thoughts go through your mind? _____ _____ _____

What do these phone calls or visits have to do with the concept of "Mindfully Protecting My Peace and Stability"? _____ _____ _____

These phone calls and visits are MAJOR DISTRESSORS that COME AT US. They GREATLY UPSET US and often lead to DESTRUCTIVE THOUGHTS and IMPULSES. Sometimes, we CHOOSE to talk with them because they're important to us, like Mom or Dad. Sometimes, we CHOOSE to talk with them because we feel we have to, like an ex who has visitation rights. When these calls or visits are a HIGH PRIORITY in our life, instead of avoiding them or allowing ourselves to be abused and upset by them, we need to get a GAME PLAN for dealing with them so we can PARTICIPATE EFFECTIVELY and MINDFULLY PROTECT OUR PEACE AND STABILITY.

These calls or visits relate to the Mindfully Protecting My Peace and Stability topic because we NEED to be MINDFUL they're COMING! We know Mom calls every night or our ex calls every Thursday. We NEED to be MINDFUL of how these calls make us feel, think, and behave...and how they THREATEN our peace and stability...and our recovery...IF WE OVER-REACT to them. We need to be Mindful that WE HAVE A CHOICE HOW TO RESPOND. We need to be Mindful that WE MUST TAKE CONTROL by SETTING LIMITS and BOUNDARIES for these calls and visits. We

We CAN choose to control these phone calls or we can choose to allow them to control us.

It's ultimately about CHOOSING to allow acceptable, life-enhancing things into our world and CHOOSING to say "HELL NO!" and not "HELLO!" to things that are NOT acceptable.

29- Script – something written out that tells you what to say, like a movie script! I write-out a script for difficult phone calls. If the call is real important, I practice reading it so it doesn't sound like I'm reading it during the call! Practicing a script is much better than trying to come up with well-thought out stuff in the Heat-of-the-Moment!

30- Rehearse – (rhymes with reverse!) - to practice, like practicing a speech or dance routine.

31- Know it's natural to get nervous and tongue-tied when you're doing this. That's why I write down what I want to say and I read it off as I need to! However, I'm so practiced with it, it doesn't sound like I'm reading it! I get nervous ....so, I REHEARSE!

32- Feel free to change the wording so it fits your personality and comfort zone!

need to be Mindful that our RECOVERY GOAL is to GET A GAME PLAN for dealing with them. We need to be Mindful that our Recovery Goal is NOT ONLY a Wise Game Plan...but FOLLOWING THROUGH WITH IT and ACTUALLY DOING IT! Our Recovery Goal is to be MINDFUL of the importance of TAKING A STAND...and Fighting for the QUALITY OF OUR LIFE.

SKILL BUILDER: Managing the Upsetting Phone Calls and Visits

The following technique is a tried n' true way of managing these unmanageable phone calls...and taking control of these Out-of-Control calls. I've tried it, many Members have tried it...and it works! When these conversations Come At Us, we've got to respond to them in a way that stops them from ruining our day and our life!

The first step in Protecting Our Peace and Stability is MINDFULNESS. We need to be MINDFUL these calls WILL BE COMING and they'll be filled with ugliness, criticism, conflict, and negativity.

The second step is...BE PREPARED. We need a Game Plan for dealing with these calls. So, WRITE A SCRIPT.[29] Not a Valium script, but something like a movie script...of what you want to say...well, not what you WANT to say, but what would be in the best interests of the Big Picture of Your Life to say! Think about what they'll say and write down what you'll say in response. Consider what they might say next and write how you'll respond. Once you get an idea of what you'll say, REHEARSE![30] Run pretend conversations through your mind. You may need to play it out in your head many times until you get pretty good at it.[31] Get ENOUGH PRACTICE so when the call Comes At You, you'll be able to ADEQUATELY control the conversation. You might have to say things in a different order than you practiced and you might add things. But, if you have a script drilled into your mind and heart, you should do just fine!

> Remember, this life ISN'T about perfection. It's about Participating Effectively and doing the best we can...and THAT MAKES "ADEQUATE"...PERFECT!

The third step is to FOLLOW THROUGH with what you've PLANNED TO DO! When the call or visit turns ugly, you might say something like,[32]

> "Mom, I love you and value being able to talk with you. However, when we talk about the past and all the upsetting things going on, that upsets me. I don't want to talk about those things every day. My Recovery Plan requires I manage my moods and avoid upsetting things that aren't necessary in my life. Talking about the past and all the rotten things I've done is of NO HELP to me today. If we've talked about everything else and now it's down to this stuff, it's best we get off the phone and catch up on things tomorrow."

33- We've used "Mom" as an example, but, this could be anyone in our life! Sorry, Mom!

Over-practice - This is a High Priority event and something very important for our recovery. It's hard to be okay with this kind of continual conflict in our life!

34- I'd say "we" instead of "when YOU can talk about things…" It'll take a little heat off of her and reduce some of her defensiveness.

35- Turn off, unplug, or set the phone on vibrate. The point is to Protect YOUR Peace and Stability. If you listen to it ringing and ringing, it's going to raise your blood pressure and upset you even more. Turn it off… and try to distract yourself by focusing on something pleasant and enjoyable!

36- You can use this skill in face-to-face conversations, too. Instead of hanging up the phone, you may end up leaving the house, the restaurant, or wherever to end the conversation… even if it means packing your suitcase and ending an out-of-town visit early.

When our people LEARN that we're serious, they'll LEARN how to have a pleasant conversation with us!

Mom[33] will be VERY DEFENSIVE and ANGRY about this BOUNDARY you set. She'll probably FUSS and CRITICIZE YOU MORE! If she does, say something like,

> "Mom, I love you and part of my Recovery Plan is that I can't do upsetting phone calls anymore. I'm going to get off the phone now. Call me back tomorrow and we can talk about things that aren't upsetting."

OF COURSE, Mom WILL BE SHOCKED at this NEW BEHAVIOR and will CONTINUE TO BE UGLY…so, CUT IN and say something like…

> "Mom, I love you too much and value our relationship too much to stay on this phone when we're yelling and screaming at each other. I'm going to hang up. Call me back when we can talk about things that aren't upsetting. I love you Mom, good night. I'm going to hang up now. We'll talk again tomorrow."

Now, hang up the phone! Expect Mom to be VERY ANGRY and to call back IN A RAGE. I'd answer it and say pretty much the same thing, like,

> "Mom, I love you and value our relationship too much to stay on the phone and scream n' fuss at each other. If you want to talk about pleasant things, then I want to talk with you. If we can't have a pleasant conversation, then, I'm going to get off the phone." (Mom WILL continue to FUSS N' YELL, so say…) "Call me back when we[34] can talk about things that aren't upsetting. I'd really enjoy talking with you, then. I'm not answering the phone again tonight. We'll talk tomorrow. I love you, good night."

That's it, be done. Unplug the phone for an hour or turn it on vibrate.[35] If she calls when you plug the phone back in and she's still raging in ugliness, say,

> "Mom, I said I wouldn't talk with you when you're being hurtful. We'll talk tomorrow. I won't be answering your call again tonight. I'll call you tomorrow and we'll start over. I love you, Mom. Good night."

Then stick to it. You'll be amazed at how effective this is. YOU'RE TEACHING HER how to have an enjoyable relationship with you. SHE'LL LEARN that if she's going to spend time with you, she'll HAVE TO BE nice. SHE'LL LEARN that IF SHE'S UGLY, YOU'LL HANG UP THE PHONE[36] and she won't have any time with you! Try it! Don't leave off the love part. It's powerful she knows YOU LOVE HER and WANT a relationship with her. SHE'LL LEARN THAT YOU HAVE NEW RULES for what you'll allow in your life. NEW RULES. NEW BOUNDARIES. NEW LIFE!

Our people DO NOT WANT the rules to CHANGE and they'll FIGHT IT BIG-TIME! THEY'LL PRESSURE US TO GO BACK TO THE OLD WAY! As hard as they push us to go back to the old way, WE HAVE TO PUSH TO GO THE RECOVERY WAY! We'll have to STICK TO these new "dance steps" until our "dance partner" learns to dance nicely with us! They'll either dance nicely or we'll leave the dance floor!

Remember, this is OUR LIFE and it's OUR opportunity to take control of an Out-of-Control situation…and to build peace and stability into OUR LIFE. We've got to do it because obviously no one is going to do it for us!

BE MINDFUL that THEY VALUE OUR RELATIONSHIP, TOO…and once they know we'll LEAVE THE DANCE FLOOR, they'll start to FOLLOW OUR LEAD and begin to DANCE NICELY…and they'll STOP STEPPING ALL OVER OUR TOES!!! But…THEY HAVE TO KNOW WE'RE SERIOUS! We'll have to SHOW THEM WE'RE SERIOUS by Following Through and hanging up the phone or leaving the dance floor EVERY TIME they get ugly! This is a very powerful technique. We need to use it…and to keep using it for ALL our unpleasant phone calls and visits!!!

We need to Mindfully Protect Our Peace and Stability. We need to control our environment and the things Coming At Us just like we would for an infant.
We need to treat ourselves with the same care and devotion.
We're special and we deserve "handling with care"!

~~~~~~~~ CHAPTER REVIEW ~~~~~~~~

1. Mindfulness is a state of _____ or _____.[37]

2. When we're trying to control how we respond to difficult situations, what sort of things should we be Mindful of?[38]

1. _____

2. _____

3. _____

4. _____

5. _____

6. _____

7. _____

8. _____

9. _____

3. The opposite of Mindfulness is M _ _ _ _ _ _ _ _ _ _ _ S .

4. When does mindlessness become a problem? _____

_____

_____

5. What is Painful Rumination? How can we stop it? _____

_____

_____

_____

_____

37- Both start with letter A.

38- Nine things were noted on the first page of this chapter. Before looking, list the ones you can remember!

6. What does "mindlessly allowing ourselves to get all stirred up" refer to? _____

_____

_____

_____

7. What does a "Joiner" do and why is it a problem? _____

_____

_____

_____

8. What does a "Fixer" do and why is it a problem? _____

_____

_____

_____

9. What does a "Dance Partner" do and why is it a problem? _____

_____

_____

_____

10. What does a "Complainer's Ear" do and why is it a problem? _____

_____

_____

_____

11. What does the "Infant Analogy" have to do with Mindfulness? What does it tell us
we need to do? _____

_____

_____

_____

_____

12. What's the point of "The Mindfully Protecting My Peace and Stability Worksheet"
...and what does it have to do with Mindfulness? _____

_____

_____

_____

_____

_____

_____

118

13. What does being "okay" mean when we're faced with a difficult situation? _____

_____

_____

_____

14. What are some steps for managing bad phone calls or visits? Write out something you could say to manage one of your bad phone calls. _____

_____

_____

_____

_____

_____

_____

FOR REFLECTION:
Take a few moments to reflect on this chapter. Some questions are listed in the margin to guide your reflection. Feel free to reflect on whatever your heart brings to mind.

What are your reactions to the material?

Which parts hit home or relate to you the most?

Which parts have helped you the most?

Which parts have helped you to understand yourself the most?

How will you use this information to feel better about yourself?

How will you use this information to improve the quality of your life...or to change how things work out for you in life?

What will you do differently based on this material?

How has this information changed the way you feel about your patterns of relapse and recovery... and your overall response to life?

What does this material motivate you to do?

~~~ For Reflection ~~~

_____

_____

_____

_____

_____

_____

_____

_____

_____

_____

_____

_____

_____

How to Mindfully Protect Our Peace and Stability

Check out Figure 4.F. This figure shows the DBT-CBT model of relapse prevention...
It's the "HOW TO" for Mindfully Protecting Our Peace and Stability.

The smallest circle in the middle is our Inner Circle. This is the inner circle from
Figures 4.D and 4.E that contains the happy-faced stick figure and the 12 small circles.
On Figure 4.E, we filled these 12 circles with things that give our life meaning and value...
the things we want to protect.

In this chapter, we've discussed the importance of
putting up a boundary or shield to protect our Inner Circle.
We also discussed the necessity of using Life-Enhancing Coping Skills
to manage and control the things Coming At Us. That's because we don't want the things
Coming At Us to GET TO US and mess up or take away the things we cherish and value.
We discussed that we must Fight for these things. This is the Fight FOR our life.
The weapons we use in this Fight are Life-Enhancing Coping Skills.

This new figure (Figure 4.F) includes the boundary or shield that protects our Inner Circle.
This shield is made up of various kinds of Life-Enhancing Coping Skills
that we can use to defend our Inner Circle.
These weapons or tools will help us to maintain our boundary...
so, we can protect the things that are so important to us.
For instance, when we start to become upset about something Coming At Us,
we can use some of our Life-Enhancing Coping Skills to calm and comfort ourselves.
The goal is to regain peace and to Think Through Before We Do...
so we don't do something destructive that jeopardizes our stability!
So, this new figure shows HOW we can go about protecting
the precious things in our Inner Circle.

A blank form of this worksheet is included in this chapter (Figure 4.G).
You'll also find it in Chapter 13, the Life-Enhancing Coping Skills chapter.
By the time you finish that chapter,
you'll have many new coping tools to add to your worksheet.

Figure 4.F: How to Mindfully Protect Our Peace and Stability (Completed)

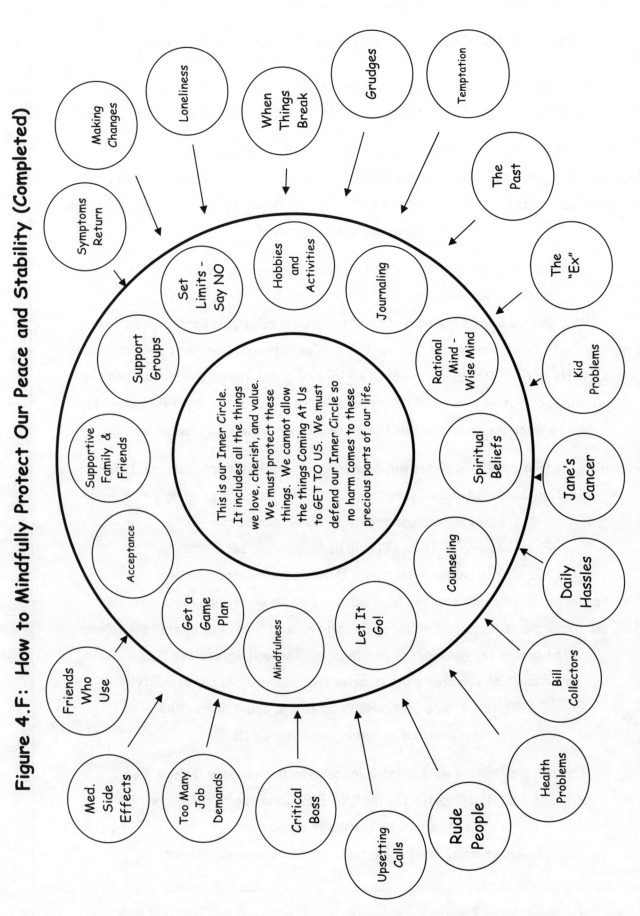

This is our Inner Circle. It includes all the things we love, cherish, and value. We must protect these things. We cannot allow the things Coming At Us to GET TO US. We must defend our Inner Circle so no harm comes to these precious parts of our life.

Inner circle items: Set Limits – Say NO; Hobbies and Activities; Journaling; Rational Mind – Wise Mind; Spiritual Beliefs; Counseling; Let It Go!; Mindfulness; Get a Game Plan; Acceptance; Supportive Family & Friends; Support Groups

Outer items: Symptoms Return; Making Changes; Loneliness; When Things Break; Grudges; Temptation; The Past; The "Ex"; Kid Problems; Jane's Cancer; Daily Hassles; Bill Collectors; Health Problems; Rude People; Upsetting Calls; Critical Boss; Too Many Job Demands; Med. Side Effects; Friends Who Use

Figure 4.6: How I Will Mindfully Protect My Peace and Stability

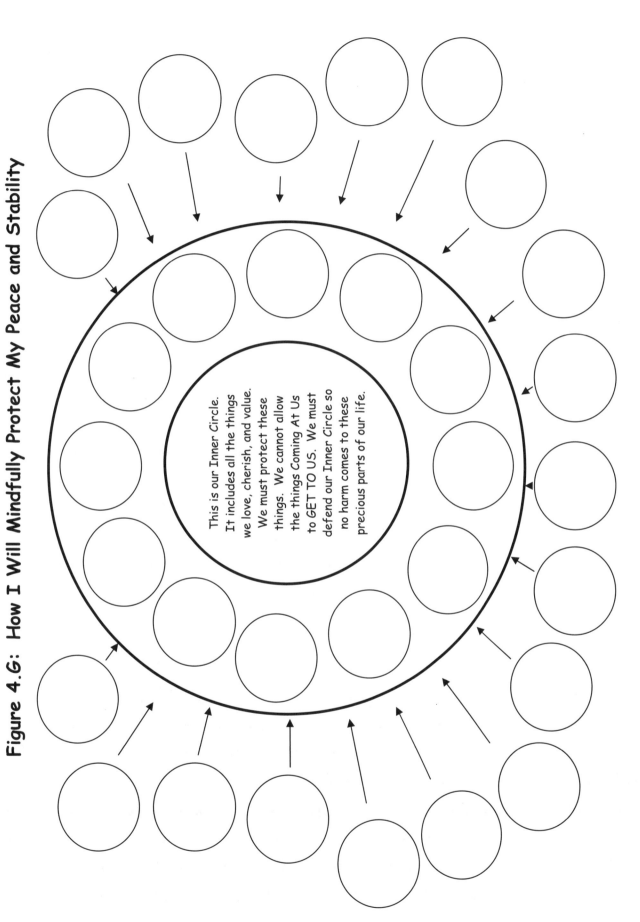

This is our Inner Circle. It includes all the things we love, cherish, and value. We must protect these things. We cannot allow the things Coming At Us to GET TO US. We must defend our Inner Circle so no harm comes to these precious parts of our life.

More on "The Concepts and Skills Tracking Sheet"

You'll QUICKLY notice that "The Concepts and Skills Tracking Sheet" for this chapter is longer than the tracking sheets for the previous chapters. This one is longer because more skills were discussed in this chapter...skills that NEED TO BE PRACTICED. This workbook is NOT meant to be JUST an intellectual pursuit. It's designed to be a LIFE-CHANGING JOURNEY. If we are to change our lives, we'll need to PRACTICE life-changing skills.

Many of the skills discussed in this chapter are BROKEN DOWN INTO STEPS. For instance, some entries will focus on BEING MINDFUL. Other entries will GO BEYOND basic Mindfulness and will focus on USING MINDFULNESS SKILLS to help ourselves. Remember...the FIRST STEP in changing our lives is MINDFULNESS. The next steps involve TAKING ACTION and doing something about the problems or issues we're Mindful of!

For an example, check out entry 4B. This one relates to basic awareness of what's going on in Emotional Mind. Notice that entry 4C goes a step further. It involves DOING SOMETHING to deal with the destructive thoughts we became Mindful of...like thinking about the consequences of acting on them! Now notice that entry 4D goes another step further. It's about USING ALL THIS INFORMATION WERE MINDFUL OF to Talk Ourselves Out of our destructive thoughts and INTO Life-Enhancing Coping Behaviors. A major Recovery Goal is to calm and soothe ourselves so we can prevent life destruction.

Breaking the skills down into steps...helps us to appreciate the steps we're taking... to learn and practice Life-Enhancing Coping Skills. The tracking sheets in the remainder of this workbook will also follow this same step-by-step learning process.

It's your decision how to use these tracking sheets. You can rate yourself on ALL the entries EVERY DAY, or part of the entries one day and others the next day. Find a way to make them work for you.

You're STRONGLY ENCOURAGED to make copies of the tracking sheets and to keep them in a notebook. That way, you can review the tracking sheets from earlier chapters to remind yourself of these skills and understandings. Also, you can check now and then to see how well you remember this information AND how well you're doing with the skills you previously learned and practiced.

Lastly, make use of the BLANK tracking sheet found in Chapter 1. When you review the tracking sheets from earlier chapters, if you find something you need to practice more, write it on the blank one. You can also list things YOU KNOW you need to practice that aren't discussed in the workbook or haven't been discussed yet! Remember, the more effort you put into this program, the more benefit you'll gain.

Figure 4.H.1: The Concepts and Skills Tracking Sheet – Chapter 4

Week # _____	Day of Week →										Notes:
	Date →										
4A. Today I listed MOST OR ALL of the nine things that we should try to become Mindful of when we need to Talk Ourselves Through desires to do something self-destructive.											
4B. When I was upset today, I stopped myself and became Mindful of the emotions I was experiencing and the self-destructive thoughts I was having.											
4C. When I was upset today and was Mindful of the self-destructive thoughts I was having, I thought about what would happen to the Big Picture of My Life and my life goals IF I acted on those thoughts.											
4D. When I was upset today, I Turned On Mindfulness and Talked Myself Out of destructive behavior and into Life-Enhancing Coping Behavior.											
4E. When I think about how I Talked Myself Through the upsetting situation today, I'm aware that Emotional Mind kept flaring up...and I went back and forth between destructive thoughts and life-enhancing thoughts. I realize I had to Fight hard to remain recovery-focused.											
4F. Today, I became aware of one or more mindless moments. I caught myself being mindless!											
4G. Today, I did something to help myself to be more mindful...like writing something down, repeating something to keep myself FOCUSED, or focusing on doing just one thing at a time.											
4H. Today, when I felt stressed-out because I had too many things to do, I decided which things were High Priorities or MUST DO's and which things were lower priorities and could wait.											
4I. Today, I became Mindful that I was ruminating about something. I realized it was causing me to be more upset.											

RATING SCALE
5 – Did Excellent in this area today
4 – Did Pretty Good in this area today
3 – Did Alright in this area today
2 – Did Only Fair in this area today
1 – Didn't Do Well in this area today
DD – Didn't Do today

124

Figure 4.H.2: The Concepts and Skills Tracking Sheet – Chapter 4

Week # _____

Day of Week →

Date →

4J. Today, when I caught myself ruminating about something upsetting, I did something to distract myself so I could get control of my mood.

4K. Today, when I caught myself ruminating, I did something to deal with the concern in a life-enhancing manner.

4L. Today, when I was faced with drama that didn't belong in my life, I got myself out of the situation so I could Mindfully Protect My Peace and Stability.

4M. Today, I reminded myself of the Infant Analogy and how it was important to soothe, care for, and protect myself like I would an infant.

4N. Today, I acted on the Infant Analogy and I soothed, cared for, or protected myself like I would an infant.

4O. Today, I thought about all the things in my life that are precious to me...and how it's important to act in ways to protect these things.

4P. Today, I realized that the things Coming At Me could get into my Inner Circle, overwhelm me, and end up messing up the things I value and cherish the most.

4Q. Today, I took action to prevent something Coming At Me from getting into my Inner Circle and upsetting my peace and stability AND my life. I did that by using Life-Enhancing Coping Skills to manage my mood, by avoiding unnecessary stress, or by taking action to deal with the problem head-on to improve the situation...like managing a bad phone call or visit!

4R. Today, I HELD FIRM to my boundaries and REFUSED to ALLOW something Coming At Me to GET TO ME. I had to Take A Stand to Protect My Peace and Stability.

Notes:

RATING SCALE

5 – Did Excellent in this area today
4 – Did Pretty Good in this area today
3 – Did Alright in this area today
2 – Did Only Fair in this area today
1 – Didn't Do Well in this area today
DD – Didn't Do today

~ 5 ~
MINDFULNESS IS A SKILL

It's a trick to get ourselves to THINK when we're used to just REACTING!

Learning and practicing Mindfulness is important because LEARNING to be IN CONTROL of what we PAY ATTENTION TO and FOCUS ON is the FIRST STEP in GETTING OUR LIFE IN ORDER. That's because when we ACT in MINDLESS, IMPULSIVE, and SELF-DESTRUCTIVE WAYS, our problems SNOWBALL, AVALANCHE, and become like a TRAIN WRECK.

WHEN WE BECOME MINDFUL of how we're FEELING, what we're THINKING, and how we're WANTING to respond...ALONG WITH Mindfulness of the REALITY of our situation, THE BIG PICTURE OF OUR LIFE, our LIFE GOALS, and the CONSEQUENCES of what we want to do...THEN, we'll be in a position to make a RATIONAL and WISE DECISION about how BEST TO RESPOND.
Our Recovery Goal is to CHOOSE HOW TO RESPOND rather than MINDLESSLY REACTING to the issues and problems Coming At Us.
Like any skill, LEARNING to be Mindful TAKES PRACTICE!

Learning Skills: From Mindful to Mindless

How many times have you suddenly snapped into Mindfulness to think, "Whoa, I don't remember going through those intersections or passing Wal-Mart!"?
I say, "Boy, I sure hope all those lights really were green!"

Think about when we were learning to drive. We were MINDFUL of EVERYTHING, like which side the gas pedal is on and where the brake is. We were Mindful of switching gears and we had to look as we shifted into park, reverse, and drive. We were VERY AWARE of the steps for making a turn, like signaling, slowing down, and cutting the turn just right. We watched closely and worried about staying in our lane. Remember all that? Now, AFTER YEARS OF DRIVING, these things have become OVERLEARNED.[1] We do them automatically or unconsciously. WE DON'T THINK ABOUT DOING THEM. WE DO THEM MINDLESSLY. We quickly shift into drive and rarely look at the dial. We sail through turns without thinking how to make a safe turn. We even drive miles without being aware of driving (scary, huh!?).

We've learned MANY skills that require A LOT OF PRACTICE and MINDFULNESS ...AT FIRST. Think about learning to write. We had to WORK HARD to make the letters just right, to make them the right height and to stay within the lines. We wrote the same letter OVER AND OVER. We labored over writing right! Now, we write sentences and paragraphs without giving any mind to writing the individual letters. OUR BRAIN JUST DOES IT AUTOMATICALLY.

1- Overlearned – very well learned. We've practiced them so much, we've overlearned them!

126

Our brain becomes programmed when we do the same thing in pretty much the same way ...many times.

Think about learning to play baseball. At first, we're concerned about our batting stance and how far apart to keep our feet, where to stand, how best to grip the bat, and how far up the bat our hands should be. OVER TIME, the BASICS become pretty mindless and we begin to focus on the MORE COMPLEX aspects of baseball. Now, instead of worrying about the mechanics of batting, we're concerned about what type of pitch is coming, how fast it's coming, and where to hit to make the best play!!! Which skills have you practiced SO MUCH that they've become rather MINDLESS or AUTOMATIC...such that you can do them now without thinking much about doing them? _____

_____

2- If we touch a hot stove, our arm jerks away before we even realize what happened. Jerking our arm away is a reflex...and a very mindless response.

> *The tasks we do that become mindless are ones we've done MANY TIMES. With repetition, OUR BRAIN REMEMBERS how to do them...then, we can do these things WITHOUT having to THINK much about doing them! They become like a REFLEX.[2]*

3- Action steps – the steps we take when we're doing something...like from Step A to Step Z.

4- Adaptive – helpful, life-enhancing, making our life better.

There are advantages to doing some things mindlessly, like driving, washing the dishes, using a computer program, and following a morning routine. We can carry out the action steps[3] QUICKLY and EASILY and WE DON'T HAVE TO THINK! THIS TYPE OF MINDLESS BEHAVIOR IS ADAPTIVE.[4] It helps us to function better. What sort of things do you do mindlessly that helps you to function better? _____

_____

APPLICATION: When the Automatic Process Goes Awry

5- Awry – (uh-wry) - to go wrong, to mess things up.

> This ADAPTIVE BRAIN PROCESS can go AWRY[5] and WORK AGAINST US, too. For instance, it CAUSES US HARM when we've done our preferred Self-Destructive Coping Behaviors over and over. When an upsetting event happens...BOOM...here comes that OVERLEARNED COPING RESPONSE. IT'S LIKE A REFLEX. We may slap or punch someone, hit the wall, say cruel things, drink more, throw something, overeat, eat for comfort, leave, or chain smoke...and we're often NOT really AWARE we're doing these things...until we're in the middle of doing them...or afterwards!

Ever hear the saying, "Be slow to speak and quick to listen"? Well, we're quite the opposite. We're quick to speak and slow to listen! We spout off and before we know it, we've said something we regret!

It's pretty much ACTION-REACTION...like we touch a hot stove and our arm flies back...or someone hurts us, so we hurt them back...or we're unhappy, so we go for the gallon of ice cream...or we're depressed, so we think about suicide...or we're nervous, so we bite the inside of our cheek or our nails. Our Self-Destructive Emotion-Driven Coping Behaviors BECOME A REFLEX. They become rather AUTOMATIC and MINDLESS. We do them WITHOUT THINKING! Now, THAT'S A PROBLEM...

It's hard to change our Emotion-Driven Behavior because we've made such a habit of doing it... and we often start to do it mindlessly.

We have to learn these skills NOW because the Heat-of-the-Moment is NOT the right time to pull out this book to read about Mindfulness. When things heat up around us, our arm is going to jerk back before we even know what happened.

Practice Life-Enhancing Coping Skills before you need them... because when you need them, you REALLY need them.

6- My sister used an anti-nail-biting product. She painted her nails with it and it tasted horrible when she went to bite her nails. The taste made her aware of what she was doing and gave her a chance to Think Through and to CHOOSE whether or not she REALLY wanted to do it. It allowed her to CATCH herself so she could CONSCIOUSLY CONTROL what she was doing. This made her Mindful of mindless behavior and conscious of her unconscious behavior. (continued)

but one WE CAN DO SOMETHING ABOUT!

Getting Control of Our Out-of-Control Emotion-Driven Reflexes

IF WE WANT TO CHANGE how things WORK OUT FOR US, we must become MINDFUL of our IMPULSIVE REACTIONS...the REFLEXIVE ACTION-REACTIONS we do! Practicing mindfulness is the first step. We MUST LEARN to BECOME AWARE OF WHAT WE'RE DOING! We must become SKILLED in this area, so when the situation is critical, we're PRACTICED and READY to manage our life. We've been learning how to become Mindful of troubling emotions and Emotion-Driven Behavior, our triggers and the things Coming At Us, the Big Picture of Our Life and what we'll lose, and the process of bottoming-out due to the Cycle of Suffering. We've studied SOME WAYS to increase Mindfulness, BUT, there's more to come!

SKILL BUILDER: An All Day Daily Devotional

AA teaches Mindfulness by encouraging folks to do a morning devotional. This STARTS OUR DAY WITH AWARENESS OF OUR PRIMARY GOAL - RECOVERY. This TURNS ON MINDFULNESS FROM THE GET-GO and FILLS OUR MIND and HEART with how WE CHOOSE TO LIVE our day AND our life. We need to ALWAYS BE MINDFUL that RECOVERY is our NUMBER ONE PRIORITY!

THROUGHOUT our day, we need to be aware of ourselves...how we're feeling, what thoughts are going through our mind, what temptations and triggers we face, what we're tempted to do, what we're starting to do, the Big Picture of Our Life, and our life goals. AS WE LIVE OUR DAY, we need to be Mindful that RECOVERY IS OUR NUMBER ONE PRIORITY...and as such, we need to CHOOSE HOW TO RESPOND TO LIFE to support our life goals...rather than JUST MINDLESSLY REACTING.

APPLICATION: From the Old to the New and Back Again

Learning new behaviors and skills REQUIRES a great deal of Mindfulness. This is especially true when we're TRYING TO BREAK old, self-defeating habits WHILE AT THE SAME TIME TRYING TO DEVELOP NEW recovery habits! This is because when we're under stress, we tend to go back to old, familiar ways. That's why we must ALWAYS be Mindful of WHAT WE'RE DOING and WHAT WE'RE THINKING ABOUT DOING. We need to CATCH OURSELVES when we BEGIN to think about doing the old behavior or we BEGIN DOING IT! We have to become MINDFUL OF OUR MINDLESS BEHAVIOR and CONSCIOUS OF OUR UNCONSCIOUS BEHAVIOR! For instance, if we're trying to quit biting our nails, we have to increase Mindfulness and catch ourselves whenever we put our nails in our mouth.[6] WE HAVE TO CATCH

(6- continued)
Don't you wish we could get a bottle of that for other self-defeating behaviors! Actually, Antabuse is a medication drinkers can take to stop drinking. It makes them very sick if they drink while taking it. But that's a bit after the fact. It's really more of a consequence than a Mindfulness tool!

7- Our fingernails are a 24-7 temptation! This is different from the gallon of ice cream in the freezer and our temptation to relapse is when we're home.

It's easier to gain control before we lose it!

It's important to realize we're human and we're not going to be 100% skilled and perfect in all we do.

Don't get discouraged. It takes time to change old ways. It may have taken 10, 20, 30, or 40 years to develop these overlearned habits. Expect it'll take a little while to change them!

OURSELVES so we can make a CONSCIOUS DECISION if we REALLY WANT to bite our nails. Nail biting is a difficult habit to break because we're around our nails 24-7.[7] When the temptation is constant, we must be CONSTANTLY aware of ourselves.

SKILL BUILDER: Catch Relapse in the Making

When we're working to CHANGE old coping habits, we need to be VERY MINDFUL to CATCH RELAPSE IN THE MAKING. We need to be aware that things are BUILDING UP and MOVING IN THE DIRECTION OF RELAPSE.
It's best to "NIP THINGS IN THE BUD" and ALTER or STOP a situation BEFORE Something Bad Happens...and WE RELAPSE.

We need to be Mindful we're GETTING upset...and we must deal with the situation EARLY ON...BEFORE it builds up and GETS OUT-OF-CONTROL. It's EVEN BETTER to be Mindful we're GOING to face a difficult situation and have a Game Plan ALREADY developed. Our Game Plan may be to AVOID the situation if it's NOT a High Priority in our life. If it's a PRIORITY, our plan will help us MANAGE the situation and MINIMIZE how upset we may become. Sometimes we get into situations unexpectedly. In these situations, our task is to apply our skills and DO THE BEST WE CAN.

As we're learning to be Mindful of what's going on within us and around us...and as we're learning other skills in this program, they may be a CHALLENGE to do...at first. At times, we'll BEGIN doing things THE OLD WAY...MINDLESSLY. We'll have to CATCH OURSELVES and MINDFULLY USE OUR NEW SKILLS. Over time, these NEW life management skills will become easier, more natural, rather automatic, and SECOND NATURE. It'll take a lot of DEDICATION and PRACTICE to change our old habits, but, the end result is WELL WORTH OUR EFFORT.

What will be the end result for you? _____

_____

I hope you wrote something like peace, balance, a stable life, having some really super things in my life, life satisfaction, happiness, etc! That's what it's all about! So, take the time it takes to LEARN more about these skills. IT'S NOT ROCKET SCIENCE. It's just PRACTICING AWARENESS!

Observing and Describing

TWO BASIC MINDFULNESS SKILLS discussed by Dr. Linehan are Observing and Describing. **OBSERVING** involves taking notice of what we see, hear, think, and feel.

Between stimulus and response there is a space. In that space is our power to choose our response. In our response lies our growth and our freedom.
Viktor E. Frankl

8- Informed decisions – decisions based on having the information we need to make a good decision!
9- DBT-CBT is about getting and maintaining peace and stability. Walking into a situation and losing our well-deserved peace and balance is a major event we want to avoid!
10- At the end of this chapter, you'll find a tracking sheet to track your practice!

Our emotional states are easily affected by what's going on around us. It's very nice to have our mood uplifted or lightened, but it's not so nice when our mood goes from neutral or happy… to angry, irritated, agitated, or depressed…just because of what's going on around us.

Our Recovery Goal is to catch situations early BEFORE we have any MAJOR mood swings.

To be Mindful, we need to be a good observer. Our observations will give us the INFORMATION WE NEED to understand our situations and to make INFORMED DECISIONS[8] about how BEST to respond. **DESCRIBING** is putting our observations into words. It's describing what we observe! It takes a little longer to do this… and this is THE TIME WE NEED TO THINK ABOUT WHAT'S GOING ON.

SKILL BUILDER: Don't Let It Get You Down

We know that things going on around us can affect our mood, for better or worse. For instance, an uplifting movie or visit can put us in a good mood. If we come across someone who's really tickled and laughing hysterically, this will make us chuckle. When we're around an inspiring person with a positive attitude, a spark of hope can flare and improve our outlook on life. Likewise, being around someone who's fussing n' moaning can get us irritated and focused on everything wrong in a situation or our life.

When we find ourselves drawn into an upsetting situation, we need to EMOTIONALLY "STEP BACK" from the situation and BECOME MINDFUL of what's going on.[9] We become Mindful by Observing and Describing. We can observe the situation as if we're watching it on TV. We can describe the situation as if we're telling a friend what happened on a TV show. Here's an example.

> "I was feeling at peace when I walked in here. I was happy. In fact, I was humming the song we sang in church yesterday! As soon as I walked in, Jan had to tell me how rude Stacy and Wanda were to her and how she's sick and tired of rude people. I was feeling pretty good until she unloaded on me for FIVE MINUTES STRAIGHT. Now I feel angry and agitated. I can't believe how strongly this has affected me."

That's an example of how we PRACTICE and how we do it in REAL LIFE. Practice Observing 5-10 times a day.[10] Observe all kinds of personal situations. We won't need to do this 5-10 times a day for the rest of our life, JUST ENOUGH so we'll become GOOD ENOUGH at it so we can use this skill when we need it!

Truth, in the Heat-of-the-Moment, we may not be as descriptive as the example above. In Real Life, with Jan CHATTERING NON-STOP, it'll be hard TO THINK STRAIGHT, so we'll probably do a shorter version, like,

> "I was feeling at peace when I walked in here. Jan is telling me all this crap and now I'm getting angry. I need to get away from her QUICK!"

Write a short story about a conversation you've had with a "Jan" in your life that TOOK AWAY YOUR PEACE…or could have if you didn't control it. This will be a conversation you DID NOT NEED TO HAVE! Describe your observations, thoughts, and feelings. _____

That's how we do it. We Talk Ourselves Through It!!!

_____

_____

_____

_____

SKILL BUILDER: Mindfully Talking Ourselves Down and Refocusing

AFTER A MOOD CHANGING SITUATION, it's helpful to run a longer version through our mind to BECOME MINDFUL about what happened and to PROCESS and LEARN FROM THE EXPERIENCE. This also helps us to Talk Ourselves Down, to CALM THE IRRITATED MOOD, and to RESTORE OUR PEACE. After we process what happened, we may need to distract ourselves so we don't ruminate or stew over what happened.[11] It may go like this...

11- By reviewing what happened, we'll have the chance to pat ourselves on the back for how well we managed an unpleasant situation.

> "I have to realize this irritation is NOT MINE. It's Jan's and I need to let it roll off me like water off a duck's back. It's NOT MY ANGER AND HOSTILITY, IT'S HERS. It does NOT belong to me. It's borrowed and I'm going to give it back!!!! I'm going to distract myself from this DRAMA and regain my peace of mind. Now what was the song I was humming?"

12- The LONGER VERSION on the previous page starting with "I was feeling at peace..."

When she spoke the long version,[12] what did she observe about her mood BEFORE she ran into Jan? _____

_____

What changes did she observe in her mood by being around Jan? _____

_____

What did she observe to be the cause of her mood change? _____

_____

13- The one on this page starting with "I have to realize..."

After Observing and Describing, she began to process the situation.[13] What truths did she tell herself that helped her to Let Go of her bad mood? _____

_____

She observed and described her mood to be peaceful and happy BEFORE she ran into Jan. She noticed her mind was focused on an uplifting song, BUT AFTER FIVE MINUTES WITH JAN, her mood CHANGED! She became aware that Jan's non-stop complaining caused her mood to change. She realized HER NEW MOOD was really JAN'S BAD MOOD...that she ABSORBED or TOOK ON JAN'S ANGER AND IRRITATION! She became Mindful of THE TRUTH and the Big Picture of the Situation. She realized the anger DID NOT BELONG TO HER, THAT IT WAS JAN'S ANGER and SHE NEEDED TO LET IT GO! Her GAME PLAN was to distract herself to

REGAIN HER PEACEFUL MOOD. She did this by "TURNING HER MIND" away from Jan's stuff and back to her own world and the special song she was singing!

SKILL BUILDER: Putting an End to a Conversation

For the sake of "How-to's" and skill development, let's get off topic a minute…and return to the Jan Story. During the Heat-of-the-Moment, the lady's Game Plan was to get away from Jan QUICK…because Jan's drama was NOT A PRIORITY in her life. The story doesn't say how she did it, but there are many ways to end a conversation. List several ways she could have ended the conversation without being added to Jan's list of rude people. _____

_____

_____

_____

She could have said, "I hate to stop you, but I've really got to go." or "Hey, I've lost track of time. I have to run. See you soon." PRACTICE "CONVERSATION ENDERS" so when you need to end one, you're ready!!! Come up with some that feel right to you!

PRACTICE Observing and Describing 5-10 times a day. BE AWARE of situations that AFFECT you. NOTE ANY MOOD CHANGES and what may have CAUSED them. PRACTICE RESPONDING to these situations EFFECTIVELY…by CONFRONTING them or REMOVING YOURSELF. PLAY OUT practice situations in your head by VISUALIZING and ROLE-PLAYING.

SKILL BUILDER: Observing Our Body

The following are some Observing exercises we do in Group TO PRACTICE Mindfulness.[14] We start by "Observing" sensations in our body.[15] Try this one!

AFTER you read this, I'll ask you to CLOSE YOUR EYES and "OBSERVE" YOUR FEET. DON'T MOVE ONCE WE START! You might notice how your feet feel inside your shoes or on the floor. You might notice some discomfort with the position they're in. You might notice the coolness or warmth of the surface they're on. You'll probably notice other sensations as well. WHEN YOU'RE OBSERVING, JUST OBSERVE. AVOID DESCRIBING what you're observing! Try to leave words out of this. Simply observe and experience your feet. IF LANGUAGE COMES IN, LET IT GO RIGHT BACK OUT. DON'T WORRY YOURSELF OR GET DISTRACTED BY IT!

Now it's time to practice. Be still and "observe" your feet for one minute. Close your eyes while you do it. Go ahead and do it NOW.

We must CHERISH and PROTECT our peace and stability. We CAN'T just let someone come across our path and take it away from us!

Our Recovery Goal is to catch situations early…BEFORE we have any major mood swings.

"Oh my! I've got to go to the bathroom!" just doesn't work for everyone, though it's highly effective! It stuns folks and is a conversation-ender most every time!

Mindfulness is the foundation for DBT-CBT and for Getting Control over our emotions AND our life! Please practice!

Practice Observing, Describing, AND Participating Effectively. TAKE Control OR BE CONTROLLED! It's YOUR CHOICE!

14- These are from Dr. Linehan's Manual.

15- This is hard to do on paper, but we'll try! I ask Members to close their eyes while I talk them through this. It's a relaxation exercise, too.

What did you observe about your feet? Now it's time to describe! _____
_____

How focused were you? Approximately how much of the time were you able to focus on your feet, like 50% of the time, 80%, 100%? _____

Other than feeling silly, what was it like to observe and be Mindful of your feet? ____
_____

16- Try focusing on your hands, shoulders, stomach, your breathing, what you're hearing, etc.

Practice again! This time, focus on your REAR END! Get all the giggles out! When it's time, close your eyes and don't move. JUST SIMPLY EXPERIENCE YOUR REAR! You might notice the contact your rear makes with the chair or sofa, maybe some warmth, heaviness, or discomfort with the position you're in. You might notice other things, too! AVOID THE USE OF WORDS AND DESCRIBING. If you begin to describe, DON'T WORRY ABOUT IT...JUST LET THE WORDS GO. Ready to try this one? Close your eyes NOW and observe your rear!

What did you observe? Now it time to describe! _____
_____

17- This includes Emotion-Driven Thoughts, excessive worrying, painful rumination, and racing thoughts.
It includes being stuck on suicidal thoughts, cutting, drinking, anger, etc.
It also includes replaying an embarrassing situation over and over in our mind and ruminating about being worthless, stupid, unloved, etc.

How focused were you on observing your rear? What percentage of the time were you able to focus? _____

Other than feeling silly, what was it like to observe and be Mindful of your rear? ____
_____

18- These are more Mindfulness exercises from Dr. Linehan's Skills Training Manual.

PRACTICE this Skill Builder several times a week. So you won't get too focused on your rear, try other body parts, too![16] Make note of how well you're able to focus. OVER TIME, you'll be able to focus LONGER, maybe 70-80% of the time...or longer. The goal is to get BETTER AND BETTER at Observing.

SKILL BUILDER: Mindfully Observing Our Thoughts

19- A thought is something we say or think inside our head.
It's usually a phrase or sentence, like, "She's not home again.", "What was I doing?", "He doesn't seem to like me.", "Wow!", ""I'll never make it.", and "I'm going to cut." These are thoughts...and some are Emotion-Driven Thoughts!

To INCREASE CONTROL OVER OUR THINKING,[17] we must be able to OBSERVE OUR THOUGHTS. The next set of Skill Builders will help us to FOCUS ON observing our thoughts.[18] I call the first one "The Next Two Thoughts" and the other two, "The Conveyer Belt" and "Put It on a Cloud."

"The Next Two Thoughts"

In this MINDFULNESS SKILL BUILDER, you'll be asked to notice "The Next Two Thoughts" that go through your mind. Notice the first two thoughts[19] or sentences, and then write them down. Start NOW.

1st _____
_____

While doing this Skill Builder, we might notice thoughts such as, "I need to mail the phone bill.", "I'm blank. I'm not having any thoughts.", "I can't think with the neighbors fighting.", "That's the first thought.", "I'm having too many to count.", or "My stomach is growling!" Those are all thoughts. Simply write the first two that go through your mind!

2nd _____

_____

Any phrase or sentence that goes through our mind IS a thought. Things like, "I'm not having a thought." and "Is that a thought?" ARE thoughts! Try it again. Before you start, say "Okay, fine"...then observe your next two thoughts. Write them down, too!

1st _____

_____

2nd _____

_____

Try it again. Say, "Almost done!"...then observe your next two thoughts.

1st _____

_____

2nd _____

_____

How was this to do? Did you get better with practice? PRACTICE observing your thoughts SEVERAL times a day until it becomes easier and MORE NATURAL to do. Our Recovery Goal is to get BETTER AND BETTER at Mindfulness!

"The Conveyer Belt"

This Mindfulness Skill Builder involves VISUAL IMAGERY.[20] Its real neat.[21] Imagine your mind to be a conveyer belt.[22] As a thought, feeling, or sensation goes through your mind, NOTICE IT and LET IT GENTLY FLOW ONTO THE CONVEYER BELT. Notice ALL things that go through your mind...and LET THEM FLOW...ONE BY ONE onto the belt. Avoid Describing. Just Observe them and LET THEM FLOW onto the belt...DOWN THE LINE...AND OUT OF YOUR MIND. If you become distracted or say something to yourself, JUST NOTICE IT and LET IT FLOW ONTO THE BELT. Close your eyes and practice this for a minute or two.

What was it like to do? _____

_____

Try it a few more times.

Did it get easier with practice? Did you have fewer distractions? Did it become relaxing? _____

_____

"Put It on a Cloud"

This is a Group favorite![23] Imagine your mind to be the sky. Notice all the

20- Imagery – (em-midge-ree) – pictures or scenes imagined in our mind. They're the things our mind "sees" when we're imagining things!

21- Another cool exercise from Dr. Linehan's Skills Training Manual. Group Members really enjoy this and find great value in it.

22- A conveyer belt is the big, wide belt that carries items down an assembly line.

23- Another great suggestion from Dr. Linehan's Skills Training Manual. I love this one! It's so relaxing!

thoughts, feelings, and sensations that go through your mind. Let them GENTLY FLOW THROUGH your mind and ONTO THE CLOUDS DRIFTING BY, ONE BY ONE. SIMPLY NOTICE THEM and LET THEM DRIFT. Try not to talk to yourself. If you do, LET YOUR WORDS FLOW onto a cloud and DRIFT BY. If you find yourself distracted, let the distraction FLOW onto a cloud and FLOAT BY. If you have a pain, LET IT FLOW onto a cloud and FLOAT BY. If you have an itch, notice it, and LET IT FLOW BY. If you scratch it, notice that, and LET IT FLOAT BY. Notice all things as they go through your mind...and LET THEM FLOW ONTO A CLOUD and PASS BY. Enjoy the RELAXATION. Practice this a minute or two. Then, do it a few more times! What was this one like to do? _____

_____

Did these Mindfulness Skill Builders become easier with practice? Did you have fewer distractions as you practiced more? Did they become enjoyable or relaxing? _____

_____

Which did you like best...the Conveyer Belt or the Cloud one? Why? _____

_____

_____

What was the hardest part about doing these? _____

_____

While you were doing these Mindfulness Skill Builders, did you find yourself describing the process and talking to yourself? Did these distractions decrease over time? It's common to get distracted A LOT at first and it's common to say things to ourselves! At first, if we go five seconds without a distraction, we've done really well! Just let those extra thoughts FLOW onto a cloud or a conveyer belt and LET THEM FLOW BY! Even if you're constantly distracted or are constantly describing, just notice...and Let 'Em Flow!!!

Other Imagery Options

Try to come up with imagery to use that's special to you. A cyclist enjoyed experiencing herself cycling down a favorite road. She'd notice her thoughts and feelings and would let them flow onto the trees and bushes as she sped by. A man worked at a water park and would imagine a lazy river setting. He'd let his thoughts and feelings flow onto a tube and float by. Try out different types of imagery. What imagery would make it fun and relaxing for you? _____

_____

24- Internal – inside. Things that go on inside us, like our thoughts and feelings.

25- External – outside. Outside of us!

26- Group Members have found this coping tool to be VERY HELPFUL for ridding their minds of unwanted thoughts and feelings. Members are excited to talk about how they've used this tool to help themselves. YEA!

27-This one reminds me of counting sheep while trying to fall asleep. I count sheep as they jump over a low fence. If you're having trouble falling asleep, try the "Put It on a Cloud" or "The Conveyer Belt" techniques for awhile! Let your thoughts flow onto them as you fall asleep!

28- Track your practice using the tracking sheets at the end of the chapter.

The best time to practice is when we AREN'T desperate for the skill.

Tips for Observing

1. To observe is to take notice. Simply observe when you're Observing. Avoid Describing. Avoid responding. JUST OBSERVE.

2. Just notice and observe. Avoid getting caught up or stuck on any one thought or observation. Just let your observations GO WITH THE FLOW.

3. Try to keep your mind on Observing. If you find yourself distracted, simply observe that…and keep on Observing.

4. Be a reporter of internal[24] events. Take note of every thought, feeling, and sensation that goes through your mind.

5 Be like a video camera of external events.[25] Take note of what you're doing and saying, how others are responding to you, and what's going on in your environment.

Using Imagery as a Coping Tool

Want to clear your mind, find some peace, and Let Things Go? "The Conveyer Belt" and "The Put It on a Cloud" imagery tools are great ways to RID OUR MIND of UNWANTED THOUGHTS and FEELINGS.[26,27] They can be VERY HELPFUL when we're worrying and ruminating, when we're anxious or our mind is racing, when we're dwelling on something painful or stewing over something that made us angry, and when destructive Emotion-Driven Thoughts fly through our mind. Just LET EACH thought, feeling, or sensation FLOW ONTO a conveyer belt, a cloud, a tree, a tube…or anything of your choosing…and LET THEM FLOW BY. DON'T HOLD ONTO ANY of these…LET THEM FLOW AWAY. AVOID interacting with these thoughts and feelings. AVOID JUDGING them as good or bad, or right or wrong. AS THEY COME INTO YOUR MIND, LET 'EM FLOW RIGHT OUT…and GET SOME PEACE…SOME PEACE OF MIND! When might this coping skill be useful to you? _____

_____

REALLY, REALLY, PRACTICE THESE EXERCISES. PRACTICE NOW,[28] so when you need these skills, you'll be practiced and can better help yourself.

Mindfully Describing Our Observations

Sometimes we'll simply observe and do nothing more. Other times, we'll observe AND DESCRIBE. We'll use words and sentences to describe our observations. A description can be in the form of a thought or something we say aloud. For instance, we may observe feelings of sadness and describe, "This is really sad. It makes me feel like crying." We may observe we're angry and describe our feelings, "I'm really angry with her. I feel like slapping the taste right out of her mouth!" When we describe

136

something, we put words to our experience. We describe it! DESCRIBING IS ANOTHER MINDFULNESS SKILL. It helps us gain MORE INFORMATION about our experiences and our world. IT TAKES MINDFULNESS TO ANOTHER LEVEL!

SKILL BUILDER: Opinions Vs. Facts

When we describe, it's important we don't confuse an opinion with a fact. That's because our goal is to be rational and to deal with reality! For example,

We sometimes confuse OUR PERCEPTIONS with the truth. We make a judgment based on parts of a situation without taking into account the Big Picture of the Situation.

> *Very kind Kim spoke a harsh word to Jim. Kim observed and described her action, "I just spoke a harsh word to Jim." She then thinks, "I'm such a mean person."*

Is Kim's statement, "I'm such a mean person." an opinion or a fact? Is Kim REALLY a mean person? Explain. _____

_____

It's an opinion because Kim is USUALLY very kind. She DID SOMETHING UNLIKE HERSELF or OUT-OF-CHARACTER when she spoke harshly to Jim. How could something like that happen? _____

_____

We're often quick to judge a person's character based on just one observation of their behavior or one piece of information.

> She may have been stressed out, tired, or too irritated with Jim and said something impulsive and out-of-character. She judged herself harshly by describing her TOTAL CHARACTER to be mean because of ONE action. Had she been Mindful of WHO SHE IS AS A PERSON and THE BIG PICTURE OF THE SITUATION, she would have been FAIR TO HERSELF and described, "*Whoa, I just did something mean. I better eat so I'm not so fussy!*" She would have RATIONALLY described her BEHAVIOR on this ONE occasion rather than JUDGING and LABELING her TOTAL SELF to be mean.

Do you do this? Do you make judgments about yourself or others based on ONE action or situation? If so, give an example. _____

_____

_____

Our behavior in one situation…and on any given day may be very different from how we usually act. Our behavior is affected by the situation we're in, who's around, our mood, and how we physically feel on any given day. That's why first impressions are usually wrong.

Our judgments are MUCH MORE ACCURATE when we observe behavior on SEVERAL OCCASIONS and in DIFFERENT SITUATIONS. This gives us more information to base our opinions on. In Kim's case, we would observe her to be a very nice person… who rarely does anything mean! Consider another story.

> *Mark quit school in the 8th grade. He is a Shift Team Leader at Taco Bell. He makes a mistake adding up sales and says, "I am SO stupid."*

Is the statement, "I am SO stupid." a fact or an opinion? Explain. _____

_____

_____

> It's an opinion! It's an Emotion-Driven Thought based on making AN ERROR!
> He may be hard on himself because he dropped out of school early. Maybe he's
> repeating what a parent or school mate said to him...something emotionally abusive.
> IT'S AN OPINION BECAUSE IT ISN'T THE TRUTH! Consider the Big Picture.
> He quit school in the 8th grade and was promoted to a Team Leader. He obviously has
> natural intelligence and ability. He has learned enough in life to be a supervisor
> with major job responsibilities. His statement is an EMOTION-DRIVEN LIE.
> It's a NEGATIVE, HURTFUL, and UNNECESSARY SELF-JUDGMENT.

How could he have more FAIRLY, REALISTICALLY, and RATIONALLY described his

mistake? _____

_____

29- I often say, "Oops, that's my first error of the day!"...and unfortunately, it usually occurs before 9AM!

He could have said, "Oops, I made an error!" The truth, most of us make MANY

ERRORS...EVERY DAY![29] Though not great, he could have said, "THAT was stupid!"

Why would "THAT was stupid!" be acceptable...but something we should still work to

avoid? _____

_____

30- Personalizing – making it personal... believing it to be about WHO HE IS AS A PERSON.

> By using the word "THAT," he'd be saying AN ACTION was stupid,
> not his WHOLE PERSON. He'd be Mindful that he USUALLY does things right.
> He wouldn't be PERSONALIZING[30] THE ERROR as if it DEFINES
> WHO HE IS AS A PERSON. It's best to AVOID words like "stupid" because
> they're NEGATIVE LABELS WE DON'T NEED IN OUR LIFE...on purpose.
> That's especially true if we have issues with labels like "stupid."

Which negative labels do you apply to yourself that DON'T REFLECT THE TRUTH

about your WHOLE PERSON? _____

_____

Consider another example.

> *Suppose a nurse at a hospital, a manager at work, or a teacher who is generally fair
> and likeable, enforces a rule we don't like. She is firm and short with us while
> doing so and we walk away thinking, "She's such a witch!"*

Is "She's such a witch!" a fact or an opinion? Why? _____

_____

138

31- Situational – (sit-you-a-shin-ull) – based on the situation.

32- Enduring personality characteristic – a personality trait that endures. It's not situational. It's the way the person is in almost all situations and almost all the time!

It's an opinion because she's usually fair and likeable...and obviously, the rule existed and she needed to enforce it! It just so happens we don't like the rule and she was very direct when she told us about it! Maybe she said it like she did because she doesn't like the rule, either! If we're Mindful of the Big Picture, we might observe that she's short TODAY because something UNUSUAL is going on. Maybe several people called in sick or the big boss is there and is griping about everything, or the air conditioner is out and it's hot. For her, being short is unusual. It's SITUATIONAL.[31] It's NOT a long-term enduring personality characteristic.[32] Here's one more,

> Debbie believes in speaking her mind even if people don't like what she has to say. She makes people mad because of her comments. Georgia is showing co-workers pictures of her new grandson and asks Debbie if she would like to see them.
> Debbie says, "I don't have time to look at baby pictures!"
> Everyone just looks at each other. Amanda says, "She is soooo rude."

Is "She is soooo rude." a fact or an opinion? Why? _____

_____

THIS APPEARS TO BE A FACT! Being rude is just how she is! She speaks her mind and doesn't care if she hurts people or makes them mad!

Consider when you judged someone based on ONE OBSERVATION or ONE THING YOU HEARD about them...and later found out you were wrong. Describe the situation and mention how you figured out you were wrong? _____

_____

_____

Usually, we find out we're wrong when we GAIN MORE INFORMATION about the person...either by more observations or hearing more about them!

Tips for Describing

1. Use words to describe what you're thinking, feeling, experiencing, and seeing. Describe what's going on INTERNALLY and EXTERNALLY.
2. Simply identify your thoughts as thoughts and your feelings as feelings. Avoid judging yourself good or bad because of a certain thought or feeling. Recognize we're human and sometimes we have "inappropriate" thoughts and feelings that are QUITE NORMAL FOR OUR SITUATION! Remember, we're working to increase insight and Mindfulness, NOT SHAME and negative self-judgment!
3. Because we observe and describe something and are aware it's going on, it DOESN'T MEAN we have to respond to it. We can choose to Let Some Things Go. We don't have to respond to everything that Comes Our Way!

Want peace? Relax and let some things pass by. Don't feel like you have to respond to everything that upsets you!

Part of being assertive is choosing when and when not to be assertive.

33 – Extreme ways – being one way or another without anything in between. It's the same as "black and white" or "all-or-none" thinking.

34- This is another major Mindfulness skill from Dr. Linehan's Manual. Being Nonjudgmental means we don't judge or label our observations when we're trying to be Mindful!

35- Clouded or distorted – we're not seeing or dealing with the Big Picture. We're only dealing with parts of the situation. We may unconsciously twist or distort the facts and see things based on our emotional state, our prior experiences, and our view of the world. Like if we're depressed, we see the world through dark, gloomy lenses. We see everything through the pessimistic and negative eyes of depression. We see and focus on all the bad, sad, and hurtful things in our life and we overlook, minimize, or ignore the good, hopeful, and positive things in our life and world.

36- It's not because he's stupid. It's because he's normal. Few people learn everything quickly. Most of us have trouble learning something now and then. Maybe it's not explained well or we don't have the knowledge base to understand it. Maybe it's complicated or we're too stressed out to focus. Maybe our anxiety about learning things gets in the way of learning things! When we have "learning issues" and "stupid issues," Emotional Mind Turns On and makes it hard to think rationally (continued)

Another Mindfulness Skill: Being Nonjudgmental

We've BEEN talking about this Mindfulness skill already. It's the one about mindlessly labeling or judging what we're observing and describing. Judging is LABELING someone or something in EXTREME WAYS[33]...like good OR bad, worthwhile OR worthless, fair OR unfair, right OR wrong, smart OR stupid, etc. Our Mindfulness goal is to TAKE IN information...and we need to do so NONJUDGMENTALLY.[34] One reason for avoiding judgments when we're observing and describing is that we're often wrong when we base them on AN OBSERVATION OR TWO. We DON'T HAVE ENOUGH information to make an ACCURATE JUDGMENT. Also, if we're in Emotional Mind at the time, our perceptions and judgments are often clouded or distorted[35] by our emotional stuff. We're not seeing things clearly or as they truly are.

Another reason to avoid Extreme Judgments is they often SHUT DOWN OUR AWARENESS! For instance, we may make an Extreme Judgment and then ignore information which contradicts or goes against it. Mark, the Shift Team Leader, has "stupid" issues and is quick to judge himself as stupid when he makes an error or doesn't learn something fast.[36] Because he's in the habit of focusing on "stupid", he fails to be Mindful of his natural intelligence, skills, leadership ability, and all the things he does right and well. He doesn't pay attention to the BIG PICTURE OF WHO HE IS and facts like his boss finds him to be bright and skillful, he's had several promotions, and has been given a lot of responsibility. When he was observing and describing his error, he didn't deal with the fact that smart AND stupid people make mistakes ALL THE TIME...that making mistakes is part of our humanity.

> We can greatly help ourselves by avoiding judgmental labels about ourselves, others, and life in general. OUR GOAL IS AWARENESS.
> We're trying to GATHER INFORMATION so we can UNDERSTAND the Big Picture of WHAT we're dealing with. The more we know and understand, the better and wiser our decisions will be about how BEST to respond to a situation.

APPLICATION: Love at First Sight or Blinded by Love

Let's apply Observing, Describing, and Judging to our perceptions of people and our relationships. This is a VERY important topic because we often end up with relationship problems when we misjudge people...AND relationship problems are often a major TRIGGER POINT FOR RELAPSE.

Perhaps you've heard of "black and white" or "all-or-none" thinking. That's when we

140

(36- continued)
and to process and learn new information. That's because our mind is filled with anxiety and "fear of failure" thoughts and emotions! Sounds like a Self-Fulfilling Prophecy in the making!

37- Idealizing - (eye-deal-eye-zing) - seeing them as ideal, perfect, and EXACTLY what we want!

38- When we're in the "all good" mode, we may overlook or excuse bad qualities. We may also tell ourselves the bad qualities aren't really so bad or the person will change for us. When they don't live up to our expectations, we're disillusioned and broken-hearted.

When we're desperately lonely, we tend to see what we want to see and we ignore, deny, or minimize what we don't want to know about. We're NOT dealing with reality. We're living a fantasy.

No one is perfect for us and no one is 100% good! To think so would be a mindless illusion!

When we do "all good - all bad" thinking, we experience our people as all good or all bad...like there's nothing in between.

view something in extreme terms such as "good OR bad," "nice OR mean," or "friend OR enemy." In reality, things are rarely 100% one way or the other. People have "good" AND "bad" qualities...AND some "okay" qualities as well! They have the black, the white, and the shades of grey. Remember "very nice Kim," she's usually very nice...but sometimes, she's mean! She isn't "all good" or "all bad." Her personality falls somewhere in the middle...in a shade of gray.

Consider "love at FIRST SIGHT" or "I knew he was MR. RIGHT the MINUTE I met him." When we have these experiences, we're IDEALIZING[37] the person and observing, describing, and perceiving their GOOD characteristics ONLY. We view them as "ALL GOOD" or "PERFECT" and we're judging them based on what we observe AT FIRST and in ONE situation or environment. We're NOT dealing with THE BIG PICTURE of the PERSON. We have NOT observed and described the WHOLE person! We base our OPINION on VERY LITTLE information. We may ONLY be around them when they're in a GOOD MOOD or when they're flirting and are TRYING to be charming. We HAVEN'T OBSERVED them when they're ANGRY, STRESSED-OUT, TIRED, or in a BAD MOOD! We MINDLESSLY FALL IN LOVE based on LIMITED information.[38] We SEE them as WONDERFUL and our SOUL MATE and we EXPECT THEY'LL BE wonderful and will fulfill us like a soul mate. As time goes by and THE NEW WEARS OFF, THINGS OFTEN CHANGE. We spend ENOUGH TIME with them to experience them in a VARIETY of SITUATIONS and MOODS. Maybe they feel secure when we're "together" and they stop TRYING TO WIN our affection or we begin to observe the FULLNESS of their personality and we see their "OTHER SIDE." Maybe they begin to act like who they REALLY ARE...and it's NOT MR. WONDERFUL or MS. SOUL MATE anymore. We're often VERY HURT AND DISAPPOINTED when they DON'T LIVE UP TO OUR FIRST IMPRESSIONS. When we're BLINDED BY LOVE, we go from an emotional HIGH to an emotional LOW and we end up DOWN IN THE DUMPS. We end up with ANOTHER break-up and the loss of our peace and stability.

When we first meet someone and start to get excited about them, we need to be Mindful that they APPEAR wonderful. We must be MINDFUL that we're ONLY SEEING ONE SIDE OF THEM. We need to be aware that THINGS ARE RARELY AS THEY APPEAR and we'll need to GET MORE INFORMATION about them BEFORE WE DECIDE to get involved OR to be in love with them.

We need to consider the Big Picture of a person's personality by observing, describing, AND experiencing the WHOLE PERSON… the black, the white, and the gray… the good, the bad, and the stuff that's just okay.

We need to be MINDFUL that when we get to know someone, we'll notice some UNDESIRABLE or BAD qualities. When we become Mindful of the BIG PICTURE of who they are…it's time to DECIDE IF we SHOULD be with them. We need to base this DECISION on whether they'll BRING PEACE and STABILITY to our life or TAKE IT AWAY.

Have you ever QUICKLY BECOME INVOLVED with someone YOU THOUGHT was Mr. Right or Ms. Soul Mate and later found out you were VERY WRONG about them? If so, what was your emotional life and behavior like during this time? How did it end up affecting you? _____

_____

_____

The problem is our MOOD SWINGS as our PERCEPTIONS SWING. We go from head over heels in love to falling flat on our face in disappointment. IF ONLY we would follow our head and not our heart. IF ONLY we would make a rational decision based on the WHOLE person.

"Once I REALLY got to know her, I didn't like her." "Things changed when we got married." "When he's in a good mood, he's really great, but when he's not, he's a mean, raging monster." Have you ever heard or said those words? When we're short-sighted and see people as "all good," everything feels great WHEN THEY'RE "GOOD." The problem is PEOPLE AREN'T "ALL GOOD." We're often DEVASTATED and BROKEN when OUR FANTASY is SHATTERED and we experience the WHOLE person and their "BAD SIDE." Consider when "Mr. Right" or "Ms. Perfect" does something "bad." We're shocked. OUR DREAM IS OVER. "Everything is ruined." Is this familiar? What do we do when this happens? We often begin to view them as "all bad," "the worst," or "just like everyone other man (or woman)." We totally dislike them or hate them…for that hour, day, or week.

The problem with Extreme Judgments, like "all good" or "all bad," is OUR MOOD often suffers EXTREME SWINGS right along with our JUDGMENTS! We can go from being "on top of the world" to being devastated and "in the pits of depression"… IN A FLASH. Extreme Judgments drive the emotional rollercoaster…up and down, up and down! These EXTREME MOOD SWINGS greatly affect our peace and stability. They sometimes occur so quickly…and are SO INTENSE…that we RESPOND TO THEM WITHOUT THINKING THINGS THROUGH. WE OFTEN DO EXTREME THINGS that throw us…once again, into the Cycle of Suffering.

To have peace and stability, we must have balance… balance in our thinking, balance in our emotions, and balance in how we view people and situations.

Mindfulness of the Big Picture of a person's personality can help us maintain peace and stability. We need to look at life in realistic ways. We need to be Mindful of the good AND the bad. Nothing on this earth is PERFECT. Even when we're tempted to

No matter how great a friend, lover, or family member is, they'll hurt and disappoint us now and then.

People who love us may hurt us now and then.
Our people aren't going to act 100% loving towards us all the time.
They're human and they deal with their own life stuff, their own moods, AND they also deal with us when we're not acting so loveable!

People who love us still love us...even when we've really upset them and they respond to us in unloving ways.
Their love for us doesn't change...but their feelings about us change in the Heat-of-the-Moment.
They get hot-headed and react with Emotion-Driven Behavior.
They still love us, but they may act pretty cold-blooded when they're burning with anger.

see a new love as PERFECT, we must be PREPARED to experience their "bad" or undesirable side as well. We also NEED to be MINDFUL that WE HAVE a good side and bad side, too. We're not "all good" or "all bad." WE HAVE shades of gray, too! What's your "bad side"? What undesirable qualities do you bring to relationships? __

_____

APPLICATION: She Loves Me, She Loves Me Not

We must understand that people WHO LOVE US WILL ACT IN UNLOVING WAYS now and then. We NEED to remain MINDFUL they STILL LOVE US but something is going on and they're NOT IN A LOVING MOOD at the time! Maybe they're mad at us or someone else. Maybe they're tired. Even the "BEST PEOPLE" AREN'T PERFECT AT LOVING and will do UNLOVING things now and then. We need to be Mindful they DON'T STOP LOVING US because they're mad at us! Remember OUR humanity. WE'RE NOT PERFECT, and the people who love us aren't either!

Do you ever feel "unloved" when someone who loves you acts in an unloving way? If so, what truths can you tell yourself so you don't HAVE TO FEEL unloved? _____

_____

APPLICATION: One Bad Apple Doesn't Spoil the Bunch

Another point to stress about judging is the difference between THE PERSON and THEIR BEHAVIOR. For instance, a NICE person will do something that's NOT SO NICE. Perhaps they're overwhelmed at work and respond to us rudely. Maybe they just received bad news about their health, a call from their kids' principal, or they were just unfairly criticized by the boss. If we make an Extreme Judgment about them IN-THE-MOMENT, we'll be WRONG about them. We MUST REMEMBER...ONE RUDE ACTION DOES NOT WIPE OUT ALL their positive qualities, especially when their rude behavior is OUT-OF-CHARACTER.
Life ISN'T "all-or-none." Most things fall somewhere in the middle.
Life ISN'T "all black or all white," either. It's made up of shades of gray.
Likewise, ONE BAD ACTION DOESN'T SPOIL the WHOLE person!

APPLICATION: "Inappropriate" Thoughts and Feelings

It's common to have the Emotion-Driven Thought, "I could just kill her!" or "I wish he would just die." After the Heat-of-the-Moment passes, we often feel guilty

Avoid the judgments. Instead, recognize a thought is a thought! It's NOT a commitment to action!

The "I could kill him." thought generally expresses a desire for someone to be OUT OF OUR LIFE and punished, rather than for them to die or to be killed!

If we shut down the process of Mindfulness and Acceptance, we open ourselves up to self-criticism, denial, negative Emotional Mind, and the Cycle of Suffering. We DON'T want to go there again!

We need to accept ourselves and understand that many forbidden, taboo, or "bad" thoughts and impulses are VERY NORMAL.

39- Dr. Linehan discusses One-Mindedness and "Turning the Mind" in her Skills Training Manual.

about these thoughts. We may label ourselves harshly...like, "I'm a terrible person. How could I have such thoughts?" We need to take a Nonjudgmental view of this and accept our humanity.

We had these thoughts because we were INSANELY ANGRY. We REALLY don't want them to die. We just wanted them REMOVED FROM OUR WORLD at the time! We were SO ANGRY with them, we didn't want them around us. We didn't want ANYTHING to do with them. We wanted them out of our life PERMANENTLY... or so we thought! If we judge ourselves to be "bad" or a crazy monster, we may begin to focus on how horrible or wicked we THINK we are. Our Recovery Goal is to AVOID getting STUCK in a SELF-DESTRUCTIVE EMOTIONAL MIND and FALLING INTO DEPRESSION or RELAPSE. To Mindfully Protect Our Peace and Stability, we need to become Mindful of the Big Picture of the Situation...that someone REALLY hurt us or wronged us...and instead of beating ourselves up, we need to get a GAME PLAN to effectively deal with the situation.

What NORMAL "inappropriate" thoughts or impulses have you had that you've felt ashamed of? Have any of these had any lasting effect on how you feel about yourself? Explain. _____

_____

_____

SKILL BUILDER: One-Mindedness and Turning Our Mind

Another skill Dr. Linehan teaches for increasing Mindfulness is "One-Mindedness."[39] This involves KEEPING our mind on ONE THING AT A TIME. When we're used to being scattered or unfocused, this seems like quite a task...especially if we have racing thoughts or attention problems! We can use this skill to "PULL OURSELVES TOGETHER" and to "THINK STRAIGHT" when we're OVERWHELMED by daily life issues and demands...and major life events. For instance, if we're ruminating and upsetting ourselves by being One-Minded about something embarrassing, painful, or worrisome, we can "TURN OUR MIND" TO FOCUS ON POSITIVE, productive things... such as the truth about our humanity and our strengths...or a Game Plan to deal with the problem! If negative thoughts are flying through our mind, we can Turn Our Mind to truth and reality. If we're filled with thoughts and impulses to do something destructive, we can Turn Our Mind to our Recovery Goals and Life-Enhancing Coping options. If we're overwhelmed at work with too much to do, we can Turn Our Mind to focus on One Thing at a Time instead of being scattered and worried about

One-Mindedness and Turning Our Mind are skills we can use when we're focused on destructive things and we need to be focused on recovery things!

We can practice One-Mindedness by Turning Our Mind to what we need to focus on... over and over... as many times as needed! As we do this more and more, we'll be distracted less and less... and able to focus longer and longer.[40]

40- The truth, we may only keep our mind turned for 5 seconds at a time the first 10 times we do it! When we keep Turning Our Mind and refuse to allow ourselves to stew on the painful and destructive... we'll stay refocused longer and longer. 5 seconds turns to 10, then 20-30 seconds, then 1-2 minutes, 5-10 minutes, 30 minutes to an hour...then longer. This gives us the time and space we need to pull ourselves together... to get rational, to Think Straight... and to come up with ways to effectively deal with whatever is going on. If we don't refocus and pull ourselves out of a negative Emotional Mind, things may spiral Out-of-Control.

EVERYTHING AT THE SAME TIME.

> When we're using this skill to help ourselves...we must be PERSISTENT! We must KEEP TRYING. We'll have to WORK HARD to KEEP OUR MIND where we want it! We may Turn Our Mind to something positive and it stays there for five seconds... and goes right back to where it was. We MUST REFUSE to ALLOW OURSELVES TO STAY THERE. We must TURN OUR MIND BACK TO the things of recovery. We MUST REFOCUS and REFOCUS and REFOCUS...for as long as needed!

One-Mindedness and Turning Our Mind are SKILLS. As such, we must PRACTICE to get good at them. Start practicing 5-10 times a day. There are many ways to practice. For instance, if we're helping our child with homework, we can turn the TV or radio off and FOCUS ON spending quality time with our child and helping with homework. When we get distracted, we can TURN OUR MIND back to our child and the homework...OVER AND OVER again! If we're eating, we can turn off the TV, put the book down, and FOCUS on eating. We can observe and describe the flavor temperature, texture, and smell of our food. We can be Mindful of cutting our meat or twirling spaghetti on our fork. We can be Mindful of each mouthful. We can chew and enjoy our food rather than gulping it down. We can focus on our dining experience IN ITS TOTALITY rather than the long list of things we need to do next!

We can practice while washing the dishes. We can FOCUS ON WASHING THE DISHES in a One-Minded manner. We can FOCUS on observing and describing the process...like the temperature of the water, the smell of the soap, the feel of the bubbles, and the sounds of the water and dishes. We can practice by WORKING to give this chore our FULL ATTENTION. This means we won't straighten the spice rack, fill the dog's water bowl, or watch TV while we do the dishes. It means we'll just relax...and focus on washing the dishes. When we're done, we can do the spice rack... and then, the dog's water...but, only ONE THING AT A TIME!

When might One-Mindedness and Turning Your Mind be helpful to you? _____

_____

_____

SKILL BUILDER: A One-Minded Solution for Chronic Worriers

A VERY EFFECTIVE therapy for intense worriers involves SETTING ASIDE A CERTAIN AMOUNT OF TIME once or twice a day TO WORRY or RUMINATE. Same place, same time, One-Minded. The goal is to FILL this time with rumination and worry. We are to be ONE-MINDED in worry! We're not allowed to focus on anything

41- This technique is described in Dr. Linehan's Skills Training Manual. It was originally published in Borkovec & Inz (1990).

We must be Mindful that every now and then, we'll be tempted to do things the old, destructive way. Therefore, we must remain One-Minded about recovery. We must be determined to FIGHT ourselves as necessary to stay well-grounded on the Recovery Path.

42- Mindset – an attitude our mind is set on or stuck on.

43- To Stand – to hold up, to dig our heels in, and to Stay in the Ring! It means we do not cower, we do not fall over, and we do not run. It means we STAND... that we take a Stand and we Stand up and Fight for our recovery and our peace and stability. We don't let people or life run us over or stomp on our Recovery Path.

We must PRACTICE recovery skills to TRAIN OUR BRAIN to respond to life in a different way... before the Heat-of-the-Moment burns us once again!

else. IT'S A TIME SET ASIDE TO WORRY.[41] We're giving ourselves time and permission to worry or ruminate. If worries CREEP UP at other times, we are to TURN OUR MIND from them and SAVE THEM for our WORRY TIME! This HELPS US TO HAVE PEACE and to be MORE RELAXED and FOCUSED. It helps us to have the MENTAL and EMOTIONAL ENERGY to Participate Effectively and to handle the PRIORITIES of our day...so worrying DOESN'T TAKE OVER our life.

APPLICATION: Being One-Minded About Recovery

In today's world, we refer to One-Mindedness as being "IN THE ZONE." For us, OUR ZONE is RECOVERY. Our mind MUST BE FOCUSED ON RECOVERY 24-7... or at least from the time we wake until we fall asleep! We NEED TO BE AWARE OF what we're DOING, how we're FEELING, what we're FEELING LIKE DOING, and what we have NO INTEREST in ALLOWING ourselves TO DO. We have to be aware of WHAT'S HELPFUL to us in recovery and WHAT'S DESTRUCTIVE. Based on this information, WE MUST MAKE CHOICES HOW WE'LL RESPOND to our life situations RATHER THAN MINDLESSLY REACTING to them.

> We must be Mindful that difficult and upsetting things will Come Our Way. We must Mindfully act in ways to MINIMIZE LIFE PROBLEMS instead of creating more problems. We must be ONE-MINDED about doing WHATEVER POSSIBLE to effectively deal with and manage what Comes Our Way. We must maintain the MINDSET[42] that we're going to STAND[43] and DEAL WITH life in a PRODUCTIVE, LIFE-ENHANCING MANNER NO MATTER WHAT.

So, LIVE, EAT, and BREATHE what we've been discussing and doing so far. REVIEW the readings and worksheets and PRACTICE the skills and attitudes. DRILL THIS INFORMATION into your head. Be able to QUICKLY name off the things that make up the Big Picture of Your Life. Be able to QUICKLY identify triggers, trouble spots, and things Coming At You. KNOW THYSELF. Know your typical reactions that cause you trouble. Know the consequences you cause yourself... and know... LIFE WILL IMPROVE WHEN WE'RE LIVING A RECOVERY LIFESTYLE. BE MINDFUL...it's UNLIKELY we'll maintain recovery MINDLESSLY.

We know Mindfulness is the FIRST STEP in GAINING CONTROL over our Emotional Reflexes. We need this control so we can MINIMIZE PAIN and PROBLEMS and MAXIMIZE PEACE and STABILITY. We know Mindfulness is a SKILL. We know that if we PRACTICE a skill LONG ENOUGH, it'll become rather automatic and natural for us to do. We know recovery IS NOT A ONE-TIME EVENT...IT'S A LIFESTYLE.

146

We must be ALWAYS MINDFUL that Recovery is Our Number One Priority.
We must be One-Minded and determined TO MAKE IT SO!

We know if we MINDFULLY RESPOND TO LIFE, WE'LL RECOVER. What a GIFT this will be. GO FOR IT! Everyday can be our BIRTH DAY...A DAY OF NEW LIFE... NEW BEGINNINGS...NEW JOY...and something to CELEBRATE!

~~~~~~~~~ CHAPTER REVIEW ~~~~~~~~~

1. Give several reasons why Mindfulness is so important? _____
_____
_____
_____

2. Why do we want to OVERLEARN recovery skills? _____
_____
_____

3. What's meant by "Our Self-Destructive Emotion-Driven Behaviors become a reflex"? Mention why this is a problem? _____
_____
_____

4. If we want to change how things work out for us, what's the first thing we need to do? What do we need to learn and why? _____
_____
_____

5. Why is a morning devotional so important? _____
_____
_____

6. What's meant by "From the Old to the New and Back Again"? How does Mindfulness help with this? _____
_____
_____
_____

7. How does a bad tasting anti-nail-biting product help someone to stop biting their nails? _____
_____

8. Why is nail biting such a difficult habit to break? _____
_____

9. Why is Observing an important Mindfulness skill? _____

Mindfulness is the first step in gaining control of our thoughts, feelings, and behavior. When we take control of our Emotional Mind, the quality of our life will GREATLY improve. That's because we won't be creating so many EXTRA problems for ourselves! Enough problems Come Our Way just because things happen. We certainly don't need to create more problems for ourselves!

_____

_____

10. How can practicing "Conversation Enders" help us to Maintain Our Peace and
Stability? _____

_____

_____

11. How can "The Conveyer Belt" and the "Put it on a Cloud" techniques help us if we're
worried or angry? _____

_____

_____

12. What problems might we have if we confuse an opinion with a fact? _____

_____

_____

Sometimes we aren't Mindful of ALL the facts. Something may get in our way of perceiving the Big Picture. Consider when we REALLY WANT a relationship. We only see the best in the person and we DON'T WANT TO CONSIDER or deal with all the negative stuff!

13. What do we need to make MANY observations of someone before making
judgments about them? What types of things cause someone to act different than
they usually are...or out-of-character? _____

_____

_____

14. Mark, the Shift Team Leader, is quick to call himself "stupid" when he makes an
error. How do you think this affects him? What truths is he ignoring or minimizing
when he calls himself stupid? _____

_____

_____

15. Why should we avoid labeling or judging? _____

_____

_____

_____

16. In what way do problems in observing lead to problems in romantic relationships...
and quite often heartbreak? _____

_____

_____

17. What is meant by the "WHOLE" person? _____

_____

18. Some people are in the habit of making Extreme Judgments. How does this affect

their mood? _____

_____

19. Do our people still love us when they're mad at us? What are some reasons that someone who loves us may act in unloving ways towards us...now and then? _____

_____

_____

20. What's the point of the "One Bad Apple Doesn't Spoil the Bunch" section? _____

_____

_____

_____

_____

21. When we say things like, "I wish he would die." what do we really want? _____

_____

_____

22. Why is it important to recognize that "a thought is a thought"? _____

_____

_____

23. What does "One-Minded" mean? _____

_____

24. What does "Turning Our Mind" mean? When should we "Turn Our Mind"? _____

_____

_____

25. At first, many people think "Turning Our Mind" doesn't work. Why might they think it doesn't work? What do they need to do to get it to work for them? _____

_____

_____

26. What is a "Solution for Chronic Worriers"? Why it is considered a "One-Minded Solution"? _____

_____

_____

27. In the "Being One-Minded About Recovery" section, many things were mentioned that we need to be Mindful of...and One-Minded about...to help ourselves maintain recovery. Which ones are most meaningful for you? _____

_____

28. What does "To Stand" mean? Try to describe it in your own words. Also mention its importance for recovery. _____

_____

_____

_____

~~~ For Reflection ~~~

_____

_____

_____

_____

_____

_____

_____

_____

_____

_____

_____

_____

_____

_____

_____

_____

_____

_____

_____

_____

_____

_____

FOR REFLECTION:
Take a few moments to reflect on this chapter. Some questions are listed in the margin to guide your reflection.
Feel free to reflect on whatever your heart brings to mind.

What are your reactions to the material?

Which parts hit home or relate to you the most?

Which parts have helped you the most?

Which parts have helped you to understand yourself the most?

How will you use this information to feel better about yourself?

How will you use this information to improve the quality of your life...or to change how things work out for you in life?

What will you do differently based on this material?

How has this information changed the way you feel about your patterns of relapse and recovery... and your overall response to life?

What does this material motivate you to do?

Figure 5.A.1: The Concepts and Skills Tracking Sheet – Chapter 5

Week # _____

Day of Week →									
Date →									

5A. Today, I CHOSE how to respond to a situation rather than JUST REACTING.

5B. Today, I remembered how awkward I felt when I tried something new in The past. I remembered that I had to pay close attention to all the steps. I realize I'll feel awkward when I try out these new recovery skills, but I know they'll get easier and more mindless to do over time.

5C. Today, Something Happened and I responded to a situation mindlessly... and in an undesirable way. I realize my response was an Emotional Reflex... an ACTION-REACTION.

5D. I did a morning devotional today. I thought about Recovery Being My #1 Priority and how I was determined to make it so!

5E. I did a morning devotional today. I thought about the things Coming At Me today and I made some plans how I would handle these in a life-enhancing way.

5F. Today, I caught relapse in the making! I caught myself in...or going into a backslide.

5G. Today, I caught relapse in the making! I caught myself in...or going into a Backslide. I pulled myself together and got right back on track.

5H. Today, I was in a situation that improved my mood. I became Mindful of how this situation affected my mood.

5I. Today, I was in a situation that brought my mood down. I became Mindful of how this affected my mood.

5J. Today, I practiced Observing and Describing several situations...just for the sake of practice!

5K. Today, I was in a situation that upset me. I described what happened, Talked Myself Down, refocused myself, and restored my peace.

Notes:

RATING SCALE
5 – Did Excellent in this area today
4 – Did Pretty Good in this area today
3 – Did Alright in this area today
2 – Did Only Fair in this area today
1 – Didn't Do Well in this area today
DD – Didn't Do today

From "Out-of-Control: A Dialectical Behavior Therapy (DBT) – Cognitive-Behavioral Therapy (CBT) Workbook for Getting Control of Our Emotions and Emotion-Driven Behavior" Copyright © 2009 by Melanie Gordon Sheets, Ph.D. (www.dbt-cbt-workbook.com)

Figure 5.A.2: The Concepts and Skills Tracking Sheet – Chapter 5

Week # _____

Day of Week →

Date →

5L. Today, I was in a situation that was upsetting me. I observed and described what was going on. I took action to change the situation or to remove myself.										
5M. Today, I thought about ways to end conversations. I practiced these Conversation-Enders so I would be good at using them when I needed them!										
5N. Today, I was Mindful that I needed...or wanted...to end a conversation. I decided to use a Conversation Ender...and I did!										
5O. I practiced the "Observing My Body" Skill Builder today.										
5P. I practiced observing my thoughts using "The Next Two Thoughts" technique.										
5Q. I practiced observing my thoughts using "The Conveyer Belt" or the "Put It on a Cloud" technique.										
5R. I practiced observing my thoughts using imagery that was special to me.										
5S. I used my own special imagery or "The Conveyer Belt" or the "Put It on a Cloud" technique as a coping tool to rid my mind of unwanted thoughts...or just to relax myself today.										
5T. I applied "Is it an opinion or a fact" to a Real Life situation today.										
5U. I caught myself using a negative label to describe myself today. I challenged it and told myself the truth and the facts!										
5V. I caught myself labeling someone's WHOLE personality based on very little information about them. I realized this judgment MAY BE VERY WRONG!										
5W. I recognized that someone else was labeling someone's WHOLE personality based on very little information. I realized their judgment was likely wrong.										

Notes:

RATING SCALE

5 – Did Excellent in this area today
4 – Did Pretty Good in this area today
3 – Did Alright in this area today
2 – Did Only Fair in this area today
1 – Didn't Do Well in this area today
DD – Didn't Do today

Figure 5.A.3: The Concepts and Skills Tracking Sheet – Chapter 5

Week # _____

Day of Week →

Date →

5X. Today, I thought about or caught myself doing the "Love at First Sight" thing. I reminded myself that there's a whole lot more to the person than I see at first. I told myself that I need to spend enough time with them to see the other side they don't show people at first. Everyone's got that type of side! I reminded myself how painful break-ups are and the importance of making a rational decision about my next relationship...not a desperate, mindless, or emotional one!

5Y. Today, I thought about times when someone was very upset with me and I felt like they didn't love me anymore. I reminded myself that my people still love me even though they're angry with me.

5Z. Today, when someone who cares about me was upset with me, I began to feel like they didn't care about me anymore. I challenged that Emotion-Driven Thought and reminded myself that they still care about me...but they're mad at me and aren't in such a caring mood at the moment!

5AA. Today, I THOUGHT ABOUT how I sometimes go from loving someone to hating someone when they do something that upsets me. I reminded myself that One Bad Action Doesn't Spoil the WHOLE Person...that people who love me will hurt me now and then.

5BB. Today, Something Happened and someone who loves me hurt me. I reminded myself that One Bad Action Doesn't Spoil the WHOLE Person...that people who love me will hurt me now and then.

5CC. Today, I caught myself having a "bad" or "inappropriate" thought. I did not allow myself to stew on it or to beat myself up about it. I "Put It on a Cloud" or on a conveyer belt...or otherwise Let It Flow out of my mind.

5DD. Today, I practiced One-Mindedness by trying to focus on ONE thing. I Turned My Mind back to this one thing as many times as was needed!

Notes:

RATING SCALE

5 - Did Excellent in this area today
4 - Did Pretty Good in this area today
3 - Did Alright in this area today
2 - Did Only Fair in this area today
1 - Didn't Do Well in this area today
DD - Didn't Do today

Figure 5.A.4: The Concepts and Skills Tracking Sheet – Chapter 5

Week # _____

Day of Week →

Date →

5EE. Today, I Turned My Mind from something upsetting or destructive to something positive. I had to do this many times, but I did it as many times as was needed to help myself.

5FF. Today, I felt overwhelmed by too many worries or demands. My mind was racing. I decided to focus on One Thing at a Time. It took some effort, but I worked to stay as One-Minded as I could. I had to Turn My Mind back to this one thing many times!

5GG. Today, I set limits for my worrying. I set aside a certain time to worry. Each time a worry came up, I Turned My Mind from it and told myself I'd worry about it during my worry time. I didn't allow myself to freely worry all day!

5HH. Today, I worked on being One-Minded about recovery! Each time Something Happened that challenged my recovery, I found a way to deal with it in a recovery way. I was focused on recovery and Mindfully Protecting My Peace and Stability.

Notes:

RATING SCALE
5 – Did Excellent in this area today
4 – Did Pretty Good in this area today
3 – Did Alright in this area today
2 – Did Only Fair in this area today
1 – Didn't Do Well in this area today
DD – Didn't Do today

154

REST STOP #1

Road Map: Where We've Been...What Ground We've Covered

CONGRATULATIONS! YOU'VE COMPLETED the first leg of our journey. The first section addressed "The Cycle of Suffering: Why is My Life So Out-of-Control." We learned this has to do with Emotional Mind Coping Behavior. Before we continue our journey, we'll take note of where we've been and what ground we've covered. Then, we'll map-out where we're going next and what we'll learn along the way.

In Chapter 1, "The Nature of the Problem," we looked at why our life ends up like a train wreck...full of problems and loss...with everything precious to us strewn about like the debris of a train wreck. We looked at what causes our life to blow up right in front of our eyes.

By way of the first two chapters, we've gained great insight into why we have the problems we have...and why our life becomes filled with pain and suffering. We've gained an understanding of why things are the way they are. We've answered the questions, "How did this happen?" and "Why me?"

> The Nature of the Problem is...THE THINGS WE DO TO FEEL BETTER END UP CAUSING US MORE LIFE PROBLEMS. We feel worse because of the painful consequences of our Destructive Coping Behaviors. When we feel worse, we do our preferred Emotion-Driven Coping Behaviors again...and we end up with EVEN MORE consequences and losses. The result...we feel WORSE. This is THE CYCLE OF SUFFERING. As this cycle runs its course, we feel worse and worse and the CONSEQUENCES of our coping behaviors become more and more severe. The losses and problems in our life become more intense and widespread UNTIL EVERYTHING WE LOVE AND CHERISH IS LOST, DESTROYED, OR FILLED WITH CONFLICT.

Self-Destructive Coping Behavior destroys our life. Everything that's been good, goes bad. Everything that once brought joy and satisfaction, brings pain and suffering.

In Chapter 2, "The Big Picture of My Life," we identified the most precious and important things in our life. These are the things that give our life meaning...and bring joy and satisfaction. We saw how the consequences of Emotion-Driven Coping Behavior lead to problems in some areas of our life. Then, like a Domino Effect, these problems cause problems in other areas of our life...and so on. This goes on until the Big Picture of Our Life is overtaken by problems, losses, emptiness, and pain.

In Chapter 3, "The Pathways of Recovery," we rationally challenged "WHY TRY? THINGS WILL GET SCREWED UP ANYWAY." We determined that MANY GOOD THINGS HAPPEN in our life WHEN WE'RE ON THE RECOVERY PATH. It's when we relapse into Emotion-Driven Coping Behavior that life takes a turn for the worst... and many bad things begin to happen again. We noted that bad things happen to all of us and it doesn't matter how good or self-disciplined we are, bad things and difficult

We've learned that some bad things happen just because bad things happen that we have NO control over. Other bad things happen because of something we have control over. Either we did something to cause a bad event or we didn't do what was needed to prevent one! Bad things happen when we don't manage our life effectively. When Emotional Mind drives, bad things happen… and our life becomes a wreck.

1- Penetrating – (pen-uh-tray-ting) – to break the surface of something and to go inside.

2- Transformation – (trans-form-a-shin) – to change from one form to another. Like the caterpillar transforms into a butterfly, we want our life of pain and suffering to transform into a life of peace and satisfaction.

We've learned that life isn't easy. It's a series of ups and downs… good times and bad …and happy times and sad.

times WILL Come Our Way. We learned that when we're faced with a difficult situation, we have TWO CHOICES. One is TO STAND and face our troubles and to Fight to stay on the Recovery Path. The other is to relapse into Destructive Coping Behavior. WHY TRY? WHEN WE TRY good things happen…and when we KEEP TRYING, we GET THROUGH tough times and good things CONTINUE to happen.

In the Mindfulness Chapters, 4 and 5, "Mindfully Protecting My Peace and Stability" and "Mindfulness Is a Skill," we learned that many of our problems are caused by mindless and impulsive behavior. We learned that MINDFULNESS IS THE FIRST STEP IN GAINING CONTROL over our life. Mindfulness is awareness in the "here-and-now" moment. It's awareness of our thoughts and feelings and the reality of our troubling situations. It's awareness of what we're doing, what we're thinking about doing, and how our behavior will affect the Big Picture of Our Life and our life goals. We also learned about MINDFULLY PROTECTING OUR PEACE AND STABILITY and the importance of being Mindful and dealing with the things Coming At Us. We learned Mindfulness is a skill that requires lots of practice.

Road Map: Where Do We Go from Here?

The first section of this workbook has answered, "WHY is my life SO TROUBLED?" and "HOW has my life become SO OUT-OF-CONTROL?" We learned that it's because of the THINGS WE DO IN THE HEAT-OF-THE-MOMENT! We went through some VERY penetrating[1] and painful material to gain this understanding. We've had to look at and process some very difficult things. However, this is PAIN FOR GAIN. This is a very therapeutic type of pain that will help to END OUR SUFFERING and bring PEACE, STABILITY, and SATISFACTION to our life. This transformation[2] DOESN'T HAPPEN OVER NIGHT, it COMES TO US as we make our way along the RECOVERY PATH.

The remainder of this workbook will focus on HOW TO GET CONTROL of our OUT-OF-CONTROL thoughts, feelings, and behavior…and HOW TO GET ON and STAY ON the Recovery Path. Emotional Mind, Rational Mind, and Wise Mind will be discussed in detail. Recovery skills such as Distress Tolerance, Acceptance, Game Plans, and Life-Enhancing Coping Skills will also be discussed. Get ready! We're getting into what this study is all about…HOW TO GET CONTROL of ourselves and our life…and HOW TO SET-UP and LIVE A LIFE that's FILLED with MEANING and SATISFACTION!

Road Map: How Do We Get There from Here?

We've learned that the reason life gets screwed up again… is because WE screwed up AGAIN. We relapsed into self-destructive behavior and we self-destructed! Our relapse behavior triggered the Cycle of Suffering AGAIN. The ONLY way to stop it…is to STOP IT. We MUST STOP responding to life in ways that cause pain and suffering.

Mindfulness is the first step for changing how we respond to life. Rather than JUST RESPONDING, we must CHOOSE how to respond. To make wise decisions, we need a good understanding of what's going on within us and in the situations we face. If we don't have enough information about the Big Picture of what's going on, we may respond inappropriately or ineffectively. Consider this example.

> Laura walks past Gina, a fairly new friend at work. A back-stabbing co-worker is talking to Gina. Laura says "Hey, what's up!" as she walks by Gina. Gina looks at Laura, but doesn't acknowledge her. Laura walks away feeling rejected.
> Her Emotional Mind perception is that Gina doesn't like her anymore and is snubbing her. Laura stews over this. Out of hurt and anger, she thinks about rejecting Gina at her next opportunity. She also fantasizes about telling others that Gina really isn't so nice and is just putting on a big show. Laura thinks, "Screw her! I didn't do anything to her and she's acting like such a snob." She decides to ignore Gina when Gina says "Hello" to her later. "I'll look right through her like she did me!"

How many times have we made an error in judgment and said, "Ooops, I didn't know that." or "Oh, I wasn't aware of that."?

DBT-CBT teaches that when we act on Emotional Mind, we most often do or say things we'll regret later! In the above example, Laura is ruminating about the hurtful situation and how best to get even. She's planning to punish Gina for snubbing her. No doubt this will cause a lot of conflict and tension and Laura may lose a good friend by judging Gina in an "all good – all bad" way.

Laura studied DBT-CBT in the past and before doing anything, she FORCED herself to STEP BACK EMOTIONALLY and to THINK RATIONALLY. She thought,

> *"It hurts my feelings that she didn't say 'Hello' or acknowledge me when I walked by. I'm not aware of anything I did to upset her. She's been so nice. I really don't think she'd be ugly on purpose…but, I don't know. I do know I'm very sensitive to rejection …BUT SHE SAW ME. I know she heard me. It's like she looked right through me. That was embarrassing. Everybody heard me greet her and saw that she ignored me. However, I can't worry about that. Friends are hard to come by. I better ask her if she's upset with me about something before I start being ugly to her!*
> *Maybe something's up that I don't know about yet. Maybe Ms. Back-Stabber is confronting her on something. I'll check with her later to see what's up."*

DBT-CBT teaches that WHEN we're having an EMOTIONAL MOMENT and it begins to turn destructive, it's ABSOLUTELY NECESSARY to TURN ON RATIONAL

MIND. Rational Mind deals with the Big Picture of the Situation in a logical, factual, and realistic way. It helps us to gain a FULL UNDERSTANDING of the situation AND the consequences we'll suffer IF WE ACT ON OUR EMOTIONS.

Which truths did Rational Mind remind Laura of? In the text box above, underline the truths Laura considered while she was Thinking Through the situation.

3- Synergy - (sin-or-gee) – when two or more things work together and create something greater than...either of the two things separately.

> Dr. Linehan's DBT teaches that when we use BOTH Emotional Mind and Rational Mind to deal with a problem, the synergy[3] creates a third state of mind, called Wise Mind. Wise Mind considers what's going on in our Emotional Mind AND what Rational Mind has to say about the situation. Wise Mind helps us to come up with a good Game Plan for dealing with our situation...taking into account OUR issues and who we are as a person AS WELL AS the Big Picture of the Situation and our life goals.

In the bottom text box on the previous page, <u>double underline</u> the Wise Mind solution or plan of action that Laura came up with?

Laura did a great job of applying DBT-CBT concepts and principles to Mindfully Protect the Big Picture of Her Life. She protected her peace and emotional stability AND she protected a friendship and her work environment. She regained her peace and avoided conflict, tension, and DRAMA. By Thinking Through the situation, she was Mindful and RESPECTFUL of her emotional issues (sensitive to rejection), her feelings (hurt, embarrassed), and her Emotion-Driven impulses to get even! She was also Mindful of Rational Mind facts and truth including,

We're hip to the problems we get into when we respond with an Emotional Reflex...when we DON'T Think Through Before We Do...when we impulsively do our preferred, overlearned, Self-Destructive Coping Responses!

Rational Mind helps us to Think Through Before We Do!

> "It hurts my feelings...I'm very sensitive to rejection..."
> "I'm not aware of anything I did to upset her."
> "She's been so nice. I really don't think she'd be ugly on purpose..."
> "I know she heard me. It was like she looked right through me."
> "That was embarrassing. Everybody heard me greet her..."
> "Friends are hard to come by."
> "Maybe something's up...Maybe Ms. Back-Stabber is confronting her...'"

When Laura Turned On Rational Mind to deal with her uncomfortable emotional state, Wise Mind was activated. She wisely thought,

> "I can't worry about that."
> "I better ask her if she's upset with me...before I start being ugly to her!"
> "I'll check with her later to see what's up."

I sure hope you're thinking, "If this is how you do DBT-CBT, it isn't too hard!" Well, this IS how you do it! This IS what helps us to GAIN CONTROL over our emotions and OUR LIFE. As Laura's story shows, the steps include:

> 1. STEPPING BACK emotionally
> 2. Being Mindful of what's going on in EMOTIONAL MIND
> 3. Being Mindful of RATIONAL MIND truths related to the situation AND the Big Picture of Our Life
> 4. Being Mindful of WISE MIND problem-solving and coping suggestions
> 5. FOLLOWING THROUGH with Wise Mind suggestions

Wise Mind is where our good judgment comes from!

How the Three Mind States Are Similar to Other Theories

The three states of mind, Emotional Mind, Reasonable Mind (Rational Mind), and Wise Mind, are classic DBT concepts. If you've studied[4] Freudian psychology (Psychoanalytic Theory) and the Id, Ego, and Superego, you'll notice these "ego states"[5] are similar to Dr. Linehan's mind states. ID is like Emotional Mind because IT'S CONSUMED[6] by our personal needs and drives. ID SEEKS TO PLEASE ITSELF no matter what! Id lives by "Since it feels good, I'll do it!" Id doesn't care about the Big Picture of Our Life or how our behavior affects others. It's very selfish and pleasure-seeking. The SUPEREGO is somewhat similar to Rational Mind. The Superego is concerned with right and wrong, morals, values, and rules. It's our conscience.[7] However, there's more to Rational Mind than the Superego part! The EGO is very similar to Wise Mind because its job is to BALANCE the needs and demands of ID while being RESPECTFUL of the rules and values of the SUPEREGO. The Ego comes up with a PLAN for PLEASING ID desires as much as possible...WITHIN THE LIMITS of what the SUPEREGO says is acceptable. That's what Wise Mind tries to do. It addresses the needs and concerns of Emotional Mind in a rational and reasonable way.

If you've studied[8] variants[9] of Eric Berne's Transactional Analysis (TA), you'll note similarity between his "ego states" and Dr. Linehan's mind states. The CHILD is similar to Emotional MIND because the Child ACTS OUT EMOTIONS without the insight and self-control of a Parent or Adult.[10] The PARENT is similar to Rational Mind because of its focus on the Big Picture of Reality! When the Parent speaks, we're reminded of right and wrong...what's good for us...and what's harmful. The Parent is the VOICE OF REALITY! The ADULT is very similar to WISE MIND because it works to come up with a PLAN to meet the emotional needs of the Child in a way that isn't harmful,

4- If you haven't studied Freudian psychology, just read through it to get the Big Picture of what's being discussed. Don't worry about the parts that don't make sense! If none of it makes sense...just move on and know that Dr. Linehan's three mind states fit well with other theories and understandings of human nature!

5- Ego States – what Freud called his mind states.

6- Consumed – to be totally focused on and interested in something. Preoccupied.

7- Conscience – (con-shints) - the part of us that thinks about...and knows right from wrong.

8- See #4 above...and apply it to this one!

9- Variants – (very-ents) – things that differ a bit from the original version.

10- Think of a 3 year old that throws a temper tantrum in the middle of a church service or funeral...or hits a bigger and meaner kid!

self-defeating, or destructive! Sounds familiar, huh?

As we discuss Emotional Mind, Rational Mind, and Wise Mind in more detail, you'll recognize the similarities between these states of mind and the ones described in other theories. Enjoy these next few chapters. They contain some very interesting concepts that MAKE GREAT SENSE. They're common sense...WE JUST DON'T COMMONLY SENSE THEM! We haven't been Mindful of these things in our everyday life...but, WE WILL BE! These three mind states are the meat and potatoes of DBT and DBT-CBT. Enjoy!

Section Two

The Three States of Mind:

"How Do I Get Control of My Life?"

~ 6 ~
EMOTIONAL MIND

In Chapter 1, "The Nature of the Problem," the two parts of Emotional Mind were introduced. These are RAW EMOTIONS and EMOTION-DRIVEN THOUGHTS. In simpler terms, they are our feelings and the thoughts we have when we're feeling a certain way.[1] When we act on our emotions, we do EMOTION-DRIVEN BEHAVIOR. When we act on upsetting emotions WITHOUT Thinking Through Before We Do, we often do SELF-DESTRUCTIVE THINGS.[2] In this chapter, we'll review these concepts and learn about other aspects of Emotional Mind.

SKILL BUILDER: The Raw Emotions of Emotional Mind

List 12 types of feelings below. Focus on negative ones rather than positive ones.[3] Group together similar emotions, like angry and mad. Extra room is provided above each line to cluster these. Try for 12 different emotions.[4]

1. _Mad, Angry, Rage, Pissed-off _____   2. _____

3. _____   4. _____

5. _____   6. _____

7. _____   8. _____

9. _____   10. _____

11. _____   12. _____

When we're upset, we GET HIT with MANY UPSETTING FEELINGS...ALL AT ONCE. These include "SURFACE" emotions and "UNDERLYING" ones. On the SURFACE, we may feel angry or depressed. BENEATH these emotions, we may feel hurt, abused, misunderstood, betrayed, disgusted, or embarrassed. There are MANY feelings UNDERNEATH the SURFACE ONES. When we TAKE TIME to EXPLORE our feelings, we'll notice we have LOTS of emotions going on at the SAME TIME![5]

SKILL BUILDER: The Depth and Breadth[6] of Our Emotions

The following questions will increase Mindfulness of the VARIETY of feelings we experience in any given situation. When you respond, list MANY feelings, not just a couple! THINK ABOUT the situations and GET IN TOUCH with the WIDE RANGE of emotions we experience.

1- If we're feeling betrayed, we may think, "I don't get mad, I get even." or "I'm going to hurt them worse than they've hurt me." If we're jealous and paranoid, we may think, "I can't trust anyone." or "I'll kill him if I catch him with her." If we're feeling empty, we may think, "I'll always be depressed." or "Life is meaningless."

2- Also known as Emotion-Driven Coping Behaviors. See Figure 1.C (in Chapter 1) for "A List of Common Self-Destructive Coping Behaviors."

3- We also experience a wide range of positive emotions, but those aren't the troubling ones that are the focus of this study!

4- If you get stuck, read on. You'll come across many emotions in this chapter. Our goal is to become Mindful of our feelings, so practice identifying these on your own before reviewing Figure 1.B: "A List of Negative Emotions." In the Heat-of-the-Moment, we won't have the list available! So, practice Mindfulness and TRY to think of as many as you can on your own.

5- This was discussed in Chapter 1. The margin text below is copied from Chapter 1.
Why do our emotions become so overwhelming?
(continued)

162

(5 - continued)
1. Because we're hit by emotions AND Emotion-Driven Thoughts. These two sources of distress feed off each other, too!
2. Because our current emotional state is driven by the here-and-now situation AND unresolved situations from the past.
3. Because of the number of underlying emotions. We're not hit by just one unpleasant feeling...but sometimes 10-20 AT ONCE! Together, these three things make for a triple whammy of distress! No wonder we get so overwhelmed! NO WONDER WE FEEL SO OUT-OF-CONTROL!

6- Depth and breadth - depth refers to how deep our feelings run. Breadth refers to the wide range of feelings we experience.

If we're angry that our friend is ALWAYS late when we do things together, what other feelings might we experience? _____ _____

If we're upset that someone we went out with last week hasn't called and isn't returning our calls, how else might we feel? _____ _____

Common feelings about the LATE FRIEND include frustration, anger, aggravation, and feeling disrespected, not taken seriously, not valued, used, and mistreated. Difficult feelings about the "NO CALL BACK" DATE may include rejection, anger, loneliness, anxiety, disappointment, desperation, hurt, sadness, feeling dumped, undesirable, unlovable, inadequate, defective, ashamed, worthless, and hopeless. These are a lot of UNCOMFORTABLE feelings to experience ALL AT ONCE. No wonder we feel so bad.

If our house burns down, how might we feel? _____ _____

If we find out our best friend has been having sex with OUR romantic partner, how might we feel? _____ _____

If our HOUSE BURNS DOWN, we may feel shocked, empty, numb, "at a loss," sad, overwhelmed, anxious, angry, devastated, hopeless, helpless, and frantic. Upsetting feelings about OUR CHEATING MATES may include rage, shock, confusion, distrust, jealousy, rejection, and disgust. We may also feel unloved, not cared for, taken advantage of, betrayed, manipulated, made a fool of, lost, alone, lonely, sad, devalued, disrespected, devastated, hopeless, worthless, and vengeful.

If we get fired from a job we REALLY like, what emotions might we experience? ____ _____ _____

If our kid keeps getting in trouble and nothing seems to help, how might we feel? ___ _____ _____

If we're pregnant (or our spouse is pregnant) and we find out something is seriously wrong with the baby, how might we feel? _____ _____

If we GET FIRED, we may feel angry, rejected, misunderstood, at a loss, devastated, unappreciated, confused, shocked, sad, discouraged, ashamed, embarrassed, incompetent, ineffective, disrespected, worthless, hopeless, worried, and scared.

7- Bombarded - (bomb-bard-ed) – when we're hit with a whole bunch of stuff at once.

In a difficult situation, we're bombarded by MANY troubling feelings. That's why we become SO overwhelmed and we feel SO pressured, crazy-like, and Out-of-Control.

There are many emotions and experiences, both past and present, which influence how we feel at any given moment.

When our KID KEEPS GETTING IN TROUBLE, we may feel angry, hopeless, helpless, ineffective, ashamed, worthless, overwhelmed, confused, worried, anxious, disrespected, and mistrusting. If something is WRONG WITH OUR BABY, we may feel devastated, frantic, scared, shocked, desperate, sad, angry, disillusioned, lost, discouraged, guilty, ashamed, empty, depressed, anxious, and worried.

Thinking about these situations no doubt brings up a VARIETY of feelings. Notice the DEPTH and BREADTH of our emotions. We're BOMBARDED[7] BY MANY DIFFERENT feelings. It's quite a challenge to PROCESS and DEAL WITH them ALL... ALL AT ONCE.

TO MAKE MATTERS WORSE, when we're upset about a CURRENT situation, not only are we FLOODED by HERE-AND-NOW feelings, but we're also FLOODED by UNRESOLVED EMOTIONS FROM THE PAST. That's why we get so overloaded and overwhelmed. We're HIT BY SO MANY uncomfortable feelings that we become DESPERATE and PRESSURED to quickly change our mood.

> We do DESPERATE things to TRY to NUMB-OUT and WHITE-OUT. We DON'T WANT TO FEEL this way and we DON'T WANT TO THINK ABOUT all the painful stuff. Drugs, alcohol, cutting, overdosing, aggression, rebound relationships, and other DESTRUCTIVE COPING BEHAVIORS provide RELIEF. They help us cope IN-THE-MOMENT. They work great for a SHORT time... but, they END UP DESTROYING OUR LIFE.

We've just described situations that clearly involve Emotional Mind. In the next seven sections, we'll explore a wider range of Emotional Mind experiences. You may be surprised that some of these are DRIVEN BY Emotional Mind!

APPLICATION: "Getting Into" a Sad Movie

Why do you think "GETTING INTO" a sad or scary movie is a major Emotional Mind experience? Think about how we are when we're "into" a sad movie. _____

_____

After a scary movie, Rational Mind would say, "Why are you freaked out and looking behind the shower curtain? It was JUST a movie!"

> When we're INTO a movie, we LOSE OUR SENSE OF REALITY. We react AS IF it's real. When folks ask, "Why are you crying? It's just a movie!"...that bit of Rational Mind can blow our emotional connection to the movie. We say, "Why do you have to RUIN the movie for me?" Familiar? We lose our emotional connection because RATIONAL MIND Turns On and tells us, "They're just actors. It's pretend!"

164

APPLICATION: Revisiting the Drama Queen

8- Arousing – (a-rouz-ing) - stirring up… or causing to happen.

We've talked about how drama-seeking people become INVOLVED IN emotionally arousing[8] situations which can TAKE AWAY their peace and stability. For them, life is about excitement, curiosity, drama, fun, and living on the edge WITHOUT MUCH CONCERN about CONSEQUENCES!

The High Drama person LIVES in Emotional Mind.

How much time do you think a High Drama person spends in Emotional Mind and Rational Mind? Is 100% of their time spent in Emotional Mind or do they live 90% in Emotional Mind and 10% in Rational Mind? Is it more like 80%-20%, 70%-30%, or 60%-40%? Circle the percent that seems most reasonable.

A High Drama person obviously spends MOST of their time in Emotional Mind. They're likely to have SOME Rational Mind time…but, not much! My guess is about 90% - 10% or 80% - 20% with the 90% and 80% being Emotional Mind!

9- The shopping high often wears off when we're leaving the mall and the, "Oh my God, what did I just do?" hits. It's a very short high followed by painful… and often long-term consequences like credit card debt, hot checks, getting behind on bills, and a MAD spouse.

APPLICATION: The Shop-a-Holic

This is the HABIT of OVERSHOPPING and spending MORE than we can afford! What are some emotional reasons we overshop? _____

_____

We overshop for many Emotion-Driven reasons. Some common ones include:

10- Deprived – (dee-prived) – not having what we need.

Emotional Mind says "Let's go shopping!" Rational Mind says, "I can't afford it. It's not worth missing a car payment."

> *I was bored. I wanted some fun and excitement![9]*
> *I was depressed. Shopping always makes me feel better.*
> *I needed to get some worries off my mind.*
> *I felt deprived.[10] I wanted to make myself happy.*
> *I shop when I'm manic.*
> *I was mad at my husband. I went shopping to get even!*

The first four are DRIVEN BY A DESIRE to change from a negative mood to a positive one. The next one is a symptom of Bipolar Disorder.[11] The last one is strongly rooted in revenge! All are DRIVEN BY Emotional Mind. We're doing what we FEEL LIKE doing WITHOUT worrying about the consequences!

11- When folks are manic, they're 100% Emotional Mind! Rational Mind is Turned Off. They live by the Pleasure Principle – if it feels good, do it. They don't Think Through Before They Do. The impulse control and good judgment part of their brain is NOT working. Medication brings their brain chemistry into balance and that part of their brain turns back on. It's like they've been in a black-out. Most don't remember the painful things they did because their brain wasn't working right.

APPLICATION: Blinded by Love

Why do you think "love at first sight" is an Emotional Mind experience? _____

_____

It an Emotional Mind experience because it's BASED on a SUDDEN feeling. It's IMPULSIVE. It's no doubt hormonal, too! It's DRIVEN BY EXCITEMENT and DESIRE. It's a "FANTASY LOVE." It's based on a FIRST IMPRESSION. It's NOT

From "Out-of-Control: A Dialectical Behavior Therapy (DBT) – Cognitive-Behavioral Therapy (CBT) Workbook for Getting Control of Our Emotions and Emotion-Driven Behavior" - Copyright © 2009 by Melanie Gordon Sheets, Ph.D. (www.dbt-cbt-workbook.com)

12- Glimpse – (glimps) –
a brief look, a glance.

13- Perceptions –
(per-cep-shins) – how we
view, see, or perceive
things. We may view
things very differently
than others!

*"Love at first sight"
is an impulsive,
Heat-of-the-Moment,
Emotional Mind
impression.
That sounds like
TROUBLE FROM
THE GET-GO!*

*We get blinded by
our desires in
Emotional Mind.*

*Rational Mind deals
with how things
really are.
Our perceptions
and reality are
often two VERY
different things.*

*Our people often see
or pick up on things
we don't see or pick
up on. These are
often things we
don't WANT to see
or know about!*

*Why do I still have
a temper if I lose it
all the time? If it
gets lost, why can't
it just stay gone!?*

14- A crash diet is very
strict and is designed for
FAST weight loss.

based on knowing what the person is REALLY LIKE and being in love with the WHOLE PERSON. It's based on a GLIMPSE[12] of their appearance, voice, or behavior. It's based on how they APPEAR to be...NOT truth and reality! It's NOT a Rational Mind decision based on facts and the Big Picture of what the person is REALLY like!

Have you ever become involved in a "love at first sight" relationship...one that VERY QUICKLY became a RELATIONSHIP? If so, how did it work out? Did the person live up to your first impressions? Explain. _____

_____

_____

Our PERCEPTIONS[13] are strongly influenced by Emotional Mind. Our needs and issues affect how we see and understand the world. Our emotional stuff influences how we think and feel about things. If we're lonely and REALLY WANT a relationship, we may SEE the POSITIVE and OVERLOOK the NEGATIVE. We may SEE them "IN A BETTER LIGHT" and a "DIFFERENT LIGHT" than others see them! We SEE and EXPERIENCE THEM through the lenses of what we WANT to believe!

Has your family or friends ever warned you about someone and told you NOT to get involved and gave you a bunch of reasons why? If so, did you get involved OR did you bail? Were they right about the person OR were you? Mention how this relationship turned out and how it ended up making you feel. _____

_____

_____

APPLICATION: Losing Our Temper

"Losing our temper"...the saying says it all! WE LOSE IT!

What is "IT" that we're talking about? _____

_____

We LOSE emotional control! We LOSE touch with Rational Mind and we're not Thinking Straight. We LOSE sight of our goals. We LOSE the ability to Participate Effectively. We're raging! We're 100% Emotional Mind. Emotional Mind is driving... and is in OVERDRIVE!

APPLICATION: Crash n' Burn Dieting

Why do you think a "crash diet"[14] is an Emotional Mind behavior? _____

_____

_____

_____

15- Deluded - (duh-lew-did) - talked ourselves or others into believing something that's not true.

16- Metabolism - (met-tab-oh-liz-em) - the process of breaking down the food we eat.

17- Famines - (fah-men's) - times when there's little or no food in a country or region.

Just like other Destructive Coping Behaviors, we want IMMEDIATE RELIEF…for our long-term weight problem. So, we do something desperate to lose weight FAST!

We're willing TO TRY to defy[18] the laws of nature to lose a ton of weight fast! A friend once said, "I've given up on dieting. Every time I go on a diet, I end up gaining 10 pounds!" After we starve ourselves, our brain pushes us to gain extra weight so our body is prepared for the next famine!

18- Defy - (dee-fi) - to go against or to challenge.

19- Replenish - (ree-plin-ish) - to restore and fill back up!

20 - (see next page)

We've all heard of these diets and most of us have done them! We see many advertised on magazine covers, "Lose 10 pounds in 10 days with the Grapefruit Diet!" Some have strict menu plans. Many limit food choices. We may be able to eat as much as we want…but ONLY lean meat and vegetables…or boiled chicken and rice all day! Consider how limited a high protein - low carbohydrate diet is. One reason these diets fail is they don't allow us to eat our favorite foods…and WE'RE NOT GOING TO STAY ON A DIET LIKE THAT…FOR VERY LONG!

Crash diets are driven by Emotional Mind because we're WILLING to do something DESPERATE to lose weight QUICK. We're IMPATIENT. We want IMMEDIATE RESULTS. We DON'T WANT TO WAIT to lose weight in a REASONABLE and HEALTHY way…even though WE KNOW it's the only way to lose weight and keep it off! We're being IRRATIONAL! We've deluded[15] ourselves! We're believing a LIE. SOMEHOW WE BELIEVE THIS CRAZY DIET WILL WORK…that we'll suddenly develop skills to control our eating…that we'll give up most or all of our favorite foods …and just eat certain foods. REALLY, IF WE HAD ALL THIS WILLPOWER, why would we need a crazy diet? Why wouldn't we just do a "normal diet" and eat like a skinny person? They eat many of the same things we eat…just smaller portions!

The problem with a crash diet is it's SO UNREASONABLE and STRICT we WON'T STAY ON IT the rest of our life! When we GET OFF the diet, we return to our old eating habits. We GAIN the weight back…AND THEN SOME! That's because we've been starving our body and depriving it of what it needs to function. Our brain sends out "I'M STARVING TO DEATH" signals that tell our body to PROTECT ITSELF FROM DYING. So, our metabolism[16] slows, we BURN FEWER CALORIES, and fat stores up for future famines.[17] At the same time, our BRAIN POUNDS on us to EAT MORE to replenish[19] our body. Finally, we GIVE IN TO TEMPTATION and the demands of our brain and body and we do a ROYAL PIG-OUT! Then we FEEL HORRIBLE physically and emotionally. We're bloated, sick, disappointed, and ashamed. WE FEEL LIKE A FAILURE. Weight loss seems hopeless, so, we GIVE UP on the diet. WE GAIN ALL OUR WEIGHT BACK…AND THEN SOME!

What kind of diet would Rational Mind suggest? ______________________________

____

Rational Mind would encourage us to EAT THINGS WE LIKE, BUT LESS! Then our stomach will shrink and we'll REDUCE CALORIES. We'll get in the HABIT of eating "SKINNY PERSON PORTIONS"[20] and we'll lose weight. Because we're still getting our

20- Ever notice how skinny people eat? They eat many of the same foods as an overweight person... just smaller portions. We had a store and I'd go there after my hospital job. I was always shocked to find half a bag of chips or half a candy bar left on the desk. I could never understand why the employee didn't eat it ALL! Obviously, their eating habits were very different from mine! They'd eat half when I'd eat two!

I'd rather lose 25 pounds a year by eating reasonably than gaining 10 with a crash diet!

21- If we're on a major weight gain cycle, we'll have to cut down even more to get our daily calories in the range for losing weight. These numbers are estimates based on someone who's maintaining their weight or is only gaining a few pounds a year.

Even though we've had many panic attacks...and we rationally know they're just scary and they don't tend to kill people... we're CONVINCED we're having a heart attack and we'll die!

22- Adrenaline – (uh-drin-uh-len).

favorite foods, we're less likely to get tired of this "eating plan!" It'll become A WAY OF LIFE...that we can LIVE WITH for the rest of our life. We'll STAY ON IT, LOSE WEIGHT, and KEEP IT OFF!

We've all heard THE BEST WAY to lose weight is to do it SLOWLY! If we're not in a major weight gain cycle[21] and we cut our food intake by one-fourth, we may lose 2-3 pounds a month. That's 24-36 pounds a year and 48-72 in two years! If we cut our intake in half, we may lose 4-5 pounds a month or 48-60 a year and 96-120 in two years! That's a lot...and we can KEEP IT OFF if we KEEP IT UP! A "three-fourths" or "halves" diet will serve us MUCH BETTER over time than a "crash n' burn" diet!

APPLICATION: Having a Panic Attack

Why is having a panic attack an Emotional Mind experience? _____

_____

When we're having a panic attack, we're Big-Time Emotional Mind. We're FREAKIN' OUT. Our mind and body "have done gone crazy." We're OUT-OF-CONTROL and we're CONVINCED some bad, horrible, rotten things will happen. We're so overwhelmed and FILLED WITH FEAR that we don't believe the rational thoughts that go through our mind...or what others are telling us. We're PANICKING! We think we're going TO DIE. Once we BEGIN to panic...we panic EVEN MORE. We're "SCARED TO DEATH" or so we THINK...and things get OUT-OF-CONTROL...FAST!

Have you had a panic attack? If so, what sort of things did you fear would happen? _
_____
_____

We FEAR we won't be able to breathe or we'll have a heart attack. We're CONVINCED we'll die THIS time. We FEAR being trapped and unable to escape. We FEAR embarrassment. We FEAR many things. We're FEARFUL of the ENTIRE EXPERIENCE because it's FRIGHTENING.

Having a panic attack is a great example of how Emotional-Driven Thoughts FUEL our emotional state. Our thoughts INTENSIFY our feelings, making them more intense and severe. AS SOON AS we think, "OH, MY GOD, I CAN'T BREATHE!" or "MY HEART IS BEATING SO FAST. I'M GOING TO HAVE A HEART ATTACK!"... BOOM...there goes ANOTHER ADRENALINE[22] RUSH. We panic EVEN MORE and this makes us SURE we're going to die, so we rush to the emergency room.

168

The second we feel anxiety, we begin to panic. Our body didn't start to panic, our mind did! It's like an Emotional Reflex. Knowing we're anxious panics us…we fear we'll start panicking and have a panic attack.

Our Emotion-Driven Thoughts and feelings feed off each other. It's like adding fuel to the fire. Our panic becomes more and more intense. What starts off as a spark of anxiety quickly ignites into a 4-alarm panic.

We Talk Ourselves Through the panic by allowing Rational Mind and Wise Mind to counsel our Emotional Mind.

Why does he need to change when he doesn't need to change? Someone's always there for Damage Control!

We may yell and scream and threaten this and that…but, they learn we won't Follow Through… because we DON'T Follow Through!

If you've had panic attacks, what Emotion-Driven Thoughts raced through your mind?

_____

_____

If your Emotion-Driven Thoughts were about something bad happening because of the panic attack, did these things ever happen or were they just something you feared would happen? Explain. _____

_____

_____

Treatment for MANAGING panic attacks involves TURNING ON Rational Mind. We're EDUCATED about panic attacks (Rational Mind facts). We're taught to TALK OURSELVES THROUGH the anxiety by reminding ourselves of the facts about anxiety and panic attacks. We're taught to CHALLENGE our EMOTION-DRIVEN THOUGHTS with Rational Mind statements. For instance, when we think "Oh my God, I'm going to have a heart attack!", we can REMIND OURSELVES of something like,

> *"I'm going to be okay. My heart always slows back down. I'm always okay afterwards. This will pass. I need to slowly breathe in my mouth and out my nose. I'm going to focus on my breathing and I'll be okay in a few minutes. This will pass."*

APPLICATION: When Help Is Destructive

If you're familiar with the psych term, "enabling," why is "enabling" someone an Emotional Mind behavior? _____

_____

> "Enabling" refers to HELPING people in a DESTRUCTIVE way. We enable or help them to continue self-destructive, irresponsible, and sometimes, even abusive behavior. A classic example involves parents who are "pushing" their adult child to be independent, productive, and out of trouble. However, the ADULT child is allowed to live in the family home WITHOUT any major consequences for irresponsible behavior other than a lot of conflict and screaming. If the ADULT child gets into financial or legal trouble, his parents bail him out. Thus, they ENABLE HIM to be IRRESPONSIBLE by BAILING HIM OUT and TAKING RESPONSIBILITY FOR HIM when he SHOULD BE TAKING RESPONSIBILITY FOR HIMSELF!

Enabling occurs in many ways. Consider the wife who phones her husband's work and says he's sick when he's really passed-out drunk! Consider the husband who buys his diabetic wife sweets so she doesn't go in a rage when he comes home without them! Consider the physically abused wife who makes "socially appropriate" excuses why they

From "Out-of-Control: A Dialectical Behavior Therapy (DBT) – Cognitive-Behavioral Therapy (CBT) Workbook for Getting Control of Our Emotions and Emotion-Driven Behavior" - Copyright © 2009 by Melanie Gordon Sheets, Ph.D. (www.dbt-cbt-workbook.com)

We enable someone to be abusive by making excuses for our injuries and by staying in the relationship.

Enabling is helping someone along their self-destructive path.

don't show up to a family reunion when it's really because of bruises. When we do these things, we ENABLE the people around us to CONTINUE IRRESPONSIBLE, HURTFUL, and DESTRUCTIVE BEHAVIOR.

In what way do you enable people? Be specific. _____

_____

_____

> Remember when everyone was talking about "Tough Love." It's the opposite of enabling. Tough Love involves setting rules, limits, and boundaries...and STICKING TO THEM. It's about allowing NATURAL CONSEQUENCES TO OCCUR. Being tough IS a tough decision. Like all Wise Mind decisions, the Big Picture of the Situation must be considered before Tough Love actions are taken. Ultimately, we have to decide what's ACCEPTABLE to us and what ISN'T...and what we're WILLING TO LIVE WITH...and what we're NOT WILLING to TOLERATE any longer. When someone's behavior is NOT ACCEPTABLE or TOLERABLE, we MUST TAKE A STAND and BE TOUGH in holding to our limits and boundaries.

I hate to admit that I take advantage of such a situation! I have a sister who can't stand disorder. When my house gets super messy, I invite her over for lunch!

Consider a wife who is obsessive-compulsive with housecleaning and organization. The family plays along with MOST of her cleaning and organization rules, like facing the milk the "right" direction in the fridge. They do this so they don't have to deal with her temper tantrums.

Is this enabling? If so, what would Wise Mind encourage us to do? _____

_____

If you said "Get her in therapy!" that's the right answer! If someone is SOOO obsessive-compulsive that others feel they MUST comply to keep peace, then the O-C person must be SERIOUSLY TROUBLED with unresolved issues.

Can you imagine being so pressured to avoid dealing with life issues that you have to work almost 24-7 to keep everything perfectly ordered and clean?

Consider how you enable others. Consider the enabling situation that upsets you the most. Then, answer...what drives your behavior? Why are you helping this person to be dysfunctional? Are you afraid something bad will happen if you don't enable them? Explain. _____

_____

_____

Rational Mind would tell us we're not just enabling them, we're DISABLING them.

What would Rational Mind say about your behavior and the situation? _____

_____

_____

23- Dire consequences –
serious consequences
such as going to jail,
losing their driver's
license or job, being
homeless, etc.

24- We're just prolonging
pain and suffering for
everyone involved. We
don't want to confront
the situation because we
don't want to go through
the heartache of the
natural consequences.
So, we enable them to be
dysfunctional and we
allow the pain and
troubles to go on and
on...and we all suffer
through it. When the
dysfunctional behavior
continues, it becomes
more and more of a
habit...and these bad
habits tend to worsen
over time. We THINK
we're helping them....but,
we're hurting them...and
us. Our "helping" is an
Emotional Mind decision.
It's NOT a Wise Mind
decision.

We enable people for many reasons. We may want TO SAVE THEM from dire consequences[23] because we love them and want the best for them. We may TRY to KEEP THEM "HAPPY" to keep the relationship...because we don't want to be alone. We may want them to be dysfunctional because we're afraid they'll leave us if they become functional. We may lie for them because we don't want people TO KNOW they have problems...and because WE don't want to look bad. Regardless of our reasons, Rational Mind would tell us we're doing MORE HARM THAN GOOD for EVERYONE involved.[24]

> When we enable our people, we TEACH them that their behavior will be TOLERATED. That's because we PUT UP WITH IT. WHY SHOULD THEY CHANGE when we're tolerating their behavior and cleaning up their messes? Rational Mind would remind us that we're enabling them to be dysfunctional by PREVENTING the NATURAL CONSEQUENCES of their behavior...and by HELPING THEM to AVOID DEALING WITH THE REALITY OF WHAT'S GOING ON.

What Did We Just Do?

We explored a variety of Emotional Mind experiences and behaviors that GO BEYOND ACTING-OUT and RESPONDING IMPULSIVELY to upsetting emotions in the HEAT-OF-THE-MOMENT. They're certainly less dramatic than throwing fits, suicide attempts, or pulling a drunk...but, they're self-defeating nonetheless!

APPLICATION: The Adaptive Nature of Emotional Mind

We seek the positive, rewarding, and inspiring Emotional Mind experiences!

We have to rid ourselves of negative emotions and fill our emotional experience with positive emotions. We have to add positive experiences to our life so we experience satisfaction, joy, and happiness.

Throughout this workbook, we've focused on the destructive side of Emotional Mind. It's important to be Mindful that Emotional Mind has a VERY POSITIVE and HELPFUL SIDE, too! For instance, an "atta-boy" from a boss or a performance award makes us feel valued, appreciated, and recognized. These positive emotions often lead to increased job satisfaction, dedication, and performance. This POSITIVE EFFECT is driven by Emotional Mind! Consider the benefits of participating in social activities... the fun, enjoyment, and a sense of belonging and being a part of something. These activities GIVE US THINGS TO LOOK FORWARD TO and to be EXCITED about. We look forward to the next meeting, get-together, or event. These things have a VERY POSITIVE EFFECT on our mood, quality of life, and life satisfaction. These things are GOOD Emotional Mind experiences!

In Chapter 3, "The Pathways of Recovery," we discussed the POSITIVE emotions and BENEFITS of being on and staying on the Recovery Path. MANY GOOD THINGS HAPPEN when we're living a Recovery Lifestyle. People begin to TRUST US and WANT US AROUND again. We have more cash flow, stable housing, transportation, a job, activities, a support system, etc. We feel joy, satisfaction, peace, pride, dignity, and self-respect. These things are SO REWARDING...THEY MOTIVATE US to stay on the Recovery Path. These positive Emotional Mind experiences are ADAPTIVE. They HELP US TO FUNCTION BETTER and to be MORE PRODUCTIVE and HAPPY!

Describe two ways that positive emotions lead you to function better? _____

_____

_____

We can no longer allow negative emotions to occupy space in our mind. We must evict them and fill the vacancy with positive tenants. That's so we can have a new lease on life!

Believe it or not, SOME NEGATIVE EMOTIONS are VERY ADAPTIVE, too!

In what type of situations can negative emotions be adaptive or helpful to us? _____

_____

_____

How can being upset and angry be adaptive or helpful? _____

_____

Our upsetting emotions push us to deal with things we'd PREFER NOT to deal with or have put off dealing with!

> Upsetting emotions PRESSURE and MOTIVATE us to CONFRONT SITUATIONS that ARE NOT OKAY! Our anger and unhappiness PUSHES us to DEAL WITH THINGS that are causing pain or distress. For instance, if our "friend" is unable to be kind and respectful...and to honor us as a friend, our anger RIGHTLY PRESSURES US TO CONFRONT THE PROBLEM...and to end the relationship, if necessary.

How about when we're angry because we feel someone is taking advantage of us? How can this anger be adaptive? _____

_____

This anger MOTIVATES US TO CONFRONT the situation and to SET LIMITS by saying "NO" as needed. THIS IS VERY ADAPTIVE. It helps us to Mindfully Protect Our Peace and Stability and to function better in OUR world.

How about when we're sad and SOMEWHAT depressed because of a loss. How can these feelings benefit us? _____

_____

_____

Our losses and hurts don't go away because we ignore them! They're always there for us ...waiting for us to deal with them!!!!

It sounds odd to say that sadness and mild to moderate depression can help us. However, these feelings SLOW us down and give us THE TIME and MINDSET TO GRIEVE and PROCESS our loss...IF we don't drink, drug, cut, or otherwise Numb-Out or White-Out. THE GRIEVING PROCESS **IS** THE HEALING PROCESS. WE MUST GRIEVE our loss SO WE CAN BE OKAY down the road. We MUST do our emotional

172

and psychological work to WORK THROUGH and GET THROUGH our loss and difficult emotions. Else, WE'LL SUFFER the same loss FOR YEARS and YEARS...until we SLOW DOWN...LONG ENOUGH ...TO PROCESS IT.

SKILL BUILDER: About Emotion-Driven Thoughts

We've learned that when we're in an emotional state, we experience Raw Emotions AND Emotion-Driven Thoughts. Emotion-Driven Thoughts are "driven by" or are caused by our emotions.[25] Each of us have CERTAIN Emotion-Driven Thoughts that go through OUR mind when we're upset. They're like attitudes...and they're based on OUR experiences and personality, like..."People can't be trusted." or "I always get hurt. I'm better off without a relationship." Some are trendy sayings, like, "I don't get mad, I GET EVEN!" Some are thoughts we've had before that we apply to new situations, like "NOBODY understands me." or "I screw EVERYTHING up." Emotion-Driven Thoughts can become a habit because we tend to use THE SAME ONES over and over. When you're depressed, which Emotion-Driven Thoughts run through your mind? What sort of things do you say? Write the SENTENCES you say. _____

_____

_____

When you're angry, what are some of your Emotion-Driven Thoughts? Write SENTENCES. _____

_____

_____

25- In Chapter 1, "The Nature of the Problem," Figure 1.A lists some common Emotion-Driven Thoughts and the emotional states they generally go with. Please review that list as needed.

Life's a beach and then you get whaled![26]

26- Whaled means beaten up and hit hard.

> When we're DEPRESSED, we have hopeless, helpless, worthless, shame and guilt, nobody loves me, cares about me, or understands me, and I'm going to leave this world or place type of thoughts. When we're ANGRY, our thoughts focus on getting even and hurting others like they've hurt us (but worse!), hurting or destroying ourselves, and thoughts about losing control and not being able to deal with whatever's going on. Some angry thoughts are similar to depressed thoughts. That's because anger and depression often go hand in-hand.

When you're faced with a challenging task, what are some of your Emotion-Driven Thoughts? Use sentences like you say in your head! _____

_____

_____

When you feel rejected, what are some of your Emotion-Driven Thoughts? _____

_____

_____

When you don't get what you want, what are some of your Emotion-Driven Thoughts?

_____

_____

When we're faced with a CHALLENGING TASK, our thoughts often center on not being able to do it and having messed up things like this before. Consider, "I'll NEVER be able to do it.", "I'm just going to make a fool out of myself.", and, "Why try, I'll mess this up like EVERYTHING else." REJECTION THOUGHTS may include, "What's wrong with me?", "No one will ever want me.", "I'm too _____. I'll ALWAYS end up getting dumped.", and, "I don't deserve to have a good friend." When we DON'T GET WHAT WE WANT, our thoughts often center on not being deserving or capable of having what we want. We may feel hopeless and helpless and believe we'll never obtain or achieve the things we desire. Thoughts may go through our mind like, "Why try, I'll never get what I want.", "I don't deserve to be happy.", "I'll never be able to have something like that.", and "I'm too _____ to get that."

27- Intensify – (in-tents-suh-fi) – to get worse or more severe.

We must challenge the lies we tell ourselves…and understand the truth behind our Emotion-Driven Thoughts.

> These Emotion-Driven Thoughts are VERY NEGATIVE and MAKE US FEEL WORSE. When we FEEL WORSE, we say these things EVEN MORE…which makes us feel EVEN WORSE THAN BEFORE! Sounds like the Cycle of Suffering! That's how our emotions and Emotion-Driven Thoughts FEED OFF each other and INTENSIFY[27] our emotional state. To STOP this CYCLE of PAIN AND SUFFERING, we MUST TURN ON Rational Mind to CHALLENGE these thoughts ONE-BY-ONE. We must CHECK the TRUTHFULNESS of these statements by LOOKING AT the FACTS REALISTICALLY, LOGICALLY, AND RATIONALLY.

APPLICATION: The Abusive Lies We Come to Believe

28- Parrot – to repeat, to say back to ourselves.

They were Emotion-Driven LIES when they came out of the speaker's mouth AND they're Emotion-Driven LIES when they come out of our mouth or mind.

These are the UGLY, EMOTIONALLY ABUSIVE statements TOLD TO US or said about us and we heard! They've NEGATIVELY affected how we feel about ourselves. We may have been told we're a SCREW-UP, we're STUPID, or WE'LL NEVER AMOUNT TO ANYTHING, or WE SHOULD HAVE NEVER BEEN BORN. These statements SOAK INTO OUR BRAIN. We come to BELIEVE them and PARROT[28] these ABUSIVE statements BACK TO OURSELVES. We HOLD ONTO these. They become PART OF our EMOTIONAL MIND and HOW WE FEEL ABOUT OURSELVES.

The truth, these statements are NOT based on reality or ANYTHING ABOUT US. They're LIES told to us by someone who's VERY EMOTIONALLY DISTURBED. These statements are NOT BASED on facts or truth. THEY'RE NOT EVEN ABOUT US!

174

They're REFLECTIONS of the emotional problems of the PERSON WHO SAID THEM.

APPLICATION: Out-of-Control Emotion-Driven Thinking

When we ruminate, we think about upsetting things...EXCESSIVELY.[29] Thoughts churn in our mind...over and over. Rumination is driven by Emotional Mind and feelings such as discouragement, vengeance,[30] desperation, depression, embarrassment, fear, and anger. The things we ruminate about are sometimes reality-based,[31] but, the ACT of rumination is an Emotion-Driven Behavior. That's because we're WORRYING and our THINKING IS OUT-OF-CONTROL...and it's making us EVEN MORE UPSET!

What sort of things do you ruminate about? _____

_____

We ruminate about MANY things. We ruminate over painful past events and personal injustices.[32] This just makes us MORE depressed or angry. We ruminate over mistakes, embarrassments, and other upsetting things we've done. In our rumination, WE BEAT OURSELVES UP mentally. This makes us FEEL WORSE...with INCREASED guilt, shame, depression, anger...and LOWER self-esteem. We ruminate about our financial and legal problems, relationship issues, job concerns, and our future when it seems uncertain or unpleasant. This just causes anxiety, panic, depression, self-doubt, indecision,[33] and inaction. Rumination becomes a problem when we get STUCK or PARALYZED in our thoughts and feelings. We end up MAKING OURSELVES SICK and MORE TROUBLED. Rumination also becomes a problem when we DWELL ON our problems rather than doing the things WE NEED TO DO to take care of them.

SKILL BUILDER: Managing Rumination

A Recovery Goal is to become Mindful of rumination and to FOCUS ON something HELPFUL. We might catch ourselves and say,

"I've been sitting here for three hours stewing over this. It's making me feel worse and worse...to the point of being suicidal and ready to say, 'Screw it, I'm gonna drink again.' Lord, look at what I'm doing to myself. I can't change what happened and it's tearing me up to keep thinking about it. I need to get out of this chair and find a way to distract myself. I'll go to Lisa's game and I'll chat with Pat afterwards. I need to Let This Go and Go On with my life!"

When we become MINDFUL of being STUCK IN NEGATIVITY and aware of the INCREASED DISTRESS it's causing...RATIONAL MIND and WISE MIND are TURNING ON. Rational Mind helps us to look at our issue realistically and logically and it brings truth to mind. Wise Mind reminds us that instead of IDLE[34] WORRY, we're better off PROBLEM-SOLVING. Wise Mind encourages us to ACT IN WAYS

Sidebar notes

29- Excessively – (ex-cess-ive-ly) – to excess, way too much.

30- Vengeance – (ven-gents) – a desire for revenge.

31- Reality-based – based on something real. We may ruminate about being unemployed and unable to pay bills...or about health problems, divorce issues, serious car problems, etc.

32- Personal injustices – things that happened to us that weren't fair or just.

33- Indecision – when we can't make up our mind and decide on something.

Rumination is a Self-Destructive Emotion-Driven Behavior. It causes us more and more distress and keeps us stuck in negativity.

When we're ruminating, we're NOT Participating Effectively. We're mindlessly hurting ourselves.

34- Idle – (eye-dull) – still, without activity.

Wise Mind encourages us to focus on what we need to do to solve the problem…and to distract ourselves from worrying while we go about it.

We're not Thinking Through Before We Do, we're just doing …doing whatever we feel like doing!

35- There are times when I'm so tired and irritable that EVERYTHING is an irritation. My favorite saying at these times is, "I'm so irritable. I don't deserve to be awake." With that moment of Mindfulness, I get ready for bed, even if it's only 6:00 pm!

36- In these situations, Emotional Mind is TURNED ON! It'll be quite a challenge to Turn On Rational Mind and Wise Mind in these situations because Emotional Mind is IN CHARGE. At times like these, we experience less control over our emotions and behaviors.

TO RELIEVE the distress INSTEAD of being STUCK in it. Wise Mind helps us to FIND PEACE by coming up with a GAME PLAN to deal with our issue. Wise Mind also leads us to Follow Through with our plan so we can Participate Effectively in our life.

APPLICATION: What Turns On Emotional Mind

When we're upset, Emotional Mind is Turned On and TURNED UP! It's also turned up when we're TIRED, SICK, or in PAIN. When we don't feel well, we're sensitive, easily bothered and upset…and QUICK TEMPERED![35] We're less likely to THINK rationally and Mindfully. Emotional Mind is also TURNED UP when we're HUNGRY, under the influence of DRUGS and ALCOHOL, when we're under HIGH STRESS, and when we're OVERWHELMED with problems and demands. Consider when we're drunk or high. We're Big-Time in Emotional Mind. We're rather mindless of the Big Picture of Our Life and WE'RE NOT THINKING rationally or wisely. We're often impulsive, reckless, angry, aggressive, paranoid, "loose," moody, or depressed. We're MUCH MORE LIKELY TO ACT ON our feelings and do self-destructive or risky things.

The statements below reflect how various physical and emotional states increase the intensity of Emotional Mind and its effect on us.[36]

> I was so drunk…I didn't know what I was doing.
> I was so stoned…I couldn't stop laughing.
> I was so coked-up…I got paranoid.
> I was so mad…I was about to explode.
> I was so scared…I just froze.
> When I was being assaulted, why didn't I scream?
> I'm so overwhelmed, my thoughts are racing.
> I'm so stressed-out…I'm losing it.
> I'm so hungry, I'm irritable.
> When I'm tired, I have zero patience.
> I was in so much pain, all I could think of was dying.
> When I was in labor, all I did was cuss my husband and the doctors.
> My husband is the biggest whiny baby when he's sick.

Under what type of physical and emotional conditions do you find yourself DEEPER in Emotional Mind? Using the statements above as examples, write some statements to describe your experiences. _____

_____

_____

_____

_____

SKILL BUILDER: Requesting Time-Out

A piece of wisdom...when we're in the Heat-of-the-Moment or otherwise in an intense emotional state,[37] we SHOULD NOT CARRY ON AN ARGUMENT and we SHOULD NOT TRY TO SOLVE A MAJOR PROBLEM. When we're living, eating, and breathing Emotional Mind, we're likely to HAVE TROUBLE Turning On Rational Mind and Wise Mind. We're likely to be MINDLESS and to SAY or DO things we'll LATER REGRET. We may make IMPULSIVE DECISIONS that greatly hurt our life and other people or we may say or do something terribly hurtful. When we're BIG-TIME IN EMOTIONAL MIND, it's TIME for TIME-OUT. If we're starting to get into an argument or heated discussion, we should say something like,

37- Like when we're very angry, hurt, in a lot of pain, or are very tired or hungry.

When we're Big-Time in Emotional Mind...Emotional Mind is driving... and Rational Mind and Wise Mind are in the trunk!

Be Rational!
Be Wise!
Don't act when you're Big-Time in Emotional Mind!

When we're getting Out-of-Control, we must TAKE CONTROL. Else, things happen and we lose control... and our life spirals Out-of-Control. A Recovery Goal is to get control BEFORE things get Out-of-Control.

When you "go back to the table" to discuss the situation, take Rational Mind and Wise Mind with you. Tell Emotional Mind to be quiet and NOT TO SPEAK unless spoken to!

> *"I really care about talking this over....but, right now I'm so hungry, I'm irritable and I can't think straight. Let me get a sandwich or three, chill-out for a few minutes, and then we'll talk."*

> *"Listen, I'm so hungry right now, I can't think about anything else. All we're doing is yelling and fussing. Let me get a bite to eat. I'll feel better and can listen to you without being so grumpy."*

> *"We're both really tired and grumpy from a long day. This problem is very important to us. I think it's best we get a good night's sleep and talk about it in the morning. Let's get up an hour early, have coffee, and go over it."*

> *"I'm so angry right now. I'm about to totally lose it. We need to stop this discussion here, right now. I need to take some time to chill-out and sort out my thoughts. We'll have to finish this discussion later."*

Consider times and situations when Emotional Mind gets the best of you. Think about the physical or mental state you're in (angry, hurt, hungry, tired, sick, overwhelmed, in pain, etc). Like the samples above, write TWO EXAMPLES of how you can REQUEST TIME-OUT in a REASONABLE and RESPECTFUL manner. Write what you can say to GET CONTROL of the situation...to PREVENT IT from GETTING OUT-OF-CONTROL!

1. _____

_____

_____

_____

2. _____

_____

_____

_____

OUR GAME PLAN FOR RECOVERY needs to include TAKING CARE OF OUR PHYSICAL AND MENTAL NEEDS so things like hunger, too little sleep, or too much stress doesn't cause major mood swings, irritability, and regretful behavior. For instance, if we have chronic pain, we shouldn't try to make major decisions or deal with major stressors when we're in a high pain state. We need to deal with those things when our pain is at a lower level. Likewise, if we're still using drugs or alcohol, we shouldn't try to deal with important problems when we're under the influence.

Time-Out...Some Steps Worth Taking

Step 1. REQUEST TIME-OUT in a reasonable and respectful manner.

Step 2. Take Time-Out to PULL YOURSELF TOGETHER! Get whatever physical, mental, or other need state taken care of[38] so you can deal with the situation rationally!

Step 3. Use your Time-Out to THINK THROUGH the situation so when it's time to discuss it, you can do so rationally and wisely. Come up with some ideas or a plan to deal with the problem. Think about how you're willing to negotiate[39] ...what you're willing to do, give up, or give in to...to do your part to bring about a peaceful resolution.[40]

Step 4. WHEN folks are CALM AND RATIONAL, DISCUSS the situation and NEGOTIATE! Listen, share your ideas, and be willing to negotiate! Remember, we're seeking peace and stability...and both people need to be SATISFIED for the relationship to be SATISFYING and LONG-TERM. It can't be ALL ABOUT US or ALL ABOUT THEM.

38- For instance, take a nap, eat, take a warm bath to relax, let your headache go away, etc!

39- Negotiate – (knee-go-she-ate) – to bargain, the give n' take process! I'll do this... if you'll do that.

40- Resolution – (rez-zuh-lu-shin) – to come to an end... a problem is solved or a course of action is decided upon. The situation is resolved!

A Recovery Goal is to be thoughtful and deliberate... and able to Turn On Rational Mind and Wise Mind to solve problems and handle situations...rather than letting Emotional Mind do all the driving.

Understanding how these three mind states work is ESSENTIAL to our recovery. We NEED TO UNDERSTAND that when we're Big-Time in Emotional Mind, Rational Mind is generally TURNED-OFF. We're NOT Thinking Straight...and we RARELY ACT WITH WISDOM or in DESIRABLE WAYS. And that's just the way things are. We're human and THAT'S THE WAY OUR BRAIN IS WIRED. As such, we need to FORGIVE OURSELVES if we didn't respond the way WE WISH WE HAD during a frightening, difficult, or traumatic situation. We need to ACCEPT OUR HUMANITY, FORGIVE OURSELVES, and MOVE ON with our recovery.

~~~~~~~~ CHAPTER REVIEW ~~~~~~~~

1. What are the two parts of Emotional Mind? _____

_____

2. Provide an example to explain what is meant by "surface" and "underlying" emotions.

_____

_____

_____

_____

3. Why is "getting into" a scary movie an Emotional Mind experience? _____

_____

_____

4. Why is overshopping an Emotional Mind experience? _____

_____

_____

What do our weight and our temper have in common? We lose these things all the time, but they keep coming back!

5. Why is a "crash diet" an Emotional Mind experience? _____

_____

_____

6. Why is having a panic attack an Emotional Mind experience? _____

_____

_____

7. Why is "enabling" an Emotional Mind experience? _____

_____

_____

8. How are positive emotions adaptive or helpful? _____

_____

_____

9. How can negative emotions be adaptive or helpful? _____

_____

_____

10. What are Emotion-Driven Thoughts? _____

_____

_____

11. What is meant when we say our emotions and Emotion-Driven Thoughts "feed off" each other? _____

_____

_____

12. Why are emotionally abusive statements really Emotion-Driven Lies? _____

_____

_____

13. In what way is rumination an Emotion-Driven experience? _____
_____

Take a few moments to reflect on this chapter. Some questions are listed in the margin to guide your reflection. Feel free to reflect on whatever your heart brings to mind.

What are your reactions to the material?

Which parts hit home or relate to you the most?

Which parts have helped you the most?

Which parts have helped you to understand yourself the most?

How will you use this information to feel better about yourself?

How will you use this information to improve the quality of your life...or to change how things work out for you in life?

What will you do differently based on this material?

How has this information changed the way you feel about your patterns of relapse and recovery... and your overall response to life?

What does this material motivate you to do?

14. How can Rational Mind and Wise Mind help us when we're ruminating? _____
_____
_____

15. List 5 types of mental and physical states that Turn Up Emotional Mind. _____
_____
_____

16. What are the four steps for using Time-Out to resolve conflict? _____
_____
_____
_____

~~~ For Reflection ~~~

_____
_____
_____
_____
_____
_____
_____
_____
_____
_____
_____
_____
_____

Figure 6.A.1: The Concepts and Skills Tracking Sheet – Chapter 6

Week # _____

		Day of Week →							
		Date →							

6A. Today, I quickly listed 15-20 different types of Raw Emotions.

6B. Today, I became Mindful that I was in Emotional Mind!

6C. When I was upset today, I listed 10 or more different types of emotions I was experiencing.

6D. When I was upset today, I became Mindful that some of my feelings were because of the here-and-now situation and some were based on the past.

6E. When I was upset today, I realized my emotional INTENSITY was because of unresolved things in the past. I realize I over-reacted to today's situation because of anger, hurt, losses, or other painful things from the past.

6F. When I was upset today, I became Mindful that my thoughts and impulses to do something destructive occurred because I didn't want to feel bad. I wanted to Numb-Out and White-Out my upsetting thoughts and feelings.

6G. Today, I became Mindful that I was "getting into" a movie or TV show. I realized I lost touch with reality and was responding to the show AS IF it was real!

6H. Today, I caught myself overshopping or being very tempted to do so. I became Mindful of what was going on in my Emotional Mind. I became Mindful of what was driving that impulse or behavior!

6I. Today, when I became Mindful of the Emotional Mind stuff that was leading me to overshop, I Turned On Rational Mind to Talk Myself Out Of overshopping!

Continued on the next page!

Notes:

RATING SCALE

5 – Did Excellent in this area today
4 – Did Pretty Good in this area today
3 – Did Alright in this area today
2 – Did Only Fair in this area today
1 – Didn't Do Well in this area today
DD – Didn't Do today

From "Out-of-Control: A Dialectical Behavior Therapy (DBT) – Cognitive-Behavioral Therapy (CBT) Workbook for Getting Control of Our Emotions and Emotion-Driven Behavior"

Copyright © 2009 by Melanie Gordon Sheets, Ph.D. (www.dbt-cbt-workbook.com)

Figure 6.A.2: The Concepts and Skills Tracking Sheet – Chapter 6

Week # _____ Day of Week →									
Date →									
6J. Today, I caught myself being "Blinded by Love." I became Mindful that Emotional Mind was driving...and Rational Mind was in the trunk! I realized I was following my heart and not my head. I realized I wasn't dealing with the Big Picture of the person. I was aware that I was seeing what I wanted to see because I wanted to be with that person or I just wanted a relationship!									
6K. Today, I Talked Myself Out Of a "Blinded by Love" relationship because "I can see clearly now!"									
6L. Today, I caught myself considering a "Crash N' Burn Diet." I Turned On Rational Mind and Talked Myself Out Of It! I decided I didn't want to GAIN weight by suffering through a diet!									
6M. Today, I reminded myself of the truths about panic attacks. I'm preparing to Talk Myself Through a panic attack...if one occurs again.									
6N. Today, I began to feel panicky. I quickly began to Talk Myself Through the anxiety. I was able to Get Through the anxiety without suffering a full blow panic attack. I took control of what could have become Out-of-Control.									
6O. Today, I became Mindful that I was tempted to ENABLE someone or I WAS enabling someone.									
6P. Today, I became Mindful of what was going on in my Emotional Mind...because I was tempted to enable someone or I WAS enabling someone. I became aware of the Raw Emotions and Emotion-Driven Thoughts that were driving my behavior.									
Continued on the next page!									

Notes:

RATING SCALE
5 – Did Excellent in this area today
4 – Did Pretty Good in this area today
3 – Did Alright in this area today
2 – Did Only Fair in this area today
1 – Didn't Do Well in this area today
DD – Didn't Do today

Figure 6.A.3: The Concepts and Skills Tracking Sheet – Chapter 6

Week # _____	Day of Week →							
	Date →							
6Q. Today, I became Mindful that Tough Love is a tough decision. I reminded myself that I must Choose My Battles and make decisions about WHETHER OR NOT it's appropriate for my life NOW to continue to enable certain people. WHEN IT'S TIME, I'll seek wise counsel about WHEN and HOW to deal with enabling in my High Priority and complicated relationships and situations.								
6R. Today, I caught myself in a positive and life-enhancing Emotional Mind state.								
6S. Today, I took time to think about the positive things in my life...and the positive things I expect as my time on the Recovery Path increases!								
6T. Today, I did something ON PURPOSE to bring positive emotions into my life. This was something life-enhancing, like a fun activity, inspirational reading, watching a comedy, and saying NO to an unnecessary demand and relaxing instead.								
6U. I took some time to think about my day...today. I became Mindful of the moments and hours that I was in a positive, LIFE-ENHANCING, Emotional Mind state.								
6V. Today, I became Mindful that a negative emotion I was experiencing was REALLY an ADAPTIVE emotion that encouraged me to do something to take care of myself and to end something painful or unwanted.								
6W. Today, I was Mindful of many Emotion-Driven Thoughts that ran through my mind.								
(Continued)								

Notes:

RATING SCALE

5 – Did Excellent in this area today
4 – Did Pretty Good in this area today
3 – Did Alright in this area today
2 – Did Only Fair in this area today
1 – Didn't Do Well in this area today
DD – Didn't Do today

Figure 6.A.4: The Concepts and Skills Tracking Sheet – Chapter 6

Week # _____

Day of Week →

Date →

6X. Today, I realized an Emotion-Driven Thought I was having was making me feel worse. I either distracted myself from that thought or I used Rational Mind to challenge it by looking at the truth. I found a way to help myself feel better and to clear my mind of negativity.

6Y. Today, I caught myself believing or repeating an ABUSIVE Emotion-Driven Lie said of me. I either distracted myself from that thought or I used Rational Mind to challenge it by looking at the truth. I found a way to help myself feel better and to clear my mind of negativity.

6Z. Today, I became aware that my mood was negatively affected by being tired, hungry, sick, or in physical pain.

6AA. Today, I became aware that my mood was negatively affected by being under the influence of drugs or alcohol.

6BB. Today, I became aware that my mood was negatively affected by being overwhelmed with too many demands or being under too much stress.

6CC. Today, I took Time-Out when I needed to...to pull myself together and to get my mood to a manageable level.

6DD. When I was upset and having conflict with someone today, I requested Time-Out to pull myself together. I thought about what I was willing to do to bring about a peaceful resolution.

6EE. Today, I discussed and NEGOTIATED a problem with someone. When my emotions began to flare, I was able to bring them down to a manageable level...so the discussion was a discussion and NOT a fight!

6FF. Today, something came up and I decided to accept my humanity, forgive myself, and move on with my recovery!

Notes:

RATING SCALE
5 – Did Excellent in this area today
4 – Did Pretty Good in this area today
3 – Did Alright in this area today
2 – Did Only Fair in this area today
1 – Didn't Do Well in this area today
DD – Didn't Do today

1- Dr. Linehan calls this mind state "Reasonable Mind." On page 65 of her Skills Training Manual, she states, "This is your rational, thinking, logical mind. It is the part of you that plans and evaluates things logically. It is your cool part."

~ 7 ~
RATIONAL MIND

We've been working with Rational Mind[1] throughout this book, so you're somewhat familiar with this mind state. Rational Mind is the part of us that processes life in a logical, legalistic, fact-driven, reality-oriented, and cut n' dry manner. In other words, Rational Mind uses reasoning, it respects rules, it's guided by truth, it deals with how things really are, and it's the calm, cool, intellectual, and unemotional part of us!

Emotional Mind is driven by HOW WE SEE AND EXPERIENCE the world while Rational Mind is driven by HOW THE WORLD REALLY IS!

The Purpose of Rational Mind

When we're in a troubling Emotional Mind state, the first step for gaining control is Mindfulness. We need to be aware of what's going on in Emotional Mind. We need to be Mindful of our Raw Emotions, Emotion-Driven Thoughts, and our desired Emotion-Driven Behavior. This includes awareness of our feelings, the thoughts racing through our mind, and what we're thinking about doing! Once we become aware of what's going on in Emotional Mind, we need to TURN ON RATIONAL MIND to look at our situation logically and realistically.

Rational Mind helps us to understand THE BIG PICTURE OF THE SITUATION and the TRUTH about what's going on. This helps us to challenge our Emotion-Driven Thoughts and to get our emotions MORE IN LINE with the REALITY of the situation. This REDUCES our emotional distress because we FOCUS on the HERE-AND-NOW situation RATHER THAN EVERYTHING that has EVER HAPPENED to us.

Rational Mind also considers the Big Picture of Our Life and REMINDS us of the CONSEQUENCES we'll SUFFER if we ACT ON destructive Emotion-Driven impulses. WHEN we're USING Rational Mind to deal with what's going on in Emotional Mind, WISE MIND TURNS ON and BRINGS US to a GAME PLAN for effectively dealing with our situation. Our Recovery Goal is to PARTICIPATE EFFECTIVELY in our life... so we're MANAGING and DEALING WITH our problems RATHER THAN CAUSING OURSELVES MORE PROBLEMS!

APPLICATION: The Meeting of the Minds

The following story, "Pete's Story," is a good example of HOW THE THREE MIND STATES WORK TOGETHER IN REAL LIFE.

Rational Mind helps us to know what is true and factual. It helps us to perceive the reality of our situations and our life. The reality of Rational Mind is generally quite different from the picture Emotional Mind paints!

A Recovery Goal is PREVENTION of Self-Destructive Emotion-Driven Behavior. We need to STOP OURSELVES before we do what we really feel like doing! Rational Mind helps us to gain control before things get Out-of-Control.

The quality of our life comes down to two choices.
We can LIVE IN Emotional Mind and ALLOW our life to fall apart OR we can TURN ON Rational Mind and Wise Mind to get a Game Plan for dealing with our problems.
The choice is to stay on the life-enhancing Recovery Path or to go the way of Relapse Route.

2- UA – urinalysis – a urine test to check for drugs or alcohol.

3- Probation revoked – to lose the privilege of being on probation. Folks have to serve their sentence in jail if their probation is revoked.

Pete's Story

Pete has a lot of stress and family conflict caused by his responses to life. His family has allowed him to stay in their garage apartment "for the last time." His probation requires him to be employed. He doesn't have a good work history so it took a while to find a job. He just bought a used car and now has visitation with his kids because he's paying child support. Things are pretty good in his life... though not the greatest. His boss accused him of doing something he didn't do. He blew up and walked off the job. He went to an old hangout and started drinking again and snorted some coke. Thoughts began churning in his mind. He is very worried and is thinking the worst, "My family is going to kick me out and I'll be homeless again. I'll lose my car without income and I'll lose visits with my kids. If I get called for a UA,[2] it'll be dirty and my probation will get revoked[3]... especially since I'm now unemployed. Then I won't see my kids for a long time." He's very upset with himself and thinks, "I am such a failure. I screw everything up. My family will NEVER let me hear the end of this. I should just kill myself. I can't handle all this crap again." Thoughts are racing through his mind. His emotions intensify and he becomes more and more upset. He begins to panic. He is desperate for a way out and considers going back to live with his ex-girlfriend. He's afraid of doing that because she still uses drugs. He panics even more and all he can think about is killing himself. He ruminates about this stuff for hours and hours. It's now 3AM and he's worried about going home...so late...so upset...and so messed up.

Does Pete's story seem like Real Life or does it seem like an exaggeration to make a good story? _____

Have you been in a state like this before about a lost job or some other major problem? If so, describe how your experience is similar to his. _____

_____

_____

SKILL BUILDER: Pete's State of Mind

Re-read Pete's story and UNDERLINE the parts that describe what's going on in his Emotional Mind. Put a BOX around the parts that are driven by Rational Mind.

You probably had no trouble identifying what was going on in Emotional Mind. You may have had some trouble deciding if his statements about getting kicked out of his apartment, being homeless...and losing his car, probation, and visits with his kids were

186

Rational Mind or Emotional Mind. What did you decide? Explain what you based your decision on? _____

_____

_____

4- Catastrophizing –
(cuh-tah-stro-fi-zing) –
when we're focusing on
the very worst things
that could happen.
It's a form of the word,
catastrophe –
(cuh-tah-stro-fee).

*When he went to the
bar, he was upset.
When he began
drinking and
drugging, he became
hopeless, desperate,
and PANICKED.*

*Isn't it odd how
we can go from
bad to worse…
and we begin to
think the worst
option is the best?*

Mindfulness of the consequences suggests he was in Rational Mind. Some think he was in Emotional Mind because it seemed like he was catastrophizing[4] how bad things could get. However, given his life situation, his worries WERE based on truth and reality!

A reason to suspect he was Big-Time in Emotional Mind is…WISE MIND DIDN'T TURN ON and OFFER LIFE-ENHANCING SOLUTIONS. All he did was ruminate for hours about consequences and finding a way out…NOT A WAY THROUGH. He was panicking! All the COCAINE and ALCOHOL did was PUSH HIM DEEPER and DEEPER into Emotional Mind…and farther and farther away from Rational Mind and Wise Mind. He couldn't think straight. The MORE he ruminated, drank, and snorted, the MORE DEPRESSED, ANXIOUS, WORRIED, and PARANOID he became.

The Big Picture of Pete's Story suggests he was Big-Time in Emotional Mind. He had SOME Rational Mind going on…but, not much. He was AWARE of the consequences of losing his job, he KNEW he should not return to his ex, and he KNEW his behavior would cause family problems. He was probably 80%-20% Emotional Mind - Rational Mind. Wise Mind flickered on and encouraged him NOT to call his ex. Not having that option…and having more time to drink and snort, he panicked even more…and came to believe that suicide was his best option.

Given Pete's story IS Real Life, how do you think this part of his story ends? _____

_____

He'll either do something MORE DESTRUCTIVE, like a suicide attempt, driving drunk, or a full-blown relapse OR he'll do something LIFE-ENHANCING like staying safe and sleeping it off in the car and TURNING ON Rational Mind WHEN HE COMES TO… TO GET HIS LIFE BACK IN ORDER.

Pete's story tells about the "Something That Happens" on the Recovery Path and the two choices we have. Pete CHOSE the RELAPSE ROUTE in the Heat-of-the-Moment. HOWEVER, he DOESN'T HAVE TO stay on that path. He can call for help at 3AM or crawl into his car and sleep it off.

SKILL BUILDER: *How to Get Control Once We've Lost Control*

Let's suppose he chose the Recovery Path at 3AM. When he comes to and is able to shake off the cobwebs later that day, what might Rational Mind say to him? _____

_____

_____

Rational Mind might lead him to think,

> *"I blew up and walked off the job and I drank and used coke last night. I was scared. I freaked out...but this DOESN'T HAVE TO BE the end of the world. It's time for DAMAGE CONTROL. MY PRIORITY RIGHT NOW is to get a job. Whether it's my old job back or a new one...I need to act fast! No doubt my folks know Something Happened because I didn't come home last night and I'm home now when I'm supposed to be at work. I need a plan for dealing with them, too, so I don't lose housing."*

At this point, Emotional Mind will probably rear up with all kinds of self-defeating thoughts and feelings. Pete MUST TURN ON Rational Mind to Fight for his peace and stability. He cannot ALLOW Emotional Mind to control the course of his life.

> When a destructive thought comes up, Pete needs to remind himself that HIS NUMBER ONE PRIORITY is to STAY ON the RECOVERY PATH and that HE CAN AND WILL HANDLE this situation. He needs to tell himself that he STRUCK OUT last night, but there's still MORE INNINGS in the game. He'll have to challenge the destructive Emotion-Driven Thoughts AS THEY COME UP and REMAIN FOCUSED on TRUTH, REALITY, DAMAGE CONTROL, and PROBLEM-SOLVING.

At this point, Wise Mind will kick in to help him with a plan of action. What might Wise Mind suggest? _____

_____

_____

Wise Mind might suggest he visit his boss to apologize for blowing up and to ask for his job back. Wise Mind might suggest he TRY to assure his boss he didn't do what he was accused of doing. Wise Mind would likely remind him if "Plan A" doesn't work, he could apply for dozens of other jobs until he gets one...and that IT'S NO TIME TO BE PICKY! Wise Mind might encourage him to explain the situation to his parents... to let them know HE SLIPPED...but was BACK ON the RECOVERY PATH. If needed, he could tell them he'll have a job quickly, REGARDLESS OF WHAT HE HAD TO DO. Wise Mind would likely inform him that it's unlikely he'll get called for a UA over the next few days and to pray on that! If he did get called for one, Wise Mind might suggest telling his probation officer what happened and the POSITIVE WAY HE'S DEALING WITH IT. Wise Mind would have MANY DAMAGE CONTROL and PROBLEM-SOLVING IDEAS for GETTING RECOVERY BACK ON TRACK!

If at the end of the next day, he didn't get his job back and he didn't get a new one, Emotional Mind could easily start the self-defeating rumination and worry process. What could he do to help himself if this starts up? _____

_____

_____

Wise Mind would strongly encourage him to chill-out and focus on Damage Control, problem-solving, and the use of Life-Enhancing Coping Behaviors[5] to avoid destructive worry.

5- Being busy with problem-solving...and working towards the solution is a powerful coping tool. Getting a newspaper and a phone book and making a list of jobs to apply for and businesses to call and visit **is** solution-focused. Visiting the employment agency and ironing a decent set of clothes for job hunting is very constructive, too!

Through Rational Mind, he could TAKE NOTE of the PRODUCTIVE things he's done the last two days INCLUDING his MAJOR SUCCESS with QUICKLY GETTING BACK ON THE RECOVERY PATH and preventing a full-blown relapse. He could LIST HIS GOALS for the next day and a PLAN OF ACTION for the rest of the week. Since money is tight, he could WORK OUT A PLAN for paying what HAS TO BE paid. He could DISTRACT himself with POSITIVE ACTIVITIES (support group meetings like AA, helping his family prepare a meal, visiting with a recovery friend, etc.). He could SEEK TEMPORARY WORK cleaning yards, painting his parents home, and whatever else he can come up with to earn money and to KEEP HIS MIND BUSY. He could even talk with businesses about hiring him for a day or two to do "odd jobs."

Rational Mind tames what comes out of Emotional Mind. Rational Mind pulls on the reins and helps to get control of what is going Out-of-Control.

This WORK-UP of Pete's story shows how RATIONAL MIND helps to CONTROL the INTENSITY and NEGATIVITY of an UPSET EMOTIONAL MIND! Rational Mind DOESN'T BUY INTO a "I'm a total screw-up. This is going to ruin everything. I can't deal with it. I should kill myself." mentality. Rational Mind CHALLENGES panic and negativity by looking at the situation in a calm, NON-EMOTIONAL, realistic, logical, and truthful manner. In the upcoming sections, we'll look at some common Emotional Mind experiences from the viewpoint of Rational Mind. We'll see how Rational Mind TAKES the POWER and NEGATIVITY OUT OF a destructive emotional experience.

SKILL BUILDER: Cutting Always Helps

What would Rational Mind say to this Emotion-Driven Thought? _____

_____

_____

"Cutting only gives me temporary relief from my problems. I never deal with my stuff head-on, I always cut. My problems are piling up. Things are getting worse and I feel so Out-of-Control."

"Cutting myself sometimes helps me to feel better. However, relief is SO SHORT-LIVED and then I have to WORRY about hiding my cuts."

"I'm getting all these cuts and scars. NOW I HAVE OTHER WORRIES...like what to say when I go for my check-up and how to explain long sleeves in the summer. I'm all scarred up. Am I going to lose my job when we switch to summer uniforms? Everyone is going to know."

"Cutting really hurts me more than it helps."

> *"My cutting is GETTING WORSE. I HAVE TO CUT MORE and DEEPER to get relief. I'm really starting to scare myself. I almost called 9-1-1 last time. They'll send me to a psych ward if they find out how bad off I am. I'll lose everything. Cutting is VERY DESTRUCTIVE and it's causing me different kinds of problems and lots of EXTRA anxiety and worry. I've got to find another way to deal with life."*

SKILL BUILDER: Just One Drink Doesn't Matter

"I'm thinking about drinking through Emotional Mind. I'm trying to get myself to believe something I know is a lie!"

What would Rational Mind say about this relapse lie? _____

_____

_____

Rational Mind would say things like,

> *"If I allow myself to start 'a little drinking', it won't be long before I'm back to old drinking habits. I know this game. One drink today pours next week's drinks... and soon, I'll be back to my old drinking patterns. I remember, 'THE MAN TAKES THE DRINK AND THE DRINK TAKES THE MAN.'"*

"I'm not foolin' myself. This is STINKIN' THINKIN'. I've already begun to relapse when I say, 'One drink doesn't matter.'"

> *"I can see what I'm doing. I'm trying to convince myself I can control my drinking SO I'LL ALLOW MYSELF TO DRINK TONIGHT! I know I've relapsed if I act on this lie. Actually, I'm already in trouble if I have to Turn On Rational Mind to challenge this Emotion-Driven Lie!"*

> *"I might be able to have JUST ONE drink tonight, but soon it'll be two drinks, four drinks, and then I'll be saying, pulling one drunk doesn't matter."*

SKILL BUILDER: I Can't Deal With This

When we're overwhelmed and say, "I can't handle this." what would Rational Mind say?

_____

_____

Rational Mind would say things like,

> *"I'm too upset right now to deal with this effectively. I need to chill-out and pull myself together. THEN I'll be able to deal with it."*

"I can't." usually means "I don't want to... but I can if I really want to!" Truth, we CAN deal with our stuff even though we aren't in any mood to do so!

> *"I'm SO overwhelmed and upset about SO many things. I FEEL LIKE I CAN'T deal with it, BUT I CAN DEAL WITH IT if I put my heart and soul into dealing with it!"*

> *"I don't know how to deal with this whole thing, but I'll seek advisors to help me. I CAN deal with it, but I WILL NEED SOME HELP."*

> *"I have so many other things to deal with that are more important. I CAN DEAL WITH THIS SITUATION, but I'm going to have to take care of some other things first. I've got to focus on priority stuff first!"*

SKILL BUILDER: I Can't Stand to Be Alone

What would Rational Mind say to this? _____

_____

_____

If we keep telling ourselves, "I can't be alone." and we do desperate things to avoid aloneness, we don't give ourselves a fair chance to practice being alone! We don't learn ways to cope with it so we CONTINUE TO BELIEVE we can't be okay when we're alone!

Rational Mind would say many things from the previous "I Can't" section...plus,

> "I CAN be alone! It'll be uncomfortable though.
> I'll have to WORK THROUGH the anxiety and distress...but, I CAN do it!"

> "It'll take A LOT OF DETERMINATION AND A VERY GOOD GAME PLAN with lots of activities, coping plans, and support to get through the first couple of weeks because I DON'T LIKE TO BE ALONE!"

> "It scares me to think about it! I know I can make it, but it'll be VERY hard at first. If I stay busy and make new friends, that'll help a lot!"

Folks who "can't"... often "do"... and what a sense of pride and mastery "doing" brings!

I've worked with many people who "can't stand to be alone" and IT IS a big deal to overcome. However, with determination, many do it! They say it's VERY hard at first, but it gets a lot easier with time. Some become comfortable with alone time...and others say they LEARN to tolerate it...but never really like it. It's LIFE-CHANGING to CONQUER such a STRONG emotional "I CAN'T." It makes us feel like we CAN DO ALMOST ANYTHING in comparison! What AWESOME EMPOWERMENT!

SKILL BUILDER: A Bad Relationship Is Better than No Relationship

What would Rational Mind say to this? _____

_____

_____

"We just can't live like this...fighting all the time. I can't have peace and stability with this constant conflict. Even though it would be awful to move out and start over, it NEEDS TO happen."

Rational Mind would say things like,

> "I don't like being without a boyfriend. That's a fact. But...this relationship is so hurtful, I'm absolutely miserable. Even though it'll be VERY HARD to be alone, I'LL be MUCH BETTER OFF without this relationship.
> I need to work on my relationship issues so next time, I'll CHOOSE a better partner. THEN, I'll have a relationship that brings MUCH MORE HAPPINESS THAN PAIN."

> "When she's in a good mood, things are really great. When she's in a bad mood, THINGS ARE HORRIBLE. She becomes so abusive to me and the kids. IT'S MAKING US SICK TO CONTINUE TO LIVE LIKE THIS."

"It's really better to end it now. We're toxic for each other and we're both so miserable."

SKILL BUILDER: I Don't Deserve Any Better than This

What would Rational Mind say to "I don't deserve..." thoughts? _____

_____

On any given day, we don't always get what we deserve, good or bad. However, over time, things tend to balance out. The outcomes of our choices WILL BE experienced... both the good outcomes and the bad. We generally reap what we sow.

_____

_____

Rational Mind would say,

> "If I'm REALLY doing the best I can, MANY GOOD THINGS will Come My Way. I have to be patient and ALLOW TIME FOR MY CHANGES TO TAKE ROOT. If I'm NOT trying and am doing self-destructive things, many bad things will Come My Way. I wasn't born deserving bad things, but bad things have been the natural consequences of the choices I've made. WE REAP WHAT WE SOW, good and bad."

> "I've been told I'm NOT DESERVING since I was young...that I don't deserve anything good. However, that's just an ABUSIVE, EMOTION-DRIVEN LIE!"

> "I WAS BORN DESERVING! I deserve good things in life like everyone else. When I treat people right, I DESERVE to be treated right. When I'm good to people, I DESERVE good relationships. When I work hard, I DESERVE to be rewarded!"

SKILL BUILDER: I'm So Fat, No One Would Want Me

What would Rational Mind say to that? _____

_____

_____

"I have many positive qualities. There's a lot more to me than my body size."

"I have to give people time to get to know my positive qualities so they can get passed 'fat' to see that I'm a great person to be around. I may be rejected by folks who can't get passed 'fat'...but that's just the way things are. There's many people who value others for more than their appearance."

Rational Mind would say things like,

> "I'm overweight and it DEFINITELY LIMITS who will be interested in me."

> "Some people judge others based on how they look and it's UNLIKELY these people will choose to be with me. These people are shallow and are missing out on a good friend, spouse, or employee. I need to stop getting my feelings hurt by NO LONGER EXPECTING these people to accept me. It's just how they are and it ISN'T WORTH my peace and stability to try to get them to like me for who I really am."

> "I need to seek companionship with people who aren't so judgmental. Many folks value a loyal friend who's fun to be around. I need to focus my energies on these people!"

> "It'll be hard to get a big job being so overweight. I may have to start at the bottom and work my way up. When they see how bright and capable I am and what a hard worker I am, they'll learn to value that. I may not get the 'in the public eye' job, but I'll move up to a good job nonetheless."

> "Being so overweight, it's unlikely that the best looking person will ask me out. I NEED TO BE LESS JUDGMENTAL...and flirt with folks who rank closer to my 'general appearance rating!'"

192

"Do I want to 'suffer'[6] through a weight loss plan… or do I want to suffer through life because of rejection, loneliness, and shame over my appearance?"

6- Truth, we don't have to "suffer" through a diet if we start with a "three-fourths" or "halves" diet. We'll still be able to eat the foods we like…just less of them! In a few days, our stomach will shrink and we'll be satisfied with less food. If we think of this "diet" as a life-long eating plan, we can still have some of our favorite foods now and then. We might gain a pound, but we'll lose it over the month…and then some. Remember, it's about losing 30-40 pounds a year…not in two months!

We should DECIDE to control our behavior before the consequences of our behavior control us! We have a choice to STOP OURSELVES BEFORE WE ARE STOPPED!

Most of us wouldn't Follow Through with violence… but we're certainly ANGRY enough that violent thoughts fly THROUGH our mind!

Rational Mind is all about dealing with truth. If we're pretty heavy, it's important to ACKNOWLEDGE THAT FACT and DEAL WITH our situation RATIONALLY. With the HELP OF WISE MIND, we can MAKE A DECISION about how to deal with it…and then, we can come up with a GAME PLAN for doing so! For instance, we may DECIDE we're NOT INTERESTED in new eating habits and we're going to STOP WORRYING about how we look. We may DECIDE we're going to seek romance with someone who is LESS ATTRACTIVE and LONELY…and okay with THEIR looks and OUR size! We may DECIDE we're going to FOCUS ON OUR POSITIVE QUALITIES and on meeting someone who places a high value on those…and less value on physical appearance.

We may also decide we're TIRED OF THE PAIN AND SUFFERING that goes with being "BIG" and that we're GOING TO DO something about it. We may decide it's better to CHOOSE to change our eating habits BEFORE WE'RE FORCED TO because of a serious medical problem. We may DECIDE it's better to develop healthier eating habits BY CHOICE AND NOT HAVE DIABETES…rather than waiting until we get diabetes and we're FORCED to change our diet! This way, we're doing NOW what we'll HAVE TO do later…BUT, we won't have diabetes, too! Thus, we can PREVENT some negative consequences. If we're GOING TO HAVE TO CONTROL our eating, it's best to do so BEFORE we get a serious medical problem to deal with, too!

SKILL BUILDER: I'd Kill Her if I Had the Chance

What would Rational Mind say about violent thoughts? _____

_____

_____

Consider the common saying, "I could just choke him!" Well, we're human and we have aggressive thoughts…even to the extent, "I'd kill him if I had the chance." The truth, these FORBIDDEN or TABOO thoughts and impulses are FAIRLY COMMON when we're VERY ANGRY. Fortunately, the frontal lobes of our brain usually KICK IN and TALK US OUT OF THIS…REAL QUICK! We feel like hurting someone, but we're NOT going to do it. Rational Mind Turns On and reminds us that we're VERY ANGRY and it's NORMAL to have violent thoughts…but, that it would be HIGHLY DESTRUCTIVE TO ACT ON THESE THOUGHTS or to spend much time RUMINATING over them. Rational Mind would also tell us things like,

"IT'S NOT WORTH IT. She's not worth it. She's not worth going to jail over or ruining my life and my family's life over."

> "HE'LL GET HIS in the end...but it won't be with my hands. He'll keep doing this to people and SOMEONE will take care of him FOR ME. I don't have to do it. Teaching him a lesson IS NOT WORTH MY peace and stability."

> "I really don't want him dead or seriously hurt.
> I just want him out of my business...and out of my life."

Once we're thinking rationally about our problem, Wise Mind Turns On and suggests some CONSTRUCTIVE, ANGER-RELIEVING, COPING ACTIVITIES and ways to MANAGE the problem.

SKILL BUILDER: I'll Show Them...They'll Be Sorry

What would Rational Mind say about that? _____

_____

_____

Rational Mind would say something like,

Getting even is NOT a wise idea, though it's SOOO tempting!

"She's VENGEFUL LIKE ME. If I take revenge on her, she'll get even. All the pain, anxiety, and conflict AREN'T worth it. I'm going to cut my losses, walk away, and focus on IMPROVING MY LIFE rather than destroying it."

"I'll just be starting a war and we'll both have battle scars to show for it!"

> "I feel like hurting them because they've hurt me. I want them to pay. I want them to be sorry they ever treated me like this. As much as I'd love to get even, I can't. I MUST Let this Go. I'd end up hurting myself EVEN MORE. I CAN'T CONTINUE TO DO THINGS THAT HURT MY LIFE. I must Let this Go and GO ON with my life. I know people will hurt me now and then and THEY sure did a fine job this time."

> "Maybe they'd be sorry, maybe they wouldn't be. They'd probably say, 'I did what I had to do. I wish he wouldn't have done that, but I had no choice.'"

> "If I ALLOW myself to ruminate over this, I'll be LIVING IN Emotional Mind. MY mental space will be FILLED with NEGATIVITY and HURTFUL memories. Anger and revenge will be MY FOCUS...and I'LL BE MISERABLE until I carry out the revenge or DECIDE to Let It Go. If I carry it out, I'll have a few moments of satisfaction and joy because I've evened the score. However, those GREAT feelings will be SHORT-LIVED because the CONSEQUENCES of revenge will SLAM me. I may get arrested or live in fear of being arrested. I may lose my job or not be able to see my kids. My people will be very upset with me. I may burn a bridge or permanently destroy a relationship. The Big Picture of My Life will fall apart. This isn't about them... and making them sorry. This is about MY LIFE. I stand to lose SO MUCH by getting even that it's NOT WORTH MY TIME and ENERGY to even think about!"

The Self-Fulfilling Prophecy of failure: I expect to fail so I don't try very hard ...so, I fail.

> "I don't HAVE TO take revenge. He's SO dirty and does this to SO many people, he'll get SOMEONE ELSE real angry and THEY'LL do it FOR ME! It's gonna happen. HE'LL GET HIS and I DON'T HAVE TO RISK ANYTHING! S-W-E-E-E-T!"

SKILL BUILDER: Failing to Succeed...or Successful Failures

Consider the lies we tell ourselves about success and failure, like, "I'll NEVER be

If we don't put forth a FULL effort, we'll never REALLY KNOW if we can succeed.

Some of our greatest leaders and wealthiest people failed many times before they achieved great success.

We never fail until we quit trying. Success comes to those who are determined to overcome obstacles in their path.

When we understand our failures are just a part of the learning process, then we can constructively accept our failures and learn from them.

7- Some say, "Been there, done 14, I've got to be real close to making it!" Folks who are new to recovery are discouraged, "I don't want to do this that many times." Be Mindful that 8-18 is an average. Some make it on the 1st try (they need to write the book!), others on the 25th. Some make it in 3 tries, others in 20. These numbers don't mean it's okay to relapse 17 times "just because we can" and then work real hard on the 18th try!

able to do it." or "Everything I try gets screwed-up somehow."

What do you say about your failures? _____

_____

_____

The truth...we MAY HAVE failed at MANY tasks. If so, we need to rationally understand why. Quite often, we fail because we DON'T TRY to succeed. We "KNOW" WE CAN'T DO IT...so we DON'T TRY, or we DON'T TRY VERY HARD.

Despite USUALLY giving things ONLY A HALF-HEARTED EFFORT, we may recall some times WHEN WE REALLY TRIED, but failed anyway. BUT, DON'T THINK we're off the hook because of some FULL EFFORT failures. WE DON'T GET TO STOP TRYING just because when we've REALLY TRIED, we've still failed! Rational Mind would inform us that MOST PEOPLE WHO SUCCEED HAVE FAILED MANY TIMES. There are many TRUE stories to support this TRUTH.

Which stories have you heard...about people who FINALLY SUCCEED AFTER A LONG STRING OF FAILURES? _____

_____

_____

Abraham Lincoln ran for MANY political positions and lost MANY TIMES before he ever WON an election. The ONE he won was THE BIG ONE...the PRESIDENTIAL election! There are MANY stories about business leaders who had MANY failed businesses before they hit it big! Henry Ford went bankrupt 5-6 times because of failed businesses before he gained success in the automotive industry. The Heinz company had the same kind of start. Have you read that Oprah was fired from a reporter's job because she wasn't right for TV? Somebody certainly misjudged her!

When we fail, we need to SEEK AN UNDERSTANDING of WHY WE FAILED. We need to LEARN FROM IT and CORRECT WHAT WE'RE DOING. We need to change or adjust our plan to deal with what went wrong. Successful "failures" start with PLAN A and go to PLAN B, C, D, E...and so on until things work out! Despite their failures, THEY KEEP ON KEEPING ON!

It's also important to be Mindful of our successes and accomplishments and to note WE'VE ALL HAD SOME! We also need to realize that WHEN WE'VE TRIED...when we've REALLY STUCK WITH IT, we've overcome challenges...and WE HAVE BEEN SUCCESSFUL. Consider the 8-18 attempts[7] at recovery that it takes people ON AVERAGE to become clean n' sober. Through our recovery attempts, we learn about

We're so willful and hard-headed about recovery that we won't take someone's advice or learn from THEIR experiences. We have to learn from our personal experiences… which is often OUR failures!

A mistake is only a mistake if we fail to learn from it! When we learn from our experiences, our failures become a stepping stone toward success!

A Recovery Goal is to Turn On Rational Mind to challenge our "failure" lies… and to Turn On Wise Mind to make some adjustments to our Game Plan! That's because WE haven't failed, our plan has!

When we're desperate, we often pressure our people to do desperate things to help us.

our triggers and relapse patterns. We learn we REALLY HAVE TO change the things in our life that we DON'T WANT TO CHANGE…things that we've refused to change, like friendships, activities, and abusive or conflict-filled relationships. Because of our repeated failures at recovery, we FINALLY SUCCEED! That's because we've revised our Recovery Plan SO MANY TIMES that we FINALLY GET ENOUGH OF THE NECESSARY CHANGES made! We're hard-headed and we've got to learn from OUR experiences…and in the world of recovery…these experiences ARE OFTEN RELAPSES. Does this information change the way you think about your "failures"? If so, explain.

_____

_____

> *Changing our LIFESTYLE and our LIFE IS VERY DIFFICULT. We need to ACCEPT OUR FAILURES and UNDERSTAND they're a NATURAL part of the LEARNING PROCESS…IF we learn from them.*

It's clear that Emotion-Driven Thoughts like, "I can't do it. Why try?" are lies we tell ourselves. What's the truth? _____

_____

> *The truth is, WHEN WE KEEP TRYING, things FINALLY work out. Sometimes, we don't succeed because we aren't going about it the right way. Therefore, we need to get a NEW PLAN. Sometimes, we try to do more than is do-able at one time. We plunge head first when we'd be better off wading in and taking smaller steps! There are many reasons why we haven't reached our goals. Fortunately, most of these problems can be overcome with PERSISTENCE and a REVISED GAME PLAN!*

SKILL BUILDER: My Family Would Be Better Off Without Me

Consider, "I'm a BURDEN to my family. They'd be better off without me." and "I'd be doing them a favor by killing myself." and "It would make them happy if I was dead." What would Rational Mind say about these types of statements? _____

_____

_____

Have you ever spoken with a child, spouse, parent, sibling, friend, or other loved one of someone who committed suicide? THEY AREN'T OKAY. THEY AREN'T PLEASED. THEY AREN'T RELIEVED. HELL HAS JUST STARTED for them. Not only do they suffer the normal DEPRESSION and GRIEF associated with a loved one's death, but, they also SUFFER OVERWHELMING GUILT. They often get stuck in EMOTIONAL

MIND with the, "IF ONLY I WOULD HAVE..." condition.

> "IF ONLY I wouldn't have worried so much about my job and stayed home with her, SHE'D STILL BE ALIVE."

"If only I would have given him more money. So what if my house was repossessed, at least my son would be alive today."

> "I told her she couldn't come back and live with us. I told her I had three kids to protect and my husband threatened to leave if I let her come back. I told her Annie still had nightmares about finding her cutting in the bathroom. I SHOULDN'T HAVE told her she couldn't come back...but what could I have done? I feel like IT'S ALL MY FAULT. I can't forgive myself."

"My Dad was under a lot of stress and I got so mad at him for taking away my car. My last words to him were that I hated him and he was a horrible father. I just can't live with myself. He was just trying to be a good father."

> "I couldn't deal with her problems anymore, so I stopped taking her calls. Now she's dead and it's all my fault. IF ONLY I had tried ONE MORE TIME."

Children suffer the "IF ONLY" condition, too. They have a CHILD'S MIND and they don't understand the Big Picture. They personalize the suicide and BELIEVE it's THEIR FAULT. They suffer guilt and shame ON TOP OF the loss and depression, too.

> "If I would have been quiet, Mommy would not have died."
> "If I would have been a good boy, daddy wouldn't have killed himself."
> "It's all my fault that Momma died."
> "I gave Mom so much grief, I wish I wouldn't have pushed her so far."

A mother of six children BELIEVED that killing herself would bring peace to her husband and kids because they would no longer have to endure her anger, moodiness, and screaming n' fussing. She had Bipolar Disorder and PTSD. She was asked to consider what life would be like for her family if she had died.

What do you think daily life would be like for the SIX kids and Dad? _____

Sometimes when folks suicide, it's like they hand off their problems to their loved ones...and then some. Suicide "kills" the family with a type of grief and suffering that people don't easily recover from.

_____
_____
_____
_____
_____

Of course the SELF-BLAME, GRIEF, and PAIN AND SUFFERING we just spoke of would be present. On top of that, the family would be thrown in a WORLD OF TURMOIL.[8] Dad would have the DOUBLE DUTY of HIS JOB outside the home and MOM'S JOB INSIDE the home. He would have the added responsibilities of housekeeping, cooking, and all the kid duties she took care of (homework, meals, kid squabbles, evening baths, the morning routine, shopping, special things for school, hauling kids to games, practices, and activities, etc). The KIDS WOULD SUFFER

8- Turmoil – severe stress and emotional pain.

We don't do our family a favor by suiciding. It just adds a whole bunch of new problems to their lives... problems that run deep and can last a lifetime.

9- Children learn from their family how to cope with problems. If momma kills herself, these kids are MUCH MORE LIKELY to attempt suicide when life gets tough. That's one reason mental health professionals ask about family history of suicide when assessing suicide risk.

What would her family rather have... Momma fussing or Momma dead?

"My life is not just about me. My family depends on me being okay and it just kills them that I keep attempting suicide."

10- A young mother spoke of being so depressed that she couldn't work. She believed she could help her child more by suiciding so her child would get a million dollars in insurance money. What do you think this child would prefer...to be rich or to have her Momma?

BECAUSE DAD CAN'T DO ALL THESE THINGS. Their activities, homework, meals, grooming and appearance...everything would suffer. It's predictable that with six kids, SOME would have FAILING GRADES and one or more wouldn't pass to the next grade because of ANGER, DEPRESSION, GUILT, and INABILITY TO CONCENTRATE in school. SOME would "ACT-OUT" THEIR PAIN and GET INTO TROUBLE (fighting, skipping school, talking back, destroying property, breaking rules, etc). SOME would get involved in DRUGS and ALCOHOL and ALL THE THINGS THAT GO WITH that LIFESTYLE and CULTURE. Some would have LONG-TERM DEPRESSION, COPING PROBLEMS, ABANDONMENT ISSUES, and NUMEROUS SUICIDE ATTEMPTS.[9]

What other problems do you expect these kids would have? _____

_____

_____

Do you think they'd be RELIEVED or HAPPY that Momma killed herself? YES / NO

How do you think Dad would deal with her suicide? _____

_____

_____

With the OVERWHELMING STRESS of caring for a large family as a SINGLE-PARENT suddenly dropped on him...IN ADDITION TO the GRIEF, ANGER, GUILT, and DESPAIR because his wife killed herself, he's very likely to be MOODY and IRRITABLE with the kids. It's expected that this family's daily life would be FILLED with OVERWHELMING STRESS and DISORDER...AND LOTS OF ANGER and DEPRESSION. It's a PERFECT SET-UP for VERBAL and PHYSICAL ABUSE. So, would the family REALLY BE BETTER OFF without Mom? I expect your answer to be a flat "NO." WILL A NEW TYPE OF HELL BE EXPERIENCED by the family? MOST DEFINITELY. When folks depart from this world by suicide, they often HAND OFF THEIR PROBLEMS to their loved ones...AND THEN SOME. No one will be happy. Stress will not be relieved. PAIN AND SUFFERING WILL HIT A NEW LEVEL...AND OF A VERY DIFFERENT KIND. Rational Mind would remind us of the consequences of suicide...and that WE'RE NOT DOING OUR FAMILY A FAVOR by suiciding.[10]

If this precious lady had rationally considered the Big Picture of her Situation, Wise Mind would have Turned On. What do you think Wise Mind would have encouraged her to do? _____

_____

_____

What would her family rather have... family therapy or Momma dead?

Wise Mind would have encouraged her to work with her doctor when her meds stopped working RATHER THAN getting off of them. Wise Mind would have encouraged her to GET IN THERAPY to work on her issues and problems and to learn positive ways of dealing with her frustrations, stress, and unhappiness. Wise Mind would have suggested FAMILY THERAPY. These things would BRING PEACE to the family, instead of the HELL of a parental suicide.

APPLICATION: The Truth, the Whole Truth, and Nothing but the Truth

We've just Worked Through some of the difficult Emotion-Driven Thoughts Group Members struggle with THE MOST. We saw Emotional Mind and Rational Mind in action. We saw how Rational Mind challenges the destructive lies that come out of Emotional Mind in a BAD MOOD! Through this workbook, we've learned that Emotion-Driven Thoughts are based on how we FEEL and SEE THINGS at any given time. For instance, if we're depressed, our thoughts are of a DEPRESSED quality.

Rational Mind is focused on the reality of our situation while Emotional Mind catastrophizes and blows everything out of proportion!

We think about ourselves, other people, and the world in a DEPRESSED way. On the other hand, when we're happy, we see things in a hopeful and positive light. We've seen that Emotional Mind thoughts are "moody"...that THEY CHANGE AS OUR MOODS CHANGE. They're based on our MOODY PERCEPTIONS in-the-moment...and as such, they're not usually based on UNCHANGING facts and truth.

Rational Mind thoughts are VERY DIFFERENT. They're driven by truth and reality...and the way things REALLY are! They're facts that DON'T CHANGE from hour-to-hour or day-to-day with our moods! Consider these Rational Mind truths,

---

We're human and we'll make mistakes no matter how hard we work to avoid them.

Our people love us...and their greatest wish for us is that we'll find peace and happiness...and that we'll be okay.

We'll be successful in recovery and in life IF we keep trying... and IF we keep Fighting to stay on the Recovery Path.

We CAN deal with a difficult situation IF we remain Mindful of our desire for recovery...IF we seek help as needed...IF we develop a Game Plan for dealing with whatever is troubling us...and IF we Follow Through with it.

With Rational Mind, the facts are the facts and the truth is the truth. Always remember... the truth shall set you free!

Those Rational Mind statements are UNCHANGING TRUTHS. NO MATTER HOW hurt or discouraged we are, THOSE THINGS REMAIN TRUE! The truth is THE TRUTH. We need to LEARN TO BELIEVE Rational Mind truths and to seriously doubt and CHALLENGE the hurtful things that come out of a "MOODY" Emotional Mind.

SKILL BUILDER: Challenging My Emotion-Driven Thoughts

In the spaces below, write three Emotion-Driven Thoughts that you tend to say when you're upset...thoughts that are destructive to your well-being and your recovery. Like we did in the previous sections, write Rational Mind truths to challenge those statements. Consider truths about the Big Picture of Your Life, the Big Picture of the Situation, and general truths about the world and human nature. Our Recovery Goal is to have the information and skills to look at things realistically...so we can pull ourselves out of a negative Emotional Mind.

Emotion-Driven Thought #1: _____

_____

Rational Mind truths: _____

_____

_____

_____

_____

_____

Emotion-Driven Thought #2: _____

_____

Rational Mind truths: _____

_____

_____

_____

_____

_____

Emotion-Driven Thought #3: _____

_____

Rational Mind truths: _____

_____

_____

_____

_____

_____

APPLICATION: When a Warped Thought Is Normal

At times, "normal people" experience extreme mood states and have hostile, warped, and forbidden thoughts and feelings. THAT'S JUST HOW WE ARE when we become VERY angry, depressed, and hurt. It's part of our humanity. Most folks

Warped thoughts are like a big red flag.
They make us Mindful of the seriousness of the situation and the need to get control over our Emotional Mind.

DON'T ACT ON THESE thoughts and feelings or spend TOO MUCH TIME BEATING THEMSELVES UP over them. They ALLOW A THOUGHT TO BE A THOUGHT and a FEELING TO BE A FEELING. They ALLOW these to be "PASSING EXPERIENCES" that come into their mind and pass through! They recognize these thoughts and impulses are extreme and will cause major problems if acted upon. Therefore, they don't hold onto these or stew over them. However, these INTENSE thoughts and feelings GET THEIR ATTENTION and RATIONAL MIND KICKS IN REAL QUICK!

> "Man, I'm way too angry! I've got to pull myself together."
>
> "Whoa, this is scaring me. I'm way too mad...I'm losing it. I better call my wife. I need to download and get some Rational Mind quick!"

APPLICATION: Red Flags for Irrational Statements

11- We discussed these statements in Chapter 5.

Statements which include words like, "Always," "Never," "All," "Every," "No one," and "Everyone," are "all-or-none" statements.[11] When we're upset, we say things like "NOBODY cares about me." or "NOTHING EVER works out for me." When we hear ourselves using "all-or-none" words, we should suspect we're NOT in Rational Mind!

When we use words like these, it's like waving a red flag and saying, "Hello, I'm way too upset. I'm exaggerating everything!"

> Consider the Emotion-Driven statement "NOBODY loves me." We often feel this way when we're lonely or we're in need...and someone has pushed us away or told us "NO." When we feel like NOBODY loves us, we're often focusing on ONE rejection event or several, but, we're NOT looking at the loving things our people have done for us over time...nor are we rationally looking at the Big Picture of the Situation.

Rarely in life are things "all-or-none," unless it's about me eating ALL the cookies or ice cream!

Rational Mind would tell us that even though, AT THE MOMENT, we FEEL "Nobody" cares about us, many people REALLY DO CARE. Rational Mind might remind us that we've done some hurtful and destructive things and our people are seriously hurt, angry, or burnt-out with us...and THAT'S WHY they have pulled away or told us to stay away...that it has nothing to do with their love for us. Rational Mind would tell us that THEY LOVE US and CARE VERY MUCH ABOUT US...but, they've HAD ENOUGH for

Our people still love us, but they can't deal with all our stuff at the time.

the time being. Maybe we've caused them SO MUCH stress and unhappiness that THEY HAD TO pull away TO PROTECT THEMSELVES from our chaos, drama, and dysfunction. Rational Mind would tell us THEY HAVE TO do things to Mindfully Protect THEIR Peace and Stability, too!

How many times have you heard divorced or separated people say, "I love him, but I can't live with him." or "I love her, but I just can't do this anymore. I can't continue to live like this."? Once time has cooled the heated conflict and hurt, many will speak of the love they have for their ex and the fond memories they shared. You may even hear them say, "I wish _____ didn't happen, we'd probably still be together."

> The TRUTH, they STILL love them. Once our people love us, they generally DON'T STOP LOVING US. They may get fed up with us, but they STILL love us. When they pull away and push us away, we FEEL UNLOVED and UNCARED FOR. However, these are Emotional Mind FEELINGS, NOT Rational Mind TRUTHS!

So, what's the truth behind FEELING "unloved and uncared for"? _____

_____

_____

> The truth, THEY LOVE US and CARE ABOUT US. They HAVE TO push us away because WE ARE one of the things COMING AT THEM and WE ARE TAKING AWAY THEIR peace and stability. Our destructive behavior has FORCED them to put up a boundary to keep us out of THEIR Inner Circle... because OUR STUFF IS WRECKING THEIR LIFE, TOO.

Consider another common all-or-none statement. What's the truth behind, "This ALWAYS happens."? Does it happen ALWAYS...or just SOMETIMES, like when we behave in certain ways or we're involved in certain types of situations? Explain. _____

_____

_____

It's a truth... when we approach life in the SAME way, we have the same outcomes.

> IF we have a HABIT of CHOOSING abusive partners, we're likely to be abused in our relationships. IF we have a HABIT of CHOOSING people who have troubled relationships with others, our relationships are likely to be troubled. IF we have a HABIT of CHOOSING people with a history of short-term relationships, our relationships are likely to be short-term. Similarly, IF we have a HABIT of DOING self-destructive things, bad things will often happen to us. When we do the SAME THINGS over and over...we're likely to EXPERIENCE the SAME THINGS over and over...and "This ALWAYS happens" will SEEM LIKE a truth for us.

Life changes when we change...it gets better when we get better!

However, the Rational Mind truth is...WHEN we make DIFFERENT CHOICES, we'll have DIFFERENT OUTCOMES...and things WON'T ALWAYS be like this...IF WE CHANGE THINGS! If we challenge the Emotion-Driven statement, "This ALWAYS happens" through Rational Mind, we'll consider the facts about the Big Picture of Our Life. We'll become Mindful that WHEN WE MADE DIFFERENT CHOICES in life, we had DIFFERENT LIFE OUTCOMES!

APPLICATION: When It's Hard to Think Straight

It's MUCH EASIER to be in Rational Mind WHEN WE FEEL GOOD...and it's MUCH HARDER WHEN WE DON'T.[12] For instance, it's difficult to TURN ON Rational Mind and to STAY IN Rational Mind when we're upset, depressed, in pain, hot, tired, hungry, or uncomfortable. Have you ever thought, said, or heard...

12- In Chapter 6, we discussed the effects of various mood and physical states on Emotional Mind. We noted that when we're upset or we don't feel well, Emotional Mind Turns On...and we're very sensitive and irritable! We're talking about the same thing here...but from the perspective of how hard it is to Turn On Rational Mind when we're in these uncomfortable mood and physical states. During these times, it's a challenge to get to Rational Mind because Emotional Mind is driving!

> I'm so hungry, I can't think straight.
>
> I'm so upset, I can't think.
>
> I was just panicking...I didn't think.
>
> My head hurts so bad right now, I can't think about anything else.
>
> I'm so hot, I'm about to come unglued!
>
> It's so noisy in here, I can't hear myself think.
>
> I'm so stressed out, I'm scattered. I can't think straight.
>
> I'm so tired, I can't think.

As mentioned in the Emotional Mind chapter, when we're in one of these mood or physical states, we should NOT try to make major decisions or handle conflicts or problems. THE FIRST THING WE NEED TO DO IS TO TAKE TIME-OUT to get whatever physical, mental, or other need state taken care of...so we can THINK STRAIGHT and DEAL WITH LIFE RATIONALLY!

> *If we don't think straight, we'll go down a very crooked and troubled road!*
> *We must Turn On Rational Mind so we can think straight...and Keep Straight*
> *SO WE DON'T STRAY OFF THE RECOVERY PATH!*

~~~~~~~~ CHAPTER REVIEW ~~~~~~~~

1. In what ways is Rational Mind different from Emotional Mind? _____

_____

_____

_____

2. What's the purpose of Rational Mind? _____

_____

_____

3. Pete was able to think rationally when the cocaine and alcohol had time to wear off. How was his thinking different from the night before? _____

_____

_____

4. What became his plan of action? _____

_____

_____

5. When Emotional Mind attempts to regain control of Pete, what can he do to PUT
Rational Mind and Wise Mind BACK in control? _____

_____

_____

6. What would Rational Mind say about cutting? _____

_____

_____

7. What would Rational Mind say about "just one drink"? _____

_____

_____

8. What would Rational Mind say about "I can't…"? _____

_____

_____

9. What would Rational Mind say about "A bad relationship is better than being
alone."? _____

_____

_____

10. What would Rational Mind say about "I don't deserve any better."? _____

_____

_____

11. What would Rational Mind say about taking revenge? _____

_____

_____

12. What would Rational Mind say about "I've failed. I'm a failure."? _____

_____

_____

_____

13. What would Rational Mind say about "My family would be better off without me."?

_____

_____

_____

204

14. What type of words are RED FLAGS that Emotional Mind is driving? _____

FOR REFLECTION:
Take a few moments to reflect on this chapter. Some questions are listed in the margin to guide your reflection. Feel free to reflect on whatever your heart brings to mind.

What are your reactions to the material?

Which parts hit home or relate to you the most?

Which parts have helped you the most?

Which parts have helped you to understand yourself the most?

How will you use this information to feel better about yourself?

How will you use this information to improve the quality of your life...or to change how things work out for you in life?

What will you do differently based on this material?

How has this information changed the way you feel about your patterns of relapse and recovery... and your overall response to life?

What does this material motivate you to do?

15. Why does it seem like "This ALWAYS happens."? _____

~~~ *For Reflection* ~~~

Figure 7.A.1: The Concepts and Skills Tracking Sheet – Chapter 7

Week # _____	Day of Week →									
	Date →									
7A. Today, I became Mindful of my mind state! I noticed myself being in Emotional Mind AND Rational Mind.										
7B. When I was in an upset or destructive Emotional Mind today, I became Mindful that I needed to get Rational Mind Turned On so things wouldn't spiral Out-of-Control.										
7C. When I was in an upset or destructive Emotional Mind today, I became Mindful that I needed to get Rational Mind Turned On. I wasn't doing such a good job on my own, so I talked with someone who helped me to Get Rational!										
7D. When I was in an upset or destructive Emotional Mind today, I took some time to Think Things Through. I Turned On Rational Mind to challenge my Emotion-Driven Thoughts.										
7E. I did something destructive today. I took some time to Think Things Through. I Turned On Rational Mind to consider the Big Picture of the Situation and My Life. I came up with some Damage Control and problem-solving ideas.										
7F. When I felt discouraged today in my recovery efforts, I took note of all the positive things I WAS DOING and all the positive things HAPPENING in my life. I reminded myself that I needed to BE PATIENT and to KEEP TRYING …that overall, things were moving in the right direction!										
7G. Today, I challenged an Emotion-Driven Lie I was telling myself so I could relapse into self-destructive behavior…thoughts like "Cutting always helps." or "One drink doesn't matter".										
7H. Today, I caught myself making an "I can't" type of statement. I challenged that statement IN-THE-MOMENT! I didn't allow myself to go there!										

Notes:

RATING SCALE
5 – Did Excellent in this area today
4 – Did Pretty Good in this area today
3 – Did Alright in this area today
2 – Did Only Fair in this area today
1 – Didn't Do Well in this area today
DD – Didn't Do today

Figure 7.A.2: The Concepts and Skills Tracking Sheet – Chapter 7

Week # _____

	Day of Week →									
	Date →									

7I. Today, I caught myself having aggressive or "get even" type thoughts or impulses. I STOPPED myself and challenged those thoughts and impulses IN-THE-MOMENT! I didn't allow myself to spend much time there!

7J. Today, I caught myself making a "I'm such a loser or failure." type of statement. I challenged that statement IN-THE-MOMENT! I didn't allow myself to go there!

7K. Today, I caught myself making a "Nobody loves me." or a "I'm too _____, no one will want me or like me." type of statement. I challenged that statement IN-THE-MOMENT! I didn't allow myself to spend any time there!

7L. Today, I caught myself making a "I'd be better off dead." or other suicidal type of statement. I challenged that statement IN-THE-MOMENT! I didn't allow myself time to stew on that!

7M. Today, I caught myself making another type of destructive statement that's not listed on this tracking sheet. I challenged that statement IN-THE-MOMENT! I didn't allow myself to go there!

7N. Today, I had a warped thought. I became Mindful that it was a BIG RED FLAG telling me I was way too upset about something or I otherwise needed to GET CONTROL FAST.

7O. Today, I caught myself making an "all-or-none" statement. I challenged that statement IN-THE-MOMENT.

7P. Today, I became aware that my ability to "Think Straight" and to TURN-ON Rational Mind was affected by being tired, hungry, sick, in pain, under the influence of drugs or alcohol, or just too upset, overwhelmed, or stressed-out.

7Q. Today, I reminded myself that my life won't change if I don't change.

Notes:

RATING SCALE
5 – Did Excellent in this area today
4 – Did Pretty Good in this area today
3 – Did Alright in this area today
2 – Did Only Fair in this area today
1 – Didn't Do Well in this area today
DD – Didn't Do today

~ 8 ~
CHALLENGING EXTREME JUDGMENTS

We've talked about "all-or-none," "black and white," and "all good – all bad" thinking and extreme words such as "Always," "Never," and "Nobody." We've become Mindful that Extreme Judgments are "red flags" that Emotional Mind is Turned On and some exaggeration is occurring! Extreme Judgments are NOT Rational Mind truths!

Extreme Judgments are often fightin' words. They make people angry! People get defensive real quick and discussions turn into arguments.

When we label people to be one way or another, they often shut down on us and become more and more like what we say they are! Why would they try to do any better when we NEVER give them ANY credit and we WON'T view them realistically anyway?

1- Discounted – not counted, noticed, or valued.

2- Nullified – (nul-if-fied) – devalued or made useless.

When we're mad, it's easy to accuse someone of NEVER saying they're sorry, or NEVER doing nice things for us without being asked, or ALWAYS saying things that embarrass us in front of others, or ALWAYS being selfish. The RATIONAL TRUTH is…we're so hurt or upset that we FEEL LIKE they NEVER or ALWAYS do this or that. Sometimes, we FEEL LIKE NOBODY cares about us or our spouse is ALWAYS taking care of friends and NEVER takes time to do special things for us. THAT'S HOW WE FEEL! That's our Emotional Mind PERCEPTION in-the-moment. That's how we're SEEING and EXPERIENCING things. However, Rational Mind would tell us…they DON'T ALWAYS or NEVER. Maybe they do it 90% of the time, but NOT ALWAYS or NEVER! So we say, "Big deal, 10% of the time doesn't matter." Well, it matters to the person we're fussing at!

APPLICATION: How Extreme Judgments Backfire and Ignite the Situation

Think about when we're trying to get someone to change their behavior. We often criticize them in an extreme way, like "You ALWAYS," "You NEVER." We may tell them they're ALWAYS selfish, irresponsible, uncaring, or thoughtless. How do people generally react when we say, "You ALWAYS" or "You NEVER"? _____

_____

Do they tend to be open to what we have to say? YES / NO   Are they usually willing to listen and hear us out? YES / NO   Does our STYLE of communication MOTIVATE them to make changes to meet our needs? YES / NO

When we label people in extreme ways, they become VERY DEFENSIVE because our statements are so ONE-SIDED and UNREALISTIC. They get angry that ALL the positive things they've EVER DONE for us are discounted,[1] nullified,[2] and ignored.

Would we really date, marry, or befriend someone who was ALWAYS uncaring or ALWAYS selfish? YES / NO   Has this person NEVER listened or NEVER cared about what we had to say? YES / NO   Has it ALWAYS been that way? YES / NO

What IS the TRUTH then? _____

_____

Extreme statements are Emotion-Driven statements. They're based on how we're FEELING in-the-moment and how we've been feeling recently. They're based on FEELINGS, NOT TRUTH.

How do you feel when someone says, "You NEVER" when indeed you do...or you have recently started to do...to PLEASE THEM? _____

_____

Our ears slam shut and our mouth opens wide and flaps full speed!

How likely are you to "hear" them and to WANT to do what they're asking of you? How are you likely to respond to them? _____

_____

3- Negotiation – (knee-go-she-a-shin) - when we bargain and come to an agreement by way of a "give and take" process.

> *We get MAD and DEFENSIVE! We DON'T LIKE IT when people ACCUSE US of things we DON'T DO! This is NOT an effective way to get us to make changes to PLEASE THEM! What they say SLAMS SHUT the doors of negotiation[3] and change. We'll either FIGHT BACK or we'll WITHDRAW and feel hurt, misunderstood, or not appreciated.*

4- Extinguishing – (ex-ting-wish-ing) - putting an end to something...like a fire extinguisher puts an end to a fire!

SKILL BUILDER: Extinguishing[4] Extreme Judgments

Consider the three sets of statements below. In each set, circle the statement that's more likely to encourage someone to LISTEN to us, to honestly LOOK AT their behavior, and to TRY to make some changes to please us.

> "You're such a cruel and mean person."
> "Your jokes tonight about my haircut were really hurtful to me."

> "You're so selfish. You only think about yourself."
> "You've gone fishing two weekends in a row. I really need some relief from the kids."

If we want someone to change, it's much better to focus on the EFFECT their behavior has on us rather than labeling their WHOLE PERSON to be "ALL this" or "NONE of that!"

> "You never think about anything before you say it."
> "I felt betrayed when you told Jack about our conversation."

The second statement in each set will be MUCH MORE EFFECTIVE! These describe SPECIFIC BEHAVIORS and the EFFECTS they have on US. The first ones are PERSONAL ATTACKS. These LABEL the person to be someone who ALWAYS acts in an undesirable way. We AREN'T GIVING THEM CREDIT for the times they HAVEN'T ACTED THAT WAY...and this makes them VERY MAD! The truth, no matter how great and Mindful we are, we're human. We're going to say things like this now and then. Our goal is Mindfulness. THE MOMENT we become aware we have used an Extreme Label, we NEED to do DAMAGE CONTROL! We need to APOLOGIZE, START OVER, and FIGHT FAIR! Here's some examples of how to do that!

We need to describe their behavior and how it affects us WITHOUT ATTACKING WHO THEY ARE AS A PERSON and without discounting or nullifying ALL the positive things they've done.

> "I'm sorry. I'm really mad right now. I know you don't ALWAYS do that! It just *SEEMS LIKE THAT* right now! You've spent the last week helping others and you haven't had time to do things around here."

> "I'm sorry. I know you care about our family and do many nice things for us. I'm just frustrated right now about the broken dryer and the water leak. I really need you to find time to get those fixed."

> "It SEEMS LIKE when I'm talking to you, you stay focused on the TV or the computer and you're not listening to me."
>
> *"I'm listening to you. I'm just looking at the TV."*
>
> "I'm glad you ARE listening. It hurts my feelings when I'm talking to you and you're not looking at me. It SEEMS LIKE you AREN'T listening, especially when you finally say 'Huh?' and I have to repeat myself. It hurts my feelings because it SEEMS LIKE the TV is more important than I am. It would be nice if you would look at me when I'm talking to you."
>
> *"You SEEM to catch me at important times in the program. That's why I keep looking at the TV."*
>
> "When I catch you at a critical time, just hold your hand up for a second, or say, 'Hold on!' and then, turn to me when you're finished. I'd rather do it that way so I know you care about what I have to say."
>
> *"YOU DO THAT TO ME ALL the time."*
>
> "When I do, bring it to my attention. I don't want you to feel that way either."
>
> *"You do it ALL the time!"*
>
> "I'll try to be more aware of myself. If I do it to you again, please bring it to my attention. I don't want to hurt your feelings, either."

When we're Mindful and carefully choose our words, even though people may not like what we have to say, they're less defensive and more open to what we're asking of them.

The examples above show how describing OUR FEELINGS and the SPECIFIC SITUATION works MUCH BETTER than using extreme words to label and criticize the person we're upset with! The two small words, "SEEMS LIKE" can make a big difference! They can help us have a DISCUSSION about our feelings and how things SEEM to be rather than A BIG FIGHT!

In the "looking at the TV" example above, the first speaker (not italics) had a good opportunity to lose their cool when they we're twice attacked with "You do it ALL the time!" However, they stayed rational and reasonable and asked the other person to bring it to their attention when they do it so they can work on THEIR behavior, too! It sure would have been easy to say, "I don't do that. You're just saying that because I brought this up." That would have turned a constructive discussion into a big FIGHT!

SKILL BUILDER: When We Apply Extreme Labels to Ourselves

We make some very unfair and hurtful judgments about ourselves. Yet, for some reason, we don't get mad and defend ourselves. We just accept these as truth.

Just like we use Extreme Labels to describe the character and behavior of other people, we use these UNFAIR labels to describe ourselves! These labels HURT us. They SHUT DOWN OUR MOTIVATION TO CHANGE. They keep us stuck in our self-defeating ways.

In each set of statements below, circle the one that's MORE LIKELY to ENCOURAGE us to Participate Effectively in our life.

"I'm so stupid."
"I've missed my appointment for the third time. I'll lose services if I don't show up."

We often overdo negative labels when we judge ourselves. Have you ever heard the saying, "We're our own worst critics"?

"I'm Borderline…I can't control my moods."
"I've been impulsive for SO LONG. It's going to take a BUNCH of practice and a WHOLE LOT of Mindfulness and Self-Talk to manage my moods."

"I've been sexually abused. I'll never get over it."
"Many people have worked through abuse issues and function ADEQUATELY. I can, too! It's just going to take some time and whole lot of determination."

5- When patients claim, "I can't read," I've learned to give them something to read! EVERYONE has read most of the words. Their reading was slow and choppy, but…THEY READ! They know the basics of reading. If they read more often, their reading would smooth out! It's not that they CAN'T read, it's that they DON'T read… and they don't improve their skills by trying!

When we destructively label ourselves, we shut ourselves down. Often, what we say becomes a SELF-FULFILLING PROPHECY. That is, WHAT WE SAY WE ARE, WE END UP BECOMING. For instance, if we say we're "stupid," why would we accept a job which requires us to learn something? Why would we go to school or learn how to use a computer? So, what happens? We don't learn new things and we BECOME more and more LIKE THE PERSON WE LABELED OURSELVES TO BE.[5]

Which labels have become Self-Fulfilling Prophecies for you? Explain. _____

_____

_____

_____

APPLICATION: Challenging Negative Judgments About Me

Over time, destructive labels START TO STICK. We come to BELIEVE these things and to think of them as TRUTH. Quite often, these LIES have DEVASTATING and LONG-LASTING EFFECTS on our self-esteem and our sense of self.

Have you been seriously hurt by Extreme Labels...ones you've applied to yourself or others have said about you? If so, which labels have had the most destructive effects on your self-esteem and the quality of your life? _____

_____

_____

When we're mad or hurt, what we say is often Emotion-Driven. We're not in Rational Mind and we're not speaking truth. We're expressing HOW WE FEEL about people and things WHEN WE'RE MAD OR HURT!

Were these Extreme Labels applied to you by someone who lived by truth and Rational Mind or someone who was impulsive and emotionally troubled? _____

_____

Are these Extreme Judgments about you facts or opinions? _____

Should you trust a hurtful opinion of someone who has major emotional problems? Explain. _____

_____

> *When we're mad or hurt, we sometimes say very hurtful things to ourselves and others. This is Emotion-Driven Behavior. Our hurtful words are based on how we're thinking and feeling in the Heat-of-the-Moment! They're ANGRY WORDS. Words driven by a heated Emotional Mind SHOULD NOT BE TRUSTED!*

SKILL BUILDER: "The Challenging Negative Judgments About Me Worksheet"

The worksheet for this chapter is a therapeutic activity developed years ago in response to being devastated by a comment a loved one said to me. They say, "Necessity is the mother of invention." Hopefully, this will be eye opening... and will lead to some major healing and personal growth for you...like it did for me.

Step 1. Read "My Story..." on the next page.

Step 2. Check out the blank worksheet in Figure 8.A and the completed one in Figure 8.B. Remember to make a copy of the blank one before writing on it!

Step 3. Identify a VERY HURTFUL judgment made about you. Choose one that has STUCK WITH YOU and has GREATLY AFFECTED your self-esteem.[6]

Step 4. Write this judgment at the top of the blank worksheet in the space next to "The Negative Judgment I'm Challenging."

Step 5. Write the opposite judgment or as appropriate, a neutral one, in the shaded box at the top of the worksheet.[7] Really think about this worksheet. If needed, ask someone to help you turn the negative judgment around so you can write a positive truth about yourself in the box.

6- Common ones are: You're stupid...worthless, or ugly...You're a loser... You'll never amount to anything.

7- If the judgment is "You're stupid." you might write, "I'm bright." "I'm capable of doing many things." or "I'm of adequate intelligence." If the judgment is "You're worthless." you might write, "I have value and worth." If it's "You're fat." or "You're ugly." you might write, "I'm desirable." or "I have many good qualities."

Step 6. In the 13 unshaded boxes, write things to support the positive statement you wrote in the shaded box. Identify MANY things to support the TRUTH! See the section, "Some Ideas to Get You Started!" on the next page for some ideas. If you get stumped, ask others for feedback.[8] Fill up all 13 unshaded boxes! Once you get going, you might have to add extra boxes!

8- Pull as many of these out of YOUR heart as you can. It's much more meaningful that way!

9- Dissertation – (dis-sir-tay-shin) – a major research project that's the final hurdle for most Ph.D. programs.

10- Statistical – (stat-tis-tickle) – a mathematical way to analyze or understand the data collected in a research project.

No matter how smart we are or how much psychological stuff we know, we can get side-swiped and wrecked-out by a hurtful comment.

My Story...Challenging a Negative Judgment of Me

I was 28 and months away from earning my Ph.D. from a well-respected southern university. It was my internship year and I was working full-time at the VA Hospital. I was also working full-time on my dissertation[9] during the evenings and over the weekends. I had been told by my professors that the ambitious Ph.D. project would take two years to complete and I was almost done in eight months. I was rockin'!

My week had been GREAT! I had just worked through a major statistical[10] problem in my research and came up with a solution that impressed my professors. I received some VERY positive letters of recommendation from my professors describing me as one of the strongest students in the program with many other very positive remarks. I received a job offer from a university to teach in their Psychology Department. A psychologist I worked with at a private hospital prior to graduate school offered me a position in his private practice. Quite a week, huh! No doubt it was a once in a lifetime type of week! An ego boost like none other!

Well, the week was coming to an end. It was Friday evening and someone very important to me, someone who CELEBRATED ALL THESE GREAT EVENTS WITH ME, began criticizing me about the music I was listening to (country music). This person asked me to go out for dinner. I told this person that I didn't want to go because I was finishing the data entry portion of my dissertation and I wanted to get it done that night. Well, my dinner refusal ENRAGED this person. Several more ugly comments were made about the music and in an intensely hateful manner, I was told, "Look what I raised, four girls, all losers."

Despite seven years of counseling others and years of course work and study, this comment DEVASTATED me. I had an image that kept flashing in my mind of a brutal type of self-harm. I felt so strongly about doing it that I acted it out many times using my hands instead of an object. I was SO DEVASTATED all I could think about was destroying myself. I wanted to no longer exist. I wanted to SELF-DESTRUCT. The person's comment penetrated me DEEPLY. I was shocked at my intense reaction. I called my sister and cried my way through the telling of the story...and about how angry and hurt I felt. After the 45-minute conversation, I rocked myself with my arms wrapped tightly around my chest, almost hugging myself...while tears streamed down my face. The event kept replaying in my mind.

I knew I needed big help and I began to pray. I cried out to God...blubbering out my words because I could hardly breathe and cry so intensely at the same time. I found Wise Mind. It occurred to me that this person was emotionally disturbed... that the remarks made were not about me at all, but reflected this person's issues and personality. In my mind, I completed "The Challenging Negative Judgments About Me Worksheet." It totally changed how I looked at such things from then on. I NEVER want to get anywhere close to experiencing the pain of that time again.

Figure 8.A: The Challenging Negative Judgments About Me Worksheet

The Negative Judgment I'm Challenging: _____

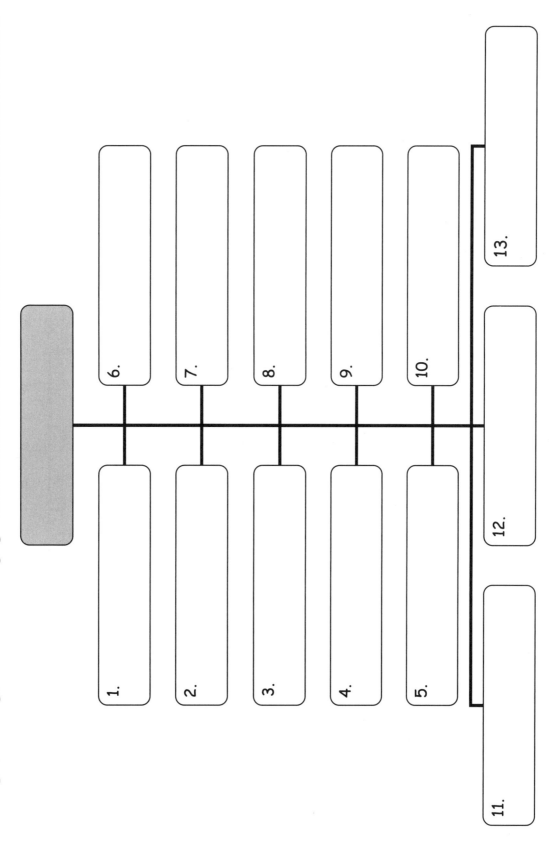

214

Figure 8.B: The Challenging Negative Judgments About Me Worksheet (Completed)

The Negative Judgment I'm Challenging: I'm a worthless piece of crap.

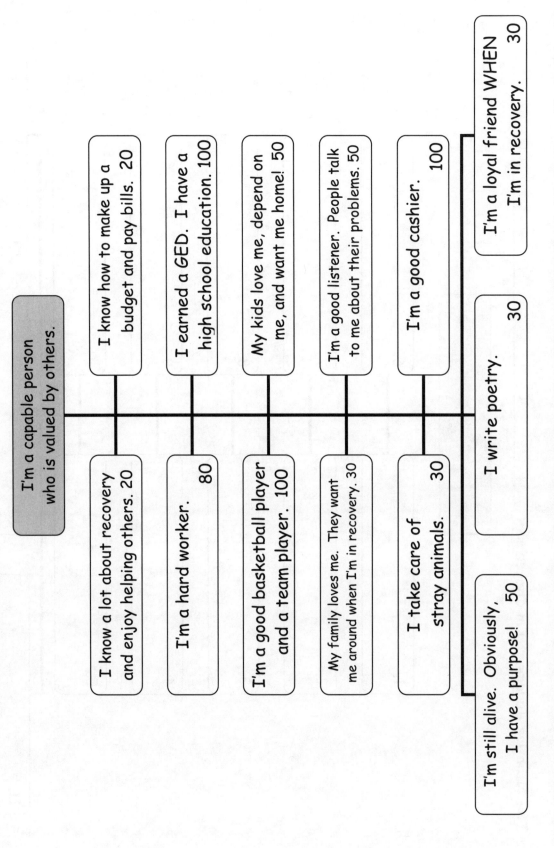

I'm a capable person who is valued by others.

I know how to make up a budget and pay bills. 20

I know a lot about recovery and enjoy helping others. 20

I earned a GED. I have a high school education. 100

I'm a hard worker. 80

My kids love me, depend on me, and want me home! 50

I'm a good basketball player and a team player. 100

I'm a good listener. People talk to me about their problems. 50

My family loves me. They want me around when I'm in recovery. 30

I'm a good cashier. 100

I take care of stray animals. 30

I write poetry. 30

I'm still alive. Obviously, I have a purpose! 50

I'm a loyal friend WHEN I'm in recovery. 30

Some Ideas to Get You Started

Our value and worth is not just about the "big stuff" or major accomplishments. In truth, it's really the small stuff that's really the BIG stuff in life!

11- When doing this in Group, Members blurt out labels to work on. A lady blurted, "You're fat." This caught me off guard! She WAS fat. I didn't know what to do on that one…so, I chose one SEVERAL Members said, instead. It bothered me all evening that I was unable to help this lady with her pain. By morning, Wise Mind hit! It came to me that when people say that, knowing they're hurting us, the message is "You're undesirable" or less than acceptable. With this insight, we challenged the "You're fat" label in the next Group!

12- I'm a realist. I believe in and often say, "Call it as you see it." I've been VERY overweight before. I would shake my head in disbelief when people said, "I don't see you as fat." My thought, "Uh, hello…I'm fat…see…wide BOTH ways…BIG…FAT." Oddly, many people said that. I think, over time, people who knew ME began to appreciate and see other things about ME. They looked passed my size and no longer judged me or interacted (continued)

To support "I'M OF ADEQUATE INTELLIGENCE," list things which prove you have intelligence. For instance, "I can read," "I can write," "I passed my driver's test," "I earned a GED," "I can cook," "I can do car repairs," "I can learn new things," "I can communicate adequately with others," "I'm a cashier and handle money well," "I can play guitar," "I do Sudoku puzzles," "I'm pretty good with the computer," etc. Fill up the circles! THINK THINK THINK!!!

To support "I'M VALUED AND HAVE WORTH," you might list, "My kids love me," "My family depends on me," "My income is needed," "I teach Sunday School," "My boss loses it when I'm not at work," "I'm a child of God and He doesn't make junk," "People ask for my advice," "I comfort others," "I'm a good friend," "I care for animals," etc. Does this seem easier now? Sometimes it's hard to think in such a simple or basic way…but, it's OFTEN the EVERYDAY THINGS we do that PROVE HOW WRONG the judgment is!

Now, for the one that weighed heavily on me…the big one, the "You're fat" one.[11] We can turn this around with, "I'm desirable. There's a lot more to me than my size."[12] To support this, we can list things like, "My children love me," "My family depends on me," "I am a good teacher," "I have a good sense of humor," "I'm a good worker," "People ask for my advice," "I'm kind to others and bring people joy," "I have pretty hair and eyes," "I have a beautiful heart," "I'm a volunteer," "God adores me," etc. Once you get the 13 boxes filled in, review them. Take some time to REALLY THINK ABOUT what you just did! Write about how this activity affects you? What truths does it help you to be Mindful of and to KNOW? _____

_____
_____
_____
_____

THESE TRUTHS SHOW HOW MUCH OF A LIE the negative judgment is…and has been. The judgment was NOT based on truth. It was an EMOTION-DRIVEN LIE MADE UP about us…and WE HAVE LIVED SO MUCH OF OUR LIFE BASED ON THIS LIE. We have believed the lie. We have NOTICED EVERYTHING that supported the lie, and discounted, overlooked, and IGNORED ALL THE THINGS that challenged the lie…all the things that prove we're NOT stupid, worthless, or undesirable. LET THAT SINK IN. What was said about you is A BOLD-FACED LIE. IT IS NOT TRUTH. We

216

(12 – continued)
with me based on my body size. I knew I had other good qualities, but, I'm human. Every day, I painfully saw a very unattractive person in the mirror. I tended to define myself as a fat person. Interestingly, many people who made up my social world didn't. The people who knew me were dealing with the whole person while I focused on one feature, the FAT one! We often make ourselves sick by our judgments. Of course, people who didn't know ME tended to judge me based on what they saw. That's because they had little information about who I was AS A PERSON. Though it hurt, in the Big Picture of My Life, MOST of these people and their opinions mattered little. What are we going to focus on ….the ugliness of people who judge us without knowing us or the positive regard people have for us who know us well and love us?!! Happiness IS A CHOICE.

13- We'll choose to Mindfully Protect Our Peace and Stability by not allowing this to make us obsessive-compulsive and crazy!!

14- It's funny how we give ourselves CREDIT for the good things that Come Our Way and blame others when bad things happen. We say, "I EARNED an 'A' on the test." and "The teacher GAVE ME an 'F.'" Really, we probably DID something to EARN the "F"! What we did was… not do our homework!

15- Verify – to say something is true.

know that now because THE FACTS PROVE IT! Anytime those old feelings come up, be ever so Mindful of the facts and the TRUTH. TAKE A STAND and RATIONALLY CHALLENGE THE LIE…right then and there. Don't EVER let yourself get away with believing that lie again. RATIONALLY CONFRONT IT and DEFEND YOURSELF!

SKILL BUILDER: The Second Part of the Worksheet

Step 1. What did you write in box number 1? _____

_____

Step 2. How many people were involved in making that judgment or would support that truth about you? _____

Count the number of people who would support that truth. To figure out how to do that, read the examples below. For the sake of Mindfully Protecting Our Peace and Stability and not driving ourselves crazy counting people, let 100 be the highest number of people. So, when you count 100 people, stop counting. Just ESTIMATE…the number DOESN'T HAVE TO BE EXACT.[13]

If you put "MY FAMILY DEPENDS ON ME" in a box, add up the number of people in your family that depend on you ALONG WITH the number of other people who would say, "YES, HER FAMILY DEPENDS ON HER." Count these people because THEY OFFER PROOF that you're valued by your family.

If you listed "GOT A PROMOTION," count the people who have said nice things about your work including folks who recommended you for a promotion. Consider your boss, co-workers, administrators, customers, and others who appreciate your work and would say, "HE DESERVED A PROMOTION!" Likewise, if you listed, "I'M A GOOD WORKER," count all the people who would say, "YES, HE SURE IS!"

If you listed, "I GRADUATED HIGH SCHOOL," count the teachers you've had over the years that gave you passing grades[14] and other people who would say, "HE'S SMART ENOUGH TO HAVE GRADUATED." If you listed "GOT A GED," count people who would say, "YEP, SHE'S GOT A HIGH SCHOOL LEVEL OF KNOWLEDGE." Count family, friends, teachers, and co-workers. Also, count the number of people who developed the GED test. Since you passed their test, they would say you have a high school level of knowledge! So, if you listed "GED," you could say at least 50 people could verify[15] your achievement, probably 100 or more. You decide!

If you listed, "I'M A GOOD BASEBALL PLAYER," estimate the number of people who would agree. Count teammates, coaches, umpires, spectators, etc.

If you put "CAN PLAY GUITAR," count the people who would say, "He plays pretty good!" Consider music teachers, band students, family, friends, an audience who has heard you play, etc.

If you listed, "IM A GOOD CASHIER," count co-workers, management, customers, and others who would say, "She's a good cashier."

If you listed, "I'M A GOOD FRIEND," count people who would say, "Yes, she's a good friend." They may not be one of your close friends, but they know how caring and loyal you are to your friends!

Hopefully, these examples explain how to add up the number of people who would verify and support the truths you wrote in each box.[16]

16- This activity is completed on a big dry erase board in Group. It's a lot easier to DO in Group than to explain on paper!

17- If you have more than 13 boxes, add more spaces…and add them to the Grand Total!

18- Write down who said it. If it's more than one person, list the ones who hurt you the most by the judgment.

19- Write the number of people listed in #18 above.

20- List the TRUTH you wrote in the shaded box on your worksheet.

21- Enter the Grand Total from above.

Step 3. In the spaces below, write the number of people who support each truth.[17] Then, add them up to get a Grand Total.

1. _____ 2. _____ 3. _____ 4. _____ 5. _____
6. _____ 7. _____ 8. _____ 9. _____ 10. _____
11. _____ 12. _____ 13. _____ GRAND TOTAL _____

Step 4. Fill in the blanks. The negative judgment about me, that I'm _____ _____ was told to me by[18] _____. A total of[19] _____ person/people in my life unfairly labeled me this way. I'm now Mindful that I'm[20] _____ _____ and I'm aware that at least[21] _____ people agree with me.

Step 5. Read that fill-in-the-blank paragraph again! How does it impact you? What does it say to you? _____
_____
_____
_____
_____
_____
_____

Who is it rational to believe? The one or two people who labeled you based on an Emotion-Driven LIE or the hundreds of people who believe just the opposite about you.

_____
_____

218

When we believe these lies and base our sense of self and identity on these lies, we're viewing ourselves through Emotional Mind. We're not dealing with the facts and the truth. We're overlooking, ignoring, and denying all the things which tell us we aren't that way… and we're focusing on ALL the things which suggest we may be that way. We're ignoring what Rational Mind is telling us and we're viewing ourselves through the distorted lenses of Emotional Mind.

22- If we're older when these lies were spoken, they usually came from an abusive spouse or romantic partner. Over time, we'll realize these people were angry, mean, harsh, moody, and unfair. We KNOW their words were Emotion-Driven. We KNOW they're abusive, mean, and critical people, but for some reason, we believe their ugly opinions. We believe they're right and other people are wrong. Go figure. The truth, we were vulnerable and they took advantage of it. Often, they were mean to "keep us in our place"… in a "downed position" with low self-esteem. They wanted us to believe we ARE stupid, unworthy, and not capable…so we would never have the strength to leave them.

Who are you GOING TO BELIEVE…people who made an impulsive, angry, or Emotion-Driven judgment about you or the hundreds of people who made rational judgments about you based on facts and truth…things that are observable or demonstrated?

_____

It should be pretty clear that IT'S RATIONAL to believe the facts and the truth… and to understand what we have believed all along HAS BEEN AN EMOTION-DRIVEN LIE! LOOK AT THE NUMBERS! 1000 or more people have RATIONALLY observed your behavior, character, personality, and accomplishments and AGREE that you're a capable, valued, and worthy person! Compare this to the VERY SMALL number of people who made an Emotion-Driven negative judgment about you. Which group SPEAKS the truth? _____

APPLICATION: The Origin of the Judgmental Lies

Most of the negative judgments made about us…were first said to us when we were young. They were NOT based on anything about us…not a character trait or a personality feature.

> When someone tells a 3 or 4 year old child that they're worthless, stupid, or will never amount to anything…or they're too much of this or too little of that… or no one will ever love them…IT'S AN EMOTION-DRIVEN LIE. How in the world can someone know something like that about a very young child? This type of meanness, ugliness, and hurtfulness SPEAKS VOLUMES about the person making the statements…AND SAYS NOTHING ABOUT THE CHARACTER OF THE CHILD.

We know that when WE make ugly and insulting comments to others, we're being verbally abusive. Oftentimes, we're mad and we say these things in anger. Likewise, THE PERSON saying ugly things to us is UPSET, too. Often, THEY FEEL stupid, irresponsible, or worthless and THEY TAKE IT OUT ON US. Most of them were emotionally abused…and are just MINDLESSLY PASSING IT ON to the next generation. Also, they may suffer the moodiness and impulsivity that goes with drugs and alcohol, Bipolar Disorder, Borderline Personality Disorder, etc. For whatever reason, they're BIG-TIME IN EMOTIONAL MIND and they're being verbally and emotionally ABUSIVE to us. When we're YOUNG or VULNERABLE,[22] WE TRUST THEIR OPINIONS and come to BELIEVE what they're saying. However, WE'RE BELIEVING AN EMOTION-DRIVEN LIE.

When we did "The Challenging Negative Judgments About Me Worksheet," we

We have thought poorly of ourselves and have treated ourselves poorly because of a lie.

CHALLENGED the EMOTION-DRIVEN LIE by looking at the Big Picture of Our Life THROUGH THE EYES AND TRUTH OF RATIONAL MIND. When we review this worksheet and consider all the things about us that support we're capable people with worth and value, we're functioning in Rational Mind. When we make a DECISION that WE'LL NO LONGER JUDGE OURSELVES in a FALSE and HURTFUL manner, we're functioning in WISE MIND. When we're DETERMINED that ANY TIME those old thoughts or labels COME TO MIND, we'll CHALLENGE THEM and REMIND OURSELVES of all the things about us that PROVE otherwise, then, we'll be USING WISE MIND TO MINDFULLY PROTECT OUR PEACE AND STABILITY.

23- Whenever a negative judgment begins to bother you, either complete "The Challenging Negative Judgments of Me Worksheet" in your mind or on paper. Use this RECOVERY TOOL to challenge those lies!

> ANY TIME, ANY ONE of those NASTY JUDGMENTS comes into our thoughts and begins to hurt us, WE NEED TO CHALLENGE THEM...right then n' there.[23]
> We need to STOMP THEM OUT and REFUSE to allow them to CONTROL US any longer. They are lies. WE HAVE BEEN LIVING A LIE. We have perceived ourselves based on a lie. DO NOT ALLOW THESE LIES TO CONTROL YOUR LIFE ANY LONGER! DO NOT ALLOW THEM TO TAKE AWAY your peace and stability!
> They're things Coming At Us that have NO PLACE in our Inner Circle.
> TAKE A STAND against these lies...and FIGHT FOR YOUR RECOVERY!

We ARE going to do some stupid and thoughtless things now and then, but that doesn't mean we're a stupid and thoughtless person. It means we DID SOMETHING that was stupid or thoughtless.

APPLICATION: Stupid Is as Stupid Does?

At this point, some folks say, "When they said that, I had done something stupid or irresponsible." Remember, we're human. We're not perfect. Things WILL happen. That's our humanity! One stupid behavior or 10 or 12 of them means we did one stupid behavior or 10 or 12 of them. Those things describe our behavior in-the-moment or the month. They DO NOT define WHO WE ARE as a person or WHAT WE'RE CAPABLE OF. They DO NOT define our character or our make-up. THEY DEFINE AN event, action, or a behavior...NOT our WHOLE person. Just because the 8th grade educated shift team leader made a mistake, that doesn't mean he's stupid. That means HE MADE A MISTAKE...THAT DAY. That mistake and an 8th grade education DOESN'T describe what he's capable of. Those things DO NOT define his character or describe everything he has ever accomplished in life. HE IS NOT STUPID. He simply made AN ERROR.[24] Stupid ISN'T as stupid does!

24- I'm pretty smart with a Ph.D...that just gives me a license to be Piled Higher and Deeper in errors! Lord knows if it's 10AM and I haven't made an error yet, I must still be asleep!

25- Dysregulated – (dis-reg-you-lated) – not in control of ourselves... we're not able to regulate or control our behavior.

There may be times in our life when we make many errors...even when we totally mess things up for a year or two by making one bad decision after another. DOES THAT MEAN WE'RE STUPID? NOOOOOO. It means we're DYSREGULATED[25] and

LIVING Big-Time in Emotional Mind. It means we're making a lot of Emotion-Driven decisions which ARE STUPID. That DOESN'T MEAN WE ARE STUPID...you know why? Explain. _____

_____

> We're NOT stupid or clueless. In our gut, we usually know our behavior is going to cause problems BEFORE we do it! We have Wise Mind going on, but we're NOT PAYING ATTENTION TO IT. We're NOT Following Through With What We Know is in our best interests...because WE'RE BIG-TIME in Emotional Mind! WE'RE DYSREGULATED...we're LIVING IN-THE-MOMENT. We're uncomfortable... we hurt...we're not worrying about tomorrow. We're living for TODAY... and if it feels good...we're going to do it!

Are we STUPID because we do it? Explain. _____

_____

We ACTED in poor judgment. We went against our good judgment.

> No, we're NOT STUPID. We're ACTING in poor judgment. We KNOW better. We know right from wrong...and good from bad. We DO stupid things because EMOTIONAL MIND IS DRIVING. That's why we SPIN-OUT and LOSE CONTROL. That's why we wreck-out and our life becomes a total wreck.

So, does that mean we have poor judgment? Explain. _____

_____

_____

"Then how do we describe this stupid, poor judgment behavior?!" We describe it as DESPERATE behavior. It's not an issue of smarts. It's an issue of being desperate and dysregulated! It's an issue of being OUT-OF-CONTROL! We know better, but we do desperate, self-defeating things anyway.

> NO...because WE HAVE GOOD JUDGMENT! We KNEW it was stupid or of poor judgment...but we did it anyway! We KNEW it was going to end poorly, but we DIDN'T CARE AT THE TIME. We just did what we WANTED to do... and no one or nothing was going to stop us. We were being VERY WILLFUL.

What we did was EMOTION-DRIVEN Behavior. We do all types of MINDLESS and IMPULSIVE things when we're acting on Emotional Mind...ESPECIALLY WHEN WE'RE IN A DESPERATE STATE, like desperate for relief, desperate for comfort, or desperate to be held and loved on. It's NOT STUPIDITY. It's DESPERATION. You've heard the saying, "Desperate times call for desperate measures." Well, desperate measures often involve risky things that are likely to have a bad outcome. So, BECAUSE WE'VE DONE SOMETHING STUPID or two years or ten years worth, that DOESN'T MEAN WE ARE STUPID. That's because WE KNOW BETTER.

WE JUST DO IT ANYWAY! Gladly, this workbook is about GETTING CONTROL of our BEHAVIOR and our LIFE! And, we do that by Turning On RATIONAL MIND and WISE MIND to REGULATE and CONTROL our dysregulated and Out-of-Control emotions and Emotion-Driven Behavior.

SKILL BUILDER: Using Our Smarts to "Dis"[26] Dysregulation

26- "Dis" is a trendy term that means...to disrespect or go against.

> IT DOESN'T MATTER HOW SMART WE ARE OR HOW MUCH WE KNOW. We're HUMAN. We're EMOTIONAL BEINGS.
> We all have emotional issues, vulnerabilities, and weaknesses.
> Therefore, we must be MINDFUL. We must be aware of how things are affecting us.
> We must CONTINUALLY APPLY RECOVERY PRINCIPLES and SKILLS to
> HELP OURSELVES maintain peace and stability, self-respect, and integrity.[27]

27- Integrity – (in-teg-gritty) – believing we're whole...that we're "okay."

When stuff comes up...use the recovery tools and principles we've been learning to regulate and manage yourself. This is YOUR LIFE...and YOUR peace and stability is WELL WORTH IT...to you...and those who LOVE YOU and DEPEND ON YOU! OUR LIFE IS NOT JUST ABOUT US. Many people and things depend on us to be okay, like our spouse, kids, family, friends, pets, employers, co-workers, teammates, and all the people we come in contact with, from waitresses to store clerks to the doctor's receptionist. Do you know why else we need to work to be stable and okay?

28- Been there, done that, wrote the book... and I'm STILL "a work in progress! I always have to deal with myself and WORK to regulate myself! I've written THREE FULL Wise Mind Worksheets so far this year! Think I don't have issues and concerns! We all do.

> Because WE'RE HERE FOR A PURPOSE! OUR LIFE ISN'T MEANINGLESS and WITHOUT VALUE. OUR ATTEMPTS TO KILL OURSELVES HAVEN'T WORKED because IT WASN'T OUR TIME. WE STILL HAVE SOMETHING TO DO... and we're A WORK IN PROGRESS.[28]

So, say this aloud: I now KNOW that the negative judgments made about me that have HURT ME for so long...were made by a VERY MISINFORMED and EMOTION-DRIVEN person or persons. What was said of me...and to me...was just an OPINION. IT WASN'T A FACT ABOUT ME OR MY LIFE. It was NOT TRUTH. It was a lie. I WILL NOW OBSERVE AND DESCRIBE MYSELF ACCORDING TO TRUTH AND I'M GOING TO PARTICIPATE EFFECTIVELY IN MY LIFE AS[29] _____

29 - What you wrote in the shaded box on the worksheet...the TRUTH about yourself!

_____

type of person. I am going to make a copy of the "Challenging Negative Judgments About Me Worksheet"...and ANY TIME I start to believe this lie...I am going to review the worksheet TO REMIND MYSELF OF THE TRUTH. I REFUSE TO LIVE MY LIFE... AND BASE MY LIFE...ON LIFE-SAPPING[30] EMOTION-DRIVEN LIES!

30- Life-sapping – to drain the life out of us.

222

~~~~~~~~ CHAPTER REVIEW ~~~~~~~~

1. Why are Extreme Labels often "fightin' words"? How do people generally respond when we accuse them of NEVER or ALWAYS? What makes them so mad about these words? _____

_____

_____

_____

2. If we want our communication to lead someone to change their behavior, what should we focus on when we're talking to them? _____

_____

_____

3. How is it that Extreme Judgments become Self-Fulfilling Prophecies? _____

_____

_____

4. Consider the negative judgment you challenged on "The Challenging Negative Judgments About Me Worksheet." Is it a fact or an opinion? If it's an opinion, what is the truth about you? _____

_____

_____

_____

5. What was the point of the second part of the worksheet (counting the people)? ___

_____

_____

_____

_____

6. Why do you think we come to believe the hurtful lies? _____

_____

_____

_____

7. Think about the person who made the negative judgment of you. What do you think led them to say it? _____

_____

_____

8. If we do "stupid" things, how is it that we're NOT stupid? _____

_____
_____

FOR REFLECTION:
Take a few moments
to reflect on
this chapter.
Some questions are
listed in the margin
to guide your
reflection.
Feel free to reflect on
whatever your heart
brings to mind.

What are your
reactions to the
material?

Which parts hit home
or relate to you
the most?

Which parts have
helped you the most?

Which parts have
helped you to
understand yourself
the most?

How will you use this
information to feel
better about yourself?

How will you use this
information to improve
the quality of your
life...or to change how
things work out for
you in life?

What will you do
differently based on
this material?

How has this
information changed
the way you feel about
your patterns of
relapse and recovery...
and your overall
response to life?

What does this
material motivate
you to do?

9. If we do things of poor judgment, how can it be that we really have good judgment?
_____
_____

10. Why do we do the Out-of-Control things we do? _____
_____
_____

11. How do we "Dis" dysregulation? What can we do to get control? _____
_____
_____
_____

~~~ For Reflection ~~~

_____
_____
_____
_____
_____
_____
_____
_____
_____
_____
_____
_____
_____
_____
_____

Figure 8.C.1: The Concepts and Skills Tracking Sheet – Chapter 8

Week # _____										
Day of Week →										
Date →										

8A. Today, I caught myself accusing someone of "Always" or "Never" or some similar "all-or-none" word. I realized it wasn't the truth.

8B. Today, I caught myself accusing someone of "Always" or "Never" or some similar "all-or-none" word. I realized it wasn't the truth and it was making the person mad and defensive. I apologized, did Damage Control, and described the actual situation and my feelings.

8C. Today, I thought about how to EFFECTIVELY talk with someone about a problem. I practiced what I wanted to say so I could do the best job possible.

8D. Today, I spoke with someone about a problem. I was Mindful of what I was saying. I did a good job of expressing myself to MINIMIZE how upset they might become. I wanted to be effective and to do the best job possible.

8E. Today, when I was talking with someone about a problem, they became mad and defensive. I did a pretty good job of staying rational and focusing on my goal. I didn't allow their comments to throw me into Emotional Mind and to turn a discussion into a big fight.

8F. Today, I caught myself making a hurtful "all-or-none" statement about myself. I described the TRUE situation or my behavior in a way that was positive and would motivate me to Participate Effectively in my life.

8G. Today, I realized that the hurtful things I say about myself or the hurtful things others have said about me can become a Self-Fulfilling Prophecy. If I allow myself to believe those lies, I'll act in ways that'll make them come true.

8H. Today, I reviewed "The Challenging Negative Judgments About Me Worksheet" that I completed. I realize the TRUTHS I listed prove that the negative judgment is a LIE.

8I. Without looking at the worksheet, I can quickly name off many truths to challenge the lie.

Notes:

RATING SCALE
5 – Did Excellent in this area today
4 – Did Pretty Good in this area today
3 – Did Alright in this area today
2 – Did Only Fair in this area today
1 – Didn't Do Well in this area today
DD – Didn't Do today

Figure 8.C.2: The Concepts and Skills Tracking Sheet – Chapter 8

Week # _____	Day of Week →								Notes:
	Date →								
8J. I really believe the negative judgment I challenged on "The Challenging Negative Judgments About Me Worksheet" is a lie. I choose to believe the facts and truths about myself that I listed...and I choose to believe the hundreds of other people who support the facts I listed. I feel so much better about myself. I WILL NEVER ALLOW that lie to get the best of me AGAIN! I'm ready to confront it to FIGHT FOR MY RECOVERY.									
8K. Today, I completed another "Challenging Negative Judgments About Me Worksheet" to challenge another lie about me...either one I've said about myself or one someone else said about me.									
8L. Today, I used the concept of "The Challenging Negative Judgments About Me Worksheet" to challenge a judgment about me in my head rather than on paper. It helped me to describe myself in a truthful manner.									
8M. Today, I understand that the hurtful judgments made of me when I was a kid or in an abusive relationship were lies. The person who said them was emotionally disturbed or Big-Time in Emotional Mind. What they said to me had a lot more to do with them than me!									
8N. Today, I made myself aware that even though I've done many "stupid" things that have been of very poor judgment...I'm NOT STUPID...and I have good judgment. I knew those things would have a bad outcome before I did them.									
8O. Today, I choose to forgive myself for the mistakes I've made. I realize I'm human and just like everyone else, I've made BIG mistakes and have done things that have hurt others.									
8P. Today, I WORKED HARD to use the recovery skills I'm learning and those I already knew...to "Dis" dysregulation and to Participate Effectively in my life. I understand my life is not ALL about me...many people and things depend on me to be okay...and to maintain peace and stability.									

RATING SCALE
5 - Did Excellent in this area today
4 - Did Pretty Good in this area today
3 - Did Alright in this area today
2 - Did Only Fair in this area today
1 - Didn't Do Well in this area today
DD - Didn't Do today

~ 9 ~

WISE MIND

1- Wise Mind is a major concept in Dr. Linehan's DBT program.

We've been talking about Wise Mind[1] throughout this workbook...and now we're to a SET of chapters devoted entirely to it! We'll be discussing Wise Mind and "The Well Analogy of Wise Mind" in this chapter...AND the completion of "The Wise Mind Worksheet" in the next. These chapters pull together so much of what we've been learning. We've been building up to these all along...so, take them slow because they're VERY IMPORTANT!

When we seek Wise Mind and ALLOW it to guide our behavior, the door for peace and stability will open for us.

"THE WELL ANALOGY of Wise Mind" illustrates the PROCESS of TALKING OURSELVES THROUGH Destructive Coping Responses and INTO WISE MIND RESPONSES using an analogy of a deep well in the ground. "THE WISE MIND WORKSHEET" WALKS US THROUGH THE STEPS TO WISE MIND – from Emotional Mind to Rational Mind to Wise Mind. These chapters provide TWO MAJOR TOOLS for Thinking Through Before We Do AND Talking Ourselves Through the Heat-of-the-Moment. OUR RECOVERY GOAL is to make WISE DECISIONS about how BEST TO RESPOND to our life situations so we can act in ways to Mindfully Protect Our Peace and Stability.

The Basics of Wise Mind

When we're in a troubling Emotional Mind state, we MUST TURN ON Rational Mind to look at our problems in a logical, factual, and truthful way. When we use BOTH Emotional Mind and Rational Mind to deal with a problem, WISE MIND TURNS ON. Wise Mind considers what's going on in Emotional Mind and what Rational Mind has to say about our SITUATION and CONCERNS. Wise Mind PULLS THIS INFORMATION TOGETHER so we UNDERSTAND THE BIG PICTURE OF OUR SITUATION. This understanding leads us to a WISE PLAN OF ACTION for dealing with our PROBLEMS, ISSUES, and IMPULSES in a way that BENEFITS US THE MOST and helps us to AVOID BAD CONSEQUENCES. Wise Mind is concerned about our BEST INTERESTS and our PEACE and STABILITY.

When Wise Mind is Turned On, we have the insight and understanding to make wise decisions for our life.

The graphic on the next page shows that when Emotional Mind and Rational Mind WORK TOGETHER, WISE MIND IS TURNED ON. To deal with our problems WISELY, WE NEED TO BE IN TOUCH WITH OUR EMOTIONAL WORLD – our emotional issues, concerns, and need states AS WELL AS THE REAL WORLD – the facts and the truth!

Emotional Mind + Rational Mind = Wise Mind

We can Participate Effectively when Wise Mind is steering our course!

The Use of Wise Mind Is a Skill

WISE MIND IS A SKILL...and like all skills, it takes PRACTICE TO GET GOOD AT DOING! It's not hard to do, it just takes some doing! Wise Mind is a SURVIVAL TOOL for daily hassles and problems and a CRISIS SURVIVAL TOOL for major life events. We know it's best to practice survival skills before we really need them...because WHEN WE NEED THEM, we need them NOW! Like the wisdom of the Boy Scouts, Wise Mind says "BE PREPARED!"

Be prepared so when Something Happens you'll be able to respond Mindfully and wisely.

SKILL BUILDER: How to Bring On Wise Mind and Live Effectively

Step 1. Observe and describe the contents of EMOTIONAL MIND.

Step 2. Take note of what RATIONAL MIND has to say.

Step 3. Take note of WISE MIND suggestions.

Step 4. MAKE A DECISION about how to deal with the situation based on what's in our best interests.

Step 5. DEVELOP A GAME PLAN.

Step 6. TAKE ACTION! Follow Through with the Game Plan!

2- Rational Mind informs us of truth about the Big Picture of Our Life and the Situation, rules and expectations, our true strengths and weaknesses, truths about human nature (such as, we're deserving, we all make mistakes, recovery on average takes 8-18 tries, and even the most loyal of friends will disappoint us now and then), and truths about life (such as, bad things happen to good people, problems will avalanche if we act in self-defeating ways, and our lives improve when we're in recovery). We need ALL this information to make an Informed Decision about how to best respond.

The **first step** in this process is MINDFULNESS OF WHAT'S GOING ON IN EMOTIONAL MIND. We do this by observing and describing our Raw Emotions and Emotion-Driven Thoughts. The **second step** is AWARENESS OF WHAT RATIONAL MIND HAS TO SAY. Rational Mind will inform us of what is truthful, reasonable, and realistic![2] We've discussed how to do the first two steps in the Mindfulness, Emotional Mind, and Rational Mind chapters 4-8. We'll further discuss these steps in the two Wise Mind chapters 9 and 10.

3- Wise Mind deals with our current situation AND the Big Picture of Our Life. Wise Mind is concerned about what's in our best interests, the things we value and treasure, our needs and desires, and our overall peace and stability.

Once we're dealing with a situation through Emotional Mind and Rational Mind, WISE MIND TURNS ON and offers suggestions for handling the situation (**Step 3**).[3] Our Recovery task is to REVIEW these suggestions and DECIDE HOW BEST TO RESPOND considering the here-and-now situation AND the Big Picture of Our Life (**Step 4**). Next, we'll come up with a GAME PLAN that lists what we need to do to wisely deal with our problem (**Step 5**). Our Game Plan will

We usually know what the best plan of action is, BUT we don't Follow Through and do what's needed to put this plan in action!

GUIDE OUR BEHAVIOR and DIRECT OUR EFFORTS so we're PARTICIPATING EFFECTIVELY in our life! The last step (**Step 6**) is...FOLLOWING THROUGH With What We Know To Do! This step is the toughest of all!

We'll be discussing Steps 3 and 4 in this chapter and the next one, Step 5 in Chapter 14 (The Game Plan), and Step 6 will be covered in this chapter and those to follow...and it has been discussed throughout this workbook!

SKILL BUILDER: Tips for Participating Wisely and Effectively

The purpose of Wise Mind is to give us the INSIGHT and UNDERSTANDING WE NEED to Participate Effectively in our life. When we Participate Effectively, we're MINDFUL and THOUGHTFUL about our behavior. Our behavior is DRIVEN BY A PURPOSE and A PLAN. We make DECISIONS about HOW TO RESPOND to our life events AND Emotional states. When we Participate Effectively...

We CHOOSE to Participate Effectively by doing things to LESSEN and RELIEVE our problems rather than making them worse.

- We DO NOT ACT IMPULSIVELY
- We STOP OURSELVES from acting in old dysfunctional ways
- We PLAY BY THE RULES
- We make THOUGHTFUL CHOICES
- We act in our BEST INTERESTS
- We Participate Effectively WHETHER OR NOT WE LIKE IT OR WANT TO

> *To GET CONTROL of our life and our life outcomes,*
>
> *we must LEARN to be IN CONTROL of our emotions...*
>
> *INSTEAD OF ALLOWING our emotions to be IN CONTROL of us!*

4- Abruptly - (uh-brupt-ly) - suddenly and forcefully.

TO CHANGE HOW WE RESPOND to upsetting situations, we may have to ABRUPTLY[4] STOP OURSELVES if we begin to do things the old way...the impulsive, destructive way. WE MUST STOP TO THINK about what's going on and what we're doing...or getting ready to do! We must make a MINDFUL DECISION about how to respond. We can NO LONGER do things just because we feel like it.

We must STOP ourselves so we don't repeat old behaviors and consequences... and fall right back into the Cycle of Suffering.

> *We must TAKE CONTROL of ourselves and DO THINGS EFFECTIVELY*
>
> *WHETHER OR NOT WE LIKE IT OR WANT TO!*

Being Effective often requires we ACCEPT rules and limits that we cannot easily change.

For instance, we MAY NOT WANT TO leave an abusive relationship that's killing us because we'll have to be alone for awhile. We MAY NOT WANT TO walk away from an argument when we're convinced we're right. We MAY NOT LIKE IT that our parents set "house rules" when we live with them because we're adults! We MAY NOT LIKE having to negotiate to resolve a problem when it's not right or fair that we should.

To be EFFECTIVE, to IMPROVE OUR LIFE, and to have PEACE and STABILITY,

WE MAY HAVE TO DO many things WE DON'T WANT TO DO!

What are some things you MUST DO to have peace and stability, but you have no interest in doing? _____

_____

Unfortunately, *BEING EFFECTIVE REQUIRES that we FOLLOW RULES we have NO INTEREST in following! That's because FIGHTING the system, PUSHING UP AGAINST the rules, and TRYING TO BEND or GO AROUND the rules causes a lot of STRESS, CONFLICT, and WORRY.*[5]
Being effective means we have to CHOOSE OUR BATTLES.
We must MINDFULLY DECIDE IF A BATTLE IS WORTH THE FIGHT.

We must decide if fighting or going against a rule is REALLY WORTH our peace of mind. Remember, part of being assertive is choosing when and when not to be assertive. Likewise, part of having peace and stability is WISELY DECIDING WHICH BATTLES will BENEFIT the Big Picture of Our Life and our overall PEACE and STABILITY and which ones will TAKE IT AWAY.

Are there some battles you're Fighting that are causing you much more PAIN than GAIN? If so, list four of the toughest battles you're Fighting in the table below.[6]

BATTLE	VHP	MPAS	Wise Mind

For each battle, put a check in the VHP column if you MUST Fight this battle because it's a "<u>V</u>ERY <u>H</u>IGH <u>P</u>RIORITY"...and your peace and stability...and the Big Picture of Your Life depends on a win. Put an "X" in this column if you CHOOSE to Fight the battle for another reason, like to make a point, to get even, it's the right thing to do, etc. **Now,** THINK about each battle and put a check in the MPAS column if you'd have "<u>M</u>ORE <u>P</u>EACE <u>A</u>ND <u>S</u>TABILITY" in your life OVERALL if you STOPPED Fighting the battle. **Lastly,** in the Wise Mind column, write "Keep at it" if Wise Mind would encourage you to continue to Fight the battle IN THE SAME WAY you're Fighting it now. Write "Change" if Wise Mind would encourage you to continue to Fight the battle, but to CHANGE YOUR BATTLE PLAN. Write "Stop" if you think Wise Mind would encourage you to STOP FIGHTING this battle.

5- A memo came out at work saying we could no longer listen to radios, iPods, or other such devices. This applied to all staff, including office workers. I've listened to music for years in my office and I couldn't imagine being without it. I began thinking of ways I could still do this and not get caught! My idea, I had a tiny iPod that I could clip to my bra and my long hair would hide the cords fairly well. I thought of other ways around this problem, too. Stress, lying, and cheating were part of every plan and that's not the way I choose to live on purpose. Honor, peace, and stability are my big things and the words "Play by the Rules" kept going through my mind. So, I went without music for days. It wasn't soooo bad. I sure was glad to get another memo saying music could be played softly as long as it didn't interfere with patient care and safety. SAVED!

6- I had a brain problem here and got a bit off topic. I like this too much to delete it. So, for this section, consider ALL the battles you're fighting, not just battles with rules! Consider battles like trying to get someone to like you or to return your love, to get a raise, to get revenge, to change someone, to get something you want, to lose weight, etc.

From "Out-of-Control: A Dialectical Behavior Therapy (DBT) – Cognitive-Behavioral Therapy (CBT) Workbook for Getting Control of Our Emotions and Emotion-Driven Behavior" - Copyright © 2009 by Melanie Gordon Sheets, Ph.D. (www.dbt-cbt-workbook.com)

Ancient Wisdom

In the textbox below, underline or highlight the parts that are similar to the teachings of DBT-CBT.

7- Attain – to get

8- Prudent - prudence - (pru-dents) - being Mindful and cautious, acting with concern for our best interests. Good judgment.

9- Simple minded – folks who are easily talked into things. People who lack judgment, knowledge, and life experience.

10- Despise – (diss-spies) – to strongly hate, to be very disgusted by.

11- Discretion – (diss-creh-shin) – having good judgment and making responsible choices.

Attain[7] wisdom and discipline...understand words of insight
Acquire a disciplined and prudent[8] life
Wisdom includes skill in living
The simple minded[9] individuals despise[10] wisdom and discipline
How long will the simple ones love their simple ways?

Turn your ear to wisdom...apply your heart to understanding
Call out for insight...cry aloud for understanding
Look for wisdom as for silver or gold...search for it as a hidden treasure

For wisdom will enter your heart...and knowledge will be soothing to your soul
Discretion[11] will protect you...and understanding will guard you

Hold onto wisdom...do not let it go
Guard it well...for it is life itself

Leave your simple ways
And you will live...and walk in the ways of understanding
For the path of wisdom is peace

Which parts of the passage speak to you or hit home for you the most? _____

_____

_____

_____

Self-discipline is hard and often uncomfortable, but much more comfortable than living in negative Emotional Mind and the Cycle of Suffering!

We need to be serious about seeking Wise Mind. It's unlikely we'll ever take control of our life and life outcomes without it.

12- Paraphrased from the book of Proverbs.

13- Offensive - rude.

The wisdom of DBT-CBT is very similar to these words of wisdom.[12] The words "simple minded" and "simple" often refer to fools and foolishness. These words are very offensive[13] when applied to us! However, let's pull out of Emotional Mind and look at this rationally. The truth, when we think of all the impulsive things we've done that have led to major life problems, most of us would consider our behaviors to be foolish. The book of Proverbs is about LIVING EFFECTIVELY. It teaches that WE CAN GET CONTROL OF OUR LIFE through wisdom, understanding, caution, good judgment, and self-control. Indeed, this workbook is all about those things. It's about NO LONGER "LOVING" our foolish ways. It's about TURNING AWAY FROM, DESPISING, and REFUSING to act in self-destructive ways. It's about SAYING "NO" to impulsive, Self-Destructive Coping Responses. It's about OPENING OUR MINDS to wisdom and knowledge to SOOTHE and BRING PEACE to our soul. It's about BEING MINDFUL and MAKING INFORMED DECISIONS about how BEST to respond to life. It's about HOLDING TIGHT TO

We've been given the gift of reasoning to reason through our problems and emotions...so WE CAN control our emotions and thought processes instead of letting them control us.

Our Recovery Goal is to leave our foolish ways so we can walk in the ways of peace and understanding.

14- "The Well Analogy" is adapted from Dr. Linehan's Skills Training Manual (page 66).

Wise Mind is more than just thinking rationally. It's an inner wisdom that lies deep within us. It's where we find peace...and feel "at peace."

We get to Wise Mind when we "get to the bottom of a matter."

By digging deep, we break through trap doors that have had us stuck and unable to achieve peace.

WISDOM AND NOT LETTING GO OF IT because wisdom GIVES LIFE to our life. Do you feel you've responded to life in a simple minded manner? If so, do you think you could increase your peace and stability by using Rational Mind and Wise Mind to walk in the ways of understanding? Explain how this would work for you? _____

_____

_____

"The Well Analogy of Wise Mind"

The following is a great analogy of Wise Mind.[14] Check out the "well" below. The arrows point to false bottoms – things that look like the bottom of the well, but really aren't.

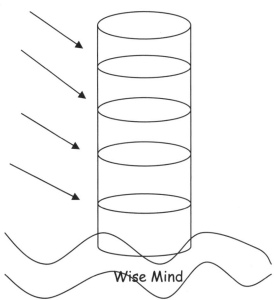

Wise Mind

Wise Mind is like a deep well in the ground. At the bottom of the well is an underground ocean. This underground ocean is WISE MIND. TRAP DOORS are at various points in the well. These trap doors are so cleverly built that when we look into the well, we think we see bottom! We THINK we've found "the solution" to our problem or the best way to respond. However, these trap doors are FALSE BOTTOMS. They're NOT the bottom of the well. They're NOT "the solution." They're NOT a wise way to respond. They're TRAP DOORS...a place where we GET STUCK...and can't move forward. We get trapped at that LEVEL OF JUDGMENT. In what ways have your behaviors and simple understandings led you to be STUCK in the SAME PLACE AND TIME...and UNABLE TO MOVE FORWARD? _____

_____

_____

We may be splashed with Wise Mind when confronted with truth. Someone may share something insightful or Rational Mind Turns On and we understand something

232

Wise Mind is sometimes the "Ah-ha" or "Oooh" moments.
It's the moments of deepening insight… when we understand something at a much deeper level.

15- First Level Coping Responses are our preferred coping responses.
They're called "First Level Coping Responses" because they're on the FIRST level or levels of the well AND they tend to be the FIRST things we think about doing in the Heat-of-the-Moment. They're our VERY WORST coping choices.

16- This example is just an example! In reality, there may be more than five levels in our well…or less!

17- A big argument with someone we live with is a critical situation. It's often a stressor that leads to desperate behavior and relapse.

First Level Coping Responses are at the top of the well and noticeably farthest from Wise Mind!

Our Recovery Goal is to Talk Ourselves Through what we feel like doing…and into what would be in our best interests!

at a different level. Wise Mind UNLOCKS the trap doors in our life and enables us to SEE THINGS CLEARLY and DEAL WITH THINGS AT A DEEPER LEVEL. We're NO LONGER STUCK! Psychological changes and GROWTH OCCURS!

> Our Recovery Goal is NOT to live on the surface of the well, but to go deep… to BREAK THROUGH THE TRAP DOORS and WORK OUR WAY DOWN TO WISE MIND…to the level of wisdom and understanding. Our goal is to go from "FIRST LEVEL COPING RESPONSES"[15] at the top of the well to WISE MIND at the bottom. Our goal is to THINK THROUGH and CHOOSE better and better COPING RESPONSES…to move ourselves from SELF-DESTRUCTIVE, First Level Coping Responses to LIFE-ENHANCING ONES. This will enable us to ACHIEVE and MAINTAIN balance, stability, and peace in our life.

SKILL BUILDER: Talking Ourselves into Wise Mind Behavior

Read through the well drawing below.[16] It applies "The Well Analogy" to Real Life. The situation involves a BIG argument with someone we live with.[17] Common coping responses are listed. Notice they become wiser and wiser as the well deepens. They go from VERY self-destructive at the top…to life-enhancing at the bottom. Our Recovery Goal is to TALK OURSELVES THROUGH impulsive, self-destructive responses by THINKING THROUGH BEFORE WE DO. This is HOW WE DO IT in Real Life!

FIRST LEVEL COPING RESPONSES: Storm out of the house and… get drunk, shoot-up, cut, overdose, or other suicidal behavior.

A BETTER RESPONSE: Threaten suicide and scare everyone by leaving… or take extra pills but don't overdose.

AN EVEN BETTER RESPONSE: Cuss them out and SLAM doors all the way to our room. Vow not to talk to them until THEY apologize. Journal for awhile.

BETTER YET: Give them a look that could kill. Shut doors with an attitude! Write in our journal until we cool down. Blow it off as if it never happened.

WISE MIND: Tell them we're too angry to discuss it any further. Suggest a cool down period and a return to the discussion later. Go to our room WITHOUT making a scene. Write in our journal. List our needs and what we're willing to do to reduce the stress or solve the problem. Return to the discussion when both are able to do so rationally and in a civil manner.

WISE MIND

From "Out-of-Control: A Dialectical Behavior Therapy (DBT) – Cognitive-Behavioral Therapy (CBT) Workbook for Getting Control of Our Emotions and Emotion-Driven Behavior" - Copyright © 2009 by Melanie Gordon Sheets, Ph.D. (www.dbt-cbt-workbook.com)

Some common **First Level** Coping Responses for this situation are listed. We may FEEL LIKE storming out of the house and getting drunk, doping up, cutting, overdosing, or doing another type of suicide attempt. Physical aggression is also a First Level Coping Response. In this example, IF WE ACT ON a First Level Coping Response, we may lose our relationship and housing...and end up in a hospital or treatment center. This may kick-off another round of the Cycle of Suffering.

Though not the greatest idea, threatening to harm ourselves is much better than actually doing it!

The Second Level is a better response. It's still VERY destructive...but less so than the First Level response. In this example, we still make a scene and storm out of the house. We may leave with a bag of pills in hand, but this time, we ONLY THREATEN suicide to scare people WITHOUT INTENT to Follow Through. We may take some pills to self-medicate, but nowhere near enough for an overdose.

It's obvious that First Level and Second Level actions are VERY BAD CHOICES that will result in VERY BAD CONSEQUENCES. In this example, the Second Level choice is MUCH BETTER than the First Level because we only THREATEN to harm ourselves rather than ACTUALLY doing it! So, it's better, right? The consequences of these two levels are similar...but, WE'LL GET SOME POINTS for not doing an actual suicide attempt!

18- When a Group Member Talks Themselves Through the First Level to the Second, it's a time for celebration! That's because instead of cutting, doing a suicide attempt, or relapsing into drugs or alcohol, they just threatened to do it! That's major progress!

Do you see recovery-in-progress when comparing First Level and Second Level responses? Why do you think going down one level is such a huge, big deal? _____

_____

_____

Because IT'S A GREAT STARTING POINT! The first steps are often the hardest![18] It's hard to break habits and to keep ourselves from doing something we REALLY feel like doing! It's a MAJOR SUCCESS when we're able to STOP OURSELVES. It takes a lot of SELF-CONTROL TO TALK OURSELVES OUT OF a First Level Coping Response and INTO a wiser response!

We must become Mindful of what we're thinking about doing, what we're getting ready to do, and what we've begun to do. Then, we must use Rational Mind to Talk Our Way Through the levels to get to Wise Mind.

First Level Coping Responses are the FIRST impulses and coping options that go through our mind in the Heat-of-the-Moment. They're the FIRST things we grab for and do. They're OUR coping habits. They're what WE DO when we're upset. Our Recovery Goal is to STOP OURSELVES and NOT ACT ON these impulses. At the soonest point possible, we must STOP OURSELVES and TALK OURSELVES THROUGH what we're planning to do or what we're in the process of doing. We've been practicing this process! It starts with Mindfulness and observing and describing how we're feeling, our Emotion-Driven Thoughts, and our desired

234

Emotion-Driven Behavior. It also includes Turning On Rational Mind to Think Through Before We Do! Consider this example.

> "I'm really mad. I'm about to explode. I can't believe he's such an idiot. How dare he? I'll show him. I'm gonna get plastered. He'll be sorry for treating me like this...Man, as much as I would like to drink, he'll leave me for sure and I really don't want to start drinking again. I should just scare the daylights out of him. I'll scare him like he's never been scared before. I'll grab a knife and run out of the house and make him THINK I'm going to kill myself! That'll scare him so bad, he'll think twice before he treats me like that again."

Wise Mind enables us to deal with a major situation by Talking Ourselves Out Of First Level Coping Responses and into a Wise Mind Coping Response. It's all about controlling our impulses in the Heat-of-the-Moment.[19]

Which emotions are "driving" in this situation? _____
_____

What did this lady talk herself out of doing? _____

Which Rational Mind "realities" helped her to decide NOT TO DO the First Level Coping Responses? _____
_____
_____

What did she decide to do instead? _____
_____

19- We may really want to storm out and use drugs or alcohol or take a bunch of pills. We may want to yell and scream. We may want to go through the house and slam every door off its hinges. We may feel like not talking to someone until they apologize! Although these behaviors provide some immediate relief, all they really do is multiply and intensify our problems.

She used Rational Mind to TALK HERSELF OUT OF drinking as a response to her anger and a desire to get even. She recognized that drinking this one time might end up in a full blown relapse AND the loss of her relationship. She decided to ACT LIKE she was going to harm herself JUST TO SCARE HIM. Even though this Second Level Response is VERY destructive, IT'S MUCH BETTER than the First! It's much better to grab a knife and threaten to kill ourselves rather than actually harming ourselves. It's also much better than relapsing back into drinking. Fortunately, this lady continued to use Self-Talk and Talked Herself Out Of the dramatic "grab a knife and run out of the house" response, too.

The Third Level in this Well Analogy is a MUCH BETTER choice than the first two! This time, we storm to our room, cuss them out, and slam every door along the way SO HARD that wall hangings and shelf items fall off and break! We promise NOT to talk to them until WE GET AN APOLOGY! We journal to express our feelings and to process the situation. This helps us to BECOME MINDFUL of what just happened and it OPENS THE DOOR to Rational Mind. Overall, Third Level behavior ISN'T a great way to deal with conflict, but it's MUCH BETTER than a suicide attempt, hitting someone, relapsing into drugs and alcohol, or threatening self-harm. Be Mindful though, if we do this type of Third Level behavior, we'll no doubt make someone REAL MAD because of our words and property damage. Also, the tension will remain high in the house if we continue the conflict by refusing to speak with them. The good part...it's unlikely we'll go to jail or the hospital at this level! Let's go down another level to one that's even better.

The Fourth Level in this example is to give them a look that could kill instead of cussing them out...and to shut doors with an attitude rather than destructive door slamming! We CHOOSE to write in our journal to cool off and process the situation. We decide to "blow off" the conflict and act as if it never happened.[20] The Fourth Level is better than the Third, but it's still not great.

What's better about this response as compared to the previous levels? _____

_____

_____

What major problem do you see with this Fourth Level response? _____

_____

_____

20- You probably realize that blowing it off as if it never happened is NOT the best idea either, especially if we're "stuffing anger." However, it's probably better than not talking to someone until we get an apology! Can you imagine the extreme tension in the house if we're refusing to speak with someone we live with?!

21-If she truly blows off the conflict and decides to Let It Go and is at peace with the situation, she may be okay. But, if she's blowing it off WITHOUT being at peace with it, it'll still be there for her to deal with down the road. It'll rear its ugly head when this person does something else that upsets her...and she'll experience a double dose of anger! That's like packing explosives and she's the time bomb... a next-time-it-happens bomb! When she finally goes off, the explosion will be VERY intense. It's dangerous to pack away anger...this can lead to an explosive Out-of-Control response!

The major problem is...we're NOT wisely dealing with our problem. We're blowing it off. We're stuffing it. We're saving our anger for the next go-round.[21] It's progress because of greater self-control. Also, the consequences of our actions will be MUCH LESS SEVERE. We've moved ourselves from a First Level Coping Response to a milder form of anger expression. At this level, we're NOT LIKELY to lose our relationship and housing and end up in jail or a hospital. We've DONE GOOD! Now, let's go down one more level and do even better!

The Fifth Level in this example is the bottom level of Wise Mind. We've Talked Ourselves Through four levels of unhealthy coping to get here. We've decided to tell them we're way too upset to discuss the problem in-the-moment. We suggest a Time-Out to calm down and process the conflict...and to return to DISCUSS the problem when we both feel better. We might say,

"I'm so angry right now I'm about to explode...and I know you are, too. All we're doing is screaming and yelling and this is getting Out-of-Control. We've talked about this before and agreed that when we get this way we're going to take Time-Out. I'm going to the bedroom to chill out and think awhile. This will give you time to think, too. When I feel better and have some ideas about what we can do to work this out, I'll come and talk with you. I hope you'll do the same. If you're still too mad, we'll talk about it when you're ready. Our relationship is too important to me to fight like this. We'll talk later."

Then, we go to our room without making a scene. We explore our needs and wants and what we're willing to do to solve the problem. Once we've cooled down, we check to see if the other person is ready to talk. We WAIT UNTIL we're BOTH able to do so RATIONALLY and in a CIVIL manner and we WORK to CALMLY SETTLE the conflict. Now, is that Wise Mind or what!?

Think of a time when you Talked Yourself Out Of a First Level Coping Response AND INTO a Wise Mind response. What did you FEEL LIKE doing...and what did you do instead? _____

_____

_____

What positive things happened as a result of your self-control? _____

_____

_____

How did you feel about yourself as a result of how you handled your problem? __

_____

If we took a Wise Mind approach to all our problems, imagine the peace and stability we would experience... and the quality and length of our relationships!

Think of another time when you Talked Yourself Out Of a First Level Coping Response AND INTO a Wise Mind response. What did you FEEL LIKE doing... and what did you do instead? _____

_____

_____

What positive things happened as a result of your self-control? _____

_____

_____

How did you feel about yourself as a result of how you handled your problem? __

_____

SKILL BUILDER: Drew Got Dumped...Talking Our Way Through It

The story on the next page, "Drew Got Dumped" is an example of Talking Ourselves Through First Level Coping Responses to Bring On Wise Mind in the Heat-of-the-Moment. This is HOW WE DO IT in Real Life! Drew Talked Himself Through the rage he was experiencing. As you read the story, UNDERLINE or HIGHLIGHT how he FELT LIKE responding in the Heat-of-the-Moment. Then, answer the following questions.

Have you been in Drew's shoes before...so hurt and angry that you REALLY wanted to hurt someone or their prized possessions? YES / NO

Did you ever act on these feelings and do something violent? YES / NO **If so**, what did you do and what were the consequences of your behavior? **If you didn't take revenge, how did you deal with your anger AND what was the outcome of your coping response?** _____

_____

_____

Drew Got Dumped

"I can't believe she left me. What trash she is. Screw it, screw her, screw sobriety. It hasn't done me a bit of good. Things never change. I'm going to drink tonight and no one's going to tell me any different. Maybe I'll down a bunch of pills too, and die. How dare she dump me for that dork? He just waves his money around. He isn't any better than me. I'm so angry, I could knock his teeth down his throat. I can't believe I fell for her. How could I have been so stupid? I don't know who I'm angrier with, her or me. I've got to get a grip before I lose it. Maybe I should pay them a visit...and knock the crap out of them. That would feel SO GOOD right now. My luck, I'll end up in jail and she'd come over here and empty this place out...my stuff and hers. Why is life so hard? Why can't I do what I feel like doing? I want to hurt them and I want to get drunk and stay that way. Maybe I should go over there and bash the windows in his perky little car. The Group lady said strenuous[22] exercise would relieve stress and tension. Swinging a sledge hammer sounds strenuous to me. That would land me in jail, though. Spray painting the car would be quiet...but, they'd know it was me. Anything I do is going to have bad consequences and she isn't worth ruining everything I have going for me. Boy, this REALLY pisses me off. I guess I better call my sponsor. I've done so well for five months, I would hate to blow it here... though I would LOVE to get even. But going to jail tonight and losing my job tomorrow isn't the way to go. She'd clean this apartment out. Man, I'm so angry I could explode. If Joe's not there, I'll call my brother, he hated her anyway."

22- Strenuous – (stren-you-iss) (iss, the sound when you take "h" off of "hiss") – takes a lot of energy to do and it wears you out!

"I'm Out-of-Control. I've got to call for help NOW. I've got to get Rational Mind Turned On...fast."

SKILL BUILDER: From One Level to the Next...Going Deep to Reach Wise Mind

Let's take a closer look at how Drew did it! Using what you underlined in the previous section, fill in the well levels below. Start with his First Level Coping Responses and try to order his coping choices[23] from worst to best all the way down to Wise Mind. Refer to the previous well example for hints.

23- The levels are based on the destructiveness of our behavior and how severely our behavior will affect the Big Picture of Our Life.

The First Level would be drinking and taking an overdose to suicide. The Second Level, the better choice, would be to drink WITHOUT taking pills. You may have put these in one or two levels, either way is fine. The next level would be physical aggression towards the EX-girlfriend and her NEW boyfriend. The next would be aggression towards the car (bash windows, spray paint). The Wise Mind Level would be reached when he decided to call his sponsor or brother. Depending on how you chose to do the first two levels, this well may have four or five levels.

238

First Level_____

Second Level_____

Third Level_____

Fourth Level_____

Fifth Level_____

To Work Through the levels, we must be Mindful of what we're thinking about doing and what we ARE doing. We must not allow ourselves to do something if it's going to hurt our life. We must stop, Say "NO!"…and hold ourselves still… long enough to come up with a better idea!

Wise Mind balances the pressures of Emotional Mind and Rational Mind …the pressure to explode and act-out with the pressure to be cool and act wisely.

24- Naïve - (nigh-eve) oversimplification – (over-sim-pluh-fi-kay-shin) – making something seem easier than it really is… out of ignorance. Not having the experience or knowledge to understand how difficult something really is.

We do these things because we don't want to NOT do them. We do them despite knowing they'll lead to bad consequences and bigger problems.

Many of Drew's DESIRED behaviors would have led to great trouble had he acted on them. He did an awesome job of Talking Himself Through a very difficult situation. He used Rational Mind and maintained self-control. His coping choices became less and less destructive for the Big Picture of His Life. He finally arrived at Wise Mind and a life-enhancing plan for dealing with his rage.

APPLICATION: Just Say "Yes" to "Just Say No"

We witnessed Drew saying "NO" to his First Level Coping Responses and "NO" to other destructive choices along the way to Wise Mind. Many have laughed at the "Just Say No" anti-drug campaign of former First Lady Nancy Reagan in the 1980's. Many believe the three words "Just Say No" are a naïve oversimplification[24] of the recovery process. However, there's a lot of wisdom in those words. Think about it… IF we don't say "NO," if we don't DENY OURSELVES, HOW ARE WE GOING TO STOP OURSELVES? If we WANT to control our life outcomes, we MUST CONTROL OURSELVES. How Drew did it…IS HOW PEOPLE DO IT in Real Life. He had destructive impulses, but, he DIDN'T ALLOW HIMSELF to act on them. He CONSIDERED the consequences of EACH impulse and he DIDN'T ACT on ones that would hurt his life. He said "NO" to destructive impulses and "YES" to Wise Mind responses. There's NO WAY AROUND saying "NO" and NOT ALLOWING OURSELVES to do as we please. SOMEONE HAS TO TAKE CONTROL…and it might as well be us! We sure hate to be CONTROLLED BY cops, jailers, doctors, and social workers!

APPLICATION: Wisdom Lies Deep Within Us All

We often believe we don't have wisdom, but WE DO! WE KNOW right from wrong…and what will help our life and what will be harmful. THE PROBLEM IS… when we're BIG-TIME IN EMOTIONAL MIND and DESPERATE for relief…

We must say "NO!" We must deny ourselves. We can't always let ourselves do what we feel like doing. There's absolutely no way around denying ourselves and saying "NO" if we want to stop the chaos and problems in our life.

Our emotions are part of us, but they don't have to define who we are as a person or what type of life we will live.

we do things WE KNOW are destructive. We say, "I did it AGAINST MY BETTER JUDGMENT." or "I KNEW IT WAS STUPID, but I did it anyway." The point is... wisdom lies deep within us all. If we set our heart to it, we CAN Think Through our choices to come up with a life-enhancing plan for dealing with our emotional impulses, even when we FEEL we CAN'T Think Straight or we FEEL Out-of-Control! What do you think Wise Mind would suggest we do in situations when we're SO OVERWHELMED that we THINK we can't Think Through? _____

_____

_____

Wise Mind would say, "DON'T DO ANYTHING in this state of mind...other than TO GET HELP." That's because we need to get Rational Mind Turned On FAST so we can come up with some Wise Mind plans for dealing with OURSELVES and the situation. Wise Mind would encourage us to visit or phone someone who will give us an emergency injection of Rational Mind! If we're TOO OUT-OF-CONTROL, Wise Mind would encourage us to CALL 911. The consequences of this are MUCH BETTER than relapsing into First Level Coping Responses.

SKILL BUILDER: "The Well Analogy Worksheet"

We've reviewed two Well Analogy examples. Now it's your turn to do one! Check out "The Well Analogy Worksheet" on the next page and follow the instructions below.[25] Complete this worksheet based on how YOU ARE, what YOU WOULD DO, and how YOU WOULD RESPOND. Maybe your First Level Coping Responses are storming out of the house and threatening to end a relationship. Maybe it's high-speed driving or physically harming yourself or someone else. Maybe a Third or Fourth Level response for YOU includes cleaning, lifting weights, working in the garage or garden, or playing video games until you cool off rather than going to your room and journaling. Maybe YOUR TRIGGER SITUATION has to do with your boss or co-workers...or a rude and uncaring caseworker, probation officer, or landlord...maybe it's the ex! PERSONALIZE this worksheet. Do it based on YOUR COPING PREFERENCES so it's MEANINGFUL to YOUR LIFE!

Instructions for "The Well Analogy Worksheet"

Step 1. Think of a current situation you're having trouble dealing with.

Step 2. List the MOST destructive things you've considered doing in the first few levels. Order them from the MOST destructive to the least destructive... with the most destructive at the top.

25- Feel free to make copies of this worksheet for personal use.

The worksheet has five levels. You don't have to use all of them and you can add more if needed... but, you'll have to draw it on another piece of paper.

Step 3. Then, work your way down the well and list better problem-solving and coping and problem-solving options. List the BEST option at the bottom Wise Mind Level. It should be a life-enhancing one that will help bring peace and stability to your life.[26]

"The Well Analogy Worksheet"

1st Level:

2nd Level:

3rd Level:

4th Level:

Wise Mind:

Wise Mind

26- Sometimes, the WISE response creates great instability and distress at first...but in the long run, it brings peace and stability. Consider leaving a very unpleasant high paying job for a lower paying job that's rewarding and MUCH LESS stressful. The major job change and reduced income will be stressful at first, but once we adjust to it, we'll have increased peace and stability. Think about leaving an abusive relationship. There's lots of stress and instability at first...but there's often an immediate sense of relief...and peace and stability down the road. Sometimes we have to sacrifice current peace and/or stability TO HAVE A BETTER LIFE DOWN THE ROAD. When we make these changes, we MUST be committed to Getting Through the temporary distress. We must use DISTRESS TOLERANCE SKILLS!

The Well Analogy helps us to be Mindful of our options for responding to an emotionally charged situation. It helps us to understand that our coping choices range from destructive to life-enhancing...and from impulsive to wise. It also helps us to KNOW that we can Think Through and Talk Ourselves Through destructive impulses...to come up with a life-enhancing way to deal with a situation. DIG DEEP INTO YOUR SOUL...WISE MIND IS THERE. You KNOW right from wrong, good from bad...what will help your life and what will hurt it...and what will give you peace and stability and what will take it away. Make use of the tools and principles in this workbook to help LIVE A LIFE that brings SATISFACTION and MEANING...and PEACE and STABILITY!

~~~~~~~~~ CHAPTER REVIEW ~~~~~~~~~

1. What two sources of information does Wise Mind pull together? _____

_____

2. What's the goal of pulling this information together? _____
_____

3. The Wise plan of action helps us to deal with our problems in a way that

b _ _ _ _ _ _ _ us the m _ _ _ and helps us to a _ _ _ _ b _ _

c _ _ _ _ _ _ _ _ _ _ _ . Wise Mind is concerned about our b _ _ _

i _ _ _ _ _ _ _ _ and our p _ _ _ _ and s _ _ _ _ _ _ _ _. When Wise Mind is

Turned On, we have the i _ _ _ _ _ _ and u _ _ _ _ _ _ _ _ _ _ _ we need to

make w _ _ _ d _ _ _ _ _ _ _ _ for our life.

4. What are the six steps for Bringing On Wise Mind?

1. _____
2. _____
3. _____
4. _____
5. _____
6. _____

5. What are the six tips for Participating wisely and Effectively in our lives?

1. _____
2. _____
3. _____
4. _____
5. _____
6. _____

6. What are some benefits of "Playing by the Rules"? _____
_____
_____

7. What is meant by "Choosing our Battles"? _____
_____
_____

8. According to "Ancient Wisdom," how will wisdom help us? _____
_____
_____

9. What is meant by a "false bottom" in "The Well Analogy"? Why is it a problem?
_____
_____
_____

10. According to "The Well Analogy," what leads to psychological growth? _____
_____
_____

FOR REFLECTION:
Take a few moments to reflect on this chapter. Some questions are listed in the margin to guide your reflection. Feel free to reflect on whatever your heart brings to mind.

What are your reactions to the material?

Which parts hit home or relate to you the most?

Which parts have helped you the most?

Which parts have helped you to understand yourself the most?

How will you use this information to feel better about yourself?

How will you use this information to improve the quality of your life...or to change how things work out for you in life?

What will you do differently based on this material?

How has this information changed the way you feel about your patterns of relapse and recovery... and your overall response to life?

What does this material motivate you to do?

11. Which Recovery Goal does "The Well Analogy" point out to us? How do we go about doing it? _____
_____
_____

12. What are First Level Coping Responses? _____
_____
_____

13. How do we Talk Ourselves Through the levels? What does that involve? ____
_____
_____
_____

14. How come "Just Say No" isn't as stupid as it sounds...or seems to be on the surface? _____
_____

15. If we're totally overwhelmed, feel Out-of-Control, and we can't Think Straight, what would Wise Mind suggest we do? _____
_____
_____

~~~ For Reflection ~~~

_____
_____
_____
_____
_____
_____
_____
_____
_____
_____
_____
_____
_____

Figure 9.A.1: The Concepts and Skills Tracking Sheet – Chapter 9

Week # _____

Day of Week →

Date →

9A. Today, the thought came up or I reminded myself that part of Participating Effectively in my life is to NOT act impulsively or in old dysfunctional ways.

9B. Today, I caught myself doing something or getting ready to do something impulsive or in an old dysfunctional way that could have caused me problems. I STOPPED myself so I could Participate Effectively in my life.

9C. Today, the thought came up or I reminded myself that I needed to Play by the Rules to Participate Effectively in my life.

9D. Today, I made a Wise Mind decision to Play by the Rules.

9E. Today, the thought came up or I reminded myself that I must make thoughtful choices in order to Participate Effectively in my life.

9F. Today, I made a thoughtful choice about something important in my life.

9G. Today, the thought came up or I reminded myself that I must be IN CONTROL of myself in order TO CONTROL how life works out for me.

9H. Today, I acted in ways to be IN CONTROL of my life so I could CONTROL how life works out for me.

9I. Today, I became Mindful I was Fighting a Battle. I thought about the Big Picture of the Situation and My Life. I made a decision about whether or not the battle was worth the Fight...and whether it was in the best interests of my peace and stability to continue the Fight.

9J. Today, I thought about how I need to use Wise Mind to get control of my life. I realize the importance of searching for wisdom because it's a pathway to recovery. I realize I need to use my Wise Mind to walk in the ways of peace and understanding rather than walking in the pathways of foolishness and destruction.

Notes:

RATING SCALE
5 – Did Excellent in this area today
4 – Did Pretty Good in this area today
3 – Did Alright in this area today
2 – Did Only Fair in this area today
1 – Didn't Do Well in this area today
DD – Didn't Do today

244

Figure 9.A.2: The Concepts and Skills Tracking Sheet – Chapter 9

Week # _____

Day of Week →

Date →

9K. Today, I thought about how self-discipline is hard or uncomfortable...however, I also thought about how it's worse to be undisciplined and to live in negative Emotional Mind and the Cycle of Suffering!

9L. Today, I forced myself to do something I didn't want to do because it was in my best interests to do it. I practiced self-discipline and did it even though I didn't like it or I didn't want to! I did it anyway to Participate Effectively in my life!

9M. I understand "The Well Analogy of Wise Mind"...about how First Level Coping Responses are my worst choices and how I need to Think Through what I'm wanting to do...so I can move myself down the well to a Wise Mind response.

9N. I understand that I get stuck in my life...and my life doesn't move forward or improve...when I get stuck in one of the trap doors in the well. I get stuck at the level of my behavior and coping responses. I realize the quality of my life will only be as good as the quality of my coping choices.

9O. Today, I used "The Well Analogy" and I Talked Myself down a level or several.

9P. Today, I used "The Well Analogy" and I Talked Myself all the way down to Wise Mind! I thought about my problem-solving and coping options and decided on a plan of action that was in the best interests of the Big Picture of My Life and the Situation.

9Q. Today, I began to Follow Through with my Wise Mind action plan.

Notes:

RATING SCALE
5 – Did Excellent in this area today
4 – Did Pretty Good in this area today
3 – Did Alright in this area today
2 – Did Only Fair in this area today
1 – Didn't Do Well in this area today
DD – Didn't Do today

"The Wise Mind Worksheet" and the Game Plan that comes out of it are major tools in the DBT-CBT program. They are our LIFELINES.

In the first Wise Mind chapter, we waded through the basics of Wise Mind and dived down the levels of "The Well Analogy" to the underground ocean of Wise Mind. Now, we're going to sail into "THE WISE MIND WORKSHEET." This worksheet is a MAJOR TOOL in the DBT-CBT program. We've been building up to this all along! This worksheet walks us through the steps to Wise Mind. This process starts with Mindfulness, so this worksheet is also a Mindfulness tool.

This worksheet helps us to become Mindful of Emotional Mind dynamics and what Rational Mind has to say. It helps us to IDENTIFY and CHALLENGE IRRATIONAL THOUGHTS and DESTRUCTIVE IMPULSES. It helps us to LOOK at a situation REALISTICALLY and LOGICALLY. When we address a problem using BOTH Emotional Mind and Rational Mind, WISE MIND TURNS ON! This worksheet is a LIFELINE.[1] It helps us to THINK THROUGH...and to GET TO...WISE MIND!

"The Wise Mind Worksheet"

1- I've used Wise Mind Worksheets many times to help myself through troubling issues. I can't stand to ruminate and tear myself up and I can't stand all the frustration and anxiety that goes with feeling Out-of-Control. Remember, we have two choices when we're upset. We can do life-enhancing things or self-defeating things. "The Wise Mind Worksheet" is a life-enhancing thing to do! Even psychologists have difficult issues and problems to deal with... and need tools to Work Through them! "The Wise Mind Worksheet" works...even for the most hard-headed among us!

2- See Figure 10.A on the next page.

Check out the sample worksheet.[2] Notice the two Emotional Mind columns. One is for listing Raw Emotions...the other is for Emotion-Driven Thoughts. On this worksheet, similar feelings and similar Emotion-Driven Thoughts are grouped together. The original, hand-written worksheet WASN'T so organized! It BECAME organized when it was typed up for this book! When we're completing a worksheet, our goal is to write down what's coming out of our mind and heart...and often, these things come out quickly! Group as you can, but don't worry about it! It's helpful, but NOT necessary!

Check out the Rational Mind column. It contains Rational Mind statements that challenge the Emotion-Driven Thoughts. It also contains other statements of truth about the Big Picture of the person's life AND the situation. These statements were grouped together to show how the Emotion-Driven Thoughts were challenged. Don't worry about being so organized. You can organize later if you choose to re-write the worksheet! The goal is to THINK THROUGH and to get this stuff on paper!

Check out the Wise Mind column. It's organized to show how WISE MIND dealt with four major issues brought up by EMOTIONAL MIND (love him, hard to leave; no one cares about me; will never have a better relationship; and problems coping with the loss). Wise Mind was RESPECTFUL of what was going on in EMOTIONAL MIND (the Raw Emotions and the fears and concerns expressed in the Emotion-Driven

Figure 10.A: The Wise Mind Worksheet: Just an Example

The Wise Mind Worksheet: Just an Example – We're Toxic for Each Other

RAW EMOTIONS	EMOTIONAL MIND — EMOTION-DRIVEN THOUGHTS	RATIONAL MIND	WISE MIND
Depressed, Sad, Hopeless, Helpless, Exhausted, Used Up	I can't leave. I love him. I can't live without him.	It'll be hard to break up, but...if there's a will, there's a way. I CAN live without him.	Even though we love each other, the smartest thing is to go our separate ways. The counseling has helped, but our personalities really clash.
Confused, "Lost", Crazy, Out-of-Control, Desperate,	I can't tolerate being alone.	It's uncomfortable, but I CAN deal with being alone if I have to.	I'll have to stay busy and be with people. I'll join the bowling league, paint, and add church activities to fill my evenings and downtime. Being busy will help me keep my mind off him.
Overwhelmed, Shocked, Feel Unreal, Numb, Empty	A bad relationship is better than no relationship.	Change is always hard, but life is full of changes. If we don't accept change, we'll stagnate and suffer. We're toxic for each other. I'm so miserable with him. Really, a bad relationship is MUCH MORE PAINFUL than no relationship!	Amanda needs a roommate. Living together would help me through the loneliness. She's good support, too!
Feel Self-Destructive, Feel Like Hurting Myself, Drinking, or OD'ing	Nobody really cares about me.	Many people have offered to help me get on my feet.	Everyone told me how difficult he was...but, I didn't listen. Next time, I'll ask folks for their opinion. If they have a bad opinion, I'll bail and not get involved! I make such poor relationship choices on my own.
Anger, Rage, Feel Hate, Resentment, Aggressive, Vengeful	No one else would want me. I don't deserve any better.	I'm a nice person. I'm loyal. I have many good qualities that a decent man would value! I deserve a good relationship because I'm good to others.	I'll stay out of a relationship until I get my relationship stuff figured out! I have to learn to THINK THROUGH BEFORE I get involved! I need to take
Nervous, Anxious, Worried, Scared, Fearful	I'll never have a better relationship.	Everyone told me he slept around and had a bad temper. I didn't listen. It's hard to have a good relationship with someone who has bad relationships with everyone!	time to find a compatible mate, one I have things in common with and one who treats people with respect!
Abandoned, Alone, Lonely, Rejected, Hurt, Betrayed, Abused, Mistreated, Unloved, Undeserving, Worthless	I hate him. All men are worthless.	I'll have a better relationship when I chose a better relationship partner! I know God has someone right picked out for me. All men aren't worthless...just the ones I keep choosing! I keep picking men that are like my father.	
Misunderstood, Ashamed, Guilty	Why try, I'm better off staying a drunk. I might as well relapse.	These Emotion-Driven Behaviors would hurt me, not help me. I refuse to go backwards because of this.	It'll be very sad to break up. I'll have to allow time to feel better... and I'll have to stay busy! I'll use Life-Enhancing Coping Activities
Paranoid, Suspicious, Mistrusting	I'd be better off dead. I have nothing to live for. I'd kill him if I had the chance.	My family depends on me being okay. Relapsing, harming myself, or doing destructive things is not an option anymore.	to get through this tough time.

From "Out-of-Control: A Dialectical Behavior Therapy (DBT) – Cognitive-Behavioral Therapy (CBT) Workbook for Getting Control of Our Emotions and Emotion-Driven Behavior"
Copyright © 2009 by Melanie Gordon Sheets, Ph.D. (www.dbt-cbt-workbook.com)

3- The ability to do a Wise Mind Worksheet is a critical skill. If it seems difficult, recall the truth about learning skills – they become easier with practice! Give yourself time to learn how to do them. They'll take a bit of working with to get good at using!

4- Use the blank worksheet (Figure 10.B).

5- If you can't think of the word for an emotion, review "The List of Negative Emotions" on page 26 for ideas. Also, don't worry about how to list an emotion, like anger or angry, rage or enraged, or hatred or hate. It doesn't matter!

6- These aren't feeling statements like "I'm so angry." They're statements of what he's thinking BECAUSE he's angry...like, "Why can't I do what I really feel like doing?" and "I want to hurt him," and "I want to get drunk." Emotion-Driven Thoughts will also reflect how he sees and understands the world... in-the-moment. They'll reflect his Emotional Mind perceptions like "What trash she is." and "He just waves his money around."[7]

7- He said she left for the money. That's an Emotional Mind perception. It's more likely she left because of relationship issues AND the money. He's mad and hurt, so he's focusing on the money right now. The money issue is less personal and hurtful than their relationship issues and what he did or didn't do in the relationship. We (continued)

Thoughts). Wise Mind was also RESPECTFUL of the logical and reality-based understandings of RATIONAL MIND. Wise Mind pulled ALL THIS INFORMATION TOGETHER and CAME UP WITH some SUGGESTIONS for DEALING WITH THE BIG PICTURE of what was going on.

This worksheet may SEEM overwhelming AT FIRST, but once you get the hang of it, it'll seem pretty easy.[3] We've been preparing to complete this worksheet throughout this workbook. This information has been drilled into our heads so it should make sense once we get started. We'll practice completing one together and several completed worksheets are provided for your review.

SKILL BUILDER: Completing Drew's Wise Mind Worksheet

Step 1. Use the "Drew Got Dumped" story on page 77 to complete this worksheet.[4]

Step 2. **In the Raw Emotions column**, list emotions HE MENTIONED and ones the story SUGGESTED he was experiencing AND ones that would be EXPECTED based on what he was going through. Think how you might feel in such a situation. List many, 10-15 or more![5]

Step 3. **In the Emotion-Driven Thoughts column**, list ones that went through his mind.[6] PARAPHRASE, don't bother writing them word for word.[8]

Step 4. **In the Rational Mind column**, list his rational, realistic, logical, and TRUTH-based statements.[9] Some will directly challenge his Emotion-Driven Thoughts and some will reflect truths about life and the world in general.

Step 5. Pick out and challenge at least five of his Emotion-Driven Thoughts. Pick ones that are the most meaningful to you. Write your challenges in the Rational Mind column. If you need to make up some story details to challenge a statement, feel free to do so!

Step 6. **In the Wise Mind column**, list the wise understandings and problem-solving ideas he came up with. Add some of your own, too. You may notice some Wise Mind ideas will come to mind as you're working with Emotional Mind and Rational Mind at the same time!

Step 7. When you're done with your worksheet, check out the one I did.[10] Mine is based on MY interpretation, so it'll be a little different from yours. Avoid looking at mine until you finish yours! However, if you need some hints, check it out!!!! It's important to THINK on your own...and practice as much as possible...so you can do one when you really need to!

The Wise Mind Worksheet: Drew Got Dumped – Short Version

Figure 10.B: Drew Got Dumped – Short Version

WISE MIND

RATIONAL MIND

EMOTIONAL MIND

EMOTION-DRIVEN THOUGHTS

RAW EMOTIONS

SKILL BUILDER: More on Challenging Emotion-Driven Thoughts

Step 1. Check out the COMPLETED "Drew Got Dumped" worksheet.[10] Notice the Emotion-Driven Thoughts are numbered 1-11. For each one, look for a statement in the Rational Mind column that challenges it. Underline the challenge and put the number of the Emotion-Driven Thought next to it… to note this Rational Mind statement challenges the Emotion-Driven Thought. I did the first two Emotion-Driven Thoughts for you![11] Notice what's underlined in the Rational Mind column and the numbers at the end of those statements. The numbers show which Emotion-Driven Thought is being challenged. You may use TWO OR MORE Rational Mind statements to challenge one Emotion-Driven Thought…AND you may use ONE Rational Mind statement to challenge MORE THAN ONE Emotion-Driven Thought.

Step 2. If there are NO Rational Mind statements to challenge an Emotion-Driven Thought, write one to challenge it! A blank worksheet is provided for extra space.[12] Put the number of the Emotion-Driven Thought next to the Rational Mind statement that you write.

Step 3. If you GET STUCK…or when YOU'RE DONE, check out Figure 10.E for some "answers" and the explanations below. I cheated though! I didn't add any new Rational Mind statements! That's because we're not finished yet!

SKILL BUILDER: What I Think

Emotion-Driven Thought #1 was challenged by four Rational Mind thoughts. Look for four Rational Mind statements that have the little number "1" next to them. He knew she wasn't a good relationship choice and he knew they were having problems. The break-up came as no surprise!

Emotion-Driven Thought #2 was challenged by one statement about why she left.

Emotion-Driven Thought #3 was somewhat challenged. It's noted that she had a good side,[13] but not much was said about it.

Emotion-Driven Thought #4 was challenged by three statements. It's noted that he has been successful with recovery for awhile and many positive things are going on in his life as a result of his recovery efforts.

Emotion-Driven Thought #5 was challenged by five statements about recovery being HIS choice and HIS #1 Priority. It's what HE WANTS to do.

Emotion-Driven Thought #6 was challenged eleven times! He recognized HE WAS THE ONE to say that he WASN'T going to relapse into Emotion-Driven Behavior! Like

(7 – continued) all know he had some role in the break-up. It's not ALL her fault or ALL about the money! This relationship loss is very fresh and it's less painful for him to blame others than to take a close look at himself! Given this is all about gaining insight and wisdom, he'll see the Big Picture as he processes the situation! We'll just have to wait for him to get rational enough to be able to acknowledge the truth!

8- Shorten the sentence. For instance, "Maybe I should just go over there and bash the windows in his perky little car." could be written "bash windows."

9- Sometimes it's hard to tell if a statement is Rational Mind or Wise Mind. Don't get stuck trying to decide which column a statement goes in. In the Big Picture of Life, it doesn't really matter. We'll CHOOSE not to trouble ourselves with such details. If the thought is rational and challenges Emotional Mind, put it in the Rational Mind column. If it's part of a good solution, put it in the Wise Mind column. If you can't decide, Wise Mind would say, "Life's too short to make a big deal of this, put it in this column, the Rational Mind column, or both…just get 'er done!"

10- See Figure 10.C.

11- If these instructions make no sense to you, skip to Step 3!

12- See Figure 10.D.

13- (see the next page)

Figure 10.C: Drew Got Dumped – Short Version – (Completed)

The Wise Mind Worksheet: Drew Got Dumped – Short Version – (Completed)

RAW EMOTIONS	EMOTIONAL MIND — EMOTION-DRIVEN THOUGHTS	RATIONAL MIND	WISE MIND
Disbelief - Shock	1- I can't believe she left me.	I knew a break-up was going to happen. We've had so many fights because she's selfish. I wanted some of my needs met, too.[1] She probably left because of the conflict and he has plenty of money to blow on her.[1,2]	Since I'm so mad and have destructive thoughts, I'll use my Crisis Survival Plan and call my sponsor and brother. They both said, "Any time, any day."
Betrayal - Hurt Anger - Rage	2- She dumped me for money. 3- She's trash.		I need to get a plan for dealing with this loss and getting my life back in order. Tonight, I'm going to chill-out. Tomorrow, I'll work on a plan of action!
Hopelessness Feel like giving up	4- Screw everything. Sobriety hasn't done me any good. Things never change.	I'm not stupid, but getting with her was a foolish Emotional Mind response to loneliness.[1] I was attracted to her GOOD side and everyone warned me about her BAD side.[1] I should have listened! I'm mad at myself for the upset I've caused myself.	
Feeling Willful Reckless - Rebellious Want to Self-Destruct Feeling Suicidal	5- Why can't I do what I feel like?	I've been successful in recovery for five months now. Recovery is too important to blow. Many great things are happening that I don't want to mess up and lose. I have no interest in doing the Cycle of Suffering again. I'm done with that existence.	Recovery is My #1 Priority so I need to make life-enhancing decisions. I'm not going to screw up my life over this. I'm going to use every skill I know... and then some...to be okay!
Feeling Desperate Preoccupied Confused Overwhelmed Pressured - Pent-Up	6- I'm going to drink tonight and no one's going to tell me any different. 7- Down pills too, and die. 8- I want to hurt them, get even. 9- Physically hurt them. Bash windows. Spray paint.	Getting aggressive would feel good, but it would land me in jail. I'd lose my job and she'd clean me out! I have no interest in losing everything again.	Knew it! Did it! Gotta suck up the consequences! I'll hurt for awhile until I get things re-organized in my life...AND while time passes. I need to stay busy so I'm not thinking TOO MUCH about this. I can get back into the hobbies I gave up for her! I've been itching to go back to school, too!
Feeling Constrained, like I can't do what I want Frustrated Aggressive Want Revenge	10- Falling for her, how could I have been so stupid?	I can do whatever I want. I can stay on the Recovery Path or I can relapse. IT'S MY CHOICE and I've made Recovery my #1 Priority. I CAN work through this and talk myself out of destructive behavior with some MAJOR effort.	
Loss of Self-Respect Feeling Stupid Ashamed Angry and Disgusted with myself	11- Why is life so hard to deal with?	I'm fixing to do something stupid over someone who isn't worth it. I've got to get a grip or I'm going to lose it. It would be too easy right now to act on Emotional Mind. When big stuff happens, my "screw it" mentality turns on. I really don't want to relapse or die. I just want the hurt and anger to go away. Life's good when I'm doing good and life gets messed up when I mess up. Drinking and OD'ing would mess things up and make my problems worse.	Do NOT get involved with another woman until I work out my issues and why I make bad relationship choices! Just say NO to romance for now! This is too destructive to keep on doing!

Figure 10.D: Drew Got Dumped – Short Version – (Extra Page)

The Wise Mind Worksheet: Drew Got Dumped – Short Version – (Extra Page)

RAW EMOTIONS	EMOTIONAL MIND — EMOTION-DRIVEN THOUGHTS	RATIONAL MIND	WISE MIND

Figure 10.E: Drew Got Dumped – Short Version – (Second Completed)

The Wise Mind Worksheet: Drew Got Dumped – Short Version – (Second Completed)

EMOTIONAL MIND		RATIONAL MIND	WISE MIND
RAW EMOTIONS	**EMOTION-DRIVEN THOUGHTS**		
Disbelief - Shock Betrayal - Hurt Anger - Rage Hopelessness Feel like giving up Feeling Willful Reckless - Rebellious Want to Self-Destruct Feeling Suicidal Feeling Desperate Preoccupied Confused Overwhelmed Pressured - Pent-Up Feeling Constrained, like I can't do what I want Frustrated Aggressive Want Revenge Loss of Self-Respect Feeling Stupid Ashamed Angry and Disgusted with myself	1- I can't believe she left me. 2- She dumped me for money. 3- She's trash. 4- Screw everything. Sobriety hasn't done me any good. Things never change. 5- Why can't I do what I feel like? 6- I'm going to drink tonight and no one's going to tell me any different. 7- Down pills too, and die. 8- I want to hurt them, get even. 9- Physically hurt them. Bash windows. Spray paint. 10- Falling for her, how could I have been so stupid? 11- Why is life so hard to deal with?	I knew a break-up was going to happen. We've had so many fights because she's selfish. I wanted some of my needs met too.[1] She probably left because of the conflict and he has plenty of money to blow on her.[1,2] I'm not stupid, but getting with her was a foolish Emotional Mind response to loneliness.[1,10] I was attracted to her GOOD side.[3,10] and everyone warned me about her BAD side.[1] I should have listened![10,11] I'm mad at myself for the upset I've caused myself.[11] I've been successful in recovery for five months now.[4] Recovery is too important to blow.[6-9] Many great things are happening that I don't want to mess up and lose.[4,6-9] I have no interest in doing the Cycle of Suffering again. I'm done with that existence.[5,6-9] Getting aggressive would feel good, but it would land me in jail. I'd lose my job and she'd clean me out![8-9] I have no interest in losing everything again.[5,6-9] I can do whatever I want. I can stay on the Recovery Path or I can relapse.[5] IT'S MY CHOICE and I've made Recovery my #1 Priority.[5,6-9] I CAN work through this and talk myself out of destructive behavior with some MAJOR effort.[6,11] I'm fixing to do something stupid over someone who isn't worth it.[6-9] I've got to get a grip[6] or I'm going to lose it. It would be too easy right now to act on Emotional Mind. When big stuff happens, my "screw it" mentality turns on.[11] I really don't want to relapse or die.[5,6-9] I just want the hurt and anger to go away. Life's good when I'm doing good[4] and life gets messed up when I mess up.[6-9,11] Drinking and OD'ing would mess things up and make my problems worse.[6,7]	Since I'm so mad and have destructive thoughts, I'll use my Crisis Survival Plan and call my sponsor and brother. They both said, "Any time, any day." I need to get a plan for dealing with this loss and getting my life back in order. Tonight, I'm going to chill-out. Tomorrow, I'll work on a plan of action! Recovery is My #1 Priority so I need to make life-enhancing decisions. I'm not going to screw up my life over this. I'm going to use every skill I know... and then some...to be okay! Knew it! Did it! Gotta suck up the consequences! I'll hurt for awhile until I get things re-organized in my life...AND while time passes. I need to stay busy so I'm not thinking TOO MUCH about this. I can get back into the hobbies I gave up for her! I've been itching to go back to school, too! Do NOT get involved with another woman until I work out my issues and why I make bad relationship choices! Just say NO to romance for now! This is too destructive to keep on doing!

13- In a longer story about Drew, we'll find out that he ignored warnings from others about her bad side. He was "blinded by loneliness" and got involved with her anyway! He does note that she had a good side, too...so, she wasn't "trash" or "all bad." In the longer story, he said his picker was broken because he keeps choosing women who hurt him. In truth, he'll keep having major relationship problems until he gains insight into his relationship choices and his role in hurtful relationships.

#5, he noted it was HIS CHOICE.

Emotion-Driven Thoughts **#7, #8**, and **#9** were challenged MANY times. These four thoughts involve Emotion-Driven Coping Behaviors (relapsing into drugs and alcohol, a suicide attempt, and violence). Some were marked as a group ($^{6-9}$) and some by their separate numbers. These statements tell why he doesn't want to act on these impulses. Notice the statement, "Getting aggressive would feel good." Rational Mind isn't going to lie. The truth about revenge feeling good "in-the-moment" was noted... but Rational Mind also brought to mind the negative consequences of revenge.

Emotion-Driven Thought **#10** was challenged by three statements which support the truth that he's NOT stupid. These statements point out that he KNEW getting with her was a FOOLISH Emotional Mind decision driven by loneliness and attraction to her good qualities. He knew better!

Emotion-Driven Thought **#11** was challenged by five statements. He noted life gets hard when he says "Screw it" and makes bad decisions that have bad outcomes. He also noted life is good when he puts in the effort to manage his life.

The Long Version of "Drew Got Dumped"

We've been working with a short version of Drew's Self-Talk dialogue. It was created by deleting parts from the "long" version so it wouldn't be so overwhelming to work with and study! The long version (on the next page) uses DBT-CBT principles in a more advanced manner. Don't panic! You won't be asked to do a worksheet on this one! We're just going to discuss it! Go ahead and read it, then answer the questions below.

That's a pretty intense story! Many people can relate to this story. Fortunately, it's not an everyday experience for most folks, but it describes a state of great anger that many of us have experienced! Have you been like that before...so filled with anger...with aggressive thoughts flying through your mind? If so, what made you so angry? _____

How much Rational Mind did you have going on when you were like that? Were you 90% Emotional Mind and 10% Rational Mind or 80%-20%...70%-30%? _____

When we're Big-Time in Emotional Mind like Drew was, we'll need a BUNCH of Rational Mind going on to TAME Emotional Mind. It's not healthy to stuff our anger, but, IT'S NOT HEALTHY TO LET IT RUN LOOSE either! We need to experience and express our anger, BUT WITH CONTROL. It's normal to have aggressive thoughts. However, IT'S NOT OKAY TO ACT ON THEM!

254

We must use Rational Mind and Wise Mind to get control of our Out-of-Control Emotional Mind!

Wise Mind is more than just coming up with a great plan of action. Wise Mind is also about Following Through with what We Know to do! Wise Mind pressures us TO ACT ON the plan. Think about it, if we come up with the greatest plan, there isn't anything wise about NOT Following Through With It! This might make us feel quite the opposite!

Drew was at the starting gate for Relapse Road. He FINALLY shut the gate and walked away! Now, his life continues along the Recovery Path and gets better n' better!

We can't allow ourselves to ruminate over aggressive thoughts. When they go through our mind …they need to GO THROUGH our mind and onto a passing cloud!

How do we Talk Ourselves Out Of destructive impulses? One Rational Mind - Wise Mind statement after another.

"Drew Got Dumped" – The Long Version

"I can't believe she left me. What trash she is. Screw it, screw her, screw this sobriety thing. It hasn't done me a bit of good. I'm right back where I started. Things never change. Screw everything. I'm going to drink tonight and no one's going to tell me any different. I'll get so plastered, I won't be thinking about her. Maybe I'll down a bunch of pills too, and die. That'll serve her right. How dare she dump me for that dork? He's nothing but a pompous idiot waving his money around. She dumped me for his money. He isn't any better than me. I work hard for my money and that spoiled jerk lives off Daddy. He hasn't worked a hard day in his life. I'm so angry I could knock his teeth down his throat. This is one of those times that was just going to happen. Bad things happen to good people. How many times did I hear that? I knew something was going to happen sooner or later and here I am ready to do something stupid over some trash I'm better off without. I can't believe I fell for her. How could I have been so stupid? 'If someone is cheating on their mate to be with you…what do you think they're going to do when they're with you?' I'm so angry. I don't know who I'm angrier with, her or me. I'm so angry, I'm disgusted. I don't know why I have to hurt like this. I'm so sick n' tired of hurting all the time. What am I going to do? I've gotta get a grip before I lose it. That two-timing trash. Maybe I should pay them a visit and knock the crap out of them, put my fist right down their throats. That would feel good right now! I'd love to see their reaction when I showed up! Right when he opens the door, I'll knock him so hard that the last thing that goes through his mind will be my fist! Oh yeah, that would be great! Real great. My luck, I'd end up in jail and she'll come over here and empty this place out…her stuff and mine. Why is life so hard? Why can't I do what I feel like doing? Why do I have to keep on the Recovery Path? I'm so sick of this recovery thing. This frustrates me to no end. I want to hurt him. I want to hurt her…and I want to get drunk and stay that way. I should bash the windows in his perky little car. That would feel good! The Group lady said strenuous exercise would relieve stress and tension. Swinging a sledgehammer sounds strenuous to me! Ka-bam…Ka-bam…I can hear it now! I can't do that either. I can't do anything I want. That would make so much noise, the cops would show up. And that dork would send HER out to see what was going on and then I'd have to smack her, too. I'm way too mad to face them. Things would get out of control fast. Hey, spray painting his perky little car would be quiet. Just beautifying the neighborhood…a mural on his little car! He would freak out! I'd love to be a fly on his windshield when he saw it. That would be good…but not as good as putting my fist down his throat! That's what I really feel like doing…but what AM I going to do? Everything has bad consequences and that piece of trash isn't worth ruining everything I have going for me. As much as I hate to, I'll call my sponsor. He's #1 on my Crisis Survival List. I've done so well for five months, I would hate to blow it…though I'd LOVE to get even. But going to jail tonight and losing my job tomorrow isn't the way to go. And her cleaning this apartment out while I sit in jail, that would give them the last laugh. If my sponsor's not there, I'll call my brother. He hates her. At least one of us will be happy. I don't know why I pick women like her. I guess my picker is broken."

SKILL BUILDER: How Drew Maintained Self-Control
Notice Drew went BACK AND FORTH between Emotional Mind and Rational Mind.

In the Heat-of-the-Moment, Emotional Mind is like a fire that's hard to put out. As soon as we think we have it under control, we get hit with another burst of flames. We must be prepared for it to flare back up…and ready to hose it down again with Rational Mind!

Emotional Mind fought to have the last word…but Rational Mind stepped up to the challenge!

We can't let these Emotion-Driven Thoughts run loose. We've got to contain them and tame them. We've got to take away their power to deceive us and to get us in trouble.

14- See Figure 10.F.

15- I've recently used these worksheets in my personal life to get myself back on track with writing this workbook, to regain control over eating habits, to make a major life decision, to help a teenager to feel like a valued part of her family, and to help some close friends with serious marital issues. This is the best tool I know of to help us Think Through our problems, to see the truth, to make decisions, and to come up with solutions! This worksheet helps us to FIND PEACE amidst the chaos. I hope they'll bring peace into YOUR life.

He'd Talk Himself Out Of something destructive and then ANOTHER aggressive impulse would pop up. Though it was usually LESS destructive…he didn't go for it! He CONTINUED to Think Through his impulses and to Talk Himself Out Of destructive behavior with the help of Rational Mind. He went back and forth and FOUGHT HIMSELF for 15-20 minutes. He WORKED HARD! Although things got intense, he MAINTAINED CONTROL by being MINDFUL of what Rational Mind was saying to him THROUGHOUT the process. He had to process his emotions and the situation for a while, but he came to a Wise Mind plan to call his sponsor and brother. He KNEW he needed help to Get Through this experience. He ended up going to his brother's house for DISTRACTION, SUPPORT, and RATIONAL MIND INJECTIONS! He did a GREAT JOB of HANDLING what COULD HAVE BEEN a relapse event.

If Drew had acted on his aggressive impulses, what consequences do you think he would have suffered? _____

_____

Being arrested would be very likely! Do you think drinking would have been involved in his aggressive behavior? YES / NO Probably both before and after! Do you think suicidal behavior would've been likely once he was good n' drunk…and maybe messed up on other substances, too? YES / NO Think about ALL the precious things in the Big Picture of His Life that would've been messed up if he did what he felt like doing. Life had really improved for him. It's awesome that he FOUGHT HARD TO STAY ON THE RECOVERY PATH. He had WAY TOO MUCH to lose.

SKILL BUILDER: Drew's Wise Mind Worksheet - Long Version

Review the "long version" of Drew's Wise Mind Worksheet.[14] It's filled with wisdom and healthy attitudes…and it tells "the rest of the story." Pay special attention to how he challenged his Emotion-Driven Thoughts and the Wise Mind plans he came up with. Wise Mind helped him to MAKE A DECISION about how BEST to respond…a decision based on the Big Picture of His Life, his life goals, and what was in HIS best interests.

SKILL BUILDER: Four More Wise Mind Worksheets

Four COMPLETED Wise Mind Worksheets are included in Figures 10.G – 10.J. They address "Having to Start Over," "Have Bipolar - Must Quit Drugs and Alcohol," "Must Stop Smoking," and "Can't Keep a Job." They provide more examples of HOW TO complete a Wise Mind Worksheet AND they show the VARIETY OF PROBLEMS that are helped by this process.[15] Even though they may not cover problems in your life, PLEASE READ THEM! They provide more examples of using Rational Mind to challenge

Figure 10.F.1: Drew Got Dumped – Long Version

The Wise Mind Worksheet: Drew Got Dumped – Long Version

EMOTIONAL MIND		RATIONAL MIND	WISE MIND
RAW EMOTIONS	**EMOTION-DRIVEN THOUGHTS**		
Disbelief - Shock Betrayal - Hurt Anger - Rage	I can't believe she dumped me.	A break-up was going to happen...sooner or later. I knew her history. She doesn't commit to relationships. She slept with me when she was living with someone else! What was I thinking?!!!	I missed the Big Red Flag! I WILL BE MINDFUL next time. I'm determined to make better decisions so I can avoid painful consequences.
Hopelessness Feel like giving up Feeling Willful Reckless - Rebellious Want to Self-Destruct Feeling Suicidal	Why is life so hard to deal with? Why do I have to hurt like this? I'm sick n' tired of hurting.	I knew a time of great distress would come across my path. That's why I have a Crisis Survival Plan. I know bad things happen to good people and things happen that are out of our control. This is hard and I'm hurting. However, I brought this one on myself. I made an Emotional Mind decision to be with her. I knew it and everyone told me, "She's going to hurt you." I'm mad at myself for the hurt and trouble I have caused myself.	Knew it! Did it! Gotta suck up the consequences! I'll hurt for awhile until I get things reorganized in my life AND time passes. I've got to make rational relationship choices. Emotional Mind ones have always ended in pain for me.
Feeling Desperate Preoccupied Confused Overwhelmed Pressured - Pent-Up	Falling for her, how could I have been so stupid? My picker is broken.	I'm not stupid, but getting with her was foolish. My picker really isn't broken. I didn't pay attention to my good judgment. I knew! I knew deep down this wouldn't last! I did it because it felt good at the time...like the famous last words, "It was fun while it lasted!"	It would do me well to ACCEPT THE THINGS I COULD HAVE CHANGED, BUT DIDN'T! I need to accept that I made a choice to be with her and now I have to live through the consequences. I'm going to be sad and lonely for awhile, but this soon shall pass.
Feeling Constrained, like I can't do what I want Frustrated Aggressive Want Revenge	She dumped me for his money.	I knew she wasn't a good pick. To make good relationship choices, I must follow my head, not just my heart! She's selfish and we've been fighting a lot about her not being concerned about MY needs. Really, it's not only about the money, but the money no doubt had something to do with it! If it wasn't him now, it would be someone else later. This has much less to do with me than her relationship patterns. I was hoping "true love" would settle her down.	Make rational relationship choices! Get to know someone...before becoming INVOLVED. Follow my head and not just my heart! We can't change people. When they're ready, they'll take hold of the good stuff in life, but...not until they're ready to get their life in order.
Loss of Self-Respect Feeling Stupid Angry and Disgusted with myself	She's two-timing trash.	She's not really trash...she's just Out-of-Control. If she were trash, I wouldn't have been with her. What she DID IS trashy, though.	IF ALL WE DO IS LIVE A "PARTY LIFESTYLE"... OUR LIFE WILL BE WASTED!

From "Out-of-Control: A Dialectical Behavior Therapy (DBT) - Cognitive-Behavioral Therapy (CBT) Workbook for Getting Control of Our Emotions and Emotion-Driven Behavior" Copyright © 2009 by Melanie Gordon Sheets, Ph.D. (www.dbt-cbt-workbook.com)

Figure 10.F.2: Drew Got Dumped – Long Version

I want to hurt them. Put my fist down their throats. Would LOVE to get even!	I feel like hurting them like I'm hurting. I know I don't have to take revenge. They'll get theirs in the end...and not of my doing. With all his money, she'll soon start the cocaine cycle again. She'll suffer at her own hands and he will too. She'll hurt him. That's just how she operates. I know getting even and taking revenge would be self-defeating. Granted, it would feel good to go off on them and release all this anger and frustration, it carries too high a price for my life. Even fantasizing about revenge is eating up my peace and stability.	Start going to the gym again to work off some of this anger. Work on "Letting It Go" to protect my peace and stability. Turn My Mind from destructive thoughts to life-enhancing ones.
Would feel good!	It wouldn't feel good to relapse. Relapsing into old ways is SO painful. IT IS the Cycle of Suffering. A few hours of relief would lead to months and years of pain and suffering. I'd rather deal with my stuff now, thank you!	Continue to be Mindful of the Cycle of Suffering and the Big Picture of My Life.
Bash windows. Get away with spray painting?	Hurting him or his favorite possession would feel good. However, it would also land me in jail. I'd lose my job, have new legal problems, and she'd have free access to the apartment. I'm not in the mood to lose everything again. I'm far too mad to be in their presence any time soon. I'd probably end up doing something I'd regret!	Avoid contact with them. If she wants to get her stuff out of the apartment, I'll let my brother or sponsor go over there to control what she takes. I'll box her stuff up and put it in one place.
Screw everything. Screw sobriety. It hasn't done me any good. I'm going to drink tonight and no one's going to tell me any different. I'll get so plastered, I won't be thinking about her.	Staying sober and on the Recovery Path has been good to me. Many great things have been happening. I was really angry and hurt when I got her note. I felt like giving up. When big stuff happens, my "Screw it" mentality turns on. I have lived like that. I've always lived like that. Get hurt, self-destruct. When I get like that, I really don't want to die, I just want the pain to go away QUICK! It's always tempting to "get plastered" so I can numb out and not think about or feel the pain I'm going through. However, I know it'll still be there for me to deal with when I come to. I know I'll have even bigger problems to deal with, the least of which will be an awful hangover! It's just the Cycle of Suffering.	I need to keep my mind focused on the Big Picture of My Life and all the good things going on in my life. I need to stay Mindful that I'll lose everything again if I act on my impulses to hurt them, drink, or OD. FOCUS ON MY RECOVERY! LIVE...RECOVERY IS MY #1 PRIORITY! Every action I take must be in line with recovery and maintaining my peace and stability.

Figure 10.F.3: Drew Got Dumped – Long Version

Why do I have to stay on the Recovery Path? I'm sick of it.	I've been successful in recovery for five months now. Recovery is far too important to me to blow it. Many great things are happening that I don't want to mess up and lose. I know I'll end up talking myself out of foolish behavior or I'll call someone who will!	Make use of AA and my support system to get through the tough time. Accept that our relationship is over and it's to my benefit. Focus on getting through this loss and finding someone who can offer me a long-term relationship AND RELATIONSHIP SATISFACTION!
Why can't I do what I feel like?	I can do whatever I feel like doing. I always have two choices - to stay on the Recovery Path or to relapse. It is always MY CHOICE. I'm committed to staying on the Recovery Path. I'll make a MINDFUL decision about how I want to respond to this. I'm perfectly capable of knocking their teeth down their throat if I CHOOSE to go that route! Drinking and overdosing would only make my problems worse...and she'd still be with that dork after they pumped my stomach. I'd lose so much by doing that again! I told myself last time that I'd never act like that again because I'm tired of living in the Cycle of Suffering. I'm done with that. I'm done. I refuse to go backwards. I refuse to do that stuff anymore. I'm smart enough to know that self-defeating behavior is self-defeating! It doesn't take a rocket scientist to figure that out!	Practice Distress Tolerance...and tolerate the pain without doing something destructive...for as long as it takes to get through this tough time. Life will only get better as my recovery time increases and I deal with whatever I have to deal with. Keep busy so I don't spend too much time thinking about her! Get back to the hobbies I gave up for this relationship and go back to school like I've wanted to do! With this relationship over, I'll have time to focus on MY NEEDS AND DESIRES!
Drink, down pills, and die.	Doing what I feel like doing has too many consequences AND she isn't worth it. Nothing is worth it. Recovery IS My #1 Priority. Falling off the Recovery Path will land me back in a hell that would be a whole lot worse than dealing with this pain. This pain will be fairly temporary. Relapsing would lead me back into Long-Term Pain and Suffering. I DON'T WANT TO GO BACK THERE. I don't want to die. I just want the pain to go away. The only thing that will truly take this pain away is time and Wise Mind! Killing or hurting myself would hurt her, but it would also hurt the people who love me and care about me. It's not worth THEIR peace and sanity to do that.	It'll be a hard few weeks, but, time will pass and I'll feel better soon!

259

Figure 10.F.4: Drew Got Dumped – Long Version

That'll serve her right!	She'd only wish bad things for me if I take revenge on them. Truly, I don't think she wants to see me destroy myself! Further, she's not concerned about me now. She's got the excitement of a new relationship, money to blow, and access to long lines of cocaine. She's into her own world now and won't feel guilty if I hurt myself. She'll just say I'm stupid and put me down because of it! I don't have to cause her any pain. She'll get hers! She's going to live a Cycle of Suffering by way of HER OWN DECISIONS, not mine!	Focus on MY Recovery, not her downfall! How she feels is no longer my concern. I don't want her back anyway. This would just happen again. Turn My Mind from focusing on her... to focusing on positive things in my life. Now that's time well spent! Thoughts of revenge and negativity take away my peace and stability.
He's a pompous idiot!	Yep, he's pompous and thinks he's better than everyone. He does wave that money around. Obviously, money doesn't buy happiness because he just bought her! Sorry, that was an Emotional Mind invasion! The point is...I'm a lot better of a person than he is. I have a lot more going for me than a stuffed wallet and a fancy car. He can lose those things, but I'll always have my strength, character, skills, personality, and people to fall back on.	Continue to remind myself of my good qualities and all the positive things in my life.
What am I going to do?	I'm thinking about doing something stupid... over someone who's not worth it. Breaking up is hard for anyone to deal with. All these emotions ARE overwhelming and they took me by surprise. Even though dealing with it productively wasn't my first thought, in the back of my mind, I knew there was a positive way to deal with this and I'd find one. It's perfectly normal to feel overwhelmed, angry, and hurt during times like these. I'll probably need some help dealing with this now and then. I have to get a grip or I'll lose it. It would be too easy to act on Emotional Mind because I'm way too hurt, frustrated, and angry right now. I'm Big Time in Emotional Mind and I could easily relapse into reckless, self-destructive, anger-driven behavior. I'm grateful that I know there are Wise Mind alternatives.	Do not act on Emotion-Driven Thoughts. Get help Turning On Rational Mind when I'm Big-Time in Emotional Mind. Call my sponsor or my brother. They'll give me an emergency dose of Rational Mind! LIVE a Recovery Lifestyle. Follow Wise Mind suggestions and GET A GAME PLAN for setting up a new life since she's out of the picture. I'm going to have to fill my time with other stuff. I need things to do so I don't sit home alone every night and on the weekends. I SEEK RECOVERY... NOT DEPRESSION AND LONELINESS.

From "Out-of-Control: A Dialectical Behavior Therapy (DBT) – Cognitive-Behavioral Therapy (CBT) Workbook for Getting Control of Our Emotions and Emotion-Driven Behavior" Copyright © 2009 by Melanie Gordon Sheets, Ph.D. (www.dbt-cbt-workbook.com)

Figure 10.G.1: Having to Start Over

The Wise Mind Worksheet: Having to Start Over

EMOTIONAL MIND		RATIONAL MIND	WISE MIND
RAW EMOTIONS	EMOTION-DRIVEN THOUGHTS		
Depressed Bummed-out Sickened Disgusted Disappointed Remorseful Ashamed	I'm so tired, I'm not in the mood to do this AGAIN. Why do I have to do this AGAIN? It would be so easy not to care. I'm really not sure I want to go through this. If I stay down, I'll have nothing more to lose.	I AM tired. I AM exhausted. I AM disappointed and disgusted with myself. My feelings are very normal given where I'm at in life and what's going on right now. This is one of those awful times when I'm looking at the debris of the train wreck of my life. I know I have to go on. There's people counting on me...but, I AM tired and exhausted.	LEAN INTO IT! I'll write a Game Plan for Starting Over. I'll start with the priorities and what needs to comes first. I'll get a foundation in place and build my life on that. Housing, food, meds, a job, and saying "NO" to self-destructive coping responses are the basics right now. Hello Salvation Army, the Mental Health Clinic, the Workforce Commission, and AA! Here I come!
Exhausted Fatigued Beaten Defeated Burdened Dreading It	I'm so disgusted with myself. Everyone is disgusted with me. Why do this AGAIN to myself and everyone else? If I just leave their lives, it won't matter.	It's normal at this point to be sitting on the fence and considering all it will take to get started again. It's normal to be struggling with the decision to go on. I obviously know what I have to do...and it's to Start Over. Else I wouldn't be having this discussion with myself...and struggling so much with the decision to go on. I guess I just need to get on with getting on...since it's obviously going to happen. I need to stop fussing with the decision...and work up a plan to get 'er done.	Participate Effectively! I'LL DO WHAT I NEED TO DO DESPITE HOW I FEEL. I'll get up...and PUT UP WITH the rules of the day and I'll find a way around the obstacles in my path. I'll put a smile on my face when I need to. IT'LL TAKE TIME to regain my independence and to feel better...and TO SMILE BECAUSE MY FACE FEELS LIKE IT! I'll have to suck up right now and work with the system. There
Apprehensive Reluctant Uncertain Overwhelmed Paralyzed	I really don't know if I have it in me to start over again. I think my starter is broken and I'm all out of replacement parts. I've lost my drive. I don't know if I can get it back into gear. This Cycle of Suffering has been more like the highway of hell.	I know many people have to start over in life. Starting over IS overwhelming. It takes a lot of energy. The hardest part of starting over IS STARTING. It's a step-by-step process. I know I have to start with the basics and one step at a time.	will be lots of red tape, rules, and inconveniences that I'll have to deal with. I'll re-read the chapters on Distress Tolerance and Acceptance...and Coping Skills!
Alienated Isolated Rejected Alone		It's painful and discouraging to look at the train wreck of my life. I know I have to ACCEPT what's happened and move on down the tracks. Sitting here and staring at the mess and ruminating about it all is destructive and just paralyzes me.	

Figure 10.G.2: Having to Start Over

My family is tired of all my ups and downs, all the drama, and all the problems and heartache I've caused them. I've made so many promises and told so many lies during the downward spiral. They're tired too...and they don't trust what I have to say anymore. Phone calls to them are hard and I feel bad afterwards. I know they love me...they're just worn out and used up from their attempts to help me when I was hell bent on destruction.

It's my choice to give up...or to go on. The pain and suffering of living like I'm living now is much greater than the pain and distress of getting my life in order. I'LL ALWAYS BE DEPRESSED, ASHAMED, AND REMORSEFUL IF I GIVE UP ON LIFE and leave my family and responsibilities. At least, BY STARTING OVER, HOPE AND HAPPINESS ARE IN MY FUTURE. I'D RATHER WORK FOR SOMETHING THAN GIVE UP FOR NOTHING.

I was in this same mood when I started over last time. I'm good at starting over. I CAN DO THIS. My biggest task is maintaining my great start and STAYING ON THE RECOVERY PATH.

I'll Turn My Mind to the steps I'm taking and the gains I'm making day-by-day. EVERY STEP I TAKE IS A TRIUMPH. I'll focus on the good things that are happening and I'll work through...whatever I must work through...to get through this tough time.

I'll make note of the steps I take each day and I'll celebrate each step even if the step wasn't "successful." I AM SUCCESSFUL WHEN I'VE TAKEN ANOTHER STEP! Putting in five job applications puts me five applications closer to a job and peace and stability in my life.

The Group lady stressed the importance of life-enhancing activities and socialization. This is the link I've left off each time. Once I get the basics down, I'll add activities to my weekly schedule. I'll go back to my support group this week. That'll be a good start.

I'll write letters to my family each week to update them on what I'm doing. That'll be easier than phone calls.

Figure 10.H.1: Have Bipolar – Must Quit Drugs and Alcohol

The Wise Mind Worksheet: Have Bipolar – Must Quit Drugs and Alcohol

EMOTIONAL MIND — RAW EMOTIONS	EMOTIONAL MIND — EMOTION-DRIVEN THOUGHTS	RATIONAL MIND	WISE MIND
ANGRY Frustrated Overwhelmed Burdened Tested Sad Upset	I don't want to give up drugs and alcohol. They make me happy and partying is FUN! People that don't party are BORING! A life without partying is boring.	Great relief comes from MAKING a decision to quit using. However, great anxiety also comes because of what I'm getting ready to do... AND ALL THAT'S INVOLVED in being clean and sober. I'll never be emotionally stable until I quit using drugs and alcohol... and stay on my Bipolar meds. I AM TIRED OF THE ROLLERCOASTER. and being in and out of hospitals, rehabs, and jail. If I continue to live FOR MYSELF, I'm going to lose my husband and kids PERMANENTLY. I do understand that this is my last chance.	I'll sign a contract with my husband and the mental health clinic to put me in treatment if I need it...even if I'm screaming and cursing them for doing so. If I get that manic or depressed again, I'll need the help. Really, I'm always glad that I've had treatment once I stabilize. 90 meetings in 90 days! I'll go to AA at least once a day. I'll go to the one on Main Street. They accept folks who take psych meds. I can't be okay without my Bipolar meds.
Feel Pushed and Forced to Quit	I feel forced to quit. It's not my choice. It's not fair that I have to give up something I enjoy so much...just to please others. If they don't like being around me, they can just leave!	I can't be mad at my husband for giving me this ultimatum – the family or drugs. He's been so patient and has stood with me for so long. He and the kids have suffered so much embarrassment and heartache and so many losses because of my lifestyle. I would've dumped me a long time ago. I'm very blessed and fortunate to have them by my side.	I'll go to church with the family. I need God-stuff and I need to be around people living a Recovery Lifestyle.
Relief Fear Anxiety Dread Apprehension Depression Grief and Loss	I'll never make it. I've been doing this too long to be straight. I get too manic and I can't control myself. I'll never have a stable life. I don't know how to be normal or to live a normal life.	Really, other than short periods of mania, I've been depressed for the past 10 years that I've been using drug and alcohol. Those years have been filled with more unhappiness and conflict than I've ever experienced before. I've been miserable...and any pleasure I've had has been short-lived. I'm not a happy drunk. I'm an angry, belligerent, and depressed drunk. I'm not high and happy on cocaine, I'm paranoid and I hear voices. When I'm clean, it's hard to see the appeal for drugs and alcohol. I guess it's the first few highs in the cycle that are good and then things get real bad, real quick. Stability is much better than the emotional rollercoaster life I've been living. I'll miss the good highs but not everything else that goes with them. It's okay to miss things because that's a normal part of life. To be healthy, happy, and to have my family, I'll have to be okay missing the highs. I'd miss my kids and husband and my home and pets a lot more than the highs. It's a matter of how I choose to look at things...and this is how I choose to look at things.	When I start missing the highs, I'll challenge those feelings with Rational Mind. I'll be Mindful of what I really value in life and what I would REALLY MISS by using again! I'll remind myself how awful it would be to be away from my husband and kids. I'll remind myself of the hell associated with getting high, both the substance high and the manic high! I have to fill my day with meaningful activities. I can't have too much down time. I'll get on the same schedule as my family. I'll see if I can work from 9-1 or something like that so I HAVE TO get up with the family.

From "Out-of-Control: A Dialectical Behavior Therapy (DBT) – Cognitive-Behavioral Therapy (CBT) Workbook for Getting Control of Our Emotions and Emotion-Driven Behavior"
Copyright © 2009 by Melanie Gordon Sheets, Ph.D. (www.dbt-cbt-workbook.com)

Figure 10.H.2: Have Bipolar – Must Quit Drugs and Alcohol

Being straight is going to be a major lifestyle change. I've pulled it off for a few weeks after rehabs and hospitals but not over 9 months at a time. I guess if I can make it 9 months, I can make it longer.

I won't be able to go around my family since they'll be using even if I ask them not to. That's going to have to be okay for now. Maybe when I get strong, we'll be able to go over there for short visits. I'll have to discuss this with my counselors when it's time.

My greatest fun has been when partying...fun until trouble starts! I have to be okay with letting that go. I have to let the fun times be a fond memory because I'm no longer able to party without problems. Something always happens...fights, people getting angry with me, threatening to hurt myself, spending too much money... It just doesn't work for me anymore. I'll have to live, "That was then, this is now" and Let It Go. The party lifestyle can't be part of my life anymore.

Parties with straight people are fun...they're just not wild n' crazy fun. I'll have to accept that and go on with life. You know, life isn't all about parties. It's about what goes on between the parties. It's about family and all the things that are important to me. It's about the Big Picture of My Life, not just the one partying piece.

I've been clean for up to 9 months at a time. I usually relapse after I get off my meds, start missing doses, or when something difficult happens. I HAVE lived a normal life during these periods, so I KNOW HOW to live a normal life. To increase my chances of staying off drugs and alcohol, I need to be on my Bipolar meds...so my brain is "normal" and I have a "normal" chance at sobriety. If my brain chemistry is off... my attitude, thinking, and self-control will be off, too. If I start to get manic, I'll have a hard time controlling my impulses because my brain won't be working right. Impulse management is gone with mania!

A part of me is sad to have to give up this part of my life... but another part is really excited to live a normal, stable life... and to do all the "boring" things that normal people do...things like Easter egg hunts, football games, community events, playing with the kids, etc. I AM excited about being a mom and wife again.

I'll allow my husband to manage and keep my meds. I surrender.

If I start wigging out, I'll call my sponsor and the mental health clinic. They're willing to work hard for me IF I'm willing to work hard for my recovery.

Recovery is a lifestyle AND an attitude. My attitude will drive my recovery!

I'll begin practicing productive coping skills NOW so when I need them, they'll already be a part of my life. I'll journal, do daily devotionals, continue the DBT-CBT worksheets, and I'll do Mindfulness stuff. I love the "Put it on a cloud and let it float away" thing. I'll continue to use that! When I miss the fun of partying, I'll put that on a cloud and let it float away!

I'll make Recovery My #1 Priority and a part of every decision I make.

I'll do my symptom and trigger checklists as part of my daily journaling. I won't fuss when my husband does one on me or notices a symptom coming back...like if I'm having trouble sleeping or I'm way too grumpy!

I'll stay in counseling for the first year. Even if there's nothing special to talk about, I'll go. I'll need the stability of a therapy relationship when something big comes up. My therapist is full of Rational Mind that I'll always need!!!!!

Start filling out that Game Plan form now! I'm ready to be a mom and wife again!

From "Out-of-Control: A Dialectical Behavior Therapy (DBT) – Cognitive-Behavioral Therapy (CBT) Workbook for Getting Control of Our Emotions and Emotion-Driven Behavior" Copyright © 2009 by Melanie Gordon Sheets, Ph.D. (www.dbt-cbt-workbook.com)

Figure 10.I.1: Must Stop Smoking

The Wise Mind Worksheet: Must Stop Smoking

EMOTIONAL MIND		RATIONAL MIND	WISE MIND
RAW EMOTIONS	EMOTION-DRIVEN THOUGHTS		
Angry Aggravated PISSED-OFF Frustrated Angry PISSED-OFF Aggravated Totally PISSED-OFF	I don't know how I'll make it. I've never been able to quit for long. I get so irritable and agitated, I always start smoking again.	Sometimes, life isn't all about us. Sometimes, the decisions we make are not about what WE want. There's a bigger picture to our life than just OUR life. I want to see my kids grow up and my kids want their Dad around. This isn't about me and what I want...it's about the kids. It's not about my wife who's griped at me for years to quit...it's about the kids.	I can still be with my friends during lunch since we can't smoke inside or outside the restaurants anymore. I'll can take my own car or go with Fred since he doesn't smoke. I just won't be able to hang out with them at work or after work anymore.
Dread Pent-Up Uptight Tense	I'm going to die if I don't quit...probably within the next few years. I love to smoke. All I do is smoke. What am I going to do instead?	Really, I don't enjoy smoking as much as before because I can hardly breathe...and I cough so much. I've had to go down to light cigarettes and they're really not a very good smoke. I enjoy the first couple drags...but, after that, it's really a drag. My chest tightens and I start coughing. Then, I get really frustrated with the "to smoke or not to smoke" conflict. It's really eating on me and making me miserable. I can hardly enjoy smoking anymore.	Get some low calorie snack foods. Sugarless gum and candy will keep my mouth busy...and sunflower seeds will keep my mouth and hands busy! Toothpicks and straws will help, too!
Worried Concerned Anxious Agitated Overwhelmed	Everyone smokes around me. How will I ever quit? We're always smoking at work.	I've quit for a week before. I CAN do that again if I really try. There's a lot of meds out now that help to take the edge off. I guess if I have to, I can take Valium for a week! It WILL be a very tough first week, but, a week's worth of chemotherapy would be a whole lot worse. Do I want agitation from not smoking...or do I want throwing up and constant nausea from chemo? Hmmm...agitation or nausea...agitation or nausea.	Get stuff for reloading this weekend! Talk with family about how to deal with my moodiness and agitation the first week or two. Ask the Doc about meds, too.
Feel Forced Pushed Feel Defiant and Rebellious	I'll have to give up everything. Everyone smokes everywhere I go.	The smartest choice is to quit on my own rather than waiting until I'm forced to quit because of cancer. That would be a double whammy of distress - having the sickness from chemo on top of the frustration of not being able to smoke! No matter what I do, I'll end up not being able to smoke. It's better to quit now while I have a choice...and BEFORE I get cancer. I'm pre-cancerous right now. Lifestyle changes may prevent this from getting any worse.	Tell my friends what I'm doing and that I can't be around smoking and that I don't want to talk about it! Be Mindful that this tough period is temporary. It'll get better after a few weeks.
A Sense of Loss Sad Depressed Broken Helpless At a Loss Very Upset PISSED	I can't imagine dying and not seeing my kids grow up. I can't imagine my kids having to grow up without me. That would be awful. My luck, I'll quit smoking and die in a few years anyway. It hardly seems worth the effort.	I'm going to be very irritable at first. I'll discuss this with my family and get a Game Plan for dealing with it. They may have to ignore me for awhile! Maybe I can get some reloading equipment and go to the garage and reload when I get too agitated. Can't smoke and reload bullets at the same time! That's interesting to think about because I stopped reloading because I couldn't smoke while doing it! Wonder what other things I have enjoyed that I gave up for smoking.	Have my wife get rid of all the ashtrays, lighters, and cigarettes while I'm at work and use a bunch of air fresheners! We'll need an industrial size bottle of Febreze!

From "Out-of-Control: A Dialectical Behavior Therapy (DBT) - Cognitive-Behavioral Therapy (CBT) Workbook for Getting Control of Our Emotions and Emotion-Driven Behavior" Copyright © 2009 by Melanie Gordon Sheets, Ph.D. (www.dbt-cbt-workbook.com)

Figure 10.I.2: Must Stop Smoking

Why do I have to give this up? It's my only source of enjoyment. Life's not worth living if I can't smoke.

I'll gain 20 pounds if I quit. I can barely fit in my clothes now.

I'm going to be such a jerk if I can't smoke. That's enough to drive my family away. I might as well smoke. They haven't left me yet for smoking!

It's just like giving up alcohol. I'm not going to be able to hang out with my friends. It's a major drag to have to give up ALL my friends. However, it would be a lot worse to have to say good-bye to ALL my kids. That would kill me. I can't tolerate thinking about that. Friends...kids... there's no comparison. Spending more time with my family would be a good thing. I could watch my boy play ball instead of spending half the time in the car smoking!

Even if I end up dying anyway from lung problems, I can do so without the guilt...and my family won't be so angry with me.

They'll know I loved them enough to quit...even if it was a little late. Gaining 5-10 years of life and a better quality of life is much better than the breathing problems I have now.

I've always enjoyed smoking...but it has taken away many joys from me. I can't enjoy a lot of things I do...because I'm always wanting to smoke while doing them...and I can't! If I choose to quit, I'll be able to enjoy going to movies, ball games, band concerts, Six Flags...etc. There's so many things to enjoy...that I've always dreaded because I can't smoke!

It'll be too hard to quit smoking if I'm around people who are smoking. The boss will have to move me to a different job or team. If I can't get to a non-smoking environment, I'll have to find a new job... which may mean a new line of work. I can finally see the benefit of non-smoking workplaces!

My family would prefer me fat than dead. At least I can always lose weight...but resurrection is just not likely for me! I guess the money I save by not smoking I can use to buy new clothes! If I'm not smoking, exercise would be more enjoyable. Imagine keeping up with my wife on a walk and being able to breathe at the same time!

Cancel all upcoming social events that I can smoke at. Guess we do New Years at home or at the pastor's house!

Take baths in the evening and go to bed early. Extra rest will help with the irritability and will give me less time in the evening to wig out over not smoking!

Avoid unpleasant tasks during the first week or two. Live a pleasure principle (minus smoking) for awhile. I bet I can get away with watching 24-7 sports for awhile. I'll use this to my advantage as long as I can!!!!!

Be busy. Plan special things. There's a gun and boat show next weekend! Get back into reloading. Buy some new computer games. Once I get done with the stop smoking meds, we'll have extra money. A good reward will be to use the cigarette money for my hobby stuff!

Talk with the boss about a non-smoking work environment.

Figure 10.J.1: Can't Keep a Job

The Wise Mind Worksheet: Can't Keep a Job

EMOTIONAL MIND			WISE MIND
RAW EMOTIONS	EMOTION-DRIVEN THOUGHTS	RATIONAL MIND	
Frustration Anger	I can't keep a job. Something always happens and I blow up or screw up.	Truth, I have trouble keeping jobs. I usually get mad and go off on someone. My mouth goes off and then I'm off permanently! I really don't like it when people watch over me and nit-pick my work. It reminds me of my father. No matter what I did, he would find fault. Even when I brought home an A-B report card, he yelled at me because a grade went down or something. He didn't comment on the ones that went up and it didn't please him that they were all A's and B's.	My father wasn't going to be pleased by anything I did or accomplished. HE'S DEAD NOW, and I have to QUIT TRYING TO RAISE THE DEAD to change him. My supervisors and bosses are NOT my father.
Hopelessness Helplessness Worthlessness	What's wrong with me? I'm not a man. I'm not responsible.		They're just checking to see that the job is being done right. I'm the new man and they don't know my skills and they don't trust my work yet.
Guilt Remorse Shame	I'm worthless. I'll never measure up.	It bothers most people to have someone stand behind them and watch what they're doing. People deal with it and I can, too. I'll just have to accept it, shut up, allow it to happen, answer their questions politely, and Put It on a Cloud and Let It Float Away!	I have to SUCK UP and GET THROUGH the "checking time" until they learn to trust my work and know I KNOW what I'm doing. I'll talk myself through the stand-overs. I'll remind myself that I'm okay and that being checked on and watched over is normal for a new employee. It's their business and they have a right to make sure the job is done right!
Pressured Conflicted Tension Worried Anxious Upset Concerned Bewilderment Confusion	I've become what my father said, "You're useless." "You'll never amount to anything." "You'll never be a man." I can't control my temper.	Now that I'm not drinking, I'll be rested when I go to work. I'll feel better and I'll be in better control of my emotions. That will help me not go off or say something that'll get me in trouble. I'm on meds now that help me feel better. I'm less moody and irritable. I have better self-control, too. I'll be better able to "SUCK UP." The boss has a right to watch me to see if I'm doing the job right. That's his job. I need to expect this and not get so upset. It's normal to get anxious and to make mistakes when the boss is watching. I'll let him know it makes me nervous. I'll normalize it because it's normal!	I have to shut my mouth, allow it to happen, answer their questions politely, and Put It on a Cloud and Let It Float Away!
Disappointment Depression Loss	Everyone makes me angry. I can't stand to be told what to do. I can't stand people standing over me while I work...nit-picking everything I do.	It's normal for a new employee to be corrected on something. I'm used to welding my way, the way I've always done it. The boss may have his own way and as a paid employee, I'm required to do it HIS way! I have to stop being so willful and hard-headed. I need to be more flexible. I'll be Mindful that I'm being paid to do things his way!	Throughout the day, I'll remind myself that I'm being paid to do things the way the boss wants them done. I'll remind myself that if his way is slower or less efficient than mine, than it's just costing him more. I still work 8 hours a day and get paid just the same!
Defective Useless Irresponsible Can't measure up Screwed up	It's not worth trying to get a good job. I'll never keep it. What's wrong with me? Why am I so defective?	I'll probably be underpaid at first and that will have to be okay. A paycheck is better than no paycheck. I have to start somewhere. There are consequences for walking off jobs all the time! I won't get the best jobs until I improve my work history!!!!	

From "Out-of-Control: A Dialectical Behavior Therapy (DBT) - Cognitive-Behavioral Therapy (CBT) Workbook for Getting Control of Our Emotions and Emotion-Driven Behavior" Copyright © 2009 by Melanie Gordon Sheets, Ph.D. (www.dbt-cbt-workbook.com)

Figure 10.J.2: Can't Keep a Job

Because I have a bad work history, I'll have to get whatever job I can get right now. Once my job history improves, I can get a better job. Employers get a million applications for a job and they toss out people who have bad work histories. My longest job has been six months and that was 10 years ago! I need to stay on one job for AT LEAST a year or two. If I do well on this job, I can get a promotion. That may be my best bet. That means I'll have to suck up and deal with jerk co-workers and bosses...they're on every job! I must do that to keep a job. Most everyone has had to SUCK UP and SHUT UP every now and then. Life's not fair and perfect - there's a jerk at every jobsite who thinks they know more than everyone else.

My dad was often wrong about people. He was overly critical. He always had something ugly to say about people. He was abusive. The things he said about me were lies just like the things he said about everyone else. He felt bad about himself and downed other people to feel better about himself. What he said has affected me BIG-TIME over the years. My self-esteem has been so low. I used to think he was right, now I know better.

I know I have trouble with authority because of my anger towards my father. I must continue to be Mindful and remind myself that my bosses are not my father and just because I'm being corrected does not mean I'm being scolded or criticized by someone hateful. It's probably not that I'm doing the job wrong, it's that I'm doing it different from how they do things. Everyone has their preferences. Five people could do the same job and do it well in five different ways. I'm being paid to do it the way my boss feels comfortable. I need to remove my ego from the job and be their servant and do it the way they want me to do it!

This isn't JUST A JOB, it's my future. My goal over the next five years is to build a decent work history.

I'll say "Yes, Sir," "No, Sir," "Yes, Ma'am," and "No, Ma'am." I'll do what I'm told and how I'm told to do it. I'll remember they're paying me to do what they want me to do. I'm their servant when I'm on the clock.

If the boss is rude, I'll suck up. I'm getting paid to suck up. Usually when a boss is rude, they're rude to many people. I have to remember it's not personal and it's not about me. It's the boss' stuff...their stupid emotional stuff. I'll let it roll off me, like water off a duck's back!

SUCK UP - Put up with difficult work situations because this isn't about a job. It's about improving my work history so I can get a better job down the road! I need time on the job...even if it's a year or two!!! I'll be Mindful that I'm using them, too!

It's better to SUCK UP than MUCK UP!

Stay on my meds! Stay sober!

REMOVE MY EGO FROM THE JOB!!!

Don't take things personally.
Get time on the job and get paid!
This is for a great purpose... my future!

Emotion-Driven Thoughts...and LOTS OF WISDOM and healthy ways of looking at life. While reviewing them, highlight things that would be helpful to apply to your life.

Concluding Remarks on Wise Mind Worksheets

Our emotions are part of us, but they don't have to define who we are as a person or what type of life we'll live.

By further studying humanity, we'll gain greater insight into our own normalcy!

The more we live, eat, and breathe Rational Mind and Wise Mind, the easier it'll be to think rationally and wisely...and the sooner it'll become a way of thinking... and a WAY OF LIFE.

"When I'm talking with my friend, I can tell her all this stuff, but when it comes to dealing with my own stuff, I'm horrible."

When we're challenging our Emotion-Driven Thoughts, we can create some emotional distance by asking ourselves "If my child, parent, or friend said this to me, what would I tell them?"

16- Make some copies of this worksheet for personal use. The form is also simple enough that you can draw it on paper as needed.

The short version of Drew's worksheet is something most of us would do. Some people MIGHT do a longer version after they've had time to process the situation... when they're less emotional and better able to think straight...and when the Heat-of-the-Moment has COOLED DOWN! The long version is something a more advanced student of DBT-CBT would do...and someone who is super organized! In reality, very few people would do such a long one...so, expect yours to be much shorter! Remember, the detailed, sample worksheets are included in this workbook because they provide lots of examples of the DBT-CBT process.

Hopefully, how to do a Wise Mind Worksheet is pretty clear...and hopefully, it's getting easier to challenge Emotion-Driven Thoughts. Truth, WE ALL KNOW this Rational Mind - Wise Mind stuff, we just DON'T THINK so rationally or wisely when we're dealing with OUR ISSUES in the Heat-of-the-Moment. Think how great we are with Rational Mind when we're counseling and advising friends and family!

Why do you think we do such a better job of dealing with other people's problems than our own problems? _____

_____

_____

It's much easier to Turn On Rational Mind when we're not caught up in Emotional Mind and the Heat-of-the-Moment. When we're talking a friend through an emotional state, we have some EMOTIONAL DISTANCE and much less emotional INTENSITY than when it's OUR ISSUE we're dealing with! When it's OUR STUFF, it's MUCH different!

Completing a Wise Mind Worksheet is a COPING TOOL. We're helped by writing out our thoughts and feelings. Also, when we look at our Emotion-Driven Thoughts ONE-BY-ONE, we're better able to STEP BACK, TURN ON RATIONAL MIND, and to go into THERAPY MODE!

SKILL BUILDER: Completing Your Own Wise Mind Worksheet

We've reviewed a bunch of completed Wise Mind Worksheets and now it's your turn to practice this skill! Use the blank Wise Mind Worksheet (Figure 10.K).[16] Choose an important situation that has been troubling you and follow the directions below. See what you can come up with. Maybe you'll come up with a way to DEAL WITH your

Figure 10.K: The Wise Mind Worksheet

My Wise Mind Worksheet for:

EMOTIONAL MIND		RATIONAL MIND	WISE MIND
RAW EMOTIONS	EMOTION-DRIVEN THOUGHTS		

problem and to find some much desired peace!

Instructions for Completing Your Wise Mind Worksheet

Step 1. **Write a title** for your worksheet in the top row. Complete the sentence... "My Wise Mind Worksheet for..."

Step 2. In the **Raw Emotions section**, list the feelings you have when you think about this situation. List 10 or more, preferably more![17]

Step 3. In the **Emotion-Driven Thoughts column**, list 8 or more Emotion-Driven Thoughts that come to mind when you think about this situation.

Step 4. In the **Rational Mind column**, write statements to challenge your Emotion-Driven Thoughts. Challenge them based on truth and how things REALLY are, NOT your Emotional Mind perceptions! ALSO, add statements that reflect rational understandings, facts, and truth about life in general, the Big Picture of Your Life, the Big Picture of the Situation, and the logical consequences of certain actions. Be sure to mention truths about your situation that should be considered by Wise Mind when trying to make a decision about the BEST plan of action.

Step 5. In the **Wise Mind section**, list WISE UNDERSTANDINGS and PROBLEM-SOLVING IDEAS that COME TO YOU as you're completing the worksheet. Wise Mind considers everything going on in Emotional Mind AND what Rational Mind has to say about the Big Picture of the Situation. Wise Mind is concerned about our best interests and our peace and stability...both in the here-and-now AND the future.

Step 6. If you're having trouble completing your worksheet, review the completed ones for ideas. You can also review your worksheet with a support person. They can use what you've written to help you complete it. We can get stuck on a detail or two and a little feedback can bring us to an Ah-ha moment! We can get unstuck...and see things clearly or at a different level. That's how we grow! This worksheet is a critical DBT-CBT skill. Get help if you need it! After you complete one, let a support person review it...maybe their Wise Mind will Turn On and they'll have some extra suggestions for you!

17- If needed, refer to "The List of Negative Emotions" on page 26 for words to describe your feelings.

Wise ideas will come to us as we're working with Emotional Mind and Rational Mind at the same time.

The suggestions Wise Mind makes... may NOT be about what will make us the most comfortable TODAY...because Wise Mind is more concerned about our TOMORROWS.

APPLICATION: Should I Follow My Head or My Heart?

Do you think that in some situations, it's appropriate to totally DISCONNECT FROM EMOTIONAL MIND and DO WHAT IS ENTIRELY RATIONAL? Do you think it's ever appropriate TO IGNORE OUR EMOTIONS and make a decision BASED ON LOGIC

ALONE? YES / NO If so, what type of situations would call for such a decision? __

_____

_____

In some situations, we may need to ignore our emotions and deal with life in an entirely logical and rational manner.
Our Recovery Goal is to act in our best interests…not only in regard to the current situation… but with respect for the Big Picture of Our Life.

> *Consider a severely abusive relationship and all attempts to change the relationship have failed. IT DOESN'T MATTER HOW MUCH WE LOVE this person or HOW DIFFICULT IT WILL BE TO LEAVE, we MUST LEAVE…NO MATTER WHAT OUR HEART TELLS US. Consider when someone's life is in danger. For instance, if a woman is 7-months pregnant and spends more than 30 minutes out of bed per day, she'll lose the baby. In this situation, IT DOESN'T MATTER how much she wants to get out of bed or whose big event she might miss, SHE SHOULD BE ENTIRELY RATIONAL, DENY HERSELF, and STAY IN THE BED! Consider someone who's trying to stay sober and is strongly craving alcohol. Should this person FOLLOW THEIR HEAD OR THEIR HEART…their Rational Mind or Emotional Mind?*

In these situations, do we do what we want to do…or do we do what's needed…no matter what? I just gave my opinion. What do you think? _____

_____

_____

APPLICATION: When Our Emotions "Have Done Gone Crazy"

Sometimes, we're hit by an overwhelming amount of emotion. The INTENSITY of our emotions and the VARIETY of emotions we experience is often caused by "Carry-Over Emotions." These are emotions that are LEFT OVER from UNRESOLVED things. Consider times of major relationship conflict. We experience many upsetting emotions because of THIS CRISIS…but, the intensity and variety of our emotions is also due to OUR HISTORY of relationship hurts and losses. For instance, our rage and mistrust is not due to the CURRENT relationship and problem ONLY, but also SIMILAR EVENTS FROM THE PAST (abandonment, rejection, abuse, affairs by our mate, break-ups, etc.). At times like these, Rational Mind would remind us that the person we're upset with IS NOT EVERYONE who has ever hurt us…and this situation IS NOT EVERYTHING BAD that has ever happened to us. Wise Mind would suggest we FOCUS ON THE HERE-AND-NOW situation and Mindfully deal with THIS ONE SITUATION in an appropriate and reasonable manner.

It's important to be Mindful that our response to a current situation may be overly intense or even inappropriate because of Carry-Over Emotions.

APPLICATION: There's an Order to Things

Consider this scenario. We're really angry or upset about something. We're BIG-TIME IN EMOTIONAL MIND and we call a trusted person. We unload our feelings on them and tell them all about the situation. They're a good listener and we talk non-stop for ten minutes. How might they respond to us at this point? _____

_____

Quite often, they begin to offer advice and tell us WHAT WE NEED TO DO.

Do we quickly and easily accept their advice? YES / NO How do we typically respond?

_____

_____

Usually, WE REPEAT PARTS OF WHAT WE JUST TOLD THEM! We remind them of how we're feeling and what we're thinking about ourselves and the situation. We tell them ALL OVER AGAIN about our Raw Emotions and Emotion-Driven Thoughts. We AGAIN dump the contents of our Emotional Mind on them.

What do they typically do now? _____

_____

THEY REPEAT THEIR ADVICE and OFFER MORE! They may change it up a little, but basically, they tell us the same things ALL OVER AGAIN! Do we accept their advice this time? NOOOO! We repeat ourselves and tell parts of the story ALL OVER AGAIN. It's like they HAVEN'T HEARD what we've been telling them. It's like, "Hello, DON'T YOU HEAR what I'm saying? DON'T YOU GET IT? CAN YOU HEAR ME NOW?"

We keep REPEATING ourselves because we want them to UNDERSTAND what we're going through. We THINK they don't understand because THEIR ADVICE MAKES NO SENSE. It seems SOOOO unreasonable and out of place. We feel they MUST BE MISSING the Big Picture of what we're telling them! They finally get mad and say something like, "If you're not going to listen, I can't help you. You're going to have to figure this out on your own." We may get in a fight with them and end up more hurt...more angry...and feeling even more uncared for and misunderstood. What do you think is going on? Why is there this break-down in communication? They're great listeners. They're trying to help...but they don't seem to get what we're telling them. It's like they're from another planet and their advice doesn't relate to our world. Have you had an experience like this with a support person? What was it like for you? How did you feel as a result? _____

_____

_____

_____

Why do you think their help wasn't helping? Why did the conversation go so bad? __

_____

_____

_____

THE REASON THIS CONVERSATION GOES SO BAD has to do with the three Mind States. When we spoke to them, we were Big-Time in Emotional Mind. They listened and gathered information. They Mindfully thought about our situation based on what they know ABOUT US, what they JUST HEARD US SAY about the situation, and what they ALREADY KNEW about the situation from previous discussions. They put it all together and came back at us with Wise Mind solutions.

Why weren't their Wise Mind solutions ACCEPTABLE to us? _____

_____

> THE REASON IS...THERE'S AN ORDER TO THINGS! We were Big-Time in Emotional Mind and they were trying to tell us Wise Mind stuff. WE WEREN'T THERE YET! We were still in Emotional Mind. We were irrational and so upset we could hardly think straight. We were 90-95% Emotional Mind! WE MUST BE ABLE TO THINK RATIONALLY BEFORE ANYTHING WISE MIND MAKES SENSE!

So, what needs to happen here? _____

_____

> Our support person needs to give us a BIG INJECTION of Rational Mind BEFORE they offer Wise Mind advice! They need to HELP US TURN ON RATIONAL MIND. They need to TALK US THROUGH Emotional Mind stuff and acknowledge the normalcy of our feelings and Emotion-Driven Thoughts. Then, they need to help us look at our situation logically and rationally by reminding us of facts and truth. They need to do the EMOTIONAL MIND - RATIONAL MIND thing with us BEFORE JUMPING THE GUN and SHOOTING WISE MIND BULLETS OUR WAY.

It's what Drew did. He VENTED his emotions and Emotion-Driven Thoughts. He REMINDED HIMSELF OF TRUTH (she sleeps around, is selfish and hurtful, he knew it would be short-lived, etc). He DEALT WITH HIS EMOTION-DRIVEN IMPULSES by considering logical consequences. He CHALLENGED NEGATIVE THOUGHTS by reminding himself of truths about his recovery and the good things going on in his life. He went BACK AND FORTH between Emotional Mind and Rational Mind for 15-20 minutes before he reached Wise Mind. Drew HAD TO TURN ON RATIONAL MIND

When we're Big-Time in Emotional Mind and we can't think straight even the wisest suggestions will seem meaningless and ridiculous. That's because we aren't there yet! Rational Mind must be Turned On so we're in a frame of mind to accept and Follow Through with Wise Mind suggestions.

We need to ask our people to learn about DBT-CBT so when we call them in an emotional crisis…they'll know what we need most is a MEGA-DOSE of RATIONAL MIND! We need to teach them how to help us …so their help helps!

to deal with Emotional Mind. ONCE HE DID THAT, WISE MIND TURNED ON!

We NEED THE SAME THING from our support people. THEY'RE RIGHT. THEY CAN'T HELP US. That's because WE'RE NOT READY TO RECEIVE the help they're offering! THEY'RE TRYING TO HELP US IN WAYS THAT DON'T HELP! Their help isn't helping. They don't know how to help us through an Emotional Mind crisis. They're trying to reason with the unreasonable. We both end up angry and frustrated.

APPLICATION: The Good Counselor

Like a good support person, a Good Counselor will ALLOW US TO VENT our Emotional Mind WITHOUT judgment. THEN, he'll hit us with a BIG DOSE of Rational Mind. When we say, "I can't deal with this." or "I'll never get over this."... he'll remind us of times we felt like this before...and we WERE ABLE to deal with it... and we GOT THROUGH IT and PAST IT. When we say, "I can't do it." or "Things never work out for me."...he'll remind us of the times when we stuck to a plan and things WORKED OUT. He'll remind us of our accomplishments and strengths, too. When we say, "I wish I was dead." or "There's no meaning in life. I should just kill myself." or "I'll never feel better."...he'll remind us of the times we felt like this...but when we got back on meds and had time to think rationally...we felt better, became hopeful, and got back in touch with the meaningful things in our life...and WE WERE GLAD OUR SUICIDE ATTEMPT FAILED. When we say, "I KNOW, BUT THIS TIME IS DIFFERENT."...he'll remind us we said that the last time we felt overwhelmed and depressed...but THINGS CHANGED and later, WE WERE GLAD TO BE ALIVE. He'll remind us of TRUTH, FACTS, and how things are for us IN REALITY.

Just like Rational Mind, the Good Counselor WON'T LIE TO US. When we say, "I'm such a screw-up. I screw everything up."...he'll be truthful. He won't sugar coat things just so we feel better IN THE MOMENT. He's concerned about our psychological GROWTH and he wants us to have insight and rational understanding. He'll tell us we've made mistakes before and screwed SOME things up...BUT, HE'LL REMIND US WE'RE HUMAN AND EVERYONE MAKES MISTAKES.

> If we've just screwed up in a BIG way, the Good Counselor will tell us that this is our "15 minutes in the spotlight"...the time when fingers are pointing AT US and we're the talk of the town. However, he'll remind us that EVERYONE has had 15 minutes in the spotlight...MANY TIMES OVER...and this is just OUR TURN now! He'll remind us that RIGHT NOW, our FOCUS needs to be on DAMAGE CONTROL, SUCKING UP THE CONSEQUENCES, and GETTING BACK ON THE RECOVERY PATH.

The Good Counselor will TALK US THROUGH Emotional Mind stuff by giving us a BIG INJECTION of Rational Mind. THEN, he'll work WITH US in Wise Mind to come up with a PLAN OF ACTION to address our problems. He'll HELP us develop a Game Plan...but, HE WON'T DO IT FOR US. He'll guide us and support us in our efforts, but he'll require WE MAKE the phone calls to find out what resources are available and what times meetings meet, etc. He'll ENCOURAGE US to do what WE NEED TO DO to Follow Through with the plan. He'll PRAISE US for the steps we take and he'll HELP us to come up with ideas to GET AROUND REAL OBSTACLES in our path and to GET PAST THE EXCUSES we give for not being able to do something. A Good Counselor COUNSELS and SUPPORTS us. He DOES NOT DO THE WORK FOR US! He may DO something now and then, but his goal is TO EMPOWER US to do what WE NEED TO DO!

Think about the support people and counselors who have been most helpful to you. How did they help you? What do you think THEY DID that helped you? _____

_____

_____

_____

What a Good Counselor does for us is exactly what we need to learn to do for ourselves. We need to implant a "MINI-ME" or a "mini counselor" in our mind...and we need to TURN IT ON when we're Big-Time in Emotional Mind!

> In the Heat-of-the-Moment, we won't always have immediate access to our counselor or support person. Therefore, we must REMEMBER THE WORDS AND WAYS of our counselors so we can TALK OURSELVES THROUGH the moment. We CAN LEARN this life stuff and WE CAN LIVE IT. We have to be WILLING TO DO IT though! We have to be DEDICATED to Follow Through with what we KNOW is in our best interests. This is exactly what this DBT-CBT program is all about. You're learning many truths about life and many ways to GET and MAINTAIN peace and stability. GO FOR IT! USE WHAT YOU KNOW, KEEP LEARNING, and GET BETTER N' BETTER ALL THE TIME! LIVE 'N LEARN!

APPLICATION: Listen to the Voice of Wisdom

When you've done things that had a very bad outcome, did words of warning or wisdom go through your mind? Did you ever hear or say things like "Don't do it." or "Say "No." or "Walk away." or "I have a bad feeling about this."? If so, describe. _____

_____

_____

_____

Do you usually follow that guidance or ignore it? _____

The Voice of Wisdom

I had an experience when my daughter was turning a year old, one I think parents go through that end up physically abusing their child. This seems horrid, but WE ARE human. Our primitive and destructive emotions do flare. Long story short. I went on a STRESSFUL trip to visit family. The TWO-PARENT LIFE turned into a ONE-PARENT NIGHTMARE. My husband couldn't go and it was JUST ME, 24-7, with a baby who DIDN'T SLEEP MUCH by her nature. There's MANY DEMANDS and LOTS OF COMMOTION when a "once every five years" family visit occurs. Everyone wants to see you, lots of running around, and lots of activity. I'M TIRED because of it all AND the BABY DOESN'T SLEEP MUCH. My Grandma is on her way to pick us up for lunch and then we'll meet my mom for studio pictures... four generations!!! The baby IS CRANKY because she's been out of her routine and environment TOO LONG. THE NEW HAD WORN OFF.

Of course, IT TAKES FOREVER to get dressed when away from home because we're OUT OF ROUTINE and stuff is not organized or handy. I'm staying UPSTAIRS and THE BATHROOM IS DOWNSTAIRS. UP and DOWN the stairs I GO AND GO getting stuff ready for baby and me. I FINALLY get the baby ALL DOLLED UP in a fancy dress and stockings for Grandma and pictures. I was FINALLY dressed, too.

I thought the baby might be CRANKY due to teething, at least I hoped that was it! MINUTES BEFORE Grandma is to arrive, I sat her on my lap to give her some Tylenol. Okay, I bet some of you are cackling...knowing what's getting ready to happen. It's funny now, but it wasn't then! I CAREFULLY got a teaspoon of cherry liquid in her mouth...and she proceeds to SPEW IT ALL OVER. Tylenol went EVERYWHERE...all over ME, HER, my glasses, my hair, my clothes, and her clothes including the FANCY dress and WHITE stockings.

AN INTENSE MOMENT OF RAGE FLARED. It happened so fast. With one hand, I grabbed her clothing in the chest area and TIGHTENED MY GRIP. Who knows what I was getting ready to do. Thank God a statement went through my mind, "JUST GET THE BABY AWAY FROM YOU."...and my own words followed, "This is how children get hurt." I was Mindful at that moment that I was getting ready to hurt her. Given I already had a MIGHTY GRIP, I lifted her off my lap with that one hand clutching her clothing and set her down on her back on the floor...with only a MINIMAL THUD. I went BACK UPSTAIRS to change my clothes and then BACK DOWNSTAIRS to rinse my glasses and the sticky splotches off my hair. Grandma got there. I CALMLY put the baby in normal clothes and told Grandma we'd have to buy a dress while we were out... because the child JUST BLEW TYLENOL ALL OVER HER FANCY OUTFIT!!!!

I never traveled alone with an infant again. I warn everyone...you take young ones out of their element and routine, YOU'LL HAVE A CRANKY LITTLE MONSTER WHO'LL SPEW STICKY RED STUFF EVERYWHERE! Live n' learn!

When have you heard the Voice of Wisdom? What did you hear? Did you follow it?

If you didn't follow it, do you wish you would have? Explain. _____

_____

_____

_____

_____

_____

I wish we'd known this stuff as kids. How our lives would be different…if we knew then what we're learning NOW.

Most every day, we have FLASHES OF WISDOM. These occur during everyday life events AND crisis situations. We hear, say, or think these words of warning. EVEN WHEN WE THINK WE AREN'T THINKING, WE OFTEN ARE. The truth, wisdom lives deep WITHIN US ALL. We all have FLASHES OF WISDOM. We all have a pretty good idea about what's helpful for our life and what's destructive…about what's dangerous and what's pretty safe…and what's a good idea and what's a bad one. WE ALL KNOW. WE JUST DON'T LISTEN OR FOLLOW OUR GOOD JUDGMENT. BE MINDFUL OF THAT SPLIT-SECOND WISDOM…AND **HEED WARNING.**

~~~~~~~~ CHAPTER REVIEW ~~~~~~~~

1. How does a Wise Mind Worksheet help us? _____

_____

_____

2. Sometimes it's hard to tell if a statement is a Rational Mind statement or a Wise Mind one. What questions can you ask yourself to help decide? _____

_____

_____

3. What should you do if you still can't decide? _____

_____

4. Wise Mind is NOT just concerned about coming up with a good plan of action. What else is it concerned about? What does it pressure us to do? _____

_____

5. Drew took about 20 minutes to Talk Himself Through a raging Emotional Mind. He went back and forth between Emotional Mind and Rational Mind. How did he maintain control? _____

_____

_____

6. How do we Talk Ourselves Out Of destructive impulses? One _____ _____ - _____ _____ statement _____ _____.

7. Why should you review ALL the completed Wise Mind Worksheets even if they don't apply directly to you? _____

_____

8. Why is it MUCH easier to Turn On Rational Mind and Wise Mind when counseling a friend than when counseling ourselves? _____

_____

_____

9. What five problems and issues in your life could be helped the most through the completion of a Wise Mind Worksheet? _____

_____

_____

10. When does Wise Mind Turn On? _____

_____

_____

11. Should we follow our head or our heart? Discuss with examples from YOUR life.

_____

_____

_____

_____

_____

_____

12. If our current problem is becoming worse due to Carry-Over emotions, what would Rational Mind and Wise Mind say to us? _____

_____

_____

13.   When we're Big-Time in Emotional Mind, why do we often have trouble accepting Wise Mind suggestions? _____

_____

_____

14. Why should we teach our people DBT-CBT? _____

_____

_____

15. What are some things a "Good Counselor" will do? _____

_____

_____

_____

16. What's the purpose of a "Mini Me" counselor? _____

_____

_____

FOR REFLECTION:
Take a few moments to reflect on this chapter. Some questions are listed in the margin to guide your reflection.
Feel free to reflect on whatever your heart brings to mind.

What are your reactions to the material?

Which parts hit home or relate to you the most?

Which parts have helped you the most?

Which parts have helped you to understand yourself the most?

How will you use this information to feel better about yourself?

How will you use this information to improve the quality of your life...or to change how things work out for you in life?

What will you do differently based on this material?

How has this information changed the way you feel about your patterns of relapse and recovery... and your overall response to life?

What does this material motivate you to do?

17. What is the Voice of Wisdom and who hears it? _____

_____

_____

~~~ For Reflection ~~~

_____

_____

_____

_____

_____

_____

_____

_____

_____

_____

_____

_____

_____

_____

_____

_____

_____

_____

_____

_____

_____

_____

_____

_____

_____

Figure 10.L: The Concepts and Skills Tracking Sheet – Chapter 10

Week # _____										
Day of Week →										
Date →										

10A. I'm able to list my Raw Emotions and Emotion-Driven Thoughts on a Wise Mind Worksheet.

10B. I can do a pretty good job of challenging my Emotion-Driven Thoughts by looking at the truth about myself, my life, other people, and the situation.

10C. I can do a pretty good job of coming up with Wise Mind suggestions for dealing with my problems and concerns.

10D. Today, I did a Wise Mind Worksheet to help myself Think Through a problem. This helped me.

10E. Today, I was talking about my problems with a support person. I realized some of their comments were from Rational Mind and Wise Mind.

10F. Today, when I was upset , I had trouble getting to Rational Mind. I got some emotional distance by considering what I would say to someone who was having the same problem.

10G. Today, I told a support person about the three mind states and how to help me get to Rational Mind when I'm upset.

10H. Today, when I was upset, I had trouble getting to Rational Mind. I asked a support person to help me TURN ON Rational Mind.

10I. Today, I had a situation come up...and I was Mindful that I needed to follow my head and not my heart.

10J. Today, I became Mindful that I was experiencing Carry-Over Emotions. I worked to focus myself on the here-and-now situation.

10K. Today, I "heard" the Voice of Wisdom. I wisely considered my situation based on the words of warning!

RATING SCALE
5 – Did Excellent in this area today
4 – Did Pretty Good in this area today
3 – Did Alright in this area today
2 – Did Only Fair in this area today
1 – Didn't Do Well in this area today
DD – Didn't Do today

REST STOP #2

Road Map: Where We've Been...What Ground We've Covered

We've covered a bit of territory since our last Rest Stop. During this part of our journey, we addressed "How Do I Get Control of My Life?" We completed a detailed exploration of the three mind states and learned HOW TO GAIN CONTROL of an OUT-OF-CONTROL Emotional Mind. We learned we can do this by using Rational Mind and Wise Mind to THINK THROUGH BEFORE WE DO and to deal with our emotional issues and concerns in a rational and wise manner.

In Chapter 6, "Emotional Mind," the two parts of Emotional Mind were discussed in detail. We gained more information about our Raw Emotions and Emotion-Driven Thoughts. We also discussed several common Emotional Mind experiences which are fueled by intense emotions and irrational thoughts. Some of these included LOVE AT FIRST SIGHT, CRASH N' BURN DIETING, PANIC ATTACKS, and ENABLING. We also reviewed some positive aspects of Emotional Mind. In addition, we gained insight into HOW WE COME TO BELIEVE the abusive and hurtful statements people say about us. We determined that these statements are EMOTION-DRIVEN LIES which say more about the speaker than us. We also discussed ways to control painful RUMINATION and ways to REQUEST TIME-OUT...so we can COOL OFF IN THE HEAT-OF-THE-MOMENT and gain control over our Emotional Mind.

In Chapter 7, "Rational Mind," we focused on how to use Rational Mind to deal with an upset Emotional Mind. Many common Emotion-Driven Thoughts were challenged, like "CUTTING ALWAYS HELPS.", "I CAN'T STAND TO BE ALONE.", "JUST ONE DRINK DOESN'T MATTER.", "I'M SO FAT, NO ONE WOULD WANT ME.", and "KILLING MYSELF WOULD MAKE LIFE EASIER FOR MY FAMILY." Focus was also given to the LIES we tell ourselves about SUCCESS and FAILURE and the irrational nature of ALL-OR-NONE thinking. We also identified emotional and physical states which make Turning On Rational Mind more of a challenge.

> We reviewed "Pete's Story" about how he relapsed into substance abuse and suicidal thinking after Something Happened. He blew up on the job and faced TWO CHOICES - TO STAY ON THE RECOVERY PATH OR TO RELAPSE. He initially chose Relapse Route. We witnessed how he rationally and wisely WORKED THROUGH his relapse and STEPPED RIGHT BACK ON THE RECOVERY PATH!

We're not stupid! We know what's wise and what's foolish. We just CHOOSE to do foolish things now and then!

When we're dysregulated and Out-of-Control, we don't control ourselves and we act in ways we KNOW are NOT in our best interests. It's not an issue of intelligence, it's an issue of impulse control!

A Recovery Goal is to come up with a wise plan of action RATHER THAN responding to a problem in an impulsive or self-destructive manner...or not responding at all.

Wise Mind comes up with a plan of action that best meets our emotional needs AND the demands and reality of the Big Picture of the Situation and Our Life.

In Chapter 8, "Challenging Extreme Judgments," we explored the destructive nature of Extreme Judgments. We took a close look at the effect OUR Extreme Judgments have on OURSELVES and OTHERS...and the effect OTHER PEOPLE'S Extreme Judgments have on US.

We determined that Extreme Judgments often become Self-Fulfilling Prophecies. This means that WE tend to become what WE CONSIDER OURSELVES to be... and OUR PEOPLE tend to become what WE CONSIDER THEM to be... and WE tend to become what OTHERS CONSIDER US to be.

We also worked with "The Challenging Negative Judgments of Me Worksheet" and rationally challenged the negative judgments made of us. We PROVED these to be EMOTION-DRIVEN LIES. We determined that these labels have little or nothing to do with us, but SPEAK VOLUMES about the emotional issues of the speaker. We also noted the difference between our BEHAVIOR and our CHARACTER. We saw that "Stupid ISN'T as stupid does." We learned we're NOT STUPID because we do foolish things. We learned WE HAVE GOOD JUDGMENT...but, we don't ALWAYS act on it!

In Chapters 9 and 10, "Wise Mind" and "The Wise Mind Worksheet," we learned about Wise Mind and two tools for getting to Wise Mind. We learned that when we use BOTH Emotional Mind and Rational Mind to deal with a situation, WISE MIND TURNS ON. Wise Mind is respectful of our EMOTIONAL ISSUES and CONCERNS and WHO WE ARE AS A PERSON...as well as the TRUTH and REALITY of the situation AND the Big Picture of Our Life. Wise Mind leads us to WISE UNDERSTANDINGS and a GAME PLAN for dealing with our situation. Wise Mind urges us to ACT IN OUR BEST INTERESTS and to gain and MAINTAIN PEACE AND STABILITY. We discussed that Wise Mind is ACTION-ORIENTED since there isn't anything wise about NOT Following Through with what We Know to do!

"THE WELL ANALOGY WORKSHEET" and "THE WISE MIND WORKSHEET" were discussed in detail in these two chapters. These are Mindfulness tools that help us to THINK THROUGH BEFORE WE DO and to TALK OURSELVES THROUGH the Heat-of-the-Moment. The story, "Drew Got Dumped," was used as an example of how to TALK OURSELVES DOWN the Wise Mind Well...out of some very desperate and aggressive impulses...and INTO Wise Mind. We also worked with Drew's story to learn how to complete a Wise Mind Worksheet.

In these Wise Mind chapters, we also discussed "Six Tips for Participating Wisely

When we're living wild n' reckless, we MUST take hold of the reins to get control. We can no longer allow Emotional Mind to stampede our life. We must "hold our horses" and Think Through Before We Do! There's a time to say "Whoa" and a time to say "Giddy-up." We must say "Whoa" to Self-Destructive Emotion-Driven Behavior and "Giddy-up" to Following Through with what We Know to do!

If we don't say "NO," if we don't deny ourselves, how are we going to STOP ourselves?

1- Disregard – (diss-re-gard) - to ignore, not pay attention to, to not value.

Can you imagine the amount of conflict in this home! I bet Joey would much rather have his parents work together than have a new pair of shoes!

and Effectively." Some of these included STOPPING OURSELVES from carrying-out destructive behavior, PLAYING BY THE RULES, and DOING WHAT WE NEED TO DO WHETHER OR NOT WE LIKE IT OR WANT TO! We also addressed FOLLOWING OUR HEAD OR OUR HEART, CARRY-OVER EMOTIONS, and how there's AN ORDER TO THINGS such that Rational Mind must be Turned On before we'll accept Wise Mind suggestions for problem-solving and coping. The ways of "THE GOOD COUNSELOR" and the importance of LISTENING TO THE VOICE OF WISDOM were also discussed.

Through **Chapters 6-10**, we learned that when we're Big-Time in Emotional Mind, we often do desperate things to relieve the emotional pressure so we can return ourselves to a more comfortable emotional state. If we allow Emotional Mind to "run its' course," we often end up acting in IMPULSIVE and DESTRUCTIVE ways. We must STOP OURSELVES and Turn On Rational Mind and Wise Mind to manage our emotional state. That's the only way to TAME A RECKLESS and OUT-OF-CONTROL Emotional Mind. That's the only way to GAIN CONTROL of our life and our life outcomes. That's the only way to Mindfully Protect Our Peace and Stability and the Big Picture of Our Life. If we don't STOP OURSELVES, our Out-of-Control behavior WILL destroy us and everything that's important to us.

Joey's Shoes…What Would You Do?

The following story is a great example of how the three mind states work. Joey's Dad LIVES in Rational Mind. His emotions are basically turned off. Logic and reasoning control his decisions and behavior. He tends to be "cold" and to disregard[1] the feelings of others. His Mom LIVES in Emotional Mind. She's an INTENSE EMOTIONAL RESPONDER. She becomes filled with emotion quickly and is quick to act on her feelings. She often acts in impulsive and irrational ways because her behavior is VERY Emotion-Driven. Read their story below.

Joey's Shoes

Joey's shoe gets torn apart by the new German Shepherd puppy. Mom tells Dad that Joey needs new shoes. Dad has developed a strict budget and keeps the family to it! OF COURSE, he checks the budget before okaying the purchase. He CALMLY tells Mom they'll have to wait six days until the first of the month to buy new shoes because the clothing allowance in the budget has been used up for the month. Mom PROTESTS his decision because she wants the boy to have a decent pair of shoes to wear. Dad won't budge because he LIVES in Rational Mind. Mom FREAKS OUT and becomes FILLED with rage. She threatens to write a hot check or to pawn off his fishing tackle because Joey WILL HAVE some new shoes!

Just like the two mind states, Mom and Dad would have much less conflict if they pulled together, worked as a team, and dealt with their problems through Wise Mind!

Our Recovery Goal is to have balance in our life.
This includes a healthy balance of Emotional Mind and Rational Mind!
We've heard a zillion times, "You've got to have balance if you want to be happy."

How could this family wisely solve this problem with respect for the logic of Rational Mind and the "heart" or feelings of Emotional Mind? List two options. _____

_____

_____

_____

They could "borrow" money from next month's clothing budget to buy shoes this month. This means they'll have less money to spend on clothes next month. They could also use money from another part of this month's budget (like Entertainment or Eating Out) to buy the shoes. This may mean dinner out on Friday night and Blockbuster movies aren't going to happen! If they "stepped out of the box," they might realize they DON'T HAVE TO BUY NEW shoes...that a DECENT pair could be purchased from a thrift shop for a dollar or borrowed from a family member or close friend until the first of the month. However the problem is solved, it's important to respect the LOGICAL, REASONABLE, and RATIONAL nature of Rational Mind and the COMPASSIONATE, NEED SATISFYING nature of Emotional Mind. That's what Wise Mind does! It comes up with THE BEST and MOST REASONABLE SOLUTION that RESPECTS and PULLS TOGETHER the needs and opinions of both mind states.

This example shows that Rational Mind is NOT BETTER than Emotional Mind. Our goal is NOT to Turn Off either mind state, but to BALANCE THEM OUT! Joey would be tripping over his torn shoes for six days if Mom didn't protest Dad's way of handling the problem! If Dad was too relaxed about the budget, they would overspend, be broke, and the whole budgeting effort would be worthless.

What would you rather be, 100% Rational Mind or Emotional Mind? Why? _____

_____

_____

_____

Who do you think will have the most stable life...someone who's Big-Time Emotional Mind or Rational Mind? Explain. _____

_____

_____

Who do you think will be the happiest or most fulfilled in their life...someone who's Big-Time Emotional Mind or Rational Mind? Mention why. _____

_____

_____

> *If I HAD TO CHOOSE, I'd rather be 100% Rational Mind because I GREATLY VALUE peace and stability. The Rational Mind person would have a lot of that, but their life would probably lack meaning and fulfillment. They'd always be missing something...like being emotionally involved with others, love and compassion, AND the passion and excitement that gives us things to look forward to in life! Although someone who's 100% Emotional Mind would have many ups, they'd also have many downs...and many periods of being "down and out" due to their Out-of-Control emotions and impulsive behavior. I DON'T THINK EITHER TYPE WOULD BE FULFILLING. Of the two, I'd prefer the flat-lined stable life! The Emotional Mind person would have a very difficult life with many losses and problems...and many periods of great turmoil and unhappiness. I just can't go there on purpose.*

Joey's parents need to work on getting some balance! Dad needs to develop his emotional side so he'll have some compassion and concern for people's needs and feelings. Mom needs to work on developing her rational side, so she'll Think Through her problems in a logical way. This will help her to manage her strong emotions and her Emotion-Driven Behavior.

BALANCE IS NEEDED in Joey's family to solve the shoe problem. A wise-minded solution would come by pulling together Dad's logic and reasoning and Mom's compassion and urgency. Either parent could have pulled in the other state of mind. Dad could have said or thought,

> "It's very important for the stability of this family that we follow a budget. However, this is a time when we have to WORK WITH the budget to meet this unexpected need. I'll move money around so we can make this happen for Joey. I'll have to be careful not to blow the budget and run out of money for the month."

Mom could have pulled in the other state of mind and thought,

> "How can I make this happen? Joey needs some shoes and money is tight this month. Sam has a million pairs. Joey could borrow a pair for a few days. I could also find a dollar or two and check out the thrift shops. Certainly, I can find something to hold him over for a week. I could take my lunch to work next week and use my lunch money now to buy him shoes. We'll figure out something."

Where Do We Go from Here...Where Is This Road Leading?

We're now about two-thirds the way through our journey! So far, we've addressed "The Cycle of Suffering: Why is My Life So Out-of-Control?" and "The Three States of Mind: How Do I Get Control of My Life?" Now, we're on the move to "Tolerating and Coping with Distress: How Do I Stay in Control?" This next section is a follow-up to the Wise Mind Worksheet. It addresses, "Okay, I got to Wise Mind and I know I need to do all these things...but HOW IN THE WORLD DO I PULL IT OFF?" Honestly, we've done the easy part...and now we're to the hardest part...it's the "Gettin' 'er done" part! It's the Following Through with what We Know to do part!

Making major life changes is VERY difficult to do. To live a Recovery Lifestyle, we're required to give up the Destructive Coping Behaviors that have provided us relief and some measure of comfort over the years. We'll experience a sense of loss when we give these things up. The experience of distress is a normal part of loss. We all know that part of giving up our Destructive Coping Behaviors is giving up the people, places, and things that go with them. Many of these things we enjoy very much! This creates another level of loss and distress. On top of all this distress, we're now required to deal with our life problems, issues, and losses WITHOUT our preferred coping mechanisms. We CANNOT Numb-Out or White-Out the pain and distress any longer. Talk about EVEN MORE distress! As a substitute, we're required to learn and practice new coping behaviors. This causes EVEN MORE distress because we have to try new things that we may not be comfortable doing. No wonder people don't want to change! No wonder recovery usually takes 8-18 tries! There's a lot of change and distress that comes with recovery. However, if we want our life to change, we've got to make life changes. Things won't change if we won't change. THE GIFT…when we make major life changes, our life changes in major ways. That's what this workbook is all about…making life changes that are life-changing!

The remaining chapters of this workbook will address HOW TO GET THROUGH THESE TIMES OF DISTRESS. It's tough, but do-able. Many people tough it out and do it! You CAN, too! We're going to discuss ways to PRODUCTIVELY COPE with and MANAGE EMOTIONAL DISTRESS. We'll discuss how to TOLERATE and ACCEPT what Comes Our Way…rather than acting in desperate or impulsive ways to quickly Numb-Out or White-Out. We'll discuss HOW TO SET-UP A RECOVERY LIFESTYLE and how to Work Through the things which get in the way of recovery. In so doing, we'll address DISTRESS TOLERANCE, ACCEPTANCE, LIFE-ENHANCING COPING SKILLS, PARTICIPATING EFFECTIVELY, and HOW TO WORK UP AND FOLLOW THROUGH WITH A GAME PLAN for living a Recovery Lifestyle. These remaining chapters contain some very helpful concepts and tools for KEEPING THINGS UNDER CONTROL while we're TRYING TO GET THINGS IN CONTROL! So, let's saddle up and hit the trail. May it lead to "Happy Trails" for you!

We're going to experience distress in life…no matter how hard we work to avoid it!

From "Out-of-Control: A Dialectical Behavior Therapy (DBT) – Cognitive-Behavioral Therapy (CBT) Workbook for Getting Control of Our Emotions and Emotion-Driven Behavior" - Copyright © 2009 by Melanie Gordon Sheets, Ph.D. (www.dbt-cbt-workbook.com)

Section Three

Tolerating and Coping with Distress:

"How Do I Stay in Control?"

~ 11 ~
DISTRESS TOLERANCE

To be human is to suffer loss
To suffer loss is to GRIEVE
To grieve is TO HEAL
HEALING comes to us
By LEANING INTO
And MOVING THROUGH
The painful process.[1]

1- Adapted from an email, reportedly created by Kathlyn S. Baldwin, a social worker from Wichita, KS.

Read that again. Then, list three major things this says to you…in your own words.

_____

_____

_____

_____

Leaning Into the Painful Situation

Healing comes to us by LEANING INTO and moving through the painful process.

What do you think "LEANING INTO" means? _____

_____

> It means we LEAN INTO, step into, face, and DEAL WITH the difficult situations that Come Our Way. Instead of trying to run, avoid, drink, drug, shop, work, or cut away our problems, WE LEAN INTO them and do WHATEVER IT TAKES to WORK THROUGH and GET THROUGH them.

We get into trouble when we keep running from our problems. We never really get passed them and they keep piling up. Our feelings get stuffed and we develop more and more issues, more and more problems, and more and more baggage to the extent we're burdened with more than we FEEL we can bear.

When you face a difficult situation or loss, do you tend to Lean Into it or avoid dealing with it? _____

Is it always bad to pull away from a difficult situation and not meet it straight on… 100% of the time? Explain. _____

_____

_____

It's NOT always bad. A balanced life is a balancing act. When we deal with difficult life situations, we need to LEAN INTO them rather than DIVING INTO them. We should WISELY PUSH OURSELVES to do and handle AS MUCH AS we SAFELY can… and, AS NEEDED, we should BACK OFF, CHILL OUT, and REST UP! Then, we need to GO AT IT AGAIN! This balancing act requires Mindfulness of our physical and

When we try to do more than we can handle, we become overwhelmed. Being too overwhelmed for too long causes us to feel Out-of-Control. That's something we really need to avoid!

We HEAL and finally Get Through our pain when we do our emotional work and whatever else is part of our HEALING PROCESS.

Running from our problems just prolongs our agony and brings us to a chronic state of suffering…a long-term condition of being overwhelmed with despair and stuck in the same place and time… and we don't move forward.

2- Totality – (toe-tal-it-tee) – all of it, the whole thing.

3- Fragile – (frah-gel) – can be broken, needs to be handled with care!

emotional states - to know WHEN WE'VE HAD ENOUGH and WHEN WE CAN DO MORE! "Leaning Into" is all about wisdom, balance, and Participating Effectively!

APPLICATION: To Be Human Is to Suffer Loss

Part of living a FULL LIFE is experiencing losses and painful situations. As time goes by, we'll undergo DAILY LIFE and MAJOR LIFE changes and events. Things are going to Come At Us and some bad things will happen. We'll lose some things we love and cherish. WE CAUSE some of our losses and painful situations…and some JUST HAPPEN. When we suffer loss, it's NATURAL to be depressed and sad for awhile. It's NATURAL to experience PAIN and GRIEF. When we ALLOW OURSELVES to grieve and experience our pain and sadness, WE WILL HEAL. The process of healing occurs when we LEAN INTO and GO THROUGH the painful process.

Because we don't like to grieve and feel bad, we do things to avoid experiencing our pain. We use Destructive Coping Behaviors to NUMB-OUT our feelings and to WHITE-OUT our thoughts. We try to EMOTIONALLY REMOVE OURSELVES from the painful situation. When we try to numb ourselves, run away from, or avoid the situation, ALL WE DO IS PROLONG OUR PAIN AND SUFFERING. The ONLY WAY to heal is to ACCEPT THE REALITY of our situation… to LEAN INTO it…to grasp it in its totality[2]…to acknowledge our fragile[3] humanity… and to ALLOW ourselves to feel…to have thoughts…to PROCESS THE EXPERIENCE… and to GRADUALLY heal and recover. We MUST EXPERIENCE and GO THROUGH the painful situation…in order to GET THROUGH it and to heal.

I hope you'll re-read that textbox several times. It carries some heavy meaning. Which parts hit home for you? Where do you find yourself? _____

_____

_____

_____

_____

List three types of DIFFICULT situations you're able to Lean Into and adequately deal with. _____

_____

List three types of DIFFICULT situations you tend to AVOID dealing with that REALLY NEED to be dealt with? _____

_____

What are the consequences of avoidance or "stuffing" for you? _____

When difficult times Come Our Way, it's normal to spend time on the pity pot. However, we ought not sit so long that we get "ring around the butt." Further, when we're done, we need to flush! We need to process, learn the lesson, "Let it Go," and MOVE ON!

We've all heard of stress management and anger management classes, workshops, and books. They're not called stress or anger ELIMINATION programs because distressing things are going to happen! Our Recovery Goal is to learn ways to prevent, minimize, manage, and cope with what Comes Our Way!

No matter how committed we are to peace and stability, distress cannot be entirely prevented.

4- Distressors - (diss-stress-ors) - things which cause distress! Yep, I think I just made that word up!! You should meet my sister, she makes up all kinds of words! :)

_____

_____

What do you do to "Numb-Out" or "White-Out" problems and emotional pain? _____

_____

_____

We'll do some pretty desperate things to AVOID EXPERIENCING pain and distress. Our desire in the Heat-of-the-Moment is to relieve emotional pressure AND TO CHANGE OUR MOOD. We don't want to PROCESS our painful emotions...so we don't DEAL WITH our painful problems. Most of these problems don't resolve themselves and just go away...especially the big ones. Our problems and worries pile up... and we have to carry these burdens day after day, year after year, and decade after decade. We become overwhelmed and weighed down by this heavy load.

Over time, our load becomes even BIGGER, HEAVIER, and MORE of a BURDEN because the things we do to TRY to feel better end up causing us MORE PROBLEMS... and MORE pain and suffering. It's the Cycle of Suffering. We're not resolving our problems...we're just PROLONGING our pain and suffering...and it goes on and on and on. Our problems MULTIPLY and INTENSIFY and we end up with severe problems throughout the Big Picture of Our Life...OR we bottom-out and LOSE EVERYTHING we love and value.

APPLICATION: Major Distressors and Everyday Distressors

When we're distressed, WE'RE UPSET. Those two words mean just about the same thing. DISTRESS IS A NORMAL PART OF LIFE. It's part of living in the world. NOBODY lives a trouble-free, conflict-free, loss-free, problem-free, or stress-free life. Remember, bad things happen to good people. Some problems we CAUSE and some JUST HAPPEN that we have absolutely no control over.

List five or more situations people face that cause MAJOR DISTRESS in their lives.

_____

_____

_____

Examples of MAJOR DISTRESSORS[4] include the death, dying, and major illnesses of loved ones; relationship losses; divorce; child custody or visitation problems; legal problems; "starting over;" stopping drugs, alcohol, or other major habits; family pulling away; adjusting to a major injury or health problems; difficult work situations, an unfair or heavy workload, or job loss; financial problems; serious relationship conflict;

Major Distressors are MAJOR life events which cause MAJOR distress.

abuse; a major move; major life changes; and dealing with our past in therapy.

Circle the Major Distressors above that you've experienced in the LAST TWO YEARS.

List Major Distressors below that you've experienced during the last two years that aren't listed above. _____

_____

Every day, we have many opportunities to get in a bad mood.

Believe it or not, the quality of our life depends on how we handle the daily hassles and irritating situations... as well as the MAJOR distressors.

In addition to Major Distressors, we're also hit by EVERYDAY DISTRESSORS. Consider how bothered we get by rude drivers, someone hanging up on us after we race to the phone, kid squabbles, a lazy or rude salesperson, long lines, slow people, dense people, being unable to find something, forgetting something and having to go BACK to the store, getting charged a late fee when we sent the payment on time, the boss giving us ANOTHER unwanted task, being denied something WE WANT, running late, a flat tire, something breaks, having to suck up and adjust to the politics of a situation, and piles of laundry after a long day at work.

Circle the Everyday Distressors above which affect your mood and can easily take away your peace and stability in-the-moment. List others ones that bother you a lot.

_____

_____

We don't like to be pushed to admit we could change things if we really tried... especially when we're NOT IN THE MOOD to try!

For each Major Distressor and Everyday Distressor you circled or wrote, put an "X" over ones you could eliminate[5] or resolve[6] IF you were WILLING TO DO what it would take to do so. The truth, sometimes we're ABLE to make changes, but we're NOT WILLING TO GO THROUGH the distress, anxiety, hassle, or discomfort to do so. Now, put a ✔ beside ones you cannot reasonably change no matter how hard you try, no matter how much distress or discomfort you're willing to tolerate, or how much hassle you're willing to Go Through.

5- Eliminate – (ee-limb-in-ate) – to get rid of.

6- Resolve – (ree-zolve) – to fix or solve.

> Our lives are FULL of daily hassles, aggravating situations, and very often, Major Distressors. EVERY DAY we're CHALLENGED to tolerate distress. How we respond will determine whether or not we're productive and have peace in our life.

What Is Distress Tolerance?

Distress Tolerance is about Participating Effectively no matter what comes across our plate!

Distress Tolerance is the ability to TOLERATE DISTRESS and to BEAR PAIN EFFECTIVELY. It involves PUTTING UP WITH painful, uncomfortable, difficult, or undesirable experiences FOR AS LONG AS NECESSARY WITHOUT doing things that cause more pain and problems!

With the concept of Distress Tolerance in mind, what are we supposed to do...just

292

Suck Up and live with all the pain and distress these situations cause? Explain. _____

_____

_____

_____

The gift…when we do these things, distressors will affect us less and less. They'll lose their destructive power and destabilizing effect on us!

> The answer is NO! If we were supposed to just LIVE WITH distress, this workbook would be very short! Our Recovery Goal is to PARTICIPATE EFFECTIVELY in our life and to MINDFULLY PROTECT OUR PEACE AND STABILITY. This involves PREVENTING difficult situations AS MUCH AS POSSIBLE…and LEANING INTO and DEALING WITH what is UNAVOIDABLE. We MUST USE Life-Enhancing Coping Tools to MANAGE OUR DISTRESS and OUR LIFE while we GO THROUGH difficult times! We MUST USE Wise Mind to PROBLEM SOLVE, PROCESS, WORK THROUGH, and GET THROUGH! We MUST DEAL WITH WHATEVER WE HAVE TO DEAL WITH TO GET 'ER DONE…to get passed, over, around, and through whatever we've got to GET THROUGH…so, we can GO ON with our life.

The truth, no matter how hard we try to change some people and situations, they won't change. No matter what we do, we're powerless to change them.

Sometimes DOING SOMETHING involves ACCEPTING THINGS we cannot change, REFRAMING situations by looking at them and thinking about them differently so we feel better, and CHANGING HOW WE RESPOND to distressors. Sometimes we're POWERLESS to change "NEVER-CHANGING" situations or people, but we're NOT powerless to change HOW WE ALLOW these people or situations to affect us! We CAN CHANGE THE WAY we deal with, think about, and respond to our distressors. Consider the wisdom of "The Serenity Prayer."[7] It's an AA prayer for peace and emotional stability. Note three major DBT-CBT principles in this prayer. _____

_____

_____

_____

7- "God grant me the serenity to accept the things I cannot change, the courage to change the things I can, and the wisdom to know the difference." Amen.

Pain and Suffering

Pain and suffering[8] are two terms which have been used throughout this workbook. They're major DBT and DBT-CBT concepts. There's a big difference between the two. What do you think it is? _____

_____

_____

8- Dr. Linehan discusses these concepts in her Skills Training Manual in the Distress Tolerance unit. Distress Tolerance is a major part of her program.

Pain is pain, that's the easy part! We're all familiar with pain, be it physical pain or emotional pain. We experience emotional pain from a major embarrassment, a broken relationship, a death, being depressed again, guilt, shame, loss of self-respect,

When we're in physical pain, we're usually VERY motivated to do what's necessary to stop the pain. Pain pushes us to respond. Pain is a CALL TO ACTION.

Unresolved pain causes people to become bitter, harsh, cold, and miserable. Something big and hurtful happened. They never processed it, so they never got passed it. They live as if it just happened yesterday.

job loss, etc. Pain is a type of distress. We CANNOT ESCAPE the experience of pain. It's a natural part of life. Pain is NOT supposed to go on and on...it's designed to be TEMPORARY. The purpose of pain is to PUSH US TO DO SOMETHING to end the pain...so we can return to a pain-free state. Alike most things in life, we have two choices when it comes to pain. We can either LEAN INTO the painful situation and problem solve, process, and Work Through it OR we can work hard to Numb-Out or White-Out to AVOID dealing with it.

If all we do is work to AVOID pain...if we DON'T Lean Into it...if we DON'T deal with it...if we REFUSE to accept it...if we REFUSE to do what's needed to Get Through it ...OUR PAIN WON'T GO AWAY. It'll be with us for a LONG time. When we don't deal with our pain in the here-and-now, our problems build up and worsen and we end up with many more problems down the road. Our pain from the ORIGINAL SITUATION that was SUPPOSED TO BE temporary turns into LONG-TERM pain and suffering which can be a part of our life...for THE REST OF OUR LIFE.

Does that describe you? Have you been suffering a painful situation for a long time? If so, do you think you've continued to suffer this pain because you haven't Worked Through it all the way? Explain. _____

_____

_____

_____

9- Bereavement – (bee-reeve-ment) – a clinical term for a grieving process that's normal in length.

10- Subside - (sub-side) - to decrease gradually.

The pain we experience in life is designed to be temporary. It's for a season. When we Lean Into and deal with our pain, it should pass or decrease to a level that's MORE TOLERABLE... and not so horribly painful.

APPLICATION: To Grieve or to Be Grieved

When a loved one dies, "Normal Bereavement"[9] occurs during the first year of our loss. During this time, a great deal of crying, anger, sadness, and worry is normal. AT FIRST, the distress is VERY INTENSE and it's about all we think about. Our life as we've known it may have ended. Our life may be in a state of chaos and disorder. However, AS MONTHS PASS, we get BACK INTO our daily lives A LITTLE AT A TIME. We eat better, care for the house better...we can concentrate enough to read a little or watch TV, we may try a hobby again, we go back to church, etc. We hold things together pretty well when we're with others, but when alone, we cry and experience the pain of our loss. Sounds very normal. This is NORMAL Bereavement. We grieve and ALLOW ourselves to EXPERIENCE and PROCESS our feelings... and the SADNESS and PAIN of it all.

AS MORE MONTHS PASS, the intensity of our sadness BEGINS to subside.[10] We may go MOST of the day without crying. We're not crying ourselves to sleep EVERY

"Complicated Bereavement" is when the INTENSE pain and depression lasts longer than a year…and continues to significantly affect our ability to function in daily life. This is a diagnosable psychiatric condition.

Instead of working to Work Through Temporary Pain, we try to shortcut the process. This lands us on the long and winding road of pain and suffering. Instead of Leaning Into our pain, we try to find a way around it. We get lost in a trail of tears and we don't find our way… to the peace that's down the road.

11- Secondary – a second layer of problems. The first layer is the Original Pain. The second layer is the negative effects the unprocessed[12] loss has on our life, like legal, financial, relationship, health, or substance abuse problems.

12- Unprocessed – (un-prah-cessed) – not processed or dealt with.

night anymore. BY YEARS' END, we're back into life…for the most part. We've developed some new routines. The INTENSE pain has lifted. We still experience pain, but daily life is becoming more "normal." During the EARLY YEARS of a loss, major holidays, anniversaries, and birthdays are a time of intense pain WHEN THE HURT AND LOSS FEELS FRESH all over again. OVER TIME though, this even lessens. Thus, the INTENSE DISTRESS in Normal Bereavement is designed to be temporary. It's for a SEASON…then it SUBSIDES.

Consider the same death, but INSTEAD OF ALLOWING ourselves to experience our pain and loss, we DROWN OUR SORROWS in alcohol or NUMB-OUT with drugs, painkillers, or Valium, or we try to CUT AWAY or SCRATCH OUT the pain when it surfaces. Maybe we try to EAT AWAY our sorrows, or OVERSHOP TO BUY a better mood, or CAUSE ARGUMENTS TO TURN sadness and emptiness into something else like anger and drama, or we STAY SO BUSY we don't have time to think and feel…or we do other things to DESPERATELY avoid experiencing the pain and sting of our loss.

> TIME GOES BY, maybe 5, 10, or 20 years…and we STILL haven't ADEQUATELY GRIEVED our loss. The quality of our life DETERIORATES and we're not functioning well. We REMAIN severely troubled and in great distress. The Original Pain has stayed with us…and it's STILL INTENSE. We CONTINUE TO SUFFER this pain YEAR AFTER YEAR. We HAVEN'T GRIEVED…so we REMAIN GRIEVED.

Due to attempts to AVOID our pain through ineffective, Self-Destructive Coping, we END UP WITH many more problems. Maybe we're going through our third divorce or our fourth DWI and we face prison time. Maybe we have a serious drug problem or because of bitterness and causing so many arguments, we've lost relationships and are now isolated. Maybe we've impulsively blown an inheritance or some insurance money and we have major financial problems. Maybe the long-term depression has resulted in hopelessness, severe underachievement, and unfulfilled dreams. THE POINT IS… THE ORIGINAL PAIN IS STILL THERE…but now, because of how we've tried to avoid dealing with it, we have a lot of SECONDARY LIFE PROBLEMS.[11] We NOW HAVE EXTRA PAIN because of the secondary life problems and EVEN MORE extra pain because we've SUFFERED all these years.

The ORIGINAL PAIN has SNOWBALLED. The life issue we NEEDED TO DEAL WITH and DIDN'T has caused problems in MANY AREAS of our life. It has brought anger, depression, and PAIN AND SUFFERING to many precious years of our life.

Sometimes we grow so tired of dealing with pain and loss that we pull away from the world and refuse relationships. This just adds to our pain and suffering. We become isolated and miserable…and we miss out on the things that bring joy and meaning to life.

The quality of life comes down to two choices. The choice to do what it takes to make it through the pain AND the choice NOT to do what it takes to make it through. If we're determined to do what it takes, we WILL make it through. If we choose NOT to do what it takes to make it through, we WILL NOT Get Through It. Instead, we'll go through it and through it…day after day, month after month, and year after year. Which route do you choose? The route of Temporary Pain or Long-Term Suffering?

> So, INSTEAD OF ALLOWING ourselves to experience TEMPORARY PAIN for a year or so, we have caused ourselves pain and suffering FOR MANY YEARS.

Have you ever been in a LONG-TERM CYCLE OF SUFFERING due to a death or other major loss? How long did you SUFFER THROUGH that loss…or are you STILL SUFFERING this loss? Explain. _____

_____

_____

APPLICATION: We Grieve Many Types of Losses

Bereavement is a term associated with grieving a death. This same process applies to grieving and Working Through other painful losses and experiences. During our life, we'll have many losses and difficult events that we'll need to GRIEVE THROUGH.

What sort of things have you grieved over in your life? _____

_____

_____

Review what you wrote above…and circle the things that still bother you a lot.

We grieve many things like break-ups, divorces, betrayals, rejection, and other relationship injuries. We grieve lost jobs, careers, businesses, missed opportunities, being passed up for a promotion, and not being suited for something we really want to do. We grieve mistakes, bad decisions, lost items, a physical deformity, mental illness, and other physical problems. WE WILL GRIEVE the loss of our preferred, Self-Destructive Coping Mechanisms when we give them up, too.

APPLICATION: Suffering Is a Triple Whammy of Pain and Distress

> Suffering = the pain and distress of the **Original Situation**
> + the pain and distress of **long-term emotional problems**
> + the pain and distress of the **negative consequences** of our Destructive Coping Responses

The state of suffering includes the pain and sting of the Original Situation **PLUS** the long-term emotional pain (depression, anxiety, shame, etc) that we experience over the years because our problem is unresolved and still bothers us **PLUS** the pain and suffering due to the problems our Destructive Coping Responses have caused. Now that's A LOT of pain and suffering.

How is the Cycle of Suffering similar to this concept of suffering? _____

_____

_____

Given what you know now, do you think it would have been less painful to have Leaned Into and dealt with your Original Situation rather than working so hard to avoid dealing with it?

They're really very similar. The Cycle of Suffering starts with an Original Situation, too. Instead of Leaning Into it and dealing with it, we use Destructive Coping Responses to avoid the pain and sting. Then, we have lots of extra problems due to the consequences of our coping responses. Our pain and distress increases because we end up with many other problems to deal with...IN ADDITION TO the Original Situation WHICH HASN'T GONE AWAY! To try to feel better about it all...to avoid the depression, pain, and anxiety, we do our Destructive Coping Behaviors again and again. This cycle CONTINUES over the years. Our lives become MESSED UP. Our problems SNOWBALL, AVALANCHE, and make a WRECK OF OUR LIFE. Would you describe the state of your life NOW to be more like a snowball, an avalanche, or a train wreck? _____

Members have described theirs to be "a BIG snowball," "an avalanche in action," "the end of an avalanche with the snow settling," and "a high speed train wreck."

Where do you find yourself? Mark ALL statements that apply to you.

_____ I'm just dealing with pain and distress as it comes my way.

_____ Old stuff still affects me, but I'm doing okay with it. It really doesn't affect my life in big, noticeable ways.

_____ Old stuff still affects my behavior and emotional life. It affects me enough that it has impacted SOME parts of my life in noticeable ways.

_____ I have lots of old stuff and current stuff that I don't deal with well. I do my best to avoid dealing with all the distress. My stuff has piled up and has started to bother me QUITE A BIT. It affects my life in major ways.

_____ My life is a grand example of the Cycle of Suffering. I've been running from and trying to avoid dealing with so much stuff that I'm overwhelmed with stuff! Many areas in the Big Picture of My Life suffer as a result.

_____ Ditto on the above...but my life is a train wreck. It's not snowballs anymore. It's like my whole world has avalanched!

When we accept our painful situation and accept we have to Get Through it... when we Lean Into it and take steps to Get Through it...at some point, we'll Get Through it. That's how folks do it! One step and one day at a time!

When we Go Through painful times, we must ACCEPT we'll be distressed, unhappy, and uncomfortable for awhile.

APPLICATION: Problem Defined, Now What?

To protect our peace and stability, we must respond to life in ways to ENSURE pain and distress will be TEMPORARY and more problems won't result. We do this by ACCEPTING that we'll be distressed and in pain when we Go Through difficult times. We must ALLOW ourselves to GO THROUGH this NORMAL human experience WITHOUT FIGHTING THE REALITY of our distress and WITHOUT DESPERATELY

TRYING TO NUMB-OUT OR WHITE-OUT. We must DECIDE TO TOLERATE the situation and feelings LONG ENOUGH to WORK THROUGH THE SEASON of distress. We must be COMMITTED to do WHAT WE HAVE TO DO to Get Through it so the distress will SUBSIDE!

This means...if we have major legal issues, we'll have to GET THROUGH THE CONSEQUENCES. If we have a new medical condition, we'll have to ADJUST OUR LIFE accordingly. If we have to quit smoking or quit drugs and alcohol, we'll have to DIVORCE ALL THINGS related to our addiction...and DEVELOP smoke-free and substance-free relationships, hobbies, and environments (job, home, etc). If we're divorcing, we'll have to RE-ESTABLISH housing, finances, relationships, etc. If we've lost our kids and want them back, we'll have to do ALL the things expected of us to regain custody.

We need to do these things to Participate Effectively in our life and to Mindfully Protect Our Peace and Stability.

The things that cause pain and suffering aren't just bad habits like drinking, temper tantrums, bulimia, or avoidance. Some very wholesome and productive things can become "bad habits" and destroy our life, too.

> This means we're going to feel STRESSED, IRRITABLE, and DEPRESSED at times. It means we'll have to use minute to minute, hour to hour, and day to day coping skills to bide our time through all the distress and changes. It means we'll HAVE TO DO...WHAT WE HAVE TO DO... to WORK THROUGH and GET THROUGH the painful times and distress.

Maybe we'll have to deal with a hurtful relationship with a parent, spouse, or friend and SET LIMITS because they say ugly things or bring up the past...and it's bringing us down. Maybe it's a physically abusive relationship we'll have to end. Maybe we'll need to ACCEPT a difficult situation we CAN'T CHANGE so we can STOP FIGHTING IT all the time. Maybe we'll need to GIVE UP an unpleasant job that pays well. Maybe it's time to LET GO of old hurts so we can GO ON with life. Maybe we'll need to GIVE UP some life consuming habits because we're tired of the problems they cause.[13] There's all kinds of things we'll need to deal with to REDUCE the conflict and unhappiness in our life.

13- Wholesome activities like collecting dolls, fishing, reading, work, sports, games, and cleaning can become destructive when we lose the ability to do them in MODERATION. Problems, conflict, heartache, and distress results. When something OVERTAKES our life, it becomes a problem. For instance, if we're golfing rather than spending enough time with family or on the job, it'll become a problem. Also consider the marital conflict, financial stress, lying, and sneaking around that goes with overshopping or Out-of-Control gambling.

> There comes a time when we have to CONFRONT WHAT'S GOING ON in our life and HOW OUR LIFE IS GOING. We become Mindful that IF ONLY we'd address these things and do what we need to do to GET OUR LIFE IN CONTROL, then we'd experience RELIEF, PEACE, and opportunities for JOY and a BETTER LIFE.

List three things you could change that would increase your peace and life satisfaction THE MOST. This doesn't include changing other people! Also mention the problems and distress you expect to experience while making these changes.

1. _____

   _____

2. _____

   _____

3. _____

   _____

It seems odd that so many things we enjoy…end up taking away our joy and peace…good and bad habits alike. They get us stuck in distress, frustration, anger, and turmoil…even something positive like golf. Many people love to golf and its good exercise, good socialization, and a "clean" activity. However, like most things in life, if we overdo it, it overtakes our life and good judgment …and it becomes a bad thing.

We're creatures of habit. We become familiar and comfortable with the way things are… and we don't want to Go Through all the stress and anxiety associated with change.

All in all, we really WANT our life to change, but we're NOT WILLING to make the changes that will change things.

APPLICATION: The Good, the Bad, and the Ugly of Change

We're usually VERY AWARE of the things we do that cause us unhappiness and pain. However, WE DON'T MAKE CHANGES for many reasons. For instance, we may like our habit and we don't want to lose the source of pleasure. We may tell ourselves it's the only thing that gives our life meaning and pleasure…and without it, life wouldn't be worth living. We may think we need it to cope and we couldn't make it without it. We may not want to give up friends who do it…and we don't want to be rejected by them because we're no longer doing it. We may lose a "sense of belonging" to a group and perhaps part of our identity, self-esteem, and social status. We may have to give up our line of work and settle for a smaller paycheck. We may have to move if there's too much temptation where we live. We may have to leave a marriage. We may have to go to therapy or take meds and deal with the stigma that can go along with treatment. We may have to find new activities to fill our time and we're shy and have great anxiety when we go to new places and are around new people. Overall, WE DISLIKE these types of changes because they REQUIRE WE DO THINGS WE DON'T FEEL LIKE DOING, things we're NOT USED TO DOING, things we're NOT CONFIDENT ABOUT DOING, and things which cause anxiety, stress, and discomfort. The truth, CHANGE CAUSES TEMPORARY PAIN AND DISTRESS. There's many reasons we don't make the changes in our life that we know we really need to make.

We WANT THINGS TO GET BETTER in our life, but we're NOT WILLING TO DO THE THINGS that make life better. We WANT LIFE TO CHANGE, but we're NOT IN THE MOOD to change! If we REALLY WANT our life to change, we HAVE TO MAKE CHANGES…DESPITE THE DISTRESS of change. Our life isn't going to get better UNLESS we DO THINGS THAT MAKE LIFE BETTER. When people make major life changes, a STRONG COMMITMENT is made, like, "COME HAIL OR HIGH WATER, THIS IS GOING TO HAPPEN. I'M GOING TO DO WHAT I HAVE TO DO, NO MATTER WHAT. I'M SO TIRED OF LIVING THIS WAY. I REFUSE TO ALLOW MYSELF TO LIVE LIKE THIS ANY LONGER."

Most often, we decide to make changes when we have NO OTHER CHOICE but to change.

We finally decide to change when the pain of living like we're living is MUCH GREATER than the pain of change.

We're hard-headed. We don't learn from experience. For us, consequences have to be so severe before we change. We have to be neck deep in hot water before we get out. For us, it's the learning from burning experience!

We're stubborn and willful. We have to bottom-out before we're willing to make changes. It's the most willful and stubborn who'll have to bottom-out and lose everything many times!

What do you think has to happen to people before they're WILLING and COMMITTED to make major life changes? _____

_____

We generally DON'T CHOOSE to make major life changes "out of the blue" or on our own. Change usually happens when SOMETHING HAPPENS and we're FORCED to make changes. We're faced with a demand like, "Stop _____ or _____." WE'RE FORCED TO MAKE A CHOICE between our habit and something we value, like our marriage, kids, job, health, freedom, etc. Either we quit drinking or our spouse will leave. Either we quit spending or we'll get cut off. Either we lose weight or we'll get diabetes. Either we spend time with our family or our family will leave. Either we stop meth or we'll lose our teeth. Either we stop the anorexic behavior or we'll end up in the hospital AGAIN. Either we venture out and add activities to our life or we'll remain painfully lonely. When we push things so far, we'll finally be faced with a choice...EITHER WE STOP THIS...OR THAT WILL HAPPEN.

Are you WILLING to make changes NOW or will you WAIT UNTIL YOU'RE FORCED TO? If you're not ready now, what bad things will have to happen before you are ready? How bad will things have to get? Explain. _____

_____

_____

_____

If you're not ready to change, what keeps you from making the changes you ought to make? _____

_____

APPLICATION: Hurry Up and Wait!

Many people STAY in a bad relationship even though they're miserable. They RATIONALLY KNOW they'd be better off ending it. They don't end the relationship because they don't want to be alone. In their opinion, NO RELATIONSHIP IS WORSE THAN A BAD RELATIONSHIP. Our time of change may require us to TOLERATE the distress of aloneness for awhile. Our change may require us to venture out and take up activities that put us with people so we can develop new relationships. This may require us to try new things that we find scary or uncomfortable. We may have to ENDURE this distress for days, weeks, or months because we generally DON'T EXPERIENCE IMMEDIATE REWARDS with changes in our behavior. We must be

Being patient is the last thing we want to do when we're used to instant gratification and immediate pleasure.

PATIENT and WAIT FOR OUR CHANGES TO TAKE ROOT. WE'RE HURTING. WE'RE DESPERATE FOR RELIEF. WHO WANTS TO WAIT?

Have you ever stayed in a bad relationship because you didn't want to be alone? If so, do you think it was a bad decision? Explain. _____

_____

_____

Do you regret your decision to stay in it so long? YES / NO

Distress Tolerance is about Following Through with goal-directed behavior LONG ENOUGH to experience relief, peace, happy times, and life satisfaction.

> Quite often, we leave one bad relationship and QUICKLY ENTER another one. We CAN'T STAND the distress of being alone so we JUMP INTO one of the FIRST relationships AVAILABLE. Often, we DON'T REALLY CHOOSE who to be with based on what type of person they are...or how much we have in common. We just HOOK UP with one of the FIRST PEOPLE WHO'LL HAVE US! We often take what we can get in-the-moment or someone who meets minimum standards... like they breathe! The truth, we don't give ourselves TIME between relationships to WORK THROUGH our relationship issues and old emotional stuff. We're UNWILLING TO TOLERATE the distress of aloneness LONG ENOUGH to do what we need to do...to have a life-enhancing relationship.

So, what type of relationship do we end up with? _____

_____

We end up with one MUCH LIKE THE LAST ONE! WE HAVEN'T CHANGED, SO OUR CHOICE OF MATES HASN'T CHANGED. We end up with another dissatisfying or abusive relationship! Over time, we end up with A SERIES OF THESE and say, "All men are..." or "All women are..." or "All relationships are..."

All men, all women, all relationships... These are stereotypes or generalizations... and quite often, they're excuses for not waiting around, looking for, and trying out another type of person!

Does this describe you at all? Explain. _____

_____

> It's not ALL men or ALL women, it's just the ones we continue to be around and choose to get involved with! We often choose a certain type because it fits our lifestyle or is comfortable for us. If we like to drink or use drugs, we choose folks who drink or use. Then ONCE AGAIN, we go through the problems of being with someone who's using AND all the problems of two people using. We ONCE AGAIN go through the insane fights, instability, and heartaches of a bad relationship choice.

We haven't changed, so our choices haven't changed... so our relationship outcomes haven't changed either.

Maybe we like the dominant or rebellious type, or the daring and exciting type. Maybe it's the needy and dependent type. When we choose certain personality types,

She walks away thinking "All men are abusive." and "All men are jerks." It's not ALL men, it's just the ones SHE KEEPS CHOOSING!

We have to give ourselves time to change... including changes in what we want out of life AND what we don't want. We have to allow time for our changes to change us!

We must practice Distress Tolerance for as long as it takes for our changes to Take Root...and for the distress to subside...and the positive stuff to come about!

14- I asked my long-time-single friend to start going to church with me. Her first question was, "Are there any good-looking single guys there?" I couldn't think of any so she didn't want to go. I was frustrated and told her, "It's not just about the good-looking men that go. It's about all the mommas, aunties, cousins, and brothers sitting in the pews who know a good-looking guy to fix you up with!" She still didn't go. She's still stays home... and...she's still single.

we're choosing the type of relationship experiences we'll have. Someone close to me likes "strong, dominant men" and she's had a series of seriously abusive relationships. She KEEPS CHOOSING THE SAME TYPE of men and has the SAME TYPE of relationship experiences. There's wisdom in AA's advice to STAY OUT of a romantic relationship during the first year of recovery.

Why do you think AA recommends that? _____

_____

It's because we need to focus on our recovery without getting distracted by a new relationship! Also, if we want to make LASTING CHANGES in our life, we need to ALLOW TIME FOR OUR LIFE TO CHANGE. This includes time for our needs and wants to change, time for our habits to change, time to work through some issues, time for personal growth, and time to improve our life so someone with a healthier lifestyle will be interested in us! If we REALLY WANT OUR LIFE TO CHANGE, we'll need to TOLERATE THE DISTRESS of being without a mate or date for awhile.

It's about HURRYING UP and making changes...and then WAITING for our CHANGES TO TAKE ROOT! We're required to practice Distress Tolerance and patience when we're VERY UNCOMFORTABLE and feeling VERY IMPATIENT!

APPLICATION: Once Is Not Enough

Folks say, "I went out with a stable guy ONCE." They didn't like the person and went back to the rebellious or exciting type they've always been with. When trying new activities, folks say, "I went there ONCE." and they didn't like it and never went back. Maybe no one talked to them much. Maybe they felt anxious, lost, or out of place. The truth, WE DON'T USUALLY EXPERIENCE IMMEDIATE REWARDS WITH CHANGES IN OUR BEHAVIOR. To reap the benefits of our change, we MUST BE PATIENT AND WAIT FOR OUR CHANGES TO TAKE ROOT.[14]

Consider the first time we go somewhere. We may feel anxious, self-conscious, awkward, and uncomfortable. We may sit apart from others and no one really talks to us. THAT DOESN'T MEAN WE STOP GOING. It means we SUCK UP and GET THROUGH the distress. It means we KEEP GOING and ALLOW TIME FOR OUR CHANGES TO TAKE ROOT. We must allow time to become more comfortable, to get to know people, and to GIVE PEOPLE TIME TO GET TO KNOW US!

It may take SIX OR MORE VISITS before we settle in and have someone to hang out with! If we quit going after the first or third visit, we miss out on an activity

Most of us have to be in recovery for 6-12 months and PROVE lifestyle and attitude changes BEFORE our people START to trust us… or want to be around us again. That's because we have to Allow Time For Our Changes To Take Root!

we would've enjoyed had we stuck with it longer. We may miss out on meeting the best friend or the great spouse the quiet, elderly lady would've introduced us to… had she got to know us better! IF WE GIVE UP TOO QUICK, we'll keep ourselves STUCK IN A RUT and we'll MAINTAIN THE SAME OPINIONS, "Nothing ever works out for me.", "All AA meetings are…", "All people are…", "All non-drinking women are…", and "All churches are…"

What positive things have you tried once or twice and stopped because you were too uncomfortable or it didn't go well…or as you expected. Describe what happened. ____

_____

_____

If you would've FORCED yourself to go 8-10 times, do you think things would've gone better? Explain. _____

_____

Just because WE make changes doesn't mean everything suddenly changes and we're problem-free, happy, and in the good graces of our people. We have to keep doing recovery things LONG ENOUGH to reap the rewards of change.

What difference do you think Distress Tolerance and "doing things anyway" would have on the overall quality of your life? _____

_____

_____

APPLICATION: Accepting the Pain and Distress of Recovery

When we have an injury or are planning surgery, we usually ACCEPT that it'll be PAINFUL…and it'll TAKE TIME TO HEAL. We EXPECT and ACCEPT the TEMPORARY PAIN. We expect to EVENTUALLY feel better. We make LIFESTYLE CHANGES to Get Through this time. We MAKE THE BEST OF THINGS, GO ON WITH LIFE, and WAIT FOR THE RELIEF that comes from TIME and HEALING. We naturally practice Distress Tolerance in these situations. We deal with what we have to deal with to Get Through the surgery, recovery, and rehab. WE EXPECT PAIN…WE ACCEPT IT…and, WE HEAL.

We must be willing to feel worse for awhile…so we can feel better down the road. We must be willing to tolerate distress and pain NOW so we can have a less painful future. Remember "No pain, no gain!"

What physical problems have you dealt with KNOWING they'd be painful and you'd have to do things differently for awhile UNTIL the pain or discomfort SUBSIDED and you RECOVERED? _____

_____

What lifestyle changes did you make during these times? What things did you do differently as part of your recovery? _____

_____

*Are you
sick n' tired
of being
sick n' tired?*

Re-read the last textbox and think about EMOTIONAL PAIN instead of physical pain. As you read the rest of this chapter, be aware that our experiences with physical pain are very similar to our experiences with emotional pain, BUT FOR SOME REASON, we often respond to the two types of pain differently. Keep this in mind, because that's where we're going with this!

APPLICATION: A Painful Plan

Consider people preparing for back surgery. The pain and distress they experience on a day-to-day basis is so great that ALTHOUGH the thought of surgery is VERY SCARY...and ALTHOUGH they realize they'll have MORE PAIN than they're used to for awhile after the surgery...and ALTHOUGH they realize it may take MONTHS before they feel better, THEY GO THROUGH WITH IT.

*The pain of living
like they were living
was greater than the
pain of change.*

*Their painful
sacrifices helped
them to feel better...
and made their
LIFE BETTER.
ALL of their pain
may not be gone,
but it's MUCH
BETTER THAN
BEFORE...and the
relief they feel has
made life MUCH
MORE BEARABLE.*

> *The DAY-TO-DAY pain they suffer is great enough that they're VERY MOTIVATED to do WHATEVER it takes to get relief! They've bottomed-out with pain and they've HAD ENOUGH! They've reached the point of WILLINGNESS to do WHATEVER needs to be done to get relief...EVEN IF it means hurting more for awhile.*

Have you reached this point? Have you bottomed-out in EMOTIONAL pain? Have you REACHED THE POINT that your pain and suffering is SO GREAT that you're DESPERATE for your life to change? Are you willing to make changes NO MATTER HOW PAINFUL it is AT FIRST? Explain. _____

_____

_____

*They planned for
and did...what they
had to do...to have
a better life.*

When people CHOOSE to have back surgery, not only do they PREPARE themselves mentally and emotionally for GREATER PAIN AT FIRST...they also get a GAME PLAN for dealing with their recovery and rehab time. They make arrangements for help with meals, errands, bathing, etc. They may put aside money to help with extra expenses like prepared food and medication. If money is short and people are few, they make arrangements with a social worker or agency for benefits and help. They may get a rolling chair to roll around the kitchen and a shower chair for bathing. They may cook in advance and freeze stuff. However they do it, they MAKE PLANS for dealing with the inconveniences, discomfort, pain, and problems involved.

*To end the cycle of
distress, we must
ACCEPT the distress,
DEAL WITH the
distress, and LIVE
WITH the distress
FOR AS LONG AS
IT TAKES to
eliminate or reduce
the distress.*

What arrangements would you have to make to Get Through your time of emotional healing and recovery? What would go in your Game Plan? _____

_____

_____

304

> *The truth, they were in SO MUCH PAIN that they DECIDED to do what was NECESSARY to relieve the pain...EVEN THOUGH what they would have to Go Through would be very painful! They PREPARED THEMSELVES for increased pain and distress. They planned out how they would Get Through the tough time. They got a Game Plan and Leaned Into their situation. They KNEW it would take awhile for their changes to Take Root, but THEY DID IT ANYWAY! They were WILLING to UNDERGO PAIN to LESSEN THEIR PAIN.*

15- Antidepressants normalize our brain chemistry. Someone with a chemical imbalance ONLY will quickly respond to the meds and feel better. This isn't the case for folks with major psychological issues. Of course, they'll feel better in some ways, like eating and sleeping better, more energy, some hope, etc... BUT, their emotional issues and troubling feelings are still there! To really feel better, they'll need medication AND therapy. Research shows that medication ALONG WITH therapy works better than medication alone. That's because most of us get depressed because of hurtful experiences and long-term emotional pain. Medication doesn't deal with that! We're still going to have to deal with our emotional stuff. However, it's MUCH EASIER to do when our brain chemistry is balanced and is working WITH US...instead of against us!

We expect treatment for physical problems to work pretty well...but we're not sure we'll get much relief from our emotional pain ...especially since we've felt this way most of our life.

Consider the changes you need to make. Will they lead to major improvements in the overall quality of your life IN THE LONG RUN? Explain. _____

_____

APPLICATION: Changing Our Attitude About Emotional Surgery

Are you more likely to "Cowboy Up" and take care of a physical condition than you are an emotional one? Explain. _____

_____

When we have physical pain and conditions, we generally Lean Into them and do what it takes to treat them and Get Through them. We do this to improve the quality of our life AND TO LIVE. THE QUESTION IS...why is it so different with our emotional pain and emotional situations? WHY DON'T WE LEAN INTO THEM and DO WHAT IT TAKES to Get Through them...to improve the quality of our life...and TO LIVE? What are your thoughts about this? _____

_____

_____

We're more likely to accept treatment for physical pain because we expect the pain of treatment and rehab to be TEMPORARY...and we expect our emotional pain to last forever whether or not we have treatment. Another reason we're more likely to accept treatment for physical pain is the PAIN MEDICATION often brings QUICK and COMPLETE RELIEF or near complete relief. Medication for emotional pain may take weeks to work well and it won't take away all the emotional pain and distress.[15] Another reason is our people better understand physical pain. They're much more comfortable dealing with us when we're in physical pain because they know more about how to help us. Our people generally don't understand our emotional pain. They don't get it. They're not sure what to say or how to help us. They're afraid they'll say something wrong. They're uncomfortable dealing with emotional pain so they may avoid us or avoid talking about it. There are MANY REASONS why WE'RE more likely to Go Through treatment for our physical pain than emotional pain.

> We NEED to deal with emotional pain and problems JUST LIKE WE DO physical pain and problems. We need to APPROACH our emotional recovery just like we do our physical recovery. We need to have the SAME EXPECTATIONS for Getting Through emotional pain that we have for physical pain. We need to ACCEPT and EXPECT WE'LL BE IN PAIN when we make MAJOR LIFE CHANGES and do our EMOTIONAL WORK. The EARLY DAYS of recovery ARE painful.
> We must Lean Into the sadness, depression, anger, shame, hurt, guilt, and other painful emotions that may arise. We must ALLOW ourselves to EXPERIENCE the experiences we MUST EXPERIENCE in order to HEAL and RECOVER.
> For example, we can't grieve someone's death UNTIL WE GRIEVE their death.
> We can't move on in life UNTIL we move on. We can't Get Through the pain and heal UNTIL we Get Through the pain. We HAVE TO GO THROUGH THE SEASON of hurt, sadness, anger, loneliness, and other painful feelings...and gradually FORCE OURSELVES to make the life changes that'll CHANGE OUR LIFE!

We need to care for our emotional pain in the same way we care for our physical conditions. If we need to undergo relationship surgery, coping style surgery, or attitude surgery, we need to do it!

APPLICATION: Dying from a Broken Heart...When the Pain Is Killing Us

Heart patients know surgery is a SCARY thing to do...and they know the risks. They also KNOW if they DON'T Go Through it, the QUALITY OF THEIR LIFE WILL RAPIDLY DETERIORATE and they'll be on a DOWNWARD SPIRAL TO DEATH. They know they're a heart attack waiting to happen. Think about folks with cancer. Think about how awful it is to Go Through radiation, chemotherapy, surgeries, and painful tests. They're WILLING to Go Through it because they know NOT DOING IT will lead to WORSE OUTCOMES and in most cases, DEATH.

How would you respond to the following statement..."We're more likely to deal with physical pain than emotional pain because some physical conditions are life-threatening and will lead to death if you don't treat them."? _____

_____

_____

16– For instance, we take a bunch of pills, go unconscious, and our rescuer gets delayed in traffic or stops to chat with someone and doesn't find us in time...or we accidently cut too deep and bleed out.

We know UNTREATED emotional pain can be life-threatening. Many people die from impulsive behavior and actions of poor judgment that are directly related to emotional pain and Self-Destructive Coping Behavior. Consider deadly outcomes from suicide attempts, suicidal gestures gone bad,[16] violence, and reckless behavior. In addition, STAYING in a physically ABUSIVE RELATIONSHIP leads to many physical

Emotional pain won't kill us, but the THINGS WE DO BECAUSE OF IT can.

17- Impure – (em-pure) – drugs "cut" or mixed with cheaper chemicals to make more money.

problems (high blood pressure, broken bones, concussions, brain damage, etc.) and in some cases, death. DRUG ABUSE (shooting up) and MULTIPLE SEX PARTNERS can lead to fatal diseases (AIDS and Hepatitis). Drugs also kill people through accidental overdoses, heart attacks, strokes, and problems caused by impure street drugs.[17] DRINKING for years leads to death (cirrhosis of the liver) and severe pain (pancreatitis). It also causes severe symptoms of mental illness (psychosis, dementia with memory loss and poor judgment, etc.). It's clear that untreated emotional pain and problems CAN BE life-threatening or fatal.

Has your emotional pain and problems avalanched to the extent recovery has become a life or death decision for you? Explain. _____

_____

_____

18- Consider the distress we experience when ending unhealthy relationships, going back to work when we don't want to, Following Through with medical and psychiatric treatment, and not just saying "NO" but "HELL NO" to drugs and alcohol and other destructive behavior.

All in all, no matter if it's physical pain or emotional pain, we need to ACCEPT IT. We also need to ACCEPT that we'll Go Through a SEASON OF DISTRESS during the EARLY DAYS of recovery. We MUST ACCEPT THE PAIN AND DISCOMFORT that's a natural part of making major life changes.[18] When we REFUSE to accept TEMPORARY PAIN...we'll end up with LONG-TERM pain and suffering. That's because we're ADDING MORE PAIN to our pain...and MORE SUFFERING to our distress. Over time, our un-dealt with pain snowballs...our distress intensifies...and our suffering builds until we feel buried in an avalanche of problems.

19- Recurring nightmares – the ones we have over and over. The dreams may seem exactly the same or they may differ in some ways...but the theme, situation, or outcome is very much the same.

> *It's really in our best interests to SLOW DOWN, HUMBLE UP, and DEAL WITH OUR STUFF! We can't run from our problems. Even when we get to the end of the road...Relapse Road, we'll find our old stuff there...WAITING ON OUR ARRIVAL. There's NO SHORTCUT to dealing with our stuff...BUT there is a LONG and WINDING ROAD. The Truth, WE'RE GOING TO DEAL WITH OUR STUFF one way or another...and either now or 5, 10, or 20 years from now. We can't run from our pain and problems. If we don't deal with our stuff during WAKING HOURS, we'll DEAL WITH IT in our DREAMS. Ever have recurring nightmares?[19] It's your psyche SCREAMING..."DEAL WITH ME...DEAL WITH ME..."*

Do you have recurring nightmares? What's the main theme...what's similar about them?

_____

_____

_____

How have these recurring nightmares changed over time? Are any parts of it

PAIN can be very difficult…and at times, almost impossible to deal with…but, SUFFERING is even MORE painful and difficult to deal with.

better…or does it end a little better? Explain. _____

_____

_____

_____

AS WE DEAL WITH our unresolved issues, our nightmares BEGIN to change. When our issues are RESOLVED, our nightmares QUIETLY FADE. Our nightmares are really a GIFT. They tell us what we need to work on. PAIN IS LIKE A NIGHTMARE. It screams, "DEAL WITH ME! DEAL WITH ME!" Pain is our CALL TO ACTION. It tells us there's SOMETHING WRONG, that SOMETHING IS HURTING US. Pain PUSHES US to deal with it…and it KEEPS BOTHERING US UNTIL WE DO. When we deal with our pain, HEALING BEGINS and our pain GRADUALLY LESSENS. Our psyche is designed to work IN OUR BEHALF…to help us come to a place of peace… PEACE OF MIND. Therefore, TURN YOUR MIND TO DISTRESS TOLERANCE and COMMIT to dealing with what you NEED to deal with…and doing what you NEED to do to have peace, stability, meaning, and satisfaction in your life.

~~~~~~~~ CHAPTER REVIEW ~~~~~~~~

1. What do we do when we "Lean Into" our problems AND how is this better than diving into them? _____

_____

_____

_____

2. The textbox in the "To Be Human Is to Suffer Loss" section notes several things involved in healing. Describe this process in your own words. _____

_____

_____

_____

3. What causes us to be stuck in the same place and time and we don't move forward? _____

_____

4. What are the two types of distressors? What would you say is the difference between them? _____

_____

_____

_____

5. Why AREN'T Anger ELIMINATION or Stress ELIMINATION classes offered?

_____

_____

6. If our goal was to just Suck Up the distress in our life, this book would be very short. What are we SUPPOSED TO DO when we're REQUIRED to tolerate distress?

_____

_____

_____

7. When we're powerless to change people and situations, what are we supposed to do?

_____

_____

8. "Pain is a call to action."...what does that mean? Mention the purpose of pain in your answer. _____

_____

_____

9. Why do some people become bitter, harsh, and cold? What's a remedy for this condition? _____

_____

10. What are some differences between pain and suffering? _____

_____

_____

_____

11. What can we do to prevent our bereavement from becoming "Complicated"? ____

_____

_____

12. Some people grow so tired of dealing with pain and loss that they pull away from the world. Why does this increase their pain and suffering? _____

_____

13. The quality of our life comes down to two choices. What are they? _____

_____

_____

14. When do we FINALLY make changes? Complete the sentence. When the pain...

_____

_____

15. Which ultimatums or demands do you face...for instance, STOP _____ or _____.
List several. _____

_____

_____

16. How does the saying, "Hurry up and wait," apply to recovery? _____

_____

_____

17. How does "Hurry up and wait" apply to YOUR recovery? What is it you want...that
you'll have to wait for? _____

_____

18. What are some benefits of waiting a year between relationships...or not starting a
new romantic relationship during the first year of recovery? _____

_____

_____

19. List some ways that healing and recovery from physical pain is similar to healing
and recovery from emotional pain. _____

_____

_____

20. To end the cycle of distress, what must we do? _____

_____

21. List several reasons people are more likely to deal with physical pain than
emotional pain? _____

_____

_____

_____

22. What is a limitation of antidepressants? What don't they do very well...that we'll
have to do once our brain chemistry is in balance? _____

_____

_____

23. Why are recurring nightmares a gift? How can we get recurring nightmares to
STOP? _____

_____

_____

_____

~~~ *For Reflection* ~~~

FOR REFLECTION:
Take a few moments to reflect on this chapter. Some questions are listed in the margin to guide your reflection.
Feel free to reflect on whatever your heart brings to mind.

What are your reactions to the material?

Which parts hit home or relate to you the most?

Which parts have helped you the most?

Which parts have helped you to understand yourself the most?

How will you use this information to feel better about yourself?

How will you use this information to improve the quality of your life...or to change how things work out for you in life?

What will you do differently based on this material?

How has this information changed the way you feel about your patterns of relapse and recovery... and your overall response to life?

What does this material motivate you to do?

_____
_____
_____
_____
_____
_____
_____
_____
_____
_____
_____
_____
_____
_____
_____
_____
_____
_____
_____
_____
_____
_____
_____
_____

Figure 11.A.1: The Concepts and Skills Tracking Sheet – Chapter 11

Week # _____

Day of Week →

Date →

11A. Today, I became Mindful that I can prevent extra problems for myself by dealing with a current situation in an effective way.

11B. Today, I Leaned Into a problem or situation that I would have avoided or ignored in the past. I reminded myself that I've got to deal with it so I can get passed, over, around, or through it...AND HAVE SOME PEACE!

11C. Today, I pushed myself to handle as much as I safely could...and I backed off, chilled out, and rested up so I could prepare myself for the next go round.

11D. Today, I reframed an upsetting situation and I felt better about it.

11E. When I experienced emotional pain today, I reminded myself that "Pain is a call to action."...it's a signal that something is wrong.

11F. When I experienced emotional pain today, I reminded myself that IF I didn't deal with what was causing the pain...my pain would likely build and life would become more painful.

11G. Today, I reminded myself that when a major loss occurs, it's normal to go through a season of pain and sadness. I was Mindful that I must allow myself to grieve and process the loss if I wanted to Get Through it and heal.

11H. Today, I became Mindful that I have a choice. I can either experience Temporary Pain by dealing with a difficult situation in the here-and-now or I can endure Long-Term pain and suffering by choosing to avoid or ignore the situation.

11I. Today, I realized I could do my life a favor by Leaning Into a difficult situation. I was Mindful that I'd have to use minute to minute, hour to hour, and day to day coping skills to get myself through the difficult time.

Notes:

RATING SCALE

5 – Did Excellent in this area today
4 – Did Pretty Good in this area today
3 – Did Alright in this area today
2 – Did Only Fair in this area today
1 – Didn't Do Well in this area today
DD – Didn't Do today

Figure 11.A.2: The Concepts and Skills Tracking Sheet – Chapter 11

Week # _____

Day of Week →

Date →

11J. Today, I made a strong commitment to recovery...something like, "Come hail or high water, I'm going to do what I have to do...no matter what. I refuse to allow myself to live like this any longer."

11K. Today, I realized I was faced with an ultimatum...either I do _____ or I'll have to Go Through _____. I realized I can CHOOSE to do _____ on my own or I'll be FORCED to Go Through something even more unpleasant.

11L. Today, I became WILLING to do _____ because I didn't want to Go Through something even more unpleasant.

11M. Today, I realized I might not experience immediate rewards from my changes. I realized I'll have to be patient and Wait for My Changes to Take Root. I made a commitment to myself that I'll do whatever I need to do ...no matter how long it takes me to reap the rewards of my changes.

11N. Today, I reminded myself that I have the same types of relationship experiences because I choose to get involved with the same types of people.

11O. Today, I decided I'd be better off without a relationship for awhile...so I can give myself TIME to meet someone who could offer me a satisfying and life-enhancing relationship experience.

11P. Today, I was Mindful that I need to focus on MY recovery and improving my life situation so someone with a healthier lifestyle would be interested in me!

11Q. I realize the nightmares I've been having are because of unresolved issues. I know I'll find some peace when I Work Through these issues. I realize I can either suffer ongoing nightmares or I can Go Through the Temporary Pain of working on these issues.

Notes:

RATING SCALE

5 - Did Excellent in this area today
4 - Did Pretty Good in this area today
3 - Did Alright in this area today
2 - Did Only Fair in this area today
1 - Didn't Do Well in this area today
DD - Didn't Do today

> ~ 12 ~
>
> ACCEPTANCE

We have a choice to accept difficulties as they Come Our Way...
To Lean Into them and to get a Game Plan for dealing with them
AND a choice to Follow Through until we can Get Through...
OR we can choose to avoid, ignore, and Numb-Out our pain and problems
And stagnate in pain and suffering.

When we choose to confront things
With an attitude of Acceptance
That gives us the serenity to change the things we can
And the wisdom to know our limits.

ACCEPTANCE is part of most every major religion and life philosophy... from Christianity to Buddhism to AA's principle of surrendering to a Higher Power and accepting things we cannot change.

1- Stagnate – (stag-nate) – when something goes bad from lack of movement (like water)... or from being stuck in an unchanging situation (like the economy).

ACCEPTANCE of our life situation and what we need to do about it... is a way of TURNING SUFFERING we CANNOT TOLERATE into PAIN we CAN TOLERATE. It's a way of turning HOPELESSNESS into HOPE. Most of us have been SUFFERING the pain of our LIFESTYLE and CHOICES for years...and SOMEHOW, we REMAIN WILLING to experience ONGOING PAIN AND MISERY because of them. We're SOMEHOW WILLING to SUFFER LONG-TERM PAIN but we're NOT WILLING to Go Through the TEMPORARY pain of change. We're SOMEHOW WILLING to dwell in a painful past, to remain in painful situations, and to continue painful addictions and impulsive behavior. We do so because we're UNWILLING to ACCEPT and UNDERGO the CHANGES that will BRING PEACE and STABILITY. Reflect on this opening information. How does it apply to you? _____

_____

_____

_____

_____

We're somehow willing to remain in the Cycle of Suffering because we don't want to Go Through what we HAVE TO GO THROUGH to get it to stop.

When we're suffering, pain builds, depression deepens, hope is quenched, and the light at the end of the tunnel is too far off to see.

> *If we want to end our pain and suffering, WE MUST BE WILLING TO ACCEPT THE PAIN OF CHANGE. We must be willing to deal with painful situations... and to make painful changes. THE ONLY WAY TO GET THE SUFFERING TO STOP is to get down to business and MAKE THE REQUIRED CHANGES even though they may be painful, undesirable, or uncomfortable...at first.*

The truth, IT'S PAINFUL TO DO OUR EMOTIONAL WORK. It's painful to address our stuff and deal with the painful situations underlying our suffering.

314

The Temporary Pain of healing is much less painful in the long run than the ENDURING PAIN of suffering.

When we're in recovery, we see light at the end of the tunnel. It's a time when suffering transforms into peace.

We've experienced many hurts and pains as we've gone through life. There's so many things we need to accept so we can be okay…and have some peace in our life.

It really doesn't matter what we've done or why we've done it. To have peace and stability we must Let It Go.

> Unlike the pain of suffering, THE PAIN OF RECOVERY EASES
> as our life-enhancing changes Take Root. It is then…when we BEGIN
> TO EXPERIENCE RELIEF, SATISFACTION, HOPE, AND JOY.

The Acceptance of Recovery

When we make the decision to change, we'll have to ACCEPT and DEAL WITH things like giving up our self-destructive addictions; Saying No to temptation; pulling away from unhealthy people; learning to enjoy being around people who live life-enhancing lifestyles; giving up our free time to participate in productive activities; and handling difficult emotions and situations in a life-enhancing manner. We'll have to accept and deal with many other painful things, too.

Review the Acceptance Statements below and circle the ones that apply to you.

Some Acceptance Statements for Recovery

There's some people in our life…that no matter how hard we try, we can't change them or make them see things our way.

There's some people in our life…that no matter how hard we try, we can't make them love us, respect us, or accept us.

All the fussing and yelling we're doing…isn't doing anything… other than pushing our people further and further away from us.

A relationship loss was mostly our fault no matter how much we blamed others.

Some of our people have pulled away from us because we haven't presented ourselves as very loveable or likeable.

Even the best of friends and family will hurt us now and then.

We have a drug, alcohol, rage, or other coping addiction that we'll have to do something about…or we'll never have any lasting peace or stability.

Someone else was right and we were wrong. We need to apologize and admit something we don't want to admit.

Some of the bad things that have happened to us are a product of the situations and people we've allowed in our life.

The state our life is in…has a lot to do with the decisions we've made and how we've responded to difficult life situations.

Some of the problems and difficulties we're having ARE our responsibility. No matter what happened to us before, being adults, WE ARE RESPONSIBLE for how we respond to life and the consequences of our actions.

Stability is often "boring" because it doesn't have all the excitement and chaos of a wild n' reckless lifestyle.

(continued)

> *We may have to take a job we don't want because it's the only one available... and we need money in a hurry.*
>
> *We have a physical limitation or condition that affects our life.*
>
> *We have a mental illness and may have to take medication for the rest of our life.*
>
> *Time has passed and life won't be the same as it was 10, 20, or 30 years ago.*
>
> *Life isn't fair and no matter how hard we push, things won't ALWAYS go our way. Our task is to do the best we can...with the way things are.*

Write other Acceptance Statements that apply to your life. _____

_____

_____

_____

Holding onto the past makes us sick and keeps us sick. It does us no good and keeps us from doing good for ourselves and others.

THERE MAY BE something we need to accept that we can't bear to put in writing. The truth, we do all kinds of horrible, rotten, shameful things when we're filled with emotion and react in the Heat-of-the-Moment...and when we're drunk, on drugs, manic, psychotic, or otherwise in an ALTERED STATE OF MIND.

> *Work to ACKNOWLEDGE and ACCEPT whatever has happened...and MOVE ON.*
> *Yesterday is THE PAST and TODAY we're setting a foundation for a better TOMORROW. Holding onto the past KEEPS US STUCK IN THE PAST...*
> *a painful place we don't want to be! REFUSE to RUMINATE and DWELL THERE.*
> *Focus on recovery and doing things TODAY that'll bring LIFE to your life.*
> *Use all the DBT-CBT tools and any other Recovery Tools in your arsenal to Turn Your Mind to NEW LIFE and a RECOVERY LIFESTYLE.*
> *Like the Nike slogan, JUST DO IT!*

There's a meaning and purpose for our life and we can't live it out...if we live in the past.

Basic Principles of Accepting Reality

Some people have big problems with the concept of ACCEPTANCE. Some have expressed outrage,[2] "How do you expect me to accept the unacceptable?" We do it with RADICAL ACCEPTANCE.[3] Radical refers to something unusual, different, or "not normal." There are radical ideas, lifestyles, and behavior, even radical religious and political beliefs. In the 1950's, Elvis was radical. In the 60's, "free love" and hippies were radical. Later, punk rock was radical. Today, all the piercings are radical. In Communist countries, democracy is considered radical. With this in mind, what in the world do you think is meant by "Radical Acceptance"?

Our task in life is NOT to focus on all the horrible, rotten things we've ever done, but to focus on all the positive and meaningful things WE CAN DO.

2- Outrage – (out-rage) - powerful anger plus shock.

3- Radical Acceptance is a major DBT concept discussed by Dr. Linehan.

_____

_____

From "Out-of-Control: A Dialectical Behavior Therapy (DBT) – Cognitive-Behavioral Therapy (CBT) Workbook for Getting Control of Our Emotions and Emotion-Driven Behavior" - Copyright © 2009 by Melanie Gordon Sheets, Ph.D. (www.dbt-cbt-workbook.com)

> *Radical Acceptance involves accepting what we'd normally consider UNACCEPTABLE. When we LIVE BY Radical Acceptance, we CAN ACCEPT something WHETHER OR NOT we approve of it and WHETHER OR NOT it's right or wrong, fair or unfair, or pleasant or unpleasant. Radical Acceptance is about CHOOSING TO ACCEPT whatever is in our best interests to accept.*

We can CHOOSE to accept something even though we don't agree with it or approve of it.

We MUST ACCEPT whatever we HAVE TO accept because NON-ACCEPTANCE keeps us emotionally TROUBLED and STUCK IN NEGATIVITY. To have peace, we MUST ACCEPT many things WHETHER OR NOT THEY'RE ACCEPTABLE. We must accept things from the past and present. Anything in the past that's unfixable, we need to LET IT GO. Anything in our current life that we CANNOT CHANGE, we need to accept that it MAY NOT change. Anything we CAN change, we must LEAN INTO...to MAKE THE CHANGES we CAN MAKE. Our Recovery Goal is to live a life that MAXIMIZES peace, stability, meaning, and productivity. To do that, we MUST ACCEPT what has happened HAS HAPPENED, what we've done, WE'VE DONE...then, we need to LET IT GO...so we can GO ON with life.

We CHOOSE to accept things because Fighting ourselves, the world, and reality keeps us sick and in pain and turmoil.

We must accept that the things in the past ARE PASSED. To Start Over in life, we MUST Start Over. To have a Fresh Start, we MUST start fresh. That means we need to bury what has been killing us. We can't LIVE and HAVE LIFE if we live, eat, and breathe what takes the life out of us.

APPLICATION: Acceptance of the Bad, Horrible, Rotten Things We've Done

We're human. We ALL make mistakes. When we've LIVED IN Emotional Mind, we've made MANY mistakes. We've acted impulsively and have made MANY regrettable decisions. We're NOT bad, horrible, rotten people. We've just done some bad, horrible, rotten things. These things happen when people are drinking, drugging, in a manic or psychotic state, or are desperately overwhelmed with painful emotion. When we're CLEAN N' SOBER, on our MEDS, making HEALTHY LIFESTYLE CHOICES, and ACTING IN WAYS to Mindfully Protect Our Peace and Stability, we're GOOD-HEARTED PEOPLE with good morals and values... and WE CARE ABOUT PEOPLE.

We're the walking wounded. We've experienced a lot of pain. Being desperate for relief, we've done a lot of painful things that have hurt ourselves and others.

> *Think of the REALLY NEAT people we've met in rehabs, AA, support groups, and hospitals. They've lived a past JUST LIKE US. They've done hurtful things to the people they love WHEN they were in the middle of their addictions and Destructive Coping Behavior. They're NOT bad people. They're the WALKING WOUNDED and IN THEIR DAYS of PAIN and IMPULSIVITY, they did some painful and impulsive things. TAKE AWAY the drugs, alcohol, mania, depression, pain, anger, and bitterness...and what's left are some PRETTY NEAT PEOPLE!*

We weren't born this way. We became this way because of an Out-of-Control lifestyle.

Our people want us ALIVE and WELL, so we need to bury the guilt and pain that's killing us. We cannot be the person we were meant to be or live the life we were meant to live if we are carrying around what makes us wish we were dead. The only way to start over is to START OVER. We do that by accepting what needs to be accepted and by moving on down the Recovery Path.

4- Reframing is a Cognitive Behavioral Therapy (CBT) technique which involves changing the way we look at things to change the way we think and feel about them. It's like putting a different frame on a picture to make the picture look better. We can reframe the picture of an unpleasant life situation by looking at it in a different way or from a different perspective. We change the way we look at it and it changes the way we feel about it!

Think of two people YOU KNOW that fit that description. What sort of bad things did they do when they were in the middle of their addictions and Destructive Coping Behavior? Also describe their character when they're living a Recovery Lifestyle. _____

_____

_____

_____

Our Recovery Task is to ACCEPT whatever we've done. Then, we must WISELY decide which things we CAN DO SOMETHING ABOUT and which ones we CAN'T. We need to focus our efforts on the things we CAN do something about that are a PRIORITY in our life. We need to DO WHATEVER WE NEED TO DO to improve these things. The things we can change that AREN'T A PRIORITY...we need to LET THOSE GO...FOR NOW.

> *The things we CAN'T CHANGE...we MUST Let Them Go. Letting Go is a CHOICE. It's a choice for FREEDOM from burden and a choice for PEACE and SERENITY. Remember, "God grant me the serenity to ACCEPT the things I cannot change." ACCEPTANCE is what gives us serenity EVEN WHEN our lives are in turmoil. It's how we CHOOSE to THINK about things and RESPOND to things that ultimately affects HOW WE FEEL about things. We can CHOOSE to be AT PEACE with our situations or we can CHOOSE to be in turmoil. We CANNOT LIVE NEW LIFE if we live in the PAST. CHOOSE to let some things go...so you can GO ON with life...and LIVE NEW LIFE!*

SKILL BUILDER: The Art of Reframing

Think of an upsetting situation that you began to THINK ABOUT DIFFERENTLY... and the new way of thinking led you to FEEL BETTER about it. What was the situation and what were the thoughts that helped you to feel better about it? ___

_____

_____

_____

Sometimes, we find peace by "REFRAMING"[4] a situation. We do this by changing the way we LOOK AT the situation. The situation DOESN'T CHANGE, but the FRAME we put around it does. The new frame CHANGES the LOOK AND FEEL of things! Consider this example of reframing shared by a Group Member who worked as an aide in a nursing home.

5- Disheartened – (dis-heart-tend) – to have lost heart, joy, or enthusiasm.

Jenna described a long struggle with emotional pain because her "beyond the call of duty" hard work NEVER SEEMED to be appreciated or rewarded by her supervisors. She described periods of becoming very disheartened [5] and angry. These feelings were especially intense when co-workers were favored and she was overlooked. During these times, she could hardly provide for her patients and did ONLY the bare minimum of what was required for their care. She described this to be a very difficult time because she was "at her happiest" when busy and doing special things for her patients. After days or weeks, something would happen to draw her back into her work. She stated her suffering finally stopped when it occurred to her, "I don't work for my supervisors. I work for my patients and God. Recognition or rewards may never come from my supervisors, but God is no doubt very pleased with how I care for His people."

Jenna was able TO TURN a very negative situation into a POSITIVE ONE. Her insight was a TURNING POINT that brought GREAT PEACE. She LOST THE BITTERNESS and NO LONGER SUFFERED the HEAVY BURDEN and PAIN of

6- Demoralized – (dee-more-o-lized) – same as disheartened!

being so demoralized.[6] Her situation DIDN'T CHANGE...the same work dynamics continued, but SHE WAS CHANGED. She ACCEPTED the REALITY of her situation...that this was the way things were and NO MATTER WHAT she did or how hard she worked, no recognition would come. THEN, she CHANGED the way she LOOKED AT and THOUGHT ABOUT the situation. She REFRAMED it and TRANSFORMED LONG-TERM SUFFERING INTO ENDURING PEACE.

What difficult situation can you reframe so you can feel better about it, too? Describe the situation and how you can reframe it. _____

If we can't change the situation, we CAN change the way the situation affects us!

_____
_____
_____
_____

Pretty cool technique. You've heard about "thinking about it differently so we feel better." Now you see it in action!

Acceptance Doesn't Require Giving Up on Something

We often believe that Acceptance REQUIRES that we back off and stop trying

Acceptance does NOT require we pull completely out of the situation and stop trying to change things.

to make changes. Sometimes that's the wisest decision...but sometimes, the wisest decision is to accept something AND STILL TRY to make important changes. That seems like an impossible task! How do you think we can accept something but STILL TRY to change it? _____

_____
_____
_____

> *We can do it by accepting that ANYTHING WE TRY probably WON'T WORK! When we accept this on an EMOTIONAL LEVEL, we can STILL TRY to change things WITHOUT being SO EMOTIONALLY TIED to the outcome that we experience pain and frustration EVERY TIME WE TRY and things don't change! Thus, we EMOTIONALLY STEP BACK without STEPPING OUT of the situation.*

Part of wisdom is knowing when and when not to give up. It's knowing when to talk, walk, and squawk. If the situation is NOT a priority in our life, it's probably best to walk. If it involves our Inner Circle, we probably want to talk. If it's real important to us and talking isn't working, we may want to squawk a bit! If all our squawking isn't working, we may need to accept we can't change the situation and go back to talking!

SKILL BUILDER: The "I Can't Win Them Over" Situation

Consider this example. We're determined to get someone to like us, respect us, love us, or want to be around us. We try and try...and when we get tired of trying, we try some more. We jump through hoop after hoop to get their attention or to please them. We're consumed by this "need." We stay angry, frustrated, and hurt because they don't respond like we want them to. It seems we can't change them no matter what we do. The relationship is so important to us, it's hard to totally give up and stop trying. We recognize our attempts to change them are making us sick. We become Mindful that a Recovery Goal is to approach this type of situation with a RATIONAL ATTITUDE and EMOTIONAL BOUNDARIES so we DON'T GET HURT and STAY HURT all the time.

How could we use Radical Acceptance to help ourselves with this situation? _____

_____

_____

How might this new understanding change our actions towards them and our feelings...when they don't respond to us like we want them to? _____

_____

_____

We have to protect ourselves emotionally by not getting our hopes up time after time just to be slammed again and again.

7- We may decide to contact them once a week (or month, or 3 or 6 months) to check in and let them know how we're doing...and that we're interested in working on a better relationship with them.

> *We can accept they're not likely to change ANYTIME SOON...and it's not within our power to change them AT THIS TIME. We can also accept we're human and we WANT TO TRY! We should fill out a Wise Mind Worksheet to THINK THROUGH the situation to come up with a Game Plan for dealing with it. We may decide the best plan is to STEP BACK from the situation without STEPPING OUT of it. We may plan to visit with them EVERY NOW AND THEN rather than AS OFTEN AS POSSIBLE...and to TRY to change them ONLY SOMETIMES when we visit...NOT EVERY TIME![7] This Game Plan will help us to MINIMIZE our pain and suffering and MAXIMIZE our peace and stability. Over time, if we're still too bothered by our interactions with them, we'll need to revise our plan!*

We can choose to LOWER our expectations, TO HAVE NO expectations, or to totally CHANGE our expectations.

Our Recovery Goal is Radical Acceptance… to have the serenity to accept the things we cannot change, the courage to try now and then, and the wisdom to know things may never happen the way we want them to!

We have to prepare ourselves to approach each visit …and to walk away from each visit with an attitude of Radical Acceptance.

We do it by accepting the situation and getting a Game Plan for dealing with it.

8- Unimpressed – (un-im-pressed) – not impressed, pleased, or excited by. Disinterested – (dis-enter-est-ed) – not interested!

With this approach to our situation, we ACCEPTED that they weren't going to change anytime soon. We decided we weren't going to make ourselves crazy with desperate attempts to change them anymore. We decided we wouldn't ALLOW ourselves to stay consumed and preoccupied with changing them. We decided to STOP FIGHTING the situation ALL THE TIME. We decided to PULL BACK and try EVERY NOW AND THEN and not to make changing them the focus of EVERY visit. WE ACCEPTED THE REALITY OF OUR SITUATION AND TOOK SOME STEPS TO PROTECT OURSELVES EMOTIONALLY. We lowered our expectations and expected nothing to change (though we hoped differently!).

Radical Acceptance in the "I can't win them over" situation involves accepting we don't like it, it may not be fair, but, IT'S OUR REALITY RIGHT NOW. It's just the way things are. It's what we HAVE TO DEAL WITH…FOR NOW. We might run Acceptance Statements through our mind like, "Guess this isn't the week she changes her mind.", "I've done my part for now.", "He's such a bitter man…a master at holding grudges!", or "I'll follow my plan and call her back in a month to let her know how I'm doing and that I hope to work this out some day. That's all I can do."

Our Rational and Wise Mind understandings change the way we feel and respond. We began to THINK RATIONALLY about the situation…which helped us to RESPOND RATIONALLY…and to have some PEACE about the situation. We're no longer devastated or seriously hurt when we try to improve the relationship, because we DON'T EXPECT any BIG or LASTING CHANGE. We're more ACCEPTING of the NEVER CHANGING SITUATION. We Mindfully Protect Our Peace and Stability by EXPECTING that, like usual, they'll continue to set limits, act unimpressed or disinterested,[8] and distance themselves from us. Our new approach helps us to deal with a hurtful situation in a way that NO LONGER causes OVERWHELMING pain and suffering.

We're not robots. We CAN'T totally THINK ourselves out of feelings. We may need to cry a few minutes while we process the visit, but OUR GOAL is to CUT THE SADNESS SHORT and to GO ON with our day. We CANNOT ALLOW THIS TO GET THE BEST OF US. We lowered our expectations so we wouldn't be so hurt and angry. If we're NOT maintaining EMOTIONAL BOUNDARIES…if we're not maintaining peace and stability while trying now and then, we'll have to seriously think about STEPPING OUT of the situation. We CAN'T HAVE SOMETHING IN OUR LIFE that continually upsets us and strips us of our peace and stability.

Our Recovery Goal is to accept whatever Comes Our Way, to do our best in each situation, and to maintain an attitude of peace and Acceptance even when things don't go our way.

Handling life is as much of an art as it is a skill! Just Think Through Before You Do AND seek advice from the wise!

TOO MUCH NAGGING NEGATIVITY…spells "RELAPSE FIXIN' TO HAPPEN."

Briefly describe a personal "I can't win them over" situation that is hurtful to you.

_____

_____

_____

Is it likely that you can Step Back from this situation and still maintain your peace and stability…without Stepping Out of it and totally giving up? If so, what would be a good plan of action? How could you go about STILL TRYING to change the situation without being devastated or hurt each time you try? _____

_____

_____

_____

Write some Acceptance Statements that would help you deal with this situation.

_____

_____

_____

SKILL BUILDER: Radical Acceptance and the Hurtful Phone Calls

Recall the upsetting phone calls or visits discussed in Chapter 4.[9] These are the ones when we get criticized, yelled at, insulted, and the past rubbed in our face. We end up angry and hurt. We can CHOOSE to never talk to them again (Stepping Out of the Situation), to do nothing and allow things to continue the way they are so we don't lose the relationship (Keep Dancing to Maintain the Status Quo),[10] or to Fight to change the situation…to reason with them or fuss at them to try to get them to be nice (Staying in the Ring).

How would you feel as a result of each choice? How would it likely work out?

Stepping Out of the Situation? _____

_____

Keep Dancing to Maintain the Status Quo? _____

_____

Staying in the Ring? _____

_____

What's the choice for peace and stability in this situation for you? Is it one of the above, a combination, or none of the above? Explain. _____

_____

_____

9- These are the frequent calls from significant others, like a parent, a brother, an ex-spouse, etc. The calls may start off nice, but they usually end up awful!

10- Maintain the Status Quo - (Stat-us Quo) - (Quo is like quote… without the "t" sound.) - to keep things the way they are…the same as usual…like "not rocking the boat."

322

Consider how we handled the difficult phone calls with Mom in Chapter 5.

> "Mom, I love you and value talking to you, but it hurts too much when we yell and scream at each other. Part of my recovery is Maintaining My Peace and Stability. We're fussing and I'm getting upset...so, I'm going to get off the phone. I'll call you when I feel better and we can focus on having a pleasant conversation then."

Which part of this response suggests Radical Acceptance? _____

_____

_____

What is the limit or boundary that has been set? _____

_____

_____

Radical Acceptance involves accepting that conversations with Mom become very unpleasant and everything we've tried to do to change this hasn't worked. It's accepting that she isn't likely to change any time soon and the only power we have over this situation is to change how we respond to it. We came up with a Game Plan to SET THE LIMIT that when she becomes unpleasant, WE WILL GET OFF THE PHONE. Our plan is to STEP BACK from the situation by getting off the phone... rather than continuing to dance the same routine with her.[11] We decided we would CONTINUE TO TRY to change her by teaching her that IF she wants time with us, she'll have to talk to us IN A WAY WE'LL TOLERATE. She'll have to be pleasant and respectful OR WE'LL HANG UP THE PHONE! We haven't Stepped Out of the situation by refusing to speak with her again...we told her we'll call her back and try to have a pleasant conversation LATER!

11- Like screaming back and forth trying to get her to be nice...or to get her to understand that the way she treats us makes us want to destroy ourselves...or that we wouldn't have so many problems if not for her!

Because we choose to accept something, doesn't mean we Step Out of it, ignore it, or deny its existence. It means we accept reality AS IT IS and we make a wise decision about how best to respond.

We Mindfully Protect Our Peace and Stability ONE SITUATION AT A TIME!

> If we KEEP DANCING to Maintain the Status Quo or if we STAY IN THE RING and continue to Fight and try to reason with THE UNREASONABLE, we'll CONTINUE to be MISERABLE. We can NO LONGER AFFORD to do things this way. We can NO LONGER ALLOW someone to upset us all the time. WE MUST DO SOMETHING to Mindfully Protect Our Peace and Stability.

We often suffer major emotional problems when we KEEP DANCING in a troubled relationship or when we STAY IN THE RING and FIGHT all the time. Because we can't do things that cause emotional problems on purpose, we have to do something different. We have some choices. We can STEP OUT of the situation and no longer interact with them...or we can STEP BACK and SET LIMITS. The decision to STEP OUT or to STEP BACK can be a tough one that depends on many things. This decision needs to be WELL THOUGHT OUT.

In the "Hurtful Phone Calls" example, since our relationship with Mom is very important to us, the best choice was to Step Back and Set Limits WITH AN ATTITUDE of Radical Acceptance. We ACCEPTED that she's a critical person who says hurtful things. We ACCEPTED that she may never change no matter how WISELY and SKILLFULLY we deal with her. We were Mindful that she's ugly to people...so we ACCEPTED that it's normal for her to be ugly with us, too! Once we ACCEPTED THE REALITY of the situation, we began to Mindfully Protect Our Peace and Stability by PARTICIPATING EFFECTIVELY when she called.

We Participate Effectively with an attitude of Radical Acceptance by CALMLY telling her we WON'T carry on unpleasant conversations ANYMORE... and by ENDING THE CALLS when she turns ugly. A Recovery Goal is to NO LONGER ALLOW HER TO RUIN OUR DAY. When she gets ugly, we'll do our BEST to CALMLY set our limit, get off the phone, SHRUG IT OFF, and GO ON WITH OUR DAY...and we'll answer her next call when we FEEL UP TO IT!
WE'LL NO LONGER ALLOW OUR FEELINGS TO GET HURT
BY THE UGLY THINGS SHE CHOOSES TO SAY TO US.

12- Her criticism and the conflict it causes may be her Destructive Coping Mechanism. She upsets people, yells n' fusses, and releases the tension and anger that builds up in her. That's why she keeps doing it...even though it causes her more problems.

Part of being wise is changing our Game Plan as the situation requires!

If Mom tries to outsmart us by BEGINNING the visit with ugliness to be sure she HAS A CHANCE TO DOWNLOAD ON US[12]...we may have some VERY SHORT conversations! We'll also have some decisions to make about whether or not we'll take her calls. A letter to explain our position may be required...to inform her that we'll ONLY take her calls once or twice a week...on certain nights...and we'll immediately hang up if she becomes ugly. We may have to STEP OUT of the relationship for awhile if she WILL NOT play nice and respond to our limits.

APPLICATION: Radical Acceptance of Serious Life Consequences
What DIFFICULT life consequences and situations do you face as a result of how you've been living life? _____

_____

_____

How have you responded to these? Have you been PARTICIPATING EFFECTIVELY and doing what you need to do to Get Through them? Have you been FIGHTING THEM? Have you been WITHDRAWING and giving up? Have you been IGNORING THEM and doing what you felt like despite them? Next to the consequences you listed above, mark PE (Participate Effectively), F (Fighting),

To Get Through the consequences, we must accept that life will be painful FOR AWHILE. We must use Wise Mind to Participate Effectively while we're Going Through this difficult time. As time passes, life will gradually improve. Temporary consequences will be over and done with …and permanent consequences will become less difficult to bear.

Distress Tolerance is about CHOOSING to ENDURE the TEMPORARY PAIN of our situation until our life-enhancing Game Plan has time to bring us through to a time of peace and stability.

We must Mindfully CHOOSE our battles and decide if the FIGHT is worth the conflict and possible consequences.

13- Physical effects like sleep problems, high blood pressures, chest pains, headaches, stomach problems, etc.

W (Withdrawing), or I (Ignoring) to note how you've responded to these. Use O for "Other response" and write it here. _____

> *We may be at a time in life when we have a lot of negative consequences and difficult situations to deal with. We may be in great pain and turmoil… and we may be suffering as a result. Though we may FEEL LIKE we have few options, we ALWAYS HAVE OPTIONS. We can CHOOSE to FIGHT THE REALITY of our situation by Numbing-Out or trying to White-Out the problems and pain. We know this is a BAD CHOICE because it causes even greater distress and turmoil…and an avalanche of painful consequences and losses across the Big Picture of Our Life. The BETTER CHOICE is to ACCEPT THE REALITY of our situation and to PARTICIPATE EFFECTIVELY in our life. This choice requires DISTRESS TOLERANCE and RADICAL ACCEPTANCE.*

Radical Acceptance of serious life consequences involves STEPPING INTO the situation and EMBRACING IT IN ITS TOTALITY. It involves Mindfulness of THE BIG PICTURE of what's going on. It involves turning on WISE MIND to determine the BEST plan of action. It involves ACCEPTING that life IS difficult at this time…and what we NEED to Go Through is uncomfortable, painful, and distressing…but, it's what we HAVE TO GO THROUGH…TO GET THROUGH IT. Our choice for ACCEPTANCE and PARTICIPATING EFFECTIVELY requires our WILLINGNESS to use DISTRESS TOLERANCE SKILLS to GET THROUGH IT!

Fighting Reality - Radical Non-Acceptance

Can you remember times when you have fought so hard or pushed things so far that they finally changed? What was it like for you while you were Fighting and pushing so hard? _____

_____

> SOMETIMES we CAN change things this way, but THE COST is our PHYSICAL[13] and EMOTIONAL WELL-BEING. When we're Fighting reality and PUSHING to IMPOSE OUR WILL onto people and situations, we're harmed by all the negative emotion and stress. We're often so filled with anger, hatred, and conflict…and so preoccupied with the Fight…it's all we talk about or think about. When we're Fighting the battle, the quality of our life is shot. Is THIS battle REALLY worth our peace and stability and all the conflict and turmoil it causes?

WE'RE GOING TO PAY A PRICE when we Fight reality and push hard to get our way. There WILL BE consequences for our "REFUSAL TO ACCEPT REALITY" BEHAVIOR. We may get a company to reverse a late fee, BUT they may close our account! We may yell at a doctor's receptionist over a "misunderstanding" about our appointment and we might be seen by the doctor THAT day, BUT, we've likely burned a bridge and will no longer receive special treatment…like being squeezed in for an appointment or free medication samples…AND, we may receive a letter telling us to find another doctor! We may make a big complaint about our child's teacher and we may get what WE WANT in THIS battle, BUT our child is likely to lose out down the road. For instance, if our child makes a 79 for a semester grade, he'll probably get a "C" and not be bumped up to a "B." If the kid's paper is late, the teacher won't let it slide and accept it without penalty. You're probably thinking, "That isn't fair and if I find out about it, that teacher is going to pay!" I know this feeling…but, HERE WE GO AGAIN! WE'RE GEARING UP FOR **ANOTHER** FIGHT. WHEN DOES IT STOP? When do WE STOP…and WHAT'S GOING ON WITH OUR PEACE AND STABILITY ALL THIS TIME…and the peace and stability of EVERYONE around us…INCLUDING OUR KID?!

The price we pay… is the undesirable consequences of our Fight… and the price of living in a state of anger, upheaval, anxiety, or conflict because of the Fight.

When we bite the hand that feeds us, it's going to hurt.

Things can get so Out-of-Control so fast…that all we're doing is Fighting the world. Are we going to Fight for EVERYTHING that upsets us?

Remember, part of being assertive… IS CHOOSING when and when not to be assertive!

Sometimes, Acceptance is the only way out of hell, the hell of suffering.

> To Mindfully Protect Our Peace and Stability, we MUST CHOOSE OUR BATTLES. We must DECIDE which things are WORTH GETTING UPSET ABOUT, angry about, and preoccupied with. We MUST DECIDE if the Fight is going to do MORE HARM than good. We MUST CONSIDER the impact of the Fight on the Big Picture of OUR Life and the lives of those we care about. In the Mindfulness chapters, we discussed CHOOSING which things to pay attention to and MAKING DECISIONS about WHAT to get involved in rather than Fighting every injustice, every jerk, and every insult that Comes Our Way. THAT'S BECAUSE THE COST OF FIGHTING REALITY IS HIGH.

SKILL BUILDER: Peace Comes by Accepting the Unacceptable

Think about when you CHOSE TO ACCEPT a situation that was NOT ACCEPTABLE to you. Was it the right decision for you at the time? Would you do it differently today? Explain. _____

_____

_____

Consider the situation of a father STRONGLY disapproving of his son's wife based on religious, racial, or other such differences. The father has several choices for responding to this "unacceptable" situation. What are they? _____

_____
_____
_____

Acceptance transforms Long-Term Suffering into a pain that is time-limited…and much less painful than the pain of endless suffering.

We're not here to live in hell. There's a world of peace meant for us and a life full of meaning and productivity.

Instead of great emotional pain and high conflict… peace, serenity, and joy become our reality!

He can STEP OUT of the situation and disown his son, emotionally divorce him, or vow to never talk to him again. He can STAY IN THE RING and fuss and Fight anytime they talk. These are NON-ACCEPTANCE CHOICES that'll leave both the father and son bitter, angry, and miserable. They'll either not visit or they'll Fight when they're together. The father has another choice…
THE CHOICE FOR PEACE AND STABILITY. He can CHOOSE TO ACCEPT the situation. It doesn't mean he likes it or approves of it. It means that he decides to STOP FIGHTING…and TO ACCEPT things as they are.
He can CHOOSE THE RADICAL ACCEPTANCE route by ACCEPTING WHAT IS UNACCEPTABLE to him. This will bring an end to suffering for his family… and over time, THE PAIN OF HIS BROKEN DREAM WILL SUBSIDE and the JOY OF ACCEPTANCE will come…sharing his life with his son and grandchildren!

Consider another situation. You HATE the color orange and you have ONE option for housing…a room painted orange. DESCRIBE the choices you have for…
Stepping Out of the situation _____

_____

Staying in the Ring and Fighting the situation _____

_____

Radical Acceptance _____

_____

Radical Acceptance is not just about accepting the unacceptable, it's also about doing something to make the situation better!

Most of us would rather have an orange room than to STEP OUT of the situation, refuse the room, and be homeless. Many of us would STAY IN THE RING AND FIGHT. We'd complain and push to have it repainted. We'd whine and fuss about how nothing ever goes our way and about all the crap we always get stuck with.
If we REFUSE TO ACCEPT the orange room by trying to deny it exists or if we go out and get drunk every night to avoid dealing with it, WE'LL NEVER PAINT IT A COLOR WE LIKE! The Wise Mind plan is RADICAL ACCEPTANCE…accepting the reality of the room and COMING UP WITH A COUPLE BUCKETS OF PAINT!!!

What would you have done IN THE PAST? Would you have ACCEPTED it or would you have thrown major TEMPER TANTRUMS? Would you have STAYED ANGRY and LET IT RUIN your days and months? Would you have Stepped Out of it and REFUSED the room or would you have given up and become depressed? Would you have MADE THE BEST OF IT until you could get it repainted? If they wouldn't allow painting, would you have been willing to do Distress Tolerance to deal with the room LONG ENOUGH for your CHANGES TO TAKE ROOT and you had enough MONEY TO MOVE?

What is your orange room in life? Think of an unpleasant situation you face...one in which the wisest response is Radical Acceptance...but YOU'RE IN NO MOOD TO ACCEPT IT! Make note of the situation and how you WILL deal with it. _____

_____

_____

_____

SKILL BUILDER: Radical Acceptance of Complicated Life Situations

It's always nice when there can be a happy ending that's FAIRLY EASY to come by...like when we're Fighting over things that AREN'T A MAJOR PRIORITY in our life...like an orange room...a teacher favoring certain kids over ours...a store not accepting our $12 return even though they advertise a return policy...or a co-worker who gets all the recognition and glory assignments. With these things, we have a choice to apply Radical Acceptance...to accept the situation, go on with life, and do what we CAN do to change things without making ourselves sick over it.

Many situations we Fight are MORE COMPLICATED. They involve things that are MAJOR PRIORITIES in our life...and their outcome MAKES A BIG DIFFERENCE in our life and the lives of those we love...often a critical difference.

Which MAJOR situations in your life fit this description? _____

_____

_____

We're faced with a choice to ACCEPT the Temporary Pain of Going Through major life changes… or to remain in a lifestyle of Long-Term Pain and Suffering.

Group Members have described some very difficult situations. Consider an abusive marriage. The decision is whether to stay in the marriage and have the kids and self endure ongoing pain and suffering from the abuse...OR to leave and risk the children ending up with the abusive spouse. Consider whether to report sexual abuse by a parent to the police. The decision is to STOP the abuse, protect others, and have justice...OR to testify against the parent and "re-live" the abuse, "causing" the parent to go to prison, "embarrassing" the family, and "causing" other consequences for self and family (loss of income, housing, emotional stress, etc).

328

Before making BIG decisions and deciding to take on a BIG FIGHT, it's best to seek wise counsel.

When we WISELY DECIDE to take on a BIG FIGHT, we must do so with the understanding that we've made the BEST DECISION possible…and that we're doing the best we can given the situation and our current physical and emotional state. We must be pretty sure we're making the best decision. We need to be at peace with our decision. We have to strongly believe it's OUR BEST CHOICE.

14- Resources like money, housing, a support system, counseling, etc.

If we're to this point in our decision making process, no doubt we haven't found peace by Stepping Back from the situation or Staying in the Ring and Fighting.

Consider whether to leave a marriage because of something unacceptable the spouse is doing that's destroying the emotional and financial well-being of the family (substance abuse, affairs, gambling addiction, etc.). The decision is to remain married and accept the unchanging situation OR to leave and undergo the emotional and financial consequences of divorce and raising the family as a single parent. Consider whether to leave a relationship or spouse because they're still using and we can't be clean n' sober living with all the temptation and chaos of the destructive environment and lifestyle.

What do you think we're supposed to do about THESE situations? _____

_____

_____

_____

Really, we MUST DO the things we've been discussing throughout this workbook. The starting point is a Wise Mind Worksheet. We must process the situation and take a hard look at THE BIG PICTURE of the situation. We must decide HOW IMPORTANT the situation REALLY is given all the other things going on in our life…including all our other priorities. WE MUST DECIDE IF THE BATTLE IS WORTH THE FIGHT. Some questions we may ask ourselves are:

Is the Fight REALLY in my best interests and the best interests of those I care about?

Is this battle REALLY WORTH my peace and stability and the peace and stability of those who depend on me?

Do I have the EXTRA ENERGY and resources[14] I need to Fight this battle WHILE Mindfully Protecting My Peace and Stability? If not, is there enough help and assistance available?

Are there any LESS COSTLY options that I can accept and be OK with?

Is this battle worth the cost?

In COMPLICATED situations, we MUST understand that NO MATTER WHAT WE DECIDE, we'll have pain and distress to Go Through. We MUST decide if we want to keep living like we're living (KEEP DANCING) or if we want to STEP OUT of the situation to STOP the Long-Term Pain and Suffering and give ourselves and others a chance at peace and stability. We must emotionally, rationally, and wisely consider the Big Picture of the Situation and decide WHAT'S REALLY in OUR best interests and the best interests of the BIG PICTURE of the situation. Whatever

The best Game Plans have back-up plans.

15- We know Long-Term Pain and Suffering worsens over time. It kills us...either physically by way of disease, injury, or Self-Destructive Coping Behaviors...or emotionally by way of an emotional or spiritual death. Sometimes, we push things so far that the decision to change comes down to a choice between LIFE and DEATH. We can choose to live and have life for ourselves and others OR we can choose to continue in the Cycle of Suffering.

decision we make, we MUST BE PRETTY SURE that we can be AT PEACE WITH OUR CHOICE. Some of the choices we make are reversible...some are not. Sometimes, if we go with Plan A and decide it's not right for us after all, we can modify our plan...or go with Plan B, C, or D instead. Sometimes, it's not that easy.

Once we CHOOSE TO FIGHT, we'll need to prepare ourselves for the Fight. We start by accepting that the Fight will be DIFFICULT and the Road to Recovery will have many "humps n' bumps" and "twists n' turns." Our Wise Mind Worksheet led us to a Game Plan or in this case, a battle plan. We must "GET OUR DUCKS IN A ROW" to ensure we have the COPING SKILLS and RESOURCES to carry out our plan. This includes HAVING OURSELVES READY and as physically, mentally, and emotionally prepared as possible. We'll also need to have a whole lot of SUPPORT lined up to help us see the Fight to the finish. These Fights will no doubt be the FIGHT OF OUR LIFE...and in some cases, the FIGHT FOR LIFE itself.[15]

If you chose to Fight a MAJOR BATTLE in your life, what would you need to do to PREPARE for the Fight so you're EQUIPPED to see your Fight to the finish? _____

_____

_____

_____

_____

We'll have to Turn our Mind and COMMIT to ACCEPTANCE over and over. The gift, when we keep Turning Our Mind BACK to Acceptance, it'll stay there longer and longer! OVER TIME, we'll notice we went a whole ten minutes, an hour, a morning, or a whole day without going back to Non-Acceptance. We'll finally have some peace... some peace of mind!

SKILL BUILDER: Turning Our Mind to Acceptance

ACCEPTANCE REQUIRES A CHOICE. It's like coming to a fork in the road and being faced with two paths. We must choose to TURN OUR MIND towards the ACCEPT REALITY ROAD...and REFUSE to go the NON-ACCEPTANCE ROUTE. When we Turn Our Mind to Acceptance, it may STAY TURNED for a second or two. Then it goes back to the Non-Acceptance route of anger and related feelings. We MUST be Mindful of our MIND SWINGS and WORK to Turn Our Mind BACK to Acceptance TIME AND TIME AGAIN! It's like changing any old habit, we'll HAVE TO WORK at it until it becomes our reality and our way of thinking.

Because Radical Acceptance is RADICAL...because it ISN'T NATURAL or EASY at first, we MUST make an INNER COMMITMENT to accept things that are difficult to accept. Sometimes, the CHOICE to accept must be made daily... sometimes, many times a day or MANY TIMES AN HOUR! AA recommends a DAILY DEVOTIONAL for this reason and saying the SERENITY PRAYER as often as necessary! It takes WORK to change the way we think so we can change the

330

way we feel. Acceptance is a way to CONTROL OUR EMOTIONS INSTEAD OF LETTING OUR EMOTIONS CONTROL US! Remember...IF CHANGE WAS EASY, we would've done it LONG AGO...AND WE WOULDN'T STRUGGLE WITH IT SO!

APPLICATION: The Baseball Analogy of Life...We're Always at the Plate

We've talked before about how life, temptation, tough times, and problems are always Coming At Us. We know our job is to Mindfully Protect Our Peace and Stability. The following is a great analogy[16] to explain the DBT and the DBT-CBT way to APPROACH LIFE and to RESPOND to what Comes At Us.

16- This analogy was suggested by Dr. Linehan in her Skills Training Manual (page 103).

During the toughest games of the season, Rational Mind will remind us that the World Champs lost some games. Wise Mind will urge us to go up to bat and to do our best EVERY TIME we're at the plate. Distress Tolerance will keep us in the game...and Acceptance will keep us at peace... even if we're five runs behind at the bottom of the first inning.

The Baseball Analogy of Life

LIFE IS like baseball and we're up to bat.

OUR JOB IS to do our best to hit the balls Coming At Us.

MINDFULNESS IS awareness that balls will be coming.
It involves keeping our eye on the ball...
and being aware of how we're holding the bat...
and if we're in a good stance to bat well.

WISE MIND PROVIDES US with a Game Plan
and suggests how to make the best plays.

WISE MIND URGES US to hit certain balls
and to let others go by.

ACCEPTANCE IS knowing that despite doing our best,
we'll occasionally strike-out and foul.

DISTRESS TOLERANCE URGES US to accept the reality of our game situation
and to stay with the Game Plan despite any fastballs or curveballs Coming At Us.

NON-ACCEPTANCE IS refusing to go up to bat
or to swing when the good balls come across the plate.

NON-ACCEPTANCE IS standing there, doing nothing, and striking out
by not Participating Effectively in the game of our life.

NON-ACCEPTANCE ALSO INVOLVES standing in the way of the ball
and getting hit, bruised, and beaten by life.

NON-ACCEPTANCE DOES NOT stop the balls from coming.
Willpower, tantrums, crying, fussing, screaming, suicide attempts, and
manipulation do not make the balls stop. They'll still be coming.

LIFE WILL COME AT US whether or not
we choose to Get in the Game and to Participate Effectively.

From "Out-of-Control: A Dialectical Behavior Therapy (DBT) – Cognitive-Behavioral Therapy (CBT) Workbook for Getting Control of Our Emotions and Emotion-Driven Behavior" - Copyright © 2009 by Melanie Gordon Sheets, Ph.D. (www.dbt-cbt-workbook.com)

Which parts of the Baseball Analogy relate to your life at this time? _____

_____

_____

_____

_____

APPLICATION: It All Comes Down to Our Will: Willingness vs. Willfulness

WILLINGNESS is ACCEPTING REALITY...and RESPONDING TO REALITY in an EFFECTIVE way. Willingness is CHOOSING to do WHAT'S NEEDED in the current situation or moment. Willingness is FOLLOWING THROUGH with what Wise Mind KNOWS TO DO.

WILLFUL-NESS involves PUSHING OUR WILL onto reality and trying to FORCE THINGS to be like WE WANT them to be. WILLFULNESS[17] involves doing WHAT WE WANT rather than what's needed. This includes DOING NOTHING when action is required. WILLFULNESS also involves REFUSING TO TOLERATE THE MOMENT so we can have a BETTER HOUR and a BETTER TOMORROW.

At this point in your life, are you a more willing person or a more willful person? Explain. _____

_____

_____

17- Dr. Linehan discussed willingness, willfulness, and tolerating the moment in her Skills Training Manual.

Many of us are still in the game despite our game play and efforts to be OUT of the game. Don't throw in the towel and cut your game short. There are many innings left! Remember, even the World Champs suffered some hard losses in their winning season. You're reading the player's manual and you're learning new skills to improve your game play. Now go on out there and play ball! Heed the call, "Batter Up!"

WHAT DO YOU CHOOSE...to be willing or willful? The QUALITY of our life comes down to these two concepts. Are you WILLING TO MAKE THE LIFE CHANGES you've considered throughout this workbook or will you be WILLFUL and STICK TO YOUR OLD WAYS despite KNOWING how destructive and hurtful they are to yourself and others. If you're not ready to change everything at once, choose where you'll start. DON'T BE WILLFUL AND THROW IN THE TOWEL. THIS IS THE GAME OF A LIFETIME. IT'S YOUR LIFE... a life VERY PRECIOUS and DEAR to many. Your people may be on the sidelines, in the stands, or watching from their living room. No matter how close or distant, THEY WANT YOU UP TO BAT and making the BEST PLAYS possible. They don't expect you to win every inning or game, but they're rooting for you to GET PASSED LIFE'S CURVEBALLS AND FASTBALLS. They'll be standing humbled, proud, and tall at the end of the season! IT'S GAME DAY... SO GO ON OUT THERE AND PLAY BALL...AND PLAY IT BY THE RULES!

The NEXT CHAPTERS of our life involve developing a GAME PLAN for living a
Recovery Lifestyle and learning ways to STICK TO IT through the wins and the
losses of the upcoming season. To ensure a pennant at the end of this race,
pre-season training will focus on skills for Getting Through the tough games.
WE MUST LEARN AND PRACTICE COPING SKILLS that work for us
and we must DEVELOP A GAME PLAN to ensure our VICTORY.
Continue to work through this playbook and practice the skills you're learning.
Time is running short but there's still time to get in on this pre-season practice.
The season is coming whether we're ready or not.

~~~~~~~~ CHAPTER REVIEW ~~~~~~~~

1. Why do we stay in painful situations? How can we get the pain and suffering to stop? _____
_____
_____
_____

2. How is the pain of recovery different from the pain of suffering? _____
_____
_____
_____

3. How do we get a fresh start? _____
_____

4. What's so radical about Radical Acceptance? _____
_____
_____

5. How is it that we're "good-hearted people with good morals and values" if we've been doing a lot of bad things? _____
_____
_____

6. What are we supposed to do about the horrible, rotten things we've done in the past? _____
_____

7. What do we do when we "reframe" something? How does it help us? _____
_____

_____

_____

8. If we've accepted an "unchanging situation" and choose to continue to try to make changes in it, how can we do this without getting hurt and upset all the time?

_____

_____

9. What is meant by Stepping Back from a situation rather than Stepping Out of it? _____

_____

_____

10. How do we Get Through difficult life consequences? _____

_____

_____

_____

11. What are some consequences of pushing too hard or Fighting too hard to get our way? _____

_____

12. Why in the world would we want to accept the unacceptable? _____

_____

13. Name one situation that's an "orange room" for you? _____

_____

14. What are "Mind Swings" and what do we do about them? _____

_____

_____

15. In the Baseball Analogy of Life, what role does Mindfulness play? _____

_____

_____

16. In the Baseball Analogy, what role does Wise Mind play? _____

_____

_____

17. In the Baseball Analogy, what role does Acceptance play? _____

_____

_____

18. In the Baseball Analogy, what role does Distress Tolerance play? _____

334

19. In the Baseball Analogy, what is Non-Acceptance? _____
_____
_____

20. In the Baseball Analogy, how do we Participate Effectively? _____
_____
_____

21. How does willingness and willfulness affect the quality of our life? _____
_____
_____

~~~ *For Reflection* ~~~

_____
_____
_____
_____
_____
_____
_____
_____
_____
_____
_____
_____
_____
_____

Figure 12.A.1: The Concepts and Skills Tracking Sheet – Chapter 12

Week # _____

	Day of Week →							
	Date →							
12A.	Today, I thought about a problem in my life that I haven't dealt with effectively. I realized that somehow I've been willing to suffer Long-Term Pain because of it. I haven't wanted to Go Through Temporary Pain to get THE PAIN TO STOP.							
12B.	Today, I realized that the only way to get my pain to stop is to accept the pain of making changes and to Lean Into it and deal with it.							
12C.	Today, I reminded myself that the Temporary Pain of healing is much less painful in the long run than the enduring pain of suffering.							
12D.	Today, I applied one of the Acceptance Statements to my life. It helped me to accept something that would've been hard for me to accept in the past.							
12E.	Today, I realized that the way my life is going is my responsibility. I'm ultimately responsible for how things go in my life...one way or another.							
12F.	Today, I forgave someone for hurting or disappointing me. I realize folks who care about me are human and may hurt me now and then...because of their own mood states and issues.							
12G.	Today, I accepted that things won't always go my way...and my job is to do the best I can with the way things are.							
12H.	Today, I Stopped Myself from thinking about the painful past. I accepted that the past is the past. I realized that there's meaning to my life and I can't live it out if I live in the past. I refocused myself the best I could on the here-and-now and the positive things I can be doing.							
12I.	Today, I Turned My Mind from negativity to NEW LIFE and living a Recovery Lifestyle!							
12J.	Today, I thought about something unacceptable from my past that's been causing me pain. I thought how accepting the unacceptable could help me.							

Notes:

RATING SCALE

5 – Did Excellent in this area today
4 – Did Pretty Good in this area today
3 – Did Alright in this area today
2 – Did Only Fair in this area today
1 – Didn't Do Well in this area today
DD – Didn't Do today

From "Out-of-Control: A Dialectical Behavior Therapy (DBT) – Cognitive-Behavioral Therapy (CBT) Workbook for Getting Control of Our Emotions and Emotion-Driven Behavior" Copyright © 2009 by Melanie Gordon Sheets, Ph.D. (www.dbt-cbt-workbook.com)

Figure 12.A.2: The Concepts and Skills Tracking Sheet – Chapter 12

Week # _____

	Day of Week →							Notes:
	Date →							
12K. Today, I reframed a situation and was able to feel better about it.								
12L. Today, I thought about an "I can't win them over" situation in my life. I accepted that I may not be able to change the situation...but I could work To change how I dealt with the situation and felt about it.								
12M. Today, I thought about a difficult situation. I accepted that I have choices about how I deal with, feel about, and respond to it. I considered some of my options...like Stepping Out of it, Stepping Back and still trying to make changes, Staying in the Ring and Fighting, or to Keep Dancing.								
12N. I made a choice about how to deal with a difficult situation. I came up with a Game Plan for how to best deal with it.								
12O. Today, I had an opportunity to deal with a difficult situation. Though there's always room for improvement, I followed my Game Plan pretty well.								
12P. Today, I worked to accept whatever came my way and I did the best I could given what was going on in-the-moment.								
12Q. Today, I accepted responsibility for one or more negative consequences in my life.								
12R. Today, I accepted responsibility for a negative consequence in my life that I've needed to deal with. I decided I would do what I needed to do to deal with it and to GO ON WITH MY LIFE.								
12S. Today, I thought about a troubling situation. I began to Think Through it to decide if it was a battle worth Fighting.								
12T. Today, I began to prepare...or continued to prepare...to Fight a battle that is WORTH the Fight. I'm working on "getting all my ducks in a row".								

RATING SCALE

5 – Did Excellent in this area today
4 – Did Pretty Good in this area today
3 – Did Alright in this area today
2 – Did Only Fair in this area today
1 – Didn't Do Well in this area today
DD – Didn't Do today

Figure 12.A.3: The Concepts and Skills Tracking Sheet – Chapter 12

Week # _____

Day of Week →

Date →

12U. Today, I thought about the Baseball Analogy. I accepted that this is my life and I need to go up to bat and do my Best to deal with the balls Coming at Me.

12V. Today, I thought about the Baseball Analogy. I reminded myself that I need to be Mindful of what was Coming at Me and how I was going to deal with these things.

12W. Today, I thought about the Baseball Analogy. I realized that I need to get a Game Plan for dealing with the things Coming at Me.

12X. Today, I thought about the Baseball Analogy. I realized I need to use Wise Mind to decide how to deal with the things Coming at Me. I realized that I must wisely decide which things to swing at, deal with, and respond to.

12Y. Today, I applied the Baseball Analogy to my life. I accepted that no matter how hard I try...I will not play the perfect game every game. I accept that I will not be perfect in recovery...but every time I'm at bat...I will do my best.

12Z. Today, I applied the Baseball Analogy to my life. I accepted that my recovery requires Distress Tolerance. I must stay in the game despite any difficult times that Come My Way.

12AA. Today, I thought about the Baseball Analogy. I realized that if I don't accept and deal with my problems, I'll continue to be beaten and bruised by life.

12BB. Today I thought about the Baseball Analogy. I reminded myself that life will Come at Me whether or not I choose to Participate Effectively.

12CC. Today, I challenged myself to be WILLING to deal with life effectively even when I was in a willful mood and didn't feel like it!

Notes:

RATING SCALE

5 - Did Excellent in this area today
4 - Did Pretty Good in this area today
3 - Did Alright in this area today
2 - Did Only Fair in this area today
1 - Didn't Do Well in this area today
DD - Didn't Do today

┌─────────────────────────────────────┐
│ ~ 13 ~ │
│ LIFE-ENHANCING COPING SKILLS │
└─────────────────────────────────────┘

Our Recovery Goal is to PROTECT our peace and stability. This involves doing things to MAINTAIN our peace and stability AS MUCH AS POSSIBLE during difficult times.

1- Normal levels - what average people experience. When things are going fairly well in life, people experience pretty good levels of peace and stability. When difficult times come, peace and stability naturally decrease.

When we get in the habit of doing Life-Enhancing Coping Behaviors, our life will begin to normalize. Over time, we'll begin to experience "normal levels" of peace and stability.

Imagine experiencing normal levels of peace and stability and living a lifestyle that brings meaning to life and a desire to LIVE LIFE!

We've discussed coping mechanisms throughout this workbook and we're finally to a chapter devoted entirely to them! We'll discuss coping behaviors in detail starting with a comparison of the two types...the Destructive Coping Behaviors and the Life-Enhancing ones. We'll also review positive things we can do to LOWER THE INTENSITY of our negative emotions so we can BETTER MANAGE our emotions and PARTICIPATE EFFECTIVELY in our life. When we STOP ourselves from doing Destructive Coping Behaviors and begin USING life-enhancing ones, the QUALITY OF OUR LIFE will steadily improve. Our Recovery Goal is to experience "NORMAL LEVELS"[1] of peace and stability during GOOD TIMES and BAD TIMES.

Hmmmm…..Which Do I Choose?

There's many reasons we prefer to use Destructive Coping Mechanisms. Review the qualities of both types below. Which type would you rather do if they both led to positive life outcomes? _____

SELF-DESTRUCTIVE	LIFE-ENHANCING
Very powerful - Numb-Out, White-Out	Reduces, doesn't eliminate distress
Immediate gratification - relief	May take longer to work
Habits - know how to do these	Must learn or try something new
Tried n' True	Less confidence in how they work
Many are single actions - less effort	A series of actions - more effort
Long-lasting relief	Short-term relief
Many are "wild n' crazy fun"	Most are less exciting
Complete Pleasure Principle	Requires self-discipline
Causes more life problems	Improves quality of life

Most of us would choose the type that's the most fun and requires the least effort! Which type is that? _____

What are the top three or four reasons you choose Self-Destructive Coping Behaviors? Mark your top reasons above.

Most of us have chosen to do Destructive Coping Behaviors for the reasons described; however, WE'VE GROWN TIRED of their devastating consequences. TO GET OUR LIFE IN ORDER and KEEP IT THAT WAY, WE'RE REQUIRED TO GIVE UP SELF-DEFEATING BEHAVIORS...and to do life-enhancing ones instead.

We're stubborn creatures and it's hard to pull us away from the Tried N' True and the familiar and habitual, but WHAT GREAT RELIEF we'll experience as a result!

"The Levels of Emotion Chart"

Check out the chart on the next page (Figure 13.A). It describes how we FEEL and FUNCTION when we're experiencing different levels of NEGATIVE EMOTION. The levels range from 0–10. At Level 0, we're at peace. At Level 10, we're desperately overwhelmed with negative emotion. The far right columns show how active Emotional Mind and Rational Mind are at each level. It's just a guess though! This chart helps to gauge or "measure" our EMOTIONAL INTENSITY and to better understand the EFFECT our emotional level has on our ABILITY TO PARTICIPATE EFFECTIVELY in our life. It also shows how the DBT-CBT Recovery Tools can help us to Participate Effectively during difficult times.

2- Remember Chapter 4 and "The Mindfully Protecting Our Peace and Stability Worksheet." Our Inner Circle contains the most important parts of our life...the things we want to protect.

3- "It" is whatever is bothering us! "It" may be sadness over a loss...or something that worries us or makes us angry.

Let's check out these levels. **Levels 0-2** fall in the range of **Mild Emotional Intensity**. **At Level 0**, we're functioning with about 65% Rational Mind and 35% Emotional Mind. That's a pretty comfortable state. We have some problems, but we're letting things roll off of us like water off a duck's back. That means we're Mindfully Protecting Our Peace and Stability and not letting things bother us or get into our Inner Circle.[2] WE'RE PUTTING HASSLES, IRRITANTS, WORRIES, AND PROBLEMS ON A CLOUD...AND THEY'RE FLOATING AWAY!

At Level 1, "it"[3] crossed our mind just once during our work day. We're able to Participate Effectively in our daily life...and we got a lot of work done!

At Level 2, Emotional Mind is now at 45% and Rational Mind is 55%. We're EXPERIENCING our emotions more at Level 2 than Level 1...like once or twice EVERY FEW HOURS rather than just once during our work day. Upsetting thoughts come to mind, but PASS THROUGH. They don't distract us from doing what we need to do. We're managing our emotional stuff VERY WELL. We're getting through our day just fine and we're getting a good amount of work done!

Despite our problems, we're able to Participate Effectively WITH SOME EFFORT. We're taking care of our priorities and the demands of life ...which include Getting Through the work day! We're tolerating our emotions...and we're DOING THE BEST WE CAN despite the upsetting things going on.

Levels 3-5 fall in the range of **Moderate Emotional Intensity**. **At Level 3**, we're experiencing our emotions, but we're still managing things and holding on to stability. Its 50-50 Emotional Mind - Rational Mind. We're upset and we KNOW we'll cry LATER when we can do so WITHOUT major consequences...like getting sent home from work or being passed up for a promotion because we're not emotionally stable right now.

340

START READING from the bottom at Level 0 and read upwards! It'll make more sense that way!

This chart is a handy reference for "measuring" our emotional intensity. It provides descriptions of how we function at different levels of NEGATIVE EMOTION. It helps us to better understand the EFFECT our emotional levels have on our ability to PARTICIPATE EFFECTIVELY in our daily life.

There are 11 levels ranging from 0 - 10... from Mild to Severe Emotional Intensity.

In the far right columns... is an estimate of the amount of Rational Mind (RM) and Emotional Mind (EM) that's active at each level. These percentages show how much influence each mind state has on our emotional experience... and our ability to function.

These levels and percentages are for descriptive purposes only! They're not based on scientific studies! They're provided as an aid to better understand DBT-CBT principles and concepts.

Figure 13.A: The Levels of Emotion Chart

			RM	EM
SEVERE EMOTIONAL INTENSITY	10	I have NO self-control. I AM having a nervous breakdown. I'm going to blow. Ain't nothing short of a miracle will help me now. I'm Big-Time Emotional Mind. I'm 100% overtaken by Emotional Mind.	5	95
	9	I'm about to lose it. I can't handle this. I'm going to cut and then call my sponsor. I've got to do something for relief. I can't deal with this anymore. I could get a 6-pack and take some pills. That would help me feel better, too. I forgot to call-in today. They're probably pissed since it's so late...whatever. Screw it. I was looking for a job when I found this one.	10	90
	8	I'm really upset. Stuff is really bothering me. I can't focus on anything else. I called in sick today. There was no use showing up to work. There's no holding it together today. I couldn't even pretend to be okay. I'm either too angry or too depressed. I really need to call my therapist or sponsor. I'm losing it. If things get too bad, I have a razor taped under the sink and I have full bottles of most of my meds.	15	85
MODERATELY SEVERE INTENSITY	7	I'm really upset. Stuff is really bothering me. I'm thinking about it almost constantly. I keep getting distracted. I'm at work, but I can't get anything done. I'm preoccupied with my stuff. I'm either talking about it or it's churning in my head. Destructive thoughts are going through my mind, thoughts of revenge and Self-Defeating Coping Behaviors. When my boss shows up, I look okay and can act productive and "with it," but, I'm really in trouble. If I don't get control, I'm headed for disaster. I'm beyond, "Fake it 'til you make it."	20	80
	6	I'm pretty upset. I'm starting to feel overwhelmed. I had three sales calls to make. I only did one. I needed to call them back with some info but didn't feel like it. I'll have to do it tomorrow. I showed up for my AA meeting late and left a few minutes early so I could avoid everyone. I went home, flipped channels on the TV, and my sponsor called. That was nice. I agreed to meet him for coffee in the morning. I fell asleep on the couch and slept there in my clothes most of the night.	30	70
MODERATE EMOTIONAL INTENSITY	5	I'm experiencing my stuff. I have a lot to do and need to focus on my work. I spent half my work day preoccupied with my stuff, but at least I got something done. I showed up for Choir Practice, that was nice. Though I had to force myself to go and wasn't in the mood when I got there, I felt better afterwards...good enough that I got through the rest of the evening without any great impulse to do something stupid. I felt lazy, lit all my candles, took a warm bubble bath, and went to bed early without straightening the kitchen.	40	60
	4	I did alright most of the day. I cried for a few minutes in the bathroom, but dried up when Gracie came in. I think she knew, but she didn't say anything. I took care of most everything that had to be done today at work. I subbed for the bowling league like I agreed to do, but I didn't feel up to going out with folks afterwards. I came home and played on the computer for a few hours before I went to bed.	45	55
	3	Upsetting thoughts, feelings, and concerns are definitely there, but, I'm okay for now. I expect to cry or to experience my feelings later, but, I'm holding together alright. I'm able to Participate Effectively with some effort.	50	50
MILD INTENSITY	2	Upsetting thoughts, feelings, and concerns are there. I notice them once or twice every few hours, but right now, they're more of a passing thought or feeling. I'm able to keep my mind on my work and I'm doing fine for hours at a time. I'm getting through my day just fine...despite it all.	55	45
	1	Upsetting thoughts, feelings, and concerns are minimal. I'm doing good. I think it crossed my mind just once today at work. That's a great change! I'm starting to get caught up at work!	60	40
	0	I'm at peace. Things are fine. As usual, there's always something going on that can be irritating or upsetting. However, I have a good attitude. I'm feeling good. Stuff's rolling off me like water off a duck's back!	65	35

From "Out-of-Control: A Dialectical Behavior Therapy (DBT) - Cognitive-Behavioral Therapy (CBT) Workbook for Getting Control of Our Emotions and Emotion-Driven Behavior" - Copyright © 2009 by Melanie Gordon Sheets, Ph.D. (www.dbt-cbt-workbook.com)

At Level 4, Emotional Mind is building (55%). It's taking over. Rational Mind is down to 45%. There's some slippage. Emotional Mind is interfering with our ability to function.

Which parts of the story suggest problems functioning ADEQUATELY? _____

_____

_____

We weren't able to hold back our emotions, but we had ENOUGH CONTROL to get ourselves to a fairly safe place to cry. Thank goodness it was a nice co-worker who saw us rather than someone who likes to tell on people and get them in trouble! We're also slipping because we didn't go out to Denny's after bowling like we usually do. We didn't feel up to socializing, so we went home instead.

At this level, what successes did we have? _____

_____

_____

Though not 100%, we did pretty good for what we were Going Through!

> We were SUCCESSFUL because WE WENT TO WORK and we MET MOST of our work PRIORITIES. We got most everything done that we needed to do! THAT'S SUCCESS WHEN BIG STUFF IS GOING ON IN OUR LIFE!
> Also, we went bowling. We had people depending on us and WE DID WHAT WE AGREED TO DO. Once home, instead of sitting around and being preoccupied with upsetting thoughts, WE DID A LIFE-ENHANCING COPING ACTIVITY. We KEPT OUR MIND BUSY by playing on the computer!

Check out **Level 5**. What slippage do you notice? _____

_____

_____

4- Based on the story, we USUALLY enjoy Choir Practice...and straightening the kitchen is part of our evening routine...(unfortunately not mine!).

We're slipping by spending HALF our work day preoccupied with our stuff. Also, we didn't feel like going to Choir Practice and we didn't straighten the kitchen.[4] These are DEFINITE WARNING SIGNS **FOR US** that we're STARTING to LOSE CONTROL. WE'RE STRUGGLING. Notice Emotional Mind is 60% and Rational Mind is 40%. THE SCALES ARE TIPPING and Emotional Mind is beginning to weigh heavily on us.

What successes did we have? _____

_____

_____

_____

Though Emotional Mind is really building, we were ABLE to do what we NEEDED TO DO TO BE OKAY… and to Mindfully Protect Our Peace and Stability.

> We SUCCESSFULLY FORCED ourselves to PARTICIPATE EFFECTIVELY in our life EVEN THOUGH WE DIDN'T FEEL LIKE IT. We MET THE PRIORITIES of the day by going to work and Choir Practice. Getting half a day's worth of work done is BETTER than none! We DID A LIFE-ENHANCING COPING BEHAVIOR AND IT WORKED! We FOUND SOME PEACE by going to Choir Practice, ENOUGH THAT WE GOT THROUGH the evening without any great impulse to do something destructive. Though we felt lazy, WE DID ANOTHER POSITIVE COPING ACTIVITY. We lit candles and took a warm bath! IT WORKED, TOO! IT GOT US THROUGH to bedtime. WE MADE IT! WE DID AWESOME!

Check out **Levels 6 and 7**. They fall in the range of **Moderately Severe Intensity**. **At Level 6**, distress is getting the best of us. Emotional Mind is 70% and Rational Mind is 30%. We're overwhelmed with our emotions and distress. What slippage do you notice? _____

_____

_____

We tried to watch TV to get our mind off our troubles. We just flipped channels. We tried a productive coping activity but couldn't get our mind into it.

Major slippage is making ONLY 1 of 3 sales calls and NOT Following Through with what We Needed to do WITH THE ONE sales call we made. We did good to force ourselves to do a Life-Enhancing Coping Mechanism…but, we didn't Follow Through with it. We ARRIVED LATE to the AA meeting and LEFT EARLY so we could avoid people. TV didn't work for us, either. WE WERE PREOCCUPIED WITH OUR DISTRESS. We weren't able to focus on a program and we didn't enjoy it. We just flipped channels. Also, we didn't or couldn't force ourselves to get ready for bed. We slept on the couch in our clothes. Major problems here.
What successes did we have? _____

_____

_____

> We made one sales call and we forced ourselves to go to the AA meeting. We agreed to meet with our sponsor the next morning and we DID NOT RELAPSE. We're STILL TRYING to hold on. WE ARE HOLDING ON, but not by much. We MUST GET HELP at this point or we're headed down Relapse Road.

At Level 7, we're only 20% Rational Mind. Emotional Mind is in the driver's seat. We're TOTALLY PREOCCUPIED WITH OUR STUFF. We're thinking about our troubles constantly. We're very distracted. We're not getting anything done at work. We're having destructive Emotion-Driven Thoughts. This marks a very

We can't have too many days in a row of not getting anything done at work. The truth, when people are going through tough emotional times, unproductive days are very normal.

We didn't call in sick…so, we may lose our job. We're in our "Screw it" mentality and we don't care.

We'll have to do Damage Control to manage the losses we're going to suffer …because we waited too long to get help.

It's much better to Go Through the consequences of hospitalization than the consequences of hospitalization AND relapse. That's a double whammy of distress that we should avoid.

critical time in our recovery. It is VERY positive that we have enough Rational Mind going on to pull it together…to LOOK LIKE we're okay when the boss sees us. It's also very positive that we're Mindful of being seriously troubled and headed for disaster if we can't overcome this emotional state.

What else is very positive? _____

_____

_____

> It's also VERY POSITIVE that we SHOWED UP FOR WORK. We're Mindfully Protecting Our Peace and Stability by going to work and pulling it together when the boss is around. WE MAINTAIN OUR JOB and we protect everything in the Big Picture of Our Life that depends on us having a job and cash flow.

Levels 8-10 hit the Severe Intensity Level. This is when bad things happen. **At Level 8**, we BELIEVE we can't hold it together to look okay at work…so we call in sick. IF WE HAVEN'T BEEN ABUSING SICK TIME, we've probably maintained our job by calling in. We still have 15% Rational Mind going on and we KNOW we need to get help, but Emotional Mind is PLANNING RELAPSE by cutting or OD'ing. If we don't make the call, we're likely to relapse into old patterns of self-harm.

At Level 9, WE'RE EMOTION-DRIVEN. We PLAN to cut BEFORE we get help. We believe the Emotion-Driven Lies that "I can't handle this." and alcohol or extra pills will "help me feel better." We have SOME Rational Mind going on because we KNOW we need help. IF we get help, we'll have a chance to do Damage Control and plead for our job back…or we can quickly find a new one. If we don't get help, THE CYCLE OF SUFFERING STARTS HERE.

At Level 10, we'll probably do something destructive. HOPEFULLY, we'll use the 5% of Rational Mind to THINK BEFORE WE DO. Hopefully, Wise Mind will kick in and urge us to act in a way to bring about the miracle…like calling for help. At this point, WE'LL PROBABLY END UP WITH SOME CONSEQUENCES and treatment…no matter what we do.

We can MINIMIZE CONSEQUENCES by calling for help and NOT DOING destructive behavior. If we call 9-1-1 and end up in the hospital, we're MUCH better off than if we O.D., cut, pull a drunk…and end up in a hospital or jail AND the Cycle of Suffering. If we act on how we feel, we'll have all the EXTRA PROBLEMS OF RELAPSE and the losses in life that a relapse causes. We need to call for help BEFORE things get really bad.

A Member suggested adding Level 11. She described times when things get SO BAD that she becomes psychotic and loses all contact with reality. This would be 0% Rational Mind. She related that she becomes VERY paranoid and hears voices saying ugly things about her. She stated that these voices encourage her to act on her paranoid beliefs and to harm herself. She told the Group that during these times, she ends up saying and doing things that cause painful losses across the Big Picture of Her Life. Several other Members shared that their Level 11 occurs when they become manic. They related that they lose their good judgment and end up doing all kinds of impulsive and irrational things. They noted that their Out-of-Control behavior causes them serious life problems and painful losses, too. Have you ever been at the 11th Level? Describe your experience. _____

The Out-of-Control behavior of Bipolar Mania qualifies for Level 11 whether or not psychosis is involved!

_____

_____

Members are asked to identify the level they were at when "Something Happened" and they ended up in treatment. If you've been in treatment, what level are you USUALLY AT right before you end up in treatment? _____

What level are you currently at? _____

What's your highest and lowest level today? _____

What level or levels are you at MOST of the time? _____

What's the level of your best functioning over the past month? _____

What's the level of your best functioning over the past year? _____

At what level should YOU seek help? _____

Most Members believe we should call our support person, sponsor, counselor, or crisis worker at Level 5 or 6. Knowing what they know now...they want to get help BEFORE things BEGIN TO GET Out-of-Control. At Levels 5 and 6, we still have a fair amount of Rational Mind going on. This helps us to seek support...and to accept the Rational Mind and Wise Mind understandings and suggestions offered to us!

APPLICATION: How Coping Mechanisms Reduce Negative Emotion

Check out "The Emotional Thermometer" on the next page.[5] Think of Columns A, B, and C to be "temperature gauges" that measure our emotional intensity.

The level of emotion in **Column A** has reached the Severe Emotional Intensity level of Level 10. This marks the absolute breaking point...when we totally "lose it"...like when the lid blows off the teapot. This is when we're experiencing SEVERE emotional distress and are Big-Time in Emotional Mind.

5- This graphic shows how low our emotional intensity goes when we use Self-Destructive Coping Behaviors and Life-Enhancing Coping Behaviors.

These levels are based on "The Levels of Emotion Chart" in Figure 13.A.

345

When we're under the influence of Self-Destructive Coping Behaviors, even though our emotional intensity is low, we're generally not doing the life-enhancing things commonly associated with a low level of emotional distress, like catching up at work and handling other priorities!

Column B shows what happens when we use Destructive Coping Behaviors. Our emotional intensity typically falls to the Mild 0-2 range. We're pretty well Numbed-Out or are otherwise experiencing little to no emotional distress.

Figure 13.B: "The Emotional Thermometer"

A	B	C
10	10	10
9	9	9
8	8	8
7	7	7
6	6	6
5	5	5
4	4	4
3	3	3
2	2	2
1	1	1
0	0	0
IN THE HEAT-OF-THE-MOMENT *we're FILLED with emotion!*	SELF-DESTRUCTIVE COPING BEHAVIORS *wipe-out or nearly wipe-out our negative emotions for awhile.*	LIFE-ENHANCING COPING BEHAVIORS *reduce our distress to levels we can better tolerate.*

Column C shows what happens to our emotional intensity when we use Life-Enhancing Coping Mechanisms. Our intensity level often falls to the 0-2 Mild range or the Moderate range of levels 3 and 4.

To get a feel for how this works, consider this scenario. We're pretty upset and our Emotional Level is a 6 or 7. It's Sunday and we love football. We're watching our favorite team on TV. Our mind wanders to our problems now and then…and we work to stay focused on the game. Our intensity level drops to a 4 or 5. The score tightens. We're finally FOCUSED on the game and our level DROPS to the 0-2 range. DURING HALF TIME and commercials, our mind turns back to our worries…and our level GOES BACK UP to a 4 or 5. When the game comes BACK ON, our mind turns back to the game and our level DROPS again. We're no longer bothered by our problems…WE'RE "IN THE ZONE," the "game zone!"

From "Out-of-Control: A Dialectical Behavior Therapy (DBT) – Cognitive-Behavioral Therapy (CBT) Workbook for Getting Control of Our Emotions and Emotion-Driven Behavior" - Copyright © 2009 by Melanie Gordon Sheets, Ph.D. (www.dbt-cbt-workbook.com)

This up and down pattern works for all types of Life-Enhancing Coping Behaviors.[6] Our emotional intensity goes down when we're involved in the activity. It often goes back up a bit when the activity stops and our attention turns back to our problems. However, this level ISN'T USUALLY AS HIGH as it was before the activity. That's because our body and mind is more relaxed. We're not as intense as we were before. We calmed down during our coping activity and it takes a little while to get ourselves all worked up again!

Do you agree with this information...about the changes in our Emotional Intensity Levels when we're doing Self-Destructive and Life-Enhancing Coping Behaviors? Is it similar to what you've experienced? Explain. _____ _____ _____

How low does your Emotional Level fall when you're doing Destructive Coping Behaviors? _____

Which types of activities are as distracting for you as football and dominoes are for other people? If you did a favorite activity when you were upset, how low could your Emotional Level go? _____ _____ _____

APPLICATION: To Eliminate or to Reduce

We often choose Self-Destructive Coping Behaviors because they're VERY POWERFUL. They generally WIPE-OUT emotional distress for AWHILE. They NUMB US (cutting, heroin, an overdose, a major drunk), RELAX US (marijuana, pills, cutting, some alcohol[7]), or cause ELATION[8] (Ecstasy, cocaine). Some DISTRACT us from our problems by providing VERY pleasurable or exciting things to focus on (sleeping around, shopping sprees, partying, and gambling).

Consider the Self-Defeating Coping Behaviors you do. How do they bring relief to you? Do they distract you, numb you, relax you, or cause elation? List the ones you do and how they affect you. _____ _____ _____ _____

It's much more comfortable to Numb-Out than to experience painful, sad, or irritating emotions. It's also more comfortable to White-Out distressing thoughts

---

Sidebar notes:

6- This pattern doesn't just apply to football fans. It works for any of our favorite activities. If we really enjoy cards or dominoes, our distress may fall to the 0-2 while we're playing or when folks are talking about something interesting. Our level will probably increase when the game is paused for bathroom breaks or when our mind drifts to our emotional stuff. It'll go up and down, but an enjoyable activity will reduce our distress so we can Get Through the day or evening.

7- Drugs and alcohol affect people differently. For instance, there are happy drunks, depressed drunks, and angry drunks. How drugs and alcohol affect us depends on HOW MUCH we use, too! A little alcohol can be relaxing and a lot more can really get us going! Likewise, a little pot can be relaxing, but a lot can cause paranoia and racing thoughts.

8- Elation – (ee-lay-shin) – great joy and happiness or a sense of extreme well-being.

If we continue to use Self-Defeating Coping Behaviors and refuse to accept and deal with our emotional reality, we'll be down, we'll stay "down and depressed" and we'll end up "down and out" until we finally get down to business and work through our problems and issues.

so we don't have to think about them. However, we MUST ALLOW ourselves to PROCESS and EXPERIENCE our normal human emotions so we can DEAL WITH, THINK THROUGH, and WORK THROUGH our issues and problems. That's the only way we GET THROUGH them! Life-Enhancing Coping Mechanisms serve us MUCH better than avoidance strategies because they allow us to think and feel…and to process and Work Through whatever we've got to Get Through!

AT FIRST, when we STOP doing our preferred coping behaviors, OUR EMOTIONS MAY BE OVERWHELMING…and life may feel Out-of-Control. When we feel this way, WE MUST USE DISTRESS TOLERANCE SKILLS. We must accept our experience and use Life-Enhancing Coping Mechanisms to lower our emotional intensity to a level we can BETTER TOLERATE and manage. We must accept that Life-Enhancing Coping Behaviors WON'T WIPE-OUT ALL OUR DISTRESS. They'll LOWER our emotional intensity…so we can HOLD IT TOGETHER…WELL ENOUGH…to do what we need to do…to Participate Effectively DESPITE WHAT WE'RE GOING THROUGH.

We want relief NOW, not 10, 20 or 40 minutes from now. When given a choice…we're going to choose NOW over later.

What sort of positive coping behaviors have helped you through tough times…so you could function ADEQUATELY despite the emotional distress? How low did your Emotional Level go? _____

_____

_____

APPLICATION: Hurry Up! I Can't Stand This Any Longer

We keep doing these things because they provide quick relief. This makes them very POWERFUL, TEMPTING, and ADDICTIVE.

In addition to the Numb-Out, White-Out factor, we also choose Self-Defeating Coping Behaviors because they're FAST-ACTING. They provide QUICK RELIEF. A few shots of whiskey, a few hits off a joint, a couple Valiums, hooking up with a new sex partner, cutting, a shopping spree, and similar things can QUICKLY CHANGE OUR MOOD. We prefer these destructive things because POSITIVE COPING BEHAVIORS USUALLY TAKE LONGER TO WORK. Think about jogging. We have to jog AWHILE before the endorphins[9] kick in and the sense of well-being occurs. We may have to pray AWHILE or read the Bible for AWHILE before we come across passages that speak to us and provide comfort. We may have to surf the net for AWHILE before we find something real interesting. In the Heat-of-the-Moment, we're VERY IMPATIENT. We're DESPERATE FOR RELIEF and we don't want to wait!

9- Endorphins – (in-door-fins) - chemicals released by the brain. They're called opiates. They're natural painkillers which cause "the runner's high." Imagine that!

List three Life-Enhancing Coping Behaviors you WOULD do and note how long they would take to bring relief. _____

APPLICATION: The Tried N' True or the Iffy N' New

In the Heat-of-the-Moment, we want something that's "Tried N' True"… something we KNOW works and WORKS FAST. We want something we have confidence in… something that rarely lets us down.

Destructive Coping Behaviors become our preferred coping mechanisms because we can COUNT ON THEM to provide quick relief. When we're desperate for relief, we desperately grab for what we KNOW works…and WORKS QUICKLY most every time. We also prefer these coping behaviors because we KNOW HOW TO DO THEM. We don't have to stress ourselves by stepping-out of our comfort zone and trying new things. In the Heat-of-the-Moment, we want to do what we KNOW HOW TO DO and what WE'RE GOOD AT DOING! We want to do what's familiar. WE WANT THE TRIED N' TRUE…not the Iffy N' New!

APPLICATION: The Long and the Short of It

Revenge can feel great for a few days or weeks. We experience great delight every time we think about it!

Another reason we prefer Destructive Coping Behaviors is that they TEND TO LAST LONGER[10] than positive ones. Many drugs provide hours of relief. Pulling a drunk can last 12-24 hours. A sexual encounter can provide hours of pleasure… and even longer if they stick around afterwards.

10- Some Destructive Coping Behaviors are very short-acting. A hit of crack lasts about 10 minutes and the relief of cutting can last only minutes or seconds.

The problem with many positive coping behaviors is THEY ONLY WORK FOR AS LONG AS WE'RE DOING THEM! Many don't have strong carry-over effects for hours after we do them. Ever said, "That was fun. Now what?" For instance, we may experience great relief and distraction while watching a favorite TV show or playing volleyball. When the activity is over, we carry SOME benefits… like relaxation, the pride and surprise of making a good play, and the "feel good" from a happy ending to our show. However, we USUALLY have to do ANOTHER coping activity TO CONTINUE TO FEEL ALRIGHT. When we get home from volleyball at 8pm, we'll probably have to do ANOTHER COPING ACTIVITY so we don't sit around ruminating about our problems or the things of relapse… for hours before we try to go to sleep. So, after volleyball, we'll have to do something else…like chatting with an uplifting friend, watching a favorite TV show we recorded, working on a hobby, playing video games, etc. Life-enhancing coping sure takes a lot of effort!

During times of distress, positive coping is like trying to entertain a kid. It's one activity after another…and if there's too much free time, we'll get cranky and irritable! A Recovery Goal is to KEEP OURSELVES BUSY!

Think about times when you've been VERY BUSY. Were you distracted from your problems while you were busy? How low did your Emotional Level go while you were in the middle of busy? _____

APPLICATION: A One-Shot Deal...I'll Drink to That!

MANY DESTRUCTIVE COPING BEHAVIORS ARE "ONE-SHOT DEALS." We do ONE THING and we feel alright for AWHILE. Life-Enhancing Coping Behaviors are different. They provide SHORT-TERM RELIEF and we have to do SEVERAL IN A ROW to maintain relief. For instance, we're NOT DONE with positive coping activities after volleyball. We'll need something else planned for the rest of the evening to MAINTAIN OUR GAINS! This is why recovery programs urge us to STAY BUSY FROM MORNING TO NIGHT!

Recovery programs often suggest starting the day with a morning devotional, and filling our day with things like volunteer or paid work, hobbies and leisure activities, support groups, and eating 2-3 meals a day. Then, we're supposed to get a full night's rest. Those things make for a FULL DAY and a FULL WEEK! Have you heard the saying that idle[11] hands lead to trouble! Recovery REQUIRES AN ACTIVE LIFESTYLE. An active lifestyle requires EFFORT and PLANNING. It starts with getting up and dressed...and showing up for activities and meetings on time. It includes being around people and socializing. It includes doing many things WE MAY NOT FEEL LIKE DOING. Until an activity becomes rewarding, we'll have to force ourselves to do it! That'll take some of the SELF-DISCIPLINE that recovery requires.

11- Idle - (eye-dull) – still, not busy.

If we're going to drink all day, we don't even have to brush our teeth. Our face is going to stink in a little while anyway and the alcohol no doubt will kill more bacteria than toothpaste! We don't even have to move around much, other than back n' forth to the porch or bathroom, whichever is closer and has fewer stairs! If we're good at drinking, we don't even have to worry about fixing a meal because we're on a liquid diet...and who in the world would want to blow their buzz by eating!

Compare a day of drinking to a day full of life-enhancing activity.
If we stay home and drink all day, we don't have to bathe and dress decent...
and we don't have to socialize and be nice to people, either. We don't have
to do much...other than drink, pee, smoke, and get more to drink.
Hopefully, we let the dog out on time and the kids can fend for themselves.
If we're living a Life-Enhancing Lifestyle, we can have a stay-home day now and
then, but otherwise, WE'RE BUSY! We're bathing and grooming. We're going
places and doing things. We're walking and talking...and moving and grooving.
The truth...if we're NOT busy, few of us will maintain recovery.

Think about these questions...then respond to the ones that apply to you. During periods of recovery, how busy were you? During your longer periods of recovery, did you STAY busier than during your shorter periods? Are YOU more likely to relapse when you slow down? Do you think being busy will help you to recover? _____

_____

_____

_____

"If it feels good, do it…and the better it feels, the more I do it!" That's the attitude of Reckless Abandon.[12]

12- "Reckless Abandon" - a saying that refers to a lifestyle of doing things without concern for consequences. It's living life according to the Pleasure Principle.

Going to a wild party and streaking through the neighborhood stoned and drunk is a lot of fun. It's a lot of laughs and a lot of excitement. However, for most of us, in between parties is Real Life …the Real Life of addictions, pain, heartache, and awful life consequences.

Today, these behaviors wreck havoc in our life. They destroy our life. We can't live like that anymore. There's a season for all things and that season has long passed for us.

APPLICATION: A Time of Reckless Abandon…
or a Time to Abandon the Reckless

We prefer Destructive Coping Behaviors because they provide "WILD N' CRAZY FUN!" Drinking, partying, sleeping around, gambling, and other reckless… pleasure-seeking behavior fit that category. When we LIVE A PARTY LIFESTYLE, POSITIVE COPING BEHAVIORS SEEM BORING. For instance, going to a movie is boring because we can't smoke or drink FOR TWO HOURS. Cooking dinner with friends and sitting around playing board games WITHOUT drugs and alcohol is for "old fogies." Taking an art class or a computer class or doing volunteer work is for people who need to get a life! We're just not interested in those things. If we can't smoke, drink, cuss, fuss, or screw around, it isn't for us. For people who WALK ON THE WILD SIDE, wholesome activities SEEM BORING! The truth, many life-enhancing activities that are part of DAILY living are less exciting, but… THEY ARE FUN AND REWARDING!

There's often a time in our lives that we would love to go back to…and live over again…if we had the chance. Many fondly remember the "wild n' crazy times"… a time of partying, good friends, and a carefree lifestyle. Many of us MIGHT choose to go back there IF WE COULD STAY THERE and not have to go through everything that happened afterwards…like the pain and consequences of our addictions and lifestyle. OTHERS WOULD NOT CHOOSE TO RELIVE THOSE TIMES ON PURPOSE because of all the heartaches, break-ups, insecurities, chaos, drama, problems, and losses THAT WERE A PART OF THOSE TIMES.

Is there a time in your life that you'd love to go back to and STAY? If so, describe that time. _____

_____

Was it a time of wholesome behavior or a time of reckless behavior before all the major consequences hit? _____

Though the days of Reckless Abandon are filled with great memories for many of us, WE CAN'T GO BACK. LIFE HAS CHANGED. If we do NOW…the things we did THEN, we'd be hit with some VERY PAINFUL consequences. We might lose our marriage, family, kids, career, job, reputation, trust, health, self-respect, brain functioning, etc. However, many folks spend a lifetime TRYING to relive the good ol' days...CHASING EARLY HIGHS and times of RECKLESS EXCITEMENT.

For many folks, contentment, stability, and peace of mind...trump the days of Reckless Abandon.

There's many reasons why we keep doing the reckless, destructive things we do. They make us feel good in-the-moment. They're Tried N' True. Many are fun and exciting...and are associated with memories of fun and excitement. We like to do them. They're old friends and habits. They provide us comfort and relief. HOWEVER...THE NATURE OF THE PROBLEM IS...the destructive things we do for pleasure and comfort cause us increased pain and suffering. These things are destroying our life. They're not making it better. If we truly want the pain and problems to stop, we must ABANDON OUR RECKLESS WAYS.

Remember These Truths:

If we want the life we live to change, we have to change the way we live life.

If we want bad things to stop, we have to stop bad things.

If we want to live a "normal life," then we have to live a normal life.

If we want peace and stability in our life, then we need to live a life that fosters peace and stability.

We have to make a choice. We can't have everything we want... and still do everything we want to do.

APPLICATION: How to Get Hooked on Normal Life

When we're addicted to a reckless, high drama lifestyle, it's hard to understand how wholesome activities can be fun!

A "normal life" is NORMAL. It's pretty predictable day-in and day-out. The same things tend to go on and happen. There's a set routine. That's what makes it stable. That's what brings PEACE and COMFORT. It's the SECURITY of KNOWING WHAT TO EXPECT in a few hours, tomorrow, and next year. Normal people live normal lives. Their lives are filled with normalcy and routine. Folks who are used to a lot of change, drama, excitement, uncertainty, and recklessness PERCEIVE normal life to be VERY BORING! The truth, MANY activities of daily living ARE boring...but, there's enough stuff to bring excitement, enjoyment, and things to look forward to. There's enough stuff to make normal life rewarding, highly desirable, and fulfilling.

We can become hooked on normal life by Following Through with a recovery-focused Game Plan...even though it may seem like a drag at first!

Do you think normal life is boring? If so, think about the normal activities you've enjoyed before and actually LOOKED FORWARD TO doing. List these and mention what you enjoyed about them. _____

_____

When we choose productive, life-enhancing ways to fill our life...our life will gradually improve. We'll be building a life for ourselves rather than destroying it.

These things FILL UP the Big Picture of Our Life rather than EMPTYING it out!

13- Normal people have a lot of stress and problems to deal with. Normal life is filled with normal life problems... like money problems, job problems, unemployment, teenager problems, health problems, and problems with too many pressures and demands. Although the "normal person" has a lot to deal with, they have an advantage over most people in early recovery. They don't have AS MANY MAJOR problems to deal with...because they don't have all the extra problems caused by Destructive Coping Behavior, like legal problems, legal histories that affect employment, bad work histories, badly damaged relationships, homelessness, addictions, etc. KEEP IN MIND that during early recovery, we'll have a VERY ABNORMAL level of problems to deal with... AT FIRST. Be Mindful that even though we're living a normal lifestyle, it'll take a while for life to normalize...and life problems to reduce to a more normal level.

Now, list some normal activities you thought would be BORING...but they turned out to be enjoyable...and you were glad you did them. _____

When we start doing normal activities, they may SEEM BORING...at first. That HAS TO BE OKAY. Remember Distress Tolerance! It TAKES TIME to develop the relationships, interests, hobbies, and lifestyle that provide the excitement, anticipation, and fun of normal life. We can get HOOKED ON normal life...by FILLING our life with positive activities...and then ALLOWING TIME for our CHANGES TO TAKE ROOT. Over time, our DISTRESS WILL SUBSIDE and life will STABILIZE and NORMALIZE. Over time, WE'LL REAP THE BENEFITS of our changes...and life will become peaceful, rewarding, and meaningful. We'll have MANY things to LOOK FORWARD TO and to be EXCITED about. We'll experience life satisfaction and PRICELESS MOMENTS OF JOY. Then, when we LOOK BACK to where we've been and how we've SUFFERED... we'll FIGHT REAL HARD NEVER TO GO BACK THERE AGAIN...because what we have now is so PRECIOUS to us. We'll BE HOOKED on NORMAL LIFE. We'll NEVER WANT to live like that again...or to lose all we've gained.

APPLICATION: How Do "Normal" People Do It?

People who live lives with normal levels of peace and stability EXPERIENCE MANY BAD, HORRIBLE, ROTTEN LIFE EVENTS like death, illness, divorce, job loss, financial problems, business loss, rejection, betrayal, trauma, etc. They also experience the frustrations and burdens of daily hassles and stressors.[13] They Go Through times of severe distress...and their peace and stability is GREATLY CHALLENGED or LOST. Life becomes filled with conflict, chaos, and instability. However, IT'S FOR A SEASON because they DO THINGS to get their life BACK in order. They do the BEST they can, even if their best isn't so great for awhile.

They do their best to MEET THE PRIORITIES of daily life and to take care of the MUST DO'S...even if it's all they do. They PARTICIPATE EFFECTIVELY by participating ADEQUATELY. They may do the BARE MINIMUM...and they may have to PUSH THEMSELVES to do that! Some days, they may not meet ALL the priorities...but, THEIR HEART AND SOUL PUSHES THEM to do so in the days to follow. Normal people Go Through tough times and they have to WORK VERY HARD TO GET THROUGH THEM.

Normal people are continually challenged to maintain peace and stability! Life is not a cake walk…it's more like walking a tightrope! It takes determination to maintain balance and to Mindfully Protect Our Peace and Stability!

14- Buffers – they're like cushions. They're things that soften the blow or reduce the impact of a hit. They "take the edge off" rough times.

They've BEEN THROUGH tough times before and MADE IT THROUGH… so even during the darkest moments they have that tiny SPARK OF HOPE and the faith to know that at some point things will get better again.

15- During tough times, many normal people use anti-depressant medication to get their brain chemistry back in balance…and to PREVENT Major Depression. They may also use anti-anxiety and sleep medication to help them function and to GET THROUGH the tough time. They use it… they don't abuse it.

People who make it through tough times EASIER THAN OTHERS…usually have many DISTRESS BUFFERS.[14] These are things that buffer or protect them from the disorganizing and destructive effects of stress, problems, and major life events. For instance, when Something Happens and a boulder falls out of the sky and lands in the middle of their life path, their DISTRESS BUFFERS will ABSORB THE IMPACT of the hit. Distress Buffers help them COPE with and GET THROUGH the difficult things that Come Their Way.

Distress Buffers are SUPPORTIVE PEOPLE like family, friends, co-workers, a sponsor, Group Members, counselors, neighbors, and people we visit with during our activities like teammates, church people, other volunteers, etc. Distress Buffers are also the ACTIVITIES and HOBBIES that keep us busy and provide distraction and pleasure when we need it…like jobs, AA meetings, volunteer work, tennis, coin collecting, bowling, scrapbooking, football games, and fishing. Distress Buffers are ATTITUDES and WAYS OF THINKING like Radical Acceptance, faith, and hope… and UNDERSTANDINGS like "Bad things happen to good people.", "Everyone has to deal with tough stuff now and then. This is just my time. This is what I have to deal with right now.", "All I can do is Lean Into it and take it one day at a time.", and "Things won't always be this bad and they could've been a lot worse. Thank God we all got out okay and no one was hurt in the fire." Distress Buffers are COPING SKILLS and BEHAVIORS like putting it on a cloud and letting it float away, reframing, prioritizing, challenging Emotion-Driven Thoughts, and seeking Rational Mind and Wise Mind. They're also RESOURCES like housing, transportation, and cash flow which help us to do what we need to do[15] AND possessions like a TV, computer, CD player, and hobby supplies which provide comfort and enjoyment.

People who Get Through tough times better than others have a coping lifestyle ALREADY set up. Distress Buffers are a NATURAL PART of their DAILY LIFE… and they NATURALLY use them to help themselves. Their lifestyle has BUILT-IN Distress Buffers which provide supportive relationships, busy-ness, a daily routine, meaningful activities, and REASONS TO KEEP GOING. When tough times hit, their support system is ALREADY IN PLACE. They have hobbies and activities ALREADY GOING ON. They have ONGOING demands and responsibilities that GET THEM OUT OF BED EVEN IF THEY DON'T FEEL LIKE FACING THE DAY. They have things going on that help them to MAKE IT THROUGH, PAST, and AROUND the boulders that slam into their path.

> Some people think a job is just about money. They're wrong. A job provides much more, like friends, a support system, self-esteem, self-respect, and productivity. Jobs can provide a sense of being valued and important...because people depend on us. We provide a service not only to our employer, but to customers, patients, co-workers, other businesses we deal with, the community, our nation, etc. Jobs provide us with distraction and busy-ness. They give us a schedule and routine. The money is great... but these other things are HIGHLY IMPORTANT in the Big Picture of Life.

Jobs get us out of bed...out of the house...and into an activity that provides meaning and purpose in life.

Do you think you could cope better with daily hassles and major life events if you had more Distress Buffers in your life? What kind of Distress Buffers do you have now? _____

_____

_____

A Recovery Goal is to fill our life with Distress Buffers so we can MAKE IT THROUGH the hail and boulders that slam into our Recovery Path!

What type of Distress Buffers do you need to add to your life to help cushion the blows of the things Coming At You? _____

_____

_____

Do you find yourself WILLING to do the things you need to do to build Distress Buffers into your life? What things would you have to do? _____

_____

_____

APPLICATION: The Destructive Coping Behaviors of Normal People

Normal people are normal. That means they're human and NOT perfect. Normal people aren't "perfect copers." Sometimes, they do self-defeating things during times of major distress. They may overeat and gain 15 pounds or not eat and lose more weight than they should. They may start smoking cigarettes again or drink a bit to relax and sleep. They may have an impulsive rebound relationship. They may yell n' scream at home, but they avoid doing this at work!

Normal people do Self-Destructive Coping Behaviors. However, they often choose "safer" ones. The ones they choose they GENERALLY don't abuse... TOO MUCH.

> During times of distress, their GOAL is to REGAIN peace and stability...so they DON'T let themselves get OUT-OF-CONTROL. They also have a support system and responsibilities that PRESSURE them to KEEP THINGS IN CONTROL.

Think about the normal people you know. What sort of self-defeating things have they done during times of major distress? _____

We were once normal people who began to do Self-Destructive Coping Behaviors during a time of major distress. We kept these behaviors under control…for awhile. But then, Something Happened and we lost control.

16- Some people quickly become addicted to things and some don't. Some can drink, drug, smoke, gamble, use addictive meds, or do other things WITHOUT becoming addicted. They seem to be able to "turn it on and off" with a little self-discipline. Some people become over-confident and believe they can handle these things. Then, Something Happens and what they thought they could control becomes Out-of-Control. Some people have "addictive personalities" and "addiction genes." They can do something once or twice and become miserably addicted. For these reasons, risky coping behaviors should be avoided because we never know which "recreational" or temporary coping behaviors will turn into a life destroying addiction.

In what ways can these behaviors harm their lives if they do them TOO MUCH, TOO OFTEN, OR TOO LONG? _____ _____ _____

Do you know people who once lived normal adult lives, but Something Happened and they LOST CONTROL OVER their self-defeating coping behavior? Describe what happened to two of these people. _____ _____ _____ _____

The self-defeating things normal people do to relieve stress CAN become LIFE DESTRUCTIVE if they're overused. These coping behaviors are risky and are NEVER RECOMMENDED. They can get Out-of-Control REAL FAST and DESTROY NORMAL LIVES.[16] Many people become alcoholics, coke-heads, and prescription drug addicts after living normal adult lives. Some end up weighing 300 pounds or become anorexic…or addicted to gambling…or with multiple affairs… or so much into pornography that "normal sex" isn't satisfying anymore. They do something a few times that was normally "off-limits." Then, they do it several more times because it brings relief, pleasure, or fun…and it takes their mind off their problems. Then, they keep doing it…because once INTO it…it becomes hard to stop doing. Then, SOMETHING HAPPENS and they LOSE CONTROL. Their life spirals OUT-OF-CONTROL and right into the Cycle of Suffering.

The Something that Happens is they let something into their Inner Circle that didn't belong. The thick boundary that once protected their Inner Circle…opened. Just like the rest of us, when they open their boundary a LITTLE, it often ends up opening A LOT. With all the pressures, demands, and distress, a small gap can become a floodgate. What they might do ONCE…they may end up doing MANY times. When they open themselves up to this ONE THING…other things associated with it FOLLOW…and like the Domino Effect more and more things get into their Inner Circle. Their life quickly fills with more problems, chaos, and turmoil. We know this pattern all too well. It's how relapse works for the rest of us. When we feel bad, our boundaries weaken…and when we open our boundaries to

356

one thing, a flood of other things follow. WE CAN'T DO THAT...and they can't either. It goes like the saying, "When you play with fire, you'll get burned."

APPLICATION: The Not So Normal "Normal Appearing People"

We've all heard the term "functional alcoholics"...but how functional are they really? They seem normal and functional to people who don't know them well. They hold down a job. Some participate in wholesome activities and popular social clubs. Some go to church. They APPEAR functional in their public roles ...because it's behind the scenes where their dysfunction is seen and felt. It's their private life that takes the brunt of their dysfunction.

We all know people who SEEM to live functional lives, however, behind the scenes they have severe addictions and highly dysfunctional lives. They may hold a GOOD JOB and LOOK OKAY in public, but they're SUFFERING IN OTHER AREAS of their life. Months ago, IN AN ODD MOMENT, a church-going lady told me she barely drank. Soon thereafter, others were talking about her Reckless Abandon lifestyle of wild parties, "way too sexualized drunk dancing," and trying to get a drunk co-worker to go home and sleep with her while her husband was drunk and asleep. Sounds like a DWI fixing to happen, major violence in the home, cops being called, job problems, divorce, family problems, AND THE CYCLE OF SUFFERING.

Think of someone you know who seems normal to most people, but a major addiction causes severe problems that most people don't know about. Describe their normal side AND the destructive behaviors they do. _____
_____
_____
_____

What consequences have they had so far because of their addiction? _____
_____
_____

What consequences do you see coming? _____
_____
_____

These are the Life-Enhancing Coping Activities that we've discussed throughout this workbook! They're the Distress Buffers that help us through difficult times. They're tools for staying on the Recovery Path! THEY'RE OUR LIFELINES!

How to Build a Normal Lifestyle

In the remaining sections of this workbook, we'll review many types of Life-Enhancing Coping Behaviors. We'll also learn to write-up and use an Activity Calendar and a structured Game Plan. These two TOOLS are our LIFELINES and GUIDELINES for setting up and living a Recovery Lifestyle. They're the FOUNDATION for BUILDING A FULL LIFE so when tough times hit, we'll have RESOURCES, COPING SKILLS, ACTIVITIES, and SUPPORT to BUFFER THE DISTRESS! A Recovery Goal is to have a lifestyle IN PLACE to manage distress when life Comes At Us. This lifestyle will lead us down the path to peace and stability and a meaningful life.

SKILL BUILDER: "The Life-Enhancing Coping Activities Worksheet"

This worksheet will be a list of Life-Enhancing Coping Behaviors. You'll prepare this list...so it'll be a list of things you CAN do and are WILLING to do. This will be a PREPARED list...so in the heat-of-the-moment, you won't have to think of what you can do, you'll already have a LONG LIST of options that are do-able for you.

This is a two-page worksheet with 20 categories of Life-Enhancing Coping Activities. It includes some of the positive coping skills discussed by Dr. Linehan[17] plus some other ones. Follow the steps below to learn more about this worksheet and to complete your own.

Step 1. Check out the completed worksheet (Figures 13.C.1 and 13.C.2). Review the 20 categories of Life-Enhancing Coping Activities and highlight or mark the specific[18] coping activities YOU'D BE WILLING TO DO.

Step 2. Fill-out the blank worksheet (Figures 13.D.1 and 13.D.2). In each category, list the activities you highlighted on the completed worksheet AND add other activities you'd be WILLING to do THAT FIT EACH CATEGORY.

Step 3. Keep YOUR completed worksheet handy[19] so when you need to do a Life-Enhancing Coping Activity, you'll have a long list to choose from!

Step 4. Begin to practice these coping activities so when you need them, you'll be better able to do them...and you'll reap the greatest benefit.[20]

Step 5. Make up a Recovery Tool Box as described below!

> Here's a neat suggestion from a Group Member. It's called a Recovery Tool Box. Write down the coping activities you're WILLING TO DO on separate slips of paper. Put them in a box, bowl, or other container. When you NEED or WANT a coping activity, pull out three slips and choose one to do. You can also use the Recovery Tool Box to choose coping activities to practice for skill building!

SKILL BUILDER: "The Activity Calendar"

We've mentioned an Activity Calendar several times during this study. This is a calendar WE MAKE UP that lists all the activities and people AVAILABLE TO US on any given day. It's a great coping tool. When we need to TURN OUR MIND to recovery and away from problems, worries, temptation, triggers, and thoughts of relapse, we can turn to this tool for help. It provides us with the INFORMATION WE NEED...to make a decision about WHAT TO DO...when we're in need of support

17- From Dr. Linehan's Skills Training Manual.

18- Don't mark the category name, like "Activities" or "Helping / Contributing." Mark the types of coping activities in each category that you'd be interested in doing, like "Creative activities" or "Cook for someone in need."

19- It would be good to put this worksheet on your refrigerator, in your car or purse, at your desk, etc! Put it in places where you can easily get to it when you need it!

20- Remember, if we PRACTICE these coping skills, we'll be better able to do them when we really need them. We have to practice skills to get good at them!

Figure 13.C.1: The Life-Enhancing Coping Activities Worksheet (Completed)

The Life-Enhancing Coping Activities Worksheet

ACTIVITIES	HELPING / CONTRIBUTING	OPPOSITE EMOTIONS	BUSY MIND	SHORT VACATION
Creative activities	Cook for someone in need	Watch a comedy	Read a book or magazine	Visit tourist spot in town
Fix something	Help a friend fix something	Go to an UPLIFTING church	Strategy game	Read a vacation book
Play on the computer	Babysit a DECENT child!	Play a silly game	Sudoku puzzles	Watch a vacation show
Support Group meeting	Help with a volunteer activity	Play with a PLAYFUL pet	Alphabet/category game	Take a short trip
DBT-CBT worksheet	Deliver Meals on Wheels	Visit or call a CHEERFUL person	Watch a favorite show	Go somewhere relaxing
Phone a friend	Play piano at the nursing home	Listen to inspirational music	Balance my checkbook	Pretend to be on vacation!
Sports	Tutor at the local school	Recite healing words / scriptures	Write a Game Plan	Take a day or two off
Dancing	Take a walk and pick up trash	Do my favorite calming activity	Write a story/song/poem	Do something different
A favorite activity	Mow a neighbor's lawn	Turn My Mind to good memories	Do therapy homework	Take some time for myself
Garage sales	Salvation Army work	Surf the net-Opposite Emotion content	Do a workbook study	Soak in the tub
Clean / organize	Help with a community event	Do something thoughtful for someone	Organize something	Try on fancy clothes!
Walk the dog	Help out at the animal shelter	Treat myself to something	Count something	Go to a fun community event
Gardening	Assist with a Little League team	Smile and be friendly ANYWAY	Word search puzzle	Take a nap or relax
Tractor work	Do a special craft for someone	Encourage someone	Memorize something	Rent several movies
Community event	Write a note to a sick friend	List things I'm grateful for	Study a foreign language	Attend a local sports event
Video games	Visit someone who needs a visit	Reframe / think of the positives	Surf the net	Spend the night out

IMAGERY	FIND MEANING IN EVENTS	PRAYER - MEDITATION	RELAXATION	ONE THING AT A TIME
Fantasize - Daydream	"This is part of the expected course of recovery."	From devotionals	Guided (tapes, CD's)	Close my eyes and listen to favorite music/sounds
Visual memories of:	"My life isn't just about me."	From the bible	Fish tanks / lava lamps	One task in a quiet house
a successful time	"Life isn't just about today."	From my heart	Massage - warm bath	Watch a favorite show and do nothing else
the best Christmas	"Getting Through this will help others down the road."	With others	Just chillin'	A mindless massage
a funny time	"My kids are learning how to handle life by watching me."	Prayer Hotline	Iced tea - cool breeze	Favorite video game
a favorite trip	"This is a spiritual battle."	The Serenity Prayer	Meditation	Sing to a favorite CD
the ocean	"This is a learning experience."	For strength and endurance	Short nap	A warm bath and incense
horseback riding	"This will make sense later."	For support people / good friends	Take Time-Out	Calmly talk my way thru one relaxing task
a motorcycle ride	"This is really the best for me."	For Distress Tolerance	Stretch	Daily siestas - nap time
a proud moment	"I know good will come of this."	For wisdom, understanding, guidance	Slow dance	Get up early for quiet time
best childhood friend	"I needed to do this long ago."	For good judgment & Thinking Through	Favorite calming activity	Cook 1 thing - notice all aspects- smell, texture, temperature, taste, etc.
serene garden	"What hurts now, helps later."	For relief, comfort, and help	Coloring/drawing/painting	
camping - fishing	"I'll get to it and through it!"	For Acceptance	Inspirational music	
the mountains		For recovery and peace	Favorite poetry / music	
autumn trees		For blessings and stability	Comfort food	
a relaxing drive		For a deeper relationship	A heartfelt embrace	

Figure 13.C.2: The Life-Enhancing Coping Activities Worksheet (Completed)

The Life-Enhancing Coping Activities Worksheet

ENCOURAGE SELF	COMPARISONS	MINDFULNESS – SENSES	CHANGING THOUGHTS	MENTAL TIME OUT
Remember successes with	Note how far I've come!	Listen to all the sounds in my	Turn My Mind	Close my eyes and relax
new recovery skills	Recall the Long-Term Pain and	environment - loud, soft,	Distraction games – count	Put everything on clouds
Write/review a list of	Suffering of destructive	constant, intermittent, once	things, list things that	Take a 20-minute nap
positive statements	behavior & times of relapse	Study my environment and notice	start with letter a, b, c...	Take a music break
about myself	Note gains in The Big Picture	different shades of a color	Set a "worry time"	Do something mindless
Review positive journal	of My Life	different sizes of a shape,	Do Rational Mind challenges	Let It Go for now
entries of hope/success	Note improved boundaries	diff. things of the same color	Count my blessings	Leave work an hour early
Read inspirational book	Note the new skills I've	unusual shapes or texture etc.	"Reframing" – find positives	Do a favorite activity
Talk with uplifting friend	developed & how I handle	Notice and touch diff. textures	Learn a lesson and benefit	Treat myself to something
Do something I'm good at	tough situations better	soft, rough, smooth, etc.	Thank God in advance for	Say "No way, not today"
Listen to inspiring music	Note changes others see in me	Find and experience smells like	making good of the bad	Do something impulsive but
Surf net focusing on	Think of the peace and hope	perfumes, spices, candles, food	Recall times of joy and hope	recovery-based!
hope and inspiration	recovering people have vs.	Enjoy outdoor movement – watch	Write a Game Plan	Talk with a pleasant friend
Make a list of sayings and	the anger, hatred, and pain of	planes, leaves, clouds, dogs, etc.	Put It on a Cloud	Play with a pet
quotes about hope	folks still stuck in addiction	Notice common shapes in clouds	Pick a coping activity	Imagery and daydreaming

FOCUS ON RECENT SUCCESSES	PRACTICE DBT-CBT SKILLS	COMPLETE DBT-CBT WORKSHEETS / ACTIVITIES	JOURNALING	OTHER
Distress Tolerance	Acceptance	Keep tracking sheets	My new understandings	Be Mindful of triggers
Use positive coping skill	Review Wise Mind Worksheets	Do a Wise Mind Worksheet	Recovery Goals for today	Be Mindful of warning
Tried something new	Distraction	Make a Recovery Tool Box for	Sayings to live by	signs - act early
Accomplishments	Catch it early - get help early	Life-Enhancing Coping Activities	My greatest priorities and	Call 9-1-1 if needed
Met a goal	Distress Tolerance	& pick some out to practice or do.	Must-Do's for today	Keep special movies, books,
Took steps towards a goal	Act in a life-enhancing way	List alternatives to Destructive	Other things I'll try to do if	games, and hobby items
Made a tough phone call	Think "Mindfully Protecting My	Coping Behaviors	time and energy permits	for difficult times
Said "No way...not today"	Peace and Stability"	List the things that currently	Special activities for today	Build a support system and
Note what I "Did Alright"	Think "The Big Picture Of Life"	fill The Big Picture of My Life	How to fill my down time	have activities as Distress
or better on a recent	Think "The Cycle of Suffering"	Do a "Challenging Negative	My successes!	Buffers
tracking sheet	Think "The Pathways of	Judgments of Me Worksheet"	Difficult things Coming My	Read/reread a DBT-CBT
Moments and areas of	Recovery" and my two choices	for hurtful statements	Way today (triggers, too)	workbook chapter
self-discipline	Think Through Before I Do	Do a "Mindfully Protecting My	Good things that happened	Teach friends and family
Compliments from others	Turn My Mind	Peace and Stability Worksheet"	Steps I'm taking today	about DBT-CBT so they
Turned on Rational Mind	Challenge emotional thoughts	and note what's Coming At Me	Today's new opportunities	know how I think now and
Got to Wise Mind	"Put It on a Cloud"	Write a Game Plan	Compliments from others	how they can best help me
Got to Wise Mind	"Put It on a Cloud"	the priorities in your life.	Compliments from others	me to help myself!

The Life-Enhancing Coping Activities Worksheet

Figure 13.D.1: The Life-Enhancing Coping Activities Worksheet

ACTIVITIES	HELPING / CONTRIBUTING	OPPOSITE EMOTIONS	BUSY MIND	SHORT VACATION

IMAGERY	FIND MEANING IN EVENTS	PRAYER - MEDITATION	RELAXATION	ONE THING AT A TIME

The Life-Enhancing Coping Activities Worksheet

Figure 13.D.2: The Life-Enhancing Coping Activities Worksheet

ENCOURAGE SELF	COMPARISONS	MINDFULNESS - SENSES	CHANGING THOUGHTS	MENTAL TIME OUT

FOCUS ON RECENT SUCCESSES	PRACTICE DBT-CBT SKILLS	COMPLETE DBT-CBT WORKSHEETS / ACTIVITIES	JOURNALING	OTHER

or a distracting activity in the Heat-of-the-Moment! It's very useful when we're upset and we NEED TO GET OUT OF THE HOUSE and TURN OUR MIND from negative things to RECOVERY things. It puts all our options in one place, so we have just ONE PLACE TO LOOK when we can't think straight. It lists the WHO or WHAT...and the WHEN and WHERE. It tells us when these people and activities are available and the place of the activity. We can also add addresses and phone numbers as needed.[21] When we're in the Heat-of-the-Moment, this Activity Calendar can be A LIFELINE. For instance, if we're freakin' out at 3pm on a Tuesday, we can look at our Activity Calendar for Tuesdays to see what activities and people are available. Alike the Life-Enhancing Coping Activities Worksheet, this calendar helps us to QUICKLY come up with many WISE MIND SUGGESTIONS for Getting Through the moment, hour, or day.

Instructions for Setting Up and Using "The Activity Calendar"

Step 1. Make AT LEAST seven copies of the blank Activity Calendar[22] before you get started. That's one for each day of the week.

Step 2. Review the completed Activity Calendar for Monday.[23] Notice "M" is shaded at the top. The "M" stands for Monday!

Step 3. Notice the four columns (up and down). The times range from 8am-9pm.[24]

Step 4. Notice the two rows (across) for 8am. One row is for 8am and one is for 8:30am.[25] This means we have four slots to list the activities available at 8am, four for 8:30...and four for all the other time slots.

Step 5. Look at the 9am row. This shows that on Mondays at 9am the Salvation Army has a sale and the Walking Club meets at the mall. As we learn about other 9am activities we're WILLING to do, we can write them in.

Step 6. Right under the 9am Salvation Army sale slot are rows of stars "******". Those show that the sale goes on UNTIL 12:00. Look at the 10:30am YMCA Open Swim entry. The stars show it goes on UNTIL 12:00, too!

Step 7. Notice the Salvation Army entry shows that the 50 cent sale is for the FIRST MONDAY of the month. Be sure to list those details so we don't think the sale is EVERY Monday. Look at the Activity Calendar for Tuesdays.[26] Notice the Women's Recovery Group meets at 9am on the 2nd and 4th Tuesdays of the month. We'll have to keep up with that so we don't show up on the wrong Tuesday!

Step 8. Notice the 12:00 entries on Monday's Calendar. Two activities are

21- You can put phone numbers and addresses on the back of your Activity Calendar. You can also make a list of numbers for support people and organizations like the Crisis Line, Mental Health Clinic, churches, etc. Keep this information handy so when you need it, you'll have it!

22- See Figure 13.E.

23- Figure 13.F.1.

24- Feel free to change the times. Some folks may start their day at 6AM or 9AM instead of 8AM!

25- "8:30" isn't written in, nor are the other ":30's". The calendar looked too crowded with those written in! It's easier to read without them.

26- See Figure 13.F.2. This calendar is for Tuesdays. Notice the "T" is shaded!

Figure 13.E: The Activity Calendar

M T W TH F SAT SUN			
8am	8am	8am	8am
9	9	9	9
10	10	10	10
11	11	11	11
12	12	12	12
1pm	1pm	1pm	1pm
2	2	2	2
3	3	3	3
4	4	4	4
5	5	5	5
6	6	6	6
7	7	7	7
8	8	8	8
9	9	9	9

Figure 13.F.1: The Activity Calendar - (Completed - Monday)

M T W TH F SAT SUN

8am Coffee-Journal / Plan my day	8am	8am	8am
9 Salvation Army Sale - 1st Monday Only / Everything 50 cents!	9 Walking Club - Mall	9	9
10 """""" """"""	10 YMCA - Open Swim - $2	10	10
11 """""" """""" """""" """"""	11 """""" """""" """""" """"""	11	11
12 AA - Abrams / DRA - Richland / Water Aerobics - YMCA $2	12 Lunch with Janet / Ladies Bible Study - Hillside	12 Lunch at Home - Favorite Soap Opera!	12
1pm """""" """""" Veterans' Home - Volunteer """"""	1pm	1pm	1pm
2 """""" """""" """""" """"""	2 Favorite Soap !!!!	2	2
3 """""" """"""	3	3	3
4 Therapy Appointment	4 Open Bowling ½ price games / Free Shoes !!! """""" """"""	4	4
5 AA - Settles	5 """""" """""" """""" """"""	5	5
6 Fellowship Meal - New Life / Weight Watchers - Carson / Book Club Meeting	6 Jeanne Gets Home / Lisa Gets Home	6 AA - Jersey Ln.	6
7	7 NAMI Meeting - Parkside	7 Volleyball with Parents Without Partners """""" """"""	7
8 DRA - Richland / AA - Settles	8	8 """""" """""" """""" """"""	8
9 AA - Goliad	9 Favorite TV	9	9

Figure 13.F.2: The Activity Calendar - (Completed – Tuesday)

M **T** W TH F SAT SUN

8am Coffee-Journal Plan my day	8am	8am	8am
9 Women's Recovery Group 2nd and 4th Tues """"""" """""""	9 Walking Club - Park """"""" """""""	9	9
10 Scrapbook Club 1st and 3rd Tues """"""" """""""	10 Open Swim - YMCA $2 """"""" """""""	10	10
11 """"""" """"""" """"""" """""""	11 """"""" """""""	11 Medication Appointment 4th Tues	11
12 AA - Abrams DRA - Richland	12 Lunch With Dawn Lunch with Mom	12 Church Meal - Bible Study Dayton Rd. Church """"""" """""""	12 Favorite Soap
1pm	1pm	1pm	1pm
$$$$ Care for Grandma $$$			
2 """"""" """"""" """"""" """""""	2 Favorite Soap	2	2
3 """"""" """"""" """"""" """""""	3	3	3
4 Get Dinner Ready for Grandpa & Ma """"""" """""""	4 Cheap Movie Rentals Overnight	4	4
5 AA - Settles	5	5	5
6 AA - Stephen's	6 Fellowship Meal - Trinity Lisa Gets Home	6 Dad Cooks!	6 Joel's and Jamie's Baseball Practice """"""" """""""
7 Free Tae Kwon Do Class 1st Tues """"""" """""""	7 Casserole Ministry Meets 3rd Tues """"""" """""""	7 Single's Night Out Check Calendar for Where! 1st and 3rd Tues	7
8 Denise Home AA - Settles	8 Poetry Reading - UTPB """"""" """""""	8 """"""" """"""" """"""" """""""	8 Favorite TV Show Favorite TV Show
9 AA - Goliad	9	9 """"""" """""""	9 Favorite TV Show Favorite TV Show

27- The things that go on the Activity Calendars occur on a regular basis. They're not one-time events. They occur each week, every two weeks, or monthly.

How to find out about available activities: Look in the newspaper for activities and meetings, like in the community calendar section. Call a crisis line and ask about support groups. Call the United Way about volunteer opportunities...**and the** activities and services available to you. Call colleges to see about non-credit classes and free classes and services. Many colleges offer counseling and support groups for community folks. Call the YMCA to see what classes and activities they offer. Call churches and ask about Fellowship Meals, self-help Bible Study Classes, and other activities. In Texas, call 2-1-1. It's a free service that answers all types of questions. They can tell you about local groups and events. See if your state or town has a number like this. Fill up the slots in your calendar! Brainstorm and ask around! The more options, the better! **Many will be free. Ask about a "sliding scale" if you need the cost reduced!**

28- Figures 13.G.1, 13.G.2 and 13.H.1 and 13.H.2. They're two-page calendars. One set is blank and the other is a sample that's filled-out.

29- Make copies of the blank calendar and fill them out in advance!

listed in each slot. That means we have a lot of options at that time on Tuesday's. Double up the entries if you need extra room. That'll give us room to list eight choices for each time rather than four!

Step 9. On Monday's calendar, the 10:30 YMCA Swim entry shows that it costs $2. The Open Bowling entry at 4pm notes that games are ½ price and shoes are free! Put that type of information on your calendar. That way we'll know we have some fun options even if we're short on money!

Step 10. Review the TYPES of activities listed on the completed Activity Calendars (Monday's and Tuesday's). They include special sales, fun activities and meetings, support group meetings, options for lunch and dinner, favorite TV shows, appointments, scheduled volunteer work and paid work, when our people get home from work, etc.

Step 11. Using copies of the blank Activity Calendar, start a calendar for EACH day of the week, including the weekends. Keep these calendars updated. Make changes as needed and add new activities and specials as they become available[27] and remove ones that are no longer available.

Step 12. Keep these calendars handy and use them when you need coping options!

These Activity Calendars are a lifeline in the Heat-of-the-Moment. When we need distraction, help, or support, we have a list of things to choose from. These calendars are about being PREPARED. If we're upset and we can hardly think straight, all we have to do is pull it out and pick something! Add as much stuff as possible to your calendar so you'll have many choices when you really need them.

SKILL BUILDER: Planning Our Day and Week

You've probably noticed another set of calendars.[28] These are Weekly Calendars that we can use to plan our day, our week, and the weeks ahead.[29] We can use the activities we've listed on our Activity Calendars to add things to our WEEKLY CALENDARS. We can pick n' choose things to fill our day and our week. Our recovery REQUIRES that we STAY BUSY. These calendars help us to set up a RECOVERY LIFESTYLE...one that's FILLED with meaningful activities and Distress Buffers. Recovery also requires some STRUCTURE AND ROUTINE in our life. If we work a regular schedule, we already have quite a bit of structure and routine in our life. If we don't work, we can BUILD structure and routine into our life by filling our day with life-enhancing activities. When we're busy in life-enhancing activities, we're filling up the Big Picture of Our Life and we're developing a lifestyle that helps us to stay on the Recovery Path. We need the people and activities to keep our mind on recovery and to fill our life with FULFILLING things.

Instructions for Setting Up and Using "The Weekly Calendar"

Step 1. Take a look at the WEEKLY CALENDARS.[28] Notice the two-page blank calendar[30] and the two-page completed one.

30- Be sure to make copies of the blank one before using it!

Step 2. Check out the COMPLETED Weekly Calendar. Notice the date at the top, "June 08." Notice the columns for each day of the week and the date (like Monday the 7th). We'll have to write the month on the blank ones as well as the date of the month, like the 7th or 8th.

Step 3. Notice this COMPLETED calendar is filled-out like the Activity Calendar. Even the stars are there to note how long each activity will last.

Step 4. Begin to fill-out a blank Weekly Calendar. Choose things from the Activity Calendars to plan your day and week.

Step 5. Add ONE-TIME events and appointments to your Weekly Calendar. These are things like a doctor's appointment at 4pm on Tuesday and Valerie's recital at 7pm on Thursday. These things are one-time events so they won't be on our Activity Calendar.

Step 6. Begin to Follow Through...and do the things on your Weekly Calendar! Begin to live and build a FULFILLING and MEANINGFUL life!

Did You Notice?

When life seems meaningless and empty…it probably is. We feel empty when we're not living a FULL life. We feel life is meaningless when we don't have enough meaningful things going on in our life. WE MUST ADD the people and activities that bring fulfillment and meaning to life… AND, WE MUST DO THESE LONG ENOUGH for our changes to Take Root. That's so we can reap the rewards of our efforts to change… to change how life goes for us!

DID YOU NOTICE...that what we do to COPE WITH LIFE is the SAME THING we do to BUILD a FULL LIFE...a life that's REWARDING and PRODUCTIVE... a life that gives MEANING TO LIFE? The activities on "The Life-Enhancing Coping Activities Worksheet" and the Weekly Calendars ARE the types of things that GIVE OUR LIFE MEANING and THINGS TO BE EXCITED ABOUT and to LOOK FORWARD to. They also put us with people so we can BUILD A SUPPORT SYSTEM and MEANINGFUL RELATIONSHIPS. These things provide a BUFFER AGAINST DISTRESS...and, they ADD LIFE TO OUR LIFE!

~~~~~~~~ CHAPTER REVIEW ~~~~~~~~

1. When we're Going Through tough times, what are some of our Recovery Goals?

_____

_____

Figure 13.G.1: The Weekly Calendar

MONDAY	TUESDAY	WEDNESDAY	THURSDAY
8am	8am	8am	8am
9	9	9	9
10	10	10	10
11	11	11	11
12	12	12	12
1pm	1pm	1pm	1pm
2	2	2	2
3	3	3	3
4	4	4	4
5	5	5	5
6	6	6	6
7	7	7	7
8	8	8	8
9	9	9	9

369

Figure 13.G.2: The Weekly Calendar

FRIDAY	SATURDAY	SUNDAY	NOTES
8am	8am	8am	
9	9	9	
10	10	10	
11	11	11	
12	12	12	
1pm	1pm	1pm	
2	2	2	
3	3	3	
4	4	4	
5	5	5	
6	6	6	
7	7	7	
8	8	8	
9	9	9	

JUNE 08   Figure 13.H.1: The Weekly Calendar - (Completed)

MONDAY 7th	TUESDAY 8th	WEDNESDAY 9th	THURSDAY 10th
8am Coffee - Journal Plan my day	8am Coffee - Journal Plan my day	8am Coffee - Journal Plan my day	8am Coffee - Journal Plan my day
9 Walking Club - Mall """"""	9 Women's Recovery Group	9 Get recycling to the curb!!! Wrap Randall's gift Chill-Out - Goof-Off !!!!	9
10 Post Office Return pants to Wal-mart	10 Open Swim - $2	10	10 Water Aerobics with Rebecca """"""
11 See Aunt Adrienne before she leaves town	11 """""" """"""	11	11
12 Bible Study (Hillside) Luncheon too! """"""	12 Lunch with Dawn at her work!	12 Meet Dad for lunch	12 See who's available for lunch or go home
1pm Veteran's Home	1pm $$$$ Care for Grandma $$$	1pm Painting Class	1pm $$$$ Care for Grandma $$$
2 """""" """"""	2 """""" """"""	2 """"""	2 """""" """"""
3 """"""	3 """""" Mom relieves me early	3 Run errands, grocery store, etc. """"""	3 """""" """"""
4 Therapy Appointment	4 Dr. McDaniel - Knee Apptm	4 """"""	4 """"""
5 Home - Let Shep outside! Chill a few minutes!	5	5 Walk Shep, Chill-out!	5 Sandra lets Shep out
6 Fellowship Meal - New Life """"""	6 Home, eat, Shep out	6 Fellowship Meal - Hillcrest	6 Dinner at Janet's
7	7 Go to Lisa's - Help with kids Chat for awhile. Leave around 8:15 """"""	7 Stop by Sandy's – pick up shoes	7 Valerie's Recital """"""
8 DRA – Richland Center	8 AA - Settles	8 DRA – Richland Center	8 """""" AA - Settles
9	9	9	9

JUNE 08   Figure 13.H.2: The Weekly Calendar - (Completed)

FRIDAY 11th	SATURDAY 12th	SUNDAY 13th	NOTES
8am Coffee - Journal Plan my day	8am SLEEP IN !!!!!	8am	
		Coffee - Journal Plan my day	
9	9 Coffee - Journal Plan my day	9 Church	
10 Open Swim – Free day!	10 Marie picks me up - Do a bunch of Garage Sales!	10 """"""	
11 """""" """"""	11	11 """""" """"""	
12 Bring lunch –Diana's	12	12 Lunch DATE with Clint !!!	
1 $$$$ Care for Grandma $$$	1pm	1pm	
2 """""" """"""	2	2 Scrapbooking with Michelle Depends on Date!!!!!!	
3 """"""	3	3	
4 Return books to library, pay on lay-away, pick up meds	4 Pick up Mara at Airport	4	
5 Home, Shep out….Chill-out	5	5 Do Bible Buddies Class for Vernie """"""	
6	6 Dinner at Mom's	6 Stay for Service """"""	
7 Shane's Game - West Field	7	7	
8 AA - Settles	8 AA - Settles	8 Coffee with Marissa AA – Cowboy Church	
9	9	9	

372

2. In "The Levels of Emotion Chart," what were some of the warning signs that the people were slipping or beginning to lose control? _____

_____

_____

_____

3. To what levels might our emotional intensity fall if we're doing Life-Enhancing Coping Activities? _____

4. If we're doing a Life-Enhancing Coping Activity, why may our level of relief go up and down...like from 0 to 4, then back to 2, and then to 4 again? _____

_____

_____

_____

5. In the "To Eliminate or to Reduce" section, several ways that Self-Destructive Coping Behaviors work were noted. What are some of those ways? _____

_____

_____

6. Destructive Coping Mechanisms were described to be "One Shot Deals," what does that mean? How are Life-Enhancing Coping Mechanisms different? _____

_____

_____

_____

7. Why do some people think life-enhancing activities are boring? _____

_____

_____

8. In what ways are life-enhancing activities rewarding? _____

_____

_____

9. When we first start doing life-enhancing activities, why do we have to practice Distress Tolerance? _____

_____

_____

10. How do we Get Hooked on normal life? _____

_____

_____

11. How do normal people handle the tough times of life? _____

_____

_____

_____

FOR REFLECTION:

Take a few moments
to reflect on
this chapter.
Some questions are
listed in the margin
to guide your
reflection.
Feel free to reflect on
whatever your heart
brings to mind.

12. What is meant by "Distress Buffers"? What sort of things are Distress

Buffers? _____

_____

_____

_____

What are your
reactions to the
material?

13. How is it that some normal people are able to do self-destructive things…

but their life isn't destroyed by them? _____

_____

Which parts hit home
or relate to you
the most?

_____

Which parts have
helped you the most?

14. Why do some people feel their life is empty and meaningless? What do they

need to do to change that? _____

Which parts have
helped you to
understand yourself
the most?

_____

_____

_____

How will you use this
information to feel
better about yourself?

~~~ *For Reflection* ~~~

_____

How will you use this
information to improve
the quality of your
life…or to change how
things work out for
you in life?

_____

_____

_____

_____

What will you do
differently based on
this material?

_____

_____

How has this
information changed
the way you feel about
your patterns of
relapse and recovery…
and your overall
response to life?

_____

_____

_____

What does this
material motivate
you to do?

_____

_____

From "Out-of-Control: A Dialectical Behavior Therapy (DBT) – Cognitive-Behavioral Therapy (CBT) Workbook for Getting Control of
Our Emotions and Emotion-Driven Behavior" - Copyright © 2009 by Melanie Gordon Sheets, Ph.D.   (www.dbt-cbt-workbook.com)

Using Distress Buffers to Mindfully Protect Our Peace and Stability

Check out Figure 13.I. You'll probably recognize this worksheet!
It's Figure 4.G found at the end of Chapter 4. It's included here, too...
because now you have knowledge of MANY kinds of Distress Buffers and Recovery Tools...
and MUCH MORE insight into the things Coming At You...
that can GET TO YOU...and wreck your world.

In Chapter 4, we discussed the importance of
putting up a boundary or shield to protect our Inner Circle.
Our Inner Circle contains all the things we love, cherish, and value in life.
These are the things we want to protect...so we can protect our peace and stability...
and our recovery. We don't want TO ALLOW the things Coming At Us to GET TO US...
and mess up or take away the things that are precious and dear to us.
We must Fight for these things. This is the Fight FOR our life.

The weapons and tools we use in this Fight
are Life-Enhancing Coping Skills and Recovery Attitudes (a.k.a. Rehab-itudes).
They make up the boundary or shield that defends our Inner Circle.
For instance, when we start to become upset about something Coming At Us,
we can use some of our Life-Enhancing Coping Skills and Rehab-itudes
to calm and comfort ourselves.
A MAJOR RECOVERY GOAL is to regain peace and to Think Through Before We Do...
so we don't do something destructive that takes away our peace and stability!

So, to complete this worksheet,
take a minute and list the things Coming At YOU in the outer circles.
These are the distressors, demands, temptations, and unpleasant situations IN YOUR LIFE
that can take away your peace and stability...IF THEY CAN GET TO YOU.

Then, think of the Life-Enhancing Coping Skills and Rehab-itudes that you've learned
from this workbook...from other recovery programs...and from general life experience.
In the middle circles, list the ones that YOU WILL USE to protect your life.

Make a copy of your completed worksheet...and post it where you'll see if often.
This will keep you Mindful of some of the weapons and tools in your RECOVERY ARSENAL!

From "Out-of-Control: A Dialectical Behavior Therapy (DBT) – Cognitive-Behavioral Therapy (CBT) Workbook for Getting Control of Our Emotions and Emotion-Driven Behavior" - Copyright © 2009 by Melanie Gordon Sheets, Ph.D. (www.dbt-cbt-workbook.com)

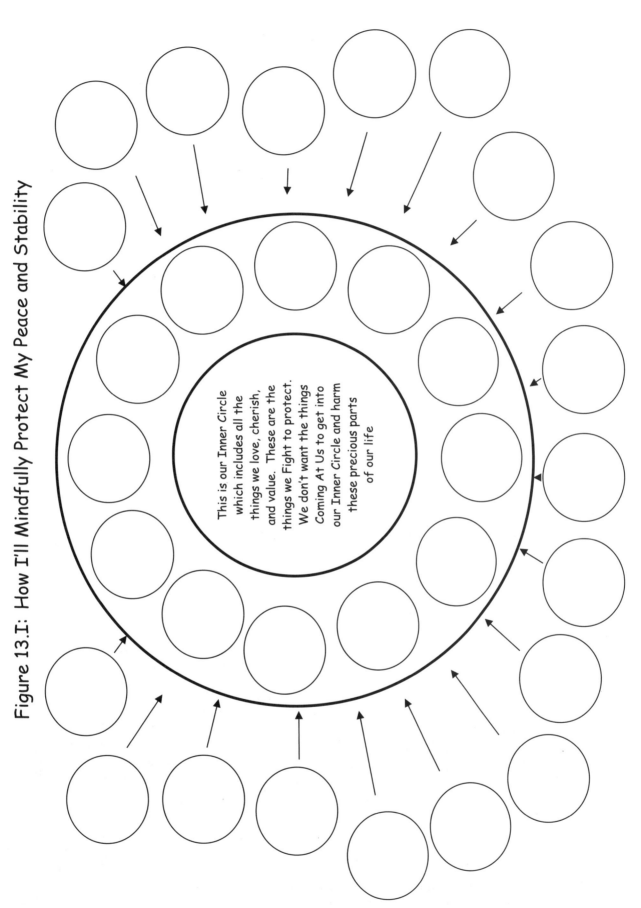

Figure 13.I: How I'll Mindfully Protect My Peace and Stability

This is our Inner Circle which includes all the things we love, cherish, and value. These are the things we Fight to protect. We don't want the things Coming At Us to get into our Inner Circle and harm these precious parts of our life

Figure 13.J.1: The Concepts and Skills Tracking Sheet – Chapter 13

Week # _____

	Day of Week →										
	Date →										
13A.	Today, I listed off several differences between Self-Destructive and Life-Enhancing Coping Mechanisms.										
13B.	Today, I used information about the differences between Self-Destructive and Life-Enhancing Coping Mechanisms to better understand why I've used certain types of Destructive Coping Behaviors.										
13C.	Today, I was Mindful that I could do positive things to lower my emotional level. I realized this would help me to Participate Effectively in my life... and to have normal levels of peace and stability during good times and bad.										
13D.	I used "The Levels of Emotion Chart" to gain information about my emotional level today.										
13E.	Today, I thought about the warning signs I show when I'm starting to slip... when my emotional level is affecting my ability to Participate Effectively and manage my life.										
13F.	Using "The Levels of Emotion Chart," I've identified the level when I need to seek help. I'm aware of what that level is like for me.										
13G.	Today, I did one or more Life-Enhancing Coping Activities to reduce my emotional level.										
13H.	Today, I reminded myself that Life-Enhancing Coping Activities will NOT WIPE-OUT my emotional distress...but they'll lower it to a level I can better manage. I'm Mindful I'll still have to tolerate SOME distress.										
13I.	Today, when I was upset, I noticed my emotional level went down when I was busy doing something positive...and went back up a bit when I wasn't busy.										
13J.	Today, I was upset about something. I noticed my emotional level went down when I was busy doing something positive. I also noticed that my coping efforts kept things from getting as bad as they would have in the past.										

Notes:

RATING SCALE

5 – Did Excellent in this area today
4 – Did Pretty Good in this area today
3 – Did Alright in this area today
2 – Did Only Fair in this area today
1 – Didn't Do Well in this area today
DD – Didn't Do today

Figure 13.J.2: The Concepts and Skills Tracking Sheet – Chapter 13

Week # _____

	Day of Week →							
	Date →							
13K.	Today, I was Mindful that when I give up Self-Destructive Coping Behavior and begin to use Life-Enhancing ones...things may feel worse for awhile until I GET GOOD AT using the Life-Enhancing Coping Behaviors.							
13L.	Today, I reminded myself that I'll have to step out of my comfort zone and try new coping activities. I know I prefer the Tried N' True, but I'll have to begin practicing the Iffy N' New!							
13M.	Today, I was Mindful that life-enhancing coping is NOT a "One-Shot Deal." I reminded myself that I may have to do several Life-Enhancing Coping Activities in a row to lower my distress to a more tolerable level... and to KEEP IT THAT WAY!							
13N.	Today, I was Mindful that I must abandon my reckless ways. I realized I can't have the type of life I want...IF I DO EVERYTHING I want!							
13O.	Today, I reminded myself that Life-Enhancing Coping Activities MAY SEEM boring at first because I'm so used to the "wild n' crazy." I reminded myself that I must do life-enhancing activities LONG ENOUGH for them to become rewarding and meaningful.							
13P.	Today, something came up and I told myself something like, "If I want the life I live to change, then I'll have to change the way I live life." or "If I want to live a 'normal' life', then I'll have to live a 'normal' life." or "If I want peace and stability in my life, I'll have to live a life that fosters peace and stability."							
13Q.	Today, I took some action to ADD Distress Buffers to my life...or to IMPROVE the quality of ones I have in my life right now.							
	(continued)							

Notes:

RATING SCALE

5 – Did Excellent in this area today
4 – Did Pretty Good in this area today
3 – Did Alright in this area today
2 – Did Only Fair in this area today
1 – Didn't Do Well in this area today
DD – Didn't Do today

Figure 13.J.3: The Concepts and Skills Tracking Sheet – Chapter 13

Week # _____

Day of Week →

Date →

13R. Today, I caught myself becoming angry or discouraged because people around me SEEM to have such perfect lives. They seem to be happy and carefree WHILE I'm burdened and struggling. I reminded myself that many of these people have a lot of major life issues and problems they're DEALING WITH... and they're working hard to Participate Effectively in their life.

13S. Today, I encouraged myself to KEEP DOING the things I need to be doing to be okay...to GO ON and to GET THROUGH whatever I need to GO THROUGH ...to GET PASSED this difficult time. I reminded myself that things WILL get better as time goes by.

13T. Today, I caught myself becoming angry or discouraged because people around me SEEM to be able to GET AWAY with doing the Destructive Coping Behaviors I can't do anymore. I reminded myself that NO DOUBT their behaviors cause them life problems that I'm just not aware of...YET. I'm aware that if they keep doing what they're doing...their consequences will get so bad EVERYONE will know.

13U. Today, I looked at or thought about the coping behaviors and activities listed on my Life-Enhancing Coping Activities Worksheet.

13V. Today, I picked out and DID a coping activity from my Life-Enhancing Coping Activities Worksheet or from the Recovery Tool Box I made.

13W. Today, I worked on my Activity Calendar or my Weekly Calendar.

13X. Today, I USED my Activity Calendar or my Weekly Calendar to help me in my recovery.

13Y. Today, I kept busy and used Distress Buffers to help me live a Recovery Lifestyle.

Notes:

RATING SCALE
5 – Did Excellent in this area today
4 – Did Pretty Good in this area today
3 – Did Alright in this area today
2 – Did Only Fair in this area today
1 – Didn't Do Well in this area today
DD – Didn't Do today

~ 14 ~

THE GAME PLAN

A Game Plan is our how-to guide for recovery. It details the Action Steps we need to take to deal with our problems and to GET ON WITH OUR LIFE!

1- Individualized – (in-di-vid-u-ol-lized) – made up for one person.

Well, we're finally to it...the Game Plan chapter! The work of this workbook comes down to the Game Plan. It's everything we've been talking about and working towards! The Game Plan is a plan of action. It's an individualized[1] recovery plan based on OUR needs. A Game Plan begins to form when Wise Mind kicks in and suggests ways to deal with our problems. Wise Mind suggests things like, "Get marriage counseling", "AA - 90 meetings in 90 days", "Stay on medication", "Add productive activities", "Get on a regular sleep schedule", etc. A Game Plan provides the STRUCTURE for living a Recovery Lifestyle! It's a written plan that outlines the steps WE NEED TO TAKE to be okay...and to STAY ON the Recovery Path.

One Plan, Two Plans, Three Plans, Four?

Game Plans can be developed for any problem or situation. A Game Plan may address just one problem like "managing my diabetes" or several problems like "Starting over, being substance free, and managing my depression." It'll be YOUR Wise Mind decision whether you write separate Game Plans for each major problem in your life or one Game Plan that combines several problems.

2- See Figure 14.A, "The Long, Detailed Game Plan." It's 11 pages long, so it's numbered 14.A.1 – 14.A.11. It's all one Game Plan.

In Group, we often include several problems in one Game Plan. That's because most Members have several major life issues to deal with early in their recovery. The sample Game Plan, "The Long, Detailed Game Plan"[2] includes the areas often addressed in these plans (substance abuse, mental illness, transportation problems, getting a job, unhealthy relationships, dealing with difficult situations, etc).

The Structure of a Game Plan

We're going to take a QUICK LOOK at a Game Plan. As we work through this chapter, we'll talk about the parts of a Game Plan in detail. As a start, check out "The Long, Detailed Game Plan."[2] DON'T PANIC THOUGH! The one we make for ourselves will be MUCH shorter. This one is a SAMPLE. It's VERY L-O-N-G and detailed to give people LOTS OF IDEAS for doing their own!

Notice the **title** of this Game Plan is "Starting Over and Living a Recovery Lifestyle...Recovery from Substance Abuse and Mental Illness."

3- Action Steps – the steps we take to do something.

Look at the **first column**. It's called "Wise Mind **Action Steps**: How Do I Go About It?" This column goes on for 11 pages! It contains 17 Action Steps[3] for

Figure 14.A.1: The Long, Detailed Game Plan

My Game Plan for: Starting Over and Living a Recovery Lifestyle - Recovery from Substance Abuse and Mental Illness

WISE MIND ACTION STEPS: "How Do I Go About It?" List the Action Steps you NEED to take and ones which would be HELPFUL for your recovery. These are the "Must Do's" and the "Would Be Helpful To Do's."	RATIONAL MIND OBSTACLES AND EMOTIONAL MIND EXCUSES: "What Might Discourage Me from Doing This?" List the major Obstacles and Excuses that will get in your way of carrying out the Action Steps.	RATIONAL MIND CHALLENGES AND WISE MIND HOW-TO'S: "Come Hail or High Water... How I'll Get Through It and Do It" Note how you'll help yourself to get passed and around the Rational Mind Obstacles and Emotional Mind Excuses.
1. DEAL WITH STUFF AS IT COMES MY WAY - I'LL LEAN INTO IT! - I'll CHOOSE what I need to deal with and what I'll walk away from. I WILL CHOOSE my battles. I WILL DEAL WITH whatever Comes My Way, good or bad, just or unjust...because I know life happens. All types of things happen...and bad things happen to good people. I know I create some of my problems and situations...and I know some things happen that are out of my control. I know some things that happen TO me have nothing to do WITH ME. I know some people will be rude and my people will let me down sometimes. I expect daily hassles and unexpected setbacks and stressors. I expect BIG AWFUL things will happen, too. I WILL DEAL WITH LIFE THE BEST I CAN. When my strength or know-how falters, I'll seek advisors. I'll work to stay balanced and WILLING to accept what Comes My Way. I'll deal with life as it presents itself. I have to deal with things like everyone else has to. I vow TO GET THROUGH what I have to Go Through and I WILL DO MY BEST!	1. Some things are very hard to deal with and accept. 2. This is a weak area for me!!!! I'm easily overwhelmed by things and I worry a lot. 3. Over-responding and going off is a hard habit to break!!!	1A. This is something I'll have to work on! Some things will be easier to accept and deal with...and others will take more work! I have NOT mastered recovery and everything isn't going to be easy! I'm in the learning phases and I'll do the BEST I can...and I'll STRETCH and CHALLENGE myself to do better n' better. When I notice I'm falling short, I'll seek support and counsel. I am a WORK IN PROGRESS! 1B. I'll make a list of what I need to deal with. I'll prioritize what to focus on based on what's most important and the order in which things make sense. I'll get a Game Plan for the priorities and I won't try to deal with everything at once. I'll Lean Into life and what I need to do to get my life in order!!!! 1C. If I find myself avoiding something and making excuses why I should avoid it, I'll catch myself and make a Rational/Wise Mind decision about whether or not I really need to deal with it. 2A. I'll get a Game Plan for dealing with my stuff. Each morning, I'll remind myself what I'm focusing on THIS day and I won't allow myself to worry about everything else. I'll have a Game Plan that's Rational and Wise and that'll be my FOCUS. If I'm Following Through with my Game Plan, I'm doing very well and there's no need to worry about all the other things. I'll remind myself that I'll get a Game Plan for those things WHEN IT'S TIME and they'll be focused on WHEN IT'S TIME and until then, it does me no good to worry about them. It only hurts me and destabilizes me. I'll put my extra worries on a cloud and let them float away! I'll remind myself there's an order to things... and I'm doing great and keeping them in order! 2B. I'll use all kinds of Life-Enhancing Coping Skills, Rational Mind thinking, and Wise Mind actions to help myself during the tough times! 3A. I'll Turn On Rational Mind to balance my Emotional Mind. I'll work on Thinking Through Before I Do so I can better control my reactions. I'll wisely CHOOSE my battles rather than fighting for everything

From "Out-of-Control: A Dialectical Behavior Therapy (DBT) - Cognitive-Behavioral Therapy (CBT) Workbook for Getting Control of Our Emotions and Emotion-Driven Behavior" Copyright © 2009 by Melanie Gordon Sheets, Ph.D. (www.dbt-cbt-workbook.com)

Figure 14.A.2: The Long, Detailed Game Plan

(Action Step 1 – continued)

that upsets me or disrespects my rights or personhood! If I choose to fight for something, I'll fight in a wise and effective way.
3B. If I find myself upset and in the process of going off, I'll STOP myself, apologize, do Damage Control, and START OVER! I'll learn from it, get a plan for next time, and move on!

---

2. DAILY DEVOTION – Meditation – Prayer. I'll spend some time each morning to remind myself THAT NO MATTER WHAT, "Recovery is My #1 Priority!" I'll seek the strength, focus, wisdom, and perseverance to KEEP Recovery My #1 Priority. I'll seek Mindfulness of recovery THROUGHOUT my day...and especially when I hit trouble spots, aggravations, and upsetting situations.

1. I'll forget to do this.

2. I'll be in a hurry and won't have time.

3. I'm not religious. I don't pray. I don't do yoga. I don't know how to meditate.

1. I'm human. I might forget at first. It takes a while to make a new behavior a habit...some say 30 days! I'll put a note on my TV, coffee pot, refrigerator, or steering wheel to remind myself to take a few minutes to get the focus and peace I need to Get Through the day. I can pray or focus many times DURING the day, like when I'm waiting for an appointment or in line or while riding in the car or bus. I'll have many opportunities if I forget!
2A. I'll get a book with short devotional readings or an inspirational reading sent to my computer each day. I'll read while I have coffee or breakfast.
2B. I'll work to set aside 5-10 minutes each morning for this VERY IMPORTANT ACTIVITY. Recovery is not easy...each morning I need to focus on my OVERALL GOAL which is RECOVERY. I'll remind myself that no matter what happens, I'll Mindfully Protect My Peace and Stability and MY RECOVERY!
3. Since I'm not comfortable with prayer or meditation, I can simply talk to myself and remind myself that Recovery is My #1 Priority! I'll do a journal entry each morning to list my goals for the day and a Game Plan for any trouble spots I see coming. I'll encourage myself to respond to the day with a Recovery Attitude by Leaning Into and responding to challenges consistent with my ultimate goal...RECOVERY, PEACE, and STABILITY!!!!

---

3. GET ON A SLEEP-WAKE SCHEDULE THAT MATCHES MY LIFE'S NEEDS – Granted I'm a night person and I can make more money working nights, recovery activities are day things. I have to adjust myself to be in sync with a Recovery Lifestyle...and that includes being awake during the day!

1. I'm a night person. I like nights. I feel better being up at night. I AM NOT A MORNING PERSON!!! I DON'T DO MORNINGS!!!

1A. DISTRESS TOLERANCE! Most night people have to conform to the world! I need to be in sync with the world to be in recovery. It's too stressful to work nights and try to take care of appointments, errands, and social activities during the day WHEN I'M SUPPOSED TO BE SLEEPING! Family and friends can help me better if I'm on a regular schedule. Part of being "normal" IS "being normal."
1B. I'll be tired at first when I change my sleep pattern. I'll accept it, go with it, and make the best of it! I'll take 20-minute chair naps if necessary to get me through the adjustment time!
1C. Having more money is MUCH LESS important than living a Recovery Lifestyle. I CHOOSE recovery!

Figure 14.A.3: The Long, Detailed Game Plan

4. MAINTAIN A POSITIVE ATTITUDE – I can improve my attitude by Turning My Mind from negative things to positive things. This includes avoiding people with negative attitudes...and spending time with folks who have a positive outlook on life. Focusing on the constructive things in life that give me pleasure will help, too. I will avoid "Digging in the Garbage" by keeping my mind on the here-and-now, not the past and painful. I'll read and watch inspirational things and I'll avoid depressing or irritating content!	1. There's so many difficult things in my life, it's so depressing. It'll be real hard to stay positive. 2. Negative thinking is such a habit for me!!!	1A/2A. I'll meditate or pray for help to see the positives and the silver linings in things and to stay focused on the here-and-now. 1B/2B. I'll challenge myself to be Mindful of my thinking. I'll Turn My Mind when I start to think negative or about the painful past. 1C/2C. I'll look for the silver lining in other people's lives and challenge them to see it, too. It's always easier to see the good in someone else's life...so this will be good practice for me! 1D/2D. Every day, I'll read, listen to, or watch something inspiring. 1E/2E. I'll work to make sure I have inspirational going on outside of me and inside me. I can inspire myself by thinking about the things I've done well each day including the new things I've tried...whether or not they worked out. If I tried, that's inspirational in itself! 1F/2F. I'll write a list of 10 positive things about myself and I'll read it 5-10 times daily. I'll post this list everywhere! 1G/2G. I'll keep re-reading this workbook to drill the recovery skills into my mind! I'll keep practicing positive thinking, thought control skills, reframing, and other skills like Distress Tolerance and Acceptance.
	3. There are so many negative people in my life. I'd have to get rid of everybody!	3. I'll "Hang Up The Phone" if people become negative around me... I'll leave or otherwise remove myself. I'll think "Mindfully Protecting My Peace and Stability" and care for myself like I would an infant!
5. SET LIMITS AND BOUNDARIES WITH OTHERS... AND SAY "NO" WHEN I NEED TO BECAUSE RECOVERY IS MY GREATEST PRIORITY – In all things and in all ways, I'll make decisions for myself based on recovery being my greatest priority. I'm going to act in my best interests even if people don't like it. It's an appropriate time to be "selfish" and to put my recovery needs before everything else.	1. I can't stand to tell people "No" and I feel so selfish by focusing on myself. I'm not sure I can do this.	1A. Recovery requires Distress Tolerance and doing things I'm not comfortable doing! I can tell people that I hate telling them NO, but for me to be in recovery, I must make decisions based on recovery being my #1 priority. Though folks may get mad or frustrated when I tell them NO, those who REALLY love me will understand and be proud of me for making such tough choices...and for taking a Stand for my recovery. They'll respect me and support me MORE knowing I'm serious about recovery! 1B. Folks who get mad at me for putting recovery first are selfish. Folks who love me want the best for me and they'll support me even if it inconveniences them. If I explain why I'm saying "NO," though they don't like it, they'll respect it. If they don't, then their part in my story is over for this time in my life. They're not right for me now... they're DESTABILIZERS. I can't have that because Recovery is My #1 Priority!!!!! 1C. If I don't maintain recovery, I won't have the focus or resources to help others down the road. I must help myself now and become stable. That's like the saying, "You must love yourself first!"

From "Out-of-Control: A Dialectical Behavior Therapy (DBT) - Cognitive-Behavioral Therapy (CBT) Workbook for Getting Control of Our Emotions and Emotion-Driven Behavior" Copyright © 2009 by Melanie Gordon Sheets, Ph.D. (www.dbt-cbt-workbook.com)

Figure 14.A.4: The Long, Detailed Game Plan

6. USE LIFE-ENHANCING COPING SKILLS AND SAY NO TO SELF-DESTRUCTIVE COPING (CUTTING, SUICIDE ATTEMPTS, DRUGS, AND ALCOHOL) AND SOURCES OF TEMPTATION – I cannot continue to respond to life in the same old ways. It's killing me and it's causing me more and more problems. I must use Life-Enhancing Coping Skills to deal with life's ups and downs. When I use life-enhancing skills, I'll have fewer problems and fewer ups and downs to deal with.

I cannot be around my old drug and alcohol friends or I'll end up using again. I cannot go to the old hang-outs because my old friends and the setting will tempt me to drink and use again. I cannot get on the chat line with my cutter friends...and I'll have to stay away from those websites. I'll have my family throw away all my possessions that have to do with a drug, alcohol, and cutting lifestyle...OUCH! I can't have my life filled with temptation and reminders of my old lifestyle. That's a needless destabilizer!

I will not be around people, places, and things associated with relapse and instability. I'll CHOOSE to be around people, places, and things that SUPPORT A RECOVERY LIFESTYLE. If I'm somewhere I think is safe and it's not, I'll remove myself as quickly as possible. If someone comes into my home environment that's a destabilizer, I'll ask them to leave or I'll have them removed!

---

1. I don't have any other way to cope with life. I need these things to be okay. They make me happy.

2. I expect periods of being very frustrated and angry that I won't allow myself to do my favorite copings. I expect to be tempted to go back to my old coping behaviors when I'm upset. I expect times of being irritable and grouchy...and times when I'll feel pretty miserable and sorry for myself.

3. When my drug friends and alcohol buddies know I'm home, they'll be coming by and calling. My cutter friends will be calling and emailing, too. They'll want me to relapse so I'll spend time with them again.

1A/2A. I'll Turn On Rational Mind to talk myself through this Emotional Mind stuff. I'll remind myself that these feelings are normal...but I'm not going to stew over them or act on them. If I'm not able to Turn My Mind quick enough, I'll call my sponsor or another support person. They have a way of talking me through tough times.
If I don't have an activity scheduled, I'll look at my calendar and pick something to go to for distraction, fun, or inspiration!
1B/2B. I'm practicing Life-Enhancing Coping Skills now. They're helping me to lower my negative emotional levels. I'll continue to use these to help myself. I'll use my Life-Enhancing Coping Behaviors Worksheet to practice new skills. Over time, I'll have a whole lot of coping skills to use during tough times.
1C/2C. I'll be developing a lifestyle to help buffer distress by following this Game Plan. Many things in here will give me ways to cope better with stress and upsetting things. I'm building a support network with co-workers, treatment providers, and AA people. A busy lifestyle will help me to focus less on negative things while giving me many positive things to focus on and enjoy. The extra distress I'll experience by NOT doing old copings will be temporary...soon, my changes will take root and things will be much better in my life.
1D/2D. My Self-Destructive Coping Behaviors help me to feel better in the moment, but they're ruining my life. I'm NOT happy. That's why I cut and try to kill myself. They make me miserable. I WILL NOT allow myself to fall back into STINKIN' THINKIN' and the ways of relapse. I'll seek strength to endure this difficult time and I'll remind myself of the light at the end of the tunnel.
3A. I'll set limits and boundaries and hold to my recovery plan. If relapse people come over, I'll ask them to leave, then insist they leave, and have them removed if needed! When they call, I'll hold a VERY SHORT conversation to tell them that I'm in recovery and I can't be around them anymore. I'll write-out how to handle this in a nice, but firm manner. I won't argue with them, I'll get off the phone and not answer if they call back. It's got to be over and I'm not doing all the drama. I'll do what's needed to Protect My Peace and Stability!
3B. Rather than having my support people run them off, I'll Take a Stand and tell them I'm in recovery and they should no longer come around or call. I'll take a firm "Don't Come Back, Don't Call" stance.
3C. I'll invite them to church, a bible study, volunteer activities, or AA. That'll run them off real fast! Wholesome, recovery-focused activities are the last things they'll want to do! That'll keep 'em away!

Figure 14.A.5: The Long, Detailed Game Plan

(Action Step 6 – continued)	4. My mother calls or comes over every day. She ALWAYS gets me upset. She's a major destabilizer!	3D. I'll cancel the email address connected to the chat websites and I'll open a new one. I'll stay away from those types of websites.
	5. I'm surrounded by all kinds of TEMPTATION!!!!	4. I'll practice the "Hang up the Phone" script and set limits for her phone calls AND visits. If she can't be nice, I can't talk with her. She'll have to learn to be nice or we won't have much time together.
	6. I'll feel lonely at times and will miss being around my old friends.	5. I know temptation will be present. I'll Mindfully Protect My Peace and Stability at all times by making decisions that honor my recovery. I'll avoid temptation at all costs. If I find myself in a tempting situation, I'll quickly remove myself!
		6A. DISTRESS TOLERANCE! I'll remind myself that I'm involved in many activities that'll help me build new friendships. I'll remind myself that this loneliness is temporary. I'll allow time for my changes to take root...and soon, I'll have people to hang out with again.
		6B. I'll remind myself that it's normal to miss the good times with old buddies, but, I'll also remind myself that I can't be around them anymore. I'll pray for their recovery and Turn My Mind to focus on something positive.
7. SECURE TRANSPORTATION – Make arrangements NOW. Talk to friends, family, and neighbors about the activities I'll need rides for. I'll see who's willing to do what. When I choose activities, I'll consider places they go, their schedules, and when they're willing to take me places. I'll choose meetings, groups, church, and activities which I can most easily get to! I'll save money to buy a $500 car to get started with. I'll babysit, do yard work, and other such jobs to put money aside for a car and insurance.	1. It's hard to ask people to do things for me and then it's hard to feel like I owe them something.	1. Distress Tolerance. It doesn't matter if I hate it. THIS IS MY RECOVERY. I'll be doing many things I'm not comfortable with, so I might as well add asking for rides to the list!! I'll ask for rides when I need them. My recovery will be a gift to those who love me!
	2. Friends and family are pretty burnt out with me. They may not be too willing to help me AT FIRST!	2. I'll take a bus. I'll check for discounts and programs for "needy" people. I'll rely on my feet, public services, and people who go to my activities for rides. I'll only ask friends and family as a back-up. When they see me trying, they'll be more likely to help!
	3. It'll be hard to have enough money to save for a car when I have meds, doctor appointments, and other things to pay for.	3. My meds and doctor appointments are necessities. A car is a luxury. I'll save for a car and insurance as I'm able. It'll take some time, but, it's a goal. I'll do the best I can and I'll see how things work out!
8. BE PREPARED – I'll set up an Activity Calendar listing the times and days activities, services, and people are available. I'll add phone numbers and addresses...so if I'm having a crisis or need extra support, I'll quickly know where to turn! If all options fail or I'm freakin' out too much, I'll call 911. I'd rather do that than relapse!	1. I'm not a good organizer!	1. I need to do this. This is about setting up a Recovery Lifestyle and preventing relapse. It's not a choice. I'll either buy a calendar, copy the calendar forms from this workbook, or I'll draw up some of my own! I'll have to make some phone calls to find out what types of things are available and when they're available.

Figure 14.A.6: The Long, Detailed Game Plan

9. GO TO MY APPOINTMENTS - I must take care of my physical and mental health. This requires I show up for appointments (Mental Health Center, diabetes doctor, medication appointments, lab work, counseling, groups, etc.). Good attendance will build good relations with my treatment providers. Good relations with them will help me to be chosen for the best programs and services. I want to be considered for those!	1. I have trouble getting rides. 2. I don't have money for everything. 3. It'll be hard to make all these appointments once I start working. 4. I'm not a morning person!	1. See Step 7, the Transportation section! 2A. Many will be free with State and Community Mental Health programs. I'll check into other public assistance and reduced fee programs. Churches and other groups may help pay for these, too. 2B. Since Recovery is My #1 Priority and this is a major priority, I'll hold money back each month as necessary. 3. I'll get appointments that work best with my job schedule. I'll look for a "Recovery Friendly" job that works with my Recovery Lifestyle. 4. I'll choose afternoon appointments or ones later in the morning. I'll refer to Step 3 about a regular sleep schedule.
10. TAKE MEDICATION - I'll take my meds as ordered. I won't take more or less or add other stuff! If I have a problem with them, I'll talk to the Doc. I'll use Distress Tolerance to Get Through the temporary side-effects of new medications. I will NOT stop my meds when I'm feeling better! I feel better because they're working! When I quit taking them, my symptoms return and I relapse into destructive behavior. Recovery is My #1 Priority and MY RECOVERY requires meds. If I begin to think I don't need them, I'll talk it over with Doc. If he agrees, he'll slowly reduce them and we'll watch to see if any symptoms return. I'll follow Wise Mind about my medication...and Wise Mind is not only knowing what to do, it's Following Through and Doing It!!!	1. I don't have the money to pay for all those meds and everything else I need. 2. I hate the side effects. Sometimes they make me very tired, thirsty, or jittery at first. 3. They don't work or they stop working after taking them awhile. 4. I always end up forgetting to take them!	1. I'll look into free and low price medication programs, like drug manufacturer programs, state programs, etc. I'll have money held from my check and I'll clean house for Jan to help pay for my meds. 2. I will NOT stop my meds if I have side effects unless my doctor tells me to. Some side effects last a few days or weeks and go away. I'll be patient because I need them to work. 3A. I'll allow new meds time to take effect before assuming they won't work. Some take months to reach full effects. 3B. I will NOT overtake medication or add other stuff if I'm feeling bad. Instead, I'll call my doctor and follow his instructions. I'll use Distress Tolerance and Life-Enhancing Coping Skills instead. 4A. I'll get a pill organizer box and set up my meds each week. I'll keep it in the kitchen so it's always in sight and I'll remember to take them! I'll take my meds with me if I'll be away from home at a medication time. 4B. I'll work with my doctor to simplify my medication schedule so I can take them once or twice a day. I'll get it as easy as possible.
11. GET AND MAINTAIN A JOB - I'll put out applications, make phone calls, and visit businesses until I get a job. The best way to get a job is to look in a phonebook and call and visit places where I'd like to work. That's because many jobs aren't advertised. This increases my chance of getting a job because I'm not competing with 150 other people! I'll dress nice when visiting businesses. A sharp appearance will help me	1. I don't have a resume.	1A. I'll get someone to help me write one. I'll ask around. The State Workforce Agency and other organizations will help. I'll put together basic information to fill out job applications, like where I've worked before, how long I worked there, why I left, etc. A typed resume will help me get a better job. I'll take copies with me when I go out, who knows when an opportunity to hand one out will come up! I'll be prepared! 1B. As appropriate, when I go out, I'll let folks know I'm looking for work. Some will tell me about job openings and they may even put in a good word for me! I'll have resumes with me so I can hand them out!

Figure 14.A.7: The Long, Detailed Game Plan

stand out and make a good first impression! To better my chances of getting a job, I'll send out applications and resumes, too. I'll take whatever work is available at first so I can get some money coming in...and I'll keep looking for a job that better suits me.	2. I have a bad work history and a legal history...and a mental health history. This stuff makes it hard to get a job.	2A. I'll talk with a job coach and other smart people to learn how to handle a bad work or legal history...and questions about mental health or medications that may come up during an interview or on an application. I'll find a way to minimize these problems and offer great reasons why they should hire me! 2B. I'll look on the internet for tips on filling out applications and interviewing. I'll seek community programs and trusted others to help with this, too. There are lots of resources out there to help me!
	3. I'M NOT A MORNING PERSON!	3A. See Step 3 about a regular sleep schedule. 3B. To be realistic, a 7AM job won't last for long! I could probably pull off a 9AM one though!
	4. Transportation problems! 5. I have a bad habit of walking off jobs when I get mad.	4. See Step 7, the Transportation section. 5. Even if I get mad or bored, I'll stay with the job until I find another one. I'll use every Life-Enhancing Coping Skill and Distress Tolerance skill possible to manage myself and the situation. I'll Mindfully Protect My Peace and Stability by maintaining my job!!! I'll remind myself that some bosses are jerks and that's the way things are. I need the money, the job, and the stability! They're paying me, so I'm their servant. I'll do as I'm asked and I'll do it their way even if my way is better...because they're paying me to do it their way! I'll say "Yes, Sir" and "Yes, Ma'am" and I'll be the best worker I can be! I'll deal with whatever comes my way. I'll work very hard to stay on the job for a year or more so I can improve my work history and get a better job next time. Developing a new lifestyle IS a process and it'll take time to get my life like I want it! Hello Distress Tolerance!
	6. Drinking and drugs are part of the jobs I'm qualified to do. I can't work at these places anymore.	6. I'll seek a job that fits a Recovery Lifestyle even if it means changing careers or my line of work. I'll do this because Recovery is My #1 Priority! I'll take less money and start at whatever level or pay is available so I can start working. I'll seek promotions and better paying jobs as appropriate.
	7. I don't have the right kind of clothes for a job interview or for working at a non-uniform place. 8. I get SO nervous during interviews. I'll mess up. It's hardly worth trying.	7. I'll go to thrift stores for nice clothes! Community programs and churches will help with this, too. This doesn't have to be a barrier! 8. Most people are nervous when interviewing. That's normal! I'll prepare myself for tough questions and problems in my resume. I'll practice pretend interviews in my head and with friends and family. I'll practice answering all kinds of questions. I'll get tips for interviewing. I could say "I'm very excited to meet with you! I would very much like to work here! I'm a bit nervous because this interview is very important to me!" Many interviewers will say something to set me at ease! If I mess up, I'll be normal! I can do damage control by

Figure 14.A.8: The Long, Detailed Game Plan

(Action Step 11 – continued)		offering a better answer as Part 2 of my response or I can throw in a better answer later. Most people will mess up during an interview... there are few PERFECT INTERVIEWS! I know I'll probably leave the interview knowing I could have said something better...and, I'll say it better next time!!! I won't sit around waiting for a call back, I'll keep applying and interviewing until I GET a call back.
	9. I can't work. If I work, I'll lose my Social Security benefits.	9. It's hard to meet my needs on Social Security. Being dependent on $700 a month is disabling! It's hard to pay for decent housing, meds, transportation, hobbies, and other stuff with so little money. I may be better off working...the extra income is quality of life. I'll find out how much I can earn without losing benefits. If I can't earn much, I may be better off with a job. I must think this through and get advice before I do anything!
	10. I can't work. I get so restless. It's hard to be still and focused.	10. I can't have a job where I sit for hours. I need one that allows me to move around. I'll ask a job coach and others for some job ideas!
12. KEEP BUSY – I'll make up a schedule to keep busy so I don't have much time to worry...or to think about things of relapse. When I'm busy, I'll meet people. I'll be choosy and develop friendships with folks who live a Recovery Lifestyle! Being busy will help me to set up a Recovery Lifestyle and to fill my life and time with meaningful activities and relationships. These activities and friendships will be a Distress Buffer to help me through difficult times. I'll call the YMCA and see if they have a Painting Class. The college sends newsletters about Adult Ed classes for fun and interest. I'll see what they have to offer. I'll check out the Community Calendar in the newspaper or online to see what's going on in town. I'll make other phone calls, too! I'll get my bike fixed up. I could ride for fun and transportation! Dual purpose!	1. Transportation issues! 2. I'm shy and I get anxious around new people. I hate going to new places alone and I hate feeling alone in a group of people. I expect to come up with "good reasons" why I should stay home when it's time to go! 3. My meds make me tired.	1. Refer to Step 7, the Transportation section!!!! 2A. I've got to go anyway! I'll use Distress Tolerance skills and I'll walk into activities like I own the place! I'll take a buddy the first few times I go somewhere new so I'll feel more comfortable. If no one is available, I'll go by myself and sit alone if I have to...and I'll keep reminding myself that I'll meet people to be with after I go a few times. I'll take control of my shyness so I can LIVE life! 2B. I'll make a list of "conversation starters" and practice things to say to start conversations. This will help me to do better in new situations and will increase my chances of having someone to hang out with quicker! 2C. I'll remind myself to be patient and Give Time for My Changes to Take Root! It'll take time to make friends, especially close friends! 2D. I'll remind myself that going is NOT A CHOICE! I've planned to go...so I'm going! I'll go whether or not I want to. I'll go because going is the only way out of hell...the hell of suffering, being alone, and experiencing little meaning in life. I won't even think about not going. I'll do what I need to do...no questions asked!!!! 3. I'll allow for tiredness and I'll take short naps as needed. A 20-minute nap can do wonders. Napping during medication tiredness periods will be a planned activity! It's an essential activity that'll allow me to live a normal life! I'll talk with my doc if tiredness continues. An active lifestyle IS a Recovery Lifestyle. A lazy lifestyle spells RELAPSE. Therefore, I'll go to activities even if I'm tired. Having fun will wake me up!!!

Figure 14.A.9: The Long, Detailed Game Plan

13. NO ROMANTIC RELATIONSHIPS FOR AT LEAST ONE YEAR – I must get a Recovery Lifestyle set up…and I must be stable BEFORE getting involved with someone. I need to work on my emotional issues and my relationship issues BEFORE starting a new relationship. I'm tired of the drama, chaos, and crises of unhealthy relationships. This is one area that CANNOT be overlooked. It's what usually triggers relapse for me. If I'm stable and living a Recovery Lifestyle, I'll have a better chance of meeting someone stable who lives a Life-Enhancing lifestyle. I'll have to deal with the sense of aloneness that comes when I have to live alone.	1. I can't stand to be alone. I become so lonely and miserable that I end up relapsing.	1A. I'll remind myself that this is an area I must master if I'm to recover. I'll talk myself through this Emotional Mind stuff. I'll use Life-Enhancing Coping Skills to Get Through these feelings. I'll get a specific plan for dealing with this…a Crisis Survival Plan! It's always possible that I'll be so tired at the end of the day that this won't bother me as much as it did before. I WILL call my sponsor or another support person IF it becomes overwhelming. 1B. I'll see about getting a roommate who is easy to get along with and DOESN'T use drugs or alcohol…someone straight and happy! 1C. I'll work on my relationship issues with my therapist. 1D. When it's time for a relationship, I'll listen to my people. If everyone warns me NOT to get involved with someone, I WILL LISTEN THIS TIME. They've ALWAYS been right and I've always been hard-headed and desperate for love! 1E. Set boundaries and let people know my plan to stay out of a relationship. This includes NO dating and no special outings with members of the opposite sex…NO TEMPTATION. Just say NO!
14. ATTEND A SUPPORT GROUP – I'll attend "90 meetings in 90 days" – AA, NA, or DRA (Dual Recovery Anonymous for mental illness and substance abuse). There's all kinds of AA type groups for problems like anger, overeating, codependency, depression, etc. I'll look into other support groups, too! I'll check with Community Health Services, the Crisis Line, colleges, and in the newspaper for groups and counseling services. I'll call churches and see what programs they have. I'll try some Groups and go to one or two I like best.	1. Transportation issues! 2. I'm shy and social stuff makes me anxious. I hate going alone and I hate feeling alone in a group of people. 3. There are lots of demands for my time. It'll be hard to fit in new stuff.	1. Refer to Step 7, the Transportation section. 2. Refer to Step 12, the Keep Busy section. 3. I'll remind myself that Recovery is My #1 Priority and support groups are ESSENTIAL to my recovery. I need to make this happen. Most things are less important. I'll remind myself that a busy life is a good life…as long as it's the right kind of busy and not too busy! Leaning Into life is important…and I must do things with moderation and balance in mind. I'll have to wisely choose a schedule that isn't overwhelming and has enough of the important stuff. I'll prioritize the demands on my time. I'll get help in this area if I need it!
15. GET INVOLVED WITH A SERVICE ORGANIZATION – A GROUP THAT SERVES AND HELPS OTHERS – GIVE BACK, MY LIFE ISN'T ALL ABOUT ME! Service will "fill me" in ways other things can't. This will hit my soul and give me satisfaction and a sense of purpose and meaning. This is big stuff! I'll try some Groups! I'll go on a regular basis and participate in the extra	1. I'm NOT a morning person! I can't get up to go to church! 2. I don't have wheels to go extra places. Getting rides to work is hard enough. 3. I'm shy and I get anxious in social situations. I hate going to new places alone and I hate feeling alone in a group of people.	1A. Refer to Step 3 about getting on a good sleep schedule. 1B. Get that way! Most churches don't pull many people for evening services. Think "Recovery or Sleep Late, Recovery-Sleep Late"! I choose recovery and a church with 11 AM services, not the 8:30 AM ones! I'll schedule volunteer work later in the day, too! 2. Refer to Step 7, the Transportation section. 3. Refer to Step 12, the Keep Busy section. Being involved in church activities or volunteer work will give me a great opportunity to develop relationships. Working with others on a project makes it easier to talk to people because we'll have something to talk about…project things!

Figure 14.A.10: The Long, Detailed Game Plan

activities. I'll allow time for people to get to know me...to trust me...and to know how best to plug me into activities. I'll allow time to make friends, too...because that's another reason I'm going!

I'll go back to my old church or I'll find a new one. I'll go to the weekly services and other activities on a regular basis. This will help me spiritually and will give me the recovery advantage of hope, faith, and belief.

I'm not a church person, so I'll get involved in volunteer work. I'll call the United Way to see what's available and what matches my interests. The VA is nearby. They'd welcome a new volunteer! I could walk there instead of worrying about a ride!

4. There's many demands for my time. It's hard to fit new stuff into my schedule.	4. Remember "Recovery is My #1 Priority!" Involvement in service activities will help me in ways other things can't. My help is needed... and I like to feel needed and valued.
5. Who wants to work for free?	5. This isn't about money. It's about developing a meaningful life, feeling good about myself, and building a support network and friendships. I should pay these organizations for all this help!!! I need to be around positive, productive people to increase my chances of having friends with emotionally healthy lifestyles. It'll help me a lot to be around people who are focused on living a meaningful life. This is also about filling up my days and evenings with things that add meaning and purpose to my life! Getting involved with a service organization is about helping people AND myself. The "pay" I receive is much greater than money. A job is important for many reasons, but, I need to choose church or volunteer activities for the reasons listed above!!!!

16. PRACTICE RANDOM ACTS OF KINDNESS

I'll look for opportunities to be kind and helpful to others. Their appreciation will help me to feel better and to experience extra moments of joy. When I touch other people's lives, I'm touched, too. It's nice to see people's faces brighten because of something I've done! Sometimes, my acts of kindness will "make their day"...and this will make my day, too! Giving back to the world...gives back to me! It's also nice to be well thought of and appreciated! I'll seek opportunities to practice random acts of kindness on a daily basis!

1. I'm NOT a nice person!	1. I'm making lots of changes and this is a great one to add! This will give me joy because smiles are contagious! Their appreciation will soften my heart and help me to feel good! It's good for the spirit!
2. I've already agreed to do volunteer work, that's enough!	1B/2. This doesn't have to be BIG stuff. I can hold the door open for someone, I can pick up something dropped, push a basket into the store, or say "Good morning" to someone who doesn't get greeted often. I can let someone with a couple items go before me in the check-out line. I can express appreciation. I can show respect. I can do many things which aren't WORK and aren't time consuming! Doing nice things helps me to feel better about the kind of person I am. People may even see me in a new light! They may return kindness to me...and to others. That's meaningful! Being kind to others helps me to connect to the world and to feel good about myself!

17. CARE FOR MY PHYSICAL HEALTH - diet, exercise, sleep schedule

I'll improve my diet a little at a time, but I'll make sure I eat 2-3 meals a day. I'll add exercise to my weekly schedule even if it means parking further from stores, walking to the mailbox, or choosing a job that requires movement rather than sitting! I'll work to get

1. I'm trying to quit drinking and using drugs. I'm trying to fill my life with productive activities and to remove negative faces, places, and things from my life. I don't need to worry about making major diet changes at this point or exercising. I can't do everything at once and worrying about this stuff is	1A. My medication causes weight gain...which increases my risk for diabetes. This medication is working like others haven't and I want to stay on it! I can help myself by doing some things to prevent too much weight gain. 1B. RECOVERY from drugs and alcohol and from the intense symptoms of mental illness is My #1 Priority. Recovery is not one action or event...it's a lifestyle. Eating well, sleeping well, and exercise are important. Even reducing caffeine is important since it interferes

Figure 14.A.11: The Long, Detailed Game Plan

with my recovery (sleep, restlessness, and anxiety levels). I can reduce caffeine by having caffeine-free soda during the day...while still having my coffee in the morning! It's all about balance and moderation!

1C. I'm willing to make SOME diet changes, I'm not THAT stubborn! I know it's important to drink water and to eat more than one meal per day! I can pull off some minor diet changes right now.

1D. I'll try to eat better and get some exercise but I'm not going to make myself crazy with this right now. It's a lower priority for me. When I get good at other parts of recovery, I can worry about this.

1E. I WILL work to get on a good sleep schedule. I'll go to bed when I need to whether or not I'm tired. My body will finally adjust.

1F. When I'm choosing my activities, I'll choose some with exercise built in, like bowling and volleyball. Also, rather than sitting and collecting tickets, I could ask to be a door greeter and show people where they're supposed to go...so I can move around!

---

not a priority for me right now. If I had diabetes or an eating disorder, it would be different.

---

on a good sleep schedule. Taking care of my physical condition will greatly help with recovery. For instance, being rested will help me to cope better and to be more focused and less irritable. Eating good food and 2-3 meals a day has the same effects!

4- Obstacles – (ob-stuh-coles) – things that get in our way, like an obstacle in our path that we have to get around.

Rational Mind Obstacles and Emotional Mind Excuses get in our way of carrying out the steps we need to take to improve the quality of our life… and to maintain recovery.

starting over and living a Recovery Lifestyle. The first Action Step is "Deal With Stuff as It Comes My Way – I'll Lean Into It." On the second page, you'll find the second and third Action Steps, "Daily Devotion" and "Get on a Sleep-Wake Schedule that Matches My Life's Needs." Check out the titles of the other Action Steps. Don't panic…your plan won't be as long as this one!

Go back to the first page and check out **the middle column**. It's called, **"Rational Mind Obstacles[4] and Emotional Mind Excuses**: What Might Discourage Me from Doing This." This column includes the excuses we give ourselves and others for not being able to do the Action Steps our recovery requires. Read through some of these to get a feel for what goes in this column.

Go back to the first page and check out **the last column**. It's called, **"Rational Mind Challenges and Wise Mind How-To's**: Come Hail or High Water…How I'll Get Through It and Do It." This column is for Talking Ourselves Through the Excuses and Obstacles we face so we can problem-solve and Talk Ourselves INTO carrying out the Actions Steps. Remember, Wise Mind is not just about knowing what to do…it's about FOLLOWING THROUGH with what We Know to do!

Uh…Can I Get a Short Version?

The Long, Detailed Game Plan is a sample. It SHOULD BE USED as an EXAMPLE of how to write a Game Plan. It has more in it than most of us will need. The plan is very long because of the L-O-N-G descriptions of the Action Steps in the first column and the number of Challenges in the last column. We won't need all that information, so our plan will be MUCH SHORTER!

5- See Figure 14.B, "A Typical Game Plan." It's four pages long, so it's numbered 14.B.1 – 14.B.4. It's the SHORT Game Plan!

Check out the "Typical" Game Plan.[5] It's called "typical" because it's more like something we would do. It's a typical Game Plan! It ONLY INCLUDES what was important to the person writing the plan. It has FEWER ACTION STEPS and A LOT LESS WORDING than the long plan. Look at the first Action Step…the one about "Dealing With Stuff as It Comes My Way." Notice they only wrote a few sentences to describe the step. They wrote what was REALLY MEANINGFUL to them, not everything on the LONG plan. In the "Excuses and Obstacles" section, three Excuses were used. Two were from the long plan…and one they came up with on their own! The CHALLENGES AND HOW-TO column is MUCH SHORTER, too. It has less than half the number of Challenges and How-To's.

Hit the Highlights for Me, Please

Because many DBT-CBT concepts and principles are discussed in the LONG

Figure 14.B.1: A Typical Game Plan

My Game Plan for: Starting Over and Living a Recovery Lifestyle - Recovery from Substance Abuse and Mental Illness

WISE MIND ACTION STEPS: "How Do I Go About It?" List the Action Steps you NEED to take and ones which would be HELPFUL for your recovery. These are the "Must Do's" and the "Would Be Helpful To Do's."	RATIONAL MIND OBSTACLES AND EMOTIONAL MIND EXCUSES: "What Might Discourage Me from Doing This?" List the major Obstacles and Excuses that will get in your way of carrying out the Action Steps.	RATIONAL MIND CHALLENGES AND WISE MIND HOW-TO'S: "Come Hail or High Water... How I'll Get Through It and Do It" Note how you'll help yourself to get passed and around the Rational Mind Obstacles and Emotional Mind Excuses.
1. DEAL WITH STUFF AS IT COMES MY WAY...I'LL LEAN INTO IT! - I'LL CHOOSE what I need to deal with and what I'll walk away from. I WILL CHOOSE my battles. I'LL DEAL WITH whatever comes my way, good or bad, just or unjust. I'll deal with my past when it gets in the way of the present. I'LL DEAL WITH LIFE THE BEST I CAN. When my strength or know-how falters, I'll seek advisors.	1. Some things are very hard to deal with and accept. 2. I'm easily overwhelmed and I'm a worrier. 3. I screw everything up. I'll screw this up, too.	1A. This is something I'll have to work on! Some things will be easier to accept and deal with...and others will take more work! I have NOT mastered recovery and everything isn't going to be easy! I'm in the learning phases and I'll do the BEST I can. When I notice I'm falling short, I'll seek support and counsel. I am a WORK IN PROGRESS! 1B. I'll make a list of what I need to deal with. I'll decide what should be dealt with first. I'll write a Game Plan as needed. I'll Lean Into my recovery. 1C. If I find myself avoiding something, I'll catch myself and make a decision about whether or not I need to deal with it. 2A. I'll get a Game Plan for dealing with major stuff. Each morning, I'll remind myself what I'm focusing on THIS day and I won't allow myself to worry about everything else. I'll remind myself there's an order to things. 2B. I'll use all kinds of Life-Enhancing Coping Skills, Rational Mind thinking, and Wise Mind actions to help myself through the tough times! 3. If I find myself upset and in the process of screwing up, I'll STOP myself, do damage control, and start over! I'll learn from it, get a plan for next time, and move on.
2. DAILY DEVOTION - Meditation - I'll spend some time each morning to remind myself THAT NO MATTER WHAT, Recovery is My #1 Priority! I'll seek the strength, focus, wisdom, and perseverance to KEEP Recovery My #1 Priority. I'll seek mindfulness of recovery THROUGHOUT my day...and especially when I hit trouble spots, aggravations, and upsetting situations.	1. I'll forget to do this.	1A. I might forget at first. I'll put a note on my coffee pot to remember. I'll hang something of my son's on my rear view mirror as a reminder...because he's really depending on me to remain in recovery. 1B. When I hit trouble spots, I'll repeat to myself..."Recovery is My #1 Priority" and "Think Life-Enhancing!" 1C. Better yet, I'll get up 30 minutes early so I'm not in such a hurry each morning. I'll start a new morning routine. I'll sit down at the table with my coffee and I'll think about my day, my goals, what I face, etc. I'll get a notebook and write stuff down.

Figure 14.B.2: A Typical Game Plan

3. MAINTAIN A POSITIVE ATTITUDE – I'll improve my attitude by Turning My Mind from negative things to positive things. This includes Ellen and Kirk. I can't stand their negativity. I'll walk away if they become needlessly negative. Same goes for my family! I will no longer "Dig in the Garbage." I'll Turn My Mind from my painful past when it's not therapeutic. I'll focus on my recovery and what I'm doing about it in the here-and-now instead. I can't continue to live like I was living...it's been killing me for years.	1. I face many difficult things. It'll take a LOT of work to stay focused on the here-and-now and the positive things. Living in the past has been my life.	1A. I'll challenge myself to be mindful of my thinking. I'll Turn My Mind when I start to think negative or about the painful past...unless it's therapy-focused. 1B. I'll try to control conversations with my brother. If he throws a fit on the phone about my past, I'll practice the "Hang Up the Phone" technique. I can't deal with the negativity anymore. 1C. When my co-workers begin to piss n' moan, I'll try to Turn their Minds to something else! I'll see if I can get the conversation to change, or I'll have to remove myself...and avoid them!
4. SET LIMITS AND BOUNDARIES...AND SAY "NO" WHEN I NEED TO BECAUSE RECOVERY IS MY #1 PRIORITY – In all things, I'll make decisions based on recovery being my greatest priority. I'm going to act in my best interests even if others don't like it. It's an appropriate time to be "selfish" and to put my recovery needs first.	1. I can tell my family NO, but I've never been able to say NO to my buddies. I work hard to please them so I'll have friends.	1A. Recovery requires Distress Tolerance and doing things I'm not comfortable doing! I have to tell my old friends NO and deal with NOT having friends right now if they aren't supportive of my recovery. I have to say NO, else they'll step all over my recovery... and I'll be right back to old ways. To maintain recovery, I must make MY RECOVERY...my #1 priority. 1B. I know my TRUE friends will be proud of me for saying NO and putting recovery first. People that get mad and reject me don't have my best interests at heart...they're just USER FRIENDS. I don't need them in my life. This will be a good way to weed out USER friends from TRUE friends! 1C. I'll run some situations through my mind to practice saying NO. I must be ready to deal with them. They'll be pressuring me.
5. USE LIFE-ENHANCING COPING SKILLS AND SAY "NO" TO DRUGS AND ALCOHOL...AND TEMPTATION – I can't be around folks who drink or drug. I can't hang out at the ballpark after the game or the pool hall. I have to give up poker night, too. I have to make major changes in who I hang with, where I go, and what I keep around me...like all the beer and whiskey wall hangings, shot glasses...and the entire décor in my house! I can't have my new life filled with temptation and reminders of my old life...that's a needless destabilizer. I'll CHOOSE to be around the people, places, and things which SUPPORT a Recovery Lifestyle. If I	1. I expect periods of being very frustrated and angry that I won't allow myself to drink or use drugs. I expect to be tempted to go back to my old coping behaviors when I'm upset...or when I'm excited about something and am in a party mood! I expect times of being irritable and grouchy...and times when I'll feel pretty miserable and sorry for myself. 2. My old friends and party people will want me back! They'll be calling, coming over, and inviting me to	1A/2A. I'll Turn On Rational Mind to talk myself through this stuff. I'm not going to stew on this stuff or act on it. If I'm not able to Turn My Mind quick enough, I'll call my sponsor or other folks who support my recovery. I'll find something to keep my mind busy and positive things to occupy my time. 1B/2B. I'll think "Big Picture of My Life" and what I stand to lose. 1C/2C. I'll avoid temptation at all costs. If I find myself in a tempting situation, I'll quickly remove myself! 2D. I'll set limits and boundaries and hold to my recovery plan. I'll ask them to leave and not call. I'll be as firm as needed. 2E. DISTRESS TOLERANCE! I'll remind myself that I'm involved in many activities that'll help me build new friendships. I'll remind myself that this loneliness is temporary. I'll allow time for my changes to take root...and soon, I'll have people to hang out with again.

Figure 14.B.3: A Typical Game Plan

find myself in a bad situation, I'll remove myself as quickly as possible. If someone comes into my house that's a destabilizer, I'll ask them to leave or I'll have them removed.	things. They'll pressure me to relapse. It'll be hard to say NO because they're the only friends I've got!	1. I need to do this. This is about setting up a Recovery Lifestyle and preventing relapse. It's not a choice.
6. BE PREPARED – I'll set up an Activity Calendar so I'm prepared for any problems. I need to be able to distract myself if I start to wig out. Sitting home and dwelling on things is the worst thing I can do. If all options fail or I'm freakin' out, I'll call 911. I'd rather do that than relapse!	1. I hate paperwork!	
7. GO TO MY APPOINTMENTS – All of them!	1. I don't have money for everything.	1A. Many will be free with state and community programs. I'll check into other public assistance and reduced fee programs, if needed. 1B. Since Recovery is My #1 Priority and this is a major priority, I'll hold money back each month as necessary.
	2. It'll be hard to make all these appointments. I'm so busy at work, it'll be hard to leave for appointments.	2. I can pull off late afternoon appointments. I have to put my recovery first. My co-workers will have to pick up the slack as needed. I always do that for them. I'm going to have to be okay with this...and okay with asking for time off even if it's a busy time.
8. ACCEPT I HAVE BIPOLAR DISORDER... A MENTAL ILLNESS...AND I NEED TO TAKE MEDICATION TO KEEP MY MOOD STABLE – I'll take my meds as ordered. If I have a problem with them, I'll talk to the doc. I'll use Distress Tolerance to Get Through the temporary side-effects. I will NOT stop them when I'm feeling better! If I begin to think I don't need them, I'll talk it over with my doctor.	1. I don't have the money to pay for all those meds and everything else I need.	1. I'll look into free and low price medication programs. Actually, I'll have extra money because I won't be buying drugs and alcohol!
	2. I hate the side effects. I don't need medication anyway.	2. I will NOT stop my meds if I have side effects unless my doctor tells me to. I'm already feeling better on them. I can see the difference. I really need them. Just like people hate to have high blood pressure, I hate to have Bipolar. Just like people take high blood pressure medication...I have to take Bipolar medication so my brain works right and I can be in recovery.
	3. I'll forget to take them! I'm awful with meds.	3. I'll get a pill organizer box and set up my meds each week. I'll keep it by the computer so I'll see it all the time.
9. KEEP BUSY AND HAVE SOME FUN! I'll skip college for now. I don't need to add unnecessary stress so early in recovery. I'll set up an Activity Calendar and a weekly one. I'll do AA every evening, but, I'd like to add some fun things, too. I need things to fill my time since I'm not hanging out at the ballpark or the pool hall anymore! I need to set up a Recovery Lifestyle and fill my life with recovery activities and relationships.	1. I don't like trying new things or meeting new people. I'm not good in conversations...unless I'm buzzed. I'll always feel out of place and anxious.	1A. I'll remind myself that going is NOT A CHOICE! I'll suck up and use Distress Tolerance skills. I'll take a buddy the first few times. If no one is available, I'll go by myself until I meet new people! Folks usually like me once they get to know me. I'll choose activities where people DO things... being on a team or working on a project together is a natural way to talk with people. 1B. I'll look over my sister's book on conversation starters to get some ideas! I can run pretend conversation openers through my mind! 1C. I'll remind myself to be patient and give time for my changes to take root! It'll take time to make friends, especially close friends.

Figure 14.B.4: A Typical Game Plan

10. GET INVOLVED WITH A SERVICE ORGANIZATION – GIVE BACK! MY LIFE ISN'T ALL ABOUT ME! Service will "fill me" in ways other things can't. It'll give me satisfaction and a sense of purpose and meaning. I'm not into church stuff, so I'll do volunteer work. I'll see what's out there to do. I'm going to prioritize and add AA and something fun first. Then, I'll add some community service type of thing. There's probably a group that gets together to fix homes for the elderly or needy. That's something to look into.	1. I don't like new people and new situations. 2. There's many demands for my time. It's hard to fit in new stuff. 3. Who wants to work for free?	1. Refer to the KEEP BUSY SECTION above! 2. I'm prioritizing things. I'll get in a good routine with AA and add something fun for my personal enjoyment. Once I adjust to this schedule, I'll add some type of service work. That'll round things out real well. 3. This isn't about money. It's about developing a meaningful life, being involved with others, meeting people with healthy lifestyles... and MY RECOVERY...WHICH IS PRICELESS!
11. PRACTICE RANDOM ACTS OF KINDNESS – I'll look for opportunities to be kind and helpful to others. I used to be like that. It'll feel good to be that type of person again. It's cool to think about this. I remember people's smiles and I knew my kindness touched their heart. I most enjoyed being nice to people who rarely had other people being nice to them. Those were the folks who needed it most!	1. I don't have a problem doing this, other than being BUSY!	1. If I'm out in the world and going to activities and being around people, I'll have many opportunities to do things that'll take only seconds of my time! I can do this! It'll be the easiest step of all!
12. CARE FOR MY PHYSICAL HEALTH – **(DIET, EXERCISE, SLEEP SCHEDULE)** – My diet has been a problem because I've been going out right after work and eating fast food and convenience store food...and ball park food...and Joe's Pool Hall food! I'll get creative and think about this. My family always wants me over, maybe I'll go from house-to-house during the week and pay them $5 for a home cooked meal! I'll see if they're interested! This will help a lot because I don't want to go home after work. I know me, I'll get lazy and want to stay there! I feel best when I go to bed by 11, so I'll make sure I'm home by 9:30 or so.	1. I don't like to cook and I don't have cooking stuff in my house. 2. It'll be too easy to stay home if I go home after work.	1A/2A. There's always Subway! I could do that once a week! 1B/2B. I'll check with my family to see which nights I could eat at their homes. That would make them happy and give me time with the nieces and nephews...and time with mom and dad. 1C/2C. Maybe AA people get together for meals. I'm sure they do. I'll ask around. I'll work to be mindful of good nutrition and eat some healthy foods at restaurants.

Game Plan, you're STRONGLY ENCOURAGED to read the WHOLE PLAN. It'll provide a good review of the things we've discussed in this workbook. While reading through this Game Plan, USE A HIGHLIGHTER to mark things that would be good to have in YOUR Recovery Plan.

This Will Take a Lot of Work!

Your Game Plan doesn't have to be written in one night! Take your time to do it...and Think Through It! Most of what you need is already in the sample plans. BEAR IN MIND that the Game Plan we're writing NOW relates to our recovery NOW...and in the next few months. We're not going to write a Game Plan for the next two years! We're going to FOCUS ON THE HERE-AND-NOW and the UP-N'-COMING in the next few months. This will cut down on our work!

> Our first Game Plan should include things related to our EARLY recovery. These are our CURRENT PRIORITIES...the HIGH priorities...the things that'll GET US ON the Recovery Path and KEEP US THERE for the next 2-3 months. When we're doing pretty well with our EARLY Recovery Plan, we can add other things to our Game Plan...the lower priority things. These are important things, but not our highest priorities at the time. Our Game Plan should deal with our priorities at any given time...not EVERYTHING we could possibly deal with and do.

This Is Overwhelming. Where Do I Start?

Well, we'll start with the parts we highlighted from the sample plan. We can COPY WHOLE SECTIONS into our plan or PARTS of a section...and we can CHANGE the wording and SHORTEN things up.[6] We'll also use the step-by-step instructions found later in this chapter. They'll TALK US THROUGH the writing of our plan. We'll start by writing in the Action Steps, then the Excuses and Obstacles, and then the Challenges and How-To's.

Stepping into Action

The Wise Mind Action Steps make up the first column. They answer the big recovery question, "How Do I Go About It?" In our Game Plan, we'll list the Action Steps we NEED TO TAKE and ones which would be HELPFUL TO DO as part of our EARLY recovery. They're our "Must Do's" and our "Would Be Helpful to Do's." Really, most of us KNOW what these things are...we just haven't wanted to do them! We've heard these things a million times in rehabs, hospitals, AA, therapy, and from our support people, books, TV...and THROUGHOUT this workbook!

Two easy places to find ideas for Actions Steps are the sample Game Plans and

Prioritize what you need to do...and make these things your starting point. Be wise and Lean Into your recovery!

6- OUR Game Plan should be SHORTENED and PERSONALIZED to meet our needs! For instance, check out Action Step #5 on the "typical" plan. It's based on Action Step #6 on the long plan. They both deal with saying NO to Destructive Coping Behavior and unnecessary temptation. However, the one on the long plan addresses cutting, suicide attempts, and drugs and alcohol. The person writing the "typical" plan addresses drugs and alcohol only... because they don't have problems with cutting or suicide attempts. So, change up the plan to meet your needs!

We'll want a Game Plan for handling the things Coming At Us so they're less likely to break through our boundaries, invade our space, and wreck our world. We need to have a plan for preventing intrusions into our Realm of Peace.

We can't get past these steps if we want our life to change. The reality is…if we want our life to change, we have to change! Our life won't change if we don't change. Don't you wish we could just skip that part!

the completed Wise Mind Worksheets. Be sure to look at the Wise Mind Worksheet YOU COMPLETED to see the Action Steps you've ALREADY identified to be important for your recovery.

Look over the Action Steps you highlighted in the long Game Plan. Which ones relate to your recovery over the NEXT YEAR? _____

_____
_____
_____
_____
_____

Look over the Action Steps you listed above. Highlight ones which would be good for your EARLY RECOVERY Game Plan…ones that are CURRENT PRIORITIES for your recovery over the next 2-3 months.

Can We Get a Bit Personal?

We'll probably have a few things to add to our Game Plan which aren't in the sample plans. In Group, Members personalize their plans by adding Action Steps to meet their specific needs. They add things like "Getting Kids Back", "Dealing With Debt and Bill Collectors", "Dealing With a Difficult Teenager", "Budgeting and Saving Up for Things", "Getting My Own Place to Live", etc.

What sort of things would you ADD to your Game Plan…one for the NEXT YEAR?

_____
_____
_____

Highlight the ones above that would be good for your EARLY RECOVERY plan… ones that are CURRENT PRIORITIES for your recovery over the next 2-3 months.

There's More to It than JUST Action Steps!

It's much better to suffer for a positive outcome than to just suffer…and live in misery because we're not willing to make the changes that'll change things.

Our recovery requires the Action Steps in the first column. Our WILLFULNESS requires the other two columns! I learned about these columns because I had to deal with myself! I'm the master of excuses. I can talk myself out of most anything I NEED to do but DON'T WANT TO DO. Sometimes, I can be prepared to do something ALL DAY…and at the last minute, I can FIND a great reason why I SHOULD NOT, CANNOT, OR DO NOT NEED to do the thing I NEED TO DO. Because I know I'm not TOO abnormal, I expect other folks have the same problem…the problem of self-sabotage![7]

7- Self-sabotage – (sab-oh-toj) – to cause ourselves to fail or mess up.

From "Out-of-Control: A Dialectical Behavior Therapy (DBT) – Cognitive-Behavioral Therapy (CBT) Workbook for Getting Control of Our Emotions and Emotion-Driven Behavior" - Copyright © 2009 by Melanie Gordon Sheets, Ph.D. (www.dbt-cbt-workbook.com)

APPLICATION: How Can I Get Out of Doing This?

The middle column covers Rational Mind Obstacles and Emotional Mind Excuses or in other words, "What Might Discourage Me from Doing This." Rational Mind Obstacles are TRUE OBSTACLES that get in our way of doing something. They're REAL OBSTACLES that we need to GET PASSED or AROUND so we can do whatever it is we need to do! They're things like transportation or money issues, having kids and being unable to afford daycare, and having panic attacks in public places. They're REAL obstacles that get in our way of doing what we NEED to do.

Most of the time, we try to convince ourselves and others that our excuses are True Obstacles when in fact, they're JUST EXCUSES!

EMOTIONAL MIND EXCUSES are NOT real obstacles.
THEY ARE LIES we tell ourselves. They're EXCUSES WE COME UP WITH so we don't have to do something! They're NOT based on truth or fact.
They're JUST EXCUSES we make-up...and they sabotage our recovery.

One of my favorite sayings has been, "I'm TOO FAT to exercise!" Is that a lie I tell myself or is it a TRUE obstacle? Does being "too fat" prevent me from exercising? Most folks would tell me, "You're not TOO FAT!" Here's how the rest of that conversation might go.

Excuse 1: I'm not TOO FAT...well, thank you.

Excuse 2: OH, I'm NOT too fat TO EXERCISE......oooohhhhhh! You mean there's exercises I can do and still be safe? Water Aerobics? That wouldn't work for me...I float WAY too much.

Excuse 3: Yea, I guess putting weights on my ankles WOULD work, but, I'm TOO FAT to get in a bathing suit.

Excuse 4: Distress Tolerance...you've got to be kidding. I DON'T DO bathing suits and the water displacement...oh, that would be TOTALLY embarrassing!

Excuse 5: Go to Curves where there are a lot of big women like me? There's NO way. I can't afford it and I don't have time.

Excuse 6: Go during my lunch hour...HELLLLOOOOOO, I'M EATING THEN!

Excuse 7: Do chair exercises at work? Oh, you've NEVER heard how my chair squeaks just from normal movement. That WOULD NOT be good!

Excuse 8: Do them for a few minutes during my lunch hour when everyone's gone? REALLY, I'm TOO pressured at work. I don't have time.

Excuse 9: Oh, a few minutes at a time...I REALLY don't think my chair would hold up to any WILD movements like THAT. If I fell off, I'd like NEVER get up, and there's NO WAY I'm going to embarrass myself by being carried out by EIGHT men on a stretcher. I don't even think my door is wide enough for that many people to get through at once.

Excuse 10: Hey, where ya' goin'? See, it's hopeless. Nothing will work. I'm just too fat to exercise.

So, in the middle column, we'll list the OBSTACLES and EXCUSES we expect to use to talk ourselves out of doing the Action Steps or to otherwise discourage ourselves from Following Through with what We NEED to do.

Take a look at the Action Steps you wrote down earlier...the HIGHLIGHTED ones. List the Rational Mind Obstacles and the Emotional Mind Excuses that might get in the way or discourage you from doing them. If you've already listed your Action Steps in a blank Game Plan form, then, list these Obstacles and Excuses in the middle column...BUT, READ STEP 7 in the Game Plan instructions first! If you haven't started a Game Plan, list them below. Remember to review the sample plans for ideas. _____

_____

_____

_____

_____

_____

_____

8- Like a machine gun, my sister can rapid-fire MANY excuses for anything she doesn't want to do. EACH excuse is pretty convincing on its' own. One day, I was gunned down by five of these "good excuses" in a row and it occurred to me that she's just full of excuses...(and I thought I WAS the Master of Excuses. I wonder who learned from who!). If she was REALLY willing to improve her life, she'd focus on ways to get around her true obstacles...instead of SO DESPERATELY and FEROCIOUSLY[9] holding onto her excuses.

9- Ferociously – (fur-oh-shis-ly) – with extreme intensity.

Most of us are very skilled at talking people into things. We can talk people into doing things for us they don't want to do...and we can talk them into NOT doing things we deserve! We've got great skills, but most of us have used them for self-destructive purposes. Now it's time to use these great skills for a life-enhancing purpose – OUR RECOVERY!

APPLICATION: The Hardest Part of Our Recovery Plan

I bet you "Yes, but" yourself and everyone in your life that gives good advice and suggestions. I'm sure you're as good at it as I am...and my sister![8]

Well, Game's Over! This "YES, BUT" tactic is NO LONGER IN PLAY. This play HAS BEEN CUT! It's time to go with another strategy! The strategy of "COME HAIL OR HIGH WATER...HOW I'LL GET THROUGH IT AND DO IT."

That's the third column. In this Game of Life, we're NO LONGER going to tolerate our lies, excuses, and roadblocks! We're masters of deceit and we can find excuses and a way around most anything. We're professional manipulators.

We're so great...we can con a con! Now it's time to use this skill to HELP OURSELVES...to talk ourselves INTO DOING what we need to do. IT'S TIME to RATIONALLY CHALLENGE those Emotion-Driven Excuses... and to USE WISE MIND to get past the TRUE OBSTACLES in our path.

This is the hardest part of our Game Plan...and our recovery.

Remember, if recovery were easy, we would've done it long ago.

In the third column, we'll come up with RATIONAL MIND CHALLENGES for our Emotional Mind Lies and Excuses. We'll also note WISE MIND SOLUTIONS for getting around or through the true, reality-based Obstacles. Where there's

No matter what kind of therapy we do, recovery comes down to looking at reality, making a decision how to adapt to reality, developing a plan of action, and then, the hard part, Following Through with what We Know to do. Make a heart-felt, gut-deep decision to Follow Through.

10- See Figure 14.C.1 – 14.C.6 for a blank Game Plan form.

11- See Figure 14.A and 14.B. These are the long and short sample plans.

a will, there's a way. That's the difference between BEING WILLING TO SOLVE A PROBLEM and willful and determined to shoot down any suggestions and play the "Yes, but" game! We're going to acknowledge the truth in our Game Plan...and we're going to get a plan for dealing with our STUMBLING BLOCKS and our LIFE! YOU'RE VERY MUCH WORTH IT and so are the people depending on you to be okay and functional!

Steps 8 and 9 in the instructions below relate to this part of the Game Plan. Write your Challenges in the blank Game Plan form when it's time.

SKILL BUILDER: Setting Up a Game Plan

Step 1. MAKE A COPY of the blank Game Plan form so you'll have a blank form for future use.[10] You may want to create a Game Plan form on your computer for personal use.

Step 2. REVIEW THE COMPLETED GAME PLANS[11] to get an idea of what one looks like and the type of information to include. USE A HIGHLIGHTER to mark things that would be good to have in your plan.

Step 3. DECIDE WHAT TO FOCUS ON in your Game Plan. Many people reading this workbook will focus on stopping a Self-Destructive Coping Behavior, managing depression and anxiety, and setting up a Recovery Lifestyle.

Game Plans can focus on ANYTHING...things like getting out of debt, losing weight, improving a relationship, leaving an abusive marriage, getting through a divorce, being "okay" in a difficult work situation, grieving a death, managing chronic pain, and regaining peace and stability when we find ourselves in a time of major stress overload.

Most of us don't have the emotional, physical, and financial resources to do everything at once...so, we must PRIORITIZE and WISELY DECIDE what MUST COME FIRST. We need to make these things our starting point...and parts of our first Game Plan for recovery.

Step 4. DECIDE HOW MANY GAME PLANS TO DO. You can do one Game Plan or several. It's easier to do one Game Plan for different problems if the Action Steps for the problems are similar. For instance, if your priorities are to stop drugs and alcohol and to manage depression or Bipolar Disorder, you could do just one plan. That because the Action Steps for both are very similar. You could do one plan for managing Bipolar Disorder and diabetes, too. The Action Steps for these are similar (attend appointments, follow treatment recommendation, manage stress, good nutrition and rest, etc.). However, you might decide to do two separate plans. Decide what's right for you.

AS A RULE OF THUMB, if you're doing a Game Plan for two or more problems and the Action Steps are very different, do separate plans. If the Action Steps are similar, do one! Don't get stuck here. You can always break them up or combine them later.

If we bite off more than we can chew… we'll choke. Take small bites and Lean Into your recovery!

12- The Mindfully Protecting My Peace and Stability Worksheet lists the things Coming At Us. The things Coming At Us that are most likely to GET TO US are things we should address in our Game Plan. Many of these are probably addressed in the sample plans in some way…like in the "Deal With Stuff as It Comes My Way," the "Maintain a Positive Attitude," or the "Set Limits and Boundaries… and Say NO" sections.

13- If the Action Step is "Get a Job," we might list, "No transportation," "I don't want to give up my free time," "Have trouble with authority," "I'd only make a little more working than staying on disability," "Poor work history," "Always walk off jobs," "My symptoms might return and I won't be able to work," "I get panicky around a lot of people," etc.

14- In the job example and the Obstacle of "No car," we might decide to get a job within walking distance of our home and work there until we can buy an ugly $500 car that runs…even if we don't want to work there or it's "beneath" us. Come hail or high water, we vow to do whatever we have to do…to work!

Step 5. DECIDE WHAT TIME PERIOD your Game Plan will cover. People who are starting over or are early in their recovery generally choose to focus on the first 2-3 months of recovery. Others may want their plan to cover a 6-12 month period. Remember, we want to be wise and to Lean Into our recovery. We don't want to sabotage ourselves by taking on more than we can handle.

Step 6. Once you decide what to focus on in your Game Plan, ADD A TITLE in the area at the top of the form, "My Game Plan for…."

Step 7. On a separate sheet of paper, MAKE A LIST OF THE ACTION STEPS your recovery requires. Start with the ones you wrote down and highlighted earlier in this chapter. It's best to sketch out a plan BEFORE putting it into the Game Plan form. That's so you can Think Through Before You Do!!

The Action Steps will include Wise Mind "MUST DO's" and "WOULD BE HELPFUL TO DO'S." The Would Be Helpful To Do's are EXTRA STEPS to MAKE SURE we reach our goal!! For instance, if our goal is to stop using alcohol, a job would be helpful to keep us busy and to provide a sense of productivity. However, a job is NOT required. We might decide to do volunteer work, go to school, or take a hobby class to stay busy instead.

If you're unsure which Action Steps to add, ask a support person for ideas. Also, get ideas from the sample Game Plans, the Wise Mind Worksheets, and "The Mindfully Protecting My Peace and Stability Worksheet."[12]

Step 8. In the blank Game Plan form, WRITE THE ACTION STEPS in the first column. There's space for 17. Put one in each space. If you have less than 17, don't use all the space! If you have more than 17, add another page!

Step 9. The middle column is for "Rational Mind Obstacles and Emotional Mind Excuses: What Might Discourage Me from Doing This." For each Action Step you wrote in the first column, LIST THE OBSTACLES AND EXCUSES that'll get in your way of carrying out the Action Steps.[13] These are OUR REASONS why we can't or shouldn't do an Action Step.

NUMBER THE OBSTACLES AND EXCUSES FOR EACH ACTION STEP. For instance, if you have two Obstacles and Excuses for Action Step #1, number them 1 and 2. If you have three for the third Action Step, number them 1, 2, and 3.

Step 10. The far right column is for "Rational Mind Challenges and Wise Mind How-To's: Come Hail or High Water…How I'll Get Through It and Do It." In this area, CHALLENGE EACH OBSTACLE AND EXCUSE. Make note of how you'll GET AROUND each one so you can do what you need to do.[14]

This part requires a lot of Rational Mind and Wise Mind. We must come up with logical, rational, and wise ways to get around the Excuses and Obstacles. If you have trouble coming up with good Challenges and How-To's, ask a support person for help.

Be Mindful of the resources and helps available in the community (like with transportation and other services). It's a matter of finding out how to get hooked up with these services and who to ask. In Texas, there's a 2-1-1 phone number to call to find out about services. Crisis Lines often have information about community programs. Check with churches, colleges, community-oriented counseling centers like Good Samaritan counseling, etc. Get some help working on your Game Plan. You might be surprised by the doors that open for you.

Bear in mind that we'll likely be frustrated or upset about having to do some of the Action Steps. That's what the Distress Tolerance chapter is all about! We'll have to use our skills and understandings to work our way through this Obstacle!

15- For instance, getting a job and housing may be some of our top priorities. If we don't have transportation, we'll have to plan where to live. We'll need to live within walking distance to possible work sites, on a bus line, or near someone who can drive us to work. At this point, we don't need to worry about BUYING a car...because we first need to focus on having enough extra income to pay for gas and insurance! Further, buying a car is a lower priority because housing and a job need to come first! Similarly, we don't need to worry about coming up with a plan to pay bill collectors if we don't have any cash flow. However, we should get a plan for dealing with calls and letters from the bill collectors! Once we get a job we can get a plan for paying them! I wonder where BUYING a car comes into the plan?

Besides housing and a job, other top priorities often include being able to get medical treatment and medication, going to AA or another support group, and having a food source. Things like developing hobbies and interests and getting a sofa and stereo will need to come later!

Step 11. Check out the NUMBERING SYSTEM used in the LONG Game Plan and NUMBER YOUR CHALLENGES and HOW-TO'S in a similar way. This numbering system is much easier to explain in Group...and much harder on paper. Don't GIVE UP because of the numbering system...that would be VERY SELF-DEFEATING. If you can't figure it out, skip the numbering and CHOOSE not to worry about it! If you can figure out an easier way to pair the Obstacles and Excuses with the Challenges and How-To's, PLEASE do it!

In the middle column, you numbered your FIRST Obstacle or Excuse for EACH Action Step #1. When you write a Rational Mind Challenge or Wise Mind How-To for these, number them "1," too because they go together. IF YOU HAVE SEVERAL CHALLENGES OR HOW-TO'S for the #1 Obstacle or Excuse, number them 1A, 1B, 1C, and so on...since they all go with the #1 Obstacle or Excuse.

Similarly, if you have TWO Obstacles and Excuses for an Action Step, you numbered them 1 and 2. When you write Challenges or How-To's for the #1 Obstacle or Excuse, number them 1A, 1B, and 1C as noted above. Likewise, when you write Challenges or How-To's for the #2 Obstacle or Excuse, number them 2A, 2B, 2C, and so on.

This next part is a bit tricky. Look at Action Step #4 on the LONG plan. Notice some of the CHALLENGES and HOW-TO'S are numbered 1A/2A, 1B/2B, 1C/2C, etc. This means the #1 and #2 Obstacles and Excuses are BOTH challenged by the SAME Challenges and How-To's. In other words, the four Challenges (meditation, challenging myself to do this, finding and talking about the Silver Lining, and every morning...read, listen to or watch something inspirational) address BOTH of the Obstacles and Excuses ("There's so many difficult things..." and "My negative thinking is such a habit..."). If this makes NO sense, skip it. It's not important in the Big Picture of Our Recovery!

Step 12. After your Game Plan is written, take time to PRIORITIZE WHAT TO FOCUS ON FIRST.[15] Most of us aren't great at doing everything at once! We must Lean Into our recovery so we don't become overwhelmed, frustrated, and discouraged. Decide which things MUST come first and start there!

Figure 14.C.1: The Game Plan

My Game Plan for:

WISE MIND ACTION STEPS: "How Do I Go About It?" List the Action Steps you NEED to take and ones which would be HELPFUL for your recovery. These are the "Must Do's" and the "Would Be Helpful To Do's."	RATIONAL MIND OBSTACLES AND EMOTIONAL MIND EXCUSES: "What Might Discourage Me from Doing This?" List the major Obstacles and Excuses that will get in your way of carrying out the Action Steps.	RATIONAL MIND CHALLENGES AND WISE MIND HOW-TO'S: "Come Hail or High Water... How I'll Get Through It and Do It" Note how you'll help yourself to get passed and around the Rational Mind Obstacles and Emotional Mind Excuses.
1.		
2.		

Figure 14.C.2: The Game Plan

WISE MIND ACTION STEPS	OBSTACLES AND EXCUSES	CHALLENGES AND HOW-TO'S
3.		
4.		
5.		

	WISE MIND ACTION STEPS	OBSTACLES AND EXCUSES	CHALLENGES AND HOW-TO'S

Figure 14.C.3: The Game Plan

6.

7.

8.

	Figure 14.C.4: The Game Plan

WISE MIND ACTION STEPS	OBSTACLES AND EXCUSES	CHALLENGES AND HOW-TO'S
9.		
10.		
11.		

Figure 14.C.5: The Game Plan

WISE MIND ACTION STEPS	OBSTACLES AND EXCUSES	CHALLENGES AND HOW-TO'S
12.		
13.		
14.		

	Figure 14.C.6: The Game Plan		
CHALLENGES AND HOW-TO'S			
OBSTACLES AND EXCUSES			
WISE MIND ACTION STEPS	15.	16.	17.

SKILL BUILDER: The Game Plan Tracking Sheets

These tracking sheets will help us to track and monitor our progress. We'll be able to see which Action Steps we're doing well...and which ones need more work! WHEN IT'S TIME, we may want to put more effort into the ones we're not doing so well. Remember, we're not going to be 100% in everything. IT'S GOING TO TAKE TIME TO BUILD A RECOVERY LIFESTYLE and to make the changes we need to make. We'll naturally get in the habit of doing some of these Action Steps fairly quickly...and some will take longer to get in the habit of doing. Also, we must PRIORITIZE which things to focus on FIRST! Our goal is to LEAN INTO our recovery and to do THE BEST WE CAN. This means we need to MINDFULLY push ourselves to do our best WITHOUT CAUSING OURSELVES to become overwhelmed or discouraged. So, TRACK YOUR PROGRESS to see which Action Steps you're doing well and which ones you need to put more energy into. Be sure to PRAISE YOURSELF for ALL progress...big and small...and ALL ATTEMPTS!

Instructions for Using the Game Plan Tracking Sheets

16- See Figure 14.D for "A Completed Game Plan Tracking Sheet."

17- From the Long completed Game Plan in Figure 14.A.

18- See Figure 14.E for "The Game Plan Tracking Sheet."

19- Write the title of YOUR Game Plan on the title line of the tracking sheet.

20- The first date to write in will be the day you begin to Follow Through with the Action Steps on your Game Plan. Then, fill in the remaining dates.

Step 1. CHECK OUT the completed tracking sheet.[16] Notice it's titled on the first row, has dates on the second row, and the 17 Action Steps[17] listed in the remaining rows. Notice the rating scale at the bottom. Each tracking sheet covers a 2-week period.

Step 2. MAKE COPIES of the blank tracking sheet.[18]

Step 3. After you finish writing your Game Plan, SET UP A TRACKING SHEET. Write in the title[19] and the dates.[20] Write in short titles for each Action Step on your Game Plan.

Step 4. Carry out Day 1 of your Game Plan.

Step 5. That evening or the next day, RATE HOW WELL YOU DID or did not do on EACH Action Step. Rate your progress using the 1-5 rating scale. If you're not sure if you earned a rating of 2 or 3, or 3 or 4 on an Action Step, go with the higher rating! Use "NA" for an Action Step you're not currently focusing on or one you didn't have a need or opportunity to do.

For instance, on Day 1, getting a job and starting AA are your priorities. Your goals for Day 2 are to continue to look for work and to make some calls about volunteer work or church. When progress is rated for Day 1, "NA" should go in the "Attend Church/Service Organization" slot because it was NOT a Day 1 event. Also, if a treatment appointment wasn't scheduled, an "NA" would go in that slot. Further, if nothing came up on Day 1 that you had to set limits for, you could put "NA" in that slot, too!

Step 6. Once you complete a tracking sheet for the first two weeks, start a new one! Keep these in a notebook or clipped together so you can watch your progress as you're SETTING UP and LIVING a Recovery Lifestyle!

Figure 14.D: A Completed Game Plan Tracking Sheet

My Game Plan Tracking Sheet: *Starting Over and Living a Recovery Lifestyle*

Date →	3-1	3-2	3-3	3-4	3-5	3-6	3-7	3-8	3-9	3-10	3-11	3-12	3-13	3-14
1. Deal with Stuff	3	3	4	3	3	4								
2. Daily Devotion	4	4	4	4	4	4								
3. Regular Sleep Schedule	1	2	2	4	3	4								
4. Positive Attitude	3	4	4	3	4	4								
5. Set Limits	3	3	4	3	2	4								
6. Do Life-Enhancing Coping	3	4	4	3	3	4								
7. Transportation	3	4	4	4	5	5								
8. Be Prepared for Crisis	3	3	4	4	4	4								
9. Go to Appointments	5	5	4	NA	NA	5								
10. Take Meds	5	5	5	4	3	5								
11. Get-Keep a Job	NA	3	4	5	3	4								
12. Keep Busy	4	5	4	4	2	4								
13. No Romance!	4	5	5	4	2	3								
14. Support Group	5	5	5	4	2	4								
15. Service Organization	NA	NA	NA	NA	NA	4								
16. Random Acts of Kindness	5	3	4	4	1	4								
17. Care for Physical Self	2	3	4	4	1	3								

Rating Scale:
5 - Did EXCELLENT in this area today
4 - Did PRETTY GOOD in this area today
3 - Did ALRIGHT in this area today
2 - Did FAIR or FAIR AT BEST in this area today
1 - DIDN'T DO WELL in this area today
NA - No Opportunity today

My Game Plan Tracking Sheet:

Figure 14.E: The Game Plan Tracking Sheet

Date →

Rating Scale: 5 - Did EXCELLENT in this area today   4 - Did PRETTY GOOD in this area today   3 - Did ALRIGHT in this area today
2 - Did FAIR or FAIR AT BEST in this area today   1 - DIDN'T DO WELL in this area today   NA - No Opportunity today

From "Out-of-Control: A Dialectical Behavior Therapy (DBT) - Cognitive-Behavioral Therapy (CBT) Workbook for Getting Control of Our Emotions and Emotion-Driven Behavior"
Copyright © 2009 by Melanie Gordon Sheets, Ph.D. (www.dbt-cbt-workbook.com)

~~~~~~~~ CHAPTER REVIEW ~~~~~~~~

1. What is a Game Plan? How does it help us? _____

_____

_____

_____

2. The LONG Game Plan is very long and detailed. In what ways will the Game Plan
we write be shorter? _____

_____

_____

_____

3. Our first Game Plan should include certain things...and a later Game Plan should
include other things? What type of things go in the first Game Plan and why? ____

_____

_____

_____

_____

4. Action Steps go in the first column of a Game Plan. What are they? _____

_____

_____

5. Excuses and Obstacles go in the middle column. What are they? Mention the
difference is between an Excuse and an Obstacle. _____

_____

_____

_____

_____

_____

6. What's the purpose of the "Rational Mind Challenges and the Wise Mind How-
To's" column? _____

_____

_____

7. What's the hardest part of the Game Plan...and our recovery? _____

_____

_____

_____

8. How will the Game Plan tracking sheets help us? Why should we do them? ____

_____

_____

_____

FOR REFLECTION:
Take a few moments to reflect on this chapter. Some questions are listed in the margin to guide your reflection.
Feel free to reflect on whatever your heart brings to mind.

What are your reactions to the material?

Which parts hit home or relate to you the most?

Which parts have helped you the most?

Which parts have helped you to understand yourself the most?

How will you use this information to feel better about yourself?

How will you use this information to improve the quality of your life...or to change how things work out for you in life?

What will you do differently based on this material?

How has this information changed the way you feel about your patterns of relapse and recovery... and your overall response to life?

What does this material motivate you to do?

~~~ For Reflection ~~~

_____

_____

_____

_____

_____

_____

_____

_____

_____

_____

_____

_____

_____

_____

_____

_____

_____

_____

_____

_____

THE FINAL REST STOP

Road Map: Where We've Been...What Ground We've Covered

Well, we've done it! We've made our way through THIS PART of our journey...and boy, have we covered a lot of ground! Through THIS LEG of our journey, we've taken many steps to get from Relapse Road to the Recovery Path. We've had to dig in our heels to Get Through some rough terrain.[1] This journey has taken us through the valley where we looked at things that brought us down and put tears in our eyes. However, our journey has landed us on a mountaintop where we can see the horizon of promise and hope. It's here that we'll find what we've been searching for...The Land of Fulfillment. Here we'll find our treasure...peace, stability, meaning, and satisfaction.

By way of THIS PART of our journey, we've packed away many souvenirs[2] and snapshots.[3] Instead of weighing us down, these prized possessions have lightened our load, reduced our pain, and have helped us to cast away many burdens.

What do you think these prized possessions are? _____

_____

1- Terrain – (tur-rain) – land or territory.

2- Souvenirs – (sue-vin-ears) – things we buy or get while on vacation. They remind us of our trip.

3- Snapshots – photos – pictures.

> They're the skills and understandings we've picked up along the way. If we've been living, eating, and breathing the principles, concepts, and worksheets that have lined the pages of this workbook, then we've tucked away many tools and resources in our recovery backpack. We've learned and practiced many skills and understandings to deal with the pitfalls, road blocks, rocks, boulders, and hailstones that WILL BE Coming At Us when we leave this rest stop and go on with our journey. This workbook has equipped us for what comes next. We've got the skills and the Rehab-itude Attitude of "Come hail or high water, I'll Get Through it and do it!" We've got the gear...we're geared up...and we're prepared to hit the road again. This time, it's the ROAD TO RECOVERY...and we're following the Recovery Path!

Our Souvenirs and Snapshots: A Time to Remember

In **Chapters 1 and 2**, we picked up the understanding that "The Nature of the Problem" is the things we do to feel better end up causing us MORE pain and suffering. We saw how Self-Destructive Coping Behaviors start "The Cycle of Suffering." The losses and problems in our life become more intense and widespread...and "The Big Picture of Our Life" fills with emptiness and pain. We learned we can stop this Cycle of Suffering by STOPPING OURSELVES from RESPONDING TO LIFE in the same

OLD WAYS...the Self-Destructive Emotion-Driven ways.

When we try, good things happen in our life. When we KEEP trying, we'll Get Through tough times...and good things will continue to happen in our life.

In **Chapter 3**, we challenged the Emotion-Driven Lie, "Why try, everything gets screwed up anyway?" We determined that many good things happen when we're on the Recovery Path. We learned that when we make a bad choice and relapse into Emotion-Driven Behavior...life takes a turn for the worst...and MANY bad things happen again. We learned that the Recovery Path is a rocky road and NO MATTER HOW GREAT OR SELF-DISCIPLINED WE ARE, bad things will happen. Some things we'll cause...and some things will JUST HAPPEN that we have no control over. We learned that when a boulder lands on our Recovery Path, we have two choices. One is to Stand and face our troubles and to Fight to stay on the Recovery Path. The other is to relapse into Self-Destructive Coping Behavior.

We aren't Masters of Recovery. We're a WORK IN PROGRESS!

In Chapter 3, we also learned that when we Go Through TOUGH times, "The least we can do...should be the most that's expected." This means we're REQUIRED to do THE BEST WE CAN...even if that means JUST SURVIVING and functioning ADEQUATELY. Our goal is to TAKE CARE of the PRIORITIES in our life so we can protect THE BIG PICTURE OF OUR LIFE. We also saw that we can turn a Partial Relapse into a "Successful Failure" by QUICKLY getting ourselves BACK ON the Recovery Path. We also learned that if we're contemplating whether we can "Safely Relapse," then we've ALREADY RELAPSED mentally, emotionally, and spiritually.

If the will is there, we CAN FIND the way.

In **Chapters 4 and 5**, we learned that it's hard to change our Emotion-Driven responses because we've made such a habit of doing them. However, we also learned that we CAN GAIN CONTROL of our Emotional Reflexes by being CONTINUALLY Mindful of ourselves, the things Coming At Us, and that Recovery is Our #1 Priority. Mindfulness is the first step in gaining control because we HAVE TO BE AWARE of what's going on AROUND US and WITHIN US before we can change anything. We practiced Observing and Describing our experiences. These are Mindfulness skills that give us a chance to notice changes in our mood and to understand what may be causing them. Observing and Describing also gives us the time we need to THINK before we respond...and to REMOVE OURSELVES from a situation before we become too upset. We also learned about caring for, protecting, and soothing ourselves like we would an infant. We discussed setting strong boundaries between the cherished things in our Inner Circle and the distressors Coming At Us. We learned that we NEED TO DEAL WITH the things Coming At Us in LIFE-ENHANCING WAYS so we can Mindfully Protect Our Peace and Stability.

Mindfulness is a skill. Like all skills we need to practice to get good at it!

Because we're human and not perfect, we need a plan for making any breaches into our Realm of Peace very temporary and a plan for minimizing any damage that may occur!!!

We often get hurt in our relationships when we follow our heart and not our head…when we impulsively become involved with someone without knowing the facts about their true personality.

We can request Time-Out in the Heat-of-the-Moment so we can cool off BEFORE we say or do things that will backfire and burn us.

We learned ways to GAIN control so we don't lose control.

Extreme Judgments often become Self-Fulfilling Prophecies. We tend to become what WE CONSIDER OURSELVES to be …and our people tend to become what WE CONSIDER THEM to be… and we tend to become WHAT OTHERS CONSIDER US to be.

We also learned how to Talk Ourselves THROUGH difficult situations, how to Talk Ourselves DOWN and to refocus, how to stop Painful Rumination, how to Let Go of upsetting thoughts and feelings, how to end upsetting phone calls and visits, and how to Turn Our Mind. We learned to prioritize our Must Do's so we don't become overwhelmed when we have too much to do! We learned about being Mindful of the Big Picture of a person's personality so we don't confuse our IMPRESSION or OPINION of someone with the FACTS of how they really are. We talked about being "Blinded by Love" and how a nice person may do something mean and that doesn't mean they're a mean person. It just means they did something OUT-OF-CHARACTER… something mean. Likewise, people who love us will act in unloving ways now and then. They still love us…they're just not in a loving mood at the time.

In **Chapter 6**, we discussed Raw Emotions and Emotion-Driven Behavior in detail. We learned that many common Emotional Mind experiences are fueled by intense emotions and irrational thoughts. For instance, we learned how a fear of panicking causes panic attacks, how we become blinded by "love at first sight,"…how we can gain 10 pounds on a "crash n' burn diet,"…and how our help and enabling can become very destructive and disabling. We also learned why we believe the Emotion-Driven Lies said about us.

In **Chapter 7**, we learned to Turn On Rational Mind to manage troubling emotional states. We challenged many Emotion-Driven Thoughts and practiced thinking about problems in a rational and life-enhancing way. We also learned that certain emotional and physical states make Turning On Rational Mind more of a challenge.

In **Chapter 8**, we took a close look at the destructive effect OUR Extreme Judgments have on OURSELVES and OTHERS…and the effect OTHER PEOPLE'S Extreme Judgments have on US. We also worked with "The Challenging Negative Judgments of Me Worksheet" and learned to rationally challenge the negative judgments made of us. We also noted the difference between our BEHAVIOR and our CHARACTER and we saw that "STUPID ISN'T AS STUPID DOES." We learned that we're NOT STUPID because we do FOOLISH things. We learned we HAVE GOOD JUDGMENT…but, we DON'T ALWAYS act on it!

In **Chapters 9 and 10**, we learned that when we use BOTH Emotional Mind and Rational Mind to deal with a situation, WISE MIND TURNS ON. Wise Mind is respectful of our EMOTIONAL ISSUES and CONCERNS as well as the REALITY and DEMANDS of our situation and the BIG PICTURE OF OUR LIFE. Wise Mind leads us

We need to figure out how BEST to respond to our life situations. Then, we need to respond the BEST we can. Our Recovery Goal is to learn from our experiences, so each time, we'll be better prepared…and can do EVEN BETTER than the time before. Our Recovery Goal is to Live n' Learn.

Emotional Mind can cloud our judgment and lead us astray …and right down Relapse Road.

When Emotional Mind drives, our life becomes a wreck. When Rational Mind takes the wheel, we'll steer clear of the road hazards on the Recovery Path.

Because change is uncomfortable and often painful… people generally don't make major life changes…UNTIL the pain of LIVING LIKE THEY'RE LIVING… is GREATER THAN the pain of change.

to wise understandings and a GAME PLAN for dealing with our problems and concerns. Wise Mind helps us to ACT IN OUR BEST INTERESTS and to gain and maintain PEACE and STABILITY. Wise Mind is ACTION-ORIENTED since there isn't anything wise about NOT Following Through with what We Know to do!

"The Well Analogy Worksheet" and "The Wise Mind Worksheet" were discussed in detail. These are Mindfulness tools that help us to THINK THROUGH BEFORE WE DO and to TALK OURSELVES DOWN and THROUGH the Heat-of-the-Moment. We also discussed six tips for Participating Effectively, such as STOPPING OURSELVES from carrying-out destructive behavior, PLAYING BY THE RULES, and doing what we need to do WHETHER OR NOT WE LIKE IT or WANT TO! We also learned about following our head or our heart, carry-over emotions, and how there's AN ORDER TO THINGS…such that Rational Mind must be Turned On before Wise Mind suggestions will be accepted. The ways of the Good Counselor and the importance of LISTENING TO THE VOICE OF WISDOM were also discussed.

Through Chapters 6-10, we learned that when we're Big-Time in a negative Emotional Mind, we become DESPERATE to relieve emotional pressure. If we let Emotional Mind "run its' course," we often act in impulsive and destructive ways. We must TAKE CONTROL BY Turning On Rational Mind and Wise Mind to manage our emotional states. That's the only way to TAME a RECKLESS and OUT-OF-CONTROL Emotional Mind. That's the only way to GAIN CONTROL of OUR LIFE and our life outcomes. That's the only way to Mindfully Protect Our Peace and Stability and the Big Picture of Our Life. If we allow Emotional Mind to run our life, it'll lead us down a path of destruction. It'll destroy us and EVERYTHING that's important to us.

In **Chapters 11 and 12**, we discussed the process of healing and recovery and how it involves Distress Tolerance and Acceptance. We learned that we must ACCEPT that pain and distress is a NORMAL part of life. We must LEAN INTO and do…whatever we have to do…to WORK THROUGH our pain and problems…so we can GET THROUGH them. We must use Distress Tolerance skills FOR AS LONG AS IT TAKES for our changes to Take Root…for the distress to subside…and the benefits of our changes to be fully experienced. We must be WILLING to feel worse for awhile so we can feel better down the road. We have a CHOICE to Go Through the TEMPORARY PAIN of dealing with our problems and losses…or the LONG-TERM PAIN and SUFFERING of avoiding and stuffing them…and carrying them with us throughout our life.

We learned to use the skill of Radical Acceptance TO ACCEPT the things that

418

To end the Cycle of Suffering, we must ACCEPT the pain and distress of change. We must DEAL WITH the pain and distress… and LIVE WITH the pain and distress… FOR AS LONG AS IT TAKES to eliminate or reduce it.

Most of us are real good at conning and manipulating others to get what we want. We can talk people into lots of things like driving us to the drug house or the beer store, to forgive us and give us another chance, to give us money, or to buy us something. We generally find ways to get what we want and we've been willing to do some pretty painful and desperate things to do so! Now it's time to use these skills to con and manipulate OURSELVES into getting what we REALLY want… a truly satisfying and meaningful life!

AREN'T ACCEPTABLE. We must accept things even if it's not right or fair that we have to…because NON-ACCEPTANCE will keep us STUCK IN PAIN and NEGATIVITY. We also learned that we can EMOTIONALLY STEP BACK from "unchanging situations" and still try to make changes…AS LONG AS WE CAN BE OKAY while doing so. If we can't be okay, we'll have to Step Out of the situation because we MUST protect our peace and stability. We also discussed "The Baseball Analogy of Life" and how our job is to go up to bat…and DO OUR BEST to hit the balls Coming At Us. Our job is to use Wise Mind to make the best play possible EACH TIME we're at bat and to use Distress Tolerance to keep ourselves in play during the toughest games and seasons.

In **Chapter 13**, we learned that we often choose Self-Destructive Coping Behaviors because they're Tried N' True, fun and exciting…they Numb-Out our emotions and White-Out our thoughts…and they give us QUICK RELIEF. We learned that when we use Life-Enhancing Coping Skills, we'll have to use Distress Tolerance skills, too. That's because Life-Enhancing Coping Skills REDUCE our pain and distress and LOWER our Emotional Intensity Level…but they DON'T WIPE-OUT our pain and distress FOR LONG PERIODS of time. We must ACCEPT and LEARN TO TOLERATE the distress of STILL HAVING SOME painful feelings and upsetting thoughts.

We learned to use "The Levels of Emotion Chart" to gain information about our emotional levels. We discussed that we ought to seek help when our emotional level is at a 5 or 6…while we HAVE ENOUGH Rational Mind going on that we CAN BENEFIT from help WITHOUT being institutionalized…and BEFORE we slip too much and cause ourselves extra problems…and BEFORE things get OUT-OF-CONTROL. We also completed "The Life-Enhancing Coping Activities Worksheet" and listed many positive coping activities that we WILL DO to reduce our emotional intensity. We learned to use an "Activity Calendar" to give ourselves many coping options in the Heat-of-the-Moment… when we really need support and distraction. We also learned how to use a "Weekly Calendar" to set up a busy Recovery Lifestyle.

In **Chapter 14**, we learned how to write-up and use a Game Plan. We identified the Wise Mind Action Steps that are critical to our recovery. We learned how we sabotage our recovery with Emotional Mind Excuses and Rational Mind Obstacles. We learned to use Rational Mind Challenges and Wise Mind How-To's…to get passed and around the obstacles and excuses that are roadblocks…and get in our way on the Recovery Path.

Where Do We Go from Here? Where Is This Road Leading?

If the road we're on isn't taking us to where we want to be…we're probably taken the wrong path.

By way of our trek through this workbook, we've learned about the Cycle of Suffering and why our life has been so OUT-OF-CONTROL. We've learned about the three Mind States and how we GET CONTROL of our life. We've learned about tolerating and coping with distress and how we can STAY IN CONTROL. Getting Through this workbook was the easy part of our recovery…and now, we're to the HARD PART. It's the "Now I know all these things…but how in the world do I pull it off?" part. What comes next is the "Following Through with what We Know to do" part! It's the "Gettin' 'er done" part!

We've been like a tourist exploring and studying the culture of life on Relapse Road and life on the Recovery Path. Now it's time to choose the route we will take…and the LIFESTYLE WE WILL LIVE. We're now at the crossroads. Will you choose the desert and poverty of Relapse Road or the green pastures and treasures of the Recovery Path? The dead end of Relapse stops when we walk the steps of Recovery. We know the pain and heartache of life in Relapse…and we know the struggles and joy of life in Recovery. Which route do you choose? The road of LONG-TERM pain and suffering or the pathway of TEMPORARY PAIN…and RECOVERY?

You've been equipped with many powerful recovery tools and skills for the next leg of your journey to Recovery. You're filled with Rational Mind and Wise Mind understandings…and Distress Tolerance and Acceptance skills. You've completed a Game Plan for your recovery. Now it's time to use what you know…and to Follow Through with your recovery plan. IT'S TIME TO PUT WISDOM INTO ACTION. It's time to go out there and build a support system, to fill your life with meaningful activities and people, and to stay busy in recovery. It's time to use your skills and understandings to MAKE the changes…and to GET THROUGH the changes…THAT'LL CHANGE YOUR LIFE. It's time to go out there and Play Ball. This is THE TIME of your life and the game of your life. IT'S GAME TIME…so follow your Game Plan…one day at a time. Keep up with your stats by tracking your progress. Practice your skills, make change-ups as necessary, and when the game is tough or you're not sure what the best play is…SEEK WISE COUNSEL. There's many coaches seasoned in the plays of recovery…and you always have this playbook to remind yourself of some tips and strategies of the game. I leave you with my hope and prayers that you'll have a long winning season…and YOUR JOURNEY LEADS YOU TO PEACE AND STABILITY ON THE RECOVERY PATH.

If you're where you're supposed to be… and doing the things you're supposed to do… things will work out like they're supposed to… and all will be well.

References

American Psychiatric Association. (2000). *The diagnostic and statistical manual of mental disorders* (Revised 4th ed.). Washington, D.C.: Author.

Hamilton, B. (1995). *Getting started in AA*. Minnesota: Hazelden.

Linehan, M. M. (1993). *Cognitive-behavioral treatment of borderline personality disorder.* New York: Guilford Press.

Linehan, M. M. (1993). *Skills training manual for treating borderline personality disorder.* New York: Guilford Press.